TRUE TO

OUR NATIVE LAND

AN AFRICAN AMERICAN

NEW TESTAMENT COMMENTARY

Shadowed beneath Thy hand,
May we forever stand.
True to our God,
True to our native land.*

———————————— ⊞⊞ ————————————

For our sons and daughters,

may they forever stand. . . .

* From "Lift Ev'ry Voice and Sing" (1900), words by James Weldon Johnson (1871–1938) and music by John Rosamond Johnson.

TRUE TO OUR NATIVE LAND

AN AFRICAN AMERICAN

NEW TESTAMENT COMMENTARY

Brian K. Blount, *General Editor*

Cain Hope Felder, Clarice J. Martin,

& Emerson B. Powery, *Associate Editors*

FORTRESS PRESS

Minneapolis

TRUE TO OUR NATIVE LAND
An African American New Testament Commentary

Cover image: *Palm Sunday* (1956) by Jacob Lawrence (1917–2000), casein tempera on paper, 30 ¼ x 22 ½". Location: North Carolina Central University Art Museum, Durham, NC. © The Estate of Gwendolyn Knight Lawrence / Artists Rights Society (ARS), New York. Photo © The Jacob and Gwendolyn Lawrence Foundation / Art Resource, NY.
Cover design: Brad Norr
Book design: Zan Ceeley, Trio Bookworks

Library of Congress Cataloging-in-Publication Data

True to our native land: an African American New Testament commentary / Brian K. Blount, general editor; Cain Hope Felder, Clarice J. Martin, and Emerson B. Powery, associate editors.
    p. cm.
Includes bibliographical references and indexes.
ISBN-13: 978-0-8006-3421-6 (alk. paper)
ISBN-10: 0-8006-3421-7 (alk. paper)
1. Bible. N.T.—Commentaries. 2. Bible N.T.—Criticism, interpretation, etc. 3. African Americans—Religion. 4. Bible—Black interpretations. I. Blount, Brian K. II. Felder, Cain Hope. III. Martin, Clarice Jannette IV. Powery, Emerson B.
BS2341.52.T78 2007
225.7089'96073—dc22

                                             2007005097

The paper used in this publication meets the minimum requirements of American National Standard for Information Sciences—Permanence of Paper for Printed Library Materials, ANSI Z329.48-1984.

Manufactured in the U.S.A.

11   10   09   08   07   2   3   4   5   6   7   8   9   10

CONTENTS

AFRICAN AMERICAN BIBLICAL INTERPRETATION

COMMENTARY ON THE NEW TESTAMENT

IMAGES

▦ Images

13. Jacob Lawrence, *Through Forests, Through Rivers, Up Mountains* (1967), tempera, gouache and pencil on paper. Smithsonian Hirshhorn Museum/The Joseph H. Hirshhorn Bequest, 1981. © 1967 The Estate of Gwendolyn Knight Lawrence / Artists Rights Society (ARS), New York. Photo © Lee Stalsworth. Used by permission.

14. Charles White, *Mother and Child* (1918–1979). Wolff crayon, 1953. Collection of Frances B. White. © 1953 The Charles White Archives

15. Charles White, *Mary, Don't You Weep.* Ink, 1956. Collection of Harry Belafonte. © 1956 The Charles White Archives.

16. Charles White, *Triumph.* Lithograph, 1956. [No provenance information.] © 1956 The Charles White Archives.

17. Charles White, *General Moses (Harriet Tubman).* Ink, 1965. Collection of Garden State Insurance Company. © 1965 The Charles White Archives. Photograph by Frank J. Thomas, courtesy of the Frank J. Thomas Archives.

18. Charles White, *Move On Up a Little Higher.* Charcoal and Wolff Crayon, 1961. Private Collection. © 1961 The Charles White Archives

Gallery following page 204

1. Henry Ossawa Tanner, *Nicodemus Visiting Christ,* 1899. Photo courtesy of the Pennsylvania Academy of Fine Arts, Philadelphia. Joseph E. Temple Fund.

2. Henry Ossawa Tanner, *The Good Shepherd,* 1920. Oil on canvas, 32" x 24". Collection of The Newark Museum, gift of Mr. and Mrs. Henry H. Wehrhane, 1929. Inv. 29.910. Photo: © The Newark Museum/Art Resource, N.Y.

3. Henry Ossawa Tanner, *The Good Shepherd (Atlas Mountains, Morocco),* c. 1930. Smithsonian American Art Museum, Washington, D.C. Photo Credit: Smithsonian American Art Museum, Washington, D.C./Art Resource, N.Y.

4. Henry Ossawa Tanner, *The Resurrection of Lazarus,* 1896. Musée D'Orsay, Paris. Photo: © Erich Lessing/Art Resource, N.Y.

5. Henry Ossawa Tanner, *Return to the Tomb,* 1914. Litho on paper, 24.2 x 28.6 cm. Smithsonian American Art Museum, Washington, D.C. Photo: © Smithsonian American Art Museum/Art Resource, N.Y.

6. Henry Ossawa Tanner, *The Miraculous Haul of Fishes,* no date. Oil on canvas, 38" x 47.5". Permanent Collection of the National Academy, N.Y., Inv. 1236-P. Photo: © The National Academy of Design, New York (1236-P). Used by permission.

7. Henry Ossawa Tanner, *Jesus and His Disciples on Their Way to Bethany (Luke 24:50),* no date. Oil on canvas, 95 x 121.5 cm. Musée D'Orsay, Paris. Photo: © Erich Lessing/Art Resource, N.Y.

Gallery following page 332

1. Funeral portrait of a young man. Egyptian-Roman period, mid-second century C.E. Tempera on wood. From Fayum, Egypt. 31.6 x 20.6 cm. Kunsthistorisches Museum, Vienna, Austria. Photo: © Erich Lessing/Art Resource, N.Y.

▦ Images

21. First-century fresco depicting the philosopher Socrates preparing for his death. Ephesus, Turkey. Ephesus Archaeological Museum. Photo: © Erich Lessing/Art Resource, N.Y.
22. Eleventh-century ivory tablet depicts Saint Paul evangelizing Saint Thecla. British Museum, London. Photo: © Erich Lessing/Art Resource, N.Y.
23. Early Christian fresco depicting female leader in her community. Second half of the third century C.E. Catacomb of Priscilla, Rome. Photo: © Scala/Art Resource, N.Y.
24. Fifth-century copy of the Acts of the Apostles written in Sahidic Coptic. MS M.910. The Pierpont Morgan Library, New York, N.Y. Photo: © The Pierpont Morgan Library/Art Resource, N.Y. Used by permission.
25. Book of Gospels in Sahidic Coptic from Monastery of St. Michael at Hamouli, Fayum, in the seventh or eighth century C.E. MS M569. The Pierpont Morgan Library, New York, N.Y. Photo: © The Pierpont Morgan Library/Art Resource, N.Y. Used by permission.

PREFACE

On a warm, clear evening in the fall of 2000, while dining outside on the deck of a Washington, D.C., restaurant near the Howard University School of Religion, Cain Hope Felder and I considered whether the timing was right to contemplate a one-volume commentary on the New Testament. Our preaching and teaching in African American churches across the country had put us into direct contact with questions that preoccupied the minds of both lay and clergy. Most of those questions centered on the particular texts or themes we happened to be teaching. Increasingly, however, most often at the end of our visits, just before we were ushered out of an assembly and hurried back to the airport, the same, provocative query emerged: when will you African American scholars of the New Testament come together and write a commentary from the perspective of our people's history and culture?

Over my fourteen years of teaching at Princeton Theological Seminary, many students have asked me about the motivations that prompted my move from a cherished vocation in the pastorate to a career in teaching. Because I speak so appreciatively and warmly about my church ministry experience (1982–1988), they are all the more eager for my response. I explain that I felt called by the opportunities to research, write, and teach about the very principles that guided the development of this work. During the years of my ministry, scholarly biblical materials written intentionally from an African American perspective were rare. There appeared to me two primary reasons for this circumstance. First, there had not yet developed a sufficient core of African American scholars who were trained in the field of New Testament studies and who had the opportunities of conversation, resources, and time afforded by libraries, faculties, and students of research institutions to consider, reflect upon, and write on the New Testament texts. Second, the push in the academy toward the value of culturally engaged readings of the biblical materials was in its initial phases of challenging the belief that historical and literary-critical readings of the Bible could yield objective conclusions about textual meaning that were not influenced by the context of the person doing those readings. It was the exciting opportunity, as one of a growing number of African American biblical scholars, to bring the impetus toward cultural readings of the New Testament together with the cultural perspective of African America that lured me back into the classroom, first as a doctoral student, and subsequently now as a professor. One of the rewarding yields of that journey is this commentary written by African American scholars with the particular concerns of the African American church in mind.

There is, of course, no single African American perspective. This is particularly the case in the twenty-first century, when African Americans are located everywhere on the U.S. economic, social, political, and religious landscape. Yet there are consistent and unique historical, social, cultural, religious, and political realities that influence the ways in which African Americans have approached and continue to approach the biblical text. Our authors have tried to draw from those realities as they have done their interpretive work.

The work begins with the editors. To Cain Felder, Clarice Martin, and Emerson Powery, I owe a great debt of gratitude for all they have done to bring this long-standing dream to reality. Professor Powery should be mentioned particularly, as he has sacrificed countless hours from his own research to ensure that this collegial work could come to fruition. Always almost immediately available to both me and the editors at Fortress Press, he has helped guide every stage of the commentary's shaping. It is impossible to think of having approached this daunting task without him.

Like my editorial colleagues, I am also appreciative of the hard work and helpful guidance rendered by the editorial staff at Fortress Press. Neil Elliott, Ron Bonner, and Michael West have been a strong source of encouragement and support throughout this rigorous process. Their expertise and, to be sure, their patience have been gifts to us. It is our hope that the work they have helped us accomplish will likewise be a gift to the African American church, especially those in the church who have over the years voiced their hope to me and others like me laboring in their midst for just this kind of resource to help facilitate their passionate study of the New Testament. To that important question "When?" we are delighted to answer, "Now!"

—Brian K. Blount,
General Editor

CONTRIBUTORS

EDITORS

Brian K. Blount is President of Union Theological Seminary and Presbyterian School of Christian Education in Richmond, Va. He is the author of *The Book of Revelation: A Commentary* (Westminster John Knox, forthcoming); *Can I Get a Witness? Reading Revelation through African American Culture* (Westminster John Knox, 2005); *Preaching Mark in Two Voices*, with Gary W. Charles (Westminster John Knox, 2002); *Struggling with Scripture*, with Walter Brueggemann and William C. Placher (Westminster John Knox, 2002); *Then the Whisper Put on Flesh: New Testament Ethics in an African American Context* (Abingdon, 2001); *Go Preach! Mark's Kingdom Message and the Black Church Today* (Orbis, 1998); and *Cultural Interpretation: Reorienting New Testament Criticism* (Fortress Press, 1995).

Cain Hope Felder is Professor of New Testament Language and Literature at the School of Divinity, Howard University, Washington, D.C. He is the author of *Race, Racism, and the Biblical Narratives*, Facets (Fortress Press, 2002) and *Troubling Biblical Waters: Race, Class, and Family* (Orbis, 1989), and editor of *The Original African Heritage Study Bible* (Winston, 1993) and *Stony the Road We Trod: African American Biblical Interpretation* (Fortress Press, 1991).

Clarice J. Martin is Jean Picker Associate Professor of Philosophy and Religion at Colgate University, Hamilton, New York. She is the author of numerous publications on early Christian origins, Greco-Roman slavery, and the religious experience of black peoples in the African diaspora (including womanist thought), including "Polishing the Unclouded Mirror: A Womanist Reading of Revelation 18:13," in *From Every People and Nation: The Book of Revelation in Intercultural Perspective* (Fortress Press, 2005); "The Eyes Have It: Slavery in the Communities of Christ-Believers," in *Christian Origins: A People's History of Early Christianity*, volume 1 (Fortress Press, 2005); and "Pentecost 2: Interpreting the Lessons of the Church Year," *Proclamation* 6, Series A (Fortress Press, 1996).

▦ Contributors

Emerson B. Powery is Associate Professor of New Testament at Lee University, Cleveland, Tennessee. He is the author of *The Gospel of Mark: A Commentary* (Pilgrim, forthcoming); *Jesus Reads Scripture: The Function of Jesus' Use of Scripture in the Synoptic Gospels* (Brill, 2003); and coeditor with Terry Cross of *The Spirit and the Mind: Essays in Informed Pentecostalism* (University Press of America, 2000).

OTHER CONTRIBUTORS

Brad R. Braxton is Associate Professor of Homiletics and New Testament at Vanderbilt University Divinity School, Nashville, Tennessee. He is the author of *Preaching Paul* (Abingdon, 2004); *No Longer Slaves: Galatians and African American Experience* (Liturgical, 2002); and *The Tyranny of Resolution: I Corinthians 7:17-24* (Society of Biblical Literature, 2000).

Michael Joseph Brown is Associate Professor of New Testament and Christian Origins at Candler School of Theology at Emory University, Atlanta, Georgia. He is the author of *The Lord's Prayer through North African Eyes: A Window into Early Christianity* (T. & T. Clark, 2005); *Blackening of the Bible: The Aims of African American Biblical Scholarship* (Trinity Press International, 2004), and *What They Don't Tell You: A Survivor's Guide to Biblical Studies* (Westminster John Knox, 2000).

Gay L. Byron is Baptist Missionary Training School Associate Professor of New Testament and Black Church Studies at Colgate Rochester Crozer Divinity School, Rochester, New York. She is the author of *Symbolic Blackness and Ethnic Difference in Early Christian Literature* (Routledge, 2002).

Allen Dwight Callahan is Professor of New Testament at the Seminário Teológico Batista do Nordeste in Bahia, Brazil. He is the author of *The Talking Book: The Bible and African Americans* (Yale University Press, 2006); *A Love Supreme: A History of the Johannine Tradition* (Fortress Press, 2005); and *The Embassy of Onesimus: The Letter of Paul to Philemon* (Trinity Press International, 1997).

Stephanie Buckhanon Crowder is Assistant Professor of Religion at Belmont University and Associate Pastor of New Covenant Christian Church (Disciples of Christ), Nashville, Tennessee. She is the author of *A Faith-Based Curriculum for Addressing Substance Abuse* (Congress of National Black Churches, 2005) and *Simon of Cyrene: A Case of Roman Conscription* (Peter Lang, 2002).

Larry George is Pathways Associate Professor of African American Biblical Faith and History at Bluffton University, Bluffton, Ohio. He is the author of *Reading the Tapestry: A Literary-Rhetorical Analysis of the Johannine Resurrection Narrative (John 20–21)* (Peter Lang, 2000) and coeditor of *What Does It Mean to Be Black and Christian?* (Townsend, 1995).

Thomas L. Hoyt Jr. is Bishop in the Christian Methodist Episcopal Church serving Louisiana and Mississippi and former President of the National Council of Churches of Christ in the USA

(2004–2005). He has served on the Faith and Order Commissions of the National and World Councils of Churches, on the National Council's Lectionary Committee on Inclusive Language, and on the Theological Commission of the Consultation on Church Union. He has taught at the Interdenominational Theological Center, Howard University School of Religion, and Hartford Seminary. Among his many publications are *"The Year of Jubilee": A Fifty-Two Week Bible Study on the Gospel of Luke* (Gilliland, 1999) and (as coeditor) *The New Testament and Psalms: A New Inclusive Version* (Oxford University Press, 1995).

Cleophus J. LaRue is Francis Landey Patton Associate Professor of Homiletics at Princeton Theological Seminary, Princeton, New Jersey. He is the author of *This Is My Story: Testimonies and Sermons of Black Women in Ministry* (Westminster John Knox, 2005); *Power in the Pulpit: How America's Most Effective Black Preachers Prepare Their Sermons* (Westminster John Knox, 2002), and *The Heart of Black Preaching* (Westminster John Knox, 2000).

Lloyd A. Lewis is Molly Laird Downs Professor of New Testament at Virginia Theological Seminary, Alexandria, Virginia. He has written contributions to *Christ and His Communities: Essays in Honor of Reginald H. Fuller* (Forward Movement Publications, 1990) and *Stony the Road We Trod: African American Biblical Interpretation* (Fortress Press, 1991).

James Earl Massey is Dean Emeritus and Distinguished Professor-at-Large at Anderson University School of Theology in Anderson, Indiana. He is the author of *Stewards of the Story: The Task of Preaching* (Westminster John Knox, 2006); *Studies in the Tuskegee Chapel: Selected Sermons* (Abingdon, 2000); *The Burdensome Joy of Preaching* (Abingdon, 1998); *The Soul Under Siege: Dealing with Temptation* (Asbury, 1987); *Spiritual Disciplines* (Asbury, 1985); *Designing the Sermon: Order and Movement in Preaching* (Abingdon, 1980); *The Sermon in Perspective: A Study of Communication and Charisma* (Baker, 1976); *The Responsible Pulpit* (Warner, 1974); and *The Hidden Disciplines* (Warner, 1972).

Guy Nave is Assistant Professor of Religion at Luther College, Decorah, Iowa. He is the author of *The Role and Function of Repentance in Luke-Acts* (Society of Biblical Literature, 2002).

James A. Noel is H. Eugene Farlough Jr. California Professor of African American Christianity at San Francisco Theological Seminary, San Francisco, California. He is coeditor of *The Passion of the Lord: African American Reflections*, Facets (Fortress Press, 2005).

Rodney S. Sadler Jr. is Associate Professor of Bible at Union Theological Seminary and Presbyterian School of Christian Education at Charlotte, in Charlotte, North Carolina. He is the author of *Can a Cushite Change His Skin? An Examination of Race, Ethnicity, and Othering in the Hebrew Bible* (T. & T. Clark, 2005) and the managing editor of *The African American Devotional Bible* (Zondervan, 1996).

Boykin Sanders is Professor of New Testament and Greek at the Samuel DeWitt Proctor School of Theology, Virginia Union University, Richmond, Virginia. He is the author of *Blowing the Trumpet in Open Court: Prophetic Judgment and Liberation* (Africa World Press, 2002).

About the Contributors

Thomas B. Slater is Professor of New Testament at McAfee School of Theology, Mercer University, Atlanta, Georgia. He is the author of *Christ and Community: A Socio-Historical Study of the Christology of Revelation* (Sheffield, 1999).

Abraham Smith is Professor of New Testament at Perkins School of Theology, Southern Methodist University, Dallas, Texas. He is coeditor of *New Interpreter's Annotated Study Bible* (Abingdon, 2003) and *Slavery in Text and Interpretation*, Semeia (Society of Biblical Literature, 1998), and author of *Comfort One Another: Reconstructing the Rhetoric and Audience of 1 Thessalonians* (Westminster John Knox, 1995).

Mitzi J. Smith is Assistant Professor of New Testament and Early Christian Origins, Ashland Theological Seminary, Detroit. Her dissertation, "The Function of the Jews, Women, and Charismatic Others in Narrative Instabilities in the Acts of the Apostles," was completed in 2005.

Raquel St. Clair is Executive Minister of St. James African Methodist Episcopal Church and Director of the St. James Christian Learning Center in Newark, New Jersey. She is coauthor of *The African Presence in the Bible: Gospel Sermons Rooted in History* (Judson, 2000).

Monya A. Stubbs is Assistant Professor of New Testament at Austin Theological Seminary, Austin, Texas. She is coauthor of *The Gospel of Matthew: A Contextual Introduction for Group Study* (Abingdon, 2003).

Demetrius K. Williams is Associate Professor at Tulane University, New Orleans, Louisiana. He is the author of *An End to This Strife: The Politics of Gender in African American Churches* (Fortress Press, 2004) and *"Enemies of the Cross of Christ": The Terminology of the Cross and Conflict in Philippians* (Sheffield, 2002).

Vincent L. Wimbush is Professor of Religion at Claremont Graduate University, Claremont, California. He is the director of the Institute for Signifying Scriptures. He is the author of *The Bible and African Americans: A Brief History*, Facets (Fortress Press, 2003); editor of *African Americans and the Bible: Sacred Texts and Social Textures* (Continuum, 2000, 2001), *The Bible and the American Myth* (Mercer University Press, 1999), and *Ascetic Behavior in Greco-Roman Antiquity* (Fortress Press, 1994); and coeditor of *Asceticism* (Oxford University Press, 1995, 2003) and *Asceticism and the New Testament* (Routledge, 1999).

ABBREVIATIONS

AB	Anchor Bible
ABD	*Anchor Bible Dictionary*. Edited by D. N. Freedman. 6 vols. New York, 1992.
ACNT	Augsburg Commentaries on the New Testament
AME	African Methodist Episcopal
AnBib	Analecta biblica
AThR	*Anglican Theological Review*
BDAG	Bauer, W., F. W. Danker, W. F. Arndt, and F. W. Gingrich. *Greek-English Lexicon of the New Testament and Other Early Christian Literature*. 3rd ed. Chicago: University of Chicago Press, 1999.
COGIC	The Church of God in Christ
ExpTim	*Expository Times*
HBC	*Harper's Bible Commentary*. Edited by J. L. Mays et al. San Francisco, 1988.
HSM	Harvard Semitic Monographs
HTR	*Harvard Theological Review*
Int	*Interpretation*
JAAR	*Journal of the American Academy of Religion*
JBL	*Journal of Biblical Literature*
JFSR	*Journal of Feminist Studies in Religion*
JITC	*Journal of Interdenominational Theological Center*
JNES	*Journal of Near Eastern Studies*
JRT	*Journal of Religious Thought*
JSNT	*Journal for the Study of the New Testament*
JSNTSup	Journal for the Study of the New Testament: Supplement Series
JSOTSup	Journal for the Study of the Old Testament: Supplement Series
KJV	King James Version
LCL	Loeb Classical Library
LXX	Septuagint

▦ Abbreviations

MFDP	Mississippi Freedom Democratic Party
NEB	New English Bible
NAB	New American Bible
NIB	*The New Interpreter's Bible*
NIV	New International Version
NovT	*Novum Testamentum*
NRSV	New Revised Standard Version
NTS	*New Testament Studies*
RevExp	*Review and Expositor*
RSV	Revised Standard Version
SBLDS	Society of Biblical Literature Dissertation Series
SCLC	Southern Christian Leadership Conference
TDNT	*Theological Dictionary of the New Testament.* Edited by G. Kittel and G. Friedrich. Translated by G. W. Bromiley. 10 vols. Grand Rapids, Mich.: Eerdmans, 1964–1976.
WBC	World Biblical Commentary
WW	*Word and World*

INTRODUCTION

Brian K. Blount, Cain Hope Felder, Clarice J. Martin, & Emerson B. Powery

"What if the reading of and thinking about the Bible . . . were read through African American experience?"[1] That is precisely the question this commentary intends to answer. In his recent volume, *African Americans and the Bible: Sacred Texts and Social Textures*, Vincent L. Wimbush offers a particular answer that also serves as one of the primary rationales for this work:

> I suggest foregrounding African American experience for the study of the Bible not because the African American experience is the one experience that finally and alone is somehow the morally right focus that will lead all to the *right* interpretation of the Bible. Nor do I advance it for the sake of ethnic cheerleading or as privi-leged insight or wisdom for the privileged few of a certain hue. What it represents is a challenge to the still largely unacknowl-edged interested, invested, racialized, culture- and ethnic-specific practice of [Eurocentric] biblical interpretation that is part of an even larger pattern of such interpretation of literatures and of history in the West.[2] (his italics)

We share that desire to challenge the largely Euro-American interpretive perspec-tive that continues to orient other one-volume biblical commentaries. Just as *The Women's Bible Commentary* was able to open up pro-vocative new possibilities for engaging the biblical writings through a unique *gender* lens, and just as the *Global Bible Commentary* has more recently interrogated the biblical texts through a variety of international voices, so our commentary engages the New Testament historically, socially, politically, and existentially through a very particular and unique *African American* lens.[3]

In 1993, Cornel West published an influential little book called *Race Matters*. West considered matters of race, but even more importantly, he reinforced the social and political thesis that race matters in the lives of individual persons and communities of people. No matter how much we hear talk of social progress, of color-blind folk and institutions, of economic advances for many middle and upper-middle class folk in ethnic and racial minorities; no matter how much we hear that the political, social, and economic playing fields are level, most persons who experience the color line personally from the minority side know that even as we anticipate the hope and promise of a new century, race *still* matters.

Space—sociocultural space—also matters. For many of us who read and interpret the texts that arise out of our biblical heritage, this thesis must be one of the primary principles by which we conduct our Christian lives

- lest, for example, we become convinced that because one is an offspring of Ham, he or she is condemned to a life of secondary and even subhuman status;
- lest, for example, we become convinced that, because an ancient author first wrote it and politically, economically, and racially interested Christians later believed and endorsed it, slaves should be obedient to their human masters as unto Christ;
- lest, for example, we become convinced that reading the Bible through the lens of African American history and culture is an illegitimate *reading into* (*eisegesis*) rather than an objective *reading out of* (*exegesis*) the text;

- lest, for example, we remain convinced somehow that the method-driven historical and critical readings of the Bible by white European and American scholars are disinterested, unbiased explorations, inoculated from the influence of those scholars' cultural and historical circumstances;
- lest, as a result, whole communities of people come to the biblical stories and find that their being and history have no place there because the stories only really make sense when they are read from the perspective of an academic, religious, and political mainstream haunted by few of the same concerns that threaten African American lives daily.

Space matters. Where we come from and who we are influence how we read the Bible and how we translate it theologically so that it becomes meaningful and effective in our lives. The alternative to this kind of understanding is that only *one* space matters, namely, the space occupied by those in positions of privilege and power, who claim that there is only one meaning in the Bible and that *they* have the tools to unearth it. They would have us believe it is a mere and fortuitous coincidence that the meaning they unearth is a meaning that applies to the needs and concerns of the space they happen to occupy.

We are protesting here the dominant paleontological perspective on biblical interpretation—or to put it more simply, the dog-and-bone theory of exegesis. On this view, meaning is like a fossil, or to bring it closer to home, like a bone that a dog buries in the back yard. The interpreter is the person who digs it up. When the interpreter lifts it up for the world to see, everyone can agree: *that's a bone*. Meaning, then, is the bone buried in the biblical text. All one need do is find the right shovel to dig it up. The idea is simple: exegetical methods are like shovels. Once one takes hold of the *right* shovel—no matter who one is, what community one belongs to, or what history one has lived—one will find the same bone that everyone from every other community or history has found, is finding, and ever will find. Even though the people doing the digging may look radically different, the bone itself will always look to each of them exactly the same.

This nefarious approach to biblical interpretation has been deployed through both church and academy against contemporary communities. Peasants in Latin America were told that biblical language both guaranteed theological justification for their impoverished existence and condemned the kinds of social and political strategies that would be necessary to challenge the systems that oppressed them. Slaves in the American North and South were taught that the Bible justified their lot in life; that God not only backed their "peculiar" situation, but encouraged it so forcefully that being religious became synonymous with being happy with one's enslavement. Through periods of reconstruction, segregation, the Civil Rights Movement, desegregation, voting rights, and demands for political empowerment, African Americans have challenged such historically and critically "objective" strategies of biblical interpretation, which remain hostile to their faith perspective and hazardous to their physical well-being. Indeed, like the slaves who, through songs and banned backwoods sermons, preached a message of liberation out of the same Bible that slaveowners and their hired evangelists proclaimed as the divine endorsement of slavery, contemporary African Americans are seeing more clearly, through their own contexts, biblical truths that the dominant biblical scholarship has heretofore refused to reveal.

Why does this sort of contextual revelation continue to meet resistance? Because

one broad community claimed the authority to privilege its own perspective on the Bible as THE accurate way to read the text and reflect theologically upon it. The "bones" its interpreters found became the bones *every* successfully objective interpreter *had* to find; otherwise, the interpreter was simply not digging the right way.

Space matters. In his book *Philosophy of Liberation*, Enrique Dussel writes: "I am trying, then, to take space, geopolitical space, seriously. To be born at the North Pole or in Chiapas is not the same thing as to be born in New York City."[4] It certainly is not. Persons born in such spaces will experience life differently. They will also read and interpret the Bible differently.

Dussel recognizes, however, that all perspectives are not considered equal when a determinative interpretation has been formulated. Instead, a collective perspective on the part of those who maintain political and numerical superiority becomes the "official" one. Minority opinions may be entertained, but they are seldom included as resources for any kind of programmatic standardization of rules and regulations. In other words, they lack political legitimation and, therefore, power.

Space is not a value-free concept. Social space has implications. The space we inhabit, where we live, has an impact on how we think, even on what we think. And whether one is in a "central" space or a "peripheral" space makes a world of difference. A person who lives in a Camden, New Jersey, slum inhabits a different space from that of a person who lives and works on Wall Street. They not only think differently but have different things to think about. And if by chance what they think and how they think should enter into conflict, *whose thought* would be considered by mainstream American society to be the most acceptable?

Space always has societal and political value. That is why theologians who perceive and think theologically through historical and cultural lenses like those of African Americans are often received skeptically by mainstream theologians. We contend, with Dussel, that it is not the case (though this is often enough alleged) that their conclusions are inappropriate and incorrect; the problem rather is that from the perspective of the mainstream, *they think from the wrong space.*

Our work in this volume directly challenges that perspective. The Euro-American, scientific, systematic, exegetical, and philosophical community has no interpretive privilege or advantage. That community, too, provides readings influenced by the space it occupies. Its readings of the biblical texts, then, are not more accurate interpretations of biblical texts; they are simply more privileged ones. *All* communities read from *their* space, interpret the text in ways that are meaningful for *their* space, and hear sermons preached and lessons taught listening for themes that will be applicable to *their* space. Any church, and the scholars and clergy who lead it, that does not operate biblically from its *own* context—its *own* space—is not a church that operates in an objective, historical manner; it is a church that adopts the contextual perspective of some other interpretive community. In so doing, such a church privileges that other community as though that other community were the gatekeeper to accurate biblical interpretation. In this work, therefore, it is our endeavor to listen for New Testament themes that speak to African American space.

But our project is about more than raising a critical intellectual and interpretive challenge. It is also about filling a void. The black church remains one of the most spiritually vital, politically successful, economically powerful, and socially transformative institutions in the African American community. And it is, as it has always been, most profoundly biblically based. In their highly regarded 1990

work on the black church, C. Eric Lincoln and Lawrence Mamiya found that African Americans donate more than 75 percent of all their charitable giving to the black church, and contribute more than 35 percent of their volunteer time to it. Those numbers translate into two billion dollars' worth of plate offerings and thirty-five billion dollars' worth of valued time. The economic numbers alone, however, do not tell the full story. Lincoln and Mamiya also found that the commitment of African Americans to religion and religious institutions consistently outranks that of other ethnicities in the United States. Seventy-eight percent of African Americans are "churched," and 37 percent are "superchurched." The weekly church attendance rates of African Americans was found to stand at 43 percent.[5] Clearly, African Americans who make up 12.8 percent of the total U.S. population, a raw figure of approximately 38 million, are a highly churched people.[6] Their involvement with a biblical faith would tend to confirm that they have at least as much interest in the biblical materials as in the institution based upon it. Given the thousands of Bible studies that take place in African American communities daily, a one-volume commentary from an African American perspective would seem to be a valuable and necessary resource.

It is most intriguing, then, that in the many centuries from that "red letter" year of 1619, when the first African slave was officially driven onto American soil at Jamestown, Virginia, to 2006, not a single one-volume commentary on the entire New Testament from the African American perspective has ever been produced. In 1993, Cain Hope Felder provided a step in this direction with the publication of *The Original African Heritage Study Bible*, which provides selected annotations on verses highlighting Africa and biblical characters of African descent. As readers of this volume will see, African American interpreters now bring questions from their African American space that shape new and provocative meanings from all these ancient texts. This commentary, like all one-volume commentaries, provides reflections on each of the separate New Testament books in canonical order.

We begin, however, by first considering several broad thematic issues sparked by questions generated from our African American space.

Certainly, for an African American, the matter of slavery is one of utmost historical importance. African American slaves are at the foundation of the Christian experience in the United States. Their tenacious faith in the liberating Exodus power that God demonstrated through the life, death, and resurrection of Jesus of Nazareth was one of the primary sources, if not *the* primary source of their endurance and resistance through centuries of wretched dehumanization. The biblical story not only fostered the hopes of the famous heroes of the tradition like Harriet Tubman, but generated the apocalyptic fervor of preachers like Nat Turner, and sustained the physical as well as spiritual being of millions of unnamed Africans enslaved on American soil. How could a volume envisioned by those who live in their courageous wake not ask questions about the matter of slavery in the early Christian church? Mitzi J. Smith offers the historical observation that slavery in the early church, as reflected through the New Testament writings, must be understood against the backdrop of Greco-Roman slavery in general. She concludes that "ancient Roman slavery ideology that required absolute submission and unyielding loyalty from slaves and freedpersons is reflected in the New Testament." Reading through their own historical lens, African American interpreters have either directly challenged such texts and the thinking behind them, or reinterpreted such texts

through the lens of more liberating New Testament materials.

Thinking even more broadly, but still about the first-century period in which Christianity found its genesis, Rodney Sadler considers the place and role of Africa and African imagery in the New Testament, introducing readers to a significant African presence that has previously been invisible to many African American churchgoers.

Knowing that the history between the writings of Paul and the sensibilities of the African American community has often been strained, Abraham Smith explains why and offers a rich introduction into the "enigma" of Paul and his place in African American text interpretation. In the end, he suggests, the "outsider" apostle has much to offer a people too often relegated to the American margins.

Vincent L. Wimbush begins his article on alternative hermeneutical approaches by critiquing commentary projects like this one because the very form limits how readers can approach the topics under their consideration. By definition, he notes, commentaries force interpreters to read not from their own context, but from the re-constructed context of the text itself. He challenges readers "to think differently about and orient ourselves differently around interpretation." This is a task the authors of the commentary sections of this volume have gladly undertaken. Though we maintain the form of commentary, we attempt to break through the limits established by that form in just the way Wimbush exhorts—by orienting our interpretations around our own African American selves.

Raquel St. Clair narrates how race, class, and gender have intersected in the context in which womanist scholars engage the New Testament materials.

Cleophus J. LaRue surveys the work of African American preachers and finds that when they are at their imaginative best, they recognize that it is not only their own context, but also that of those who hear the word that is important.

James A. Noel recognizes that a cultural investigation of the New Testament is not limited to the written word. He explores, with the aid of fine examples of African American art, how African American folk culture has operated through artistic inspiration to bring rich, new meanings to the biblical story.

The commentary sections follow a similar, though not uniform structure. Each chapter reflects on the designated text with the affirmation that African American space matters, presenting the special theological and ethical emphases that the biblical book receives from an African American perspective. These emphases play a significant role in influencing the questions the authors ask of the text and, therefore, the answers the authors receive. The bulk of each chapter is commentary on the biblical book. Short bibliographies for further study are also provided.

Because African American space matters in the work of biblical interpretation, we want to pay tribute here to the highly trained African American interpreters of the New Testament who are now working in universities, seminaries, and churches across the United States. Though many of them have in some way participated in this volume, there are others who either were unable because of (happily!) too many publishing commitments, administrative duties, or ecclesial commitments, or had not yet finished their doctoral training when this project began. In regard to the latter group, because we knew their dissertations must be their primary objective, we resisted the temptation to invite yet more work from them. We want you to know who they all are and where they trained for the important work that lies before them and all of us. We therefore offer at the end of this volume a list of African American Ph.D.s in New

Testament study. We have made every effort to be as exhaustive and as up to date as possible, and pray fervently that after our research we have not omitted anyone's name. Through simple library or bookstore searches, readers can find these authors' works and take advantage of their scholarly acumen. Their work will offer not only the excellence expected from persons so highly trained, but also a contextual perspective that will add a unique window into the New Testament materials they survey. That window promises a unique look precisely because African American space matters.

Finally, we would like to comment on the title of this volume, *True to Our Native Land*. To many of our readers, that title needs no explanation. It is, of course, the last line in the final stanza of James Weldon Johnson's "Lift Ev'ry Voice and Sing." Originally written in 1899 and set to music by James Weldon's brother, John Rosamond Johnson, this hymn was performed by schoolchildren at an annual celebration of Abraham Lincoln's birthday. Since then it has taken on a history of its own, coming to be known most affectionately as the "Black National Anthem."

This anthem is promptly developing an effective history within African American biblical scholarship as well. In 1991, Cain Hope Felder edited a collection of essays by African American scholars titled *Stony the Road We Trod*, words derived from the second stanza of Johnson's hymn. Indeed, stony the road has been. "Somehow," Felder explained, "these words seem to epitomize our struggle as African American scholars who have made biblical interpretation a daily vocational struggle." In his introduction, Felder shared some of the contributors' testimonies to this "stony" path. In 2003, Randall Bailey selected *Yet with a Steady Beat*, also from the second stanza of Johnson's lyrics, as the title of a collection of essays from a new generation of African American scholars. This *Semeia* volume represents, in Bailey's words, "the persistent march of our people on the 'Freedom Trail.'"

By titling our commentary *True to Our Native Land*, we recognize continuity with those who have preceded us in African American biblical scholarship. Indeed, several of them—including two of our editors—contributed in significant ways to those earlier collections. We stand proudly and boldly in that tradition. Furthermore, this title depicts well our desire that this publication, as a labor of love, may continue our struggle of interpreting the biblical texts in a way that is sensitive to our own heritage, that is, *True to Our Native Land*.

> *Shadowed beneath Thy hand,*
> *May we forever stand.*
> *True to our God,*
> *True to our native land.*

Notes

1. Vincent L. Wimbush, ed., *African Americans and the Bible: Sacred Texts and Social Texture* (New York and London: Continuum, 2000), 8.
2. Ibid.
3. Carol A. Newsom and Sharon H. Ringe, eds., *Women's Bible Commentary* (Louisville: Westminster John Knox, 1998). Daniel Patte, gen. ed., *Global Bible Commentary* (Nashville: Abingdon, 2004).
4. Enrique Dussel, *Philosophy of Liberation,* trans. Aquilina Martinez and Christine Morkovsky (Maryknoll, N.Y: Orbis, 1985), 2.
5. C. Eric Lincoln and Lawrence H. Mamiya, *The Black Church in the African American Experience* (Durham: Duke University Press, 1990), 260–61.
6. Figures calculated from 2004 U.S. Census Bureau Reports. Entire U.S. population as of 2005 estimated at 296,410,404. See http://quickfacts.census.gov/qfd/states/00000.html.

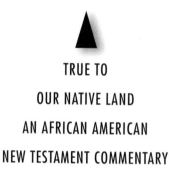

TRUE TO

OUR NATIVE LAND

AN AFRICAN AMERICAN

NEW TESTAMENT COMMENTARY

AFRICAN AMERICAN
BIBLICAL INTERPRETATION

SLAVERY *in the* EARLY CHURCH

Mitzi J. Smith

> If we are free, then I don't think you're supposed to tell
> me how much of my freedom I'm supposed to have.
> —**Fannie Lou Hamer**[1]

INTRODUCTION

The pervasive significance of slavery in the first century of the Common Era is reflected in the numerous references to slavery woven throughout the New Testament. These references reflect the social reality of ancient slaves and slave ideologies. For example, some parables in the Synoptic Gospels (Mark, Matthew, and Luke), such as the parable of the wicked tenants and the slaves dispatched to collect the master's share of the crops, portray slaveowners who expect loyalty and conscientious subservience and who violently punish noncompliant slaves. Such narrative portrayals have aroused relatively little objection among African Americans. African Americans have historically focused critically on Pauline texts containing slave mandates.

Paul's metaphorical use of slavery and slavery/freedom, slave/master polarities demonstrates that he is a man of his times. Orlando Patterson asserts that "Paul neither defended nor condemned the system of slavery, for the simple reason that in the first-century Roman imperial world in which he lived the abolition of slavery was intellectually inconceivable, and socially, politically and economically impossible."[2] At times Paul seems unable to empathize with the slave's socially and physically annihilating condition. For example, Paul arguably advises slaves and circumcised or uncircumcised men to be content with their present state (1 Cor 7:21). He also

11

returns the "runaway slave" Onesimus to his master, Philemon, whom Paul diplomatically urges to embrace Onesimus "no longer as a slave . . . but a beloved brother" (Philem 16) Whether one contends that Onesimus was a potential "apprentice to Paul" for gospel ministry, a runaway slave, or Philemon's brother, Onesimus's lack of agency is clear.[3] He has no voice and no say in the matter of his return.

The apparent ambiguity of Paul's position on the institution of slavery in the first century and the use of Pauline texts to support modern pro-slavery ideologies have caused concern for many African Americans. One of the most quoted examples is the outright rejection of the Pauline corpus, except for 1 Corinthians 13 (the "love chapter"), by Howard Thurman's illiterate grandmother. In spite of Paul's use of slave–master relations as a metaphor for the Christian's relationship to Jesus, and in spite of Paul's rhetorical attempts to equalize relations between slaves and freeborn persons (i.e., Gal 3:28, "there is no longer slave or free . . . in Christ Jesus . . ."), the apostle, because of "accommodation to the slave regime signaled elsewhere in the Pauline corpus," remained unacceptable reading in the Thurman household.[4] Thurman's grandmother, a former slave, recalled that the white minister whom the master commissioned to preach to the slaves three or four times a year always recited the Pauline text, "Slaves, be obedient to them that are your masters . . . as unto Christ." Even in freedom, Thurman's grandmother vowed she would never read from "that part of the Bible."[5]

GRECO-ROMAN SLAVERY IN GENERAL

We must understand New Testament references to slavery and freedom against the historical backdrop of Greco-Roman slavery.

The slave population in the Roman Empire included any and all peoples whom the Romans conquered, for example, Syrians, Jews, Egyptians, Ethiopians, Thracians, and Asians. Romans rarely enslaved other Romans. "The earliest Roman law code explicitly provided that if a Roman was subject to enslavement as a punishment, [she or he] had to be sold abroad."[6] Yet slave breeding, kidnapping, infant exposure (the abandonment of and sale of infants into slavery), and the selling of oneself or one's family members for the payment of debts all augmented the slave population.

The slave population consisted of two types of slaves (*servi*) distinguished by the tasks they performed. Agricultural slaves who resided in rural districts of the city (*polis*) were called *rustici*. *Rustici* performed duties associated with the cultivation and maintenance of the land. They accounted for the vast majority of slaves. *Rustici* lived "in relative seclusion, at subsistence or near subsistence level" with few prospects for social mobility.[7] Bailiffs (*vilici*) were farm managers responsible for the oversight of *rustici* (similar to overseers on southern American slave plantations). A second type were domestic slaves (*urbani*) who generally served in households of the city districts of the *polis*. *Urbani* were responsible for maintaining the family and the household.

SLAVE IDEOLOGY AND TREATMENT

Regardless of whether slaves served in the *pater familias* (ordinary patriarchal Roman household) or in the *Familia Caesaris* (Caesar's/ruler's household), the master expected absolute loyalty and submission from them. Slaveowners required that slaves put their master's welfare above their own well-being. The objective of both "humane" and inhumane treatment of slaves was to assure the physical and economic well-being of the master and his household. Slavery served to "validate and enhance the status of those who were free."[8]

Slavery under the Roman Empire was no different from other slave societies in the cruel and inhumane treatment of slaves. Seneca wrote that "we Romans are excessively haughty, cruel, and insulting" in the treatment of slaves.[9] Vedius Pollio, a friend of Emperor Augustus, punished his slaves with impunity by feeding them to his lamprey (bloodsucking fish).[10] Slaveowners regularly forced slaves and criminals to fight against gladiators and wild beasts in the arena.[11] Even the passing of legislation against cruel treatment of slaves did not dramatically alleviate arbitrary cruel treatment of slaves.[12] Slaveowners, not slaves, determined what constituted extreme cruelty.

Some utilitarian slaveowners encouraged the fair treatment of their slaves in ways that might maximize their investment. Columella (middle to late first century C.E.), the family agriculturalist, advised that rural slaves (*rustici*) should be cared for and clothed to enhance their "usefulness" rather than their appearance. Slaves' clothing should protect them from the "wind, cold, and rain" so that no matter how "unbearable" the weather, they might be able to work in the field uninterrupted. Slaveowners admonished overseers to restrain themselves when dealing with slaves. The overseer should exact the necessary labor from slaves without resorting to "cruelty," for slaves "when smarting under cruelty and greed . . . are more to be feared."[13] The extent to which Columella's advice was heeded is not known.

Many slaveowners attempted to achieve the optimum usefulness from their slaves by doling out concessions or benefits (*beneficium*). These concessions or benefits for slave loyalty (*fides*) and obedience (*obsequium*) ranged from permission to enter into de facto marriages to the promise of manumission. Slaveowners rewarded "unusually prolific"

females slaves who gave birth to a certain number of children with "exemption from work and sometimes even freedom after they reared many children," and perhaps were no longer physically able to bear children.[14] After a slave woman bore three sons, she might be exempted from work; for bearing more than three sons, she might be manumitted. Such anticipation contributed to the profitability of the estate.[15]

Some slaveowners found it beneficial to educate their slaves in certain occupations so as to produce a more economically viable commodity. For instance, Cicero trained some of his slaves to be scribes. The slaves and freedmen of Cicero about whom we have any record "are almost always administrative staff, such as secretaries and literary assistants," and letter carriers.[16] Of the slaves Cicero freed, "some left Cicero and some worked for him temporarily, occasionally, or permanently."[17] Cicero set high standards for manumission. In order to be considered for manumission, Cicero's slaves had to demonstrate loyalty, devotion, and culture.

> In Cicero's house a high standard of education made for efficiency in the master's work. A contribution of that kind meant that the value of the man's work was increased, rather than diminished, by manumission. For the master could to some extent compel the freedman's continued service and to a great extent make it desirable for his ex-slave to go on working for him.[18]

We have the "most intimate knowledge" about one of Cicero's freedmen named Tiro. The quantity of work he performed for Cicero was "phenomenal" both before and after his manumission.[19] Highly trained freedmen like Tiro were more useful to their masters. "The patronage of a man like Cicero also gave his freedmen the entrée to the society of other Romans in cultured or political circles, *not as equals but as friends and clients.*"[20]

SOCIAL MOBILITY AND THE SLAVE/FREEDPERSON

A slave was a slave and seldom more than a slave regardless of the position she or he held or any material wealth amassed or how much she or he contributed to the master's wealth. A hierarchy of "estates" existed in the Roman empire (early and late), which from top down consisted of "senatorial and equestrian orders, the free-born plebs [common masses] and rural peasantry, the slave-born freedmen (*liberti*) and those still of slave status (*servi*)."[21] However, juridical status was not always an indicator of social status. Persons on the lower rung of the ladder with low juridical status could achieve higher social status based on training and/or education, position and wealth, and by being sold to a master of greater social rank. "Social mobility in Rome is thus seen as a process of status dissonance by which persons rate highly on some criteria of status, such as ability, achievement, wealth, but low on others, such as birth or legal condition."[22] This status dissonance is most striking among the slaves and freedpersons (*liberti*) in the household of Caesar (*Familia Caesaris*). Slaves and freedpersons in the imperial household possessed greater social status than their counterparts in the wider Roman Empire because of the elevated status of their master/ patron, the emperor. Imperial freedmen and slaves "had access to positions of power in the state which were totally inaccessible to other slaves and freedmen outside the *Familia*."[23]

Freedmen did not always hold higher posts than slaves. Two notable exceptions and examples of status dissonance in which slaves held higher positions than freedmen were the *dispensatores* and the *vicarii*.[24] As powerful financial officers the *dispensatores*, all of whom were slaves, supervised cash receipts and payment transactions. Slaves were deemed more suitable for these positions because the emperor could exercise greater control over the slave and thus over the monies. The *vicarii*, also slaves, were the assistants or deputies of the *dispensatores*. Thus, the *vicarii* were slaves of slaves (of the *dispensatores*). The *vicarii* wielded "considerable influence in the financial administration" and were destined to be promoted to the grade of *dispensatores*.[25] While these slaves experienced status dissonance relative to freedpersons, imperial freedpersons rarely experienced this same type of status dissonance relative to freeborn persons. In general the emperors refused to risk the alienation of the upper echelons of society by the "massive promotion of freedmen to equestrian dignity."[26] "Upward mobility between the equestrian and senatorial orders was regular and common, indeed inevitable."[27] But the upward mobility of imperial freedpersons to equestrian status, regardless of their higher status relative to most other slaves and freedpersons, constituted a mere trickle.[28]

THE AMBIGUITIES OF MANUMISSION

A freedperson did not automatically become a Roman citizen. In the first century C.E. a slave owner could manumit a slave and simultaneously confer Roman citizenship upon the freed slave by one of two legal instruments, (a) by *vindicate* (the rod or wand) through which the owner declared his or her intention before the appropriate magistrate or (b) by last will and testament. The *Lex Fufia Caninia* (2 B.C.E.) required that the specific names of slaves to be manumitted must be written in the will, and it limited the number of slaves a slaveowner could manumit at one time.[29] Formal manumission was subject to taxation, and this was a means by which the Roman state further exploited slavery to its own pecuniary advantage. The slave might be required to pay the price of manumission as well as the extra burden of the tax.[30]

In theory, manumission released the slave from involuntary bondage, but in practice the slave–master relationship continued wherein the freedperson did not rise above his or her inferior status to the former master and to most, if not all, freeborn persons. Legal obligations (*operae*) continued to bind freedpersons to their former masters. Under these obligations, the freedpersons were largely obligated to perform certain services for a specified period of time. The freedperson became the client of the former master (patron). Theoretically, this new relationship was to be characterized by mutual respect. If a freedperson's patron (former owner) fell into poverty, the freedperson was expected to support the patron. Any delinquency in performing services due to the patron could result in punishment or even a return to slavery.[31]

It is striking that in ancient sources freedpersons are often referred to as "the freedman/woman of" someone. The freedperson did not cease to be viewed in relation to the former master; she or he remained an extension of the former master.[32]

Freedpersons were also expected to maintain an air of humility before freeborn persons, especially their former masters, regardless of any higher economic or social status the slave achieved. In a speech, Nero boasts of the many gifts he lavished on Seneca, but he adds that "numbers of men, not comparable to you in character, have held more. Shame forbids me to mention the freedmen who flaunt a wealth greater than

yours!"[33] Susan Treggiari notes that "in the actual business of administration, Cicero . . . openly recommended the ancestral practice of using [the services of] one's own freedmen . . . because they could most easily be controlled. . . . But he recommended also that a magistrate's reliance on his freedmen should be discreet and not such as to give offence. . . . Unlike Sulla or Pompey, Cicero never offended by allowing his freedmen to make a display of their influence."[34]

Some elite members of Roman society believed that the threat of revocation of manumission should remain an option to guarantee that freedpersons should never forget their place in the order of things. Tacitus relates how the Senate, during Nero's reign, discussed the iniquities of freedpersons (*fraudibus libertorum*) and sought to give patrons (*patronis*) the right to annul a freedperson's manumission. The proposal attracted a number of supporters, but Nero's advisors were divided on the issue. Some urged that "insolence, grown harder with liberty, had reached a point where freedmen were no longer content to be equal before the law with their patrons, but mocked their tameness and actually raised their hands to strike [their patrons]" with impunity or with self-prescribed punishment. The supporters of the measure reasoned that it would place no greater burden on freedpersons to require that they retain their freedom by the same obedience that it was earned. "Notorious offenders" should be re-enslaved "so that fear might coerce those whom kindness had not reformed." The opponents argued that only the guilty freedperson should be punished and not the entire "class of freedmen," since certain administrative positions relied upon the abilities of the freed class. "If the freed were set apart, the paucity of the free would be apparent! . . . Two forms of manumission have been instituted in order to allow for a change of mind. 'All, whose patron had not liberated them by the wand, were still, it might be said, held by the bond of servitude.'" In the end, Nero commanded the Senate to consider each case individually.[35]

SLAVERY IDEOLOGY AND THE BIBLICAL TEXT

Ancient Roman slavery ideology that required absolute submission and unyielding loyalty from slaves and freedpersons is reflected in the New Testament. These reflections of the social reality of slavery and slave ideology are not limited to Pauline texts. But the Pauline and deuteropauline texts that mandate the submission of slaves and women certainly have evoked creative responses from African Americans, forcing us either to reinterpret oppressive texts or to find refuge, affirmation, and hope in other, more liberating texts.

Confronted with the potential obstacle of oppressive Pauline texts, African American women appropriated other texts to support God's call on their lives. The black feminist Baptist preacher and theologian Virginia Broughton understood Paul's assertion that the woman is the glory of the man to refer to women preconversion. Broughton supplemented her interpretation of Paul with the Joel prophecy in Acts 2:17 that both women and men would prophesy.[36] African American women engaged in the civil rights movement appropriated Luke 4:18 (which cites Isa 61:1-2), "the Spirit of the Lord is upon me," rather than acquiesce to Pauline mandates not to suffer a woman to teach a man. Black women appropriated Luke's recontextualization of Isa 61:1-2, which legitimated Jesus' ministry, to authorize their own calls to teach men and women how to read, to vote, to protest, and to publicly exercise their own prophetic voices.

Fannie Lou Hamer often quoted Luke 4:18 as divine authority for her own empowerment for ministry and for that of other Christians, as well as a testimony to the indissoluble link between Christ and freedom.[37]

As Allen Callahan points out, African Americans trumped one scripture with another, more liberating text:

> When Paul's anti-emancipatory pronouncements threatened to compromise the freedom he proclaimed in Christ Jesus, the words of the Christ were used to trump those of the servant, for Christ's sake. African American women were particularly constrained to use Scripture against Scripture to overcome the Pauline mandates that served as gag rules against their witness to the truth of Gospel.[38]

Certainly, many Pauline texts are ostensibly antithetical to the claims of Gal 3:28 and have been used to oppress women and others. But the Pauline texts are not the only texts that reinscribe and fail to challenge prevailing ancient slavery stereotypes and ideologies. For example, several parables in the Synoptic Gospels reinscribe ancient slave ideology. The parables about slave–master relationships promote proper servile behavior and condone severe punishment of noncompliant slaves.

Why is there not as much indignation expressed toward slave language in the Gospels as in the Pauline texts? Jennifer Glancy makes a helpful point: "Slavery in the parables typically functions metaphorically, representing the Christian's relationship to God. Perhaps because of this theological displacement, New Testament scholars have been slow to interrogate the ideology of slavery in the parables."[39]

The parable of the master/landlord who sends several slaves and then finally his son to collect his rent (Mark 12:1-12; Luke 20:9-19; Matt 21:33-46) reflects the social reality of the *pater familias*. The slave occupied the bottom tier of the household structure, below the master's children. It is well within conventional understandings of the hierarchical patriarchal household for the master to send his son, after all his slaves are beaten, stoned, or killed. After a proven pattern of dispatch and physical assault, the master sends his son to face potentially the same fate as his slaves. But the slaves are more expendable, which is reflected in the fact that they are sacrificed first. With each emissary, the master calculated the "opportunity cost," that is, the sacrifice necessary to gain access to his revenues. The potential monetary gain outweighed the loss of lives. Slaves were less than children, but both could be expendable.

As Glancy further points out, "The representation of the slave's body as the locus of abuse is thus pervasive in the Matthean parables, constituting the most prominent aspect of Matthew's ideology of slavery."[40] In the Matthean slave parables, slaves are rewarded for their loyalty, demonstrate "absolute corporal vulnerability," fear retribution, and are subject to attack by persons outside the household.[41] The reflection of first-century slave ideology in Matthew's Gospel does not necessarily mean Matthew condoned such treatment of slaves. But Matthew's "inscription of this image assumes and participates in the normalcy of such terror in slaves' lives. The Matthean parables liken divine punishment to a slave owner's punishment of his (or, presumably, her) slaves."[42]

In the case of the parable of the unforgiving slave whom the master/king forgave for "cooking the books" (Matt 18:23-31), the imperial slave is characterized as a *dispensator* entrusted with the financial responsibility of handling cash receipts and payments. When the books do not balance, the king/master resolves to sell the slave, his wife, and his children. However, after some pleading by the slave, the king decides to forgive the slave and presumably give him a second chance. The slave, however, adopting the less generous, more traditional ways of the master, demands payment from a fellow slave for a debt owed him. When news of the incident reaches the king via other slaves, the king, who is likened to God, tortures the slave until the debt is fully satisfied. The social reality of the dominant master/slave relationship is reinscribed in the parable as an exemplar for the Christian's relationship with God the Father.

In Luke's Gospel, the centurion who pleads with Jesus to heal his servant (Luke 7:2-10; cf. Matt 8:5-13) admits that when he orders his slave to perform certain tasks, he expects immediate and absolute compliance. The centurion demonstrates no real affection for the slave as an individual. When the centurion describes his slave as "highly valued" (*entimos*), he refers to the slave's socioeconomic value. The owner is eager for Jesus to heal his servant because of the loss of revenue resulting from the slave's sickness and inactivity. And Jesus heals the servant because of the master's "worthiness"—not the slave's. Luke's Jesus maintains the social boundaries between himself, the master, and the slave when he heals the slave.

In John 4:46b-53, the royal official's slaves meet him as he is returning home to check on his sick son, whom he had asked Jesus to heal. The slaves report the exact hour when the son was healed, and subsequently John reports that the "entire household believed." Such reports of household conversions that include slaves may not reflect voluntary slave conversions but may testify to the master's absolute control over his household (cf. Matt 10:24-25; Acts 10:1—11:14; 16:15, 31-33). Albert Harrill argues that the language of subordination in the household codes containing rules for both masters and slaves (Colossians, Ephesians, the *Didache*, the

Doctrina Apostolorum, and the *Epistle of Barnabas*) has a sociological origin in ideologies about "slave management widely diffuse in classical antiquity," particularly as promoted in ancient agricultural handbooks addressing household management.[43]

The writer of the Gospel of John also employs slave language to refer to the transformation of the relationship between Jesus and his disciples. The Johannine Jesus announced to his disciples, "I do not call you servants any longer . . . but . . . friends" (John 15:15). Similarly, the Persian king Cyrus the Great admonished some new captive slaves that if any of them behaved amicably toward their captors, "doing or teaching us something [new], we will embrace that one as a benefactor (*euergetēs*) and a friend (*philos*), not as a slave (*ouk hōs doulon*)."[44] As noted above, the labeling of a slave as a friend did not mean that she or he had attained equality with freeborn persons. Thus, John 15:15 may also reflect the social reality of the ancient slave.

In the Acts of the Apostles we find this same reflection of ancient slave ideology in depictions of slaves. Albert Harrill and Russell Morton have pointed out how the slave girl Rhoda (12:13-16) is representative of the comic stock character of the running slave who is so fickle as to forget the task at hand.[45] Rhoda's report that Peter, whom Herod had imprisoned, is at the door is met with the assertion that she is mad. Luke depicts Rhoda and the high priest's slave girl similarly (Luke 22:56) in recognition scenes involving Peter. In both cases their recognition is denied as false. These depictions reinforce notions of slave testimony as credible only under torture. Luke's characterizations of slaves are not meant to subvert stereotypes of slaves and masters.[46]

In Acts we also find the Pythian slave girl whom Paul rebukes simply because her repetitive oracle annoys him (16:16-19). The slave girl repetitively prophesies that Paul and Silas are "slaves of the Most High God." Perhaps what disturbs Paul most is that the slave girl identifies him as a fellow slave. Paul responds by exorcizing the spirit that inspires her speech, thereby destroying any hope of potential profits for her master. In reality such a reaction could also affect any potential profit to the slave. Masters sometimes set aside profits for a slave's use (*peculium*), which the slave could later use to purchase his/her freedom. The story reinscribes attitudes toward slaves as tools subject to arbitrary assaults by freeborn citizens.

African Americans must reconsider the appropriateness of master/slave language, biblical or extra-biblical, that reinscribes oppressive ideologies. African Americans must equally reject a "master/slave" mentality toward traditional scholarship that ignores the oppressive existential impact of such texts and repressive hermeneutics extracted from these texts. Brad R. Braxton is on point: "A liberating African American hermeneutic is not comfortable with a 'master-servant' relationship in the world of interpretation, even if by some coup or whim of fate African Americans were to become the 'master.'"[47] An African American hermeneutic will interrogate texts and interpretations by asking, "How does this text speak directly or indirectly to the struggle for being black in America?"[48]

God's intervention in history, through God's Spirit and through Jesus, reminds us, as James H. Cone declares, that God stands firmly on the side of the oppressed.[49] Slaves, ex-slaves, and their progeny can boldly demand to be treated *not* as slaves and *not* as freedpersons. In the context of the ambiguous and dissonant social status of the freedperson, "no longer slaves" is no longer emancipatory if it means we are to be considered as freedpersons. We are more than "freedpersons." This does not mean we erase the history of our ancestors. But, challenged and ignited by that history, we embrace the present possibility of full emancipation in Jesus Christ without the stigma of color prejudice, biases, and shackles of the past.

CONCLUSION

Slavery in first-century Roman society was no less cruel and inhumane than in any other slave society. Ancient Roman slavery was a self-serving institution in every respect. Slavemasters sought to instill a sense of loyalty, a self-negating work ethic, and a consciousness that the exercise of proper slave virtues could ultimately be rewarded with manumission. But this manumission, when (or if) conferred, did not necessarily mean absolute freedom for freedpersons.

In general the oppressive ideals of ancient Roman slavery are reinscribed upon some biblical texts. The social reality of ancient Roman slave ideology is reflected in biblical texts in spite of attempts by biblical authors to recontextualize master/slave relations in parables and other narratives by employing them as exemplars for the Christian's relationship with Jesus and/or God. African Americans have historically considered as offensive and unconscionable Pauline and deuteropauline texts mandating slaves to be content and servile in their legal status. African Americans have reinterpreted, trumped, and rejected such oppressive texts and the oppressive hermeneutical maneuvers that have relied on such texts. But African Americans must treat with suspicion other biblical texts, such as parable narratives that also reinscribe ancient slave/master ideology. Therefore, African Americans

- cannot uncritically appropriate metaphors for slavery just because they are theologically contextualized as part of exemplars for the Christian's relationship with Jesus and/or God.
- must acknowledge that legal emancipation is never the end of the story. Emancipation, de facto, existentially, is an ongoing struggle.
- must guard our own souls by refusing to adopt or reinscribe the enslaving ways of our former masters. Black men must learn to treat black women as equals in every aspect of black life. Black women and men cannot afford to step on each other in order to climb the corporate ladder or to step on others, of whatever race they may be, on the rung below us.
- should acknowledge the merit in Audre Lorde's admonition that "the master's tools will never dismantle the master's house."[50] But this affirmation should not presuppose that every tool the master uses belongs solely to or was conceived of or
— created by the master. When white slavemasters claimed sole authority over the Bible and its interpretation, our ancestors creatively seized and reappropriated some of the very tools the master used against them.

Notes

1. Bob Moses, "Mississippi Movement," *Southern Exposure* 9 (1981): 47. Fannie Lou Hamer was a social activist during the civil rights era. Among other things, Hamer served as field secretary of the Student Nonviolent Coordinating Committee (SNCC) and an officer of the Mississippi Freedom Democratic Party (MFDP).
2. Orlando Patterson, "Paul, Slavery and Freedom: Personal and Socio-Historical Reflections," *Semeia* 83/84 (2004): 266.

3. Most scholars argue that Onesimus was a runaway slave. Albert Harrill, *Slaves in the New Testament: Literary Social and Moral Dimensions* (Minneapolis: Fortress Press, 2006), 14, argues that Onesimus was an apprentice. Allen Dwight Callahan, *Embassy of Onesimus: The Letter of Paul to Philemon* (Valley Forge, Pa.: Trinity Press International, 1997), 69, contends that Onesimus was not a slave but Philemon's estranged brother.

4. Allen Dwight Callahan, "'Brother Saul': An Ambivalent Witness to Freedom," *Semeia* 83/84 (2004): 235.

5. Howard Thurman, *Jesus and the Disinherited* (Boston: Beacon, 1976), 30, 31. Howard Thurman was a mystic, preacher, and former Dean of Howard University's Rankin Chapel.

6. M. I. Finley, "The Extent of Slavery: M. I. Finlay [*sic*]," in *Slavery: A Comparative Perspective*, ed. Robin W. Winks (New York: New York University Press, 1972), 5–6.

7. Keith Bradley, *Slavery and Society at Rome* (Cambridge: Cambridge University Press, 1997), 71.

8. Ibid., 29.

9. Seneca, *Epistulae Morales* 47.11, trans. Richard M. Gummere, LCL. Seneca the Younger (4 B.C.E.–65 C.E.), a rhetorician and philosopher, served as chief advisor to Emperor Nero.

10. Joseph Vogt, *Ancient Slavery and the Ideal of Man* (Cambridge: Harvard University Press, 1975), 104.

11. Naphtali Lewis and Meyer Reinhold, eds., *Roman Civilization, Sourcebook II: The Empire* (New York: Harper & Row, 1966), 229.

12. Keith Bradley, *Slaves and Masters in the Roman Empire: A Study in Social Control* (Bruxelles: Latomus Revue d'Etudes Latines, 1984), 129.

13. Columella, *Rustica*, vol. 1, §1.8.9, 10, trans. Harrison Boyd Ash, LCL.

14. Ibid., §1.8.11, 16, 17.

15. Ibid., §1.8.18, 19.

16. Susan Treggiari, "The Freedmen of Cicero," *Greece and Rome* 16 (1969): 196.

17. Ibid., 197.

18. Ibid.

19. Ibid., 200.

20. Ibid., 202, emphasis added.

21. P. R. C. Weaver, "Social Mobility in the Early Roman Empire: The Evidence of the Imperial Freedmen and Slaves," *Past and Present* 37 (1967): 3.

22. Ibid.

23. Ibid., 5.

24. Ibid.

25. Ibid., 12–13.

26. Ibid., 17.

27. Ibid.

28. Ibid., 19.

29. Alan Watson, *Roman Slave Law* (Baltimore: Johns Hopkins University Press, 1987), 24–34. An owner of three to ten slaves could manumit up to one-half of them; an owner of eleven to thirty could manumit one-third; an owner of thirty-one to one hundred could manumit one-fourth at one time. A person owning one or two slaves had full freedom to manumit.

30. Bradley, *Slaves and Masters*, 104–6.

31. Lewis and Reinhold, *Roman Civilization, Sourcebook II*, 256.

32. Tacitus, *Annals*, 4.13.19, 44; 4.14.9; 4.15.35, 45, trans. William Jackson, LCL.

33. Ibid., 4.14.55.

34. Treggiari, "The Freedmen of Cicero," 203–4.

35. Tacitus, *Annals*, 4.13.26–27.

36. Evelyn Brooks Higginbotham, *Righteous Discontent: The Women's Movement in the Black Baptist Church, 1880–1920* (Cambridge: Harvard University Press, 1993), 133. Virginia Broughton, an 1875 graduate of Fisk University, is claimed to be the first woman of any race to earn a college degree from a southern institution.

37. Jacquelyn Grant, "Civil Rights Women: A Source for Doing Womanist Theology," in *Women in the Civil Rights Movement: Trailblazers and Torchbearers, 1941–1965*, ed. Vicki L. Crawford, Jacqueline Anne Rouse, and Barbara Woods (Bloomington: Indiana University Press, 1993), 45–46.

38. Callahan, "'Brother Saul'," 242. "African Americans have made a tacit distinction between these divergent Pauline registers

[Pseudo-Pauline correspondence such as Ephesians], but making a difference with a difference. Whereas German higher criticism has tended to privilege Paul's European correspondence over the Lukan portrait of Acts and the Asian letters, some black folks have given Luke's narrative profile pride of place. They have concurred with the Lukan insight that Paul was, after all, a man of suffering acquainted with grief" (244).

39. Jennifer A. Glancy, "Slaves and Slavery in the Matthean Parables," *JBL* 119 (2000): 68.

40. Ibid., 72.

41. Ibid., 73–81. One of Jesus' disciples severed the high priest's slave's ear (Matt 26:51; Mark 14:47; Luke 22:50; John 18:10). In Luke's Gospel, Jesus immediately restores the slave's ear (22:51). John's Gospel identifies the slave as Malchus.

42. Ibid., 82.

43. Harrill, *Slaves in the New Testament*, 97. Admonitions to individual masters to exert control over their households in obeisance to a "higher authority, were part of the control that non-household church leaders began to exert." Similarly, at 1 Tim 1:9-10 the author draws upon "characterization of stock criminals" in antiquity in polemics against his opponents; he does not attack the institution or slavery ideology (141).

44. Xenophon, *Cyropaedia,* 4.4.12, trans. Walter Miller, LCL.

45. Albert Harrill, "The Dramatic Function of the Running Slave Rhoda (Acts 12:13-16): A Piece of Greco-Roman Comedy," *NTS* 46 (2000): 150–57; Russell Morton, "Acts 12:1-12: Life in the Midst of Death," *Int* 55 (2001): 67–69.

46. Harrill, *Slaves in the New Testament*, 82, 83, argues that both Rhoda and the dishonest manager "are dramatic fictions of Roman slave comedy." "The dishonest manager functions as a catalyst for the recognition scene involving the more fragile and serious character of the rich man in the Lazarus parable."

47. Brad R. Braxton, *No Longer Slaves: Galatians and the African American Experience* (Collegeville, Minn.: Liturgical, 2002), 16.

48. Ibid., 20.

49. James H. Cone, *God of the Oppressed* (Maryknoll, N.Y.: Orbis, 1997).

50. Audre Lorde, *Sister Outsider: Essays and Speeches* (Berkeley: Crossing, 1984), 110–13.

For Further Reading

Bradley, Keith R. *Slavery and Society at Rome.* Cambridge: Cambridge University Press, 1994.

———. *Slave and Masters in the Roman Empire: A Study in Social Control.* Bruxelles: Latomus Revue d'Etudes Latines, 1984.

Braxton, Brad R. *No Longer Slaves: Galatians and African American Experience.* Collegeville, Minn.: Liturgical, 2002.

Callahan, Allen Dwight. "'Brother Saul': An Ambivalent Witness to Freedom." *Semeia* 83/84 (2004): 235–50.

———. *Embassy of Onesimus: The Letter of Paul to Philemon.* Valley Forge, Pa.: Trinity Press International, 1997.

Garnsey, Peter. *Ideas of Slavery from Aristotle to Augustine.* Cambridge: Cambridge University Press, 1996.

Glancy, Jennifer A. "Slaves and Slavery in the Matthean Parables." *JBL* 119 (2000): 67–90.

Harrill, J. Albert. *Slaves in the New Testament: Literary, Social, and Moral Dimensions.* Minneapolis: Fortress Press, 2005.

———. *The Manumission of Slaves in Early Christianity.* Tübingen: Mohr, 1995.

Jones, Amos, Jr. *Paul's Message of Freedom: What Does It Mean to the Black Church?* Valley Forge, Pa.: Judson, 1984.

Martin, Clarice J. "'Somebody Done Hoodoo'd the Hoodoo Man': Language, Power, Resistance, and the Effective History of Pauline Texts in American Slavery." *Semeia* 83/84 (2004): 203–34.

Patterson, Orlando. "Paul, Slavery and Freedom: Personal and Socio-Historical Reflections." *Semeia* 83/84 (2004): 263–79.

———. *Slavery and Social Death: A Comparative Study.* Cambridge: Harvard University Press, 1982.

Thurman, Howard. *Jesus and the Disinherited.* Boston: Beacon, 1976.

Treggiari, Susan. "The Freedmen of Cicero." *Greece and Rome* 16 (1969): 195–204.

The PLACE *and* ROLE *of* AFRICA *and* AFRICAN IMAGERY *in the* BIBLE

Rodney S. Sadler Jr.

If you open a concordance and look for the term *Africa* in the Bible, you would be disappointed to see that the term occurs not once in either the Old Testament or the New Testament. Similarly, there are no accounts of people who self-identify or are identified as "Africans" on the pages of scripture. From the perspective of contemporary biblical interpreters, this may appear to be an odd omission; after all, how could an entire continent, full of diverse peoples and important ancient cultures, which was apparently a stone's throw from the Holy Land, evade attention in the Bible?

Because the word *Africa* is not found in Scripture or in most scholarship addressing Scripture, some might suppose that the continent was considered an afterthought in the biblical narratives. This omission, however, is due not to Africa's unimportance but to at least two significant concerns. First, the continent was not yet called Africa. The name *Africa* may be derived either from Africanus, a late-third-century B.C.E. general of the Roman armies charged to pursue Hannibal to Carthage, or from a Berber tribe called the "Afri," the plural of the term "Afer." This group hailed from the North African region around what is now Libya. In either instance, one of these sources subsequently lent its name to the Roman colony that gave its name to the continent.

The latter theory raises questions about the connection of that North African ethnic group and the biblical group identified by their eponymous ancestor, a man called 'eper or "Epher" (*Apher* in Greek) from Gen 25:4. Biblical Epher was the son of Midian, himself a son of Abraham and his wife Keturah. Inasmuch as the provenance of the biblical group would likely be the deserts of North Africa, the Genesis account may reflect the same group. Such is the conclusion of the historian Josephus (ca. 37–100 C.E.), who in *Antiquities* 1:239–41 describes Epher, there transliterated Eophren/Ophren, making war against Libya. According to the historian, after Eophren conquered the region, it was identified by his name. Josephus also cites a work by Alexander Polyhistor (ca. 105–35 B.C.E.) wherein a similar account is related.

Second, because there was yet no continental designation "Africa," there could not have been any "Africans" identified as such. There could have been no biblical figures who would have identified themselves as African, because the term was not applied to the continent until the postbiblical period. During the biblical period, identity tended to be based on tribal and national identity markers; thus, it is unlikely that any biblical figure would have conceived of his or her identity with as universal a self-designation as "African." "Africa" and "Africans" are terms that would have been meaningless in the biblical period.

Nonetheless, the Bible highlights countless places and people that moderns would deem "African." Contemporary readers would consider many of the countries mentioned in the Bible—such as Cush, Ethiopia, Egypt, Seba, and Put—continental African nations because they are both fixed firmly on what we understand to be the African continent and populated by deeply pigmented people. These nations frequently recur in biblical narratives as allies and enemies of the people of Israel/Judah and their God. Similarly, nationals from these countries serve as heroes (e.g., Ebed-melech, Jer 38–39; Tirhakah, 2 Kgs 19:91;

Isa 37:9), villains (e.g., Pharaoh, Exod 1–19; Zerah, 2 Chr 14:9), and pivotal characters (e.g., Moses' Cushite wife, Num 12:1; David's Cushite courtier, 2 Sam 18:21-32) in many of the stories about the survival of YHWH's people.

AFRICA REDEFINED

Despite the absence of the name "Africa," nations within the borders traditionally ascribed to this continent are well represented in scripture. Nations such as Cush (translated as "Ethiopia" in many English versions of the Bible and also associated with the kingdom of Nubia), Egypt, Put, Seba, and Sheba tend to be identified as African nations by some Afrocentric scholars.[1] Such interpreters have compellingly demonstrated that Africa and Africans figure prominently on the pages of the Judeo-Christian scriptures, countering the impact of Eurocentric scholarship, which tends either to equate biblical characters with proto-Europeans or to overlook the contributions of African figures in the biblical story. Afrocentric scholars have tended to be conservative in their assessments of "Africanness," however, focusing on the aforementioned nations because of their geographical provenance in what is traditionally deemed Africa or because their people have distinctive "black" phenotypes.

The traditional boundaries for Africa and African people, however, may be too narrowly defined, curtailing the continent in the northeastern corner of Egypt, near the Sinai Peninsula. Due to certain geographical factors, there are legitimate reasons to question the validity of the traditional boundaries and to argue for the inclusion of the Levant as a part of continental Africa. Though it is deemed the bridge "between" Asia and Africa, rarely has Western scholarship seriously addressed the location of this region "within" Africa.[2]

Typically described as a narrative of the Levant, the Near East, or the Middle East, the story of the Bible unfolds principally in Africa. The land of Palestine actually sits on the two continental plates that comprise the African continent. The line where these plates converge is marked by an enormous valley, the Great Rift Valley, which begins in the north as the Jordan Valley and extends through the Red Sea as far south as Lake Tanganyika in southeastern Africa. Israel/Judah is on the African continental plate, as is the rest of the landmass west of the Jordan Rift, while Trans-Jordan is situated on the Arabo-Nubian continental plate. Consistent with this fact are the indigenous flora and fauna of Palestine, which are typical of African botanical and zoological forms. Similarly, climate and geology are also akin to other portions of the African continent.[3]

In fact, the designations "Near East" and "Middle East" are synthetic Eurocentric concepts, defining the world from the perspective of Europe. It is only from a European orientation that these imprecise designations have meaning. More problematic is the separation of not just Libya and Egypt but all of Palestine from its African context, as though the Near or Middle East was a continental unit unto itself. This tendency has made it more difficult to explore the commonalities between Israel/Judah and other African cultures, usually directing readers to assume greater cultural continuities between the biblical peoples and Mesopotamians.[4] Maps of the biblical world tend to reinforce such thinking, having as their southwestern extreme Lower Egypt, and rarely go beyond Upper Egypt as far as Cush. The result of this "de-Africanization" of the Bible has been the perpetuation of the myth of Africa as a primitive continent that has contributed little to the progress of the world or to the biblical narratives.

TRADITIONAL STRATEGIES FOR DISCERNING AFRICANNESS IN THE FIRST TESTAMENT

Although the term "Africa" does not occur as such in the Bible, there are a few typical strategies for addressing the role that Africa and Africans play in the First Testament. One strategy has been simply to deny that the Bible addresses Africa at all. Proponents of this opinion tend to deny that known African peoples in scripture are actually African, choosing instead to label them "Semitic" or "Near Eastern" to separate them from their contexts. Charles Copher deems this perspective either the "pre-Adamite" (i.e., blacks were the product of a failed pre-creation) or the "New Hamite view" (i.e., none of Ham's children were progenitors of black peoples) and emphasizes that adherents of these strategies generally viewed the Bible as void of nonwhites or, if they acknowledge a nonwhite population, it was only due to graphic depictions of the singular Cushites.[5] The principal result of this line of reasoning has been the creation of a zone devoid of continental affiliation, called the Near or Middle East. While this view has been helpful for demonstrating certain cultural continuities between Levantine societies over time, it has also served to isolate these peoples from other African cultures that share similar traits and social structures.

Another strategy, developed around the lineage of Noah's second son, Ham, introduced in Gen 10:6-20, is to determine that this line, and generally this line alone, pre-sents characters that moderns would deem African. Works emphasizing the Hamite origins of African peoples tend to misapply the anachronistic concept of "race" to the Bible, suggesting that the "Table of Nations" in Genesis 10 represents an accurate assessment of the development of human racial subspecies groups. Though this argument has proved useful to diaspora

Africans arguing for a "stolen legacy" of great-ness,[6] it has also been used by their ideological foes to justify their oppression.[7] By misappropriating the "Curse of Canaan" from Gen 9:18-27 and transforming it into a "Curse on Ham," Europeans were able to justify theologically the enslavement of all African people as Ham's descendants. The combination of these two passages, the biblical curse on a distinctive ethnic group and a genealogical table identifying the descendants of this group, has caused insurmountable harm to diaspora Africans in the Americas by implicating Israel's God in the debasing of phenotypically black peoples and has also caused insurmountable harm to Judeo-Christian Euro-Americans whose dependence on the harmful curse replaced Israel's God with the God of white supremacy.[8]

A third strategy has been to associate all of Africa with Cush or its equivalent in Greek translation, Ethiopia. Favored by "Ethiopianists"[9] and many other diaspora African groups, Cush or, more commonly, Ethiopia became synonymous with the entire continent, in a similar manner to the way Ethiopia was used as a globalizing term for dark-skinned Africans by Hellenistic authors. In this way the glorious story of the Cushites/Ethiopians becomes the history of contemporary diaspora African peoples. For these groups, passages like Ps 68:31 [Hebrew 68:32]; Amos 9:7; and Zeph 3:10 signify the special relationship YHWH has with Africans. Yet this strategy also presents difficulties as it universalizes the narrative of a particular east African group by applying it to all contemporary diaspora Africans, although most diaspora Africans in the Western world are descendants of people from western African nations (with their own distinctive histories). By elevating Cush as the African quintessence, the histories of other African nations in the Bible, such as Egypt, Put, Seba, Sheba, and even Israel/Judah, are ignored.

THE PRESENCE OF "AFRICAN" PEOPLE AND PLACES IN THE NEW TESTAMENT

The New Testament has references to what is traditionally understood as the African continent, including Mary and Joseph's flight to Egypt (Matt 2:13-23), the accounts of Simon of Cyrene (Matt 27:32; Mark 15:21; Luke 23:26), the Pentecost story (Acts 2), and the baptism of the Ethiopian eunuch (Acts 8:27-40).

Matt 2:13-23 records the story of Mary and Joseph's flight to Egypt, where they took Jesus to escape from one of Herod's infamous murderous rages. In a story reminiscent of Exod 1:16, 22, Herod determines to kill all the children two years old or younger in an effort to eliminate his potential royal rival. Egypt, ironically, does not function as the site of danger, as in the Exodus narratives, when its king was oblivious to the significance of Joseph and hence imperiled his offspring. Here Egypt is the place of sanctuary for another of Joseph's offspring, fulfilling the "prophetic" pronouncement of Hos 11:1, "Out of Egypt I called my son," or, as Cain Hope Felder modifies it, "Out of Africa I called my son."[10] The gist of the Matthean appropriation of Hosea's

The History of Targeting Males

The strategy of targeting males of oppressed populations has been employed throughout time. How our young men fare in this world says a great deal about how we will fare as a people. Should we choose not to address the preponderance of crises such as violence, drug abuse, under-education, unemployment, and rising rates of HIV, as they affect our young men, we will be undermining the future of our people.

words is that the Lord sheltered the Christ child in the bosom of one of Africa's most prominent nations, making it a critical part of the story of salvation.

Simon of Cyrene is a prominent figure in the Passion narratives, appearing in each of the Synoptic Gospels (Matt 27:32; Mark 15:21; Luke 23:26), for he literally embodies the essence of discipleship. In each of the Synoptics, Jesus proclaims that those who would be his disciples and follow him must "take up their cross" (Matt 10:38; 16:34; Mark 8:34; Luke 9:23). Simon, said to have been seized by the Romans as he returned from the fields and forced to bear the cross (likely the cross bar on which the crucified's arms would be fixed) is described as a Cyrenian. Cyrene was the capital of the North African Roman province of Cyrenaica in what is now Libya; thus, the bearer of Jesus' cross and the symbol of true discipleship was likely a Jew or a proselyte on Passover pilgrimage from this North African country.[11] Though it is difficult to determine whether North African origins would have necessarily meant "black" African identity amid the complex ethno-political dynamics of the Hellenistic world, Boykin Sanders argues persuasively that Simon was a man with "black skin color."[12] And Cain Hope Felder remarks that "indeed, Matthew, Mark, and Luke report that an African helped Jesus to carry his cross."[13]

Africans are also present at one of the most significant moments in the history of the church, as Acts 2 attests. This chapter records the events surrounding the advent of the Holy Spirit, whose presence was made evident by the miracle of (mainly) Galilean Jewish Christians proclaiming God's praise in "other tongues" presumably unknown to them. Their audience was a host of Jews and proselytes from across the Mediterranean basin. Acts 2:10 specifically mentions that there were pilgrims who came from "Egypt and the parts of Libya belonging to Cyrene." The passage describes Peter's preaching and the eventual conversion of some three thousand persons. Though the tradition often presents the Ethiopian eunuch of Acts 8 as the first "African" convert to the faith, it is likely that the pilgrims from North Africa (in Acts 2) were among the earliest converts and recipients of the Holy Spirit. Thus, we can imagine that the ideal communion described at the end of chap. 2, where all goods were held in common and all needs were met in a divine fellowship of equals, included many early "African" Christians as well.

Acts 8:26-40 describes the account of the most familiar "African" figure in the New Testament. The story of the Ethiopian eunuch, a high official of the Nubian *kandake* ("queen"), raises several interesting questions, including: Was this man a Jew? Did he genuinely convert to Christianity? And was he actually a eunuch? Because of the significance of this passage, these questions have been addressed more thoroughly in other key resources.[14] I will, however, reflect briefly on some of the apparent implications of the text.

The text assumes that the man is either a Jew or a proselyte by the declaration that the man "had come to Jerusalem to worship" (8:27). This statement implies that a community of Yahwists existed in Nubia, as suggested in passages such as Ps 68:32; Isa 11:11; 18:7; and Zeph 3:10[15] and by the fact that Beta Israel, or Ethiopian Judaism, is still extant.[16] Given the attestation of Yahwists from the region of Cush (translated "Ethiopia"), it is plausible that the official is a Nubian Jew making pilgrimage to the temple. As such, he is not a Gentile like Cornelius (Acts 10), hence there is no need to provide the extensive detail for his authentic conversion to the new way in Christ, because he is not unlike the other Jews mentioned in Acts who become followers of Jesus.

I will not venture much by way of comment on his sexual status, except to say that the details given about this aspect of his identity are ambiguous. Acts 8:27 uses two different terms that could both suggest his position of high authority: *eunouchos* (eunuch) and *dynastēs* (court official). Because both occur, the narrative seems to imply that he is a male with his testes removed. Castration was a physical imperfection that would impede him from worshiping at the Jerusalem temple, making his lengthy trek a vain exercise. Though it is uncertain what to make of the conflicting details, perhaps the point of the narrative was to emphasize that figures whose position in mainstream Judaism was tenuous were welcomed without qualification into this new manifestation of the faith.

The implications of this brief narrative are significant. First, we recognize that this East African figure, who presumably was phenotypically black, would have been one of a number of Nubians who were Yahwists, who viewed the Jerusalem temple as their chief locus for worship, and who would be deemed Jewish. Second, the fact of his conversion extends the scope of the early gospel message into the sub-Saharan regions of Africa, not just to its North and Eastern Mediterranean coasts. Third, that he was converted indicates that black Africans were never excluded from full participation in the promises of Christianity because of their supposed "racial" designation. Finally, the official's conversion is a testimony to the openness of the new expression of Yahwism in Christ to people who may have been alienated from their faith because of their sexual status and their physical imperfections.

These are just a few of the instances in which people and places traditionally identified as African occur in the text of the New Testament. Other important texts are the reference in Acts 13:1 to Simeon who was called Niger (meaning "dark-skinned person")

and Lucius of Cyrene and various references to Alexandria (Acts 27:6; 28:11), including one to Apollos, a man with the status of an apostle, who was a native of that important Egyptian city (Acts 18:24). Even the reference to Rufus (Rom 16:13)—who may be the same person as the son of Simon mentioned in Mark 15:21—could also suggest that this prominent early Christian, with whom Paul attests to sharing the same mother, was a descendant of African peoples.

RE-ENVISIONING AFRICA

To appreciate fully the role Africa and its people play in scripture is to move beyond Western stereotypes of the "dark continent" and embrace the diversity of what is Africa and African. African nations consist of more than just Cush; they include Egypt, Canaan, Edom, Libya, Arabia, Midian, and even Israel and Judah. African peoples not only are those who are deeply pigmented with broad facial features but have various hues, different phenotypes, and varying somatic traits. A globalizing African identity cannot be assumed to have imposed certain distinctive ways of being on those from this vast continent; instead people from Africa should be appreciated for the multiplicity of ways in which they express their identities on the pages of the Bible. In this regard, as we interpret the Bible, we should recognize that the "promised land" itself is a prime piece of African real estate, at the very heart of the biblical story.

Notes

1. For example, see Charles B. Copher, *Black Biblical Studies: An Anthology of Charles B. Copher* (Chicago: Black Light Fellowship,

1993) or Cain Hope Felder, *Troubling Biblical Waters: Race, Class, and Family* (Maryknoll, N.Y.: Orbis, 1989).

2. Neville J. Price, *Major Impacts and Plate Tectonics: A Model for the Phanerozoic Evolution of the Earth's Lithosphere* (New York: Routledge, 2001), 200–204, describes this region as breaking away from continental Africa as a result of the forces that formed the Great Rift Valley, which also contributed to the development of the Red Sea.

3. See C. Nicholas Raphael, "Geography and the Bible (Early Jewish)" *ABD* 2:964–77. See also Price, *Major Impacts and Plate Tectonics*, 200–204, for a discussion of the rifting of the African and Arabo-Nubian plates; cf. Ron Redfern, *Origins: The Evolution of Continents, Oceans and Life* (Norman: University of Oklahoma Press, 2001), 61, for an alternate theory of the rift's origins.

4. Against this trend see Jan Assmann, *Moses the Egyptian: The Memory of Egypt in Western Monotheism* (Cambridge, Mass.: Harvard University Press, 1997) and Karl W. Lukert, *Egyptian Light and Hebrew Fire: Theological and Philosophical Roots of Christendom in Evolutionary Perspective* (Albany: State University of New York Press, 1991).

5. Charles B. Copher, "The Black Presence in the Old Testament," in *Stony the Road We Trod: African American Biblical Interpretation*, ed. Cain Hope Felder (Minneapolis: Fortress Press, 1991), 149–53.

6. For example, see Rufus L. Perry, *The Cushite or the Descendants of Ham as Found in the Sacred Scriptures and in the Writings of Ancient Historians and Poets from Noah to the Christian Era* (Springfield, Mass.: Willey, 1893). Perry declares that "the most favored race of men [whites] preach about their own superiority till it becomes a kind of second nature. Then they piously incorporate it in their religion, and put it in their schoolbooks to be imbibed by their children. . . . They have egregiously falsified the true history of the Cushites, or the Hamitic branch of the human family." Noting this, his clearly political aim is to inspire "the

thoughtful Negro to look back to his remote progenitors and trace up his lineage in the hope of finding something of ancestral greatness with which to . . . kindle in his breast a decent flame of pride of race" (12).

7. For example, see Josiah Priest, *Slavery as It Relates to the Negro, or African Race* (New York: Arno, 1977 [1843]), 76–78. Priest declared that the very name Ham implied that this son of Noah was

> exceedingly prone to acts of ferocity and cruelty, involving murder, war, butcheries, and even cannibalism, including beastly lusts, and lasciviousness in its worst feature, going beyond the force of these passions, as possessed in common by the other races of men. . . . The word signifies deceit, dishonesty, treachery, low mindedness, and malice. What a group of horrors are here, couched in the word Ham, all agreeing in a most surprising manner with the color of Ham's skin, as well as with his real character as a man, during his own life, as well as with that of his race even now. (33)

Priest contrasts the blackness of Ham with Japheth, the "fair white man . . . the progenitor of a race who were to fill the world with their glory . . . ; for the white man, and the white woman are paramount in all the improvements of the earth" (36).

8. Stephen R. Haynes, *Noah's Curse: The Biblical Justification of American Slavery* (New York: Oxford University Press, 2002), explores the impact of the combination of these passages at length in this helpful review of the history of the interpretation of these passages.

9. See Perry, *The Cushite*, and Edward W. Blyden, *Christianity, Islam and the Negro Race* (Edinburgh: Edinburgh University Press, 1967 [1887]).

10. Felder, *Troubling Biblical Waters*, 13.

11. W. Ward Gasque, "Cyrene," *ABD* 1:1230–31.

12. Boykin Sanders, "In Search of the Face for Simon the Cyrene," in *The Recovery of Black Presence: An Interdisciplinary Exploration*, ed.

Randall C. Bailey, Charles B. Copher, and Jacquelyn Grant (Nashville: Abingdon, 1995), 51–63.

13. Cain Hope Felder, *Race, Racism, and the Biblical Narratives* (Minneapolis: Fortress Press, 2002), 33.

14. See the discussion in Felder, "Race, Racism, and the Biblical Narratives," 141–44. For a fuller treatment and more extensive bibliography, see Cottrel R. Carson, "'Do You Understand What You Are Reading?' A Reading of the Ethiopian Eunuch Story (Acts 8:26-40) from a Site of Cultural Marronage" (Ph.D. diss., Union Theological Seminary, New York, May 1999); Clarice J. Martin, "The Function of Acts 8:26-40 within the Narrative Structure of the Book of Acts: The Significance of the Eunuch's Provenance for Acts 1:8c" (Ph.D. diss., Duke University, Durham, N.C., 1985); and Clarice J. Martin, "A Chamberlain's Journey and the Challenge of Interpretation for Liberation," *Semeia* 47 (1989): 105–35.

15. See the sections that address these verses in Rodney S. Sadler Jr., *Can a Cushite Change His Skin? An Examination of Race, Ethnicity, and Othering in the Hebrew Bible*, JSOTSup 425 (Edinburgh and New York: T. & T. Clark, 2005).

16. Beta Israel is the preferred name for Ethiopian Jewry, literally meaning "House of Israel" (and not "second Israel" as the Greek "beta" might suggest).

For Further Reading

Adamo, David T. *Africa and Africans in the Old Testament.* Eugene, Ore.: Wipf and Stock, 2001.

Bailey, Randall C., and Jacquelyn Grant, eds. *The Recovery of Black Presence: An Interdisciplinary Exploration.* Nashville: Abingdon, 1995.

Copher, Charles B. *Black Biblical Studies: An Anthology of Charles B. Copher.* Chicago: Black Light Fellowship, 1993.

Dube, Musa W., ed. *Other Ways of Reading: African Women and the Bible.* Geneva: WCC, 2001.

Felder, Cain Hope, ed. *Stony the Road We Trod: African American Biblical Interpretation.* Minneapolis: Fortress Press, 1991.

———. *Troubling Biblical Waters: Race, Class, and Family.* Maryknoll, N.Y.: Orbis, 1989.

Getui, Mary, Knut Holter, and Victor Zinkuratire. *Interpreting the Old Testament in Africa.* New York: Peter Lang, 2001.

Holter, Knut. *Yahweh in Africa: Essays on Africa and the Old Testament.* New York: Peter Lang, 2000.

Sadler, Rodney S., Jr. *Can a Cushite Change His Skin? An Examination of Race, Ethnicity and Othering in the Hebrew Bible.* New York: T. & T. Clark, 2005.

West, Gerald O., and Musa W. Dube, eds. *The Bible in Africa: Transactions, Trajectories, and Trends.* Boston: Brill, 2001.

PAUL *and* AFRICAN AMERICAN BIBLICAL INTERPRETATION

Abraham Smith

Although a man of prodigious output, relentless resolve, and careful thought, the apostle Paul remains an enigmatic—even contradictory—figure in African American biblical interpretation. As a mysterious figure, moreover, he has been received by African Americans with ambivalence—with the highest veneration on the one hand and grave suspicion on the other.

PAUL, THE TOWERING FIGURE FROM TARSUS

Though he probably did not know the earthly Jesus and lacked the credentials of a card-carrying member of the earliest Jesus move-

ment, Paul is a towering figure in the history of Christian thought. At least three factors account for this estimation. First, he wrote more letters preserved by early Christians than any other writer in the New Testament canon. Second, he was driven by a restless desire to spread his gospel despite geographic barriers and cosmic or human opposition. Third, when we view the body of his collected works, we see a systematic thinker, one who reads life deductively from a set of basic principles, thus revealing a man of careful thought.

PRODIGIOUS OUTPUT

Thirteen letters bear Paul's name (1 Thessalonians, Galatians, 1 and 2 Corinthians, Philemon, Philippians, Romans, 2 Thessalonians,

Colossians, Ephesians, 1 and 2 Timothy, and Titus), even if some letters (the last six in the aforementioned list) are disputed, that is, not incontestably from Paul or an amanuensis authorized to write for him. It appears, moreover, that Paul wrote other letters that are not extant (see, e.g., 1 Cor 5:9), and one of his canonical letters, 2 Corinthians, bears signs of being a composite of at least two letter fragments.

On the one hand, the full volume of canonical letters attributed to him attests to the high regard the early church had for Paul. This regard continued because of the esteem that prominent Christian writers and theologians have had for him, from the second-century Syrian bishop Ignatius (who imitated Paul's habit of writing letters to churches; see Ignatius, *Romans* 5.1) to the fourth-century African Aurelius Augustine (who, in his controversy with Pelagius, used Paul to develop such doctrines as original sin and free will) to the sixteenth-century Protestant reformer Martin Luther (who found in Rom 1:17 a "liberating gospel" that freed him of a morbidly guilty conscience).

On the other hand, the undisputed letters themselves amply supply a sufficient base for working through the varying social and ethical issues of early believing assemblies (e.g., marriage and sex, 1 Cor 7:2-5; slavery, Philemon and 1 Cor 7:21-22; divorce, 1 Cor 7:10-16; ethnic relations, 1 Cor 7:17-24 and Gal 3:28), thus granting Paul a certain towering prominence by canonical default.[1] When other writers may have been silent on the weighty social and ethical issues of life, Paul seems to have covered these issues sufficiently for later Christians to find in him a moral guide for centuries to come. And where the undisputed letters were not clear on these matters, subsequent Christians found in the disputed letters both Paul's voice and more fodder for the aforementioned issues.[2]

RELENTLESS RESOLVE

From the undisputed letters and the book of Acts, the relentless resolve of Paul is a considerable and important theme. Hardships buffet his life, hindrances constantly stymie his goals, and heartbreak or heartache over his assemblies weighs heavily upon him. Yet the book of Acts and his letters are peppered with notices about his die-hard determination and his relentless resolve to spread his gospel.[3] In part, his relentless resolve is evident in his constant travels. By one estimate, Paul traveled ten thousand miles during the course of his career.[4] In part, one can see his relentless resolve in the optimism of his expressions, such as the following: "The one who calls you is faithful, and he will do this" (1 Thess 5:24). "I am confident of this, that the one who began a good work among you will bring it to completion by the day of Christ" (Phil 1:6). "Thanks be to God, who gives us the victory through our Lord Jesus Christ. Therefore, my beloved, be steadfast, immovable, always excelling in the work of the Lord, because you know that in the Lord your labor is not in vain" (1 Cor 15:57-58). In part, one can also see Paul's drive in the *peristasis* catalogues (catalogues of hardship; cf. 2 Cor 4:8-9; 6:4-10; 11:23-29), which show his indefatigable spirit in the face of repeated opposition.

CAREFUL THOUGHT

Paul was a man of careful thought. His apocalyptic thinking (about the cataclysmic in-breaking of the reign of God to subdue strangleholds of oppression, vindicate the just/righteous, and annihilate evil) both framed his pastoral care and assisted him in a critique of "empire." As an apocalyptic thinker, Paul considered the death and resurrection of Jesus as a turning point between two ages: an old age or aeon (Gal 1:4) in which sin had held sway on all of God's creation, whether human beings or the earth itself (Rom 8:18-23), and a new aeon in which believers receive renewed minds (Rom 12:2). The persisting realities of sin (e.g., disease, derision, and death), however, assured Paul that the old aeon, though dealt a mortal blow by the death and resurrection of Jesus, stalked on and would do so until the parousia (the return of Jesus, 1 Thess 4:13-18; cf. 1 Cor 7:31b; Rom 16:20). The parousia would then be a culminating moment, when the old aeon would come to a complete end and the new aeon would be fully consummated (1 Cor 15:24-26).

Between these two horizons, the death and resurrection of Jesus on the one hand and his parousia on the other, believers *walked* (Paul's word for living transformed moral lives).[5] As the first-century equivalent of a pastor, Paul thus offered his various assemblies "pastoral care," assistance in their *walk* before God.[6] His pastoral care was always tailored to the particular needs of an assembly and the individuated needs of its members. Sometimes it came in the form of exhortation, that is, with reminders of the great rescue operation that God had commenced in Jesus' death and resurrection or the inherent power of the parousia, an event that guaranteed the unbreakable bonds of the believers' unity beyond present forms of separation caused by geographical distance or by death.[7] At other times Paul would apply correction when the deportment of individual believers strayed from communal values *at best*, or beyond the pale of acceptable behaviors for persons entrusted by God with holiness as an identity marker of distinction *at worst*.[8]

Yet Paul's apocalyptic thought was not confined to pastoral, to the edification of believing assemblies. A fundamental function of his apocalyptic thought was critique of "empire." Viewing Paul as standing in "opposition to the Roman imperial order" is not tantamount to seeing him as a "rabble-rousing

revolutionary," a thesis that would strain credulity in the light of Rom 13:1-7.[9] Nor does this view imply that Paul was outspoken or strident in his responses to "empire."[10] Resistance, however, may be manifested in multiple forms, many of which are subtle or indirect. Accordingly, in line with the practices of his larger culture, Paul's apocalyptic rhetoric deployed "arts of resistance":[11] (1) His use of *apocalyptic traditions* incorporated political diction and presupposed a "critique of this age and its values," including those of the Roman imperial order.[12] (2) He *cultivated "assemblies"* (*ekklesiai*) whose apocalyptic orientations resisted—on many fronts—the ideologies of the cultures around them.[13] And (3) he fostered a *subtle political critique of local accommodationist practices* through admonitions of community self-sustenance apart from the Roman patronage systems on which most of the urban cities of Paul's world depended.[14]

PAUL, THE MYSTERIOUS FIGURE

Towering though he may be, Paul is at the same time an enigma, perhaps even a protean figure.[15] The mystery about him is not solely a factor of disputable texts within the body of letters attributed to Paul, though there is as much difference between the undisputed Pauline texts and the disputed ones as there is between vintage jazz and jazz fusion. Nor is the mystery purely a factor of the temporal distance of his ancient thought, a factor that is not distinctive to any figure of the past. Indeed, even in the ancient world, he was not clearly understood. About his letters, the writer of 2 Peter declared that "there are some things in them hard to understand" (3:16).

Paul seems, however, to fall apart when one looks for a social program that would match his egalitarian vision on every side. Paul himself was a Jew, but he fought with considerable passion to include Gentiles in the family of God, an inclusion that had no entrance requirements other than faith. The passion he displayed for this struggle and the limited or ambiguous level of passion he displayed toward other kinds of inclusion, however, lie at the heart of the ambivalence with which many have approached Paul.

Thus, if Paul embraced all three parts of the egalitarian ethos of Gal 3:28—"There is no longer Jew or Greek, there is no longer slave or free, there is no longer male and female; for all of you are one in Christ"—his energies manifestly were directed more toward race/ethnicity; and his references to class/status and sex/gender reveal the lack of a "practical program" on both of these fronts.[16]

Paul, for example, does not explicitly call Philemon to free Onesimus, although he applies some "social and community pressure" on Philemon.[17] When Paul states in 1 Corinthians 7 that believers should live according to their calling, he neither endorses "the mass rebellion of slaves" nor views the "call" here as relative to social status.[18] Rather, he refers to God's call upon each believer's life, even while he encourages the possibility of emancipation for the enslaved persons for whom that possibility may arise.

Likewise, the intensity with which he theologically argued for the abrogation of ethnic distinctions is not represented in his stance on gender. While his admonition for unmarried women to remain celibate may be considered anticonventional, 1 Cor 11:2-16 shows a patriarchal bias (Paul's dictum that woman was created "for the sake of man" [1 Cor 11:9] shows his dependence on "the [patriarchal] Genesis [2:18] account of creation"); 1 Cor 14:33b-36, if Paul wrote it, is an even more radical concession to patriarchy.[19]

Paul's failure to furnish a social program for all three parts of the egalitarian ethos of Gal 3:28, moreover, laid the basis for the accommodationist readings of Paul that appeared in the disputed Pauline texts, especially in the Pastorals (1–2 Tim and Titus). Whereas Paul's restrictions on women were limited in 1 Cor 11:2-16 and perhaps altogether absent from 1 Corinthians 14 (if one or more of the misogynistic parts of 1 Cor 14:33b-36 were, in fact, added later to Paul's original letter), 1 Tim 2:11-15 wholly and explicitly prohibits "women not only [from] speaking in church but also teaching and exercising any kind of authority over males."[20] Furthermore, both Colossians (3:4—4:7) and Ephesians (5:21—6:9) domesticate Paul by reading him as constrained by ancient "household codes" (the *Haustafeln*), that is, codes commanding a social conservative ethic for the various members of ancient households (husbands and wives; parents and children; masters and slaves).[21]

PAUL'S MIXED RECEPTION IN AFRICAN AMERICAN BIBLICAL INTERPRETATION

Though Paul has certainly had a place in African American preaching,[22] citations of Paul or allusions to his life, ministry, and letters span a wide range of genres in African American arts and letters: autobiographies,[23] novels,[24] essays,[25] and music.[26] A cursory and representative sifting of these genres reveal at least *five* hermeneutical approaches to Paul taken by African Americans, some of which involve a degree of overlap. The approaches altogether, moreover, are not necessarily informed by critical biblical scholarship on Paul, and thus the "Paul" appropriated has been drawn from the undisputed texts, the disputed ones, and even Hebrews, which does not bear Paul's name but has been attributed to Paul by many African Americans on a popular level.[27]

RADICAL REJECTION

Not all African Americans have embraced Paul. Some African Americans found in Paul a corrupter of an erstwhile pristine Jesus movement. In his book *The Black Messiah* (1968), Albert Cleage laid the blame for the corruption of Christianity squarely upon the shoulders of Paul.[28] Cleage insisted on the blackness of Jesus, pictured the Romans as white Gentiles, and averred that both the Hebrew Bible and the New Testament focused on nation building, not on individuals—with the exception of Paul and a few others who (according to Cleage) distorted the teachings of Jesus.[29] Notwithstanding the citation of Paul by some of his characters,[30] James Baldwin took the same hermeneutical tact in *The Fire Next Time*. Baldwin writes: "The real architect of the Christian church was not the disreputable sun-baked Hebrew [Jesus] but the mercilessly fanatical and self-righteous Saint Paul."[31]

Although the received tradition averred that Howard Thurman's grandmother squarely rejected Paul, Allen Callahan has persuasively argued that Thurman's grandmother advocated the selective citation of Paul, not the rejection of Paul altogether.[32] That is, Thurman's grandmother would not allow Thurman to read passages from "Paul" that included the dictum "Slaves be obedient to your Masters" (Eph 6:5), because so many missionaries had preached this dictum to sanction slavery with biblical authority.[33] Yet, Thurman was allowed to read 1 Corinthians 13.[34] Paul was not completely rejected, just the parts of Paul deemed distasteful.

REVERENTIAL APPROPRIATION

Overwhelmingly, Paul has been appropriated to provide suasion, encouragement, and insight in the face of black struggles. In the pre–Civil War period, during a speech delivered at Exeter Hall (London, England, 1843), J. W. C. Pennington looked reverentially toward Paul. To support the idea of the common family of humankind, Pennington cited Paul's egalitarian ethos in Gal 3:28 and alluded to Paul's metaphorical statement on the importance of each part of the human body in 1 Corinthians 12.[35] Likewise, Henry Highland Garnet, in a speech delivered to the U.S. House of Representatives, drew reverentially on the "Paul" of Acts 17:26 to highlight the contradiction of Christians supporting slavery.[36] Frederick Douglass repeatedly cited the "Paul" of 1 Timothy to denounce slavery, which he equated with the word "menstealing" in 1 Tim 1:10.[37] Likewise, he drew on the "Paul" of Heb 13:3 to enlist support not for slaveholders but for "those in bonds as bound with them."[38]

In the post–Civil War period, in an obvious reverential reading of Paul, Charles H. Mason established the Church of God in Christ by appeal to 1 Thess 2:14, which speaks of the "churches of God in Christ."[39] In the same period, in a fight against the notion of blacks as beasts, black clergy took up the mantle of God as universal parent with a vengeance.[40] In doing so, moreover, black clergy frequently cited the "Paul" of Acts 17:26. Thus, South Carolina Baptist M. W. Gilbert could write: "A true believer in the Scriptures must be equally a believer in the fatherhood of God and the brotherhood of all men. For the divine record declares that God 'hath of one blood created all nations of men for to dwell on the face of the earth.'"[41] Likewise, Baptist minister Butler Harrison Peterson asserted: "True merit will yet be the worth of the man, under the wise and just government of a beneficent God and Father, who 'of one blood made all nations for to dwell upon the face of all the earth.'"[42] S. G. Atkins, a North Carolina African Methodist Episcopal Zion preacher also wrote: "There is still a higher authority for a negative answer to the question, 'Should the Negroes be given an education different from that given to the Whites?'" His answer was: "God hath made of one blood all nations of men for to dwell on the face of the earth."[43]

In more recent times, the reverential hermeneutical approach to Paul was taken by Fannie Lou Hamer. In responding to her struggle as a sharecropper involved in the freedom movement, she cited the "Paul" of Eph 6:11-12.[44] The next verse of Ephesians (6:13), with its commendation "to stand," would also become the basis for the Christian singer/songwriter Donald McClurken's "Stand." His *Psalms, Hymns and Spiritual Songs* CD is also dependent upon the "Paul" of Eph 5:19.

In his essays, speeches, and sermons, Martin Luther King also repeatedly drew reverentially on Paul.[45] King's essay "An Experiment in Love" cites 1 Cor 10:24 for an understanding of love as *agape* or what King called "disinterested love."[46] In his speech "The Ethical Demands for Integration," King appealed to the "Paul" of Acts 17:26. He writes: "Paul's declaration that God 'hath made of one blood' all nations of the world is more anthropological fact than religious poetry."[47] Likewise, in *Strength to Love*, King's "A Transformed Nonconformist" relies on Rom 12:2.[48]

INTRA-CANONICAL CORRECTION

African Americans often critiqued Paul or interpretations of him through appeals to other portions of the biblical canon. In support of her role as a female abolitionist, Maria Stewart corrected "Paul" by appealing to Jesus, her "High Priest and Advocate": "St. Paul declared that it is a shame for a woman to speak in public, yet our great High Priest and Advocate did not condemn the woman for a more notorious offence than this; neither will he condemn this worthless worm."[49]

Likewise, Julia Foote Moore, a traveling minister of the AME Zion Church, used some parts of Paul's own oeuvre to correct interpretations of Paul based on 1 Cor 14:34. She notes:

> The Bible puts an end to this strife when it says: "There is neither male nor female in Christ Jesus" [Gal 3:28]. . . . Paul called Priscilla, as well as Aquila, his "helper," or, as in the Greek, his "fellow-laborer." Rom xv.3; 2 Cor viii.23; Phil ii.5; 1 Thess iii.2. The same word, which, in our common translation, is now rendered a "servant of the church," in speaking of Phoebe (Rom. xix.1 [*sic*]) is rendered "minister" when applied to Tychicus. Eph. vi.21. When Paul said, "Help those women who labor with me in the Gospel," he certainly meant that they did more than to pour tea. In the eleventh chapter of First Corinthians Paul gives directions, to men and women, how they should appear when they prophesy or pray in public assemblies; and he defines prophesying to be speaking to edification, exhortation and comfort.[50]

Furthermore, in a speech delivered to the American National Baptist Convention in Mobile, Alabama, on August 26, 1887, Mary V. Cook challenged the use of Paul to silence women in any venue. To make her case, Cook offered a litany of women noted throughout the Bible (Eve, Sarah, Deborah, Naomi, Ruth, Hagar, Hannah, and others), including those associated with Jesus. More directly, she noted Paul's laudation of women in his own ministry and Paul's own words about equality in Gal 3:28: "There is no longer Jew or Greek, there is no longer slave or free, there is no longer male or female; for all of you are one in Christ Jesus."[51]

[handwritten: → Insert ANY noun and this sentence remains true.]

EXTRA-CANONICAL CORRECTION

African Americans have never relied solely on the Bible as a source of authority.[52] That is, African Americans have often appealed to an extra-biblical authority as a basis for their critique of Paul or corrections of interpretations of Paul.[53] Lemuel Haynes, an eighteenth-century minister in New England, appealed to the "unchangeable Laws of God," laws he deemed to be against slavery, for his critique of pro-slavery interpretations that found support for their cause in 1 Cor 7:21.[54]

Again, in her effort to fight opposition to her role as a *female* abolitionist, Maria Stewart critiques Paul by drawing on noncanonical authority. She argued: "Did St. Paul but know of our wrongs and deprivations [i.e., the experiences of black women], I presume he would make no objections to our pleadings in public for our rights."[55]

Lauryn Hill, in her *Miseducation of Lauryn Hill*, draws on the Paul of 1 Corinthians 13 for the lyrics of "Tell Him," but she changed Paul's words in accordance with the harsh realities of urban life.[56] Paul's declaration of what love is ("Love is patient; love is kind," 13:4) becomes more of a plea in Hill's lyrics ("Let me be patient; let me be kind"). In the bridge to the song, moreover, Paul's words are adjusted so that the singer's kindness is not taken for granted: "I'll never be jealous; and I won't be too kind."[57]

TYPOLOGICAL CORRELATION

One of the key uses of Paul in African American biblical hermeneutics is the correlation of the experiences of African Americans with those of Paul. This typological approach was used by John Marrant, who depicted his life "in the missionary role of St. Paul who spread Christ's teachings."[58] Paul's "labor in vain" imagery (1 Thess 3:5; 1 Cor 15:58; Gal 4:11)

was used by James Gronniosaw and Maria Stewart, while John Jea, George White, and Maria Stewart all adopted the form of "Paul's" farewell address to the Ephesian elders (Acts 20) for their own speeches.[59] Before the Civil War, in a defense of her call, a black woman known only by her first name, Elizabeth, repeatedly alludes to "Paul" both to describe her conversion ("immediately a light fell upon me," cf. Acts 9:3; "I felt like a new creature," 2 Cor 5:17) and her call ("not by the commission of men's hands," cf. Gal 1:1).[60]

In much more recent times, Malcolm X also used "Paul's" light imagery (more specifically, a "blinding light") to describe what he would call the "true knowledge of the black man" as taught by Elijah Muhammad.[61] Paul's letter form, moreover, was used by Martin Luther King Jr. in "Paul's Letter to American Christians."[62] Likewise, in his "Letter from Birmingham Jail," King compared himself to the apostle Paul: "Just as the Apostle Paul left his little village of Tarsus and carried the gospel of Jesus Christ to practically every hamlet and city of the Graeco-Roman world, I too am compelled to carry the gospel of freedom beyond my particular hometown. Like Paul, I must constantly respond to the Macedonian call for aid."[63]

CONCLUSION

African Americans were not the first persons to give Paul an uneven reception. His own assemblies adjusted his thought, sometimes painfully for Paul (1 Cor 5:9; cf. Gal 1:6), as they dealt with the lived realities and miseries of their urban Mediterranean settings in the Roman Empire. Ironically, though, Paul's greatest appeal *among* African Americans may also be the basis for the occasional rejection or correction of his thought *by* African Americans, that is, his role as an outsider. He was not one of the "pillars" in Jerusalem (the acknowledged principal leaders of the Jesus movement there, Gal 2:9). Some persons in his assemblies judged his speech to be contemptible (2 Cor 10:11). With regard to the earliest members of the Jesus movement, Paul speaks of God's revelation to him as one that came "last of all, as to one untimely born" (1 Cor 15:8). With his previous role as a persecutor of the church still hovering over him, Paul considered himself "the least of all the apostles" (1 Cor 15:9).

Given the miseries and harsh lived realities that African Americans have faced in the rural, urban, and suburban settings of their country, perhaps many can empathize with Paul's "outsider status." Venerated or treated with suspicion, Paul remains an important figure within African American arts and letters. As William Shakespeare once noted, "Misery [still] acquaints a man [or woman] with strange bedfellows."[64]

Notes

1. On Paul's treatment of varying social and ethical issues, see Brad R. Braxton, "The Role of Ethnicity in the Social Location of 1 Corinthians 7:17-24," in *Yet With a Steady Beat: Contemporary U.S. Afrocentric Biblical Interpretation*, ed. Randall C. Bailey, Semeia Studies (Atlanta: Society of Biblical Literature, 2003), 24.

2. Note, for example, how the author of 1 Timothy radically revises Paul's advice to young widows. Though vintage Paul advised young widows to respond to sexual passions through abstinence (1 Cor 7:8), 1 Timothy designates marital intercourse as the best arena for control of this appetite (1 Tim 5:14).

3. After his cameo appearance at the stoning of Stephen (Acts 7:58—8:1) and his dramatic Damascus encounter that follows a little later (Acts 9), Paul is clearly the main character in the book of Acts. In Acts 13–28, readers can

follow his various journeys, his hardships, and finally his appearance in Rome as a prisoner. From his letters, we learn that Paul relentlessly advanced a house-church movement that eventually took root in at least four Roman provinces: Galatia, Asia (e.g., Colossae and Ephesus, cf. 1 Cor 16:19), Macedonia (Philippi and Thessalonica), and Achaia (Corinth). See Wayne Meeks, *The First Urban Christians: The Social World of the Apostle Paul* (New Haven: Yale University Press, 1983).

4. Ron Hock, *The Social Context of Paul's Ministry: Tentmaking and Apostleship* (Philadelphia: Fortress Press, 1980), 77.

5. For example, see the "walk" diction in 1 Thessalonians, translated variously in the NRSV as "lead" (2:12), "live" (4:1), or "behave" (4:12); cf. Rom 6:4; 8:4; 14:15; 2 Cor 5:7. This short review of Paul's apocalyptic thought is largely dependent on J. Paul Sampley's *Walking Between the Times: Paul's Moral Reasoning* (Minneapolis: Fortress Press, 1991).

6. On Paul's "pastoral care," see Abraham Malherbe, "'Pastoral Care' in the Thessalonian Church," *NTS* 36 (1988): 375–91.

7. On the tailor-made deliverance of ancient moral exhortation, see Clarence Glad, *Paul and Philodemus: Adaptability in Epicurean and Early Christian Psychagogy* (New York: Brill, 1995), 137–52; cf. Seneca, *Epistles* 52.3–4. The church at Corinth seemed particularly to stray away from *communal values* that edified its assembly (1 Cor 6:1-8, 12; 10:23). Likewise, Paul's correction of the Corinthians is directed toward a person who is committing an act beyond acceptability—"a man [who] is living with his father's wife" (1 Cor 5:1).

8. On Paul's different types of moral counseling ("exhortation, edification and correction"), see Glad, *Paul and Philodemus*, 7; cf. Abraham Malherbe, "Exhortations in 1 Thessalonians," *NovT* 25 (1983): 238–56, esp. 241.

9. Richard A. Horsley, "Introduction," in *Paul and the Roman Imperial Order*, ed. Richard A. Horsley (Harrisburg, Pa.: Trinity Press International, 2004), 3.

10. Abraham Smith, "Unmasking the Powers: Toward a Postcolonial Analysis of 1 Thessalo-

nians," in Horsley, *Paul and the Roman Imperial Order*, 54.

11. On the different paths by which resistance might take place, see James C. Scott, *Domination and the Arts of Resistance: Hidden Transcripts* (New Haven: Yale University Press, 1990).

12. Sampley, *Walking Between the Times*, 108.

13. On Paul's development of *ekklesiai* as an alternative movement, see Richard A. Horsley, "Submerged Biblical Histories and Imperial Biblical Studies," in *The Postcolonial Bible*, ed. R. S. Sugirtharajah (Sheffield: Sheffield, 1998), 165.

14. Smith, "Unmasking the Powers," 54.

15. The idea that Paul was a Christian Proteus emanates from both Amos Jones Jr., *Paul's Message of Freedom: What Does It Mean to the Black Church?* (Valley Forge, Pa.: Judson, 1984), 16, and Wayne A. Meeks, ed., *The Writings of St. Paul: A Norton Critical Edition* (New York: Norton, 1972), 437. As Jones writes, "Proteus, a sea god [in *The Odyssey*], had the uncanny ability of changing forms at will and escaping the grasp of his would-be captors" (16). The same seems to be true of Paul.

16. Demetrius K. Williams, *An End to This Strife: The Politics of Gender in African American Churches* (Minneapolis: Fortress Press, 2004), 36.

17. Ibid., 34.

18. Ibid., 36.

19. Ibid., 45–52.

20. Ibid., 57.

21. On the domestication of Paul's erstwhile egalitarian ethos, see Clarice J. Martin, "The *Haustafeln* (Household Codes) in African American Biblical Interpretation: 'Free Slaves' and 'Subordinate Women,'" in *Stony the Road We Trod: African American Biblical Interpretation*, ed. Cain Hope Felder (Minneapolis: Fortress Press, 1991), 206–31.

22. A few examples of African American sermons that mention "Paul" are Daniel Alexander Payne, "Welcome to the Ransomed" (1 Tim 2:1-4), in *The Heart of Black Preaching*, ed. Cleophus J. LaRue (Louisville: Westminster John Knox, 2000), 172–79; Elias C. Morris, "The Brotherhood of Man" (which mentions the Paul of Acts 17:26), in LaRue, *The Heart*

of Black Preaching, 182; C. L. Franklin, "Pressing On" (Phil 3:4-14) on 519–29 in Cécile Coquet, "My God Is a Time-God: How African American Folk Oratory Speaks (of) Time," in *African Americans and the Bible: Sacred Texts and Social Textures*, ed. Vincent L. Wimbush (New York: Continuum, 2000), 514–36; J. Alfred Smith, "Songs of Hope from Dungeons of Despair" (Acts 16:25), in *Preach On!* ed. J. Alfred Smith (Nashville: Broadman, 1984), 115–22; Henry H. Mitchell, "Epistle to the Young, Gifted and Black" (2 Tim 1:6), in *Preaching for Black Self-Esteem*, ed. Henry H. Mitchell and Emil M. Thomas (Nashville: Abingdon, 1994), 122–30.

23. See, for example, the reference to "in season and out of season" from the "Paul" of 2 Tim 4:2 in Booker T. Washington, *Up from Slavery* (New York: Airmont, 1967), 48.

24. See, for example, "Paul's" expression "It is hard to kick against the pricks" (Acts 26:14), in James Weldon Johnson, *The Autobiography of an Ex-Coloured Man* (New York: Vintage, 1989), 177; and Paul's expression "the right hand of fellowship" (Gal 2:9), in Zora Neale Hurston, *Their Eyes Were Watching God*, with a foreword by Edwidge Danticat and an afterword by Henry Louis Gates Jr. (New York: Harperperennial Modern Classics, 2006), 42.

25. See, for example, W. E. B. Du Bois, "In Season and Out of Season" (2 Tim 4:2) and "Live, Move and Have Their Being" (Acts 17:26), in *The Souls of Black Folk* (New York: Vintage, 1990), 45, 145.

26. See, for example, William Herbert Brewster's "I Have Never Reached Perfection" (which seems to emanate from Phil 3:12-16) in his "Lord, I've Tried," cited in *"We'll Understand It Better By and By": Pioneering African American Gospel Composers*, ed. Bernice Johnson Reagon (Washington, D.C.: Smithsonian Institution, 1992), 215–16, and Thomas A. Dorsey, "When I Choose to Do the Right Thing, Evil's Present on Every Hand" (Rom 7:21), in his "The Lord Will Make a Way Somehow," cited in Reagon, *We'll Understand It Better By and By*, 161.

27. For further study of Paul by African American biblical scholars, see Vincent L. Wimbush,

Paul, the Worldly Ascetic: Response to the World and Self-Understanding According to 1 Corinthians 7 (Macon, Ga.: Mercer, 1987); Martin, "The *Haustafeln* (Household Codes) in African American Biblical Interpretation" in Felder, *Stony the Road We Trod*, 206–31; Clarice J. Martin, "'Somebody Done Hoodoo'd the Hoodoo Man'": Language, Power, Resistance, and the Effective History of Pauline Texts in American Slavery," *Semeia* 83/84 (1998): 203–33; Lloyd A. Lewis, "An African American Appraisal of the Philemon-Onesimus Triangle," in Felder, *Stony the Road We Trod*, 232–46; Ann Holmes Redding, "Together, Not Equal: The Rhetoric of Unity and Headship in the Letter to Ephesians" (Ph.D. diss., Union Theological Seminary, New York, 1999); Allen Dwight Callahan, *Embassy of Onesimus: The Letter of Paul to Philemon*, The New Testament in Context (Valley Forge, Pa.: Trinity Press International, 1997); Cain Hope Felder, "Philemon," *NIB* 11 (Nashville: Abingdon, 2000), 881–906; Abraham Smith, "First and Second Thessalonians," in *NIB* 11: 739–72; Brian K. Blount, "Paul: Theology Enabling Liberative Ethic—Sometimes," in *Then the Whisper Put on Flesh: New Testament Ethics in an African American Context* (Nashville: Abingdon, 2001), 119–57; Brad R. Braxton, *No Longer Slaves: Galatians and African American Experience* (Collegeville, Minn.: Liturgical, 2002); and Williams, *An End to This Strife*.

28. Albert Cleage, "The Resurrection of the Nation," in *The Black Messiah* (New York: Sheed and Ward, 1968), 85–99.

29. See Dwight Hopkins, *Black Theology USA and South Africa: Politics, Culture, and Liberation* (Maryknoll, N.Y.: Orbis, 1990), 36–39.

30. "Paul" is cited repeatedly by characters in James Baldwin, *Go Tell It on the Mountain* (New York: Dell, 1985), 56, 81, 93, 103, 185, 221.

31. James Baldwin, *The Fire Next Time* (New York: Dial, 1963), quoted in Allen Dwight Callahan, "'Brother Saul': An Ambivalent Witness to Freedom," *Semeia* 83/84 (1998): 247.

32. Callahan, "'Brother Saul,'" 241.

33. As Frederick Douglass stated, "This [dictum] is the Alpha and the Omega, the beginning and ending of the religious teaching received by slaves of the United States" (quoted in *The Frederick Douglass Papers, Series One: Speeches, Debates, and Interviews, Vol. 1: 1841–46*, ed. John W. Blassingame (New Haven: Yale University Press, 1979), 404–5.

34. Howard Thurman, *Jesus and the Disinherited* (Nashville: Abingdon, 1949), 30–31.

35. J. W. C. Pennington, "Speech by J. W. C. Pennington, Delivered at Exeter Hall, London, England, 21 June 1843," in *The Black Abolitionist Papers*, vol. 1: *The British Isles, 1830–1865*, ed. C. Peter Ripley (Chapel Hill, N.C.: University of North Carolina Press, 1985), 130–32.

36. Henry Highland Garnet, "Discourse Delivered in the House of Representatives," in *Let Your Motto Be Resistance: The Life and Thought of Henry Highland Garnet*, ed. Earl Ofari (Boston: Beacon, 1972), 189.

37. Douglass, *The Frederick Douglass Papers, Series One*, 49, 50, 230, 235, 247, 256, 286, 297, 298, 315, 363, 459, 451, 427, 448.

38. Ibid., 382, 427.

39. Elsie Mason, *The Man, Charles Harrison Mason (1866–1961)*, quoted in *Afro-American Religious History: A Documentary Witness*, ed. Milton Sernett (Durham, N.C.: Duke University Press, 1985), 288.

40. Edward L. Wheeler, *Uplifting the Race: The Black Minister in the New South, 1865–1902* (Lanham, Md.: University Press of America, 1986), 46.

41. Ibid., 47.

42. Ibid., 51.

43. Ibid.

44. Vincent Harding, "The Anointed Ones: Hamer, King, and the Bible in the Southern Freedom Movement," in Wimbush, *African Americans and the Bible*, 542.

45. Examinations of Martin Luther King Jr.'s biblical rhetoric usually focus on King and the prophetic tradition, for example, his use of mountaintop imagery that associates him with Moses, his reliance upon the "suffering

servant" tradition to understand theodicy, his references to prophets of justice like Amos or the infusion of Jeremiah's spirit of criticism in King's challenge to the United States to live up to its ideals. Yet King frequently also appealed to the apostle Paul.

46. Martin Luther King Jr., "An Experiment in Love," in *A Testament of Hope: The Essential Writings and Speeches of Martin Luther King, Jr.*, ed. James M. Washington (San Francisco: Harper & Row, 1986), 19.

47. Ibid., 121.

48. Martin Luther King Jr., *Strength to Love* (Philadelphia: Fortress Press, 1981), 21–29; see Harding's discussion of this sermon in "The Anointed Ones," 538.

49. Maria Stewart, quoted in *Maria Stewart: America's First Black Woman Political Writer*, ed. Marilyn Richardson (Bloomington: Indiana University Press, 1987), 68.

50. Julia Foote Moore, quoted in *Sisters of the Spirit: Three Black Women's Autobiographies of the Nineteenth Century*, ed. William L. Andrews (Bloomington: Indiana University Press, 1986), 209.

51. Mary V. Cook, "Women's Place in the Work of the Denomination," in *Lift Every Voice: African American Oratory, 1787–1900*, ed. Philip S. Foner and Robert James Branham (Tuscaloosa: University of Alabama Press, 1998), 663–76.

52. Thomas Hoyt connects the authority of scripture to the authority of black culture, that is, the authority of a fairly common story of black experience in the United States. The common story includes suffering, exodus, creation, eschatology, and larger mythic constructions of what God has done and will do in the world for black people and others. See Thomas L. Hoyt Jr., "Interpreting Biblical Scholarship for the Black Church Tradition," in Felder, *Stony the Road We Trod*, 17–39.

53. So endowed with a hermeneutics of suspicion was Sojourner Truth that she resisted the practice of adults reading the Bible, opposed literal interpretations of the Bible, and acknowledged the possibility that scripture itself was a mixture of truth and the ideas of those who recorded scripture. Truth did not want adults to read the Bible to her because most would add their own commentary. See Karen Baker-Fletcher, "Anna Julia Cooper and Sojourner Truth: Two Nineteenth-Century Black Feminist Interpreters of Scripture," in *Searching the Scriptures*, ed. Elisabeth Schüssler Fiorenza (New York: Crossroad, 1993), 49. According to Baker-Fletcher, Truth, acknowledging the hegemonic tendencies of the biblical writers themselves, would "compare the teachings of the Bible with the witness within her" (47).

54. See John Saillant's discussion of Lemuel Haynes in "Origins of African American Biblical Hermeneutics in Eighteenth-Century Black Opposition to the Slave Trade and Slavery," in Wimbush, *African Americans and the Bible*, 241.

55. Maria Stewart, quoted in Richardson, *Maria Stewart*, 68.

56. Lauryn Hill, *The Miseducation of Lauryn Hill* (New York: Ruffhouse/Columbia Records, 1998).

57. Ibid.

58. Angelo Costanzo, *Surprising Narrative: Olaudah Equiano and the Beginnings of Black Autobiography* (New York: Crossroad, 1987), 103.

59. See Abraham Smith, "Putting 'Paul' Back Together Again: William Wells Brown's *Clotel* and Black Abolitionist Approaches to Paul," *Semeia* 83/84 (1998): 255–56.

60. Elizabeth, "Not by the Commission of Men's Hands," in *Can I Get a Witness? Prophetic Religious Voices of African American Women, An Anthology*, ed. Marcia Y. Riggs (Maryknoll, N.Y.: Orbis, 1997), 3–4.

61. Malcolm X [Malcolm Little], *The Autobiography of Malcolm X* (New York: Ballantine, 1992), 189; cf. Acts 9:3-9; 22:6-11; 26:13. On "the true knowledge of the black man," see *The Autobiography of Malcolm X*, 187.

62. King, *Strength to Love*, 137–45.

63. Martin Luther King Jr., "Letter from Birmingham Jail," in *I Have a Dream: Writings and Speeches That Changed the World*, ed. James M. Washington (San Francisco: HarperSanFrancisco, 1992), 84–85.

64. William Shakespeare, *The Tempest* (Act 2, Scene 2).

For Further Reading

Braxton, Brad R. *No Longer Slaves: Galatians and African American Experience.* Collegeville, Minn.: Liturgical, 2002.

———. *Preaching Paul.* Nashville: Abingdon, 2004.

Callahan, Allen Dwight. *Embassy of Onesimus: The Letter of Paul to Philemon.* The New Testament in Context. Valley Forge, Pa.: Trinity Press International, 1997.

Redding, Ann Holmes, "Together, Not Equal: The Rhetoric of Unity and Headship in the Letter to Ephesians." Ph.D. diss., Union Theological Seminary, New York, 1999.

Smith, Abraham. *"Comfort One Another": Reconstructing the Audience of 1 Thessalonians.* Louisville: Westminster John Knox, 1995.

Williams, Demetrius K. *Enemies of the Cross of Christ: The Terminology of the Cross and Conflict in Philippians.* Sheffield: Sheffield Academic, 2002.

Wimbush, Vincent L. *Paul, the Worldly Ascetic: Response to the World and Self-Understanding According to 1 Corinthians 7.* Macon, Ga.: Mercer, 1987.

"WE WILL MAKE OUR OWN FUTURE TEXT": AN ALTERNATE ORIENTATION *to* INTERPRETATION

Vincent L. Wimbush

Jes Grew . . . is a psychic epidemic. . . . [It] is seeking its words. For what good is a liturgy without a text? . . . Jes Grew has no end and no beginning. . . . Jes Grew is life. . . . They will try to depress Jes Grew but it will only spring back and prosper. . . . Jes Grew needed its words to tell its carriers what it was up to. Jes Grew was an influence which sought its text, and whenever it thought it knew the location of its words . . . it headed in that direction. . . . If it could not find its Text then it would be mistaken for entertainment . . . merely a flair-up. The Blues is a Jes Grew, as James Weldon Johnson surmised. Jazz was a Jes Grew which followed the Jes Grew of Ragtime. Slang is Jes Grew too. . . . We will make our own future text.

—Ishmael Reed, *Mumbo Jumbo*

It is a tribute to the fairness and large-mindedness of the editors of this commentary that they would solicit and accept as part of this project this trenchant anti-commentary essay. I share the interest held by all contributors to this project (and many beyond it) to contribute to the ongoing political-ideological uplift work of African Americans. But I propose here to contribute to such work through a questioning of and challenge to the traditional and still dominant discursive formation—the commentary—that this larger project reflects and within which the Bible and other scriptures are generally thought about and engaged, and to offer at least the outlines of a different orientation and approach to interpretation. Every discursive formation is political. My basic argument is that the commentary as intellectual project is (politically) very problematic, not because of any specific substantive arguments on the part of commentators—such arguments may run widely within a certain spectrum—but because the commentary necessarily forces a certain delimitation and qualification of questioning and probing. It forces the interpreter to begin not in his or her own time, not in or with his or her own world situation, but in another one—that (one that is imagined or assumed to be) of the text. This orientation to the beginning or first step in interpretation is critical. To be sure, since Origen, biblical exegetes or commentators have tended to range widely with their questions and issues. But the point here is that a dangerous game is set up whereby the commentator feigns to be faithful "to the text" while dancing with another set of issues. This game can—in fact, has—become so twisted and dizzying that it is for the most part and for too many interpreters no longer even recognized for what it is; the game and its effects are acutely and profoundly and with devastating social-political effects obfuscating. There are high stakes in such practice for peoples on the periphery. At the very least, it keeps them distracted, unable to focus on their world situation.

I am not recommending that texts not be engaged. What I am suggesting is that we question taking up the master discursive intellectual project developed by masters in relation to the master text. I want to challenge us to think differently about and orient ourselves differently around interpretation, about what to interpret, where and how to begin, how to proceed, with what approaches, and with what agenda.

My own way of addressing this phenomenon has been through focused attention on the history of the conjuncture of African Americans and the Bible. I continue in this essay with the questions that have haunted and inspired and challenged me—not so much about the meaning of this or that text but about this phenomenon that involves the invention and uses of texts as scriptures. What psycho-social-cultural work is done in relationship to this phenomenon? With the focus on scriptures and peoples I show my interest to be in the archaeology and politics of interpretation. The phenomenon we call "scriptures" and the people we call African Americans are for me emblematic of the problematics of interpretation and consciousness. So in this essay I want to address some of the larger implications and ramifications of such an interpretive history. What does it teach us—about African Americans and other peoples, and about "scriptures"? About interpretation? About interpretation and power—psychosocial, sociocultural power? About interpretation and/as consciousness? About who and what we are, how we are, what we do—including the range of the complex good and ill as consequences and effects—as interpreters in relationship to "scriptures"? What does it mean to have and to engage scriptures? I begin—perhaps somewhat defiantly—not with a text but with social (viz., African American) textures.

DUBOIS AND THE VEIL

Because of his prescience and sharp sensitivity to issues having to do with interpretation and/as consciousness, I find still challenging and useful as an expansive, critical, and sensitive perspective on the existence and challenges of persons of African descent in the United

States the language and argumentation found in W. E. B. DuBois's classic collection of essays, *Souls of Black Folk*, originally published in 1903.[1] As part of his attempt to name the major challenges faced by the "folk"—or perhaps, more accurately, the challenges faced by the type of black person he knew himself to be, thereby speaking in complicated ways for so many others—DuBois refers again and again in these essays to the "veil."[2] Notwithstanding their internal differentiations and infra-politics, about which he as historian and social scientist was very much aware, all black folks, he argued, had been placed, no, forced, behind the "veil." Referred to (by my count) more than thirty times, the metaphor of the veil in *Souls of Black Folk* is DuBois's attempt to define the existence of black folks in the United States as those forced into divided consciousness. Thus we have the poignant significance of the plural term *souls*—not *many* souls, as in *many* persons, but two "souls" in the one representative black body, or in each black body, warring against each other. This division was for DuBois the deep internal psychologically felt reflection of the external social-political existence of black folks as the chronic persistent other, as the subaltern, as the enslaved/colonized living next to, and reduced to looking at themselves through the gaze of, the enslaver/colonizer. Recall one of the most famous of references: "Then it dawned upon me with a certain suddenness that I was different from the others . . . shut out from their world by a vast veil. . . . After the Egyptian and Indian, the Greek and Roman, the Teuton and Mongolian, the Negro is a sort of seventh son, born with a veil" (2–3).

Modified variously in terms of the "veil of Race" (55, 56), "Veil of Color" (127, 142), as that which imprisons (64), as that within which black folks are born and in which they grow up (147, 148, 150, 156, 159, 165),

as that which casts a shadow (149), as that against—above and beyond—which the black self strives to live (76, 153), as that world beyond and above which white folks live (56), as that which the black self overcomes only in death (151), and that which, based on hope, is to be rent (187), references to the "veil" were varied and complex in function.

Literary critics Shamoon Zamir[3] and Arnold Rampersad[4] have argued that, in the metaphor of the veil, DuBois drew most directly from Plato via G. W. F. Hegel, then from Ralph Waldo Emerson and some other construals of late nineteenth- and early twentieth-century letters, psychology, and interpretation of the Bible. These two scholars suggest that DuBois took from Hegel the idea of the veil and its effects on consciousness and wedded them to the Bible's stories regarding transformation. DuBois needed language and concepts through which he could articulate the reality of the crisis of divided consciousness as well as the aesthetics and performativity of transformed consciousness. The turn to Hegel had to do with the interest in finding language through which DuBois could express the poignancy of divided consciousness. Hegel's concern had been about the "unhappy consciousness" as part of the dialectics of the master-slave relationship and that moment in which such consciousness is transformed, when self-consciousness discovers itself beyond the realm of appearances, that moment in which the "curtain" is drawn aside.[5]

The pertinent references from the Bible in relationship to the "veil" also, according to DuBois, have to do with "transformation," but in a different discursive domain. In Exod 26:33 the "veil" (*to katapetasma*) separates the Holy of Holies, the sanctuary for the Ark of the Covenant, from everything else. In 1 Cor 13:12 Paul makes reference to humans, even repentant ones, being able to see only partial truths—"darkly as through a veil" (*en ainigmati*). In Heb 6:19 the writer refers to entering into the domain of the "veil" (*eis to esoteron tou katapetasmatos*) to mark the change in those who, although having been enlightened, have in the face of persecution nevertheless "fallen away." And, perhaps most poignantly, Matt 27:50-54, having depicted Jesus crying out loud and dying on the cross, indicates that "the veil" (*to katapetasma tou vaou eschisthe eis duo apo anothen hoes kato*) of the temple was "rent in two" from top to bottom.

A great part of the purpose of *Souls of Black Folk* was to celebrate the social power and social gifts and contributions of the people forced behind the veil. The way of doing this was through emphasis placed upon the forms of black expressivity—music, literature, religion. To be sure, DuBois understood the veil itself and black folks' forced positioning behind it as problematic, to be gotten rid of, ripped. He and others during his times challenged black folks to strive to rend the veil. Although after many decades of intense engagement and strivings DuBois removed himself from the United States, there is no doubt that the legal changes that were wrought here in the civil rights struggles of the 1950s, 1960s, and 1970s represented a degree of the rending of the DuBoisian veil.

Yet, even as the matter of the degree of amelioration of social-economic position among black folks continues to be debated, it is clear that "the veil" as a metaphor for black existence has proved to be elastic and expansive. At the end of *Souls of Black Folk*, after having consistently and dramatically used the term to describe and provoke strong emotions about the separation and hegemony of black folks from "the kingdom of culture," DuBois used it in a more positive sense, as the language of the slave songs that encodes or conceals the most profound and sensitive sentiments:

> In these songs . . . the slave spoke to the world. Such a message is naturally veiled and half articulate. Words and music have lost each other and new cant phrases of a dimly understood theology have displaced the older sentiment. . . . The music is distinctly sorrowful. [They] tell in word and music of trouble and exile, of strife and hiding; they grope toward some unseen power and sigh for rest in the End.
>
> The words . . . cleared of evident dross . . . conceal much of real poetry and meaning beneath conventional theology and unmeaning rhapsody. . . . Over the inner thoughts of the slaves and their relations one with another the shadow of fear ever hung, so that we get but glimpses here and there, and also with them, eloquent omissions and silences. . . .
>
> The things evidently borrowed from the surrounding world undergo characteristic change when they enter the mouth of the slave. Especially is this true of Bible phrases. (182–85)

These songs seemed to have been for DuBois evidence of a serious grappling with the "veil" of the other negative valence, the veil that was to be overcome. The point seems to have been that a certain kind of veiling—or critical interpretive strategy—was needed by those forced behind the veil. Such folk thought that for the sake of safety—physical and psychological—they had to express their deepest sentiments in veiled terms, indirectly, "in other words."

Some of the implications of this thinking were not lost on critics and scholars of African American culture and its forms of expression. Zora Neale Hurston comes immediately to mind as a well-known and provocative representative of folklorists, historians, literary critics, and others who have picked up on the veiling characteristic of African American expressivities. Most interesting for me, these critics, without consistent elaboration and problematization, without attempts to explain what was at issue, have nonetheless noticed the uses of the Bible and other sacred texts—in the "sorrow songs" and in so many other forms of black expressiveness—as part of the agenda of veiling about which DuBois argued. That veiling, indirection, encoding, and signifying are prominent in the interpretation of the folk is powerfully indicated in the saying that Hurston picked up in her field work and offered as handle for "reading" the world and the self—"hitting a lick with a crooked stick." In the manner in which she picked up on the full array of the lore and rhythms, the textures and gestures of black folk, and in the connection she made between the use even of the Bible and their liquid interpretations—"even the Bible was made over to suit our vivid imagination"[6]—Hurston named for critics of black culture to follow some of the poignancy involved in critical interpretation about and among black folks. Her rendering of black readings of the world points to the mysterious, the elusive, the uncanny:

> "Now all y'all heard what Ah said. . . . Dat's just an old time by-word. . . ." "I done heard my gran'paw say dem very words many and many a time. . . . There's a whole heap of them kinda by-words. . . . They all got a hidden meanin', jus' like de Bible. Everybody can't understand what they mean. Most people is thin-brained. They's born wid they feet under the moon. Some folks is born wid they feet on de sun and they kin seek out de inside meanin' of words."[7]

MORRISON AND THE (UN-)VEILING OF THE VEIL

We cannot fail to notice Hurston's representation of the Bible as a depository of the uncanny, the mysterious, the "hidden meanin'." Toni Morrison picks up on the connection between the DuBoisian metaphorical use of the veil and the uses of the Bible in terms of the folkways illuminated by Hurston in order to problematize black existence and interpretation. Regarding the veil, she deepens and widens DuBois's metaphorical rendering. For her the veil has to do not merely with racial segregation and other-ing. She expands the DuBoisian notion of the attendant/resultant divided consciousness into an argument about a type of shutting off, occlusion, and silencing of the interior life/self. In an essay titled "The Site of Memory," published in 1987, Morrison addresses the matter of the veiling of the interior life for the black self—the muting or encoding of deeply felt sentiments, pain, stresses, and trauma. With special attention to the autobiographical works that were the slave narratives of the eighteenth and nineteenth centuries she identifies what is for black folk the perduring poignant problem of uniting the divided consciousness and accessing and probing and articulating the movements of the interior life:

> No slave society in the history of the world wrote more . . . about its own enslavement. The milieu, however, dictated the purpose and the style. . . . Popular taste discouraged the writers from dwelling too long or too carefully on the more sordid details of their experience. Whenever there was an unusually violent incident, or a scatological one, or something "excessive," one finds the writer taking refuge in the literary conventions of

the day. "I was left in a state of distraction not to be described" (Equiano). "But let us now leave the rough usage of the field . . . and turn our attention to the less repulsive slave life as it existed in the house of my childhood" (Douglass). "I am not about to harrow the feelings of my readers by a terrific representation of the untold horrors of that fearful system of oppression. . . . It is not my purpose to descend deeply into the dark and noisome caverns of the hell of slavery" (Henry Box Brown).

Over and over, the writers pull the narrative up short with a phrase such as, "But let us drop a veil over these proceedings too terrible to relate." In shaping the experience to make it palatable to those who were in a position to alleviate it they were silent about many things, and they "forgot" many other things.[8]

Although it is clear enough that in the slave narratives the phenomenon of the silencing, hiding, and forgetting about which Morrison argues was much in evidence, it is less clear that in every instance of the narration of the experiences of slavery the term *veil* was referenced as euphemistic registration of or allusion to the phenomenon. Not all of Morrison's examples quoted above include the term itself. Yet there is no doubting their support of her general argument. She used the pointed metaphor of the veil as a way to think and make the point about the occlusion. The one narration from which she quotes that includes actual reference to the term comes from Lydia Maria Child's introduction to Linda Brent's "tale" of sexual abuse. It seems to be the reference that for Morrison makes clear the problem faced and suggests the language with which a solution can be found:

I am well aware that many will accuse me of indecorum for presenting these pages to the public; for the experiences of this intelligent and much-injured woman belong to a class which some call delicate subjects, and others indelicate. This peculiar phase of Slavery has generally been kept veiled; but the public ought to be made acquainted with its monstrous features, and I am willing to take the responsibility of presenting them with the veil drawn [aside].[9]

Morrison goes on to make her most important point: it was striking to her that in the narratives there was "no mention of [the slaves'] interior life." As a writer thriving "not much more than a hundred years after Emancipation, a writer who is black and a woman," she saw her job to be "to rip that veil drawn over 'proceedings too terrible to relate.'" She argued that this work was "critical" for all who belong to the "marginalized category" in society, because "we were seldom invited to participate in the discourse even when we were its topic."[10]

Morrison's research into the slave narratives surely did allow her both to problematize and to provoke more thinking about divided black consciousness. But it seems to me that notwithstanding her lack of acknowledgment of it—at least in "Site of Memory"—Morrison was surely aware of DuBois's uses of the "veil." She was, if not dependent on him, at least in conversation with DuBois. Here I have in mind in particular her conversation with him about his intimation of what the "sorrow songs" signify, what they beckon, what they hold out as possibilities in helping to "rend the veil," to unite a divided consciousness, to articulate powerful sentiments and yearnings. As I have pointed out, it is ironic that the term DuBois used to point to this work/office is *veil*. That is, he thought that one powerful response on the part of black folks to the dividedness of the black soul was the music—especially, but not exclusively, the "sorrow songs." The music was understood to be evocative and powerful. DuBois found himself undone by it; he first experienced and then understood it as powerful carrier of veiled sentiment. The music, then, should be compared to the slave narratives as expressive form—with the obvious different and shared possibilities and limitations respected.

From her different social historical positioning Morrison saw more sharply the limitations of both music and the literature that was the slave narrative. Regarding music, she argued in an interview that it "kept us alive, but it's not enough anymore."[11] No surprise that she favors literature: she has made it clear that she thinks that fiction—in particular, the novel—can now speak most directly and powerfully to and for the people having migrated to the cities:

> I write what I have recently begun to call village literature, fiction . . . for the village, for the tribe. Peasant literature for my people. . . . The middle class at the beginning of the industrial revolution needed a portrait of itself because the old portrait didn't work for this new class. Their roles were different; their lives in the city were new. The novel served this function then, and it still does. It tells about city values, the urban values. Now my people, we "peasants," have come to the city. . . . We live with its values. There is a confrontation between old values of the tribes and new urban values. It's confusing. There has to be a mode to do what the music did for blacks, what we used to be able to do with each other in private and in that civilization that existed underneath the white civilization.[12]

Morrison here seems to see music, including the music DuBois discussed, as a continu-

ing part of the veiling, needing to be ripped. The veiling here is that which keeps black folks from probing their interiority—on their own terms. Such a problematic and the way outward (or inward, really) seem to be precisely what Morrison addresses in most of her novels, most profoundly in *Beloved*.[13]

Beloved has been and continues to be interpreted in myriad ways, with many different types of interpreters representing many different angles, agendas, and perspectives, responding to what appears to be the author's invitation to read and probe and discuss the book. There is raging debate still about the character Beloved—whence she comes, who or what she represents, the meaning or import of this or that statement or action attributed to her/it, whither it/she goes. But all interpreters generally agree that *Beloved* is a story about a haunting, the haunting of those who are survivor-heirs of the "sixty million and more" made to undergo the Middle Passage (and to whom the book is dedicated). It is a story about the failure on the part of all of us to remember those who died in such an experience. It is about the refusal of those who died to go away and remain forgotten; it is about the haunting of the memory of those who died. It is about why and how the memory of those who died is prevented, held back, made difficult or impossible to embrace. Why the memory persists. Why it hurts, traumatizes. It is about consciousness, the impact the haunting has on the black soul, on the black consciousness. It is about the impact of the loss of memory, the prevention and refusal of memory upon the black soul. It is also ultimately about how the black soul may be reconstituted, healed, and united. So it is also consciousness, interpretation, and articulation about the terms on which, and the framework within which, the black self, the one who is survivor-heir of the Middle Passage may now look back, remember, interpret, negotiate, and speak to the world about what it thinks, how it feels, and how it travels and experiences. It is about "ripping the veil" that prevents the black self from remembering and healing itself. It is a pointing in the direction in which the psycho-social-cultural stitching, weaving work can be carried out.

Although it is clear what character in the book does the haunting, not entirely clear in every part of the book is the matter how the haunting is to be understood, that is, how the haunting works, why it persists, what the haunting is really all about. It should occasion little surprise that I would notice and want to exploit, as very few other interpreters have, Morrison's epigraph, which is taken from Paul's letter to the Romans (9:25), and which also supplies the name of the character for whom the book is named:

> I will call them my people,
> Which were not my people;
> and her beloved,
> which was not beloved.

No argument need be made about the importance of epigraphs in summing up a writer's agenda. What I want to stress here is the importance of the epigraph in naming the issue behind the (narrative plotline) issue. In order for this is to be made clear, it is important that the larger context of Paul's statement (actually a quotation of Hos 2:25, with word agreement with the LXX of 1:9) be established. The larger discursive-argumentative context is Paul's effort to address the believers at Rome of mixed background, viz., Jews and Gentiles, regarding what appears to be, in light of the success of the Pauline mission, an ironic, even paradoxical twist of fate and circumstance—the phenomenon of the turning to God in great numbers on the part of Gentiles. Since the promise of God's favor was given first to the Jews, how has it come about that the

non-Jews, the Gentiles, are turning in what seems to be great numbers and so many Jews in comparison seem not to be accepting God's "call"? Paul's tries his best to clarify matters; it does not work. His arguments are halting, elliptical, and confusing.[14]

I think it important to note that the end of the larger section, Romans 9–11, in which the prophetic statement that Morrison used for her epigraph is found, Paul sums up how he thinks the matter having to do with the turning and selection should be understood: "I do not want you to be ignorant of this *mystery* . . ." (11:25). At the beginning of the larger section Paul engages in a wonderful play on the word "call" (*kaleo*) before he draws a conclusion regarding the "mystery." It is this word and Paul's play with it—that is, signifying on it as marker of "hidden meanin'," of paradox—that seem to draw Morrison's attention and inspire her usage.

Morrison seems to have applied the Pauline "mystery" that equated "the call" (as election) and being called "beloved" to her book and black existence. She renders the historical and perduring exclusion and marginalization; the historical enslavement, other-ness, and subjugation; and the hoped-for elevation and self-possession in society and culture of black peoples mysterious. Paul's rendering of Hosea's being called "beloved" is translated by Morrison as black folks' coming to be loved. So it seems that what is most mysterious is the matter of *how* they were first enslaved and *how* they can or may come to be healed, elevated. In Morrison's thinking—through Paul—black peoples are the Gentiles, the ones thought at first to be outside, at first considered marginals, slaves, in terms of some grand design. And just as a mysterious thing happened with the Gentiles of Paul's day, as *even* they were brought into the fold, so black folks, according to Morrison, are destined to be "called," *to be loved.*

Morrison presents the challenge of addressing the mystery of black existence—how it evolved, survival strategies, the power dynamics involved, the self-acceptance. But what is first required (her essays and novels, especially the book *Beloved*, seem to suggest) is the work of identifying and "ripping the veil." With *Beloved* Morrison makes narratological, thus more complex and emotional, the identification of both the problem and the direction of the healing for the characters. Whatever is *Beloved* the book, it is not a "straight stick" that hits a "clean lick." Whatever *Beloved* means, it means not in a straightforward manner. The story that is *Beloved* cannot possibly be represented or understood as a line. And the story that the characters of the story tell is the scrambling of a line. Instead of a line circles come to mind—the characters tell versions or aspects of the same story; or they tell multiple stories, stories that are varied and overlapping. For all of the characters, but most especially for the main character, Sethe, language, certainly, the language and narratives, the "symbolic order" of the master, cannot transmit or translate her experience. In order to prevent her from having to undergo the humiliation of slavery, Sethe killed her baby girl. This experience was deemed by Sethe and by all observers to be horrible. But it was also representative. And it was precisely as horrible representative act that it was traumatic, "unspeakable."

It is the master language, the "symbolic order," that Morrison stresses must be ripped in order for black folks to come to be called beloved. Not just the slave narrative, but dominant Western discourse itself, with its need and tendency, as Pierre Bourdieu puts it, to "occult the aphasia,"[15] to veil the veiling, as Morrison might put it—this must be ripped. This ripping is signaled in the book not only by the multiple repetitive and varied tellings of the horrible experiences and hauntings by different characters but also by Sethe's effort finally to come to speech about what happened. It is Morrison's description of Sethe's movements as she comes into speech that is important to notice here: "She was spinning. Round and round the room . . . turning like a slow steady wheel. . . . Circling [Paul D] the way she was circling the subject" (151, 153). This spinning seems to reveal Morrison's understanding of knowledge, self-awareness, self-consciousness, critical interpretation in terms of indirection, and fragmentation, perhaps, functioning in terms of therapy or psychoanalysis. It is both critique of master narrative as the reflector and confirmation of fixed position in society and a pointing toward reconstitution and healing. The circling and spinning suggest a critique of and resistance to linear discursivity and politics. It also reflects an effort to reconstitute the self. This difference in movement and orientation suggests that the ripping of the veil is accomplished not so much by a refusal to engage language and texts and textuality but a refusal to accord them the power to carry meaning in the same way, on the same terms, that is, in uncritical naturalized terms, as though they were part of what Bourdieu termed the realm of *doxa*, the domain of the taken for granted, the undiscussable,[16] and what Houston Baker referred to as critical "silence."[17]

Here are the radicalism and power of the interpretive stance taken and shared by Morrison and DuBois and so many other critics of African American life—that for black and subaltern critical consciousness there is no meaning in any Western-translated narrative, script, text, and tradition unless such is first ripped, broken, and then "entranced," blackened, made usable for weaving meaning.[18]

The metaphors here and throughout my article are mixed; they rather deliciously and poignantly run amok. Speaking so—"in other words"—is necessary in order to address complexity and pain and trauma. "Ripping the veil" means refusing to think according to and live dreamily within the realm of *doxa*, the realm of the canonical. It means accessing the sites of memory. Social therapy can begin only when these memories on their own terms—not behind the "veil" of canonical texts—are woven together or "(re)textualized" (in the original meaning of that term) as "scriptures" in critical/signifying relationship to other "scriptures." And in agreement with writer-critic Ishmael Reed, it may mean, with ramifications most radical, that ultimately "we will make our own future text."[19]

Notes

1. W. E. B. DuBois, *Souls of Black Folk* (New York: Bantam, 1989 [1903]); all quotations are from this edition.

2. The term *veil* has interesting etymology: Middle English *veile*, taken from old North French, taken from the Latin *vela*, plural of *velum* (sail, awning). It has been used allusively in various prepositional phrases, such as behind, beyond, or within the veil: William Tyndale 1528; William Wollaston 1722; Alfred Tennyson 1850; E. Fitzgerald 1859; A. J. Ross 1877; to conceal from apprehension, knowledge or perception; to disguise: Benjamin D'Israel 1841. At the time of DuBois's writing, these uses were very much in the air of popular discourse and in letters. See *The Oxford English Dictionary*, sub verbo, 3c, vol. XIX, 2nd ed. (Oxford: Clarendon, 1989).

3. Shamoon Zamir, *Dark Voices: W. E. B. DuBois and American Thought, 1888–1903* (University of Chicago Press, 1995), esp. part 2.

4. Arnold Rampersad, *Art and Imagination of W. E. B. DuBois* (Cambridge Mass.: Harvard University Press, 1976), esp. chap. 4.

5. "This curtain [of appearance] . . . hanging before the inner world is withdrawn, and we have here the inner being gazing into the inner realm. . . . What we have here is Self-consciousness. It is manifest that behind the so-called curtain, which is to hide the inner world, there is nothing to be seen unless we ourselves go there, as much in order that we may thereby see, as that there may be something behind there which can be seen." Georg Wilhelm Friedrich Hegel, *Phenomenology of Mind*, trans. J. B. Baillie (New York: Harper Torchbooks, 1967 [1807, trans. 1910]), 211, 212–13, quoted in Zamir, *Dark Voices*, 135.

6. Zora Neale Hurston, *Mules and Men* (New York: Perennial Library, 1990 [1935]), 3.

7. Ibid., 125.

8. Toni Morrison, "The Site of Memory," in *Inventing the Truth: The Art and Craft of Memoir*, ed. William Zinsser (Boston: Houghton Mifflin, 1995), 109–10.

9. Ibid., 110.

10. Ibid., 110–11.

11. From Thomas Leclair, "'The Language Must Not Sweat': A Conversation with Toni," in *Toni Morrison: Critical Perspectives Past and Present*, ed. Henry Louis Gates Jr. and K. A. Appiah, Amistad Literary Series (New York: Amistad, 1993), 371.

12. Ibid., 370–71.

13. Toni Morrison, *Beloved* (New York: Penguin, 1987).

14. See Romans 9:22-26 for the larger context:

> What if God, wishing to display . . . wrath and to make known [God's] power, has endured with much patience the objects of wrath that are made for destruction; and what if [God] has done so in order to make known the riches of [God's] glory for the objects of mercy, which [God] has prepared beforehand for glory—including us [believers] whom [God] has called, not from the Jews only but also from the Gentiles? As indeed [God] says in Hosea,
> "Those who were not my people I will call 'my people,'
>   and her who was not beloved I will call 'beloved.'"
> "And in the very place where it was said to them, 'You are not my people,'

> there they shall be called
> children of the living God."

15. See Pierre Bourdieu, *Outline of a Theory of Practice*, trans. Richard Nice (Cambridge: Cambridge University Press, 1977), 170.

16. Ibid., 168.

17. It is really functionally much like the "silence" that Houston A. Baker Jr. discusses in his *Afro-American Poetics: Revisions of Harlem and the Black Aesthetic* (Madison: University of Wisconsin Press, 1988), in particular, the essay "Lowground and Inaudible Valleys: Reflections on Afro-American Spirit Work" (chap. 3). Baker argues that the interpretive orientation he associates with black folk culture is to be understood as "silence"—that is, as holding back from normal/traditional uses of language, turning away from the regular forms in order to express critique and healing. Drawing upon Susan Sontag's essay on silence, "The Aesthetics of Silence," in *A Susan Sontag Reader* (New York: Vantage, 1983), 181–204, he calls for a "criticism of silence" (106) to "match the depths of a magnificently enhancing black sounding of experience" (109).

18. "Merely arranged in a traditional Christian problematic . . . words are ineffectual. Only when they enter into entranced performance . . . do they give birth to sounds of a new order" (Baker, "Lowground and Inaudible Valleys," 106). The entranced performance about which Baker speaks is realized only when there is an addressing of the "lowground and inaudible valleys" of experiences of black folks. Then the canonical arrangements and structures are exploded, the veil is ripped.

19. Reed is widely published. See *The Reed Reader* (New York: Basic, 2001) for a selection of his writings.

For Further Reading

Gates, Henry Louis, Jr. *Signifying Monkey: A Theory of African-American Literary Criticism.* Oxford: Oxford University Press, 1988.

Reed, Ishmael. *The Reed Reader.* New York: Basic, 2000.

Sugirtharajah, R. S. *Postcolonialism and Biblical Intepretation.* Oxford: Oxford University Press, 2002.

WOMANIST BIBLICAL INTERPRETATION

Raquel St. Clair

Koala Jones-Warsaw defines the task of womanist biblical hermeneutics as "discover[ing] the significance and validity of the biblical text for black women who today experience the 'tridimensional reality' of racism, sexism, and classism."[1] For African American women, the significance and validity of the Bible are founded in its affirmation of God's solidarity with and commitment to them. Specifically, it is God's commitment to their survival and wholeness, a commitment that womanists uphold in their theological formulations and praxis. Whereas some feminists employ a hermeneutics of suspicion,[2] I suggest that a womanist biblical hermeneutic be characterized as a hermeneutics of wholeness. I begin with a brief overview of womanist theology

and Christology as a means of laying a foundation for understanding the unique perspective of womanist biblical interpretation. I conclude by positing four principles for a womanist hermeneutics of wholeness.

OVERVIEW

In 1983, Alice Walker prefaced her prose collection, *In Search of Our Mothers' Gardens*, with the definition of a word that would revolutionize the theological landscape:

> Womanist.
>   1. From *womanish*. (Opp. of "girlish," i.e., frivolous, irresponsible, not

serious.) A black feminist or feminist of color. From the black folk expression of mothers to female children, "You acting womanish," i.e., like a woman. Usually referring to outrageous, audacious, courageous or *willful* behavior. Wanting to know more and in greater depth than is considered "good" for one. Interested in grown-up doings. Acting grown up. Being grown up. Interchangeable with another black folk expression: "You trying to be grown." Responsible. In charge. *Serious.*

2. *Also:* A woman who loves other women, sexually and/or nonsexually. Appreciates and prefers women's culture, women's emotional flexibility (values tears as natural counterbalance of laughter), and women's strength. Sometimes loves individual men, sexually and /or nonsexually. Committed to the survival and wholeness of entire people, male *and* female. Not a separatist, except periodically, for health. Traditionally universalist, as in: "Mama, why are we brown, pink, and yellow and our cousins are white, beige and black?" Ans.: "Well, you know, the colored race is just like a flower garden, with every color represented." Traditionally capable, as in: "Mama, I'm walking to Canada and I'm taking you and a bunch of other slaves with me." Reply: "It wouldn't be the first time."

3. Loves music. Loves dance. Loves the moon. *Loves* the Spirit. Loves love and food and roundness. Loves struggle. *Loves* the folk. Loves herself. *Regardless.*

4. Womanist is to feminist as purple is to lavender.[3]

Although the term bears no explicitly theological or Christian meaning[4] apart from "lov[ing] the Spirit," it aptly describes the reality of African American women. It is important that, even though Alice Walker's definition is the touchstone for womanist theology, its usage has not been without debate. In the formative years of womanist theology, Cheryl Sanders questioned whether or not Walker's term had been "misconstrued" to "suit our own [theological] purposes."[5] Despite Sanders's concerns, the nomenclature remained. Walker had constructed a label for and description of the unique social, cultural, historical, and theological experiences and understandings of African American women. The term *womanist* resonated with African American women because it gave them a way "to name themselves and their experiences without having to depend on either the sexist views of men (of all races) or the racist views of white women and white men."[6] "Womanism" provided an opportunity for African American women to "be and write out of who [they] are."[7]

The coining of the term *womanist* and the publication of full-length texts on womanist theology[8] proved to be a decisive moment in the development of African American women's self-understanding and theological perspective. Delores Williams identifies three major turning points that led African American women to this juncture. First, she notes that womanist thought and theology reach as far back as the nineteenth century. The work of the 1980s was the result of a retrospective outlook in which African American women saw and embraced their connection to foremothers such as Anna Julia Cooper,[9] Maria Stewart,[10] and Ida B. Wells.[11] They saw in them the nascent characteristics of womanism only recently defined. They also saw the potential to work for the rights of both women of all races and African Americans of both genders.[12]

The second turning point was the civil rights movement of the 1950s and early 1960s. The hallmark of this movement was its communal focus on the racial issues that affected African American life. However, this "communal way of thinking obscured Black women's oppression and Black male sexism."[13]

On the heels of the civil rights movement came the third turning point, the "second wave of feminism" in the late 1960s. Feminism served to make people in general and African American women in particular aware of the oppression of women.[14]

Although each of the above liberation movements included and benefited African American women, African American women had to deny a part of themselves to participate in them. The civil rights movement sought to liberate African Americans from the racial oppression experienced in a racist society. With the emphasis on race, gender issues were ignored. The liberation of women was not included in the agenda to liberate African Americans. This placed African American women in a "precarious situation" in that they "needed to maintain a partnership with black men in the struggle against white racism . . . [and] also realized . . . black men did not respect them as equals."[15]

The feminist movement, on the other hand, addressed sexism separate from racism, as its constituents were overwhelmingly white women. Although African American and white women were united in their struggle against sexism, racism divided them. White women in the feminist movement failed to see how they had universalized their experience and made it *the* experience of womanhood.[16]

Given the particular emphases of both the feminist and the civil rights movements, African American women had to choose whether they were first African Americans or women. Instead, they chose to create for themselves the opportunity to be both black and female and to work toward the liberation of all African Americans. Thus, "womanist theology arose out of the feminist movement and the Black Power/Black liberation movement."[17] Alice Walker's nomenclature furnished them with the language and framework to be who they are and pursue liberation from sexist, racist, classist, and heterosexist oppression.

African American women's insistence that their experience was just as valid as the experience of white women also necessitated the creation of their own theological voice. M. Shawn Copeland states, "Womanist theology claims the experiences of Black women as proper and serious data for theological reflection."[18] By reflecting on their experiences, African American women needed to and could "affirm different cultural foundations for identical assertions made by both feminists and black women."[19] Womanist theology, then, expanded Walker's definition in order to create a space in which Christian theology and the experiences of African American women could connect. As Stephanie Mitchem puts it, "Womanist theology is an opportunity to state the meanings of God in the real time of black women's lives."[20]

The "real time" of African American women's lives occurs at the nexus of gender, race, and class. Womanist theology, then, engages each of these facets of African American female life simultaneously. To neglect any area of oppression that affects their lives is to "deny the holistic and integrated reality of Black womanhood."[21] Therefore "womanist symbolizes black women's resistance to their multi-dimensional oppression."[22]

Renita Weems asserts that it has only been within the context of the African American female interpretive community that African American women have been allowed to "hold in tandem all components of [their] identity."[23] This interpretive community includes the church and the academy, as well as civic organizations. Womanist theology creates another opportunity for African American women to occupy their particular gender, racial, and economic spaces and be wholly human.

The attention given to gender issues is evident in womanist theology, but womanists do not stop there. They are committed to the "wholeness of entire people":

> Womanists are particularly concerned with the 'isms' that oppress African American women. Our work unmasks, disentangles, and debunks religious language, symbols, doctrines, and socio-political structures that perpetuate the oppression of African American women in particular, but also African American men, children, humanity in general, and nature.[24]

The struggle of womanist theologians against oppression has to go beyond the survival to the liberation and well-being of women.[25] Gender, race, and class intersect and reinforce each other in the lives of African American women. Therefore, womanist theology does not limit itself to sexism and an "analysis of white racism,"[26] but also includes issues of class.

Classism can be defined as "the systemic tendency of ruling classes to reinforce the distance between themselves and ruled classes by preventing the dispersal of power through a restructuring of wealth, privilege and access to resources and technology."[27] In her article "Racism and Economics: The Perspective of Oliver Cox," Katie Cannon explores the connection between racism and classism. Cannon's work builds on the thought of Oliver Cox, who argued that capitalistic expansion requires the "core system to breed universal contempt for those exploited by the system,"[28] especially people of color and specifically people of African descent. Racism becomes the means by which contempt for African Americans is bred. Lies of inferiority and media portrayals that cast people of color as "uncivi-

lized" infer that "capitalists have the right to hold people of color in subjection until they are 'civilized.'"[29] Because "civilization" equals "white power" in this schema, people of color must permanently be held in subjection. Cannon concludes: "Racism supports the belief, conscientiously held, that poverty and ignorance sustained by force and fraud are desirable for people of color and that white power and prestige must remain at any cost."[30]

The social, economic, political, and spiritual location of African American women necessitates a theological perspective that seriously considers gender, race, and class and the interplay among them. Consequently, womanists intentionally try to "produce a theology whose construction, vocabulary and issues [take] seriously the everyday experiences, language and spirituality of women."[31]

Womanist theology is predicated upon the "experience of being Black and female in the United States."[32] Therefore, womanists bring a different lens to the theological and biblical enterprise by beginning with the uniqueness of their experience. This need to start from the foundation of African American women's experience was the catalyst for developing womanist theology[33] and womanist biblical interpretation.

Womanist biblical interpretation, then, is the result of the interplay between African American women's experience and scripture. Old Testament scholar Renita Weems claims that, although the Bible has been used to subjugate African Americans, it is "still extremely influential in the African American religious life."[34] One reason for the Bible's continued influence is that for African American women "the Bible still has some power of its own."[35] In other words, African American women view the Bible as authoritative for their lives.[36] Moreover, African American women have accessed meaning in the text that contradicts the racist, sexist, and classist interpretations of their oppressors. Weems writes, "Outlook plays an important role in how one reads the Bible."[37]

On the one hand, the Bible informs African American women's experience and their understanding of the Christian faith. On the other hand, African American women's experience also affects how they read the text. In no way do I wish to suggest that this interaction between experience and text is peculiar to African American women. Everyone enters the interpretive process with certain questions and presuppositions that are a result of his or her experience.[38] What I do contend, however, is that this interaction between the text and African American women in particular represents another vantage point from which to view the Bible.

WOMANIST CHRISTOLOGY

Central to the theology of African American women and their understanding of scripture is the person of Jesus Christ. Because Jesus is an intrinsic part of African American women's spirituality, he is also central to womanist theology and biblical interpretation. Womanists identify two primary reasons for Jesus' critical role in the theological understanding of African American women. First, womanists contend that Jesus makes God real to African American women. Second, womanists assert that the interpretations of Jesus that African American women accept will also be the interpretations they accept about their own lives and selves.

Kelly Brown articulates well the first reason for Jesus' centrality: "Jesus of Nazareth makes God real, brings God down to earth, for black women."[39] Neither Jesus' maleness nor the fact that he has been historically depicted as a white man rather than a man of color nullifies his ability to make God real for African American women. Brown asserts that African American women identify with what Jesus has done in their lives, not with how he looks.[40] Jesus is the one that African American women refer to as healer and provider.[41]

Elaine Crawford voices the second reason for Jesus' centrality in the theology of African American women. She writes, "for black women, the hermeneutical key or 'interpretive reality' is the life of Jesus Christ. One's interpretation of Jesus bears a direct relationship to one's understanding of self. And one's understanding of self is directly related to one's understanding of Jesus."[42] The relationship between African American women's perception of Jesus and their perception of themselves is a critical issue since Jesus as the divine co-sufferer is one of their dominant understandings of Jesus.[43] By espousing an understanding that makes suffering a sole or necessary point of identification with Jesus, African American women cast themselves into the role of a perpetual sufferer. To remedy an identification with Jesus that perpetuates the suffering of African American women, womanist theological constructions of Jesus bear four basic principles in mind.

First, womanist theological explorations "look beyond the static absolutism of classical Christology to discern and celebrate the presence of Jesus in the lives of the abused and the oppressed.[44] The meaning of Jesus for African American women cannot be merely theoretical postulations, but concrete affirmations grounded in the everyday experiences of their lives. This involves discovering the "presence and participation of Jesus in [their] own particular existential reality."[45]

Second, womanist Christology must dismantle interpretations of Jesus Christ that "aid and abet the oppression of black women."[46] Womanist Christology examines the ways in which traditional Christian doctrines of Jesus

Christ have affected African American women in negative ways. For example, Brown notes that because they connect the significance of Jesus to maleness, many male preachers refuse to ordain women.[47] In similar manner, biblical texts that are held to advocate the subordination and silence of women must also be challenged by womanist scholars.[48]

Third, womanist Christology "must also affirm black women's faith that Jesus has supported them in their struggles to survive and be free."[49] This affirmation is essential. If Jesus does not support African American women's struggles, then they are forced to either give Jesus up or fight against rather than in solidarity with him. Womanists, therefore, affirm his support. They affirm his support based upon a particular understanding of traditional African American women's affirmation of Jesus as the divine co-sufferer.

The affirmation of Jesus as the divine co-sufferer declares that Jesus is the one who is present with them and "empowers them in situations of oppression."[50] However, it is important to note with JoAnne Terrell that the divine co-sufferer motif is in no way to function as a legitimization of anyone's suffering or oppression.[51] In other words, African American women are not to pursue or embrace suffering in order to be Jesus' co-sufferer. Instead, they affirm that Jesus is their co-sufferer. He knows their suffering and does not abandon them but rather empowers them in their struggle for freedom.

Finally, womanist interpretations of Jesus "must always make it clear that [Jesus'] ultimate significance is predicated upon . . . his sustaining and liberating activity."[52] Although African American women have a tradition of acknowledging Jesus as the divine co-sufferer, womanists emphasize that his significance for them is not found in his suffering. For womanists, Jesus' significance is found in his ministry. In other words, womanists acknowledge

that there are definite points of connection between Jesus' suffering and that of African American women. They recognize that African American women point to these similarities as proof that Jesus knows about and can identify with their suffering and conclude that God has not abandoned them. However, womanists affirm that similarity does not automatically translate into significance. Just because African American women identify with Jesus in his suffering, does not make suffering the significant aspect of who Jesus is or what Jesus did.

A HERMENEUTICS OF WHOLENESS

Using the four christological principles outlined above, I posit the following tenets for a womanist biblical hermeneutic.[53] First, a womanist hermeneutics of wholeness must promote the wholeness of African American women without prohibiting the wholeness of others. Stated negatively, a womanist biblical hermeneutic cannot aid or abet the oppression of African American women or anyone else. Womanists recognize the interrelatedness of all people. Therefore, African American women will not accomplish individual or community wholeness by the destruction or bondage of others. Womanists are "committed to the wholeness of an entire people."[54] This commitment transcends the boundaries of racism, sexism, classism, and heterosexism. In this way, womanists will reflect the nature of Jesus, whom we describe as "inclusive, relational, particular and, yet, universal."[55]

Second, our interpretive procedure must be grounded in the concrete reality of African American women's lives. It is "grounded" in that it does not simply postulate theoretical formulations but also seeks to assist African American women in living out the gospel message and addresses issues that affect them. This requires that any methodology employed take seriously the unique perspective African American women bring to the text as well as the situations to which they will apply the interpretation.

Third, a womanist hermeneutics of wholeness affirms that God supports African American women in their commitment to and struggle for wholeness. God in the person of Jesus Christ exemplifies this commitment. I affirm this commitment based on the testimony of Gospel accounts that depict Jesus' ministry as ministry to the "least of these." I agree with womanists—Jesus makes God real to African American women. However, I maintain that it is the Bible that makes Jesus real. Therefore, the biblical record is indispensable for womanist reflection.

Finally, a womanist hermeneutics of wholeness asserts that Jesus' significance is his life and ministry without excluding his suffering and death. This perspective is exemplified in the work of Karen Baker-Fletcher, who advocates a "both/and approach."[56] Recognizing the Synoptic Gospels as fruitful sources for womanist interpretations, she notes that both womanists and African American women in general "identify Jesus by his work in the synoptic Gospels."[57] Although she believes that African Americans will always have a deep connection to the cross,[58] Baker-Fletcher maintains that it is ultimately the lives of those who have been "crucified, lynched of bullet-ridden" that we should not forget.[59] With regard to Jesus, it is his life—not his crucifixion—that must remain foremost in our memories. Baker-Fletcher's approach allows one to see the causal relationship between Jesus' ministry and suffering. Jesus' life becomes the key to understanding his suffering and his death.

In sum, womanist theologians and biblical scholars use African American women's experience to produce an experiential lens that challenges both traditional African American and Eurocentric interpretation. Stephanie Mitchem is correct: "Exploring black women's unique interpretations or hermeneutics of scripture will most likely lead to new expressions of womanist theologies. The area of womanist biblical scholarship has great promise."[60]

Notes

1. Koala Jones-Warsaw, "Toward a Womanist Hermeneutic: A Reading of Judges 19–21," *JITC* 22 (1994): 30.

2. Elisabeth Schüssler Fiorenza, *Bread Not Stone: The Challenge of Feminist Biblical Interpretation* (Boston: Beacon, 1984), 15–18.

3. Alice Walker, *In Search of Our Mothers' Gardens: Womanist Prose* (San Diego: Harcourt Brace, 1983), xi–xii.

4. For a discussion on the appropriateness of using Walker's definition for specifically Christian theological endeavors, see Cheryl J. Sanders et al., "Roundtable: Christian Ethics and Theology in Womanist Perspective," *JFSR* 5 (1989): 83–112.

5. Ibid., 85. Sanders writes, "The fact is that womanist is essentially a secular category whose theological and ecclesial significations are rather tenuous. Theological content too easily gets 'read into' the womanist concept, whose central emphasis remains the self-assertion and struggle of black women for freedom, with or without the aid of God or Jesus or anybody else" (86).

6. Rufus Burrows Jr., "Toward Womanist Theology and Ethics," *JFSR* 15 (1999): 83.

7. Jacquelyn Grant, *White Women's Christ and Black Women's Jesus: Feminist Christology and Womanist Response* (Atlanta: Scholars, 1989), 205.

8. Grant, *White Women's Christ and Black Women's Jesus*; Delores S. Williams, *Sisters in the Wilderness: The Challenge of Womanist God-Talk* (Maryknoll, N.Y.: Orbis, 1993); Emilie

M. Townes, ed., *A Troubling in My Soul: Womanist Perspectives on Evil and Suffering* (Maryknoll, N.Y.: Orbis, 1993).

9. Karen Baker-Fletcher, "'Soprano Obligato': The Voices of Black Women and American Conflict in the Thought of Anna Julia Cooper," in Townes, *A Troubling in My Soul*, 172–88.

10. Clarice J. Martin, "Biblical Theology and Black Women's Spiritual Autobiography: 'The Miry Bog, the Desolate Pit, a New Song in My Mouth,'" in Townes, *A Troubling in My Soul*, 13–36.

11. Emilie M. Townes, *Womanist Justice, Womanist Hope* (Atlanta: Scholars, 1993).

12. Delores Williams, "Womanist Theology," in *Women's Visions: Theological Reflection, Celebration, Action*, ed. Ofelia Ortega (Geneva: WCC, 1995), 117.

13. Ibid., 118.

14. Ibid., 117.

15. Kelly Delaine Brown, "God Is as Christ Does: Toward a Womanist Theology," *JRT* 46 (1989): 12.

16. A. Elaine Crawford, "Womanist Christology: Where Have We Come From and Where Are We Going?" *RevExp* 95 (1998): 371.

17. Ibid., 370.

18. M. Shawn Copeland, "Wading through Many Sorrows: Toward a Theology of Suffering in Womanist Perspective," in Townes, *A Troubling in My Soul*, 111.

19. Williams, "Womanist Theology," 115.

20. Stephanie Mitchem, *Introducing Womanist Theology* (Maryknoll, N.Y.: Orbis, 2002), 60.

21. Grant, *White Women's Christ and Black Women's Jesus*, 209.

22. Brown, "God Is as Christ Does," 8.

23. Renita J. Weems, "Reading *Her Way* through the Struggle: African American Women and the Bible," in *Stony the Road We Trod: African American Biblical Interpretation*, ed. Cain Hope Felder (Minneapolis: Fortress Press, 1991), 70.

24. Crawford, "Womanist Christology," 375.

25. Williams, "Womanist Theology," 115.

26. Ibid., 121.

27. Mark Kline Taylor, *Remembering Esperanza: A Cultural-Political Theology for North American Praxis* (Maryknoll, N.Y.: Orbis, 1990), 122.

28. Katie Geneva Cannon, *Katie's Canon: Womanism and the Soul of the Black Community* (New York, N.Y.: Continuum, 1995), 156.

29. Ibid., 157.

30. Ibid., 160.

31. Ibid., 115.

32. Brown, "God Is as Christ Does," 8.

33. Crawford, "Womanist Christology," 367.

34. Weems, "Reading *Her Way* through the Struggle," 57.

35. Ibid., 63.

36. Weems writes, "It is certainly true that [the Bible] has been able to arrest African American female readers and persuade them to make their behavior conform according to its teachings" ("Reading *Her Way* through the Struggle," 63).

37. Ibid.

38. "No exegesis is without presuppositions, inasmuch as the exegete is not a tabula rasa, but on the contrary, approaches the text with specific questions or with a specific way of raising questions and thus has a certain idea of the subject matter with which the text is concerned." Rudolph Bultmann, "Is Exegesis without Presuppositions Possible?" in *New Testament Theology and Mythology and Other Basic Writings*, ed. Schubert M. Ogden (Philadelphia: Fortress Press, 1989), 145.

39. Brown, "God Is as Christ Does," 15.

40. Ibid., 16.

41. Ibid.

42. Crawford, "Womanist Christology," 368.

43. Grant, *White Women's Christ and Black Women's Jesus*, 212.

44. Crawford, "Womanist Christology," 370.

45. Ibid.

46. Brown, "God Is as Christ Does," 14.

47. Ibid.

48. An example of such a challenge is Clarice J. Martin's "The *Haustafeln* (Household Codes) in African American Biblical Interpretation: 'Free Slaves' and 'Subordinate Women,'" in Felder, *Stony the Road We Trod*, 206–31.

49. Brown, "God Is as Christ Does," 14.

50. Grant, *White Women's Christ and Black Women's Jesus*, 212.

51. JoAnne Marie Terrell, *Power in the Blood? The Cross in the African American Experience* (Maryknoll, N.Y.: Orbis, 1998), 124.

52. Brown, "God Is as Christ Does," 16.

53. For further discussion, see Raquel A. St. Clair, "Call and Consequences: A Sociolinguistic Reading through a Womanist Cultural Lens of Mark 8:31-38" (Ph.D. diss., Princeton Theological Seminary, Princeton, New Jersey, 2005), 125–28.

54. Walker, *In Search of Our Mothers' Gardens*, xi.

55. Crawford, "Womanist Christology," 375.

56. Karen Baker-Fletcher and Garth Kasimu Baker-Fletcher, *My Sister, My Brother: Womanist and Xodus God-Talk* (Maryknoll, N.Y.: Orbis, 1997), 78.

57. Ibid., 75.

58. Ibid.

59. Ibid.

60. Mitchem, *Introducing Womanist Theology*, 118.

For Further Reading

Baker-Fletcher, Karen, and Garth Kasimu Baker-Fletcher. *My Sister, My Brother: Womanist and Xodus God-Talk.* Maryknoll, N.Y.: Orbis, 1997.

Douglas, Kelly Brown, *The Black Christ.* Maryknoll, N.Y.: Orbis, 1994.

Martin, Clarice J. "Womanist Interpretation of the New Testament: The Quest for Holistic and Inclusive Translation and Interpretation." *JFSR* 6 (1990): 41–61.

St. Clair, Raquel A. "Call and Consequences: A Sociolinguistic Reading through a Womanist Cultural Lens of Mark 8:3-38." Ph.D. diss., Princeton Theological Seminary, Princeton, New Jersey, 2005.

Weems, Renita J. "Reading *Her Way* through the Struggle: African American Woman and the Bible." In *Stony the Road We Trod: African American Biblical Interpretation.* Edited by Cain Hope Felder. Minneapolis: Fortress Press, 1991.

Williams, Delores. "The Color of Feminism: Or Speaking the Black Woman's Tongue." *JRT* 43 (1986): 42–58.

———. "Womanist Theology." In *Women's Visions: Theological Reflection, Celebration, Action.* Edited by Orfelia Ortega. Geneva: WCC, 1995.

AFRICAN AMERICAN
PREACHING *and the* BIBLE

Cleophus J. LaRue

Taking a text from scripture and announcing a sermon title when preparing to preach continue to be the two clearest signals a preacher can send to a black congregation that he or she understands the importance of the primacy of the Word. Black congregants, by and large, go to church to hear the preacher expound on the written Word, and they don't really get a feel for the sermon until they hear the scriptures or sense some connection between the scriptures and what the preacher is saying.

Thus, black preaching is inextricably tied to scripture. In the eyes of the black church, a preacher without scripture is like a doctor without a black bag. What one needs to get the preaching job done comes with some kind of encounter with scripture. Any preacher who seeks to be heard on a regular basis in a black church must learn some method of engaging the scriptural text and drawing from that encounter some sense of the Word of God revealed *to* and acting *upon* the present-day human situation of the black listeners. Effective preachers recognize that this daunting task of creatively engaging the scriptures and pairing them to some aspect of lived experience are at the center of their weekly sermon preparation task. Therefore, the preacher must be familiar with the Bible. A well-worn saying continues to hold true in the black church: Whatever they say about you, don't let it be said that you can't preach. The in-depth knowledge of scripture required of the preacher cannot simply be a task-oriented familiarity with scripture, for the Bible does not fully yield its treasures as the Word of God to those who merely visit it from time to time when fishing for a sermon. One has to live with the scriptures and walk up and down the streets of the texts in order to have those texts speak with power and conviction.

It is both unwise and inaccurate to speak of a single way in which African Americans preach from the scriptures in their quest for God. The danger lies in any claim to single-ness of expression that purports to speak for an entire group of people with a four-hundred-year history on American soil. African Americans are diverse and complex in their makeup, religious beliefs and practices, and most certainly construal and use of the scriptures. Black preaching and teaching are of necessity multifarious in their depths and expressions. Therefore, any attempt to outline the broad parameters of an African American use of the Bible must be qualified with words on the order of non-monolithic, multifaceted, and diverse. Such words help to remind us that every rule has an exception and no group can ever be said to do any one thing a certain way.

THE FOUR ESSENTIALS OF THE BLACK SERMON

There are four essentials that come together in the best of black preaching. They are God, the Scriptures, the preacher, and black lived experience. These rudimentary components interact with one another in a manner that is evident in end-result yet most difficult to dissect and set apart, even for the purpose of establishing a framework for study. Yet these four essentials are at the heart of the black

construal and use of the Bible, and they aid blacks in their quest to know what God has done *for* us and, of equal measure, what God requires *of* us. On the basis of these four fundamentals, blacks bring certain expectations to the preaching moment. First, when the scriptures are being proclaimed, blacks believe that they are being addressed by God. Second, they expect that this address will come through the preacher of the Word after the preacher has faithfully explicated the text and sought in meaningful and relevant ways to wed that text to the lived experience of the black congregation.

GOD

At the heart of the black search of the scriptures has been an unceasing quest for God and the things of God. Unlike many who claim a deep-seated love for the Bible, blacks typically have not made the mistake of worshiping the Bible, but they have sought in their preaching and teaching to probe the unsearchable riches of God's grace as those riches are witnessed to and attested in the Bible. So intense has been the black search for a divine encounter with God that in their early history in America, some former slaves were said to value their *experience* of God's power as the norm of Christian truth rather than the Bible itself.[1] In contemporary times, the Bible's importance for a large number of African Americans has been more functional than revelatory. That is, blacks have viewed the Bible as the primary way for them to encounter God. Thus it is the way the scriptures function in their lives that is of the utmost importance for blacks. In its functional import, the Bible does much more than simply witness to God's past acts on behalf of others; it actually speaks to blacks about who God is today and how God effects God's will and purpose in their present situations in life.

There is in black preaching a predominant interpretive strategy that shows up time and time again when one examines historical and present day black uses of scripture. That biblical hermeneutic concerns itself with God and God's actions especially as they are most fully and finally manifested in Jesus Christ. Many blacks are convinced that God is for them. They have historically believed the acts of God to be favorable and intentional on behalf of all those who, like themselves, have been marginalized and oppressed, neglected and looked over. Blacks believe God has continually championed their cause in spite of those who sought to relegate them to an inferior standing unworthy of the full force of God's providential care and concern. To this day, even among upwardly mobile blacks who consider that they have moved further in from the periphery of marginalization, some understanding of a God who is at work on their behalf continues to govern their construal of scripture. While in some black circles this understanding has taken a very selfish, narcissistic turn, it is nonetheless a dimension of the interpretive strategy blacks have employed. Blacks believe that God is for them—even when being for them is understood in a very provincial, restrictive, and selfish manner. It is this template that governs their explication of scripture.

It is not by accident that a popular refrain—mantra even—among the black religious public is: God is good all the time; all the time God is good! Blacks truly believe this about God. The God of power and might is good to them and good for them. Even when a particular text could conceivably be interpreted to the contrary, blacks do not despair, gloss over, or misread; they simply turn their view to the grand sweep of their eschatological hope, which is to say, they look to God's overall performance and promises—in and through human history. That

grand view of God, which has stood the test of time, grounds them both in their backward look and in their forward glance (what God has done and what God has promised). The interpretive strategy that blacks employ allows them to say with confidence to any and all who doubt their understanding of God: Come see what great things the LORD has done!

A central truth blacks quickly came to embrace when they were allowed to read and interpret for themselves is that scripture revealed a God of infinite power who could be trusted to act on their behalf. Historically blacks embraced the Christian God in large numbers only after they were able to make a connection between God's power and their servile situation in life. This direct relationship between black struggle and divine rescue colors the theological perceptions and themes of black preaching in a very decisive manner.[2]

A God who is unquestionably *for* them is what blacks see when they go to the scriptures. Thus a distinctive characteristic of black preaching is that which blacks believe scripture reveals about the sovereign God's involvement in the everyday affairs and circumstances of their existence. African Americans believe that the sovereign God acts in very concrete and practical ways in matters pertaining to their survival, deliverance, advancement, prosperity, and overall well-being. This is not to suggest that God is at work only for blacks, but it is to say with power and conviction that blacks have not been left out of the redemptive purposes of almighty God.[3] This is what blacks see when they open the pages of the written Word of God.

THE SCRIPTURES

There is in black preaching a high regard for scripture. Black preaching has historically been noted for its strong biblical content. In many black churches, biblical preaching, defined as preaching that allows a text from the Bible to serve as the leading force in shaping the content and purpose of the sermon, is the type of preaching considered to be most faithful to traditional understandings of the proclaimed word.

Indeed, it is no secret that the Bible occupies a central place in the religious life of black Americans. More than a mere source for texts in black preaching, the Bible is the single most important source of language, imagery, and story for the sermon. Though biblical literacy in black churches is greatly diminished from earlier years, it has yet to reach the state where the Bible's primacy as a rich resource for black preaching is no longer the case.

A noted white homiletician recently found it comical that blacks still draw many of their examples and illustrations in preaching directly from scripture. He wanted blacks to broaden their reading circle to include examples and illustrations from literature and modern-day life. While I agree that the reading circle should be broadened, I do not agree that it should come at the expense of our love and high regard for scripture and our ability to continue to find our lives and examples of our lives therein. The scriptures still matter in black preaching. They are our guide and source to life as it is meant to be lived before God. One is hard pressed to make his or her case in a black pulpit if the congregation comes to believe that the scriptures do not have primacy.

Blacks, like other interpreters of the Bible, rarely operate with an explicitly formulated theory of the text. Yet their theoretical assumptions are undeniably present. The black belief that they are being addressed by God in the preaching of the Word is the foremost theoretical assumption in their construal of the scriptures. This understanding of scripture has been characterized as the *divine oracle paradigm*.[4] Several basic principles inform this paradigm. First, there is the conviction that the Bible constitutes one single genre. In the view of many blacks, while the Bible is composed of diverse materials, when properly arranged as a completed collection, it is seen as unfolding a single, continuous, coherent story of salvation history.[5]

Second, God is believed to be the author of scripture, which is to say, the scriptures were written by numerous authors speaking, in some direct sense, on behalf of God. Thus, by extension, God may be viewed as the real author. Without apology, large numbers of blacks continue to believe this about the scriptures. An often-cited passage is 2 Tim 3:16-17: "All scripture is inspired by God and is useful for teaching, for reproof, for correction, and for training in righteousness, so that everyone who belongs to God may be proficient, equipped for every good work" (NRSV).

Third, there is a uniformity of revelation. If the black Bible is assumed to be a unified, coherent collection of writings that directly derive from God, it naturally flows that God is speaking in all its parts. In any given verse we can hear God's voice, and we can expect it to resonate with all the other parts to some degree. The idea that certain parts of the Bible can be cast aside and treated as something less than God's word is anathema to large numbers of blacks. A harmonious thread runs throughout the whole of scripture, and, while some passages may be a bit distant from that melody, they are a part of God's overall song.[6]

Fourth, scripture is directly expressive of divine will. This principle presupposes a direct correspondence between scripture and divine intent and assumes that the will of God is somehow embodied within and expressed by the text. The text becomes the primary focus of the interpreter's attention and the primary locus of revelation. The place the preacher looks for, or listens to, the Word of God is within the sacred pages of the Bible. Blacks believe that the attentive interpreter can hear God speaking directly through the text. So, often in black preaching there will be little distance between the preacher and the events of the text. It is not uncommon to hear the preacher proclaim, "I heard Paul say the other day . . . ," as if the preacher and Paul had recently been in conversation; the preacher believes that God is speaking in the here and now, directly through the text.[7]

Blacks are often not given credit for the nuancing they do in this paradigm. To say that one expects to be addressed by God through scripture is not to suggest that scripture must be taken literally in all its parts. It is to say that the search that drives the desire to understand and interpret the scriptures grows out of the belief that somehow, in some manner God is speaking through a particular text. The very helpful finds of the historical-critical methodology are of immense benefit to blacks in their quest to hear the voice of God. Blacks simply refuse to relegate that voice strictly to the historical past.

THE PREACHER

Without question, the black preacher has been at the center of defining the black religious experience as it has existed in this country since its inception in the seventeenth century.

Early on, the black preacher took the lead in refashioning the Christian gospel in ways that made it contextually relevant to those who hungered to hear the gospel proclaimed in an idiom they could understand.

The exact time and place of the black preacher's origin in this country is difficult to determine. We do know that, beginning in the late eighteenth and early nineteenth centuries, southern evangelicalism gave rise to large numbers of black preachers who exhorted and preached without the requirements of formal training. Albert Raboteau and Nathan Hatch are among those who have documented the appeal of southern evangelicalism's more informal approach to religion.

Hatch cites three obvious reasons why blacks, slave and free, swarmed into Methodist and Baptist folds, spurning the more high-church traditions. First, early Baptists and Methodists earned the right to be heard. They welcomed African Americans as full participants in their communions and condemned the institution of slavery, even though there was an eventual retreat on these issues by white Baptist and Methodists. The second reason for the enormous influx of black converts into the Methodist and Baptist camps is that these groups proclaimed a Christianity that was fresh and capable of being readily understood and immediately experienced. The third and most important reason for the great influx, however, was the emergence of black preachers and exhorters. Blacks for the first time were granted the right and the responsibility of openly and publicly interpreting scripture for themselves. That hard-won right to interpret and to proclaim the scriptures has never been relinquished by blacks. Then and now, in black preaching the text matters. The surge of African Americans into the Christian faith between the Revolution and the War of 1812 paralleled the decisive rise of the black preacher. Virtually unknown in colonial America, black preaching exploded in the experimental climate generated by passionate Baptist and Methodist evangelicals.[8]

By the 1830s most southern evangelicals had thoroughly repudiated a heritage that valued blacks as fellow church members.

Pushed to the fringes of white churches, African American preachers asserted the autonomy of black Christianity overtly and in secret. What preserved the black church as the first public institution over which blacks had control was nothing but the courage, foresight, and determination of the black preacher.[9]

Blacks continue to attach great importance to the one who proclaims the message. Any ol' individual will not do. The person up before them must have been called by God from the midst of the congregation to stand and proclaim the Word of God. Blacks have never been huge fans of preaching roundtables or conversational preaching. The sermon is not simply information being disseminated by a people-friendly individual who by some luck of the draw happens to be up before them on any given morning. The person who stands to preach is not there because it is his/her *turn*. Rather, the person stands to preach because it is their *time*—a time that has been set and ordered by God. The one who stands before them has been called by God and selected by the congregation to perform this task each Sunday. This is one of the primary reasons the black preacher continues to be held in such high esteem in many church circles. Black preachers are still considered to be God's anointed ones who bring to the waiting congregation the Word from God. The genre of the selected or assigned text notwithstanding—narrative, epistle, or apocalyptic—the expectation among the listening congregation is the same: They expect to be addressed by God when the preacher stands to preach the gospel.

BLACK LIVED EXPERIENCE

Fourth, the preacher must make a connection between the God who acts in scripture and the God who acts in their present-day life. Some refer to this dynamic as concretizing the gospel. In the call and response that is so much a part of traditional black preaching, one can hear a congregant shout out and say, "Make it plain, preacher!" In other words, make that connection between the God of the scriptures and the God who is at work in my life this day. The connection does not always have to be explicit, and in many instances the listening congregation can make their own connection if the preacher is sufficiently skilled in painting the picture.

When examining the structure of a traditional black sermon, one can see that its initial formation comes to life through reflection on the common life experiences of people of faith as well as people of no faith. Consequently, a sermon is best heard when an insightful perspective on lived experience and/or scripture takes the lead in creating and organizing the sermon and not the specific enunciation of a theological formulation. For this reason an understanding of "situations," or domains of experience, and how to name them and build upon them is crucial in the development of the black sermon.

A domain is a sphere or realm that covers a broad but specified area of black experience, and also provides a category for sermonic reflection, creation, and organization. Domains are based on and grow out of long-standing beliefs and experiences in black secular and religious life. An awareness of these broad areas is immensely important for understanding how scripture and black experience come together in the preaching moment.

The five broad domains of experience that appear often enough in black life and preaching to constitute a pattern are: personal piety, care of the soul, social justice, corporate concerns, and maintenance of the institutional church.[10]

Personal Piety

The first and most common domain that reflects black experience and provides a framework for the creation and organization of the black sermon is personal piety. Pietism emphasizes "heart religion," the centrality of the Bible for faith and life, the royal priesthood of the laity, and strict morality. The black attraction to personal piety can be traced in this country to the evangelical revivalism that swept America in the late eighteenth and early nineteenth centuries. In this era of religious fervor the evangelicals' demands for clean hearts and righteous personal lives became the hallmarks of African American religion in the South.

The more narrow understanding of personal piety that concerns itself with faith and personal formation is the dimension that has had and continues to have the greatest impact on black preaching. A large number of contemporary blacks experience life in this broad domain. There is an emphasis on prayer, personal discipline, moral conduct, and the maintenance of a right relationship with God. Many are convinced they have not heard the gospel if it does not address some aspect of life as it is lived in this domain. Even ministers who are known for their active participation on the social justice front preach sermons from time to time that have as their central focus some matter related to personal piety.[11]

Care of the Soul

The second domain of experience (belief and practice) on which black preaching reflects and to which it is directed may be characterized as "care of the soul." Care of the soul describes that area of experience that focuses on the well-being of individuals. It is, however, more than mere comfort for the bereaved, forgiveness for the guilty, and help for the sick and needy; it is preeminently the renewal of life in the image of Christ. Thus it has as its purpose not only the giving of comfort but also the redirection of life. The preaching that grows out of reflection on this domain concerns itself with the healing, sustaining, guiding, and reconciling of persons as they face the changes and challenges of common human experiences; experiences that are exacerbated in black life through systemic and capricious discrimination and prejudice.

Preaching that centers on experiences in need of healing aims to overcome some impairment by restoring a person to wholeness and by leading them to advance beyond their previous condition. Sustaining seeks to help persons overcome an overwhelming sense of loss. Guiding helps one determine what they ought to do when they are faced with a difficult problem wherein they must choose between various courses of thought or action, while reconciliation helps alienated persons to establish or renew proper and fruitful relationships with God, family, significant others, friends, and neighbors. The function of sermons created out of reflection on this domain is to salve or heal the wounds and brokenness of life through some form of encouragement, exhortation, consolation, renewal, instruction, or admonishment.[12]

Social Justice

The third domain centers on social justice. Matters pertaining to racism, sexism, ageism, and other forms of discrimination fall under the scope of this particular domain. Social justice is defined as a basic value and desired goal in democratic societies that includes equitable and fair access to institutions, laws, resources, and opportunities without arbitrary limitations based on age, gender, national origin, religion, or sexual orientation. Racial justice, defined as equal treatment of the races, has been the most prominent component of the social justice domain in black experience. Discrimination and prejudice are the twin evils the black preacher has spoken out against most vociferously since the inception of the black church.

Those who preach out of this domain view God as the source of social justice and are absolutely certain that God's power is on their side in their quest for social reform. They do not seek necessarily to overthrow the societal system per se but to reform it so that it conforms once again to fundamental principles of fairness and equality. Their preaching aims at constructive social change. Consequently, God's power is believed to be made available in the present order to bring about fair and just treatment in systems and structures that negatively affect all people, including blacks.[13]

Corporate Concerns

The fourth domain has to do with corporate concerns. Preaching that grows out of reflection on this domain recognizes that there are in black life certain issues and interests that arise out of its unique history and cultural experiences in this country. Because such matters are believed to pertain uniquely to blacks, many believe they are best addressed by blacks. Inasmuch as this domain has at its center matters that pertain specifically to blacks, it tends more toward exhortations of self-help, uplift, and racial solidarity.

While it often concerns matters of social justice for black people, it is not confined to social justice. Its primary distinction is that it speaks to matters that particularly and peculiarly affect black life. Unlike the domain of social justice, which seeks the common good of all, corporate concerns is specifically geared to black interests.

Matters of vital importance in black life

are thought by many to be best dealt with by other blacks. For example, teenaged pregnancy, exhortations to blacks to lift themselves from the welfare rolls, black-on-black crime, calls for educational excellence, etc. There are some things that can best be said to blacks by other blacks. More pointedly, there are some things that should only be said to blacks by other blacks. Issues and concerns that fall within this realm have historically been addressed from black pulpits.[14]

Maintenance of the Institutional Church

The fifth domain, characterized as maintenance of the institutional church, is vastly important to the ecclesiastical life of the faith community as institution. Since it is more concerned with ethos than specific acts, it operates at a higher level of abstraction and is more inclined to be coupled with one or more domains in a sermon. Owing to the historical importance of the black church in the African American community, blacks, by and large, experience "church" not simply as a place to attend worship but as a way of life. Church is more than a once-a-week encounter; it is an affirming presence that shapes and molds self-understanding, self-worth, behavior, and lifestyle. For this reason, African Americans tend to identify more strongly with a denomination, a specific fellowship, and a specific location than their counterparts in the majority culture.

Sermons in this domain reflect on the work of the people as a gathered fellowship; thus the teachings of the faith with respect to discipleship, missions, evangelism, Christian education, benevolence, etc., usually find expression in this realm. Sermons that speak to the promotion, building, and upkeep of the physical plant are also common. How members are to behave and interact with one another and the requirements for spiritual growth and maturity within the church's many departments and auxiliaries are also addressed. This, however, is more than stewardship preaching or catechetical indoctrination. It is preaching that gives continued life and sustenance to the institutional church, which in turn reaffirms and upholds its participants.

Because these domains represent ideal types, it is seldom the case that any one sermon is purely of one particular domain in the strictest sense of the term. In fact, it is quite possible for a given sermon to have some characteristics from one or more of the domains cited. The overall focus of the sermon, the primary situation in life to which it is addressed, and the makeup of the intended listeners will ultimately determine the domain that most fittingly characterizes the sermon.

Text and lived experience as outlined in the aforementioned five domains of experience are brought together and held in tension in the best of black preaching. The preacher skillfully employs both in the structuring of a sermon that must have at its central core some understanding of who God is and what God has done for us and for our salvation. The black use of scripture is functional, and it is an absolutely essential component in the creation of the black sermon. Scripture does not stand alone; it is a part of a continuous interpretive dance between the preacher, God, and black lived experience.

Notes

1. Albert J. Raboteau, "The Black Experience in American Evangelicalism: The Meaning of Slavery," in *The Evangelical Tradition in America*, ed. Leonard I. Sweet (Macon, Ga.: Mercer University Press, 1984), 181.
2. Cleophus J. LaRue, *The Heart of Black Preach-ing* (Louisville: Westminster John Knox, 2000), 2.
3. Ibid., 3.
4. Carl R. Holladay, "Contemporary Methods of Reading the Bible," in *NIB* 1 (Nashville: Abingdon, 1994), 126.
5. Ibid.
6. Ibid.
7. Keith D. Miller, *Voice of Deliverance: The Language of Martin Luther King, Jr. and Its Sources* (New York: Free Press, 1992), 23.
8. Nathan O. Hatch, *The Democratization of American Christianity* (New Haven: Yale University Press, 1989), 102–6.
9. Ibid., 107.
10. LaRue, *The Heart of Black Preaching*, 21–29.
11. Ibid.
12. Ibid.
13. Ibid.
14. Ibid.

For Further Reading

Crawford, Evans E., and Thomas H. Troeger. *The Hum: Call and Response in African American Preaching*. Nashville: Abingdon, 1995.

Forbes, James. *The Holy Spirt and Preaching*. Nashville: Abingdon, 1989.

LaRue, Cleophus J. *The Heart of Black Preaching*. Louisville: Westminster John Knox, 2000.

———, ed. *Power in the Pulpit: How America's Most Effective Black Preachers Prepare Their Sermons*. Louisville: Westminster John Knox, 2000.

McMickle, Marvin. *Preaching to the Black Middle Class: Words of Challenge Words of Hope*. Valley Forge, Pa.: Judson, 2000.

Moyd, Olin. *The Sacred Art: Preaching and Theology in the African American Tradition*. Valley Forge, Pa.: Judson, 1995.

Proctor, Samuel D. *The Certain Sound of the Trumpet: Crafting a Sermon of Authority*. Valley Forge, Pa.: Judson, 1994.

Taylor, Gardner C. *How Shall They Preach?* Elgin,
Ill.: Progressive Baptist, 1977.

Thomas, Frank A. *They Like to Never Quit Praisin'
God: The Role of Celebration in Preaching.*
Cleveland: United Church Press, 1997.

AFRICAN AMERICAN ART *and* BIBLICAL INTERPRETATION

James A. Noel

INTRODUCTION

When African American artists made the bold and courageous decision to paint black subjects, they necessarily had to devise ways of depicting their religious experience, because religion was one of the most characteristic features of black life. The paintings in this volume are by no means exhaustive of all the artists who were able to successfully capture the power and vitality of African American religion. Many important works are absent because of space limitations and our desire to convey the breadth of themes and styles employed by black artists over the years to invoke and depict African American religion—particularly African American Christi-anity. The earliest artist represented is Henry Ossawa Tanner (1859–1937). A number of contemporary African American artists are also included, showing that the meaning of Christianity is still a potent subject and inspiration for their creative output. Because of the extreme deprivation to which Africans were subjected during and subsequent to their arrival in the Americas, their artistic products required a tremendous feat on their part to muster and assert a humanity that was on the brink of annihilation. Hence, when studying African American art we must always bear in mind not only the work under interpretation but the creative act itself. In analyzing the creative act of black artists within the histori-cal context of physical, psychic, and spiritual oppression and dehumanization we can easily see the relationship between it and religious experience. Since this volume is an African American New Testament commentary, it is only fitting that the art included in the volume be introduced by a theological analysis of its meaning. I do this by discussing the religious experience of African Americans in terms of their aesthetic experience. At their fundamental core, both religious and aesthetic experience pertains to what we perceive prior to discursive thought and speech—as in the black vernacular, "I know that I know that I know." I will speak of the place from whence that perception arises as the *arche*.

I

In 1970 James H. Cone enumerated the sources and norm of black theology in *A Black Theology of Liberation*. For Cone the terms *norm* and *hermeneutical principle* are synonymous, whereas *sources* are the items or categories of reflection that determine any theology's character. Cone argued that for African American theologians and biblical scholars to successfully relate the biblical tradition to the black condition their hermeneutical activity needed to include among its sources—in addition to scripture and tradition—three other categories of reflection: the black experience, black history, and black culture. The genius of this method is that it combines the two diametrically opposed theological methodologies of Friedrich Schleiermacher and Karl Barth, who respectively privileged experience and revelation. Subsequent generations of black theologians and biblical scholars have adopted Cone's method either implicitly or explicitly in pursuing their various projects, not always, however, possessing the methodological sophistication required in the study of black history and the interpretation of the black experience and black culture. The reflective categories of black history, black culture, and black experience have rarely been sufficiently "problematized" in such a way as to indicate how even African American scholars lack direct access to one of the fundamental categories Cone specified, namely, experience. Hence, much of black theology and African American biblical scholarship has dealt with this source or category in an a priori fashion and one that inadvertently situated it outside the communal encounter with scripture and tradition.

The weakness in a superficial application of Cone's method is when his sources are regarded as distinct moments or stations the interpreter visits along the hermeneutical circle and not as categories that exist in terms of what I call "multi-dialectical reciprocity." For example, scripture and tradition are not items that reside outside black culture and the black experience since, historically and phenomenologically, these categories were constitutive of the appearance of black identity on this side of the Atlantic. What allowed for the appearance of this identity formation was a newly constructed shared cosmos and worldview structured, in part, through scripture and tradition. While this occurred, African Americans refashioned their material reality to signify, express, and locate themselves in time and space. These artistic signifiers pointed at once to their imagined past and future by articulating what I have referred to elsewhere as their memory and hope.[1] Therefore, the art African Americans made and continue to make serves as a potent site of accessibility to their symbolic systems of meaning. It provides the occasion and possibility for an aesthetic experience commensurate with those aesthetic perceptions through which they originally appropriated and interpreted the biblical message. African American art, in other words, exemplifies the creative modality through which African Americans made their world while appropriating the Bible.

II

The inclusion of black art in this African American commentary raises the question of the relationships among the aesthetic experience of African Americans, African American biblical hermeneutics, and the black religious experience. The act within consciousness common to both aesthetic perception and religious experience is imagination. Perhaps it would be more phenomenologically accurate to view the imagination as something that registers aesthetic perception and religious experience. This conceptualization distinguishes imagination from the actual and precise moment of aesthetic perception and religious experience while still lodging it at a deeper level of awareness than what is normally expressed through discursive thought and speech. In *Significations: Signs, Symbol, and Images in the Interpretation of Religion*, Charles H. Long, a historian of religion, has discussed this in terms of the "archaic." I argue that African American art is one of the most productive sites for excavating the "archaic" dimension of African American consciousness, because the black religious experience is a form of aesthetic experience. "Archaism," according to Long, "is predicated on the priority of something already there, something given. This 'something' may be the bodily perceptions, as it is for Alfred North Whitehead and Maurice Merleau-Ponty, or *a primal vision of aesthetic form*, as it is for the artist" (emphasis added). Long writes:

Numerous problems are associated with the archaic. The epistemological problem has to do with the possibility of even

grasping what is primary in thought and experience—we might push it further to think in terms of the stuff that makes thought and experience possible and therefore is prior to thought and experience. If this level of reality is grasped at all it will be done through the activity of interpretation. Thus the epistemological problem is related to the problem of hermeneutics. The interpreter will then discover the inadequacy of the language of interpretation or, we should say, the inadequacy of language per se. Language is an inadequate interpretation and expression of the archaic because the archaic first takes shape and form as symbol.[2]

The way Long suggests for bridging the gap between the archaic and its interpretation is to enter into a participatory mode of conscious whereby "the interpreting subject [is] pushed back to a level of consciousness commensurate with the forms that the subject wishes to understand."[3] The problem with language in this modern period is that it obscures this level of experience. Long sees the history of religions as offering a possibility for overcoming the dogmatic categories of what he terms the discourses of contemporaneity—"history, ethnology, linguistics, psychoanalysis, and so on."[4] Even though it invites thought, the symbol can never be reduced or equated with a rational category. Even African American biblical hermeneutics cannot assume immunity from this linguistic predicament of having to communicate via the "discourses of contemporaneity" about something that forever escapes this mode of discourse. The biblical text must be reflected on through a consciousness that has assumed the form of its original intuition by its original African American interpreters. The Bible was not originally received and interpreted by African Americans in a discursive linguistic mode of epistemological understanding but through the aesthetic mode of epistemological understanding.

Black art provides the biblical interpreter with an occasion to have an aesthetic experience that places him or her within the same or similar realm of apprehension as the text's original African American recipients. Immanuel Kant, in his *Critique of Judgment*, referred to this nondiscursive mode of perception in terms of aesthetic.[5] It is something through which one apprehends a sense of underlying order in nature and art—the "supersensible substrate" of reality. Think of the lines in the Negro spiritual, "Steal Away": "My Lord he calls me, he calls me by the thunder; the trumpet sounds within my soul." For Kant this mode of apprehension presumed a free play of the faculties and serves as the primordial ground of human freedom. When Kant's insight is applied to the religious experience and expressions of African Americans, we can see how the black aesthetic constituted one of the most fundamental practices of freedom for the enslaved community. And, as I already stated, it was through this aesthetic that the Bible was appropriated and interpreted.

A little more needs to be said about the aesthetic mode of apprehension as it relates to the appropriation of Jesus within the black religious experience. One of the distinguishing features of a certain kind of wood sculpture extant throughout western Africa from the Gulf of Guinea down to the Kongo Kingdom prior to and during the nineteenth century was the binding of carved figures with cords. These figures were also sometimes pierced with nails. Carvings of this type, called *boci*, fall into the category of what the Fon[6] termed *kannumon* or things belonging in cords (see figs. 1, 2 in gallery following page 76). Although this kind of sculpture predated the slave trade, they assumed an unusual poignancy as a result of the terror and trauma this commerce inflicted on African societies. In her study of these sculptures, *African Vodun: Art, Psychology, and Power*, Suzanne Preston Blier wrote: "Whereas Fon royal *boci* arts conform in essential ways to local beauty criteria, commoner works emphasize counter esthetic, even anti-aesthetic values and features of ugliness."[7] These objects served as signifiers of the fate feared by most commoners and, as such, functioned to displace or ward off the potential evil. According to Blier, these sculptures not only reflected the violence endemic of western African societies because of the slave trade but functioned also "as a means of readdressing wrongs and dissipating attendant anxiety."[8] In *Astonishment and Power*, Wyatt MacGaffey and Michael D. Harris have produced a masterful study and analysis of this same type of art created by the BaKongo people of the Kongo, which are called *minkisi* (plural) or *nkisi* (singular).[9] Michael Harris documents the continuity and reappropriation of the *boci* art form in the works of a contemporary African American artist, Renée Stout (see fig. 3 in gallery). This art provides the aesthetic lens through which we might see the way African slaves imagined and interpreted the significance of Jesus' crucifixion as they were undergoing their own. This art suggests that through their aesthetic mode of religious apprehension they "got it" all at once and understood Jesus hanging on the cross as their *nkisi*.

John M. Janzen's studies of "affliction cults" in western Africa are also suggestive in this regard.[10] These cults posited a special relationship between specific afflictions conceptualized as spiritual entities (for example, smallpox) and the afflicted person. Hence, a person who had been successfully cured from a specific affliction was qualified to undergo the initiation process that would equip the person to function as a healer of the specific form which he or she formerly suffered. Without elaborating on all the ramifications of this phenom-

Fig. 1. Fon *boci*, accumulating and binding together powerful objects to aid their maker. Fon culture, Benin Republic. Ben Heller Collection, New York. Photo: © Werner Forman/Art Resource, N.Y.

Fig. 2. Iron, representing Gu, vodu of war, is bound in with the figures in this powerful Fon *boci* medicine. Fon, Southern Benin. Ben Heller Collection, New York. Photo: © Werner Forman / Art Resource, N.Y.

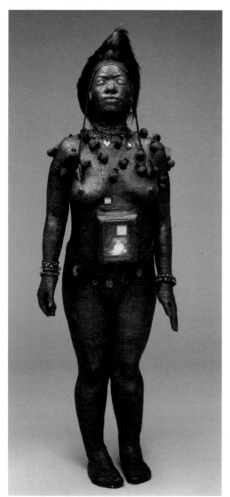

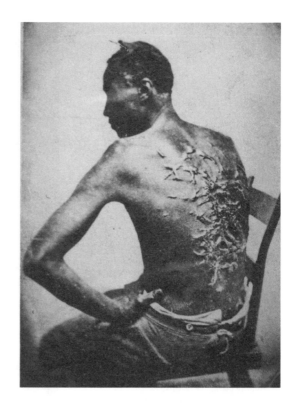

Fig. 3 (above). Renée Stout, *Fetish 2*. Mixed media with plaster body cast. 1988. Dallas Museum of Art, Metropolitan Life Foundation Grant. © Renée Stout, Washington, D.C. Photo © Dallas Museum of Art. Used by permission.

Fig. 4 (above right). Scars from whipping on the back of a black man identified only as "Poor Peter." The photograph was taken by the War Department, Baton Rouge, 1863, and was captioned, "Overseer artayou carrier whipped me. I was two months in bed sore from the whipping. My master come after I was whipped; he discharged the overseer. The very words of poor peter, taken as he sat for his picture." Courtesy of National Archive and Records Administration.

Fig. 5 (right). Scars on the back of a man about to be lynched. This man is identified as Frank Embree, and the photo was taken near Fayette, Missouri, July 22, 1899.

Quilts by Harriet Powers from 1898 (fig. 6, above) and 1886 (fig. 7, below) displaying stories from the Bible. These are among the best known and best preserved examples of the Southern American quilting tradition. Fig. 6: Museum of Fine Arts, Boston. Bequest of Maxim Karolik; photo copyright © Museum of Fine Arts, Boston. Fig. 7: Photo © Smithsonian Institution. 75-2984.

Figure 8. Harriet Powers (1901), identified as born a slave in Georgia in 1837. Photo copyright © Museum of Fine Arts, Boston.

Fig. 9. Paul Goodnight, *Links and Lineage*. © Paul Goodnight. Used by permission.

Fig. 10. Romare Bearden, *Prevalence of Ritual: Mysteries,* 1964. © Romare Bearden Foundation / Licensed by VAGA, New York, NY.

Fig. 11. Joe Overstreet, *Justice, Faith, Hope, and Peace.* © Joe Overstreet. Used by permission.

Fig. 12. William H. Johnson, *Swing Low, Sweet Chariot*. Ca. 1944. Smithsonian American Art Museum, Washington, D.C. © William H. Johnson. Photo © Smithsonian American Art Museum, Washington, D.C. / Art Resource, N.Y. Used by permission.

Fig. 13. Jacob Lawrence, *Through Forests, Through Rivers, Up Mountains* (1967), tempera, gouache and pencil on paper. Smithsonian Hirshhorn Museum / The Joseph H. Hirshhorn Bequest, 1981. © 1967 The Estate of Gwendolyn Knight Lawrence / Artist Rights Society (ARS), New York. Photo © Lee Stalsworth. Used by permission.

Fig. 14. Charles White (1918–1979), *Mother and Child.* Wolff crayon, 1953. Collection of Frances B. White. © 1953 The Charles White Archives.

Fig. 15. Charles White, *Mary, Don't You Weep.* Ink, 1956. Collection of Harry Belafonte. © 1956 The Charles White Archives.

Fig. 16. Charles White, *Triumph.* Lithograph, 1956. No provenance information. © 1956 The Charles White Archives.

Fig. 17 (above). Charles White, *General Moses (Harriet Tubman)*. Ink, 1965. Collection of Garden State Insurance Company. © 1965 The Charles White Archives. Photograph by Frank J. Thomas, courtesy of the Frank J. Thomas Archives.

Fig. 18. Charles White, *Move On Up a Little Higher*. Charcoal and Wolff Crayon, 1961. Private Collection. © 1961 The Charles White Archives.

enon, let it suffice to juxtapose several other images to those of the *nkisi* and Stout's sculpture. The aesthetic I am trying to communicate can be intuited if we juxtapose the photo taken of the scarifications from previous whippings on a former slave's back (fig. 4 in gallery) with that of a photo showing the scars inflicted on a man about to be lynched (fig. 5 in gallery). These juxtaposed images might correlate with the stream of African American collective consciousness that made connections among their scarred and battered bodies, Jesus' crucifixion, and their memory of *boci* or *nkisi* carvings.

III

The African American artist helps the biblical interpreter get in touch with the aesthetic experience of African Americans because he or she necessarily operates more closely at the level of the symbolic. This contains an ethical dimension. According to Mikhail Bakhtin, the artist, in creating, transcends the immediacy of the present situation and is addressed by the reality of an "ought" that critiques his or her life in its situation.[11] Russian philosopher Nicholas Berdyaev has reminded us that the creative act itself is the occasion of the divine-human encounter wherein one's humanity is asserted.[12] Here I am not only referring to the specialist but also to the creative products of ordinary African Americans whose art asserted their humanity amid the experience of extreme dehumanization. For example, in the quilts of Harriet Powers we see the symbolic universe she created to posit something else beyond her enslaved circumstance (see figs. 6, 7, 8 in gallery). According to Gladys-Marie Fry, quilt making was one means for African American women to engage in the cathartic process of storytelling. African American women were not only piecing together quilts

that had the practical function of providing warmth, but also fashioning meaning and selves from the fragmented experiences produced by suffering and depravation. The clothes ordinary African Americans wore on the plantation often looked like quilts from having to be patched so frequently; it would be interesting to study this more thoroughly in relation to the Negro spiritual "I Got a Robe." Some contemporary African American female artists have adopted the technique of quilt making as their mode of creative expression. A member of the Sankofa Collective in Denver created a quilt titled "Jacob's Ladder." When she displayed this quilt at an elementary school classroom, the children in the class spontaneously started singing "Jacob's Ladder" before she even had a chance to tell them the quilt's title. The children did not have to have the meaning of the quilt explained to them. The work itself communicated directly with the children's aesthetic sensibility. The importance of quilt making and its evocative power are expressed in Paul Goodnight's painting *Links and Lineages* (see fig. 9 in gallery).

The black artist must reflect on himself or herself in the process of creating. It is also true that the artist must be able to lose the self in the process of creating only to rediscover it in the completed work. However, the self's redefinition is ongoing, because the work is open to constant reinterpretation even by the artist. The work is rooted in the primal symbols, intuitions, and images that constitute the artistic urge. The artist, with the language of the archaic, interprets the archaic, and this interpretive language produces—in the case of genius—a fresh archaic strata. The symbol that every African American must struggle to transform and give meaning to—that which represents and defines their social and existential location in the political economy—is their blackness. Blackness has served as a potent symbol in the semiotics of Western racism. This fact imposes on black persons in general, and African American artists in particular, the task of deciphering the symbolism of their own materiality. Although the negative symbolism of blackness was achieved through linguistic means, among others, becoming freed of this symbolism is difficult to achieve through the use of language because the symbol operates at the level of the archaic whereas discursive language does not. Identity is archaic, and the transformation of identity, therefore, must occur at this level where symbols first make their appearance. For African slaves, their bodies and the material with which their bodies were forced to interact—the soil, cotton, tobacco, wood, and iron—took on symbolic significance through their labor. As they transformed their material surroundings, they were also transforming themselves or delivering themselves from "thinghood" into the human realm. In *Economic and Philosophical Manuscripts* Karl Marx analogized "labor to creative production by the artist, who in his works externalizes his own essential powers and appropriates the product once again in rapt contemplation."[13] Nat Turner, for example, saw hieroglyphic images on ears of corn.

When the producer is separated from his or her product through slavery or the intervention of the wage, the producer becomes self-alienated. Without necessarily having become acquainted with the above theories, the African American artist Romare Bearden showed an acute intuition of the relationship between labor exploitation and artistic practice in his 1946 article "The Negro Artist's Dilemma," in which he wrote:

The Negro, aside from his folk expressions, is a latecomer into the visual arts in America. As slave and serf, the Negro has had to struggle for his very existence. The visual arts are in a sense a sophisticated expression. . . . That the innate capacity existed is evidenced in the elegant iron-grill work created by Negro slave artisans. About the only expression allowed the Negro was religion, so it is understandable that his first artistic achievement would be a vocal one—the spirituals.[14]

In his collages Bearden revealed the symbolic nature of the black anatomy and everyday objects from black life. A social theorist, Walter Benjamin, who experimented with this medium, observed how the collage is able to "interrupt the context into which it is inserted."[15] The objects inserted into Bearden's collages interrupt their context and take on a numinous quality that provokes narration; at the same time, however, these objects remain recognizable to the black viewer. The importance of this is that it leads to self-discovery. Interpreting the meaning of objects associated with one's everyday reality elicits self-interpretation. For example, one writer said Bearden's 1964 collage *Mysteries* (11¼" x 14½") (see fig. 10 in gallery) was "no mystery to the black viewer—Jesus, watermelon, 'Alaga Syrup' (only the word 'syrup' is visible, but readers of *Ebony* magazine will recognize the lettering from the advertisements) are but stereotypes at best of the black world to the white viewer, but completely real to the black viewer."[16] Each of the objects shown in the collage has a history of its own, a history of their use and the desires projected onto them by their users.

Although many past and contemporary African American artists have chosen to depict blacks attending worship, celebrating baptisms, holding funerals, etc., these subjects do not exhaust the range of religious signification in their art. Bearden's collages cannot be read strictly in this manner of looking for explicit religious or Christian symbols, since he was more interested in the mythic element found in the mundane rituals of black folk culture than in what we usually define as religious. Therefore, when Christian symbols appear in Bearden's collages they are part of and belong to the context of neighboring objects that would customarily be seen as profane. The same can be said also of other African artists, as in the case of artists whose utopian vision is expressed in the genre of abstract art (see Joe Overstreet's *Justice, Faith, Hope, and Peace*, fig. 11 in gallery).

IV

Many African American artists, however, have made their religious themes quite explicit. This was unavoidable when, beginning in the 1920s during the New Negro Movement, African American artists focused intentionally on the black experience as their subject matter. What they sought to capture was not only what African Americans did in daily life and leisure but also their aspirations. What African Americans aspired to was not the world of appearance—the world of their enslaved, Jim Crow conditions—but rather, the world they could imagine and wanted to make. They imagined another world. Some African American artists have depicted that other world coming toward the viewer, as in William H. Johnson's *Swing Low, Sweet Chariot* (fig. 12 in gallery), while other African American artists have captured the migration theme in black history and depicted the African American trek toward freedom, as seen in Jacob Lawrence's *Through Forests, Through Rivers, Up Mountains* (fig. 13). Hence, African American art depicts what W. E. B. DuBois would term the "spiritual strivings" of black folks. Charles White's drawings capture this elusive quality of African American humanity in the faces of his subjects. The faces of the ordinary

black subject in his drawings, who could be every African American viewer's relative or acquaintance, are transformed into biblical personages through his artistic genius. White's drawing *Mother and Child* (fig. 14) invoke the image of the Virgin Mary and Jesus. His *Mary, Don't You Weep* (fig. 15) invokes the image of Mary and Elizabeth or Martha. *Triumph* (fig. 16) might easily be seen as depicting Mary and Joseph characters. Because of its title, White's *General Moses (Harriet Tubman)* (fig. 17) requires no interpretation. However, while *Move On Up a Little Higher* (fig. 18) is equally as powerful, it is much more nuanced. This image could be saying to us, among other things, that, although our bodies are no longer fettered by chains, we nevertheless remain inwardly enslaved within the system through the foreshortening of our vision. Now that we are allowed to pursue the things our former masters enjoyed, our desire is confined and limited to the commodities he dangles before us. Thus our striving has ended before fulfillment and our foreparents' dreams lie stillborn.

African American people's oppression in America entails not only joblessness, prison incarceration, substandard housing, and inadequate education but also a deeper spiritual dehumanization and the deadening of their sensibilities through drugs, despair, and hopelessness. But the technological society that would crush the black spirit has already had a negative impact on white sensibilities. The pragmatist philosopher and educator John Dewey complained in 1935: "We undergo sensations as mechanical stimuli without having a sense of the reality that is in them and behind them. . . . We see without feeling, we hear, but only a second hand report, second hand because not reinforced by vision."[17]

The spiritual question for black theology and black religious studies is how to prevent the above diagnosis from becoming truer of

African Americans than it may be already—albeit for different reasons. Part of the solution again brings us back to aesthetics, because the new vision Dewey spoke of cannot be signified with the categories of the old discourse. Breaking from the parameters of the old discourse requires a return to the counter-hegemonic language of African American slave religion and then its improvisation and re-creation to meet present-day requirements for faith and hope. In this undertaking African American art is indispensable. With African American art contributing to both the archaic and the modern symbols of black religious consciousness, it provides black theology and black religious studies with interpretive visual metaphors for developing what Charles Long called "a new and counter-creative signification and expressive deployment of new meanings expressed in styles and rhythms of dissimulation."[18] As black theology and black religious studies work toward the construction of a new emancipatory discourse, African American art will be indispensable as a dialogue partner.

CONCLUSION

The art included in this commentary shares several features: the return to African American folk culture as a source of artistic inspiration and content, the centering of the black subject in their canvasses, stylistic innovations both embodying and interpreting the aesthetic experience of African Americans, and creating artistic products through intertextual influences from the black experience. In making these observations we can see how African American art not only provides material for reflecting on the black religious experience but also models a hermeneutic for interpreting that experience and therefore serves as an essential source for black theology and African American biblical interpretation. It provides the biblical interpreter with an additional site for entering into their sources, that is, black culture, the black experience, and black religion. Additionally it reinforces the methodology advocated by these disciplines as an intertextual dialogue partner. African American art furthermore provides a mirror for scholars of black religion to see their own efforts reflected and consequently acquire new understandings of their disciplines.

Notes

1. James Noel, "Memory and Hope: Toward a Hermeneutic of African American Consciousness," *JRT* 47 (1990).
2. Charles H. Long, *Significations: Signs, Symbol, and Images in the Interpretation of Religion* (Philadelphia: Fortress Press, 1986).
3. Ibid., 54.
4. Ibid., 55.
5. Immanuel Kant, *Critique of Judgment* (Indianapolis: Hackett, 1987), 59.
6. Fon refers to one of the major ethnic/linguistic groups of western African that is found primarily in Benin (Dahomy) and southwestern Nigeria. Along with the Yorouba, Ibo, and KiKongo peoples, the Fon peoples were carried to the New World in significant numbers and have place an endurable religio-cultural stamp upon the cultures of the African Diaspora.
7. Suzanne Preston Blier, *African Vodun: Art, Psychology, and Power* (Chicago: University of Chicago Press, 1995), 30.
8. Ibid., 27.
9. Wyatt MacGaffey and Michael D. Harris, *Astonishment and Power: The Eyes of Understanding: Kongo Minkisi / The Art of Renée Stout,* ed. Dean Trackman (Washington, D.C.: Smithsonian, 1993).
10. John M. Janzen, "Drums of Affliction: Real Phenomenon or Scholarly Chimera?" in *Religion in Africa: Experience and Expression,* ed. Thomas D. Blakely, Walter E. A. van Beek,

and Dennis L. Thomson (Portsmouth, N.H.: Heinemann, 1994), 160–81.

11. M. M. Bakhtin, *Art and Answerability: Early Philosophical Essays by M. M. Bakhtin*, ed. Michael Holquist and Vadim Liapunov, trans. Vadim Liapunov (Austin: University of Texas Press, 1990), 119.

12. Nicolas Berdyaev, *The Destiny of Man* (London: Geoffrey Bles, 1948), 127.

13. Karl Marx, *Economic and Philosophical Manuscripts* in *Social Theory: The Multicultural and Classic Readings,* ed. Charles Lemert and Steve Catalano (Boulder, Colo.: Westview, 1999), 34.

14. Romare Bearden, "The Negro Artist's Dilemma," *Critique* (November 1946): 16–22.

15. Susan Buck-Morss, *The Dialectics of Seeing: Walter Benjamin and the Arcades Project*, Studies in Contemporary German Social Thought (Cambridge, Mass.: MIT Press, 1989), 67.

16. Phyllis Rauch Klotman, *Humanities through the Black Experience* (Dubuque, Ia.: Kendall and Hunt, 1977), 179.

17. John Dewey, *Art as Experience* (New York: Capricorn, 1958), 21.

18. Long, *Significations*, 9.

For Further Reading

Bearden, Romare, and Harry Henderson. *A History of African-American Artists: From 1792 to the Present*. New York: Pantheon, 1993.

Blier, Suzanne Preston. *African Vodun: Art, Psychology, and Power*. Chicago: University of Chicago Press, 1995.

Crown, Carol, ed. *Coming Home! Self-Taught Artists, the Bible and the American South* (Jackson, Miss.:University of Mississippi Press, 2004).

Fry, Gladys-Marie. *Stitched from the Soul: Slave Quilts from the Antebellum South*. New York: Dutton, 1990.

Lewis, Samella. *Art: African American*. Los Angeles: Hancraft Studios, 1990.

Powell, Richard J. *Black Art and Culture in the Twentieth Century*. New York: Thames and Hudson, 1997.

———. *Homecoming: The Art and Life of William H. Johnson*. New York: Rizzoli, 1991.

Rozelle, Robert V., Alvia Wardlaw, and Maureen McKenna eds. *Black Art, Ancestral Legacy: The African Impulse in African-American Art*. New York: Abrams.

Thompson, Robert Farris. *Flash of the Spirit*. New York: Vintage, 1983.

Trackman, Dean, ed. *Astonishment and Power: The Eyes of Understanding: Kongo Minkisi* by Wyatt MacGaffey / *The Art of Renée Stout* by Michael D. Harris. Washington, D.C.: Smithsonian, 1993.

White, Charles. *Images of Dignity: The Drawings of Charles White*. Los Angeles: Ward Ritchie, 1967.

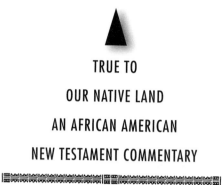

TRUE TO
OUR NATIVE LAND
AN AFRICAN AMERICAN
NEW TESTAMENT COMMENTARY

COMMENTARY ON
THE NEW TESTAMENT

The GOSPEL *of* MATTHEW

Michael Joseph Brown

INTRODUCTION

"Do not think," says Jesus, "that I have come to abolish the law or the prophets; I have come not to abolish but to fulfill" (Matt 5:17). This statement, so characteristic of Matthew's Gospel, is familiar to many of us. In truth, Matthew is so familiar to Christians that early on it was dubbed "the church's gospel." It is a well-deserved designation.

> **Matthew at a Glance**
>
> Date: 80–85 C.E.
> Original language: Greek
> Place of writing: most likely Antioch in Syria
> Author: Unknown

Matthew's Gospel serves as the framework for most of our reconstruction of the life and ministry of Jesus. Because Matthew contains more than 90 percent of the material found in Mark, to many Christians the story of Jesus is really that of Matthew with additions from Luke and maybe a hint of John. The star, the Magi, the little town of Bethlehem, the baptism in the Jordan, the Sermon on the Mount—these are but a few of the components of the gospel story that Matthew has shaped for us. Yet, if we dig into the grand story of Jesus of the first Gospel, we find that Matthew has a perspective and presentation not found in Mark, Luke, and John.

We can find Matthew's fingerprint on the Jesus story in at least five major themes that pervade the Gospel. First, for Matthew, Jesus is a teacher, a theme found throughout the Gospel—even at the end (28:19-20). The emphasis in the Great Commission is on teaching, not preaching. Even the Sermon on the Mount is a teaching moment more than a preaching occasion. The purpose behind Matthew's emphasis on teaching is to transmit wisdom, to give us the information we need to live productive lives as disciples. Like the griots and sages of West Africa, Matthew presents to us a Jesus who is preeminently a teacher.

Second, Matthew places less emphasis on miracles than do the other Gospels. He places almost all his miracle stories in chapters 8 and 9, and he shortens many of them. In fact, unlike the other Gospels, Matthew uses the miracle stories as a way to introduce questions about the nature of discipleship. For Matthew, miracles are not as important as mission.

Third, Matthew has a strong Jewish orientation—stronger than that found in most of the other Gospels. Matthew emphasizes that Jesus is the Jewish Messiah, sent by the Jewish God, in fulfillment of the Jewish scriptures, who advocates adherence to the Jewish law. One cannot read Matthew without feeling this strongly. African Americans have understood throughout their history that "where we are" influences greatly "who we are" and "what we can become." Matthew makes it clear to us that the context for Jesus' ministry was early Judaism.

Fourth, Matthew places emphasis on what can be called superabundant righteousness (5:20). He says that a disciple's righteousness, by which he means the words and deeds that proceed from faith, must be better, greater, more excessive than that of whom many would consider righteous. It is a radical understanding of discipleship. Unlike those who have claimed the title Christian but acted in ways that oppressed others, African Americans see in Matthew's Jesus and his teachings

one who looks beyond a surface understanding of scripture into the vision that God has for all human beings.

Finally, throughout Matthew's Gospel there is a constant tension between the universal and the particular. It is not always clear in a casual reading of Matthew how he sees the relationship between the local mission of Jesus and his first disciples, on the one hand, and the universal mission that the Gospel envisions in the Great Commission, on the other. Matthew appears to be telling us that the universal is found and cultivated in our concern for the immediate issues in our life setting. To put it another way, instead of missing the forest for the trees, Matthew is saying that we understand the forest adequately only when we give attention to the trees that comprise it. Again, African Americans understand that every advance for human liberation has come one act at a time within specific settings in history.

1:1-25, Roots

1:2-17, The Genealogy of Jesus

Matthew demonstrates Jesus' authenticity by connecting him to Abraham, David and the kings of Judah, and Zerubbabel, the leader of the Jews after the Babylonian exile. Matthew tells us that the generations from Abraham to Jesus can be divided into three sets of fourteen, the numerical value of the Hebrew letters in the name of the great king, David (1:17). This schema, however, is artificial.

Matthew makes clear to the reader that in the family history of Jesus there is the ongoing influence of the past on the present. Jesus is who he is because of who his ancestors were. We are led to believe that what marks the Messiah is a distinguished family history. In earlier days, people might have said that Jesus comes from "people like us."

Matthew connects Jesus to the Old Testament covenants made with Abraham and David (see Gen 12:1-3; 17:1-8; 2 Sam 7:12-17). Paul, on the other hand, repeatedly emphasizes Jesus' connection to Abraham but not to David, except in Rom 1:3.[1] The genealogical link raises the question of authenticity or legitimacy for readers. Why is it so important that "heroic" human beings come from legitimate and verifiable bloodlines? In the recent past, those involved with social empowerment movements in the African American community were often fond of saying, "We were kings and queens." This was meant to emphasize the honorable, even venerable bloodline that runs through the veins of contemporary African Americans. We have survived, it presumes, because we come from the best Africa had to offer. Although empowering in many ways, this idea is also dangerous. It smacks of a social Darwinism ("the survival of the fittest") that attempts to play the same game white Westerners have been playing on Africans in America for centuries.

One of the widespread justifications for slavery was the superiority of Europeans and their descendants to the Africans whom they enslaved. Many saw it as their religious duty to civilize these so-called uncivilized Africans. Even after the end of slavery, many believed themselves to be superior to their former captives. The ugly history of Jim Crow is a shining example of what happens when one group believes that biology confers superiority. Although Jim Crow is no longer legal, social Darwinism still exists. Are we to believe that Matthew wants readers to accept the idea that what makes Jesus the legitimate Messiah is that he comes from the right bloodline? No.

Matthew makes clear that the birth of Perez and Zerah occurred because of the coupling of Judah and Tamar (1:3; see Gen 38:1-30). This incident should disturb the reader for several reasons. First, Tamar is not an Israelite. Second, Tamar is not Judah's wife, but his daughter-in-law. Third, the event

challenges our idea of how families should operate, because the story is full of deception and inappropriate sexual interaction that cannot fit with our idealized models of biblical families.

Matthew goes on to name Rahab, Ruth, and "the wife of Uriah" (Bathsheba) among the ancestors of Jesus (1:5-6). Matthew's theological point becomes clearer as we reflect on the significance of these women. Each one is of questionable social and ethnic background, which highlights the interesting mix of Israelites and foreigners, individuals of unquestioned and questionable backgrounds, in the family history of Jesus. Now the whole issue of legitimacy is in question!

Jesus descends not only from a distinguished bloodline full of kings and queens but also from outsiders and persons of questionable character and practice. Even the patriarchs and kings in Jesus' bloodline are not above reproach (e.g., Judah and King David). And the grouping of the generations into sets of fourteen is flawed (1:17). The number of generations named by Matthew actually amounts to sets of fourteen, fourteen, and thirteen. Even if we restored King Jehoiakim to his rightful place in the genealogy, it would give us the needed forty-two names, but only in sets of fourteen, fifteen, and thirteen.

Matthew challenges our idea of "the survival of the fittest," the idea that we are who we are because we come from the right kind of people, with the idea that even the Messiah descended from a flawed family line. History is not the record of the survival of the fittest but the record of "the survival of the survivors." Matthew goes on to highlight this idea forcefully in his account of the events surrounding the birth of Jesus.

1:18-25, The Birth of Jesus

Unlike Luke, Matthew does not describe the birth of Jesus. He focuses instead on the events leading up to the birth (1:18-25). Mary's pregnancy calls into question her legitimacy as a wife for Joseph, who is described as a righteous man (1:19). She is in the same dangerous position that threatened Joseph's ancestor Tamar. Although Joseph's compassion prevents Mary from being put to death for this scandal, his decision to divorce her sharply raises the issue of legitimacy that runs through his family history. The angel's appearance to Joseph helps him see that God's purposes are advanced not only by those considered the "fittest" but also by those who find themselves in a survival crisis (1:20-21). Joseph's adoption of Jesus makes clear to the reader that God's purposes are fulfilled not only by those whom we call "righteous," like Joseph, but also by those

whose character can be questioned, like Mary. (See sidebar.) In short, what makes Jesus legitimate is not his bloodline—the pedigree that goes back to David and Abraham—but that he will be an agent for God's purposes, "he will save his people from their sins" (1:21). Our identities are determined more by the kinds of people we seek to be in the world than by our bloodlines.

2:1-23, Out of Egypt

2:1-12, Recognition from the East

The story of the Magi is a familiar one. They come from the east, possibly Persia, and were most likely ancient astrologers. They go to Jerusalem looking for Jesus, assuming that the king of the Judeans would be living in the capital. When they arrive, they announce that they saw a star announcing the birth of the king. When the text says the Magi saw the star "in the east," it means they saw it "at its rising" (2:2, NRSV). They also announce that they have come to "worship" this new king. Matthew highlights that outsiders recognize the importance of Jesus' birth, but the Jews, Herod in particular, did not.

Herod the Great was the king of the Judeans at the time. The Romans had placed him in power some three decades earlier. He is disturbed by the news of the birth, and "all Jerusalem" along with him. Herod's response is typical of people in power. Martin Luther King Jr. once wrote, "History is the long and tragic story of the fact that privileged groups seldom give up their privileges voluntarily."[2] Yet, as King knew as well, God is often the source of unrest in the universe. God challenges those in power. We see this repeatedly in the Old Testament: God raised up prophets to challenge the power of wayward kings. In this case, the birth of a child disturbs the existing power structure and forebodes its ultimate collapse.

The Silence of Mary

When we read passages such as Matt 1:18-25, we should not overlook those whose voices are not heard and who have no agency whatsoever, like Mary. Joseph is allowed to make his own decision. Mary, however, is at the mercy of others. We know nothing of her suffering, except through the eyes of Joseph. Renita Weems reminds us, "The voice of the oppressed in the end is not the predominant voice. In fact, theirs is a voice that could be viewed as random aberrant outbursts in a world otherwise rigidly held together by its patriarchal attitudes and androcentric perspective."

—Renita Weems, "African American Women and the Bible," in *Stony the Road We Trod: African American Biblical Interpretation*, ed. Cain Hope Felder (Minneapolis: Fortress Press, 1991), 76.

The birth of the Messiah, according to the quotation from Mic 5:2, was to occur in Bethlehem (Matt 2:6). Contrary to the expectations of the Magi, the king who is to rule Israel will be born not in Jerusalem but, like his ancestor David, in Bethlehem, among the insignificant clans of Judah. The least of these, a little child, is now among the prominent. Matthew informs readers that those we consider to be insignificant, unworthy of any serious consideration, can turn out to be the very agents God chooses to lead us.

2:13-23, God's Protection from Herod's Anger

Again the issue of survival arises in the narrative. Herod calls the Magi secretly, and pretends that he also wants to worship Jesus (2:8). In reality, Herod wants to kill him. Like the Pharaoh of Egypt in the Exodus story, Herod sees the child as a threat. To save the child's life, Joseph is told in a dream to take Jesus and Mary to Egypt. The land of Egypt was often used as a place of refuge, as we see from the Old Testament (see Gen 47:27). Who can forget Joseph's memorable words to his brothers, "Even though you intended to do harm to me, God intended it for good, in order to preserve a numerous people, as he is doing today" (50:20)? Jesus' flight to Egypt was to preserve his life. Some believe that the reason for choosing Egypt had to do with Jesus' color.[3] This is not necessarily true. In the time of Jesus people from all over the world lived in Egypt, especially in its largest city, Alexandria. There were at least two prominent Jewish communities in Egypt, one in Alexandria and the other in Leontopolis. Cain Hope Felder points out that "when Jesus' parents felt the need to flee Herod's domain in order to protect the innocent 'sweet lil' Jesus boy,' they followed the established trail to Africa—not Europe!"[4] It is more likely that they chose Egypt because of its status as a place of refuge,

because there were Jews already living there, and because it was beyond Herod's reach.

The Magi bring expensive gifts that would finance the journey. Frankincense, in particular, was prized in the ancient world as an important component in worship. It came from Marib, an ancient city that many believe served as the capital of the kingdom of Sheba (now part of Yemen).[5] After the death of Herod, Joseph is instructed in a dream to take Jesus and Mary back to the land of Israel. He decides that they should settle in Nazareth in the Galilee.

3:1—4:25, OUT OF THE WRONG PLACE

3:1-12, John's Announcement of God's Kingdom

Matthew's story begins to move quickly at this point. When he says "in those days," he may be implying that Jesus had already become an adult (Matt 3:1). If Luke is correct that Jesus began his ministry when he was "about thirty," then he was an old man for his day (see Luke 3:23). Seventy-five percent of people in Jesus' day died before they saw the age of thirty.[6]

> ### Male Life Expectancy
>
> Census data from Egypt tell us that in the time of Jesus male life expectancy at birth was twenty-five years.

At any rate, the scene opens with the preaching of John the Baptist. John is described as some sort of ascetic or prophet. His location in the wilderness is the first indication of this. To the ancients, the wilderness was a place beyond human habitation, dangerous, and inhabited by evil spirits. Second, John's diet suggests his status as a prophet. It appears that John consumes only God-given foodstuffs, things that are found naturally, not cultivated, one of the characteristics of an ascetic lifestyle (3:4). John's preaching of repentance appears to be advocating a transformation of society as a whole under the rule of God (3:1-2).

People came to John to be baptized. John's charge, "brood of vipers" (literally, "children of vipers"), suggests that the "Pharisees and Sadducees" dishonor God, and that God will regain God's honor. John dishonors the Pharisees and Sadducees, possibly because they rely upon their status as descendants of Abraham to save them from God's vengeance.

3:13-17, The Baptism of Jesus

In contrast to the harsh words to the Pharisees and Sadducees, when Jesus approaches John for baptism, John ultimately consents (Matt 3:13-17). Upon coming out of the water, Jesus is honored by God, who says, "This is my Son, the Beloved, with whom I am well pleased" (3:17). Again Matthew shows that we cannot be certain whom God uses. The same is true in our own experience. Who would have thought that a preacher in his mid-twenties would lead a movement that would garner him a Nobel Prize and change the character of a society? Or who would have thought that a former hustler would become a powerful and enduring figure for self-determination and social change? God, Matthew tells us, often uses outsiders. The Pharisees and Sadducees, the likely candidates to be honored, are not, and Jesus, the outsider, is shown to be the one on whom the blessing of God is bestowed.

4:1-11, Testing Jesus as God's Son

The trial in the wilderness is really a challenge to Jesus' status as the Son of God. The devil (literally, "the adversary") challenges Jesus around three areas: (1) food, (2) protection, and (3) power. Cain Hope Felder addresses how seductive these things can be:

> The temptation episodes of Matthew and Luke have captured, in a symbolic form, different aspects of evil that perennially undermine human aspirations. Whether the need is for food (daily sustenance and material possessions), magical powers (including "black" magic), or political power, a person should always be aware of potential enslavement by evil.[7]

The adversary is a figure found repeatedly in the Old Testament (e.g., Job). He comes to Jesus after forty days (4:2). This number, however, is not meant literally. In the Bible, the number forty generally means "a lot." The description here recalls the fasting of Moses (Exod 34:28), implying that Jesus is a new Moses. At any rate, the adversary first challenges Jesus' relationship to God (4:3). Jesus responds by appealing to God. This confrontation goes back and forth, each citing biblical passages for support. Finally, the adversary offers Jesus tremendous power, "the kingdoms of the world and their splendor" (Matt 4:8). Jesus again appeals to God, quoting Deut 6:13. Matthew shows here that the Messiah confirmed his status as the Son of God by resisting the temptation to capitalize on it. He highlights that our own relationships with God should not be measured by what we have. Although food, protection, and power may be influential motivators, they should not divert us from our dedication to God. Our status as children of God does not depend upon these things. In fact, many of the individuals we regard highly today were not persons of great wealth, for example, Malcolm X, Sojourner Truth, Frederick Douglass, and Martin Luther King Jr.

4:12-25, The Beginning of Jesus' Ministry

Hearing that John has been arrested, Jesus pursues his own ministry (Matt 4:12). He goes to Capernaum, a major commercial and population center on the northwest shore of the Sea of Galilee, from where he recruits his first disciples. Matthew says that this move was a fulfillment of prophecy (4:15). Quoting Isa 9:1-2, he tells us that "Galilee of the Gentiles" is the place where Jesus' ministry will unfold. This prophecy is a powerful first indication that Jesus' message will reach beyond the confines of Judaism. Further, this prophecy, one that indicates that a new era has dawned, also marks the character of Jesus' ministry. Jesus does his work among a mixed group of Jews, Greeks, Romans, Egyptians, immigrants, and others that constituted the region of the Galilee. Jesus advocates the same message of social transformation that was earlier proclaimed by John the Baptist (4:17; see 3:2). God's message is not just one of individual conversion but one of transforming the entire social structure. It was a message that attracted others who caught a glimpse of what society could be (4:18-25).

5:1—7:28, The Persecuted as Salt, Light, and Prophets

5:1-12, The Beatitudes

The Sermon on the Mount is the first of five major discourses made by Jesus in this Gospel. It begins with a series of "blessings" we call the Beatitudes (5:1-12). In reality, this is honorific language. When Jesus says someone is "blessed," it means something like "honorable" or "worthy of honor." The "poor in spirit" are those who are oppressed by the rich and powerful (see Pss 91:13; 34:10; Isa 49:14). As Felder makes clear, "Matthew 5:3 refers to the poor with respect to their spiritual status in

terms reminiscent of the *'anawim* (the collective pious poor of the Babylonian captivity)."[8] They are not just the financially destitute. People who are maimed, lame, blind, and the like were considered poor. They are those who have been misused by the powerful. For example, a widow owning millions without a son would have been considered a "poor widow" in Jesus' day. One example: a wealthy Egyptian woman named Apollonarian calls herself poor, because she is "a woman without a husband or helper."[9] Poverty was a social category and not just an economic one. The poor are those for whom "the system" does not work. By contrast, being "rich" meant having the power to get or take whatever you wanted. It was often synonymous with greed. Jesus assures the "poor in spirit" that under God's rule they are protected: "theirs *is* the kingdom of heaven" (5:3; emphasis added).

The Beatitudes between the first and the last guarantee something for the future (5:4-10). Being merciful, pure in heart, or a peacemaker refers to moral qualities disciples are expected to acquire. If a person is "pure in heart," it means that she thinks and does what pleases God (5:8). In a similar fashion, "peace" refers to the presence of those things necessary for a meaningful life. As Felder again makes clear, "The vision and promise of peace are calls to action on the part of persons seeking to participate in God's Kingdom (reign)."[10] The list ends with Jesus speaking of the "blessedness" of being persecuted (5:10-11). It appears odd to us that Jesus would say such a thing, but persecution has often been a consequence of righteousness. Nelson Mandela was locked in jail for decades because he spoke out against an evil system. Disciples should not be afraid to sacrifice creature comforts and even their own reputations for the sake of the mission of God. This should not be confused with the misguided notion that oppression is necessary, and it is certainly not an excuse to promote suffering for its own sake. Theodore Walker makes this clear when he says that "liberation struggle is inevitable because people never get used to being oppressed."[11]

5:13-20, Salt and Light

The section that follows the Beatitudes further outlines the idea of discipleship. The disciples, those who can expect persecution, are described as salt and light (5:13-14). As salt, they preserve the earth from final judgment; as light, they serve as examples to others. What Jesus calls for in this section is a radical form of discipleship, one characterized by superabundant righteousness (5:20). Brian Blount explains quite nicely what Matthew meant: "'Better' righteousness begins from the inside; it is integrally linked to an interior disposition wholly subservient to God's will as this will is authoritatively presented in Jesus' person and ministry."[12] The meaning of righteousness, as Matthew describes in the following section, is about more than personal piety; it is about how we conduct our relationships as well as our behavior. This is what the antitheses demonstrate (5:21-48).

5:21-48, Strategies to Overcome Ancient Practices of Violence

What these various scenes describe are alternatives to retaliation and dishonoring others. The disciple is to practice repentance, reconciliation, and generosity, and allow for the intervention of others instead of seeking to "win" or press her case at all costs. For example, Jesus says that reconciliation with a brother or sister is more important than worship obligations to God (5:23-24). In other words, Jesus redefines what kinds of behavior are worthy of honor among his disciples. Retaliation is to be replaced by reconciliation. Selfishness is to be replaced with generosity. In fact, when Jesus talks about tearing out your right eye, he is saying that it is better to be dishonored

yourself than to dishonor another and destroy the peace of the community (5:29). Another way to think about this passage is through the womanist practices of survival and community building.[13]

6:1-18, Almsgiving, Prayer, and Fasting

The next section in the Sermon on the Mount involves teaching about our religious obligations (6:1-18). Almsgiving, fasting, and prayer form the central acts of every disciple. Jesus makes a distinction here between the proper and improper performance of religious acts. He begins with a solemn warning to be careful about practicing one's religion (6:1). If special attention is not paid to how one performs these acts, they are then done improperly. Righteousness is not decided on the basis of conviction (faith) but on proper and careful performance.

When Jesus says, "Truly I tell you, they have received their reward," he is using economic language (6:2). The Greek term *apechousin* is often used in receipts. It means "paid in full." What the Sermon on the Mount says, which may appear peculiar, is that all rewards, even trivial ones, count. To put it another way, if one can only be punished once for a bad deed, then one can only be rewarded once for a good one. The disciple must be very careful regarding her religious acts in order to ensure that she gets her reward from God. The "hypocrite" then is not the person who is morally dishonest or a "faker," but the "typical" religious person who prays, fasts, and gives without thinking. People of such character, says Jesus, love to "perform" their religion. The true religious person might appear to be irreligious to everyone else.

Prayer is a topic of particular importance here (6:5-13). Foremost, prayer is described as a private matter between the person and God (6:6). Apparently, the disciples live in their own houses in which they would have a "room" to themselves. The "middle class" attitude of this Gospel may account for its historic lack of popularity among African Americans. Almsgiving, to cite another example, assumes that you have something to give. Nevertheless, the intimacy of prayer described here is similar to the African American slave practice of retiring to the "hush arbor" to pray. In this intimacy, asking God for anything is unnecessary because "your Father knows what you need before you ask him" (6:8). Prayer is not just a matter of asking for "things;" it is about cultivating a relationship with the creator.

A Summary of the Gospel?

The African Christian theologian Tertullian of Carthage believed that the Lord's Prayer was a shorthand version of the Gospel as a whole. He says, "How many edicts of prophets, Gospels, and apostles, how many discourses, parables, examples, and precepts of the Lord, are touched upon in the brevities of a few short words, how many duties summed up all at once?"

—Tertullian, *Prayer* 9.1–3

The Lord's Prayer serves as the model of what Christian prayer should be. As such, it defines what God regards as the real needs of human beings. As a consequence, the prayer is based not on human desires, ambitions, or selfishness but on God's wisdom. When we pray the Lord's Prayer, then, we affirm that God knows what we need and our confidence in the goodness of God's actions.[14] The first three petitions of the prayer (the hallowing of God's name, the coming of God's kingdom, and the doing of God's will) have to do with God's "needs." This is not to say that God is deficient or unrighteous, but that these

three things have been left unfulfilled. The continued presence of evil in the world is the ultimate testament that these "needs" have not been fulfilled. Disciples are important agents in accomplishing these petitions. When we pray the Lord's Prayer, we remind ourselves of what we need to do to assist God in creating a good society. For centuries, African Americans have realized that evil continues because those who could do something do nothing. Ralph Ellison once wrote, "There are few things in the world as dangerous as sleepwalkers."[15]

The next three petitions have to do with the needs of human beings. The first, the request for "daily bread," is particularly valuable (6:11). Notice it is not "my" bread but "our" bread for which we ask. When I ask for daily bread, I am asking not just for myself but for everyone. In fact, strictly speaking, God does not provide us with bread at all. Through nature God provides the ingredients from which we can make bread. It then is "our bread" because we make it. Even more pointedly, many of us do not make the bread we consume. We rely on others who then supply us with what we need. Yet what this petition acknowledges is that none of the suppliers of bread could "give," if God did not give beforehand. The request for bread asks then

---

A Womanist Understanding of Mutuality

Renita Weems explains the concept of mutuality as the realization that "as human beings we are all mutually connected to each other and dependent upon one another for our emancipation and our survival."

—Renita J. Weems, "Womanist Reflections on Biblical Hermeneutics," in *Black Theology: A Documentary History*, ed. James H. Cone and Gayraud Wilmore (Maryknoll, N.Y.: Orbis, 1993), 2:218.

---

for two things. First, it recognizes that if God does not supply the necessary ingredients, there is no way human beings can survive. Second, it asks that God motivate all those involved in the process of supplying human needs to complete their roles as well. What the petition for bread recognizes is that mutuality is necessary for human survival. (See sidebar on p. 93.) Until and unless individuals come together and share their gifts, says the prayer, we will all continue to suffer and struggle for what we need to survive. A similar conclusion can be drawn from the petition for forgiveness (6:12). It recognizes that mutuality is necessary for any society that seeks to fulfill the will of God (see also 6:14-15).

After the Lord's Prayer, the Sermon advances to the subject of fasting (6:16-18), which is a venerable practice in the African American community. According to Jesus, it should be inconspicuous. Thus, the teaching about fasting is analogous to the teaching about almsgiving and prayer. All of them are meaningful only if the disciple does them in a way that suggests to others that they are not doing them.

6:19-34, Practices of Discipleship

The Sermon abruptly shifts to more everyday topics. The first is that of treasure (6:19-21). Our predecessors understood something that is often overlooked by readers today: materialism has spiritual implications. Elias Farajaje-Jones makes the point more directly for African Americans, "With all of the Biblical injunctions against amassing wealth, it is still rare to hear a sermon [in the Black Church] on economic injustice as sin."[16] The decisions a person makes about how to conduct life when it comes to material wealth determine life here on earth and in the hereafter (6:21). How does one, though, lay up treasures in heaven? It is accomplished by performing good deeds here on earth, in particular through the sharing of

one's possessions with others. Martin Luther King Jr. understood this and exemplified it when, upon winning the Nobel Peace Prize, he decided to donate all of the monetary reward to the cause of human freedom.

After a proverb about a person's inner light and another statement about the danger of materialism (6:22-24), the Sermon focuses intently on the topic of anxiety (6:25-34). In truth, people tend to be anxious about all sorts of things. (1) There is a generalized anxiety, fear of something although we are unaware of what it is. (2) There is the more serious anxiety regarding the fragility of the human condition. The Beatitudes detail the daily troubles of poverty, sorrow, brutality, injustice, lack of mercy, impurity of heart, war, persecution of the righteous, and even martyrdom (5:3-12). The double parable at the end of the Sermon outlines the unpredictability of nature: torrential rains, flood, and storm (7:24-27). Jesus proclaims that in the face of such disasters, God's benevolence allows the world to endure, and that the possibility exists of finding a way through it all. "So," he declares, "do not worry" (6:34). The poet Gwendolyn Brooks said it poignantly, "Not that success, for him, is sure, infallible. / But never has he been afraid to reach. / His lesions are legion. But reaching is his rule."[17]

7:1-29, The Challenge of Discipleship

The Sermon ends by addressing the topics of judgment (7:1-5), profaning the holy (7:6), giving and receiving (7:7-11), and the Golden Rule (7:12), and giving intense warnings about what it truly means to be a disciple (7:13-23). Space does not permit a detailed examination of these themes, but what is apparent throughout this section is that it matters what the disciple does. Jesus tells his disciples, "Enter through the narrow gate" (7:13). The idea of the Two Ways is ancient, and it was especially prominent in Egypt. That the "hard road" indicates that travel will be difficult, even hazardous, is to be expected. Yet this is not because of what Jesus says in the Sermon on the Mount. It is the result of the difficulties of life itself. Struggles for the disciple include the external as well as the internal troubles that arise daily (6:34). To overcome these was to find "the narrow gate." In this we hear the words of Maya Angelou,

You may write me down in history
With your bitter, twisted lies,
You may trod me in the very dirt
But still, like dust, I'll rise.[18]

8:1—9:38, OUTSIDERS BECOME INSIDERS

8:1-17, Identifying the "Poor," the Outsiders
Almost all of the miracle stories in the Gospel of Matthew are found in chapters 8–9. Jesus begins his explicit miraculous activity in and around Galilee. The healing of the leper is the first detailed account we have in this Gospel. This story is peculiar in that it mediates between the little faith of the disciples (8:26) and the great faith of the centurion (8:10). The leper, because of his disease, is a social outcast. He is among the poor that Jesus referred to in the Sermon on the Mount (5:3). The healing of this leper constitutes a challenge to the temple authority. In Jesus resides the power that once belonged exclusively to the priests. Again, we see that the power of God can disrupt existing power structures. Most importantly, through his divine power Jesus restores this outcast as an insider.

We confront another outsider in the story of the healing of the centurion's son (8:5-13).[19] Unlike the leper, who was an outcast because of his disease, the centurion is an outsider because of his ethnicity. This provides us with another perspective on what it means

to be "poor." As a centurion and potentially a Roman citizen, many would consider him socially superior to Jesus and other Jews. Yet, because of his son, he must humble himself and become "poor." Jesus agrees to heal the man's son, but he is amazed at the centurion's response (8:7-10). The centurion actually verbalizes his "poverty," his need for Jesus' assistance. The recognition that he is one who needs the assistance of someone greater touches Jesus, and it serves as our first indication in the Gospel that outsiders, in this case Gentiles, will join the movement. In many respects, this story is about leveling social status. More importantly, this story is about

---

A Lukan Addition to Inclusivity

Cain Hope Felder points out that Luke's version of this incident is more inclusive than Matthew's: "The pattern is an elaborated re-presentation of Luke 13:29, where Luke amends the Q saying about those who will come and sit at Abraham's table (Matthew 8:11, 12) by adding 'north and south.' Luke is consciously more inclusive."

—Cain Hope Felder, *Troubling Biblical Waters: Race, Class, and Family*, The Bishop Henry McNeal Turner Studies in North American Black Religion 3 (Maryknoll, N.Y.: Orbis, 1989), 13.

---

interdependence. When Martin Luther King Jr. said, "I want to be the white man's brother, not his brother-in-law," he was pointing to the need for all persons to recognize their mutual need and dependence.[20]

The next miracle story occurs in a private home. Here Jesus takes the initiative. He decides to heal another outsider, a woman. Women were not considered as important as men in Jesus' day. The imposed inferior status of women, particularly women of color, has been an unfortunate experience that continues until this day. Sojourner Truth's remarks from 1851 still carry the disturbing ring of truth (see the sidebar below). Jesus' actions here suggest that under God's reign all individuals will be insiders.

Matthew finishes this set of miracle stories by saying that Jesus continues to heal and restore those who are outcasts (8:16). He quotes Isa 53:4 to help the reader understand the nature of Jesus' ministry (8:17). The Messiah overcomes the difficulties that often stigmatize our lives. The Messiah practices inclusion. In the new community created by Jesus, the social boundaries that marked one group as insiders and another as outsiders are redrawn so that all are insiders. Countless people can reiterate Sojourner Truth's question in numerous ways: persons living with HIV/AIDS, migrant workers, gay people, and victims of disaster—to name just a few. Aren't they people? Aren't they deserving of sacred worth? Yes. In a recent project I concluded the following: "Another theme found in some womanist theology is an innate sense of dignity in the face of oppressive social structures. In the presence of taunts, slurs, and physical abuse these [transvestites] 'are unanimous in their belief that they are human beings who deserve respect.' Monique's plea may be the most poignant: 'Let me be.'"[21] Notice also that Jesus heals *all* who come to him, whereas in the parallel passage in Mark, Jesus heals *many* who come to him (8:17; Mark 1:34).

8:18-22, The Seriousness of Discipleship

Jesus gives the order, apparently to his disciples, to move to the other side of the sea. Both a scribe and an unnamed disciple attempt to follow. The scribe calls Jesus "teacher," while the disciple calls him "Lord" (8:19, 21). The scribe does not fully understand who Jesus is. Jesus' response, when read with Christian eyes, underlines what appears to be a paradox: the one who is risen and will come as the judge of the world had to live in absolute poverty and homelessness (8:20). The early church, primarily through its sermons and contrary to the prevailing attitudes of the surrounding society, created a vision of God's kingdom that recognized the anonymous masses of those who were destitute. The Christian leadership gave these people a face: the face of Jesus. Ever since, the church has been committed to the poor because in the poor it sees the condition of the Savior.

Ain't I a Woman?

Dat man ober dar say dat womin needs to be helped into carriages, and lifted ober ditches, and to hab de best place everywhar. Nobody eber helps me into carriages, or ober mud-puddles, or gibs me any best place! And a'n't I a woman? Look at me! Look at my arm! I have ploughed, and planted, and gathered into barns, and no man could head me! And a'n't I a woman? I could work as much and eat as much as a man—when I could get it—and bear de lash as well! And a'n't I a woman? I have borne thirteen chilern, and seen 'em mos' all sold off to slavery, and when I cried out with my mother's grief, none but Jesus heard me! And a'n't I a woman?*

—Sojourner Truth

*One of Truth's historical biographers, Nell Irvin Painter, questions the historicity of the dialect used here. Painter suggests that this is not the way Truth spoke; this dialect was based on one white woman's portrayal a dozen years later and then the "myth" carried on. There is evidence of other reports that do not record Truth's dialect in this manner (Painter, *Sojourner Truth: A Life; A Symbol* [New York: Norton, 1966], 170–71, 174).

When Jesus tells the disciple to "let the dead bury their own dead," it sounds scandalous (8:22). The ancient African bishop Augustine said this about the statement, "One should love the begetter but prefer the creator." Without a doubt, Jesus' call to discipleship is deeply serious and uncompromisingly radical.

8:23-27, The Earthquake on the Water

The storm that follows Jesus' entering the boat is instructive because of Matthew's peculiar language. He does not call it a storm but an "earthquake" (*seismos*, verse 24). Many commentators believe that Matthew may have in mind the persecutions that "shook" the church after its inception (see 5:11-12; 10:16-39; 23:34-37). If this is true, the central issue in this passage is the fear of the disciples. Jesus calls their fear "little faith" (8:26). What is this little faith? Faith without action? In Matthew's Gospel faith must always be active, but that is not the primary issue. What makes their faith a "little faith" is that the disciples stop thinking about the power and presence of their Lord and then no longer *can* act.

Whenever the church cowers in fear at its obstacles, it is practicing "little faith." There is nothing passive about discipleship. Now Jesus' comments to the scribe and disciple become clear. What distinguishes little faith from unbelief is that little faith is the despair that can overwhelm those who have *risked* something for the sake of God's mission. It is the experience of fear among those who have witnessed the Lord's power.

8:28-34, The Fear of the Gadarenes

Once again we see that Jesus' ministry is not carried out in a homogeneous environment. Here he enters the predominantly non-Jewish area of the Gadarenes. Again Jesus comes into contact with social outsiders. He expels the demons from two men, but by doing this he rouses the fear of the Gadarenes (8:34). They want no part in Jesus' mission to redraw the social boundaries. Far too often, those for whom it would be most valuable fear change. Alice Walker correctly admonishes, "In our particular society, it is the narrowed and narrowing view of life that often wins."[22]

9:1-8, Disrupting the Recognized Power Structure

Upon his return to Capernaum, Jesus confronts a lame man (9:2). He says, "Take heart" (*tharsei*). The reader can understand this statement as Jesus' judgment on the previous two scenes, in which fear predominated. Even in the face of opposition, Jesus and his followers are to be courageous in their actions (9:3-6). At its beginning, this Gospel presented Jesus as the one who would save his people from their sins (1:21). Such a mission was bound to create conflict, but the in-breaking of God's kingdom often disrupts the established power structure. Here the words of Frederick Douglass remain incredibly powerful:

> If there is no struggle, there is no progress. Those who profess to favor freedom, and yet deprecate agitation, are [people] who want crops without plowing up the ground. They want rain without

---

Conjuring Righteousness?

Brian Blount says this about Matthew's idea of faith: "Why does he stress *doing* so emphatically? Is it because the doing creates, or, in the language of many African American slaves and their progeny, *conjured* something?

—Brian K. Blount, *Then the Whisper Put on Flesh: New Testament Ethics in an African American Context* (Nashville: Abingdon, 2001), 73.

thunder and lightning. They want the ocean without the awful roar of its many waters. This struggle may be a moral one; or it may be a physical one; or it may be both moral and physical; but it must be a struggle. Power concedes nothing without a demand.[23]

9:9-13, Tax Collectors as Outsiders

The meal that Jesus shares with Matthew and other tax collectors and sinners attracts the attention of the Pharisees, who heap scorn upon him (9:11). How did they even know Jesus was sharing a dinner with tax collectors? In Jesus' day, privacy as we know it did not exist. In a village like Capernaum, others would know about it and thus could comment on such a dinner. Their question, "Why does your teacher eat with tax collectors and sinners?" is a challenge to Jesus' honor. His response is in the form of a proverb (9:12). These are people in need of a physician. As social outcasts, they are seen as collaborators with an evil and oppressive government and are in need of social acceptance. Furthermore, Jesus' citation from Hos 6:6—only in Matthew—supports Jesus' behavior as a practice of mercy, not "sacrifice," the ritual slaughter of an animal in the temple. Mercy is to have precedence over sacrifice, as in the parable of 5:23-24. Mutuality means more than even worship.

9:14-17, Recognizing the Proper Time for Fasting and Rejoicing

It is not clear whether the disciples of John approach Jesus during or after the dinner. Jesus' response indicates that their question is inappropriate. It would be an insult to fast (a practice of mourning) during a time of celebration.

9:18-38, The Rich as Outsiders and the Harassment of the Crowds

A leader of the synagogue appeals to Jesus, asking him to intervene in the death of his daughter (9:18). Such a tragedy would have been common in Jesus' day. Nearly half of all children died before they reached the age of five.

Falling at the feet of someone was a gesture acknowledging social inferiority. As a ruler of the synagogue and thus a powerful person, he would have had the resources to

---

Female Life Expectancy

Census data from Egypt tell us that a female's life expectancy at birth was only 22.5 years.

—Roger Bagnall and Bruce Frier, *The Demography of Roman Egypt*, Cambridge Studies in Population, Economy and Society in Past Time 23 (Cambridge: Cambridge University Press, 1994), 87.

---

seek out professional physicians. Again, in the actions of the ruler we see (indirectly) the plight of the poor. Likewise, the woman who suddenly appears is among the poor. A person, especially a woman, with a flow of blood would have been considered unclean, and would have been ostracized from the community. Mark 5:26 reports that the woman had spent all of her wealth on professionals and had only grown worse. Since such care was expensive, the woman may have been initially wealthy. Matthew avoids mentioning that Jesus recognized the woman's touch (cf. Mark 5:30). This section of the narrative ends with Jesus healing two blind men and a person possessed by a demon (9:27-31). The response of the Pharisees is an attempt to undermine Jesus' credibility and authority by labeling it the power of evil (9:32). After this series of miracles, Jesus feels compassion for the crowds (9:36). He sees them as "oppressed" ("harassed," NRSV; Greek: *skyllō*) and "thrown on the ground" (*rhiptō*). Throughout 8:1—

9:38 Jesus performs miracles that transform the social conditions of the poor.[24] Outsiders are made insiders.

10:1-42, A Charge to Keep

10:1-4, Jesus' Core Group of Disciples, the Apostles

In the second major discourse in the Gospel, Matthew provides a list of Jesus' disciples (10:1-5). Jesus started recruiting core disciples at 4:18-22. He gives them power (*exousia*) to do the very things he accomplished (cf. 8:1—9:38). Further, it underscores what was said in 9:38. The disciples' mission will be like that of Jesus, to meet the needs of the "crowds," specifically the poor. The only part of Jesus' ministry that they are not yet given authority to duplicate is his teaching (see 28:20).

10:5-15, The Mission of Jesus' Group

Jesus charges his core disciples, now called apostles, to imitate his own ministry (10:5-15). Only Matthew emphasizes Jesus' commission to the Twelve to remain exclusively within "Israel," his technical term for the people of God (10:5-6). Such a command highlights the attitude of many in Jesus' day. They would have made a distinction between their group and other groups. These, however, were shifting designations. Outsiders could join their group, but they had to abide by certain expectations.

10:16-42, Commitment and Conflict

Jesus says to his disciples, "See, I am sending you out like sheep into the midst of wolves; so be wise as serpents and innocent as doves" (10:16). This makes their mission sound perilous. The joining together of doves and serpents is curious as well. The dove was a model of integrity, defenselessness, and purity. By contrast, the serpent was a model of craftiness (see, e.g., Gen 3:1). The disciples are assured, however, that they will be able to endure it all (10:23). The idea that family members would turn on each other says something quite radical (10:35-37). In the first century, one's family deserved paramount loyalty and total attachment. To turn against one's family was something almost unthinkable. Jesus' words here anticipate an alternative family that he will outline in 12:46-50. If Jesus' disciples choose their new family over their own, they must expect that their (former) family members will retaliate. Commitment will bring conflict. Such a situation can only be understood within the context of Marcus Garvey's words, "Men [and women] who are in earnest are not afraid of consequences."[25]

11:1-30, Jesus' Liberating Proclamation

11:1-19, Understanding the Nature of Jesus' Ministry

The disciples of John come to Jesus asking, "Are you the one who is to come, or are we to wait for another?" (11:3) This sounds curious to many readers who remember the baptism scene, where John appears to recognize who Jesus is (3:11, 13-15). Jesus' response may help us understand. He describes his ministry as one of "liberation" and restoration (11:4-5). John had expected it to be a ministry

---

Compensatory, *Not* Retributive Justice

Cain Hope Felder writes, "Through healings, acts of mercy and forgiveness, or direct confrontations with the conventional authorities, the ministry of Jesus in each gospel constitutes the paradigm of divine compensations."

—Cain Hope Felder, *Troubling Biblical Waters: Race, Class, and Family*, The Bishop Henry McNeal Turner Studies in North American Black Religion 3 (Maryknoll, N.Y.: Orbis, 1989), 73.

---

of judgment and condemnation (3:12). In many respects, Jesus' ministry is one of judgment. Yet it is largely a positive judgment. Jesus' ministry, instead of merely condemning people, sees the possibility for their redemption. It is often difficult for persons who have been oppressed and mistreated, like John, to see beyond their own pain and desire for divine judgment. King pointed this out when he wrote,

> In struggling for human dignity the oppressed people of the world must not succumb to the temptation of becoming bitter or indulging in hate campaigns. To retaliate with hate and bitterness would do nothing but intensify the existence of hate in our world. We have learned through the grim realities of life and history that hate and violence solve nothing. They only serve to push us deeper and deeper into the mire. Violence begets violence; hate begets hate; and toughness begets a greater toughness. It is all a descending spiral, and the end is destruction—for everybody.[26]

Jesus' subsequent statements about John honor him as a great prophet, but they also demonstrate that he does not believe that John truly understands the kingdom (11:7-15). By calling the present generation a group of "children," Jesus is in effect insulting them (11:16). Children lack wisdom, and their behavior can often be disruptive and inappropriate (11:17). The proverb "wisdom is vindicated by her deeds" points to the importance of practical outcomes. Wise people prove their abilities by the outcomes of their behavior. John's fasting behavior and Jesus' non-fasting behavior, although criticized, have had positive practical outcomes (11:18-19). This may remind the reader of Jesus' words in the Sermon on the Mount advocating inconspicuous religious practices (see 6:1-18).

11:20-24, Judgment on Unrepentant Cities

In a stunning apparent reversal, Matthew's Jesus pronounces judgment on three cities for their lack of "repentance" (11:20). Is this statement a denial of the potential for persons to repent? Possibly not. Jesus' ministry is about judgment. Without correct assessment (judgment) and often-difficult pronouncements, repentance is not possible. Evil cannot be destroyed by ignoring it. We must speak to it.

11:25-30, A Final Word of Invitation

This chapter ends with Jesus calling on God (11:25). He announces that God's favor is not revealed to the "wise" or "intelligent" but its opposite, the infant. God bypasses the wise and intelligent in favor of the simple. Who are these simple people? They are women, Galileans, and the poor of the land. Jesus then invokes a proverb that is analogous to our phrase "like father, like son" (11:27). Finally, there is the appeal to accept Jesus' "yoke" in place of the one they now bear (11:28-30). "Yoke" is a metaphor for what controls people as they make their way through life. Thus, this final statement made by Jesus in this section is one of invitation, not rejection.

12:1-50, Jesus Inspires Controversy

12:1-14, Controversy over the Sabbath

At issue in these two scenes (eating the grain and healing the man) are not the acts themselves but the deeper cultural issue of what is appropriate and what is inappropriate, and when. Jesus' response indicates that it is the task of the disciple to determine which religious obligation is appropriate at that particular time. Again, Jesus quotes Hos 6:6 as a guiding principle in such matters. The practice of mercy should be central to determine the appropriateness of any act, even if it creates controversy. Take, for example, the Truth and Reconciliation Commission in South Africa. Archbishop Desmond Tutu believed that the Commission was to uncover the ugly truth of apartheid, even if that meant offering amnesty to those who had committed heinous crimes. Truth, he believed, was more important than revenge. It stirred up considerable controversy in South Africa and the United States. The archbishop remained firm in his resolve, and, even with ongoing controversy, the truth was uncovered.

12:15-21, Controversial Silence

Even though Jesus healed "all" who came to him in Galilee, it appears that his fame was still limited. Matthew provides two reasons for this. First, Jesus "ordered them not to make him known" (12:16), which is odd in light of the spread of Jesus' fame (see 4:24-25). Second, the "servant" described by Isa 42:1-2 does not make himself fully known "until he brings justice to the nations" (12:20). In other words, it is only after the resurrection that Jesus makes himself known to "all nations" (28:19). Such a situation is not uncommon in our community as well. Often the greatness of our leaders is not perceived by the larger society. The true importance and courageousness

of Malcolm X, for example, was not appreciated until after he died.

12:22-45, Controversy with the Pharisees and Scribes

In the ancient world people were expected to behave in accordance with their social standing. People who violated these patterns of behavior were labeled "enemies" of the established order. They were people who "got out of their place." J. Edgar Hoover, for example, labeled Martin Luther King Jr. a "Communist"! Here the Pharisees label Jesus a deviant, claiming that the source of his power is Satan. Like John, Jesus calls them a "brood of vipers" (see 3:7-9; 23:33). By calling the scribes and the Pharisees an "evil and adulterous generation," Jesus says they are wicked bastards with no legitimate claim to be called the offspring of Israel. He turns their accusations against them by saying that one greater than Jonah or Solomon has come.

12:46-50, A Controversial Definition of "Family"

This incident is crucial for Matthew, who sees the good news centering in the household of those who accept Jesus and his message of the kingdom and loyalty to God the Father. The household provided the early church with one of its basic images of identity and cohesion. (I use the word "household" instead of "family" because there is no word in Hebrew or Greek that corresponds to our modern term *family*.) In Jesus' day, the "extended family" was all-important. It was the source of one's status in the community as well as the primary network for economic, religious, educational, and social functions. Leaving the family meant losing one's very identity. In contrast, a surrogate household, what anthropologists label a fictive kinship group, could serve the same function, if necessary. Matthew sees the church as such a surrogate household. It acts in the place of the household of birth. It is the locus as well as formation of the good news proclaimed by Jesus. The followers of Jesus are "brothers" and "sisters." They are supposed to act as a "family" would in such matters: supporting one another, correcting one another, and so forth. For the poor or those who had lost their households of birth (e.g., widows and orphans), this surrogate household would have been a place of refuge. For the wealthy, the well-connected, and those with strong ties to their households of birth, giving up one's birth household for the surrogate household of Jesus was a decision that could cost dearly (see 8:18-22; 10:34-36, 37-39; 19:23-30). Becoming a member of Jesus' household meant breaking ties not only with family but with the entire community of which one had been a part. The importance of extended families, as well as surrogate families, is well known in the African American community. For many slaves who were torn away from their biological families, the surrogate family was invaluable. Likewise, the network of the extended family, particularly after Emancipation, was crucial for the sur-vival of many. Even today, it is not unusual for grandparents, aunts, uncles, cousins, and others to care for family members who have fallen on "hard times."

13:1-58, The Gospel in Parable

13:1-23, The Parable of the Sower

This is the third major discourse in Matthew. A parable is a literary form or oral utterance in which its teller describes a scenario while intending the scenario to refer to something more and/or something other than what is actually being described. In this scenario, the seeds were sown before the land was plowed. This was not unusual. However, it is clear that the sowing was carelessly done. Perceptions of the sower would differ at this point depending on the status of the person. If the sower were a small landholder, he would appear to be stupid. If the sower were a hired laborer or a tenant farmer, who often struggled with difficult conditions, then he would be viewed with sympathy. Consequently, the fantastic yields would underscore that God is a generous provider (13:8). Jesus tells the disciples that parables are insider language (13:11; see the comments on 10:5-15). He goes on to speak poetically, using Isaiah to reinforce his teaching (13:14-15). Matthew is well-known for its use of the Old Testament (e.g., 1:22-23; 2:6, 18; 3:3; 4:15-16; 12:18-21; 13:14-15; 15:8-9; 21:5, 16, 42; 22:44). In these instances, the poetry that is invoked is from the biblical tradition of Israel used to underscore what Jesus does and says.

13:24-30, The Parable of the Wheat and the Tares

This is the first of many parables in Matthew beginning with the phrase, "The kingdom of heaven may be compared to . . ." or "The kingdom of heaven is like. . . ." This parable is also one of those that only appears in Mat-

---

What "Counts" in God's Family?

Cain Hope Felder says, "Jesus was not so much concerned with traditional family arrangements as he was with the in-breaking of the Kingdom of God (*Basileia tou Theou*) and how this anticipation required a new kind of household. *Blood relatives and language were no longer decisive criteria for the new Household that God and the ministry of Jesus make possible.*"

—Cain Hope Felder, *Troubling Biblical Waters: Race, Class, and Family,* The Bishop Henry McNeal Turner Studies in North American Black Religion 3 (Maryknoll, N.Y.: Orbis, 1989), 157.

thew. Harvesting is a familiar image of judgment (see 3:12). Since this parable describes how God acts, one way to understand the parable is to translate the first phrase as: "The way God acts, relates to, and affects his followers is like the following story." What is described here is a situation between feuding families. When he was born into a family, a person inherited the family's friends and its enemies. He could expect his enemies to do things to dishonor and hurt him (see the comments on 5:21-48). The parable helps to explain the continued existence of evil and why God's needs have not been met completely (see the comments on 6:1-18). God delays the judgment for the sake of the good (wheat) because they may be hurt in the process. It is only after the wheat matures that the harvesting can be conducted safely.

13:31-35, The Mustard Seed and the Leaven

How God relates to and affects his followers is like the sowing of the smallest of seeds, which later flourish into strong shrubs. Black mustard is the most likely plant referred to in this passage (13:31). It is the tallest of the mustards in Israel, at times reaching more than six feet tall. Black mustard was cultivated and used both as a condiment and as a medicine. It can also be found in many parts of the United States. The message appears to be that something different from what you expect will flourish into God's kingdom. Inconspicuous beginnings can yield unexpected results. Something similar can be found in the parable of the leaven (13:33). A very small amount of leaven is hidden in a large amount of flour, but it irresistibly expands it in excess. Jesus underscores that parables are used for outsiders and not insiders (see the comments on 10:5-15). To clarify why this is the case, something missing from the parallel in Mark 4:33-34, Matthew provides a citation from Ps 78:2.

13:36-43, Interpreting the Parable of the Wheat and Tares

This interpretation of the parable of the wheat and tares (13:24-30) does not describe the action in the scenario, and many scholars believe it was added later by the evangelist or someone else. Instead of following the action of the story, each element of the story is said to refer to something else. In short, the parable has been turned into an allegory. Allegorical interpretation was common in early Christianity. Like the Br'er Rabbit stories of the slaves and their descendants, this kind of story made it easier for insiders to speak to one another without attracting the retribution of outsiders.

13:44-52, Pictures of the Kingdom

Matthew offers three distinct pictures to characterize how God's kingdom operates. The metaphors are drawn from the everyday experiences of three types of people: tenant farmers, merchants, and fishermen. The point seems to be that the kingdom presents us with unexpected surprises in the first two pictures (hidden treasure and pearl), and that judgment is an inescapable consequence (fish). The introduction of the scribe is curious (13:52). One would expect Jesus to speak of discipleship, but he speaks of the scribe instead. The scribe (*grammateus*) was a privileged figure because he was "biblically literate." Thus, Matthew may be underscoring the importance of biblical literacy in the church.

13:53-58, Trying to Keep Jesus in His Place

We are told that Jesus is now in his hometown, presumably Nazareth. Jesus' teaching rouses the suspicion and rejection of the very people who know him best.

They ask, "Where then did this man get all this?" (13:56). In antiquity, status was ascribed at birth based primarily on family standing (see 13:55). At first the crowd in the synagogue responds positively, but they quickly question whether Jesus is really that different. Their questions all point to his family's unremarkable status. In asking whether Jesus was Joseph's son, the people question how such teaching could come from an artisan's son. Jesus' response, saying that others may be better equipped to realize who he is, would have been considered an insult (13:57). As many of us know, a sense of place can be good, offering comfort and familiarity. It can be stifling as well, keeping us from growing and limiting our opportunities. African Americans have long been ambivalent around the issue. The Great Migration to the North at the beginning of the twentieth century promised opportunity to many. Many left to escape often-vicious racism. But for many not all experiences were bad ones. In some of the very cauldrons of racism, many of our great educational institutions developed and produced some of our greatest minds. What is being described here is more of an inscribed institution, one in which those in power determined one's place. It was the kind of status that made your first name "'nigger' and your middle name becomes 'boy' (however old you are) and your last name becomes 'John.'"[27] This is why Jesus could not do any deeds of power

there; they could not see him for who he truly was (13:58; see the comments on 12:15-21 and 12:22-37).

14:1-12, Remembering John the Baptist

We finally find out what happened to John the Baptist. The subject arises because Herod is worried about Jesus (14:1). The description of the circumstances surrounding the death of John is suggestive of shameful activity. Allowing a daughter to dance before persons not in the family was often considered shameful.

The action of Herodias, the mother and primary agent in the story, indicates that she understood the threat John represented to her household, even if her husband did not. In

---

We Can't Always Be Winners

In 1966 Martin Luther King Jr. decided to take on the slums of Chicago, believing, "If we can break the backbone of discrimination in Chicago, we can do it in all the cities in the country." However, the Chicago campaign failed. He could never get the support of enough African Americans and others to make an impact. (Martin Luther King Jr., "A Proposal," MLK Papers, box 5–27, MLK Library, Atlanta, Ga., 6 January 1966, 3).

Redeeming Salome's Dance

Womanist theologian Cheryl A. Kirk-Duggan raises issues with the negative stereotype placed on Herodias's daughter. She says, "Was [Herod] a proud step-parent or a lascivious male or both? Was the dance sensuous, erotic or pornographic? (That is, in modern terms did she do a break dance, a pole dance or a lap dance?) Was this a young woman coming of age? Could it or did it arouse Herod? Lois Miriam Wilson claims that the causes of John the Baptist's beheading are beyond any dance Salome would have done." (Cheryl A. Kirk-Duggan, "Salome's Veiled Dance and David's Full Monty: A Womanist Reading on the Black Erotic in Blues, Rap, R&B, and Gospel Blues," in *Loving the Body: Black Religious Studies and the Erotic*, ed. Anthony B. Pinn and Dwight N. Hopkins [New York: Palgrave, 2004], 220.)

many ways, this story underscores the mutuality that pervades our lives. As Martin Luther King Jr. said, "We are caught in an escapable network of mutuality, tied in a single garment of destiny. Whatever affects one directly affects all indirectly."[28] What we do always influences others, for good or bad, and we can easily find ourselves to be agents of an evil that we did not intend or design.

14:13-36, ADDRESSING HUMAN NEED

14:13-21, Feeding of the Five Thousand

This meal is conducted in the wilderness (i.e., a deserted place; see the comments on 3:1-12), an unusual setting. A crowd of more than five thousand would have been larger than the population of all but a handful of settlements in the region. In providing this miracle Matthew may have the church in mind. Early Christians frequently took their meager resources, brought them together, and did miraculous things with them. In the sixth century, for example, we know that the Christians of Alexandria, under the leadership of their bishop John the Almsgiver, provided for more than seven thousand people. Such an experience is not unusual among African Americans as well. Out of the nickels and pennies, dimes and quarters placed repeatedly in offering plates and raised from bake sales and other enterprises, African Americans built educational institutions like Wilberforce University, denominations like the African Methodist Episcopal Zion Church, health care institutions like Meharry, great houses of prayer like Mother Bethel in Philadelphia, and countless other establishments. This story challenges the church not to be overwhelmed by fear, but to trust in the power of God to provide.

14:22-33, Jesus Walks on Water

In this story Peter becomes afraid when he "sees" the wind (14:30). Peter expresses "little faith" because he allows the external circumstances of the storm to overcome him, as though God did not exercise power over the wind (14:31). The disciples were "terrified" at seeing Jesus walking on the water (14:26). Fear can paralyze the disciple, but the message of Jesus is "Take heart . . . do not be afraid" (14:27; see the comments on 6:19-34; 8:23-27; and 9:1-8).

14:34-36, Jesus Continues His Healing

This summary passage underscores the fact that Jesus did not heal anyone magically. People asked to touch "the fringe of his cloak" to be healed (14:36). This fringe consisted of a blue tassel (there were several at the corners of the cloak) that served as an amulet against the evil eye, not unlike the phylacteries (prayer boxes) used by the Pharisees (see 23:5).

15:1-20, ADDRESSING TRADITION

Jesus turns the tables on those who would condemn him and his disciples. Condemning the condemners was an important strategy in the ancient world. Jesus condemns them (1) for undermining the word of God through their traditions (15:4-6) and (2) for their hypocrisy as unthinking religious practitioners (see the comments on 6:1-18). The passage from Isaiah demonstrates both points. Jesus categorically denies the position of the Pharisees. His rationale is called a parable (15:15). The explanation may appear a bit odd, but it makes sense in the context of the first century. They believed that whatever one puts in one's mouth is evacuated, and whatever is evacuated is not unclean in terms of purity rules. Fecal matter may be offensive, but it is not unclean in terms of the purity system. By contrast, what comes out of the mouth defiles a person, as the list in 15:19 demonstrates. These things are morally defiling because they promote social disorder, revenge, and violence.

15:21-39, Re-Addressing Human Need

15:21-28, The Canaanite Woman's Daughter

This story is somewhat disturbing, because Jesus initially refuses to assist this woman, calling her one of the "dogs" (15:26). She calls upon Jesus as the "Son of David" to assist her (15:22). This designation shapes the unfolding of the conversation. As the Son of David, Jesus' obligations are to Israel and not to outsiders. He is, in effect, precluded from helping her. She will not give up, however. She demonstrates great faith by humbling herself, identifying herself as one of the poor, and "demanding" mercy (15:27-28). The Canaanite woman, like the centurion, is an outsider who humbles herself. This is why she is the only other figure in the Gospel whose faith is described as great (see the comments on 9:9-13). This scene also highlights another theme we have encountered before in the Gospel, namely, survival. This woman acts on behalf of her daughter, both outsiders, and places her own life on the line to secure the survival of her family.

15:29-31, Another Summary of Jesus' Healings

This account of Jesus' healing activity is that the crowd gave praise to the "God of Israel," as fits with Jesus' description of what a disciple does (see 5:16).

15:32-39, The Feeding of the Four Thousand

This is another story about how God, through Jesus, feeds a large group of individuals who come to hear him (see the comments on 14:13-21).

16:1-12, Addressing Teaching

16:1-4, Discerning the Times

The first four verses repeat 12:38-39, forming

A Womanist Concern for Family?

"Womanist, from *womanish*. (Opp. of 'girlish,' i.e., frivolous, irresponsible, not serious.) A black feminist or feminist of color. From the black folk expression of mothers to female children, 'You acting womanish,' i.e., like a woman. Usually referring to outrageous, audacious, courageous or willful behavior. Wanting to know more and in greater depth than is considered 'good' for one. Interest in grown-up doings. Acting grown up. Being grown up. Interchangeable with another black folk expression: 'You trying to be grown.' Responsible. In charge. Serious."

—Alice Walker, *In Search of Our Mother's Gardens: Womanist Prose* (xi), quoted in Jacquelyn Grant, "Womanist Theology: Black Women's Experience as a Source for Doing Theology, with Special Reference to Christology," in *Black Theology: A Documentary History*, ed. James H. Cone and Gayraud Wilmore (Maryknoll, N.Y.: Orbis, 1993), 2:277.

---

a literary bracket to the section (see the comments on 12:38-43). The figures of speech used here appear to be exclusive to the land of Israel, because they more or less adequately reflect the weather conditions of the region. The west wind brings the breezes from the Mediterranean, which spreads moisture inland. The south wind comes from the Negev desert. It brings a very hot wind that can raise temperatures thirty degrees in an hour.

16:5-12, Teaching for Insiders

Leaven or yeast is used here as a metaphor for what corrupts because it can cause leavened dough to ooze out beyond the boundaries of its container. It is no respecter of boundaries or limits. It is, in effect, impure.

16:13—17:23, Jesus on His Way to Jerusalem

16:13-20, The Clarification of Jesus

In the ancient world, the question raised here is not the modern one of identity (Who am I?), but the position or status others could perceive (Who do you say that I am?). The most obvious reply was to identify the individual by her family or place of origin (e.g., Jesus of Nazareth, James son of Alphaeus). People generally felt that embedded in such an identification was all the information one needed in order to know the individual. Since Jesus' behavior deviates so greatly from that of an artisan's son, other means of identifying his power and status are proposed (16:14). The final designation, "The Messiah, the Son of the living God," is confirmed as the correct status, but one that only came about through revelation (16:16-17). Jesus' designation as "Son" places him in relationship to his surrogate household (see the comments on 12:46-50). There is a scene at the end of Spike Lee's *Malcolm X* in which various individuals proclaim, "I am Malcolm X." We understand that these individuals are not the actual Malcolm X, who was assassinated, but that they claim his status as an agent of social change. The same thing is happening in Matthew. The designation "Messiah" or "Christ" is a status, not an indication of a person's psychological state. This is why asking questions about how Jesus understood himself (his psychology) are misguided. None of the ways Jesus is described in this Gospel reveals that information to us. They are identification markers, status claims, and not insights into the psychological makeup of Jesus.

16:21-28, The Way of the Cross

The clarification of Jesus' status sets the stage for the fulfillment of his mission.

Peter's plans for Jesus differ from what Jesus perceives as necessary. Peter's rebuke is interpreted then as a test of Jesus' loyalty to God. This is why Peter is called "Satan," the adversary (see the comments on 4:1-11). Discipleship as described here by Jesus is a serious act that requires a great deal of sacrifice. The promise of the kingdom, however, is the benefit and reward that makes such an act meritorious (see the comments on 6:19-34 and 10:16-42).

17:1-13, Jesus Will Be Vindicated!

The assertion made at 17:5 is precisely what was affirmed by the baptism scene (see 3:13-17) and questioned by others (see 4:1-11; 9:11, 14; 11:3; 12:2, 9-14; 13:55; etc.), the ultimate status of Jesus. The assertion at the beginning of Jesus' ministry is recapitulated here as his ministry draws to a close. This preemptory scene of the resurrection functions to give the reader a preview of the final vindication of Jesus. Moses and Elijah are significant because they are two other figures in the biblical tradition whose burial places are unknown.

17:14-20, The Man with the Epileptic Son

A man with a demon-possessed son was in danger of ostracism. Since his son could not marry, the entire family and its name were in jeopardy. In fact, the entire extended family was in peril. Restoration of the boy would mean the restoration of all. (On "little faith" see the comments on 14:22-33.)

17:22-23, A Second Prediction of Jesus' Fate

This is the second of the Passion predictions, so typical of Mark's story of Jesus. Jesus repeats his conviction that his actions will bring about his betrayal and death. Yet his confidence in God is unshaken. God will raise him from the dead.

17:24-27, Paying Taxes

This scene involves the collection of the temple tax (the *didrachma*). Matthew's use of that Greek term, along with the additional term *stater* ("coin") for the coin in the fish's mouth, indicates that the author is writing for individuals who know these types of coins. These would be non-Jews probably not living in Israel. The tax, to pay for the upkeep of the temple and to support its personnel (priests, Levites, etc.), was to be paid annually by all males of the "house of Israel," that is, persons affiliated with Judaism and its temple. It had to be paid whether one lived in Israel or not. What Jesus says is that if earthly kings do not expect their subjects to pay taxes, but rather the people they conquer, the same should be true for the king of heaven. (Roman citizens, for example, were not required to pay certain taxes.) In other words, non-Israelites should pay the temple tax for the benefit of the house of Israel. The sons of the kingdom should be free from the burden of taxation. This is a curious scene that appears only in Matthew.

18:1-35, Members of the Kingdom

18:1-10, Who Is the Greatest in Our Group?

This discussion begins the fourth major discourse of the Gospel. Disagreement about status within the community is not unusual, and it would have been common in the time of Jesus. Once the pecking order was sorted out, people in Jesus' day would normally accept the decision. Here a difference in phrasing is very important. The phrase "to be humble" meant staying in your "place," not trying to upgrade oneself at the expense of another. The phrase "to become humble" meant to yield one's precedence to another, to accept a lower status and its treatment—here, to become

like a child (18:3). We should dismiss ideas of childhood bliss when we read this passage. Childhood in antiquity was difficult. Fifty percent of children died before the age of five. They were the weakest members of society. They were fed last, and received the smallest and least desirable portions of food. They were the first to suffer from famine, war, disease, and natural disasters. Many, some say more than 70 percent, would have lost one or both parents before reaching puberty. A minor had the same status as a slave, and it was not until adulthood that he would be considered a free person. Calling an adult a child or "childish" was seen as a great insult (see the comments on 11:1-19). This is not the final word, however. Children were, indeed, loved. A woman's children would have been one of her closest emotional supports. Thus, to tell his disciples to become like children is to ask that they renounce their privileges as adult men and make themselves some of the most vulnerable people in society. Again, we are confronted with the serious consequences of discipleship.

18:12-14, Straying Sheep

The image of the shepherd is surprising. Shepherds were a despised group. They could be romanticized, probably because of the status of King David, the shepherd king. David was made an object of hope in the prophecies of Zephaniah (3:19-20) and Micah (5:2-5). In truth, shepherding was among the most despised jobs. They could not protect the honor of their families, since they had to be away from home at night. Often they were seen as thieves, because they grazed their flocks on other people's property. Here, however, the shepherd plays the role of validating an important event. The large flock described would either have belonged to a large household or to several. For losing one sheep, a shepherd would have to answer to other members of the community. Thus, the celebration upon finding the sheep is understandable. Because sheep that have strayed often sit down, refuse to move, and bleat incessantly, the shepherd would have to carry it back to the flock. There are many songs, sermons, and testimonies in the African American community that refer to this scene of being "that one lost sheep." In this sense, being found means adding value back to the community. Profoundly, these songs point to the diminishment of identity that the community experiences after the loss of one of its members. All members of the community are valuable, and none should be excluded or allowed to "stray."

18:15-22, Conflict Resolution

Matthew presents a procedure for conflict resolution that does not involve merely "turning the other cheek" (5:39). Instead, three forms of conflict resolution are presented: confrontation (18:15), negotiation (18:16), and adjudication (18:17). "Brother" refers to a member of the community (see the comments on 12:46-50). All disciples have the authority to bind and loose (the "you" here is plural). The background is legal; the "anything you ask" (*pragma*) refers to legal cases (18:19). Thus, if two or three gather to hear such a case, Jesus is there as well. Yet this is not the end. The requirement to forgive another follower of Jesus (brother) is constant. Reconciliation and mutuality are dominant features of Jesus' teaching in Matthew.

18:23-35, The Parable of the Unmerciful Slave

The parable of the unmerciful slave has long been troublesome for scholars, and it is one that only appears in Matthew. It is Jesus' response to Peter's query (18:21). The idea of a king or official settling accounts often points to a scene of final judgment. The consequences of indebtedness could include the loss

of property, family, and much more. In short, indebtedness limited an individual's ability to actualize her existence. The remission of debt meant the restoration of an individual's ability to maintain his standing in the social order, and potentially to improve it. Keeping a person in debt, therefore, meant the diminishment of an individual's life chances. One of the often-overlooked aspects of this parable is its implication that forgiveness is an act that affects more than just two individuals. The parable of the unmerciful slave highlights the idea that life should be understood as interconnected. Practices of social interaction that maintain the dominance of some over others, or that liberate some to the detriment of others, are to be renounced as immoral and inconsistent with the divine character. It is not enough that God has forgiven us; we must live and act out of that forgiveness in ways that make it meaningful. Without an ethic of mutuality we cannot truly understand how to be the church, whether black or otherwise, in a world where the masses continue to writhe "silently under a mighty wrong."

19:1—20:34, Discipleship

19:1-12, A Question about Divorce

Divorce, as the dissolution of a marriage, was really a contractual matter between families.[29] In other words, individuals did not get married; families did. Divorce then meant the dissolution of family ties, which often resulted in feuding. Jesus transformed the understanding of this relationship from a legal one into a "blood" one ("no longer two, but one flesh"). A blood relationship, like the relationship one has to mother and father or siblings, cannot be dissolved. What is prohibited here is divorce *and* remarriage or divorce *in order to* marry again. The exception is the case of "unchastity" (*porneia*), which probably refers to a list of behaviors discussed in Lev 18:6-23. To divorce in order to remarry is labeled adultery. The disciples interpret this as a prohibition of divorce. Whether or not this is true is debatable.

Christian Divorce

Contrary to the popular imagination, early Christians did divorce. Divorce, in cases of "domestic violence," appears to have been quite common. Evidence from Egypt, for example, tells us of women who left their abusive husbands, some with the direct assistance of the church.

—Oxyrhynchus Papyrus L 3581 (J. F. Oates, et al., *Checklist of Editions of Greek and Latin Papyri, Ostraca and Tablets*, 4th ed., Bulletin of the American Schools of Oriental Research: Supplement Series 7 [Atlanta: Scholars, 1992]).

19:13-15, Suffer the Children

On the vulnerability of children, see the comments on 18:1-10. Jesus lays his hands on children in order to protect them from evil external influences. Jesus' statement means that God's favor belongs to those ready and willing to be under his protection.

19:16-30, Riches and Loyalty

By calling Jesus "good" the young man put Jesus on the spot. Jesus responds by saying that such a compliment should only be offered to God alone. Jesus makes two demands on the young man: to sell what he owns and to follow Jesus. The demand to sell what one possesses, if taken literally, is the demand to part with the dearest of all, the family home and land. The statement "For mortals it is impossible, but for God all things are possible" indicates the seriousness of this decision (19:26).

20:1-16, The Parable of the Laborers in the Vineyard

Day laborers were among the poorest people in ancient society. Life for them was often a bitter struggle. In the story no one goes looking for work, which would have been dishonorable. People had to be approached and asked to work (20:3, 7). The householder pays all as agreed. He shows uncharacteristic generosity by giving "to this last the same as I give to you" (20:14). What is often missed is what is said in 20:15. The NRSV translates it, "Or are you envious because I am generous?" A literal translation is more instructive: "Is your eye evil because I am good?" In other words, the upset laborers attempted to cast an evil eye (a serious matter) on the householder, but it is ineffective because he is good.

20:17-19, A Warning of Trouble to Come

Not only is the death of Jesus anticipated, but the degradation ritual he will have to endure is spelled out as well (see the comments on 26:67-68).

A Womanist Act?

Kelly Brown Douglas writes, "Not only has Black women's experience been characterized by their complex and determined struggle for freedom, but most significantly by their ability to survive with dignity in spite of demeaning social-historical circumstances, and their extraordinary commitment to the survival of their families."

—Kelly Delaine Brown Douglas, "Womanist Theology: What Is Its Relationship to Black Theology?" in *Black Theology: A Documentary History*, ed. James H. Cone and Gayraud Wilmore (Maryknoll, N.Y.: Orbis, 1993), 2:296.

20:20-28, Competition for Honor

Seeking status, the mother of these two brothers approaches Jesus. His response has two aspects. First, can they share his fate ("cup" is often a symbol for fate)? Second, he says that any honors handed out come from the Father. Jesus then sets out to reverse the normal status order. The great are now those who function as servants (*diakonoi*), and the first are those who occupy the status of slave. To further clarify, Jesus says that the new pattern of status in the community is based on his own actions (20:28).

20:29-34, Jesus Heals Two Blind Men

The healing of these men is a further amplification of the preceding story. Instead of grasping for status and honor, the disciple, like Jesus, is to use her ability to assist the poor (see also the comments on 5:1-12).

21:1-17, Jesus Arrives in Jerusalem

21:1-11, The Triumphal Entry

The horse was the customary war animal. The ass, by contrast, was a draft animal, used to carry persons and goods. Zech 9:9 indicates that for a king (essentially a military figure) to ride on an ass was beneath his status. Jesus had humbled himself. The response of the crowd is to treat him as an arriving king, spreading their garments and branches. This is similar to "red carpet" treatment in our own society. The city is in "turmoil" because of this event, outsiders approaching the city hailing this "Son of David" (21:10). The last time Jerusalem was in turmoil was at the time of Jesus' birth (2:3). Jesus' entry into Jerusalem disturbs the citizens because it challenges the power structure.

21:12-13, Jesus Opposes the Temple, the Symbol of Priestly Power

Jesus' actions are directed at people who performed a legitimate function in the temple. They enabled the performance of sacrifices commanded by God in the Old Testament. To drive them away is equivalent to putting a halt to such divinely ordained temple sacrifices. Jesus' statement clarifies his action. A "den of robbers" is the place where robbers store what they have taken from others. Calling the temple a den of robbers is to judge it to be a place where people are extorted and abused. This act would have enraged those at the heart of Jewish power, the priests. This act, more than any other, would have been the basis for his crucifixion. Attacks on the existing power structure, especially when it is oppressive, often bring death-dealing retaliation.

21:14-17, A Further Challenge to Priestly Power

After "cleansing" the temple, Jesus heals the blind and lame in the temple, another act that would have enraged the establishment.

An African Christian Perspective

Clement of Alexandria writes of the cleansing episode: "But those who act contrary to these things—the avaricious, the liars, the hypocrites, those who make merchandise from the truth—the Lord cast out of his Father's court, not willing that the holy house of God should be the house of unrighteous traffic either in words or in material things."

—Clement, *Paedagogus* 3, in *Ante-Nicene Fathers*, ed. Alexander Roberts and James Donaldson (Peabody, Mass.: Hendrickson, 1994 [1885–1887]), 2:290.

The blind and lame are categories of persons who, along with others, were not allowed to approach the altar in the temple (Lev 21:16-24). Jesus, through his actions, openly opposes the priests' authority to determine who is worthy of God's favor and who is not.

21:18—22:46, JESUS' AUTHORITY AND CHALLENGES TO IT

21:18-22, The Fig Tree

A curse is a meaningful set of words that produce some negative outcome on a person or thing. We only have a few situations that are comparable to a curse in the ancient world. When a judge pronounces a sentence, for example, his "curse" upon the person is carried out. "I sentence you to life in prison" means that the individual is immediately transported, as if by magic, to a place of punishment for the specified time. It takes the right words by the right person in the right context. The fig tree withered because of Jesus' total loyalty (faith) to God and his lack of hesitation in what God asks him to do. This is "having faith and not doubting."

21:23-32, A Challenge to Jesus' Authority

As Jesus is teaching, his authority is challenged by the chief priests and elders of the people. Authority is the ability to have influence on the behavior of others. Jesus' refusal to provide any additional legitimation for his authority appears to be based on the fact that, like John, he had credibility with the people.

21:33-46, The Parable of the Tenants

This parable is disturbing for a number of reasons but especially because it makes no sense to suppose that such a scenario would unfold in this way.[30] The church used this parable as an allegory for how God's favor was passed from the Jewish authorities to the church.

22:1-14, The Parable of the Wedding Feast

This is another parable directed at the Jewish authorities. This is a royal wedding for which invitations are sent out to invited guests, probably people of status and privilege. The invitation also allowed potential guests to find out who else was coming. If the right people were coming, all would come. If the right people were not coming, they would stay away. The excuses are indirect ways of signaling disapproval of the dinner arrangements. Further, the king's slaves are treated shamefully, an insult to the king's honor. Thus, the response would have been appropriate (22:7). The king now invites others—anyone the slaves can find—to the feast. This would have been a remarkable scene; people of different social status rarely ate together in antiquity. The idea of a king eating with someone "off the street" would have been unthinkable. This parable serves to highlight the inclusiveness of the Christian community, where slaves ate with masters, the rich and the poor sat at the same table. The bliss of this scene is broken, however, when the man is cast out (22:11-13). The king would have had the appropriate garments ready for his guests. This individual did not put on the garment provided, thus shaming the king. Inclusiveness does not mean there are no standards. The man is cast out not because of who he is, but because of what he refuses to do. He does not honor the king.

22:15-22, A Challenge over Taxes

A new set of opponents attempt to trap Jesus. The question of taxes is always volatile. Jesus asks his opponents to produce the "coin used for the tax," a Roman denarius. The irony is that *they* have the coin. They are asking if it is right to participate in a system in which *they* already participate. Jesus answers their original question with a curious answer: "Give therefore to the emperor the things that are the emperor's, and to God the things that are

God's" (22:21). The answer puts the responsibility on the individual to sort out the issues. These opponents will later claim that Jesus disapproved of paying the tax (see 23:2).

Why Taxes Are Volatile

Martin Luther King Jr. wrote, "Further, the federal government collects taxes from all citizens, Negro and white, which it is constitutionally obligated to use for the benefit of all; yet, billions of these tax dollars have gone to support housing programs and hospital and airport construction in which discrimination is an open and notorious practice."

—Martin Luther King Jr., "Equality Now: The President Has the Power," in *A Testament of Hope: The Essential Writings and Speeches of Martin Luther King, Jr,* ed. James M. Washington (San Francisco: Harper & Row, 1986), 153.

22:23-33, A Challenge over the Resurrection

Another set of opponents come forward; these are Sadducees who say "there is no resurrection" (22:23). They were the aristocratic and priestly group that controlled the temple and its lands. Their question is sarcastic and mocking, rooted in Deut 25:5-10, which lays out a system of handing on property rights through a procedure called levirate or brother-in-law marriage. Jesus' answer is equally sarcastic. He says that normal human social structures do not exist in the resurrection (22:30).

22:34-40, A Challenge over the Greatest Commandment

The Pharisees put forward a challenge that concerns the principles by which one directs one's life. Jesus answers by quoting Deut 6:5 and Lev 19:18, on love of God and neighbor. Cain Hope Felder says quite plainly that "*neighbor* means another human being, irrespective of the person's race or class."[31]

22:41-46, A Challenge from Jesus

This is a counter-challenge to the previous one. Jesus' challenge is about who the messiah is. They answer "the Son of David" (a common understanding found throughout Matthew). Jesus' response is that the messiah must be greater than David (22:43-45). Jesus challenges a prevalent ideology of his day. He calls into question the model they have for the messiah. The messiah, according to Jesus, will be something greater than a mere king. Jesus demonstrates that we far too often accept traditional understandings and patterns of behavior without testing their propriety (about hypocrites see the comments on 6:1-18).

23:1-39, Jesus Calls His Opponents to Account

Jesus issues a series of public challenges regarding the authority of "the scribes and Pharisees," while speaking "to the crowds and to his disciples." It is a serious list of challenges, piled

---

A "Subversive Memory" for the Church

Diana Hayes writes, "Black Catholics in the United States share the tradition of the church from its earliest beginnings but they also bring a critique of that tradition, serving as a 'subversive memory' within the church itself and calling it to live up to its proclamation of Scriptures that reveal God's consistent option for the poor and the oppressed but which have been, too often, submerged by a praxis which ignored the plight of those same poor and oppressed."

—Diana L. Hayes, "Feminist Theology, Womanist Theology: A Black Catholic Perspective," in *Black Theology: A Documentary History*, ed. James H. Cone and Gayraud Wilmore (Maryknoll, N.Y.: Orbis, 1993), 2:332.

---

up to suggest a very serious conflict between Jesus and his opponents. One is of particular interest. Tithing had as its purpose the support of persons in Israel who had no land with food "from the land" (e.g., priests, Levites, the poor). It had its root in Lev 27:30-31; Num 18:21-24; and Deut 14:22-29; 26:12-14. Tithing was a way all Israel could be nourished on the produce of the "holy land," the property of the God of Israel. Jesus says that the Pharisees refuse to address the real question, which was why the needy of Israel did not have land at all. It was the loss of their land that required the "tithe for the poor." They are hypocrites, unthinking religious practitioners, because they avoid the serious question of "justice, mercy, and faith" (23:23-24).

24:1—25:46, SHEEP AND GOATS

24:1-51, Warnings and Assurances

This discussion of the end of the world is the final major discourse in Matthew. The disciples are told the signs of Jesus' coming as Messiah in power (24:3-36). He warns them against deception (24:5-8) and opposition (24:9-13). Jerusalem, in particular, will suffer (24:15-22). In fact, the signs will be quite public (24:27-28). The disciples are told to remain vigilant (24:44). They are to live with a view to a soon and sudden coming of the Messiah. Those who live otherwise will be punished (24:45-51).

25:1-13, The Ten Bridesmaids

Jesus offers another parable about the sudden end. The scenario is a wedding, a time of celebration. The bridesmaids were expected to wait at the groom's home to greet him. The dull-witted bridesmaids did not plan for the task at hand and were shut out of the festivities. As a parable about the soon and sudden coming of the Messiah, the point is: be ever prepared.

25:14-30, The Rich Get Richer

This is a difficult parable to accept outside of its context. It is about two slaves who use their master's money to make him wealthier, and one that does not. In Jesus' day, these slaves would have been seen as greedy and dishonest. Here in Matthew, the parable is about how to behave in the period before the Messiah's coming, not to be lazy or useless persons.

25:31-46, The Parable about the Last Judgment

The basis for the division in this parable is compassionate action toward the poor (see the comments on 5:1-12). The judgment takes place like a shepherd's separation of sheep and goats. Sheep are on the right; they usually belong to males. Goats, the source of milk and cheese for the family and usually belonging to females, are on the left. This is similar to the earlier parable of the sorting of the fish (13:47-50). Jesus says that the soon and sudden coming of the Messiah in power will be marked by judgment based on one's behavior to those in need.

26:1—28:20, THE PASSION AND RESURRECTION

26:1-5, Trouble Is Coming

The Jewish leaders decide to take their revenge against Jesus. They follow the normal practices of people in that day: stealth (depicted in this passage), bribery (26:14-16), false witnesses (26:60), trumped-up charges before government officials (27:12), inciting the crowd (27:20), and mocking him (27:41-42). Pilate correctly determines that this is revenge prompted by "envy" (27:18).

26:6-13, The Anointing of Jesus

The disciples are rebuked by Jesus because they fail to recognize the significance of what is about to happen. They are still concerned

What Am I Required to Do?

Benjamin Mays said, "What can we, as blacks, do? It may be that God has called upon black people, black Americans to be a special people. It is my belief, it is my firm conviction, that God has sent every man and woman into the world to do something unique, something distinctive, and that if he or she does not do it, it will never be done and the world will be the loser. The call to do this unique thing does not go to the crowd or to the multitude but to the individual or a specific nation—mainly to a particular person and often a particular race. Yes, I do believe that God has sent every man and every woman into the world to do something unique and something distinctive, and if he or she does not do it, it will never be done."

—Benjamin E. Mays, "Thanksgiving," in *Outstanding Black Sermons*, ed. Milton E. Owens Jr. (Valley Forge, Pa.: Judson, 1982), 3:50.

about the poor and their treatment, as was described in the preceding parable (25:31-46).

26:14-16, Judas Is Disloyal

Betrayal was considered one of the lowest acts, one of the greatest sins in antiquity. In addition, thirty pieces of silver was not a great sum of money. Matthew never explains why Judas betrayed Jesus. The condemnation for such an act, however, would be severe.

26:17-29, The Lord's Supper

The critical importance of table fellowship cannot be overestimated. It was an act of social cohesion and shared values. Further, since the Passover meal was a family meal, eating it with his disciples is recognition of this group as a surrogate household in the deepest sense of the term.

26:30-35, Peter Will Be Disloyal

Peter, as well as the other disciples, vow that they will not be disloyal to Jesus, but we see that Jesus is privy to all the events that will unfold in the near future. These, he tells them, will happen as expected (see 26:56).

26:36-56, Jesus' Arrest in Gethsemane

The religious authorities make their move led by Judas and armed with swords and clubs. The depiction indicates that they expected a fight with Jesus' followers. Indeed, Jesus did have armed followers (26:51). Jesus says, "Have you come out with swords and clubs to arrest me as though I were a bandit?" (26:55) The Greek term used here, *lēstēs*, can mean "robber," "bandit," or "thief" in the ordinary sense. The circumstances suggest something else. A *lēstēs* was also the term used for a "social bandit." These were people who created social disorder by disrupting normal society. A modern analogue would be the street gangs that infest many large cities and create havoc and inflict violence on its residents. Jesus, of course, is not such a person. Social bandits often hid. He was in the temple every day,

The Solitude of Gethsemane

L. Vanchael Booth wrote, "The greatest loneliness in the world is to discover that one is lost from the presence of God. The agony was great in the Garden of Gethsemane, but Jesus even then was not alone. It was dark, cold, and cruel Calvary that evoked the cry: 'My God, my God, why hast thou forsaken me?' When [a person] faces the gravity of solitude, he [or she] needs a frame of reference that has power enough to pull him [or her] through."

—L. Vanchael Booth, "Are You Looking for Jesus?" in *Outstanding Black Sermons*, ed. Walter E. Hoard (Valley Forge, Pa.: Judson, 1979), 2:18.

where he could have been arrested easily
(26:55-56).

26:57-68, Jesus before Caiaphas
The authorities look for false testimony and
are not able to find any (26:60). The charge
that Jesus said he would destroy the temple,
not made in Matthew, can be found in the
Gospel of John (2:19). Contrary to many
attempts by scholars to treat this as a trial (a
legitimate legal proceeding), it is really an act
of humiliation. The authorities have already
determined that they will kill him.

26:69-75, Peter's Disloyalty
Peter uses deception to keep himself independent of association with Jesus. Lying to
others about his relationship to Jesus would
not be considered wrong. The problem is
that Jesus said Peter would behave like that,
and Peter insisted that he would not. It is the
fact that he did not fulfill his word of honor
in the presence of others that is shameful
(26:35).

27:1-10, Judas's Demise
Judas's acts are an attempt to redeem his
behavior. He repents and acclaims to the Jewish religious authorities that he betrayed an
innocent man (27:3-4). His hanging of himself was a public act of repentance.

27:11-31, Jesus before Pilate
The chief priests practice revisionist history,
attempting to claim that Jesus was subversive
all along (27:11-14). Pilate recognizes that the
actions of the leaders are prompted by revenge
(27:18). In this public spectacle, the rulers
and crowd cry out for Barabbas (literally, "son
of the father," Aramaic: *Bar 'Abba*). Jesus has
been dealt the supreme insult; he is considered
less than a criminal. This is confirmed by the
dream of Pilate's wife informing her of Jesus'
innocence (27:19). According to Matthew, the

Jews are not without shame in this process as
well. The Roman soldiers mock Jesus as "King
of the Jews," an insult to the very crowd calling for his death (27:27-31).

Pilate's Trial

Strobridge Hoard once said, "By judging
Jesus, he became judged himself. He was
the real defendant on trial. Not Jesus, but
Pilate! He who would have gained much by
this transaction stands out as the despised,
the smitten, the lonely and rejected. And no
longer Jesus, but the Romans, the Jews, the
Sanhedrin Court, and Pilate are on trial."

—Strobridge E. Hoard, "Following Pilate's Path of Futility," in
Outstanding Black Sermons, ed. Walter E. Hoard (Valley Forge,
Pa.: Judson, 1979), 2:37.

27:32-66, The Crucifixion
Crucifixion was a form of capital punishment
reserved for individuals who were not Roman
citizens. It was meant to be humiliating and
painful. The beating was so brutal that Simon
of Cyrene was forced to carry his cross (see
the comments on Mark 15:21). The charge
against Jesus, "King of the Jews," was meant
to show what happened to people who challenged Roman power (27:37). For Jesus, this
is the final act of humiliation. For his enemies,
it is the point of their greatest satisfaction.
Their enemy has been nailed to a cross, naked
and on public display. They drive home the
humiliation by gloating and taunting him
(27:38-43). It is curious that Matthew says
that even the others being crucified taunted
him as well (27:44). The force of this scene is
to demonstrate that Jesus' humiliation is complete. This is counteracted by various cosmic
events that demonstrate that God is still present in Jesus' humiliation (27:45-54).

Jesus in the Womanist Tradition

"They identified with Jesus," writes Jacquelyn Grant of black women in slavery, "because they believed that Jesus identified with them. As Jesus was persecuted and made to suffer undeservedly, so were they. His suffering culminated in the crucifixion. Their crucifixion included rapes, and husbands being castrated (literally and metaphorically), babies being sold, and other cruel and often murderous treatments. But Jesus' suffering was not the suffering of a mere human, for Jesus was understood to be God incarnate."

—Jacquelyn Grant, "Womanist Theology: Black Women's Experience as a Source for Doing Theology, with Special Reference to Christology," in *Black Theology: A Documentary History*, ed. James H. Cone and Gayraud Wilmore (Maryknoll, N.Y.: Orbis, 1993), 281.

28:1-10, The Resurrection

While the women are approaching the tomb, there is an earthquake caused by a heavenly being. He is apparently responsible for the moving of the tombstone and the disabling of the guards. It is not done, however, to let Jesus out but to allow the women to look in to see the empty tomb. He orders the women to remind the disciples that Jesus would see them in Galilee (see 26:32). Jesus then appears and delivers the same message (28:9-10).

28:11-15, The Great Cover-up

Matthew appears to be addressing a claim he has heard that Jesus' body was stolen by his disciples. He denies it and argues that the motivation for the creation of the story was the embarrassment of the Jewish authorities. African Americans are familiar with such conspiracy theories in our own community. They are used to rationalize an event or occurrence that contradicts our accepted worldview, or they can be used for the purpose of deception. When James Chaney, Michael Schwerner, and Andrew Goodman were killed in Mississippi in 1964, local authorities concocted outlandish theories to divert attention away from the real conspirators. Difficult as it may be for us to accept, many African Americans constructed similar conspiracy theories to rebut the evidence against Orenthal James (O. J.) Simpson in 1995.

28:16-20, The Great Commission

This is the scene of Jesus' vindication: "all authority in heaven and on earth has been given to me" (28:18). The location of the disciples is difficult to determine. They are in Galilee, but they are present on a "mountain to which Jesus had directed them" (28:16). The Greek (*etaxato*) suggests that this place had been selected in advance. But no such scene is found in the Gospel. At any rate, Jesus now turns over his teaching authority to his disciples (28:20). Their status of apostles/disciples is now complete (see the comments on 10:1-4). They are told that this gospel can now be carried to "all nations" and not just the house of Israel, marking the final move from the particular ministry of the Son of David to the universal witness of the Son of God.

Evangelism as Community Building

Suppose evangelism was understood as community building, rather than just "saving souls"? Delores Williams tells us that the "goal of this community building is, of course, to establish a positive quality of life—economic, spiritual, educational—for black women, men, and children." Imagine.

—Delores S. Williams, "Womanist Theology: Black Women's Voices," in *Black Theology: A Documentary History*, ed. James H. Cone and Gayraud Wilmore (Maryknoll, N.Y.: Orbis, 1993), 269.

Notes

1. Paul connects Jesus to Abraham in Galatians 3 (calling Jesus Abraham's offspring) and Romans 4 (saying that the birth of Isaac was analogous to Jesus' resurrection). These are the two most important connections.

2. Martin Luther King Jr., "Equality Now: The President Has the Power," in *A Testament of Hope: The Essential Writings and Speeches of Martin Luther King, Jr,* ed. James M. Washington (San Francisco: Harper & Row, 1986), 292.

3. For a discussion of the color of the family of Jesus, see Cain Hope Felder, "Cultural Ideology, Afrocentrism and Biblical Interpretation," in *Black Theology: A Documentary History,* ed. James H. Cone and Gayraud Wilmore (Maryknoll, N.Y.: Orbis, 1993), 2:194.

4. Ibid.

5. For an in-depth discussion of Sheba and its queen, see Cain Hope Felder, *Troubling Biblical Waters: Race, Class, and Family,* The Bishop Henry McNeal Turner Studies in North American Black Religion 3 (Maryknoll, N.Y.: Orbis, 1989), 30–36.

6. Roger Bagnall and Bruce Frier, *The Demography of Roman Egypt,* Cambridge Studies in Population, Economy and Society in Past Time 23 (Cambridge: Cambridge University Press, 1994), 100.

7. Felder, *Troubling Biblical Waters,* 105.

8. Ibid., 124.

9. Jane Rowlandson, ed., *Women and Society in Greek and Roman Egypt: A Sourcebook* (Cambridge: Cambridge University Press, 1998), 203.

10. Felder, *Troubling Biblical Waters,* 169.

11. Theodore Walker Jr., *Mothership Connections: A Black Atlantic Synthesis of Neoclassical Metaphysics and Black Theology,* SUNY Series in Constructive Postmodern Thought (Albany: State University of New York Press, 2004), 50.

12. Brian K. Blount, *Then the Whisper Put on Flesh: New Testament Ethics in an African American Context* (Nashville: Abingdon, 2001), 71.

13. See Delores S. Williams, "Womanist Theology: Black Women's Voices" in Cone and Wilmore, *Black Theology,* 2:168.

14. Michael Joseph Brown, *The Lord's Prayer through North African Eyes: A Window into Early Christianity* (New York: T. & T. Clark, 2004), 242.

15. Janet Cheatham Bell, ed., *Famous Black Quotes and Some Not So Famous* (Chicago: Sabayt, 1986), 2.

16. Elias Farajaje-Jones, "Breaking Silence: Toward an In-the-Life Theology," in Cone and Wilmore, *Black Theology,* 2:152.

17. Bell, *Famous Black Quotes,* 59. See Gwendolyn Brooks, "The Womanhood - II," *Annie Allen* (New York: Harper and Row, 1949). Reprinted by consent of Brooks Permissions.

18. Ibid. "Still I Rise," copyright © 1978 by Maya Angelou, from *And Still I Rise* by Maya Angelou. Used by permission of Random House, Inc.

19. Although almost all translations render this individual in need of healing as the centurion's servant, an alternative reading is possible. The Greek word here (*pais*) can also be understood as the centurion's son. In the Greek version of the Old Testament, it is almost always translated "servant," which explains the popular understanding in the KJV, RSV, and other translations. The degree of affection demonstrated here by the centurion makes one wonder if this individual had been a mere slave. And so, my designation of this individual as the centurion's son attempts to capture the close bond between the two, even if this "son" was not the centurion's biological son."

20. King, "Equality Now." Quoted in Richard Lischer, *The Preacher King: Martin Luther King Jr. and the Word That Moved America* (New York: Oxford University Press, 1997), 144.

21. Michael Joseph Brown, *Blackening of the Bible: The Aims of African American Biblical Scholarship* (Harrisburg, Pa.: Trinity Press International, 2004), 180.

22. Bell, *Famous Black Quotes,* 4.

23. Ibid., 13.

24. Rowlandson, *Women and Society in Greek and Roman Egypt*, 82.

25. Bell, *Famous Black Quotes*, 17.

26. Martin Luther King Jr., "The Current Crisis in Race Relations," in *A Testament of Hope*, Washington, 87.

27. King, "Equality Now," 293.

28. Ibid., 290.

29. See Rowlandson, *Women and Society in Greek and Roman Egypt,*, 208–9.

30. See Brown, *Blackening of the Bible*, 162–68.

31. Felder, *Troubling Biblical Waters*, 70.

For Further Reading

Bagnall, Roger, and Bruce Frier, *The Demography of Roman Egypt*. Cambridge Studies in Population, Economy and Society in Past Time 23. Cambridge: Cambridge University Press, 1994.

Bell, Janet Cheatham, ed. *Famous Black Quotes and Some Not So Famous*. Chicago: Sabayt, 1986.

Blount, Brian K. *Then the Whisper Put on Flesh: New Testament Ethics in an African American Context*. Nashville: Abingdon, 2001.

Booth, L. Vanchael "Are You Looking for Jesus?" Pages 15–20 in *Outstanding Black Sermons*, vol. 2. Edited by Walter E. Hoard. Valley Forge, Pa.: Judson, 1979.

Brown, Michael Joseph. *Blackening of the Bible: The Aims of African American Biblical Scholarship*. Harrisburg, Pa.: Trinity Press International, 2004.

———. *The Lord's Prayer through North African Eyes: A Window into Early Christianity*. New York: T. & T. Clark, 2004.

———. "Matthew, Gospel of." In *New Interpreter's Dictionary of the Bible*. Edited by Katharine D. Sakenfeld. Nashville: Abingdon, 2007.

Douglas, Kelly Delaine Brown. "Womanist Theology: What Is Its Relationship to Black Theology?" Pages 290–99 in *Black Theology: A Documentary History*, vol. 2. Edited by James H. Cone and Gayraud Wilmore. Maryknoll, N.Y.: Orbis, 1993.

Farajaje-Jones, Elias. "Breaking Silence: Toward an In-the-Life Theology." Pages 139–59 in *Black Theology: A Documentary History*, vol. 2. Edited by James H. Cone and Gayraud Wilmore. Maryknoll, N.Y.: Orbis, 1993.

Felder, Cain Hope. "Cultural Ideology, Afrocentrism and Biblical Interpretation." Pages 184–195 in *Black Theology: A Documentary History*. Edited by James H. Cone and Gayraud Wil-more. Maryknoll, N.Y.: Orbis, 1993.

———. *Troubling Biblical Waters: Race, Class, and Family*. The Bishop Henry McNeal Turner Studies in North American Black Religion 3. Maryknoll, N.Y.: Orbis, 1989.

Grant, Jacquelyn. "Womanist Theology: Black Women's Experience as a Source for Doing Theology, with Special Reference to Christology." Pages 273–289 in *Black Theology: A Documentary History*. Edited by James H. Cone and Gayraud Wilmore. Maryknoll, N.Y.: Orbis, 1993.

Hayes, Diana L. "Feminist Theology, Womanist Theology: A Black Catholic Perspective." Pages 325–35 in *Black Theology: A Documentary History*, vol. 2. Edited by James H. Cone and Gayraud Wilmore. Maryknoll, N.Y.: Orbis, 1993.

Hoard, Strobridge E. "Following Pilate's Path of Futility." Pages 33–40 in *Outstanding Black Sermons*, vol. 2. Edited by Walter E. Hoard. Valley Forge, Pa.: Judson, 1979.

King, Martin Luther, Jr. *A Testament of Hope: The Essential Writings and Speeches of Martin Luther King, Jr.* Edited by James M. Washington. San Francisco: Harper & Row, 1986. See especially "Equality Now: The President Has the Power," 152–59.

Kirk-Duggan, Cheryl A. "Salome's Veiled Dance and David's Full Monty: A Womanist Reading on the Black Erotic in Blues, Rap, R&B, and Gospel Blues." Pages 217–34 in *Loving the Body: Black Religious Studies and the Erotic*. Edited by Anthony B. Pinn and Dwight N. Hopkins. New York: Palgrave Macmillan, 2004.

Malina, Bruce J., and Richard L. Rohrbaugh. *Social-Science Commentary on the Synoptic Gospels*. Minneapolis: Fortress Press, 1992.

Mays, Benjamin E. "Thanksgiving." Pages 47–54 in *Outstanding Black Sermons*, vol. 3. Edited by Milton E. Owens Jr. Valley Forge, Pa.: Judson, 1982.

Painter, Nell Irvin. *Sojourner Truth: A Life, a Symbol*. New York: Norton, 1996.

Rowlandson, Jane ed. *Women and Society in Greek and Roman Egypt: A Sourcebook*. Cambridge: Cambridge University Press, 1998.

Walker, Theodore, Jr. *Mothership Connections: A Black Atlantic Synthesis of Neoclassical Metaphysics and Black Theology*. SUNY Series in Constructive Postmodern Thought. Albany: State University of New York Press, 2004.

Weems, Renita J. "Reading *Her Way* through the Struggle: African American Women and the Bible." Pages 57–78 in *Stony the Road We Trod: African American Biblical Interpretation*. Edited by Cain Hope Felder. Minneapolis: Fortress Press, 1991.

———. "Womanist Reflections on Biblical Hermeneutics." Pages 216–24 in *Black Theology: A Documentary History*, vol. 2. Edited by James H. Cone and Gayraud Wilmore. Maryknoll, N.Y.: Orbis, 1993.

Williams, Delores, S. "Womanist Theology: Black Women's Voices." Pages 265–72 in *Black Theology: A Documentary History*, vol. 2. Edited by James H. Cone and Gayraud Wilmore. Maryknoll, N.Y.: Orbis, 1993.

The GOSPEL *of*

MARK

Emerson B. Powery

INTRODUCTION

Mark is the earliest written Gospel of Jesus'
earthly mission. Most scholars suggest Rome
as its place of origin, but a few have recently
argued for Syrian Antioch, on the eastern side
of the Mediterranean, as this story's provenance. The weight of the evidence still supports the former, more traditional location.
Mark, then, is one of the early Christian writers who transported the message of the gospel
westward (toward Rome), with intentions of
making the story of Jesus compelling for a
more Latinized (i.e., European) population.
A number of stories highlight Jesus' contact
with non-Jewish people as one example of this
effort.

Specific indicators of this Gospel's affect
on African American Christianity are mini-
mal. Much attention has focused on Simon of
Cyrene, the African cross-bearer. In addition,
it was Howard Thurman's favorite Gospel,
because of its early dating and emphasis on
Jesus' life and mission. Recently, Mark's story
has received attention as one of the most
significant Gospels for liberation (e.g., Brian
Blount and Joanna Dewey).[1]

Mark's message of Jesus' life and actions
as representative of the coming reign of God
should be read in light of Mark's context,
especially the Roman-Jewish War (66–70
C.E.). How should followers of Jesus live in a
world in which Rome, the ruling elite, was in
direct conflict with leading members of the

Jewish community? Whose side should they take? Should they "give unto Caesar" or "give unto God"? Jesus' life-giving activity among the villages of Galilee had implications for the early Christian communities of first-century Rome and continues to have consequences for all who desire to follow the one who proclaimed that God's reign is near!

1:1-8, Introducing John

"The wilderness" location helps establish John as a prophetic outsider (1:2-3; cf. Isa 40:3; Mal 3:1) who challenges the status quo of urban political centers. His nontraditional clothing and eating style reinforce his populist persona while reminding many of Elijah (cf. 2 Kgs 1:8). John's prophetic spirit lived on in David Walker of nineteenth-century America, a person whom W. E. B. DuBois also called "a voice crying in the wilderness."[2]

David Walker as Forerunner

In 1829, David Walker, born free, published one of the greatest abolitionist documents to date, *Walker's Appeal*. He wrote, "Have not the Americans the Bible in their hands? Do they believe it? Surely they do not. See how they treat us in open violation of the Bible!! . . . But an American minister, with the Bible in his hand, holds us and our children in the most abject slavery and wretchedness."

—David Walker, "Walker's Appeal," in *Afro-American Religious History: A Documentary Witness*, ed. Milton C. Sernett (Durham, N.C.: Duke University Press, 1985), 191.

In addition to preaching repentance (1:4), John announced the coming of one "stronger" than John himself. This mysterious person would outshine John in the significant act of baptism, John's signature act. Unfortunately, Mark never records Jesus baptizing anyone with the Holy Spirit.

1:9-15, Introducing the Spirit, Satan, Jesus, and God's Reign

Jesus' narrative entrance is not nearly as dramatic as John's. He is not introduced by prophetic texts. His geographic reference is not the famed Jerusalem but his insignificant hometown village, Nazareth (cf. John 1:46). Amazingly, Jesus is "baptized by John." The other Gospel writers, possibly scandalized by this event, either qualify this baptism or completely omit it. Nonetheless, Jesus' baptism was an act of "solidarity with the rest of the community"[3] in the spirit of John's transforming mission.

Clearly, the characters in Mark's story are confused. Much happens before some recognize who Jesus is. Some never do. Jesus himself is reassured by a private vision (in Mark) about his status as the "stronger one," during which the Spirit descends "into him" (*eis auton*) and God declares him "my Son, the Beloved."

The Spirit then "forcefully drives" (*ekballo*) Jesus into the wilderness. The dramatic verb, altered in the other Gospels to lessen its intensity, suggests some reluctance on Jesus' part. And why not? Waiting for him in the wilderness was a lengthy period of temptation from Satan (forty days), who also makes his first appearance at this point.

Jesus' public mission does not begin, however, until John's imprisonment, another hint at the political ramifications of the John/Jesus mission. The unjust imprisonment of John reminds many of the numerous incarcerations of African Americans on trumped-up charges. (See sidebar on p. 123.) *Euangelion* ("gospel") was a term of great sociopolitical import. Jesus' gospel celebrates the moment ("the time has been fulfilled"); God's empire is near.

Justice and the Prison System

"We must strive for justice in the legal system. One-third of all young African American men are currently in jail or prison, on probation, on parole, or awaiting trial. The U.S. prison-industrial complex has become a vast warehouse for millions of the poor and unemployed. In the past ten years, the number of black women in prison has more than doubled. Any black person is four times more likely to receive the death penalty than any white person convicted of the same crime. For these reasons, we should be in the forefront of the campaign to call for the abolition of the death penalty, the twentieth century's version of lynching."

—Manning Marable, "Black Leadership, Faith, and the Struggle for Freedom," in *Black Faith and Public Talk: Critical Essays on James H. Cone's* Black Theology and Black Power, ed. Dwight N. Hopkins (Maryknoll, N.Y.: Orbis, 1999), 85.

God's imperial reign is more about a holistic, societal, communal transformation than about individual salvation. The communal nature of the first-century culture would not expect nor understand otherwise. Yet reception of such a message was as difficult for first-century followers as it is for twenty-first-century followers. This vision inscribed in the message requires a restructuring of the sociopolitical standing of those living life on the margins.

So Jesus proclaimed the nearness of God's justice *after the unjust imprisonment of John.*

1:16-20, The Call of the Disciples

Jesus' first activity, in Mark, was to seek followers. Rabbis rarely selected their own students. The radical social reorientation championed by Jesus' mission continued when he encouraged these young men to leave their

family businesses, a disrespectful act in first-century Jewish culture. These initial followers first witness what will become Jesus' signature activity, exorcism.

1:21-28, A Sign of God's Reign: A Synagogue Exorcism

Instead of working from the margins, like John, Jesus' mission invades the synagogue, the sociopolitical religious center. The African American church—where issues as diverse as health, civics, politics, election campaigning, banking, housing, commercial development, social critique, etc., are routinely considered as worship—is not unlike the ancient synagogue, where there was no real disjunction between matters "sacred" and "secular."

In performing a healing exorcism that also significantly alters a person's social status, Jesus exhibits an authority radically different from that of the scribes. According to James Cone, it "disclosed that God in Jesus has brought liberation to the poor and the wretched of the land, and that liberation is none other than the overthrow of everything that is against the fulfillment of their humanity."[4] Brian Blount's analogy of an escaped slave is apropos: "Each successful escape was as damaging to the system of institutionalized slavery as each one of Jesus' successful exorcisms or healings had been to the continued dominance of the realm of the 'strong man.'"[5]

1:29-31, Healing of Simon's Mother-in-Law

In Jesus' first narrative encounter with a woman, he demonstrates that God's rule is space- and gender-inclusive: it transforms the home and the family as well as the synagogue and the religious outcast. Mark describes the healed woman's response with the same verb used of the angels in 1:13, *diakoneo.* In Mark's Gospel only women, angels, and the Son of Man act the role of "deacon," who "serves," "waits upon," and "ministers."

1:32-39, General Activity of Healing, Preaching, and Prayer

The disruptive disciples, no doubt seeking further miracles, disturb Jesus' time of prayer and meditation. They fail to understand what Ralph Ellison's narrator of *Invisible Man* made so plain: "Hibernation is a covert preparation for a more covert action."[6]

1:40-45, Healing of the Nameless Leper

Ironically, in the Gospel of Mark it is often the nameless who best exemplify good discipleship. Although the "unnamed" are being restored as signs of God's reordering, they are not now receiving their "names" in the story! The narrator does not always go far enough; that is, he fails to provide the full restoration of humanity that naming provides. James Baldwin epitomizes the African American struggle with namelessness: "their very names were nothing more than dust blown disdainfully across the field of time."[7]

Though Jesus appears to be a law-abiding healer-prophet who is faithful to the traditions of the ancestors (e.g., "show yourself to the priest, and offer for your cleansing what Moses commanded"), he often flaunts the "rules." He touched an unclean person. He was also "angry."[8] But why? Some insight may be gained from the contemporary discussion surrounding the idea of "black rage." In an interview, Jamaica Kincaid admitted, "I realized that in writing that book [*A Small Place*] that the first step to claiming yourself is anger. You get mad. And you can't do anything before you get angry. And I recommend getting very angry to everyone, anyone."[9]

Following the 1960 riots in Watts, Newark, and Detroit, William Grier and Price Cobbs published *Black Rage*, a classic analy-

---

The Psychology behind Black Rage

"Slip for a moment into the soul of a black girl whose womanhood is blighted, not because she is ugly, but because she is black and by definition all blacks are ugly.

"Become for a moment a black citizen of Birmingham, Alabama, and try to understand his grief and dismay when innocent children are slain while they worship, for no other reason than that they are black.

"Imagine how an impoverished mother feels as she watches the light of creativity snuffed out in her children by schools which dull the mind and environs which rot the soul.

"For a moment make yourself the black father whose son went innocently to war and there was slain—for whom, for what?

"For a moment be any black person, anywhere, and you will feel the waves of hopelessness that engulfed black men and women when Martin Luther King was murdered. All black people understood the tide of anarchy that followed his death.

"It is this transformation of *this* quantum of grief into aggression of which we now speak. As a sapling bent low stores energy for a violent backswing, blacks bent double by oppression have stored energy which will be released in the form of rage—black rage, apocalyptic and final."

—William H. Grier and Price M. Cobbs, *Black Rage* (New York: Basic, 1968), 176–77.

sis of the psychological-cultural ethos that explores what it means to be African American in a predominately white society (see the sidebar). In an attempt to understand the origins of such rage, the final few pages are still relevant more than thirty years later: "Observe that the amount of rage the oppressed turns on his tormentor is a direct function of the depth of his grief, and consider the intensity of black [people's] grief." Cornell West reminds us to (re-)focus the rage in appropriate ways, so that "visions, analyses, and strategies never lose sight of black rage, yet they focus this rage where it belongs: on any form of racism, sexism, homophobia, or economic injustice that impedes the opportunities of 'everyday people' . . . to live lives of dignity and decency."[10]

Jesus refocuses his "rage" to reinstitute this "exiled" Jew, a leper—whose "whiteness" would be even more pronounced among the darker skinned Afro-Asians like Jesus and his contemporaries—back to his rightful, sociopolitical and religious position.

2:1-12, Healing of the Person with Paralysis

The narrative returns to a "home," which was an important place for Jesus' healing activity (cf. 1:29-34). After Jesus sees the "faith" of the four friends (and the paralytic's own faith?), Jesus forgives the paralytic's sins. Of the healings reported thus far, this is the first time "faith" is mentioned.

By forgiving this man's sins, Jesus again functions as "priest" (cf. 1:40-45). This is the only time *in the entire narrative* that Jesus forgives anyone's sins. Forgiveness is not restricted to Jesus' timely death but included in Jesus' active life.

Furthermore, the scribes' disturbance expresses the unusual nature of this scene. These law experts judge Jesus' "forgiveness" blasphemous and, in light of their definition of blasphemy ("Who can forgive sins but God

alone?"), they are right to do so. Of course, *authorized* persons (the priests) could "forgive" on behalf of God. So the charge of blasphemy is due to Jesus' (apparent) lack of authority. His response highlights a special "authority" granted to the "Son of Man." Such "authority" is confirmed by Jesus' healing ability: the paralytic walks!

2:13-17, Calling of Levi and Other Tax Collectors

Earlier Jesus entered Simon's house; now, he also dines at Levi's. House settings are important for the movement, but occasionally a controversy arises because of Jesus' table-fellowship practices. (The shock white folks expressed in the classic film *Guess Who's Coming to Dinner*, starring Sidney Poitier, is a contemporary analogy to how the "scribes" felt about Jesus' dinner guests.) Scribes exclude both "tax collectors" (whom they view as a visible extension of Rome) and "sinners" (whom they consider lawbreakers) from any religious privileges. Jesus overhears their concern and states: "I have come to call . . . sinners." As Jesus redefines the meaning of a "sinner" against the traditional opinions of the day, so has black theology redefined the concept of "sin" for our day.

What black theology and Jesus share is a sincere critique of the traditional "theologies" of their days, which tend to establish categories, definitions, and "sins" that dehumanize and ostracize the other.[11]

2:18-22, Fasting

In this passage Jesus first suggests that his presence, as "bridegroom," is a time of celebration; this links fasting to sorrow (cf. Zech 8:18-19). He does not view fasting the way he views prayer, which he practices regularly (cf. 1:35; 6:46; 14:32). Jesus' final reaction is even more radical than his initial one. The appearance of God's reign in the person and presence of

Jesus challenges the traditional practice of religion. From the beginning of the narrative, examples of this newness have been the thrust of the story: he touched a woman for healing; he touched a leper for healing; he forgave a paralytic's sins; he ate with "sinners." Likewise, Richard Allen, Absalom Jones, and others initiated independent African American churches because the "old wineskins" could not contain the "new wine."[12] Racism mixed with Christianity was and is an odd mixture indeed.[13]

"Sin," Meals, and Race

The correlation between "sin" and meals (and its corresponding relationships) was critical to the critique by Harriet Wilson (the first African American female novelist) of northern abolitionists. In her work *Our Nig* the narrator describes one character's (Frado's) situation: "She passed into the various towns of the State she lived in, then into Massachusetts. Strange were some of her adventures. Watched by kidnappers, maltreated by professed abolitionists, who didn't want slaves at the South, nor niggers in their own houses, North. Faugh! To lodge one; to eat with one; to admit one through the front door; to sit next to one; awful!"

—Harriet Wilson, quoted in *The African American Archive: The History of the Black Experience through Documents*, ed. Kai Wright (New York: Black Dog & Leventhal, 2001), 294. The novel *Our Nig* was originally published in 1859.

2:23-28, Jesus and the Sabbath

Historically, common folk viewed the Pharisees more favorably than other Jewish sects because of their intentions to make Torah applicable to all areas of life. This intention is behind their question of what is "lawful" to Jesus. First, Jesus recalls a scriptural story, but the Markan Jesus fails to show good

"Unlawful" in African American Interpretation

In the antebellum South, it was *unlawful* "to teach a slave to read" (Frederick Douglass, *Narrative of the Life of Frederick Douglass*, 49). Because African Americans have had to disregard so many "laws" that were established for their dehumanization, African American theologians have begun the difficult theological and biblical work of re-interpreting many categories of the "inherited" Christian tradition.

interpretive skills here; the issue of Sabbath is absent from 1 Sam 21. Second, Jesus offers a more direct response in 2:27-28: God made the Sabbath on behalf of humanity and not the other way around. It is a liberating and humanizing word. Jesus may have misappropriated the first text, but he provides good theology.

The solution of verse 27 is distinctive to the second Gospel and is democratizing! It is not only the Son of Man who had authority over the Sabbath (v. 28), but *all* humans *also* do. African Americans, such as Mary Shadd, the first African American female newspaper editor, have depended on this freedom of action on the Sabbath. (See sidebar on p. 127.)

3:1-6, The Man with the Withered Hand

The controversy over Sabbath practices continues, as Jesus beckons a man with a deformed hand. Jesus becomes "angry" with the silence of the synagogue leadership (3:4)—or perhaps with what he knew they would say. His anger turns to "grief" as he recognizes that their lack of understanding is not self-imposed; it is due to their "hardness of heart" (on Jesus' anger, see the comments on 1:40-45).

But Jesus does not stop by the synagogue *only* to have a Sabbath debate; nor does he

The Sabbath and Freedom

"There is too a fitness of time for any work for the benefit of God's human creatures. We are told to keep Holy the Sabbath day. In what manner? Not by following simply the injunctions of those who bind heavy burdens . . . but combining with God's worship the most active vigilance for the resurrector from degradation, violence, and sin of his creatures. In these cases particularly is the Sabbath made for man and *woman* if you please. . . . Christ has told us as it is lawful to lift a sheep out of the ditch on the Sabbath day, . . . a man is much better than a sheep."

—Mary Shadd, "Break Every Yoke and Let the Oppressed Go Free," from *Lift Every Voice: African American Oratory 1787–1900*, ed. Philip S. Foner and Robert James Branham (Tuscaloosa.: University of Alabama Press, 1998), 318.

allow his anger to hinder him from "doing good" and "saving life" on the Sabbath. He restores the man's withered hand. For physical needs (hunger or a deformed hand), the Sabbath represents a time for the healing and wholeness of humanity. Not everyone views Jesus' action favorably; the Pharisees plot to destroy God's liberating agent (3:6).

3:7-12, Summary Statement

Before the story of Jesus' appointment of the Twelve, Mark depicts the increasing numbers of interested persons. The presence of a large "multicultural" crowd suggests that Jesus' influence was expanding exponentially. Unique to the second Gospel is the "crushing" potential of the crowd, the possibility of an unwieldy force with a different agenda from Jesus. Jesus apparently senses this as well and gives his disciples their *first* specific assignment in the story: "prepare a boat" (3:9).

3:13-19a, Appointing Twelve

The scene changes drastically, as Jesus ascends a mountain for the first time in Mark (cf. 6:46; 9:2; 13:2; 14:26). Many scholars assume that such mountain excursions recall Mount Sinai, Moses' place of revelation. Certainly, the vantage point of the "mountain"—as Martin Luther King Jr. imagines—allowed Jesus to view things from a different perspective.

From among the large group of "disciples," Jesus distinguishes twelve with the title "apostle," a word that means "one who is sent." The apostle's function is twofold: (1) to be with him and (2) to be sent out to preach and to have authority to exorcise demons. Jesus' choice of "twelve"—although the names and order are slightly different in Matthew and Luke—symbolizes the "twelve tribes of Israel" and is thus representative of the whole people of Israel. The new mission of the reign of God would not overlook the traditional people of God. W. E. B. DuBois's controversial "talented tenth" theory was also intended to be representative of the larger African American community.[14] Borrowing the idea from Alexander Crummell, DuBois wrote:

The Negro race, like all races, is going to be saved by its exceptional [people]. The problem of education, then, among Negroes must first of all deal with the Talented Tenth; it is the problem of developing the Best of this race that they may guide the Mass away from the contamination and death of the Worst, in their own and other races.[15]

DuBois later, in 1948, critiqued the implied elitism in his earlier proposal.[16] Even as the Gospel of Mark makes little distinction between the "apostles" and the "disciples," so should the African American community make little distinction between the so-called talented and others. What is critical is the struggle for justice, the struggle for God's liberating rule evident in the righteous seeking activities on behalf of all.

The last word of this section is not a sign of hope but the indication of a traitor. African Americans have also had their "traitors." Who is the one who forgets about the struggle on behalf of the whole community? Who is the one who forgets that God's message is an inclusive message for the disenfranchised? Before anyone points a finger at the "uncle Toms" and "aunt Jemimas" among us, remember, as Cleophus J. LaRue preaches, "We've all got a little Judas in us."[17]

3:20-35, Jesus, Satan, and His "Family"

Jesus returns to his headquarters, a home (Simon's) in Capernaum. Home, food, and family: what could be more (un)settling? At this point in the story, however, even "home" is not isolated from the struggle against the opposing forces (cf. 2:1-12). The presence of the "crowd" suggests that something was underway.

The crowd was composed of several groups, each with its own assessment of Jesus. The "family" (lit., "those alongside him") said "he's crazy,"[18] an assessment that explains why they arrive "to seize" him. With such negative intentions—"seizing" people is usually negative (cf. 6:17; 12:12; 14:1)—the family's *first* appearance in the story is surprising. Furthermore, the Jerusalem scribes attempt to undermine Jesus' life-altering exorcising activity by claiming that evil forces (Beelzebul) sponsor this action. Analogously, one way to discredit the civil rights revolutionary nonviolent movement was to tie some of its leaders (like Martin Luther King Jr.) to the negatively portrayed communist movement, as FBI director J. Edgar Hoover attempted to do.

Such a charge from a *Jerusalem* "association of lawyers" needed to be challenged. Jesus replies "in parables," his most effective form of communication. From the familiar metaphors of kingdom and house, Jesus creates an analogy. That Satan's "end has come" indicates the destruction of Satan's power. This "destruction" is in process. First, as suggested in v. 27, someone needed to "bind" this "strong one," so that his house could be "plundered." Jesus' exorcising activity, which represents the removal of extreme spiritual, psychological, economic, and sociopolitical evil "bonds," is the manner for this destruction.

The family's attempt to cease Jesus' activity is not resolved until the end of this chapter. In contrast, the crowd serves as buffer to the opposing forces and desires of the family.[19]

Even after the recent selection of the twelve (3:16-19), Jesus widens his circle again. Although Jesus uses *adelphoi* ("brothers and sisters") at first, in the end of his speech he separates the individual "sister" from individual "brother," providing direct approval of female participation in "doing the will of God." Like the women of the civil rights movement (e.g., Ella Baker and Fannie Lou Hamer), these "sisters" in the second Gospel are charged to continue the liberating activity of God's reign.[20]

For Jesus, "family" is anyone who stays in the struggle, anyone who does "the will of God," who continues to fight against the dehumanizing forces of evil, who engages head-on the societal institutional structures of deprivation that keep humans down. This is an inclusive message based on legitimate acts of liberation for the disenfranchised. The Markan Jesus is not anti-family; a broader sociopolitical reality, the rule of God, has subsumed the local family unit.

4:1-20, A Story about a Sower and His Seed

For the first time in the Gospel, Jesus explains his opening message, "the kingdom of God has come near." He draws on the familiar experience of his listeners in an agrarian society. Although a lot of seed is apparently wasted, the productive seed—supported by good soil—is quite abundant. But the simplicity of this parable does not detract from its profundity, as is attested by the disciples' incomprehension (see below).

Because the disciples fail to grasp the import of this story, Jesus provides an explanation, an *allegory* of sorts. In 4:13-20 Jesus suggests that there are external factors—such as Satan (like "devouring birds"), troubles and persecutions (like the "scorching sun") and the "cares of the world," the "lure of wealth," or the "lust for other things" (like "thorns")—that distort the fruitful development of the *logos* ("word"; cf. 2:2), the "message" of God's reign. Although Jesus predicts the self-destructive activity of Satan (3:23-27), Jesus still conceives of Satan as an active force distorting and even removing the *logos* from potential listeners (4:15). Although human and nonhuman forces oppose Jesus, the Markan story is a message of hope. Despite the opposition, fruitful seed would produce, in manifold words and actions, the reign of God and its justice-seeking activity reordering the world.

4:10-11, The Disciples Alone with Jesus

Here is the first question the disciples ask Jesus in the entire Gospel. It follows Jesus' longest "teaching moment." In a significant way, their general question about parables represents "our" question—and, in many ways, it is.

Jesus delineates "insiders," those to whom the "mystery" has been given, and "outsiders," those to whom parables are spoken. This is the only time that the word *mysterion* ("mystery") occurs in Mark, and it stands in direct correlation with the reign of God. Mystery is the insight into *what* this reign looks like—Jesus' release of the oppressed—and *how* this reign occurs—through Jesus' coordinated efforts. This insight into the plan of God has already been provided for Jesus' "insiders." Similarly,

the "sorrow songs" of the enslaved operated on two levels, for insiders and outsiders. As James Cone concluded, "the slave knew that a too obvious reference of a condemnation of whites or a slight reference to political freedom in the presence of white people could mean his or her life."[21]

"Outsiders," however, receive simple, but not simplistic, parables. To explain the purpose for speaking in this manner, Jesus alludes to Isa 6:9. Isaiah's message would lead to hardening hearts and words of judgment, even to the point that Isaiah must ask, "How long, O Lord?" (Isa 6:11). Jesus appropriates this harsh reality of disbelief. As the parable of the sower suggests, Jesus' parables, too, would bring loss, as in seeds that fall on "rocky ground."

4:21-34, More Stories (Parables?) about God's Reign

The parable of the sower is the interpretive lens through which we understand the following shorter parables. The "lamp," as the earlier "seed," would become useful once what is hidden has been disclosed, once what is secret has been revealed. The third parable addresses human involvement in the mission, so that as one participates with success (i.e., "fruitfulness"), so would one be rewarded (cf. 4:8, 20). Also, as with the parable of the sower, there is a word of judgment as well, since inactive participants would jeopardize what they have (cf. 4:15, 19). This final word is a challenge to naïve notions that the human dimension is unnecessary.

Yet the next parable de-emphasizes the human dimension. Instead, the movement grows automatically (*automate*). (It is analogous to the surprise the enslaved Frederick Douglass sensed when he heard of the development of an "abolitionist" movement in the North.)[22] The final parable provides a description of the "mustard seed," symbolic of God's reign or the Jesus movement, a struggle that would become quite "large" in comparison to its origins. Analogously, one would never imagine a liberation struggle that began with a few escaped slaves would lead to insurrections that led to the abolitionist movement that led to the Civil War that led to the Reconstruction era that led to the Harlem Renaissance that led to the civil rights era. God's liberating reign has certainly become large enough "that the birds of the air can make nests in its shade" (v. 32).

The summary (4:33-34) focuses on why Jesus tells stories as his main source of instruction. Like the spiritual, the parable is not for those on the "outside." As Dwight Hopkins suggests, "Black folk related to one another in a religious cultural medium that befuddled the normative white English and circumvented standard (white) expressions."[23]

4:35-41, "Who Then Is This?"

A nature miracle leads to a question about Jesus' identity. Healings and exorcisms do not raise issues of identity, because healers and exorcists are not uncommon in Jesus' day. Even the disciples are granted authority to cast out demons (cf. 6:13)! But one who could command "the wind and the sea" would demand particular attention. In Jesus' day, people thought that such authority over nature, especially a chaotic sea, is unique to God (cf. Ps 89:9). The verb "rebuke"—usually reserved for "spiritual" dissonance (e.g., 1:25; 9:25; cf. 8:32-33!)—suggests the "spiritual" nature of the conflict.

In Mark's account, Jesus reserves nature miracles for close followers only. People in the "other boats" are apparently unaware, although they experience the storm. Why? Apparently, as with his earlier commands to silence (e.g., 1:34; 1:44), Jesus is not willing to reveal his full identity to many.

Jesus' authority over nature precipitates a condemnation of the disciples, whose lack of faith is exposed. Among the Synoptic Gospels,

the sharpest tension between Jesus and the disciples occurs in the second Gospel. Only in Mark is the disciples' question so harsh, "Teacher, do you not care . . . ?" Only in Mark does Jesus charge the disciples with having "*no* faith." If Jesus' closest followers misunderstand who he is, how will others comprehend?

5:1-20, Exorcism on the Gentile Side: The Crossing of Social Boundaries

This is the first occasion in which Jesus, the Jew from Nazareth, enters Gentile territory. As he begins his mission in Capernaum, his first act in Gentile country is also an exorcism. The pronouncement of the name "Legion" (5:9) makes explicit what had only been festering underneath this narrative's portrayal. This term

---

"I Am a-Trouble in de Mind"

"'I am a-trouble in de mind,
O I am a-trouble in de mind;
I ask my Lord what shall I do,
I am a-trouble in de mind.'"

"The troublesome quality of black life in slavery was psychologically disturbing. This does not suggest a condition of neurosis; rather the indication is that one's psychological well-being was continually challenged by constant confrontations with the insanity of slavery. The assaults upon human dignity by the slavocracy were immense and could leave their victims reaching for sane solutions within an insane situation."

—David Emmanuel Goatley, "Godforsakenness in African American Spirituals," in *Cut Loose Your Stammering Tongue: Black Theology in the Slave Narratives*, ed. Dwight N. Hopkins and George C. L. Cummings (Louisville: Westminster John Knox, 2003), 142. For "I Am a-Trouble in De Mind," see Miles Mark Fisher, *Negro Slave Songs in the United States* (New York: Russell & Russell, 1968), 92.

is the common word for a Roman military cohort of about five thousand soldiers. In that case it is unusual why some contemporary interpreters do not surmise what Obery Hendricks states clearly, "How can the possessive demonic presence called 'Legion' in Mark 5, the occupying presence that wrought the bitter pathology of oppression in Mark's community and sought to remain in possession of the *country*, not the *man* (v. 10), be anything *but* the Roman military?"[24] Furthermore, by permitting Legion's request to stay in the country, does the Markan Jesus—unlike the Matthean or Lukan one—imply a caution toward the colonizer that is in tension with other liberating parts of the narrative? Perhaps, as some suggest, in order to publish this Gospel, the author's sponsorship depends on Rome. Yet Jesus allows the drowning of the demon in the sea!

Nonetheless, the reaction of the villagers is odd. Why are they *not* pleased when they "witness" the new condition of the man? Do they prefer the man's constant disturbance *and* the legion's disruption? Their "fear" is pronounced, a fear that links this story with the preceding one, in which the disciples too are "afraid" of Jesus. The narrative shifts, at this point, as Jesus becomes a person to fear as well as to respect.

Before Jesus leaves this territory, at the request of its "citizens," the spiritually and emotionally stable man requests one thing: to be with Jesus. One cannot blame him for not wanting to stay among folk who wish to send away his restorer. One cannot blame him for not wanting to stay among folk who cannot see when oppression is thrown off for their own good. But Jesus denies the request. Although the text provides no rationale, Jesus may have wanted to seize this opportunity to begin the cross-cultural mission. According to Mark, such diversity does not begin with Paul! It begins right here with Jesus. So Jesus sends him back among his people to tell "how

---

Going from Grace to Dignity

"I see a black and white parallel here. As long as we were struggling in the cotton fields of Tennessee, Georgia, Alabama, and Mississippi with our cotton sacks across our shoulders and to our sides, picking cotton and having our fingers burning from stinging cotton worms that would hide under the cotton leaves; as long as we were barefoot, actually and symbolically, laughing when we were not tickled . . . America was satisfied. . . . But one day America saw us marching to the voting booth, sitting down at lunch counters, and all of America became afraid."

—Otis Moss, "Going from Grace to Dignity," in *Preaching the Gospel*, ed. Henry J. Young (Philadelphia: Fortress Press, 1976), 52–53.

---

much the Lord has done for you" (5:19). This formerly possessed man announces throughout the Decapolis the news of victory over the forces of evil, representing not only Satan's power but also Rome's.

5:21-43, Jairus's Daughter/Jesus' Daughter

This author often relates two stories as if they occurred simultaneously, a technique called intercalation. The author intends for readers to interpret one passage in light of the other. After returning from instigating a "Gentile mission," Jesus is confronted by a crowd. Surprisingly, a "ruler of the synagogue," Jairus, seeks Jesus' assistance. Not all of the Jewish leadership oppose Jesus. Yet, before Jesus arrives at Jairus's house, an unnamed woman, who—unlike the established religious leader—arrives secretly because of the socioreligious dynamics of the day, also seeks his (unattended) assistance.

This is a "bodacious" female. Mary Ann Tolbert describes the scene in this manner:

"That a woman, who at least at one time had some wealth (5:26), should be seen in such a public place evidently unaccompanied by protectors and that she should dare to touch a strange man without his consent are extraordinary events in an ancient cultural context."[25] But, since her condition cut her off from the religious community and from financial stability (cf. Lev 15:25-30), she may have had no choice but to act daringly. The need to act bravely has a long history in African American tradition. Phillis Wheatley's published poems were scrutinized by Thomas Jefferson, Voltaire, and other (white) intellectuals of the day. Sojourner Truth challenged male-only suffrage of blacks. Jarena Lee pursued her God-given call to preach. Rosa Parks would not give up her seat on the bus.

Just as the woman understood ("knew") changes in her body, so Jesus recognized ("knew") changes in his body. The drying up of her blood flow (i.e., her "discharge") is due to the "discharge" of Jesus "power" (*dynamis*). But no one else—including the disciples—recognizes what has transpired. Not even Jesus is fully aware of the recipient of this "dynamite." So he stops the crowd in order to find out. Out of "fear" (5:33) she comes forward to reveal the "truth." Mark reserves the term *truth* only for Jesus—who "teaches the way of God in accordance with *the truth*" (12:14)—*and* for this woman, the first woman to speak in the story! "Daughter," a familial term for

one whose blood cut her off from family, "your faith has made you well!"

Then Jesus continues his journey to Jairus's house. The delay, to "heal" *and* "converse" with the unnamed woman, leads to a disturbance from Jairus's household. While Jesus is speaking "good news," words of affirmation and confirmation to the daring woman whose "faith" has made her well, bad news arrives: "Your daughter has died." Jesus' reaction to this news reminds us of a black gospel tune derived from "slave wisdom," "God may not come when you call him, but he'll be there right on time!"[26] Jesus' progress is not hindered by this report. He challenges Jairus to hold on to his faith ("only believe"), a faith that led him to the healer in the first place.

While the story ends with "ecstasy" (*ekstasei*), Jesus makes a significant request of food for the raised girl; food that suggests a holistic mission that cares for all needs—spiritual, physical, emotional, psychological, and political. This twelve-year-old daughter of Jairus was born in the same year when the older woman began incessant bleeding. Both are now healed in the same year.

6:1-6, Perception and Rejection at Jesus' Hometown

The audience's "amazement" (5:42) is vocalized in a series of questions leading them to consider Jesus' own human origins. They—hometown folk—know all too well from where he comes. Their description of him, "the carpenter," "the son of Mary," ignores any mention of a father figure. Such would have been a direct insult on Jesus' character in first-century culture, hinting at one conceived illegitimately (i.e., out of wedlock). (Mark reports no birth narrative; yet this omission is one reason why Howard Thurman preferred it!)[27] This type of "biography" is offensive or "scandalous" (v. 3, *skandalidzo*) to them.

Sojourner Truth

"Afterward I told the Lord I wanted another name, 'cause everybody else had two names; and the Lord gave me Truth, because I was to declare the Truth to the people."

—Sojourner Truth, quoted in *Can I Get a Witness? Prophetic Religious Voices of African American Women: An Anthology*, ed. Marcia Y. Riggs (Maryknoll, N.Y.: Orbis, 1997), 21.

The absence of a father figure in this account has caused concern among African American commentators, in light of current discussions about (and policies against!) the "absent father" in African American families.[28] Partly due to the biased treatment Sojourner Truth received from her male contemporaries, she utilized this idea in defense of a woman's right to preach: "And how came Jesus into the world? Through God who created him and a woman who bore him. Man, where is your part?"[29] Cain Hope Felder suggests, "The only reason we hear so little about Joseph is that in the emerging new Household, the focus becomes fixed on God as a loving parent whose Household Jesus opens so widely."[30] While this may be generally true about the early Jesus movement, the Markan narrative never mentions Jesus' earthly father at all, nor does it positively promote Jesus' family.

In Mark 6 the lack of faith amazes even Jesus! Furthermore, it challenges Jesus' ability to perform healing miracles. At first, the text said that he "could do no deed of power there"; then it adds an exception. On the one hand, Jesus' healing ability is closely aligned with the faith of others (cf. 5:34, 36). On the other hand, Jesus could (reluctantly) overcome the lack of faith when he desired to do so.

6:7-13, The First Mission of the Disciples

Two points deserve mention. First, the disciples are to continue the Jesus movement in *households*. This is not unanticipated, in light of Jesus' own success in homes and rejection in his hometown synagogue. Synagogues (like many antebellum white congregations and some contemporary black churches), with all of their religious traditions and authorities, are not always susceptible to new ideas and activities that represent a new move of God!

Second, while they should continue Jesus' message of "repentance," their use of "oil" as a mediating "medicine" is odd. Since Mat-

thew and Luke omit the reference, its use may actually reflect a later practice in the Markan community. But it is a custom known in the culture (cf. Luke 10:34) and in some circles of early Christianity (cf. Jas 5:14). A number of African American religious communities utilize the unction as well, although its use may be due more to the relevance of such medicines in African heritage than to its use in the New Testament.

6:14-31, The Death of John the Baptist

In light of John's death at the hands of Herod, no reader should ignore the connection between Jesus' life and mission and first-century sociopolitical affairs. In fact, Mark places this story between the commission and return of the disciples to suggest its significance for the expansion of Jesus' mission. John's message met with political obstacles, and so would Jesus' and his followers'. The report of the death of John, Jesus' mentor, was the "end" of the innocence of Jesus' mission. The length and detail of this account are not insignificant. I cannot here explore Luke's omission of this story or Matthew's abbreviated version. Mark's version is filled with detail and intrigue, and his "Herod" is a much more sympathetic figure whose "oath" becomes his own demise.

Zora Neale Hurston's imaginative depiction must have preferred Mark's account to Matthew's. (See sidebar on p. 134.)

Mark's portrayal of women deserves mention. Mark's more sympathetic depiction of Herod does not carry over to Herodias. Her grudge against John finally finds its satisfaction—by means of her daughter's entertainment value—as she becomes the one most responsible for John's death. While most positive examples of women in Mark's story are unnamed, this woman of high standing receives her prize on a "platter" as well as her name on the page. Her "reward," unfortunately, halts God's messenger.

Zora Neale Hurston's Herod and Herodias

In this fantastic love story between Herod Antipas and Herodias, Hurston plausibly imagines an argument over John:

"Of course, you will order this monster slain for the insults that he has offered to you as the ruler of Galilee and to your wife."

"Oh no, my beloved Herodias. I cannot lay violent hands upon such a holy man."

"Holy man!" Herodias leaped to her feet. "What sacrilege! Do you no longer love me, my beloved?"

"More than anybody or anything else on earth, Herodias. But I revere him. . . . I fear to touch that man. Let him scold away. I will never put you away. You can be sure of that, but I will never slay this prophet either."

"Then I will!" Herodias screamed.

—Zora Neale Hurston, "The Seventh Veil," in *The Complete Stories* (New York: HarperCollins, 1995), 252.

6:32-44, First Feeding of the Crowd

This story shows just how large Jesus' following has become. Not only is the mission expanding—as the work of the apostles indicates—but many attempt to locate Jesus. Yet, once again, no one—besides the disciples—recognizes Jesus' miraculous power. Apparently, he reserves his power over nature, a sign that reveals his divine authority, for the disciples (and readers!) only. Such miracles are not meant as evangelistic tools, as proof to outsiders. God's agent does not work that way. Those who wish to turn the miraculous power of God into a circus sideshow have misunderstood the function of this power in the Christian community. These signs are to *increase* faith, not *initiate* faith. This is one reason why Jesus regularly attempts to keep healings silent.

6:45-52, Crossing the Sea Again: Jesus Walks on Water

The third nature miracle reminds us of the first, Jesus' control over the sea. This time he strolls on it as if it were sand. In order to depict the scene, contemporary artists usually draw on Matthew's version, which includes Peter's bold attempt to walk on the water. Privileging Peter's role is absent from Mark's account. Rather, Mark emphasizes that "all saw him" (v. 50), a phrase omitted by Matthew. This democratization of the disciples' astonishment will also be the downfall of "all," for none of them "understood about the loaves." The disciples are still clueless. Unlike the earlier sea miracle, which concludes with a question about Jesus' identity, this story ends with Mark's assessment that their "hearts were hardened."

7:1-23, (Un)clean Hands, Food, and People

The issue, at stake, is not just (un)clean hands and food, but also people (cf. 7:24-30). Once again, Pharisees and scribes are on the scene, questioning Jesus about his disciples' hands (cf. 2:23-28). The Pharisees' concern is reasonable, since it was not too long ago that the disciples were handling fish (6:32-44)![31]

Using scripture, Jesus argues that financial support of parents is more important than any "tradition of the elders." Economic care for the elderly is more fundamental than "tithes" for religious institutions! Then Jesus answers the original question: defilement does not stem from external things. This liberating word must have shocked Jewish crowds and Jewish readers or hearers in Mark's audience. The disciples themselves fail to understand it (their misunderstanding is an ongoing theme in the story; cf. 4:13; 6:52). But they receive private instruction (v. 17), a lesson in biology. Jesus identifies the origins of defilement, that is, the heart, from which can stem "evil," and "evil" brings corruption.

Finally, in 7:19, Mark highlights the point of the story: "Thus he declared all foods clean." For Mark's cross-cultural audience of Gentiles and Jews, such a declaration would have been freeing, such that Gentiles would not be excluded from table fellowship. Some may find in these words potential for the "integration" of contemporary races, and so it may apply. Yet, before we apply it to the contemporary situation too quickly, especially in light of the expected increase in multicultural communities in the twenty-first century, what might be the (negative) effect on African American institutions like the black church

and historical black colleges and universities? Such institutions have always had critics, even from members of the African American community, like Frederick Douglass, E. Franklin Frazier, and Malcolm X. On the other hand, as Marcia Riggs emphasizes, "whereas integration seeks the inclusion of blacks in terms of reform within U.S. society, black liberation seeks the inclusion of blacks in terms of radical change in society itself."[32]

7:24-30, The Syrophoenician Woman and Her "Crumb-like" Faith

There is a short leap from the Markan Jesus' pronouncement "all foods are clean" to "all people belong to God" (cf. Acts 10). This story, then, has implications for Mark's cross-cultural community not only in what it affirms (i.e., entrance of non-Jews) but what it implies (i.e., Jesus learns from the non-Jewish woman). Just when you thought this Jesus was safe, Mark tells the story of a Phoenician woman! Jesus has a cultural mission geared toward Jews; that is clear. Nonetheless the implication that this foreign woman

---

"Clean and Unclean" in *The Bluest Eye*

There is a fascinating analogy to Mark's un/clean story in Toni Morrison's *The Bluest Eye*. She describes the character Maureen Peal as a "disrupter of seasons," whose "beauty" was defined by cultural standards: "high-yellow dream child with long brown hair braided"; "rich"; "quality of her clothes threatened to derange" others; "a hint of spring in her sloe green eyes" (47–48). And, yet, what comes "out of her mouth" defiles, as if from the heart as Jesus suggests, when she screams at Claudia and Frieda, "I *am* cute! And you ugly! Black and ugly black e mos. I *am* cute!" But, the narrator—reflecting Claudia's thoughts shortly after the shouting match—reveals philosophical insight: "And all the time we knew that Maureen Peal was not the Enemy and not worthy of such intense hatred. The *Thing* to fear was the *Thing* that made *her* beautiful, and not us" (58; emphasis in the original). Analogously, in Mark's story, the "*Thing* to fear was the *Thing* that" defiled "hands" and "food."

—Toni Morrison, *The Bluest Eye* (New York: Holt, Rinehart, and Winston: 1970).

is a "dog" is harsh. His "good news" is not as far reaching as one might have hoped. Jesus' words have placed this woman, already twice removed from the "center," into a position of being thrice removed. Not only is she a "female" in a patriarchal society, she is a foreigner in a Jewish oriented symbolic world, and, now, the primary agent of God's liberation, Jesus, has just implied that she is a "dog" (among sheep!). Imagine the inhuman slurs African Americans have heard—"coon," "gorilla," "ape," "baboon" (and others)—and we may get a sense of this woman's feelings.

Yet, in ironic fashion, the movement of God's reign is carried on *by this foreign woman*! The woman's sass saves her daughter! Her "word," her sass, her *logos*, provides the good news of salvation. It is an outspoken proclamation—an outright challenge to the cultural and religious roadblocks—that recognizes that desired power comes through this reluctant one. She may only receive a "crumb" from the bread provider, but the leaven from that crumb develops into a survival faith that allows her to track down a foreign exorcist on behalf of her kin. Her action, indeed her word, expresses most clearly that God's reign is far-reaching even to the uttermost.

Womanists have rightfully seized this story. She seeks healing for *her daughter*, so it is a story about family. Although all of the cultural, sociopolitical, religious odds—and even the "liberator" himself—appear to be against her, she had inner resources that not even Mark can depict! Yet, through the method of "sassing," a common womanist device necessary in the struggle for survival, the Syrophoenician woman secures healing for her daughter (see the sidebar at right).

7:31-37, Healing a Deaf Man

In this final story of the chapter, Mark seems to emphasize Jesus' continual work in a "Gentile" area. Jesus puts his "unwashed hands"

inside a man's ears. Despite the Jewish leadership's concern about his "unclean hands," the crowd still desires his "touch." In addition, the involvement of Jesus' own "spit," while debated as to its medicinal value, may be the express reason why Matthew and Luke omit this story (as well as Mark 8:22-26!).

Sassing as a Survival Technique

After one failed attempt to run away, Mary Prince—in the first slave narrative by a female of African descent—responded to her "Captain," who suggested that she ought to be punished: "I then took courage and said that I could stand the floggings no longer, that I was weary of my life, and therefore I had run away to my mother. . . . He told me to hold my tongue and go about my work, or he would find a way to settle me. He did not, however, flog me that day."

—Mary Prince, "The History of Mary Prince: A West Indian Slave (Related by Herself)," in *Six Women's Slave Narratives*, ed. Henry Louis Gates (New York and Oxford: Oxford University Press, 1988 [1831]), 9.

The incompleteness in the world, and the reason for the coming of God's reign in Jesus, is most astutely depicted in Jesus' "sigh" or groan (*estenaxen*). Even on behalf of the non-Jew, Mark's Jesus groans. Jesus breaks the "binding" (*desmos*) on this man's tongue (that he, too, may "groan"). Furthermore, he does so in "impure" ways. Sometimes the community of Jesus must be more concerned with its results than its methods, especially if they are crossing social boundaries to provide restoration of "sound" and "voice." Bodily involvement for full restoration of the disenfranchised is critical to the reign of God, even when this mission is not understood by others. Analogously, physically freeing African Americans (some already legally "free") imprisoned because of the passing of the Fugitive Slave Law of 1850 and Harriet Tubman's Moses-like deliverance activity were both necessary to fulfill *bodily* the justice of God in the nineteenth century.[33]

8:1-10, Second Feeding: Jesus Feeds This "Crowd with Crumbs"

This second feeding (cf. 6:32-44) of a large crowd shows Jesus' continual cross-cultural work among Gentiles. This feeding of four thousand apparently occurs in the Decapolis, where Jesus has been since 7:31, following the controversial scene in which Jesus confesses his mission among Jews only (see 7:27). Perhaps there are some "crumbs" leftover for this eager Gentile group that has been with him "three days" (8:2). It appears that yet more credit is due the Syrophoenician woman and the effect her words had on Jesus.

As some scholars suggest, there are potential links between these two feeding narratives and the Last Supper. Language of "blessing," "giving thanks," "bread," and so on recall the significance of the final meal. Reflection on the value of meals in the mission of God's reign is important. Without vision the people perish, but without *food* there is no vision. Jesus' passion drives him to provide the vision of the new order, but his compassion causes him to provide "daily bread."

The "Justice" of Food

It was common for the enslaved to reflect on their rations, especially in relationship to their ability to envision a new future or to critique particular slaveholders. Henry Bibb considered an Indian slaveholder more humane simply because he allowed sufficient food.

—See *Narrative of the Life and Adventures of Henry Bibb, an American Slave* [1849], in *I Was Born a Slave: An Anthology of Classic Slave Narratives*, ed. Yuval Taylor (Chicago: Lawrence Hill, 1999).

It is unfortunate, then, that in the "Christian" United States the poverty rate of the overall population continues to rise: from 11.7 percent in 2001 to 12.1 percent in 2002. More alarming, poverty rates are drastically race-related: while the rate of poverty remained unchanged for whites, Asians, and Hispanics, it steadily increased from 22.7 percent in 2001 to 24.1 percent in 2002 for African Americans.[34] Perhaps Jesus' miraculous provisions on *both the Jewish and the Gentile sides* might offer contemporary folk guidance in today's struggle against poverty among all ethnic groups.

8:11-13, The Sign of the Pharisees

One reason that Mark describes tension between Jesus and the Pharisees and not others, like the Sadducees or the Zealots, is that this sect holds views similar to Jesus. Jesus and the Pharisees believe in the resurrection, unlike the Sadducees, but do not believe in violent revolt against the Romans, unlike the Zealots. The Pharisees and Jesus also believe that the law is applicable to all of life. They differ, however, on how to appropriate it. Both believe in angels, demons, and rewards/punishments in the afterlife. Finally, and most importantly, both attempt to persuade others ("the people of the land") that their view of God's work in the world is the more accurate portrayal of the Jewish faith.

8:14-21, The "Hard Heads and Hearts" of the Disciples

In the final story of this section, "bread" again is the main theme. Jesus associates the disciples directly with the "yeast" of the Pharisees and Herodians, a leaven that reveals (in)directly the desire for selfish "signs." Some folk never notice God's activity in their midst, even though they stare directly at it.

In 6:32—8:21 the author develops an increasing tension, called narrative irony. While readers gain insight into Jesus' miraculous power, the disciples—who recently completed a successful mission (6:7-13)—are described as having "hardened hearts" because of their failure to grasp Jesus' full purpose. Such irony forces readers to distance themselves from Jesus' "closest" followers, the insiders—or so readers have thought of them. But, if the disciples could be fooled, perhaps readers can too. So the final question of the section—"Do you not yet understand?"—is one with which readers must also wrestle.

8:22-26, A Non-Instantaneous Healing

In recent scholarship, many have interpreted this healing story as a symbol of the ignorance of the disciples, who do not yet "see" clearly (cf. 8:21). If read this way, it provides one particular way to understand the disciples' "hardness of heart." Only "God" could remove such hardness/blindness.

This is the first of two "blind" healing stories, which frame this large section (8:22-26 and 10:46-52). Jesus performs this healing "outside of the village," perhaps because of his method. In the Gospel narratives, this is the only time that Jesus inquires whether the person has been healed. After Jesus touches him, the man's sight is fully restored. Not all healing is instantaneous. This story provides an example of progressive healing.

8:27—9:1, "You Are the Messiah!"

In Caesarea Philippi, Jesus is interested in how others view him. Peter's representative confession is so accurate that Jesus charges them not to share this insight. Yet their "blindness," also represented by Peter, was so acute that Jesus challenges this "satanic" viewpoint.

This tension must be viewed within its first-century context. For Peter and most Jews, "messiah" (*christos*) refers to a militaristic, political figure who would overthrow Rome's power and establish a new Davidic kingdom, which itself would inaugurate the kingdom

of God. Such a divinely authorized figure could not be one who, in Jesus' words, would "suffer many things . . . and be killed." This heated debate between Peter and Jesus takes on spiritual dimensions, as Mark describes their actions toward one another with the verb *epitimao* ("to rebuke"), a word common in reports of Jesus' exorcisms. Finally, Jesus charges Peter with having "demonic" thoughts, that is, views of the messiah as one with earthly power.[35]

Turning to the crowds, Jesus provides additional insight. Since he has come to suffer, true followers should *not* ignore the struggle; they should "bear the cross." Just because one believes correctly and occasionally acts justly does not mean that one grasps the commitment necessary for the continual struggle of God's reign in the world. The splits between William Lloyd Garrison and Frederick Douglass *and* between Frances Ellen Watkins Harper and leading white feminists in the nineteenth century are classic analogies for Jesus' conflict with Peter.

But neither do Jesus' words mean "suffering for the sake of suffering" or the "redemptive value of suffering in itself." Womanists rightly warn us against such "spiritual" notions, which are also "satanic" ideas full of abusive potential.[36] Instead, as Howard Thurman suggests, one who follows Jesus "will choose rather to do the thing that is to him [or to her] the maximum exposure to the love and therefore to the approval of God, rather than the things that will save his [or her] own skin."[37]

9:2-13, Transfiguration, the Prediction of Resurrection

This is the first time that God transfigures Jesus' whole person before the eyes of the inner circle of his disciples. No other story is comparable to it. Yet the revelation is reserved for only a few! Even though a transfiguration in the presence of a large crowd would be, presumably, convincing of Jesus' high status, it is not Jesus' preferred option for securing followers.

In light of the story's peculiarity, Peter's words and actions should not be surprising. Peter's unsuitable address of Jesus, "Rabbi," coincides with the "three dwellings" to mark the location. Traditionally, such markings commemorated both the transitory (exilic?) nature of the people of Israel during their wilderness wanderings following God's liberation from Egypt (cf. Lev 23:43; Neh 8:17) *and* rest from working the land (cf. Lev 23:39-42). Yet Peter's request is misguided. The presence of Elijah and Moses and the "voice from heaven" highlight the apocalyptic nature of this event.

9:14-29, "I Believe; Help My Unbelief!"

In Jesus' fourth and final exorcism of the Gospel, the activity of this "unclean spirit" has hindered the speech and hearing of a boy. His father sought help from the remaining disciples—not privileged to witness the transfiguration—who have apparently performed successful exorcisms on their earlier mission (see 6:13). But they are unable to exorcise this "spirit."

The father, then, reports this failure to Jesus. The disciples act, but they do so without faith. The father, too, has difficulty with faith: "I believe; help my unbelief!" There is a thin line between having and not having faith. Or, to put it differently, one might possess faith *and* doubt simultaneously. That is truly the human condition. Nonetheless, faith, according to Jesus, makes all the difference (cf. 6:5-6). In private, the disciples (and readers) learn that some exorcisms require different strategies. If "faith" is the issue, then Jesus must mean that there was a kind of "faithful" prayer that is required to exorcise certain spirits (cf. Jas 5:15).

9:30-37, The Second Prediction and Misunderstanding

From 8:27 and on, Jesus concentrates his teaching efforts on the disciples. This *second* prediction of his death and resurrection is comparable to 8:31-33. Although the disciples misunderstand again, they are too afraid to ask. Perhaps, Jesus' earlier identification of Peter as "Satan" was enough to deter them.

Returning to his "headquarters" in Capernaum, Jesus proceeds to deal with what the disciples *were* discussing on the journey *while* he was predicting his death. The disciples, embarrassed perhaps, refuse to explain their selfish interests. But Jesus knows. He challenges their notions of "greatness" with the image of a "child." Here, it is not that one must become *like* a child. Rather, one's willingness to "receive" a child is the decisive issue. In first-century culture, such a "reception" of one who would be considered property (nonhuman?) is striking indeed. Jesus' teaching challenges the general negative cultural assessment of the humanity of the young.

9:38-41, "Whoever Is Not against Us Is for Us"

The disciples—represented by John this time—and Jesus also disagree about the liberating activity of one who "was not following us," exorcising demons in Jesus' name.

Old John Brown's body lies a-mouldering
    in the grave,
While weep the sons of bondage whom
    he ventured all to save;
But though he lost his life in struggling
    for the slave,
His truth is marching on.

John Brown was a hero, undaunted, true
    and brave;
Kansas knew his valor when fought her
    rights to save;

And now though the grass grows green
above his grave,
His truth is marching on.[38]

As various versions of "John Brown's Body," including Julia Ward Howe's Union marching song, recalled and celebrated the spirit of white John Brown, so Jesus' words about this "strange exorcist" continue to ring true: "Whoever is not against us is for us." May the African American church be perceptive enough to notice the good deeds of black Muslims, black Jews, and all of those "not following us" who are in the struggle for justice and righteousness in the land.

9:42-50, Warnings on Discipleship

The chapter ends with a series of seemingly loose sayings that address several themes: hindering others (v. 42), hindering oneself (vv. 43-48), and effective discipleship (vv. 49-50). For Mark, these words emphasize that causing others to stumble should not be the life of the disciple, as in John's example of attempting to stop the strange exorcist. Rather, the followers of Jesus should concentrate on being at "peace" with one other, not stirring up trouble. Such activity, as indicated in 9:50, might also be a response to debates about the greatest, a misguided discussion for all involved in the struggle. Such debates about whether Washington[39] or DuBois, or Malcolm or Martin were more significant leaders are ill-advised, since beneficial ideas for the purpose of the struggle come from both sides.

10:1-12, Jesus on Divorce and Remarriage

Foul intent surrounds the Pharisees' initiative to discuss a family matter, that is, divorce and remarriage. In the Gospel of Mark, no one "tests" Jesus except the opposition: the Pharisees, the Herodians, and Satan. The issue turns into a discussion on the intent of scripture.

Jesus argues that God's original creation was the ideal order, despite the commandment of Moses, which made adjustments to the original order as a result of the changing human condition. The new order of God reactivates the original created order. Also, at the heart of Jesus' teaching is a statement of equality that should not be overlooked: "they are no longer two, but one flesh." Dividing the mystical, spiritual union of two human beings, even a hierarchical division should be anathema.

In private instruction for the disciples (10:10-12), Jesus takes his position further. Divorce should not be an option because "remarriage" equals adultery for the one, whether male or female, who initiates the divorce. For Mark's Jesus, unlike for Matthew's Jesus, there is *no exception clause*.[40] Jesus criticizes equally the female who could also initiate a divorce (a practice more common for females in the Western part of the Mediterranean world, where Mark probably wrote his Gospel).

10:13-16, Do Not Hinder the Children

The disciples' attempt to stop people from bringing children to Jesus is surprising in light of Jesus' recent teaching on true leaders as those who "receive" such ones (9:36-37). As they return to common cultural practices, the disciples' forgetfulness continues—as does ours, a society in which, as Marian Wright Edelman writes, "The state of millions of children in the richest most powerful democratic nation in the world is morally shameful, economically costly, and politically hypocritical." She then provides the following embarrassing statistics about children in the United States:[41]

- One is reported abused or neglected every eleven seconds.
- One is born into poverty every forty-three seconds; nearly twelve million are poor.
- One is born without health insurance every minute.

- One child (or teenager) is killed by gunfire every two hours and forty minutes.

Yet Jesus warns the disciples that those who receive his mission *must* be willing to receive the children. To receive one is to receive the other, and to receive Jesus and the one who sent him (9:37). "Leave No Child Behind" is also the motto of Edelman's Children Defense Fund.

10:17-31, A Rich Man, Eternal Life, and the Disciples' Sacrifice

From familial issues to wealth, Mark continues to describe Jesus' position on very practical matters—even from a twenty-first-century mind-set—related to his mission. Marriage and divorce include economic affairs, since issues of inheritance and land are central to these unions. The rich man's question, however, confronts directly the relationship between financial status (wealth as a sign of God's blessing) and following Jesus. Furthermore, Mark mentions the "poor" for the first time. Yet, out of this love comes Jesus' challenge: "sell . . . and give." The man, as most people who face this difficulty would be, is "stunned." Wealth itself is not the problem, but the desire to hold on to wealth for oneself is problematized. Economic (in)justice is not overlooked by Jesus. Redistribution of goods among the deprived is a sign of one's commitment to God's reign in the world (cf. 10:23-27, 28-31). The complex discussions regarding reparations for African Americans are not misguided, in light of the history of the U.S. economy's dependence on the enslaved labor force in the seventeenth through nineteenth centuries.[42]

The commandments, according to Jesus, are a sufficient guide to "eternal life" for the sincere pursuer. There is no reason to question the man's sincere allegiance. It is unclear why Jesus "loved" this man, but he does. In fact, this is the *only time* in Mark that the author describes Jesus' love for anyone.

10:32-45, The Third Prediction and Misunderstanding

Jesus' metaphors of the "cup" and his "baptism" both represent his coming death, about

Love and Nonviolent Resistance

From the beginning a basic philosophy guided the movement. This guiding principle has since been referred to variously as nonviolent resistance, noncoöperation, and passive resistance. But in the first days of the protest none of these expressions was mentioned; the phrase most often heard was 'Christian love.' . . . It was Jesus of Nazareth that stirred [African Americans] to protest with the creative weapon of love.

As the days unfolded, however, the inspiration of Mahatma Gandhi began to exert its influence. I had come to see early that the Christian doctrine of love operating through the Gandhian method of nonviolence was one of the most potent weapons available to the [African American] in his struggle for freedom. . . . Nonviolent resistance had emerged as the technique of the movement, while love stood as the regulating ideal. In other words, Christ furnished the spirit and motivation, while Gandhi furnished the method.

—Martin Luther King Jr., *Stride toward Freedom: The Montgomery Story* (New York: Harper & Row, 1958), 84–85.

which the disciples seem clueless. Despite numerous predictions about a "suffering messiah," they fail to comprehend the implications of this type of leader.

This passage ends with language of service and ransom (10:45), a theological idea that traditional scholarship generally assumes points toward Jesus' death. But womanist scholars have rightly questioned the dangerous teaching of a "commitment of service" *combined with* the necessity of suffering *for redemption*. First, Clarice Martin rightly rejects the euphemistic translation of *doulos* as "servant," preferring the word "slave" (in 10:44). Yet she wonders whether these "potential 'texts of terror' for black people can in any way portend new possibilities for our understanding of what actually constitutes the radicality of the good news of the gospel" and argues that they do not.[43] This raises the troubling aspect of a liberative Jesus who is also, in cases like this, a "product" of his culture with his use of servant / slave language.

Second, in Mark, Jesus' redemption is not confined to the crucifixion scene. In fact, his liberation comes as much from his life (-giving activities) as it does from his death. Oftentimes, the emphasis on suffering histori-cally has had damaging effects, as suffering (on behalf of a cause) has often become the rhetoric of the powerful—who tend to "suffer" little. Perhaps James Cone's observation on this passage is correct: "The struggle for liberation is the service the people of God render for all, even those who are responsible for the structure of slavery."[44]

10:46-52, Blind Bartimaeus Follows "On the Way"

This section of Mark's story begins (see 8:22-26) and ends with the healing of a blind person. The man did not have sight, but he had ears and a voice, and he used what faculties he had to express his "faith" (as Jesus said) to secure his healing. If the initial blind story depicts the partial "sight" of the disciples, then this person depicts a drastic change in their ability to "see," for he regains his sight and follows Jesus on the way up to Jerusalem. So do the disciples!

11:1-11, The Humble, "Triumphal" Entrance into Jerusalem

Jesus enters Jerusalem, and the entire tone of the story narrative changes. No longer are there exorcisms, parables, and healings. No longer

---

Blind Bartimaeus in the Sorrow Songs

"The slave singers did a strange thing with this story. They identified themselves completely with the blind man at every point but the most crucial one. In the song, the blind man does not receive his sight. The song opens with the cry; it goes through many nuances of yearning, but always it ends with the same cry with which it began. The explanation for this is not far to seek; for the people who sang this song had not received their 'sight.' They had longed for freedom with all their passionate endeavors, but it had not come. This brings us face to face with a primary discovery of the human spirit. Very often the pain of life is not relieved—there is the cry of great desire, but the answer does not come—only the fading echo of one's lonely cry."

—Howard Thurman, *Deep River: Reflections on the Religious Insight of Certain of the Negro Spirituals* (New York: Harper and Brothers, 1955), 34.

are there private instructions for the disciples. Instead, what dominates the story now is the conflict with the Jerusalem leadership.

The entrance into Jerusalem has been traditionally described as a "triumphal" entry. Indeed, Matthew's and Luke's versions are more triumphal than Mark's. Mark's narrative focuses less on conquest and victory (which a triumph suggests) than on humility and royalty (i.e., riding on a donkey). Yet, as Brian Blount highlights, this entrance occurs during the Passover, which "was celebrated as a remembrance of socio-political liberation," a time "when the people were celebrating the historical extension of God's liberative power through the Exodus event."[45]

In a time of war, as in Mark's historical context, the retelling of this story is critical because of its potential for (mis)understanding. Mark downplays, in comparison to the other Synoptic writers, Jesus' messianic status and elevates the serenity of this entry. In fact, when Jesus enters Jerusalem, and, more importantly, the temple area, *nothing* happens.

11:12-25, The Temple, Its Restoration, and the "Fig" Metaphor

Mark provides another intercalation here. He surrounds Jesus' action in the temple precincts with the cursing of the fig tree. In the Old Testament, the fig tree was often a symbol for the people of Israel (cf. Jer 8:13; Hos 9:10, 16; Mic 7:1), so it is Mark's intention to interpret the temple scene, especially the critique of its leadership (cf. Hos 9:15), in light of the fig tree passage. The notice that the tree bears no fruit is a word of judgment, though Mark's side comment that "it was not the season for figs" complicates interpretation. How could Jesus have expected "fruit" from this tree in an off-season? Because of this Markan note, Jesus' condemnation appears harsh (cf. 12:1-12).

Jesus' citations from Isaiah and Jeremiah are prophetic challenges to the temple, which

intend to *correct* those practices and not *replace* them. The scene in Mark is thus a "cleansing" episode, in the sense of *restoring* and not *replacing*. God's reign would include a restored future temple; Jesus' action symbolizes that design.

The phrase "for all nations" (only in Mark) might hold special significance for Jesus' challenge to the temple. Brian Blount thinks this phrase highlights the "eschatological emphasis on the Gentiles and their equal inclusion into the worship of the Lord [as] . . . Jesus' primary interest."[46] For Mark's prominent Gentile community, these words would not be overlooked.

11:27-33, The Day After: A Challenge from Temple Leadership

The temple leadership, who vow to destroy Jesus, return when Jesus revisits the scene. The confrontation begins with a question from leaders responsible for disruptive actions within the temple area: "By what authority are you doing these things?" (The issue of authority [*exousia*] has been part of Mark's story since Jesus' initial exorcism in the synagogue [cf. 1:22, 27].) These are politically sensitive leaders, so they allow the crowd's opinion to affect their actions, whether the leaders agree with them or with Jesus.

Mark provides no further rationale for Jesus' refusal to answer their question other than their refusal to answer his. Jesus' own question about the origins of John's baptism *is* an indirect response especially since, in Mark, Jesus received his own baptism under John. Recalling the divine approval in the earlier baptism scene, readers know exactly from whom Jesus' authority came!

12:1-12, Parable of the Vineyard: Prophetic Judgment against Temple Leaders

Jesus' prophetic judgments often come in parables. This parable, a denunciation of temple leadership, flows naturally from

11:27-33. While many scholars recognized an allusion to Isaiah 5, a "love song" about a "vineyard," such a connection is not explicit in Mark. The vineyard was a metaphor for "the house of Israel" and "the people of Judah," the Northern and Southern Kingdoms of ancient Israel. In Isaiah's prophecy, the *vineyard* was destroyed (Isa 5:5).

In Mark's account, Jesus' parable portrays the "owner" of the vineyard as patient, almost to a fault, as he tolerates the killing of several slaves. Then he decides to send his "beloved son," an apparent allusion to Jesus (cf. Mark 1:11; 9:7; also cf. Rom 4:13; Gal 4:1; Heb 1:2). As the parable shifts to the future tense, the patient "lord" will destroy these unfaithful tenants and deliver the vineyard to others. In other words, as the temple leaders grasp (12:12), by way of comparison to Isaiah 5, Jesus condemns their care of the people of Israel, and, concurrently, their custody of the temple. Unlike in Isaiah, the vineyard (i.e., people) in Jesus' parable is *not* destroyed, but the leaders are.

12:13-17, Paying Taxes to Caesar: God or Caesar

The temple leadership, in the guise of Pharisees and Herodians, continue their challenges. Herod and his appointed heirs—his three sons—maintain strong, viable relationships with Rome, under whose authority they rule. For the Herodians, then, payment of taxes would not be a difficult issue. While individual Pharisees might have occasionally opposed taxation laws, Mark depicts a unified temple leadership in favor of paying taxes.

Jesus manufactures an object lesson to demonstrate their hypocrisy. He then adds a theological idea that has political ramifications: "give . . . to God the things that are God's." What would happen when Caesar's policies oppose God's, or vice versa? African American history is filled with examples of this tension between the demands of justice (i.e., abolitionism, civil rights) and the legal requirements of the state (i.e., slavery, segregation).

12:18-27, The Sadducees and the Resurrection

This is the first and only appearance in Mark of the Sadducees, the aristocracy in Jesus' day. This Jewish sect was most firmly attached (in their practices and beliefs) to the stability of the temple, so Jesus' action in the temple probably precipitated this confrontation.

Most Jews believed in the general resurrection (cf. Acts 23:8). The Sadducees, Mark reports, were an exception. Citing no supporting text at first, Jesus claims that no marriage "certificates" would be reviewed in the afterlife, because humans would be "like" angels (i.e., sexless beings). (Jesus' response provides a liberating word for females who would no longer be considered "possessions," but he fails to read this eschatological view back into his present debilitating cultural setting.) Jesus, then, turns to the issue of resurrection, an issue that the Sadducees do not specifically raise. He believes in the miraculous power of a God who is God of the living and not the dead.

12:28-34, A Scribe Not Far from the Kingdom

A temple scribe overhears the debate between Jesus and the Sadducees and acknowledges Jesus' "correct" response; he, too, is probably a believer in the general resurrection.

His question is a different one, one more fundamental than hypothetical. It was common in the first century for Jews to discuss and debate the foremost commandment. Jesus' response draws on scriptural traditions, citing Deut 6:4-5, which had become the standard daily prayer, and Lev 19:18. The addition of "love for neighbor" is not common and provides Jesus' theological understanding that love for the other elucidates most clearly one's love for God.

The scribe agrees, setting up a moment in which Jesus and a scribe concur on a fundamental belief (cf. 1:22)! In fact, the scribe goes one step further by adding that such is "more important than . . . sacrifices," a conclusion, in this context, that is an implicit temple critique (cf. Hos 6:6). Jesus positively acknowledges the scribe's well-spoken assessment with his own opinion that this scribe was "not far from the kingdom of God." Why does Jesus not invite this scribe in completely? Mark leaves us once again with a narrative gap.

12:35-37, 38-40, Challenges to Scribal Teaching and Actions

The positive atmosphere from the previous scene does not last long. In the final verses of chap. 12, Jesus challenges scribal teaching (12:35-37) and scribal lifestyles (12:38-40).

It is difficult to determine what Jesus' intentions are in his distinction between the "messiah" (christos) and David. It could not be to question the lineage of David, since Jesus himself does not refuse earlier uses of the title "son of David" (cf. 10:47-48; 11:10). Perhaps Jesus attacks here the development of a more militaristic messianic figure associated with the kingdom of David (cf. 11:10). He appropriates Psalm 110 to establish, despite David's claim of "Lord," that there is a creative distance between the two. Analogously, the debate about the different strategies used by Martin and Malcolm cannot be reduced simply to nonviolent resistance or more activist (even violent) resistance; Gayraud Wilmore rightly recognizes the radical faiths and value of each.[47]

12:41-44, The Widow's Mite: An Example of Faithfulness?

Finally, Mark provides an example of what Jesus means by how the scribes "devour wid-

ows' houses" (v. 40). The association of the scribes and the temple becomes clear. While the rich give "much," this poor widow gives all, even her very subsistence. Generally, this story has been viewed as an example of faithfulness. But Jesus does not say so. In light of the context of conflict between Jesus and the temple leaders, this story is more likely a condemnation, rather than a commendation, of the ways the "treasury" (of those scribes responsible for determining financial requirements) consumes the means of the poor.[48]

13:1-8, Prediction of the Timing of the Temple's Demise

Whoever Jesus is, he is foremost an apocalyptic, eschatological prophet. This is not missed by one of the most revolutionary statements in the early history of African American political discourse, David Walker's Appeal (see sidebar below). "Apocalypticism" literally means "revelation"; "eschatology" means "understanding" (-logy) of the "end" (eschato-). These concepts are central to Jesus' teaching. They are present in Jesus' opening "sermon": "The time is fulfilled, and the kingdom of

---

Walker's *Appeal* and Apocalyptic Ideas

Know this, my dear sirs, that although you treat us and our children now, as you do your domestic beasts—yet the final result of all future events are known but to God Almighty alone, who rules in the armies of heaven and among the inhabitants of the earth, and who dethrones one earthly king and sits up another, as it seemeth good in his holy sight.

—"Our Wretchedness in Consequence of the Preachers of Religion," in *Afro-American Religious History: A Documentary Witness*, ed. Milton C. Sernett (Durham, N.C.: Duke University Press, 1985), 191.

God has come near" (1:15). His exorcisms are signs of the end.

Here Jesus predicts the final destruction of the temple, the center of religious life in first-century Judaism. Legitimately, the disciples wonder when this might occur, providing one more example that they themselves do not understand Jesus' earlier actions as representing the obliteration of the sacred center. As clear as Jesus is about its final devastation, he is ambiguous about the timing of this event.

13:9-13, Forewarning of the Persecution of the Disciples

Persecution is inevitable for Jesus' disciples. Their role, when brought to trials, would be to allow the Spirit to provide the content "against" (not "to," as in the NRSV) the magistrates. Proficient rhetorical training is not necessary beforehand. The vital presence of the Spirit indicates to them that they are living in the period near the end, and the Spirit would sustain their political dissent.[49] Such is apparently part of the experience of the members of the Markan community.

The language about familial divisions, common language within eschatological discourse, should *not* be taken literally as a "principle" for normal family commitments (or lack thereof) for those who follow God. Yet, Jesus' earlier definition of family as anyone who "does the will of God" (3:35) coincides with this message of familial distrust. As Cain Hope Felder rightly remarks, "Mark's 'little apocalypse' (chapter 13) attempts to alert an ancient congregation to the ways the suffering witness of believers will disrupt traditional family loyalties and behavioral patterns."[50]

13:14-27, Desolation of Sacred Space, Ensuing Suffering, and False Messiahs

Some scholars have attempted to locate the historical event that precipitated Jesus' prediction of a "desolating sacrilege" (13:14). One common suggestion is Emperor Caligula's desire to place his image in the temple (ca. 41 C.E.), an attempt that failed because of the wisdom of Caligula's representative, Petronius.[51] No historical event quite captures Jesus' apparent intention. Mark's own ambiguous depiction is due to the tense atmosphere in which he wrote. To be more specific may have brought unwanted Roman attention to Mark's sectarian community. Yet Mark beckons "the reader" to pay close attention to the sign, and the ensuing suffering. Additional signage would include "false prophets" and "false messiahs." Total destruction would be inevitable, according to Jesus, if not for God's mercy for God's chosen. The term *elect* is used only three times in the Gospel of Mark (13:20, 22, 27), providing a statement of hope, an election not determined by "ethnic or racial criteria."[52]

The Morality of Nonviolence

"Over the past few years I have consistently preached that nonviolence demands that the means we use must be as pure as the ends we seek. I have tried to make clear that it is wrong to use immoral means to attain moral ends. But now I must affirm that it is just as wrong, or perhaps even more so, to use moral means to preserve immoral ends."

—Martin Luther King Jr., "Letter from Birmingham Jail," in *Afro-American Religious History: A Documentary Witness*, ed. Milton Sernett (Durham, N.C.: Duke University Press, 1985), 444.

13:28-37, Another Fig Tree Lesson, and the Final Warning

Jesus brings this teaching to a close with a reminder: "Be alert." It is the nature of apocalyptic language to remind listeners that what you see is *not* what you get. Such descriptions intend to challenge the status quo. The message for Mark's community, through Jesus, is to "watch." It is a sober, though apparently passive, message for a community living through the Roman-Jewish War. In Jesus' final image, the "homeowner" grants "authority" to his "slaves"[53] to carry out their "tasks" (*ergon*), so as not to be discovered asleep when the owner returns. What this "work" would look like has been usually interpreted as proclaiming the good news. Within this apocalyptic context, the struggle for the justice of the reign of God would also be part of this necessary work. Although Howard Thurman de-emphasized the future orientation of the "Day of Reckoning" type language, he rightly interpreted its earthly relevance: "Anticipation of the awesome vision should order a life for right living."[54]

Mark retells this story to his contemporaries so that Jesus' actions and words would be understood as opposed to any direct "Christian" involvement in the war with Rome. As God's representative, Mark's Jesus, too, is interested in how to change the world, but his means to do so is not like that of the contemporary zealots or like Toni Morrison's "Seven Days" in *Song of Solomon*.[55] "For the master's tools will never dismantle the master's house," as Audre Lorde rightly contends.[56] Nor should we conclude that it is by changing hearts only, since first-century folks did not separate the internal from the external so neatly. Jesus, like his contemporaries, desires a radical, revolutionary change.

14:1-11, An Unnamed Woman Anoints Jesus' Head for Burial

It is time for the Passover feasts, a time when Palestinian and diaspora Jews commemorate the release of their ancestors from Egypt. Not all are celebrating. "The chief priests and the scribes" are plotting the death of Jesus, because of his disturbance in the temple area. But the feast—and the crowds it attracts—deter their desires, that is, until Judas's visit!

Between the Jewish leaders' scheme and Judas's consultation with them, Mark sandwiches the depiction of the anointing of Jesus' head. Compared to Simon, in whose house they dine, this woman is known *only* by what she possesses, an alabaster box of expensive ointment. She arrives with *no* name and the wrong gender. Culturally, the public appearance of this woman without a male figure would be a shameful act. But her presence at the dinner apparently does not shame Jesus or others, who *are* dining with a former (we presume!) leper. Her "valuable" possessions are her identification. Yet she gives them all (cf. 12:41-44)![57]

In light of Jesus' earlier conversation with the "rich man," his statement about the poor should not be interpreted as an excuse *not* to do good for the less fortunate. But rendering assistance to the poor should *not* be an excuse not to do good to Jesus either. In other words, to fail to provide some comfort for the "neighbor," while using resources for "the poor" is also a failure to live out one's religious responsibilities (cf. Deut 15:11).

While this unnamed female stranger commits this faithful act, Judas—Jesus' own disciple—commits the most faithless act of the story. No clear rationale is mentioned. Many suggest finances as the cause, as in Matthew's Gospel. If correct, this would be a powerful point of comparison between the woman guest, who considers no expense too great to sacrifice, and a disciple, who cherishes the payoff. One of the "forerunner(s) for womanist biblical interpretation," Virginia Broughton, called the "forerunner for womanist biblical interpretation" by Marcia Riggs, described this woman's act as an act of supreme love, and found *the anointer* as one example of God's calling of women ministers.[58]

14:12-25, The Final Meal with the Disciples

In Christian tradition, this final meal (i.e., "The Lord's Supper," "The Eucharist," etc.), which Jesus shares with his disciples, is the most significant in a story filled with meals. At this meal, Jesus predicts the act of treachery. Readers are more informed of Judas's recent schemes than are the disciples. Jesus also provides a mystical interpretation of the "bread" and the "wine," relating them to his body and blood, respectively. Using the word for "covenant" (*diathēkē*) only once in the entire Gospel, Mark's Jesus suggests an extension of the traditional Jewish (i.e., Abrahamic, Mosaic, and Davidic) covenants. Jesus' final word ties his futuristic eschatology, prominent in chap. 13, to this eucharistic meal.

14:26-31 Prediction of the Disciples' Desertion

After the meal ends, they sing a hymn. Citing Zech 13:7, Jesus shows that death looms. But he also predicts a miraculous reunion with his disciples (14:28).

"Take My Hand, Precious Lord"

"When my way grows drear,
Precious Lord, linger near,
When my life is almost gone,
Hear my cry, hear my call,
Hold my hand lest I fall.
Take my hand, Precious Lord,
Lead me home."

The great African American hymnist Thomas A. Dorsey, the "Father of Gospel Music," wrote this classic hymn in 1932, when his wife, Nettie, died after giving birth to their son.

— "Precious Lord (Take My Hand)" by Thomas A. Dorsey © 1938 Unichappell Music Inc. (Renewed). International Copyright Reserved. Used by Permission.

14:32-52, Gethsemane and Arrest

The uniqueness of Gethsemane ought not to be overlooked. All Gospel authors, except John, include this agonizing scene. Their Jesus, like the one African Americans epitomize, understands the psychological turmoil of expected physical suffering and its aftermath. Mark portrays Jesus' personal struggle before a privileged group of disciples: Peter, James, and John (cf. 9:2-8). *Only* the folks who witness the transfiguration, which was a mystical alteration of reality, *might* be able to handle the darkest moments of Jesus' anguish. Instead, their exhaustion from following Jesus has taken its toll. Indeed, even Jesus' prayer, as Arna Bontemps poetically describes, receives nothing but silence in reply:

> I stretched full-length upon the grass and there
> I said your name but silence answered me.[59]

The plot of the temple leadership develops through the active role of Judas, "one of the twelve." Judas leads a "crowd with swords and clubs" to Gethsemane and betrays his "Rabbi" with a kiss. Oh, the irony. Up until this point, the "crowd" tends to be faithful followers of Jesus. But Judas alters their view.

In Mark, unlike the other Gospels, Jesus completely ignores the disciple's violent reaction, implicitly approving the act. Jesus reacts, however, to the apprehenders. Their weapons puzzle him, since he has never shown himself to be a violent person. (But, in light of the disciples' own arms, the weapons of the temple police seem justified.) Jesus resigns himself to the necessity of scriptural fulfillment. Finally, Mark includes one more "disciple," an unnamed "young man," who symbolically represents the departure of *all* disciples, leaving Jesus in isolation at the mercy of his adversaries.

14:53-71, The "Trials" of Jesus and Peter

The opening scene, vv. 53-54, shows Mark's narrative skills again, as he intersperses the trial of Jesus with the "trial" of Peter. The prominence of Peter in the second Gospel is most clearly evident in this passage.

The trial of Jesus begins in front of the Sanhedrin, a group of priests (some Pharisaic and some Sadducean), scribes, and elders whose primary task in the first century is to adjudicate the affairs of the priests surrounding the temple practices. They are the power-brokers, the Jewish elite. Yet they are unable to locate proper witnesses against Jesus. As Mark stresses, "false witnesses" continue to come forward.

Finally, guards take Jesus to the high priest, who requests Jesus' response to the false charges. Jesus remains silent. The high priest then asks directly whether Jesus is the Messiah. Only in Mark's narrative is Jesus' response so clear: "I am." It is the clearest Jesus has spoken about his identity. "Tearing his clothes," the priest's reaction is a sign of alarm and sorrow. Blasphemy is the charge (cf. 2:1-11). Before the high priest, Jesus identifies himself as the Messiah, an expected eschatological figure.

As Jesus trial ends with physical abuse, despite the false charges, Peter's "trial" ends with emotional shame, because of his response to the valid charges of his association with the Galilean. Mark's readers are also on "trial" as they try to determine whether their following of this Galilean has brought them into conflict with the ruling elite of their day.

15:1-15, Trial before Pilate

Either the Sanhedrin, which has condemned Jesus to death (14:64), does not have the authority to carry out the sentence, or, more likely, their trumped up charges are insufficient accusations for a death sentence. So they lead Jesus to Pilate, the Roman governor and highest ranking Roman official in the territory.

The initial meeting between Jesus and Pilate is a brief "trial" surrounding one primary issue: whether Jesus claims to be "king." On the one hand, Jesus does *not* deny Pilate's assessment; on the other hand, Pilate fails to find the claim worthy of death, "religious" blasphemy or not. From Pilate's perspective, in the Markan account, Jesus' death sentence is due to tension with the priests (i.e., their "jealousy," 15:10). It is a struggle between religious figures. At first, Mark's Pilate looks like a sympathetic Roman governor.

Then the politically charged atmosphere forces Pilate's hand. Rather than reserving crucifixion for Barabbas, a state criminal, Pilate—pressured by the crowds and the priests—requests it for Jesus. Crucifixion is a political death reserved for state criminals and slaves, particularly those charged with insurrection. Someone—the priests, the crowd, Pilate, or Mark—appears to understand the title of "king" as one worthy of political death! It may be surprising for those who view Jesus as apolitical. Jesus accepts the political title. The religious significance of Jesus' death comes later in the chapter in Mark. Here, the outcome is political to the core! The one whose initial message is "the reign of God is near" is now charged with the title "king."

15:21, Simon of Cyrene

Mark 15:21 has caught the attention of numerous African American scholars. Cyrene was a city in North Africa, and so provides direct evidence of African presence in the second Gospel. While much scholarly attention has focused on origins, a recent issue of contention is whether Simon's action of carrying the cross is a true action of discipleship (so Brian Blount) or not (so Boykin Sanders).[60] Can one be "forced" into discipleship action?

The text does *not* support the prejudice that Simon's "Africanness" is the reason the

Romans chose him for this task. In fact, the scholarly debate continues whether there was "color prejudice" in the first-century Greco-Roman world.[61] It would be appealing to suggest that a favorable attitude toward Africans is why the Roman soldiers sought this trustworthy candidate to assist at this point. But the text cannot corroborate this interpretation.

Instead the text provides a crucial piece of information significant to the discussion: the names of his sons, Alexander and Rufus. It is striking information, in light of so many unnamed minor (but more significant) characters in the Gospel of Mark. Also, it is an aside, which suggests that the author is sharing information pertinent to the audience: "It was Simon . . . the father of Alexander and Rufus [whom all of you know]." These children of the African Jewish cross bearer obviously become believers and are well-known to the community to whom the author writes. If not present themselves, they probably have family members—daughters and sons—in Mark's audience.

However we decide on Simon's "cross carrying" activity, two things are certain. First, his action, despite the ambiguity of its coercion, establishes a lineage of African Christ followers for the movement. Second, the Roman compulsion of Simon to carry this cross is more evidence of the powerful encroachment of Roman extension into all (socioreligious, psychodynamic, and economic) affairs of the Palestinian judicial system.

15:22-32, Reactions to Jesus' Public Crucifixion

The political rationale for a Roman public crucifixion is to forestall any future criminal activity against the state. Part of the maintenance of the *pax Romana* is the policy of public humiliation of renegades. Of course, such public acts of persecution dishonor the punished individual and bring shame upon the individual's family and community.

Furthermore, the political nature of this death is evident throughout this section, from the inscription ("king") to the final ironic derision from fellow sufferers. These two "bandits"—real opponents to the state—join their voices with the leadership of the Jewish socioreligious establishment *and* those "who passed by" (15:29) because of their united expectation that the true Messiah would be a political figure who could "rescue" (*sodzo*) himself, and, in turn "save" (*sodzo*) all others. Mark's Christian readers would catch the irony.

15:33-41, Jesus' Death and Its Theological and Political Effect

Were you there when they crucified my Lord?

Finally, at 15:34, Mark most poignantly describes Jesus' final cry. Although bystanders misunderstand his Aramaic, Jesus speaks the words of Ps 22:1, an individual lament of isolation and abandonment. In the psalm, the lamenter wonders aloud about God's absence in the present conflict while recalling the faithfulness of God through past struggles. Mark's analogy is an attempt to describe Jesus' final emotional and psychological torment, in addition to his physical suffering.[62] The enslaved African American had no problem grasping this type of abandonment. As Shawn Copeland's study shows, "the enslaved Africans sang because they saw on the rugged wooden planks One who had endured what was their daily portion. The cross was treasured because it enthroned the One who went all the way with them and for them."[63]

There is more. The earliest story about Jesus' mission depicts *three* crucial events surrounding his final earthly breath.[64] First, *the tearing of the veil* symbolizes a new age in which the holy place would no longer be divided from the most holy place. Whether hope (for all nations) or judgment (against Israel) is the foremost meaning of this act is uncertain from the narrative. Perhaps both are intended.

Second, *the confession of the Roman centurion* is the *first* human confession about Jesus *as Son of God* in Mark's narrative. While the sincerity of the centurion's words is less clear in Greek than in English translations, readers of Mark's Gospel will generally find here a fitting summary of Mark's story. With the veil torn, a non-Jew can "see" and confess precisely who Jesus is. It seems, however, rather unfortunate that, as Cain Hope Felder rightly describes Mark's ideological slant, "the immediate significance of this New Testament tendency—to focus on Rome instead of Jerusalem—is that the darker races outside the Roman orbit, by modern standards, seem circumstantially marginalized by New Testament authors."[65] Such "hope," while intended for all, becomes more and more exclusive (i.e., reserved for Western, more Europeanized persons), and Mark's portrayal is not excused from the charge.

Finally, *the presence of the women disciples* concludes the events of hope after Jesus breathes his final breath. These women—some named, most unnamed—provide examples of faithful, committed disciples from the beginning of Jesus' mission in Galilee. Unlike Jesus' chosen twelve male disciples, these women witness the death, and will later witness the burial and the empty tomb, providing more positive gender inclusiveness than anywhere else in the narrative.

15:42-47, The Burial of Jesus

Jewish tradition stipulates proper burials for its adherents (cf. Deut 21:22-23), but state criminals rarely receive such. The oddity of this burial is that an apparent stranger, Joseph—not one of Jesus' close followers—secures the body for burial, further suggesting Jesus' isolation at the end of his life. Mark's ambiguous description of this stranger is "clarified" in the later Gospel tradition, so

that Joseph becomes a "disciple of Jesus" (cf. Matt 27:57; John 19:38), one more suited for the task at hand. Reading only Mark's account leaves readers with a number of unanswered questions, especially *why* "a member of the council" (assuming the same "council" that condemned Jesus in 14:64) would feel compelled to complete this pious act. The act is rushed, however, since proper burial ointments are apparently not used, making necessary the women's return on the following day. Perhaps, it is Joseph's anticipation of God's reign that attracted him to Jesus. If so, this member of the condemning council, anticipating the "kingdom," may have regretted his earlier sentiments and returned to restore a sense of honor to the occasion.

Were you there when they laid him in the tomb?

16:1-8, When the End Is Only the Beginning

The faithful women—Mary Magdalene,[66] Mary, James's mother, and Salome—witness Jesus' death and burial. Now, they arrive to prepare the body with appropriate ointments. Such ointments would assist the gradual decomposition of the body *and* reduce the stench of the decay. One year after burial, family members would retrieve the bones of the deceased for final security.

The women are less concerned with how they might find Jesus' body than they are with the "very large" stone at the tomb's entrance. But, to their surprise, the stone had been rolled away. Their amazement is increased when an angelic looking "young man" speaks to them. Mark's humanlike figure, dressed in an angelic "white robe," reminds readers of an earlier "young man" who escaped during Jesus' arrest (cf. 14:50-51). Mark's use of such figures highlights the extraordinary nature surrounding these significant scenes.

As the women observe, the tomb is empty. Instead, the mysterious "young man" speaks the final words of hope of the entire story. "He has been raised. . . . Go, tell his disciples to meet him in Galilee." The final words of the Gospel of Mark are words of re-gathering, reunion, and hope.

So the women depart and proclaim all that is told to them. Right? Not at all! Instead, their fear overwhelms their speech, and the story ends with a final note of inaction, "they said nothing to anyone, for they were afraid."

This is Mark the storyteller at work. He writes for believers who know part of the story already. One significant component they know is that someone, one of these women, had to tell someone else. If not, then they would have never heard. They would not be gathered together, and Mark would not be writing this story. But Mark's ending provides his readers, and all subsequent readers, with a challenge. He does not provide a "happy ending." As descendants of the enslaved, we, too, understand how some stories do not "end" with simplistic conclusions, as if things "were happy ever after." As David Goatley's studies of the spirituals show, "They normally end with Jesus dying, dead, or buried. There are selections that focus on the crucifixion and end in the resurrection, *but they are rare.* This does not suggest that the slaves were resigned to accept their lives in slavery without protest. Instead the songs indicate the intimacy and intensity with which the slaves related to the agony of the crucified Jesus."[67] How apropos to the one Gospel that does not, in its original edition, include a resurrection account! The greatest story ever told is also the most startling, that is, that Jesus, brutally beaten, crucified, and put to death, was not found in his tomb. So what will any reader of this account do with this story? How will any "hearer" of this message, having also "heard" the song of the enslaved, react to the "end" of the story? Since Jesus has died under the decisions of the primary political and religious authorities

of his day, what will Mark's readers do with the story of his ongoing life and spirit among them, so as to oppose those sociopolitical powers?

If the story ends at Mark 16:8, as the earliest manuscripts attest, then hope is not defined by a resurrection or a physical appearance *but* by an empty tomb and a promised re-gathering. In this story, despite the absence of Jesus, hope derives from the bond of those relying on his promised return. Hope comes to those who do not ignore that each person needs the other. The absence of Jesus, with the prospect of his return, opens up the possibility that humans will rely on one another to participate in the liberation of those on the margins. The mission of Jesus, in Howard Thurman's word, is a "technique of survival for the oppressed."[68] The women left "with fear and trembling," because they, too, may have realized that this is only the beginning of something new, a newness that will require mutual effort, from all available intellectual, spiritual, economic, cultural, and other sociopolitical resources, from all, female and male, African, Asian, European, Latin, and North American persons. "Keep hope alive!" Stay in the struggle! "[P]eople who die bad don't stay in the ground."[69]

16:9-20, The Longer (Additional) Ending

In the history of early Christianity, several individual scribes had difficulty with the ending of Mark. It is no surprise, since even Matthew and Luke chose to end their accounts in more positive ways! Ending the story about Jesus with "fear" appeared unseemly (cf. Mark 16:8). At least two "endings" have become part of the published accounts of the Gospel of Mark from the early centuries. Most English translations include the "longer ending of Mark"; some also include the "shorter ending of Mark." The latter, added no earlier than the fourth century, suggests that the women reported their experience to "those around Peter," after which the message of "eternal salvation" went out "from east to west" into the whole world. The "longer ending," generally recorded as vv. 9-20 of most English Bibles, was not added to the Gospel until the middle of the second century. While its opening verse coincides with, and probably depends on, other Gospel accounts, it does not flow neatly from 16:8. In fact, it seems not to flow at all! The language, ideas, and theology of this longer account do not fit neatly with what comes prior in the Gospel of Mark. All subsequent attempts to end Mark's Gospel more "suitably" will, unfortunately, hinder the overarching, and startling, challenge of Mark's ending: the women departed with fear. What will you do?

Notes

1. Brian K. Blount, *Go Preach! Mark's Kingdom Message and the Black Church Today* (Maryknoll, N.Y.: Orbis, 1998); Joanna Dewey, "Mark," in *Searching the Scriptures: A Feminist Commentary*, vol. 2., ed. Elizabeth Schüssler Fiorenza (New York: Crossroad, 1994), 470–509.

2. W. E. B. DuBois, "The Talented Tenth," in *The Negro Problem* (New York: Arno, 1969 [1903]), 38.

3. John S. Pobee, *Toward an African Theology* (Nashville: Abingdon, 1979).

4. James Cone, *God of the Oppressed* (Maryknoll, N.Y.: Orbis, 1977), 77.

5. Brian K. Blount, *Then the Whisper Put on Flesh: New Testament Ethics in an African American Context* (Nashville: Abingdon, 2001), 61.

6. Ralph Ellison, *Invisible Man* (New York: Vintage, 1972), 13.

7. James Baldwin, *Go Tell It on the Mountain* (New York: Dell, 1953), 137–38. The exploration of namelessness is a common interest in Baldwin's other writings: *Nobody Knows My Name: More Notes of a Native Son* (New York:

Dial, 1961) and *No Name in the Street* (New York: Dial, 1972).

8. Following the text-critical rule of accepting the more difficult reading in the manuscripts, "being angry," is to be preferred to "having compassion."

9. "An Interview with Jamaica Kincaid," interview by Donna Perry, in *Reading Black, Reading Feminist: A Critical Anthology*, ed. Henry Louis Gates Jr. (New York: Meridian, 1990), 492–509, at 497–98.

10. Cornell West, *Race Matters* (New York: Vintage, 1994), 150.

11. For a definition of *sin* as a breakdown in communal relationships, see John Mbiti, "God, Sin, and Salvation in African Religion," *JITC* 16 (Fall 1988–Spring 1989): 59–68; Blount, *Go Preach!*, 80; and Katie G. Cannon, "Sin," in *Dictionary of Third World Theologies*, ed. Virginia Fabella and R. S. Sugirtharajah (Maryknoll, N.Y.: Orbis, 2000), 184–85.

12. C. Eric Lincoln and Lawrence H. Mamiya, *The Black Church in the African American Experience* (Durham, N.C.: Duke University Press, 1990), 50–52.

13. Richard Allen, "Life Experience and Gospel Labors," in *Afro-American Religious History: A Documentary History*, ed. Milton C. Sernett (Durham, N.C.: Duke University Press, 1985), 135–49.

14. "The Talented Tenth theory was a strategy to win democracy for all black Americans"; Manning Marable, *W. E. B. DuBois: Black Radical Democrat* (Boston: Twayne, 1986), 51.

15. DuBois, "The Talented Tenth," 31–75, at 31.

16. Speech delivered at Wilberforce University, Pennsylvania, in 1948. See Marable, *W. E. B. DuBois*, 147–48.

17. Cleophus J. LaRue, e-mail correspondence, September 2003.

18. The NRSV shifts the subject of the verb in v. 21 from "the family" to "the people." But in the Greek text the subject of the last clause remains the "they" of "they were saying," for which the most immediate antecedent would be "the family."

19. For an enlightening treatment of the "crowds" in Mark, see Ahn Byung-Mu, "Jesus and the

Minjung in the Gospel of Mark," in *Voices from the Margins: Interpreting the Bible in the Third World*, ed. R. S. Sugirtharajah (Maryknoll, N.Y.: Orbis, 1995), 85–104.

20. See Rosetta Ross, *Witnessing and Testifying: Black Women, Religion, and Civil Rights* (Minneapolis: Fortress Press, 2003).

21. James Cone, *The Spiritual and the Blues: An Interpretation* (Maryknoll, N.Y.: Orbis, 1991), 40. Cf. Howard Thurman, *Deep River: Reflections on the Religious Insight of Certain of the Negro Spirituals* (New York: Harper, 1945), 44–45, and Cheryl Kirk-Duggan, *Exorcising Evil: A Womanist Perspective on the Spirituals* (Maryknoll, N.Y.: Orbis, 1997), 13–14.

22. Frederick Douglass, *The Narrative of the Life of Frederick Douglass, An American Slave: Written by Himself*, ed. Houston A. Baker Jr. (New York: Penguin, 1982 [1845]), chap. 7, esp. 85–87.

23. Dwight N. Hopkins, "Slave Theology in the 'Invisible Institution,'" in *Cut Loose Your Stammering Tongue: Black Theology in the Slave Narratives*, ed. Dwight N. Hopkins and George C. L. Cummings, 2nd ed. (Louisville: Westminster John Knox, 2003), 16.

24. Obery Hendricks, "Guerrilla Exegesis: A Post Modern Proposal for Insurgent African American Biblical Interpretation," *JITC* 22 (Fall 1994): 78 (emphasis in the original).

25. Mary Ann Tolbert, "Mark," in *Women's Bible Commentary*, ed. Carol A. Newsom and Sharon H. Ringe (Louisville: Westminster John Knox, 1998), 355.

26. Derivation from "slave wisdom" is suggested by Dwight N. Hopkins in "Slave Theology in the 'Invisible Institution,'" in *Cut Loose Your Stammering Tongue*, 31.

27. According to Thurman's biographer, Thurman viewed this omission as an attempt to emphasize Jesus' significant life and ministry (Luther Smith, *Howard Thurman: The Mystic as Prophet* [Richmond, Ind.: Friends United, 1991], 234n101).

28. Cornel West and Sylvia Ann Hewlett charge Aid to Families with Dependent Children with establishing regulations "to deliberately exclude fathers. The rules held that if an 'able-bodied man' resided in a household, a woman with dependent children was unable to claim benefits for herself and her children. This caused men to be literally pushed out of the nest. . . . These government-sponsored rules help explain why out-of-wedlock births in the black community leapt from 21 percent in 1960 to 69.8 percent in 1996" ("Parents and National Survival," in *The Cornel West Reader*, ed. Cornel West [New York: Basic Civitas, 1999], 336–37).

29. Sojourner Truth quoted in *Can I Get a Witness? Prophetic Religious Voices of African American Women: An Anthology*, ed. Marcia Y. Riggs (Maryknoll, N.Y.: Orbis, 1997), 22.

30. Cain Hope Felder, *Troubling Biblical Waters: Race, Class, and Family* (Maryknoll, N.Y.: Orbis, 1989), 159.

31. Fish were not ritually unclean, according to the law of Moses.

32. Marcia Y. Riggs, *Awake, Arise and Act: A Womanist Call for Black Liberation* (Cleveland: Pilgrim, 1994), 11.

33. Cf. James Brewer Stewart, *Holy Warriors: The Abolitionists and American Slavery*, rev. ed. (New York: Hill and Wang, 1997), 127–49, and David Swift, *Black Prophets of Justice: Activist Clergy before the Civil War* (Baton Rouge: Louisiana State University Press, 1989), 260–62.

34. U.S. Census Bureau, rev. and released September 26, 2003; www.census.gov/hhes/www/poverty/histpov/hstpov2.html.

35. Zilpha Elaw thought she, an African American preacher from the North, would be taken into slavery and so—alluding to this biblical scene—questioned Satan's authority: "My faith then rallied and my confidence in the Lord returned, and I said '*get thee behind me Satan*, for my Jesus hath made me free'" (quoted in Riggs, *Can I Get a Witness?* 18 [emphasis added]).

36. Cf. Jacquelyn Grant, "Womanist Jesus and the Mutual Struggle for Liberation," in *The Recovery of Black Presence: An Interdisciplinary Exploration*, ed. Randall C. Bailey and Jacquelyn Grant (Nashville: Abingdon, 1995), 129–42, and Joanne Marie Terrell, *Power in*

the Blood? The Cross in African American Experience (Maryknoll, N.Y.: Orbis, 1998).

37. Howard Thurman, The Creative Encounter: An Interpretation of Religion and the Social Witness (Richmond, Ind.: Friends United, 1972), 123. In direct reflection on this passage, he continues, "Perhaps this is what Jesus meant when he raised the question as to what a [person] would give in exchange for his [or her] life. The profoundest disclosure in the religious experience is the awareness that the individual is not alone."

38. Julia Ward Howe, "His Truth Is Marching On," in The African-American Archive: The History of the Black Experience through Documents, ed. Kai Wright (New York: Black Dog & Leventhal, 2001), 292.

39. On Booker T. Washington, Lerone Bennett emphasizes, "Important as Washington's role was, it has been greatly misunderstood and exaggerated. For he was neither new nor revelatory. He was simply the most celebrated of a long line of accommodators, reaching into the present, who have articulated the view that it is better to buy peace by accommodating, working and studying than to disturb the peace by protesting, demanding and resisting. As a matter of fact, it is better to do both, to work and protest" (Before the Mayflower: The History of Black America [New York: Penguin, 1988], 267).

40. According to Jesus' position in Mark 12:18-27, only if a spouse dies could the other spouse remarry.

41. Marian Wright Edelman, "Foreword," in The State of Children in America's Union: A 2002 Action Guide to Leave No Child Behind (www.cdfactioncouncil.org/actionguide/2002.pdf), iv–v.

42. The bill, proposed by Rep. John Conyers (D-Mich.) since 1989, for the government to examine the case of reparations has been continually rejected.

43. Clarice Martin, "Womanist Interpretations of the New Testament: The Quest for Holistic and Inclusive Translation and Interpretation," in Black Theology: A Documentary History, vol. 2, 1980–1992, ed. James Cone and Gayraud

Wilmore (Maryknoll, N.Y.: Orbis, 1993), 239–40.

44. Cone, God of the Oppressed, 150–51.

45. Blount, Go Preach! 144.

46. Ibid., 151.

47. Gayraud Wilmore, Black Religion and Black Radicalism: An Interpretation of the Religious History of Afro-American People, 2nd ed. (Maryknoll, N.Y.: Orbis, 1983), 191.

48. R. S. Sugirtharajah, The Bible and the Third World: Precolonial, Colonial, and Postcolonial Encounters (Cambridge: Cambridge University Press, 2001), 263.

49. See Blount, Go Preach! 204.

50. Felder, Troubling Biblical Waters, 157.

51. Josephus, Antiquities of the Jews 18.8.2.

52. Felder, Troubling Biblical Waters, 46.

53. Although the use of the term slaves is less frequent in Mark—perhaps suggesting something about his particular community—he depicts Jesus' use of the term in common stories, showing Jesus to be a product of the cultural setting in which the slave system was a major part. Apparently, despite Jesus' apocalyptic imagery, some things would stay the same.

54. Smith, Howard Thurman, 64.

55. Toni Morrison, Song of Solomon (New York: Penguin, 1977), 155–62.

56. Audre Lorde, "The Master's Tool Will Never Dismantle the Master's House," in Audre Lorde, Sister Outsider: Essays and Speeches (Berkeley: Crossing, 1984), 110–13.

57. Other, later traditions, like the Gospel of Luke, exploited the potential shame factor by labeling her a "sinner."

58. Broughton's essay is cited in Can I Get a Witness? 41; for Riggs description of Broughton, see 31.

59. Arna Bontemps, "Gethsemane," in Black Voices: An Anthology of African-American Literature, ed. Abraham Chapman (New York: Signet, 2001), 421–22. Reprinted here by permission of the author's estate.

60. Brian K. Blount, "A Socio-Rhetorical Analysis of Simon of Cyrene: Mark 15:21 and Its Parallels," Semeia 49 (1991): 171–98; Boykin Sanders, "In Search of a Face for Simon of Cyrene," in The Recovery of Black Presence,

51–64. Stephanie Buckhanon Crowder, *Simon of Cyrene: A Case of Roman Conscription* (New York and Oxford: Peter Lang, 2002), 96, offers an ideological interpretation of this character in light of *Luke's* depiction. The distinction between Mark and Luke is not unimportant. In her reading of Luke, Buckhanon Crowder concludes, "Simon of Cyrene . . . was not a disciple but a victim of corruption."

61. For a recent installment, see Gay L. Byron's sophisticated ethnopolitical study, *Symbolic Blackness and Ethnic Difference in Early Christian Literature* (London and New York: Routledge, 2002).

62. Smith, *Howard Thurman*, 59–60, sums up Thurman's views on the meaning of Jesus' crucifixion:

Good Friday is not, for Thurman, an event which informs doctrines of atonement. Jesus is never mentioned as the sacrifice for humankind's sins. Thurman stresses two meanings of the crucifixion: (1) when Jesus cried out "My God! My God! Why hast thou forsaken me?" he declared the need to feel God's presence in that moment of terrible pain and anguish. Jesus wanted to be certain that the source of his life (God) was as available in this cataclysmic moment, as during the other times of his life. In this cry Jesus again confesses his dependence upon God. Good Friday is a sign that life must ultimately rest, not in comfort, but in "commending our spirits" to God. And (2) rather than the crucifixion being a God initiated event to redeem humankind, it is the logic of what happens to love in the world. To give one's self to God does not assure success, prosperity, or popularity. Since the social order contains evil, and since evil works against community, love faces immense difficulties. Good Friday is a statement about the nature of society, and the fate of the disciple of Jesus. Thurman affirms: "The crucifixion of Jesus Christ reminds us once again of the penalty which any highly organized society exacts of those who violate its laws . . . those who resist the establishment order because its requirement are too low, too unworthy of the highest and best in man."

63. Shawn Copeland, "Wading through Many Sorrows," in *Troubling in My Soul: Womanist Perspectives on Evil and Suffering*, ed. E. M. Townes (Maryknoll, N.Y.: Orbis, 1993), 120.

64. As Brian Blount aptly writes in *Then the Whisper Put on Flesh*, 60, "this kingdom-driven, boundary-breaking ethics . . . does not result in an ethics of suffering. Suffering, even Jesus' suffering on the cross, is the consequence, not the goal of his boundary-breaking ministry." On the following page, he continues, "Never mind that Mark never, even in the Supper recounting, argues that Jesus must die in order to save humankind from sin."

65. Cain Hope Felder, *Race, Racism, and the Biblical Narratives*, Facets (Minneapolis: Fortress Press, 2002), 36.

66. Mary Magdalene made Maria Stewart's 1833 list as one of the leading biblical female "activists" given divine sanction (Marilyn Richardson, ed., *Maria W. Stewart, America's First Black Woman Political Writer* [Bloomington: Indiana University Press, 1987], 22).

67. David Emmanuel Goatley, "Godforsakenness in African American Spirituals," in *Cut Loose Your Stammering Tongue*, 153.

68. Howard Thurman, *Jesus and the Disinherited* (Boston: Beacon, 1976), 29.

69. Toni Morrison, *Beloved* (New York: Plume, 1987), 188.

For Further Reading

Blount, Brian. *Go Preach! Mark's Kingdom Message and the Black Church Today.* Maryknoll, N.Y.: Orbis, 1998.

———. "A Socio-Rhetorical Analysis of Simon of Cyrene: Mark 15:21 and Its Parallels." *Semeia* 49 (1991): 171–98.

———. *Then the Whisper Put on Flesh: New Testament Ethics in an African American Context.* Nashville: Abingdon, 2001.

Byron, Gay L. *Symbolic Blackness and Ethnic Difference in Early Christian Literature.* London and New York: Routledge, 2002.

Cone, James. *God of the Oppressed.* Maryknoll, N.Y.: Orbis, 1977.

Crowder, Stephanie Buckhanon. *Simon of Cyrene: A Case of Roman Conscription*. New York and London: Peter Lang, 2002.

Felder, Cain Hope. *Race, Racism, and the Biblical Narratives*. Facets. Minneapolis: Fortress Press, 2002.

———. *Troubling Biblical Waters: Race, Class, and Family*. Maryknoll, N.Y.: Orbis, 1989.

Grant, Jacquelyn. "Womanist Jesus and the Mutual Struggle for Liberation." Pages 129–42 in *The Recovery of Black Presence: An Interdisciplinary Exploration*. Edited by Randall C. Bailey and Jacquelyn Grant. Nashville: Abingdon, 1995.

Hendricks, Obery. "Guerrilla Exegesis: A Postmodern Proposal for Insurgent African American Biblical Interpretation." *JITC* 22 (Fall 1994): 92–109.

Kirk-Duggan, Cheryl. *Exorcising Evil: A Womanist Perspective on the Spirituals*. Maryknoll, N.Y.: Orbis, 1997.

Lincoln, C. Eric, and Lawrence H. Mamiya. *The Black Church in the African American Experience*. Durham, N.C.: Duke University Press, 1990.

Riggs, Marcia Y., ed. *Can I Get a Witness? Prophetic Religious Voices of African American Women: An Anthology*. Maryknoll, N.Y.: Orbis, 1997.

Sanders, Boykin. "In Search of a Face for Simon of Cyrene." Pages 51–64 in *The Recovery of Black Presence: An Interdisciplinary Exploration: Essays in Honor of Dr. Charles B. Copher*. Edited by Randall C. Bailey and Jacquelyn Grant. Nashville: Abingdon, 1995.

Sugirtharajah, R. S. *The Bible and the Third World: Precolonial, Colonial, and Postcolonial Encounters*. Cambridge: Cambridge University Press, 2001.

Terrell, Joanne Marie. *Power in the Blood? The Cross in African American Experience*. Maryknoll, N.Y.: Orbis.

Thurman, Howard. *Jesus and the Disinherited*. Boston: Beacon, 1976.

West, Cornell. *Race Matters*. New York: Vintage, 1994.

The GOSPEL *of* LUKE

Stephanie Buckhanon Crowder

INTRODUCTION

The Gospel of Luke begins by presenting Jesus as a Savior accessible to all people. This Jesus not only transcends race and ethnicity but also wealth and poverty. Luke's Jesus confronts the rich so that rich and poor are given equal footing (6:24-26; 12:13-21; 16:1-13, 19-31). Women, the lame, the hungry, and those deemed "other" are brought to the forefront by Luke presenting Jesus as one of and for the oppressed. Lukan theology is grounded in a Jesus who comes not just to offer compassion to those who are wounded but to speak to the evil of those who wound.

Lukan theology is congruent with African American "God-talk" that emanates from and bears degrees of suffering and oppression. Just as African American faith is not solely a belief of and for spiritual development but also a belief of and for social, political, and economic enhancement, so does Luke use faith to speak to the contextual reality of believing readers and imperialistic leaders. Faith is not simply for faith's sake, but for the holistic well-being of those who have such faith. African American followers of Jesus believe in a complete approach to finding God, and the Gospel of Luke as a document of African American faith aids in this approach.

The author of the Gospel of Luke writes to a community of Gentile believers and Roman officials. While exhorting believers, the Gospel attempts to avert persecution and further political oppression. In order to communicate to both audiences, those within and those without, Luke uses a rhetoric of subversion or hidden/coded language. This cryptic literature, while opening the door for Gentile acceptance of Jesus Christ, uses subtlety as it speaks against Roman control.

The Gospel of Luke also speaks to African American spirituality, sociology, and history. Its imagery is reminiscent of the coded nature of the spirituals and other slave songs. While these songs speak of a people's love and belief in the God of heaven, they are also replete with messages of a God who rules over the earth and who can do something about earth's sorrows and pain. Just as Luke addresses Roman domination, so did the spirituals address slave domination. Just as Luke employs a rhetoric of subversion, so do the spirituals employ hidden melodies of freedom and liberty.

Although the author probably did not name the work "Gospel of Luke" during its original composition and circulation, the book nonetheless bears the name of one who was deemed a companion of the apostle Paul and a physician (Acts 16:10-17, 21:1-18; Col 4:11-14). Nothing in the work itself, however, declares the author to be Paul's companion or a physician. Nor is there much to substantiate the time it was written. Yet references to the destruction of the second temple and Jerusalem by the Romans in 70 C.E. (19:41-44, 21:20-24) aid in narrowing the time of composition to ca. 80–90 C.E.

While the structure of the Gospel of Luke is similar to Greco-Roman history and biography, its content makes it apparent that the writer had access to Mark's Gospel and to a sayings source, often labeled simply as "Q" (from *Quelle*, the German word for "source"). In addition to material from Mark and Q, much of the content of this Gospel is unique to Luke (chaps. 22–24); this is often labeled "L."

The Gospel of Luke uses refined Greek literary style. The author, while giving a second-hand account of the ministry of Jesus Christ (1:1-2), shows throughout the ability to code-switch from the common language to a more sophisticated Greek format.

1:1-4, Prologue

Luke begins this account by acknowledging that this is not the first record of past events. In fact many before this author have told the story. The events have not only taken place but have been fulfilled (*plērophoreō*) or thoroughly accomplished. Thus, the writer indicates a historical-theological underpinning for what has occurred. The past acts were not just another form of social, political, or cultural history but indeed divine in nature and purpose.

Luke's intentions are not based on personal gain, but for the sake of Theophilus. Most scholars agree that "Theophilus" (the Greek word means "God lover") was a common name that had also been adopted into Jewish culture. Because Luke gives him the title "most excellent," some say that he was a patron of Luke. The title was used by Romans to refer to those of the equestrian order. It was also used in literary dedications to persons who were not necessarily of a high social ranking.

Luke employs "most excellent Theophilus" as a symbol that represents and pays tribute to his entire "God/gospel-loving" community of believers. This literary technique is similar to the one used in the Uncle Remus folktales, in which author Joel Harris uses animal characters to symbolize human individuals and communities. The protagonist Br'er Rabbit and his nemesis Br'er Fox signify the racial conflict between slave and master. In such tales as "Tar Baby" and "Why the Negro Is Black," Br'er Rabbit as the underdog (like the slaves) uses trickery to defeat Br'er Fox (the master).

Luke 1:5—2:52, The Infancy Narratives

Before detailing the circumstances related to Jesus' announcement, birth, and circumcision, Luke introduces John the Baptist as the one who would go before Jesus to prepare a people for the coming of the Lord.

The events detailing the arrivals of Jesus and John the Baptist are structured in the same way as an African American worship experience, where crowds of neighbors, relatives, and unknown folk rejoice with parents as their children are dedicated to the service of God. There is prayer, proclamation, prophecy, singing, call and response, and audience participation. There is even an offering: human gifts in the form of baby dedications. Those assembled with Zechariah *pray* outside as he performs his priestly duties inside. The angel Gabriel *proclaims* news of John's arrival to Zechariah and the good news of Jesus' coming to Mary. Angels *proclaim* Jesus' birth to shepherds. Zechariah *prophesies* about his son's future; Simeon does the same about the baby Jesus. Mary, Elizabeth, Zechariah, and the angels *sing* praises of God's favor and manifested glory as revealed through the infant boys. Through Gabriel and other heavenly hosts, God *calls*; Mary, Zechariah, Elizabeth, and the shepherds *respond*.

1:5-25, Zechariah and Elizabeth

African theologian Itumeleng Mosala maintains that Luke's birth narrative provides a study in ruling class discourses—their form, their intentions, and their possible effects.[1] Rich people are expected to have it all, while the poor have nothing. In Luke, these expectations are reversed.

Luke identifies Zechariah and Elizabeth as well-to-do persons of Jewish ancestry. They belong to the upper class, yet not even their status can stop the aging process or give them children. They are both old and without heirs when God sends the angel Gabriel to speak to Zechariah. As the people are praying outside the temple, Zechariah is having a personal encounter inside. Zechariah's prayers have been answered; he and his wife will have John ("God has shown favor").

Luke draws from the birth announcement of the prophet Samuel to Hannah and Elkanah (1 Sam 1–2) when he announces the birth of the latter-day prophet John the Baptist. Both Elkanah and Zechariah are priests. Both Hannah and Elizabeth are barren. Both Samuel and John the Baptist are to be nazirites, persons who abstain from certain physical and social activities for religious and spiritual purposes.

After his encounter with Gabriel in the temple, Zechariah returns to the crowd silent. The text does not say how Elizabeth became aware of what was to happen. Gabriel does not speak to her, and Zechariah cannot speak. She also experiences "silence." Yet God does what God promised. When Elizabeth conceives, she praises God; the shame of her barrenness has been removed.

Luke uses the birth of John the Baptist to narrate social reversal. Zechariah, a member of the elite, was made an outcast by his speechless, voiceless state. Though rich in status, Elizabeth was poor in honor. Her high social standing could not erase the humiliation of her childless state. The conception and birth of John the Baptist did.

1:26-38, Favor on Mary from Nazareth

Mary's home, Nazareth, is a small town in southern Galilee so obscure that it rarely appears in historical accounts. Already one can see contrasts between Mary and Elizabeth: one resides in a major city, the other in an insignificant rural area. Elizabeth is old; Mary is young. Elizabeth cannot bear children because she is too old; the young Mary is a virgin.

Elizabeth is of high status; Mary's social standing is quite low. Elizabeth's pregnancy will enhance her status; Mary's pregnancy promises to lower her status even further, at least initially. But there is reversal. Mary is given a privilege far beyond that of her well-to-do cousin: the birthing of God's Son. Luke connects the status reversal to a gender reversal; two *women* become the center of God's attention. Gabriel silenced Zechariah, and Luke is silent about Joseph's whereabouts.

The reversal continues when Mary is told that the child, whom she is to name Jesus, will be a great ruler in the line of David forever. An impoverished Mary is to give birth to royalty. Yet Mary does not readily accept the prophecy. She asks what many would ask: "How?" Renita Weems states, "Mary was not questioning the wisdom of her age. Instead she questions the inconvenience of it all. . . . She knew enough to realize that being betrothed and pregnant by anyone other than the man she was to marry was dangerous in her society."[2]

The angel assures Mary that God is orchestrating this birth and offers further proof of God's involvement by informing Mary of barren Elizabeth's conception. Barrenness and virginity prove fertile ground for what God wants to accomplish. Nothing is impossible with God. Unlike Zechariah, Mary is not punished for questioning. Her submissive words of "let it be" indicate that she is perhaps more willing than Zechariah to allow God's will to be done.

1:39-56, Mary, Elizabeth, and Worship

Mary's praise of God, commonly referred to as the *Magnificat*, bears much resemblance to the song Hannah sang in response to the coming birth of her son, Samuel (1 Sam 1–2; see also the Song of Miriam, Exod 15:21).[3] The same God who enabled Hannah to conceive Samuel empowers a woman of Mary's low status to

conceive one greater than Samuel. Luke did not compose this song. It is a hymn of the *'anawim*, the "poor" of the Lord, fashioned for God's use. The "poor of the Lord" was a designation for children, widows, foreigners, and others who were economically and socially impoverished. According to the hymn, the Lord uplifts the poor and lowly and brings down the rich and mighty.

Renita Weems states that the *Magnificat* emphasizes Mary's blessedness: "The Magnificat is also important because of what it tells about Mary. It portrays Mary as a woman of deep passion. She expresses her gratitude to God for elevating her, a poor girl from the working-class town of Nazareth, for making her name known throughout the generations, for working wondrously on her behalf and for doing so not only for her, but for others like her as well."[4]

1:57-80, The Birth of John the Baptist

Luke turns back to the birth of the son of Zechariah and Elizabeth, narrating the event as a communal moment when all who had been aware of Elizabeth's barrenness come to rejoice with her. The parents carry the child to be circumcised on the eighth day, as was the custom according to the Abrahamic covenant (Gen 17:11). In true patriarchal form, Elizabeth and Zechariah's neighbors wish to name the child Zechariah. The child's mother insists on naming him John. Finally, after experiencing such humility of tongue and of spirit, Zechariah speaks, praises God, and even prophesies what will become of John. Zechariah's song, the *Benedictus* or blessing (vv. 67-79), like the *Magnificat*, is based on the hymn of the *'anawim*, or poor ones of the Lord. The *Benedictus* contains both history and prophecy. It recalls a powerful, warring God who helped to defeat Israel's enemies and forecasts what God will do with John.

The Negro spiritual "I've Been 'Buked" bears striking similarities to the hymn of the 'anawim. Like the *Magnificat* and the *Benedictus*, the song conveys the sentiments of people down below. It is a song that comes from the experience of mistreated and abused slaves. The slaves refuse to give up on God and "lay their 'ligion down." Much like the ancient "poor ones," the slaves expressed hope in God despite their present browbeaten condition.

2:1-20, The Birth of Jesus

Providing a historical as well a political backdrop, Luke sets the birth of Jesus during reign of Emperor Octavian Augustus (31 B.C.E.–14 C.E.). The author further adds that a registration for the purpose of taxation took place under Quirinius of Syria. Luke's narration about the tax has a theological motive—to get Mary and Joseph to Bethlehem, the city of David—and a political one—to situate the birth of Jesus in a context of imperialism. He does, however, make a mistake: Quirinius's registration did not take place until 6–7 C.E.; Jesus was born ca. 3–4 B.C.E.

In Bethlehem, the Son of the Most High is born to a woman of a lowly state, in a lowly place, surrounded by lowly barn animals and persons of low socioeconomic status. The first to witness the birth are persons engaged in a lowly profession, shepherds. Shepherds were considered unclean, dishonest, lower-class persons of ill repute. Shepherds were also chosen as official beneficiaries of the good news. They are told to seek the child in the city of David, the great king who himself began life as a lowly shepherd.

Though Luke includes another song of praise and more worship as the shepherds seek and find Mary, Joseph, and the newborn Jesus in a manger, Joseph remains silent. Luke centers the birth of Jesus on Mary as a means of bringing a woman to the forefront. The Gospel's portrayal of Mary should empower present-day women to speak, not because

some men may be silent but because the reversal of one's political, economic, and social status depends on such utterances. Sojourner's Truth's bold declaration "Ain't I a Woman?" is such an utterance.

Ain't I a Woman?

That man over there says that women need to be helped into carriages and lifted over ditches, and to have the best place everywhere. Nobody ever helps me into carriages, or over mud-puddles, or gives me any best place! And ain't I a woman? Look at me! Look at my arm! I could have ploughed and planted, and gathered into barns, and no man could head me! And ain't I a woman? I could work as much and eat as much as a man—when I could get it—and bear the lash as well! And ain't I a woman? I have borne thirteen children, and seen them most all sold off to slavery, and when I cried out with my mother's grief, none but Jesus heard me! And ain't I a woman?

—Sojourner Truth, May 1851, Akron, Ohio. Cited from *Crossing the Danger Waters: Three Hundred Years of African American Writing*, ed. Deirdre Mullane (New York: Anchor, 1993), 186.

2:21-40, The Public Presentation

Simeon and Anna are devout, righteous Jewish temple-goers who confirm Jesus' glorious future role: he is the long-awaited Messiah of Israel. Simeon lifts up a fourth song of praise. This *Nunc Dimittis* ("now you are dismissing") is Simeon's farewell and offering of thanks to God for allowing him to see the One who would save and give glory to Israel. Luke includes the two to establish Jewish continuity, as Jesus is the fulfillment of the line of David and the rightful Jewish heir.

After leaving the temple, Mary, Joseph, and Jesus return to Nazareth. The favor initially bestowed upon Mary (1:28) is transferred now to her son. The lowly child receives wisdom and *charis* (favor or God's undeserving love). Luke's infancy narrative demonstrates that God's love is rooted in neither social status nor gender nor geography.

2:41-52, Rites of Passage

Twelve years after his birth, Jesus goes with his parents on their customary trip (v. 42) to Jerusalem for Passover. The journey was a rite of passage, similar to ceremonies held in some African American communities that celebrate a boy's passage from childhood to adulthood. After spending much time learning from men and other boys, a special feast was held to acknowledge a boy's transition. In a similar fashion, Jesus now moves from early childhood to a pre-teen boy who must now learn what it means to take on adult responsibilities. This journey to Jerusalem is not merely physical but one that mentally and spiritually prepares the boy Jesus for his ministry as an adult among adults.

Jesus spends an unapproved three days away from his parents in the company of teachers. The boy who has the favor of the Lord upon him not only learns but teaches. For the first time in Luke's narrative, Jesus clarifies his identity and mission. As did Gabriel, Simeon, and Anna, he declares that he has been sent by his Father, God.

3:1—4:13, Preparation for Ministry

3:1-20, The Ministry of John the Baptist

Luke juxtaposes the ministry of John the Baptist with that of Jesus. Chapter 1 begins with the birth of John the Baptist and concludes with his residing in the wilderness.

Chapter 2 switches to the birth of Jesus and ends with his teaching in the temple at age twelve. Luke makes another literary change in chap. 3 by going back to an adult John the Baptist as the voice crying in the wilderness. This comparison and contrast is similar to that of W. E. B. DuBois and Booker T. Washington. Both men had the same goal of racial progress but, because of their different backgrounds, different methods of achieving this goal. DuBois focused on higher education and civil and political action. Washington concentrated on trade schools and accommodation. Similarly, both John the Baptist and Jesus had the same goal of bringing salvation to God's people. John the Baptist did this through preaching repentance for the forgiveness of sin. Jesus, on the other hand, preached good news to the poor and the year of the Lord's favor.

The message of John the Baptist pushes further against the divisions caused by differences in social status. Those who have must share clothing and food with those who have not; those who have must cease cheating and extorting. For Luke the gospel of repentance is not merely a spiritual changing of mind or a turning from one's former ways; it has at its core the obligation and duty to empower all to complete living.

3:21-38, Jesus Eighteen Years Later

In the early 1970s Alex Haley's book and subsequent television series *Roots* spurred many African Americans to search for their familial roots. Many even today are tracing genealogies back to various countries in Africa for the sake of ancestral and cultural connection. Luke includes the genealogy of Jesus as a means of making this kind of familial connection. By tracing his line back to Adam, Luke shows that Jesus is not merely God's Son but a son of humanity. God's work in Jesus is God's work with and in all humankind.

4:1-13, Temptation in the Wilderness

Luke continues the presentation of Jesus' inaugural ministry by taking him from baptism (God's Son) to his genealogy (son of humankind) to temptation (human testing). Like John the Baptist (1:80), Luke's Jesus has a wilderness experience orchestrated by the leading of the Spirit as a time of physical isolation and spiritual preparation and maturation.

While in the wilderness Jesus undergoes three different levels of temptation by the devil (cf. 8:29, where Luke also associates the devil with the wilderness). The devil tempts Jesus to look selfishly *within*, to lift him (the devil) *up*, and to throw himself *down*. As the newly announced Son of God who descends from the human ancestry of Joseph, Jesus is tempted physically, tempted to hoard materially, and tempted to test God's divinity. Each time Jesus uses scripture, "it is written," to thwart the devil's efforts. However, Luke warns us, the enemy departs only to return at a more convenient time, at a time when the child of God least expects it (4:13; 22:3).

4:14—9:50, Ministry in Galilee

4:14-44, To Set the Captive Free

Following his temptations in the wilderness Jesus returns home to Nazareth in Galilee. While demons recognize him, many people are skeptical about this man who is merely "Joseph's son." In the synagogue on the Sabbath, he declares his mission: to bring good news to the poor, release to the captives, and sight to the blind, and to set the oppressed free.

Jesus comes to bring spiritual release and political, physical, and social refuge to those on the margins. He brings release by exorcising the demon-possessed and by curing through his touch. He risks being accused of breaking prime ordinances when he "works" or uses his hands on the Sabbath. Jesus pushes against the boundaries that limit Sabbath

Captives to Set Free

Though African American chattel slavery is no longer in existence, there are still captives to be set free: for example, refugees in Guantanamo Bay, Cuba, and the displaced in Darfur, Sudan. Many of the poor need the good news of job availability, housing, and health care. African Americans who are mentally oppressed should no longer be ashamed of their need for the liberating care that goes beyond prayer, fasting, and the laying on of hands.

"work" so that physical, mental, spiritual, and social needs can be met. The Sabbath must serve not only as a period of physical rest but as a time of spiritual work and worship. This worship must also include addressing the political and social needs of humankind. Jesus is the fulfillment, the completion of this holistic ideology.

5:1-11, A Call to Discipleship

After Jesus uses the boat of one Simon to address a large crowd, he confronts the professional need of the fisherman who has been toiling all night with little result. Simon's address of Jesus as "Master" implies a servant-lord relationship. In other words, Simon the servant will do whatever and go wherever his Lord tells him. This reference is only used in Luke (8:24; 9:33; 17:13); in parallel passages, Matthew and Mark employ "Teacher" or "Rabbi." Perhaps Luke's Simon uses the title because he witnessed Jesus heal his mother-in-law.

Initially, even though he calls Jesus "Master," Simon challenges Jesus' request to lower his nets into the deep. After seeing the great haul of fish, a repentant Simon confesses himself a sinner. Because he gives an honest assessment of his personal crisis, he is no longer "Simon" but "Simon Peter," one who is strengthened and made tougher due to personal revelation and struggle.

Luke closes this call to discipleship with Simon, James, and John returning to shore. Having just made the great catch for which they had long been working, the fishermen abandon it in order to follow the one who enabled it. Their new call to fish and catch people is so overwhelming that not even professional or familial duties can impede it. The great catch of fish portends just as great a human haul.

5:12-26, More Healings

Leprosy was the term for a range of diseases from house mold to ringworm, from psoriasis to what is termed Hansen's disease (modern-day leprosy). The common symptom was the breaking of the skin. The resulting impurity and the stigma that went with it prevented the infected person from fully participating in society. For the man who now seeks a cure from Jesus, this social barrier is as damaging as the physical malady. Jesus brings "release" to this particular "captive" by touching his untouchable skin. The embrace disrupts the social-religious boundary that ostracized him. The eventual healing makes the break permanent.

In the next story, the healing focus shifts from a physical to a spiritual emphasis. After witnessing the faith of the men who bring their friend through the roof for healing, Jesus immediately tells the man that his sins are forgiven. For the first time, Jesus initially addresses an ill person's spiritual being, not his physical brokenness.

One cannot but wonder about the presumed correlation between sickness and sin in Jesus' day. Such a connection has to be carefully and contextually analyzed today so that those with contemporary illnesses are not spiritually harassed. For example, more than one million Americans live with HIV/AIDS and the disturbing stigma attached to it. The

people of God must shift focus from "how" or "why" they contracted it to "why" they must be touched and "how" they can be healed. This transfiguration of attitude is particularly important in the African American community, which accounts for 50 percent of new HIV cases even though African Americans make up only 12 percent of the population.

5:27-39, A Call to the Unlikely

In another call scene, Jesus seeks a tax collector named Levi and commands him to follow. Like Peter, James, and John, Levi too leaves everything, his booth and his business, to follow Jesus. While, as fishermen, Peter, James, and John held what were considered noble professions, Levi's detested position aligns him with the imperial interests of the Roman government and therefore places him at odds with those suffering under Roman rule.

Luke's narration implies that those who follow Jesus are pleased with their decision; Levi gives a banquet and celebrates his new-found calling. This banquet is attended by many of Levi's colleagues as well as some disgruntled Pharisees and scribes. These leaders shun such "secular" employment. Jesus, however, inaugurates a new, inclusive way of life, a new wine; all are welcome to feast at the Lord's banquet table.

6:1-11, More on the Sabbath

Luke includes two Sabbath stories that depict Jesus in violation of the sacred law: one narrates his disciples plucking grain; another shows him healing on the Sabbath, during which only life-saving activities were permissible. Plucking grain and healing damaged limbs did not meet such a standard. Jesus obliterates the need for such a standard when he declares himself the Son of Man, who is lord of the Sabbath. He, not tradition, decides now what is acceptable or permissible on this day. His behavior indicates that not the law but meeting the needs of human hunger and wholeness is the new standard. His behavior also contributes to the rising conflict between Jesus and the Pharisees.

The Sabbath and its call to service are an integral part of the black church. Corporate worship seeks to prompt attendees not only to praise and honor God, but to become disciples, followers, and even to be sent out for the cause of Christ. Luke's Jesus redefines what had been the Sabbath norm for the sake of urging those who would follow him to cater to the needs of the de-centered. Addressing hunger and the right to use one's hands to provide for one's self and others must be the work of the church even if this intervention causes conflict. Did not the work of Martin Luther King Jr. and the civil rights movement cause conflict with proponents of segregation like Bull Connor? Did not Malcolm X's voice for the liberation of African Americans by any means possible pose problems for the Kennedy administration? The cause must be worth the conflict it causes.

6:12-16, The Twelve Apostles

Luke lists the remaining eight disciples (apostles) without mentioning the details of their calls. Unlike Matthew (10:1-4) and Mark (3:13-19), Luke does not use nicknames for some of the twelve, for example, "Sons of Thunder." He does not mention Levi the tax collector, although most identify him as the person called Matthew in the Markan and Matthean versions. Luke lists a second Judas and distinguishes the two by stating that one is a traitor.

Only after Jesus has separated himself from others and has had time in prayer does he call those who are to share closely with him. Luke implies that such a call was not to be made lightly, but only after much reflection and meditation. In the words of many African American Christians, Jesus has just had a

"sweet hour of prayer" moment (referring to the gospel song with that title).

6:17-49, Various Teachings

After descending from the mountain with his newly appointed apostles, a larger group termed "disciples" and an even greater multitude of people from Jewish and Gentile areas come to hear Jesus and to be healed. Jesus engages in a series of teachings that address the social dislocation of the masses.

Unlike Matthew's Sermon on the Mount (5:1—7:29), Luke's "Sermon on the Plain" (Luke never uses the word "sermon," and his compilation of Jesus' sayings is one-fourth the length of Matthew's) begins not with nine blessings but four. His Beatitudes address the causes of social, political, and economic oppression: poverty, hunger, sadness, and hatred. In Luke, Jesus never strays from his messianic declaration to bring release and to set free. Luke's presentation of the blessings also differs from Matthew's end-times approach. Marginalizing circumstances must not be ignored, because they affect those who would follow Jesus. Jesus counters the blessings with here-and-now woes or warnings to those who experience richness, fullness, happiness, and love. Their time to experience the opposite is coming now, not in a future, heavenly setting.

Through a series of teachings, or "neighborly advice," Jesus addresses relationships. The oppressed must not become the oppressor. Love must not be limited or confined to those would return love. Help must be extended to all and not taken by force, as in the Roman way of conscription or forced hospitality. Those who would follow him must examine their own lives and behavior before instructing or disciplining others. Those who have left family, businesses, and other possessions must realize that it is simply not enough to leave; they must remain committed.

7:1-10, The Centurion and the Ill Slave

This story, also found in Matt 8:5-13 and John 4:46-53, centers on social and class location. The centurion is a Roman official who values a slave under his political and social authority. Some Jews who had great respect for the centurion approach Jesus on his behalf. The centurion, however, does not feel "worthy" enough to host Jesus in his home. Recognizing the power of a truly authoritative word to work across even great distance, he insists that Jesus command the healing from outside the house. Luke has fashioned out of this story an instructive narration about social reversal. The powerful and respected centurion rightly sees in the lowly Jesus a power greater than his own. For that insight he is praised. The pericope is reminiscent of slave stories that narrated the complex relationship between slaves and their masters. Like the centurion, the masters were the recognized powers. And yet slaves serving as midwives and those who had knowledge of healing roots and cures that an ailing "massah" might need held a certain power of their own. In such "reversal" instances when an infirm master depended upon a healthy and knowledgeable slave, class dynamics succumbed to human frailty.

7:11-17, In Nain

In a town southeast of Nazareth Jesus encounters the funeral procession of a mother's only child. Because her son was probably her primary means of support, she has lost all economic security. The social security he provided as "family" was lost as well. Both her well-being and her identity were jeopardized.

The story resembles the Elijah (1 Kgs 17:17-24) and Elisha (2 Kgs 4:32-37) narratives, which involve widows, prophets at the city gates, and sons returned to their mothers. As in the case of the centurion story, Jesus issues a verbal order and resurrects the widow's son at a distance. For the first time Luke refers

to Jesus as the "Lord" who shows compassion. The crowd reinforces the Elijah and Elisha connection by calling him a prophet.

7:18-35, More on Jesus and John

After witnessing Jesus' restoration of the widow's son and, apparently, many other miracles and healings, the disciples of the imprisoned John the Baptist (cf. 3:19-20) inform him of all Jesus has done. John's request for information from Jesus about his identity is not one of doubt but anxious messianic expectation.

After confirming his messianic status, Jesus affirms John's ministry. John's proclamations about a coming one (3:4) were correct; Jesus is that one. In addition, Jesus notes the division not only over John's activities but also over his own ministry. John was allegedly too ascetic, Jesus too "extravagant." Schisms caused for such childish reasons are indicative of those who lack wisdom or God's divine guidance and instruction.

7:36-50, A Woman Needing Forgiveness/ Release

When Jesus dines with one Simon the Pharisee, a woman described only as "sinful" comes to the table from behind Jesus to anoint his feet (Matt 26:6-13//Mark 14:3-9//John 12:1-8). Though Luke does not state the nature of the sin, many have assumed it to be prostitution because of her free-flowing hair and her alabaster jar of ointment. She could just as easily have been a liar or thief or married to someone who engaged in unethical behavior. Luke's point is that her sin warrants a great emotional and public display of need.

What upsets Simon is not just the woman's presence but her behavior and Jesus' willingness to allow it. To defend himself, Jesus uses an illustration of debt cancellation that brings to the surface the woman's and (covertly) Simon's need for forgiveness and release. In this case Luke's reversal works by lifting the woman up and bringing Simon down, so that they meet on an equal plane of divine disfavor. In God's sight both are sinners; both require messianic intervention. Jesus provides that intervention for the woman by forgiving her sins. The story resonates with the one about the four companions who lower their friend through a roof to Jesus. When the man's sins are forgiven, many question Jesus' behavior as arrogantly blasphemous (5:17-26). In both cases, the Greek word for forgiveness, *aphesis*, is the same root used for "release" in Jesus' inaugural proclamation (4:18-20). Despite the consternation this kind of behavior brings, Jesus must keep performing it because it represents the kind of ministry for which he has been sent.

The series of stories narrated in chap. 7 share much in common with the life story of the African American church. Like the Roman centurion, the black church, even with its history of political fortitude as shown during the civil rights movement, must recognize that, when it faces great political obstacles in the future, there is a force even more powerful upon which it can rely. Like the widow of Nain, who acknowledged her dependence on her son for economic and social well-being, the black church must recognize that its future and perhaps the future of black society as a whole are dependent on the restoration and revival of struggling, oppressed, and ever more desperate African American men. Like John the Baptist, the black church must seek out and respond to the one who represents God's future rule in this present age. Like the sinner woman, the black church must do whatever it takes to catch hold of that messianic representative and use his power to free itself and others from whatever sin or dysfunction that binds and hinders its work.

8:1-3, Women on the Journey

Not only does Jesus cure Mary Magdalene, Joanna, and Susanna; they also become co-laborers with him. Moreover, the women provide for Jesus and the disciples out of their own material and financial resources. With the inclusion of this story, Luke provides countercultural information about the status of women during the author's time. When he portrays these women as followers who are free from physical and spiritual exigencies and have the means to support men, he portrays Jesus' ministry as one that redefines the social status and role of women.

Many have used this text in the black church to affirm the role of women as pastors, preachers, and/or other types of church leaders. Though there may be dispute over whether the women only served the disciples or also spread the good news, it cannot be overlooked that these women were a visible and necessary force within the Jesus movement. African American women are just as visible and necessary a force in the life of the black church. The number of African American women in seminary alone increased by more than 600 percent during the years 1972–1984.[5] Instead of fighting the numbers, the black church must do as Jesus did: embrace the presence of women and accept the resources they have to offer.

8:4-21, Of Seeds and Soil

Using a second parable of sowing and harvesting (6:39-42), Jesus explains how persons could respond to his ministry in one of four ways. (1) Like the seeds eaten by birds, persons could receive the message of Jesus only to have Satan stunt their growth. (2) Like seeds on rocky, rootless, dry places, persons could allow life's difficulties to harden their hearts toward God and cease believing. (3) Like seeds among thorns, persons could allow riches, fame, and pressure to prick their faith and impede spiritual growth. Or (4) Like seeds on good soil, people could respond to the mes-

Black Soil

The concept of harvesting and plowing is not foreign to African or African American culture. Rice, tobacco, cotton, and yams are only a few of the fruits of African and African American agricultural labor. Forced into agricultural labor as slaves on southern plantations, the "stolen" labor of African Americans became the economic foundation of the ante-bellum American South. Free blacks maintained a productive connection with the soil following the Civil War. George Washington Carver's cultivation and seemingly infinitesimal use of the peanut speaks to the strong relationship between land and people. Even today African American farmers steadily till the land and make it right and ripe for the seed. Just as Jesus used this imagery of land and people to speak two thousand years ago, African American preachers can call upon the same imagery in a way that speaks from and to the African American context.

African American preachers, if they are to follow Jesus' model of using the context of his people as the foundation for his parables, should also not only repeat Jesus but follow his lead into new symbolic territory. After all, the majority of African Americans today live in the urban centers of the United States. African American preachers must find equally potent urban images to convey their thoughts about the movement of God's rule into the human arena if they hope to connect their listeners to the Word of God in the same way that Jesus did in his primarily agricultural context. How do sowers sow on an urban landscape?

---

sage of Jesus by growing and producing the fruit of faith.

8:22-55, More Personal Healings

How powerful is Jesus? When this sower encounters a man possessed with a legion of demons, he restores his right mind and his rightful place in society with a healing word (vv. 26-39). Not only does his word reverse the man's expulsion from "acceptable" society, but it also reverses the social and political understanding about the strength of Rome and Roman arms. As the representation of its power and might, the "Legion" (v. 30) was Rome. Rome took over whole countries, disrupted their peace, and destroyed their communities in the same way that this Legion took over, disrupted, and destroyed the life of the man it possessed. But when Rome, like the demon, faced the word of God, Rome could not and would not stand.

The Jesus who was not afraid to face a Legion was certainly not afraid to be touched by a bleeding and therefore ritually unclean woman (vv. 43-48). In her story, Luke reaches through social barriers to address gender and physiology. The heart of the matter is not the source of the woman's "issue" or hemorrhaging, but the fact that because of her faith she pushes her impure body boldly into an arena where even a healthy woman should not have been. It is a similar context for a little girl whom custom would dictate to be seen and not heard (vv. 40-42, 49-56). On the contrary, Jesus orders her to "get up and eat." Jesus releases persons in bondage because of spirits, societal fences, and gender constructions.

9:1-27, Identity Crisis

In an episode of *Roots*, Alex Haley's main character, Kunta Kinte, refuses to adopt his slave name. In a public spectacle that all the slaves on the plantation witness, Kunta Kinte's master brutally beats him while repeatedly asking, "What is your name?" In the end, a bloodied Kunta Kinte is compelled to grudgingly accept the new name, Toby.

In Luke's narration, Jesus faces a comparable type of identity crisis. What do people think of him. Who is he? What is his name? Although his miraculous feeding alludes to his divine nature, substantial questions remain about this suffering Son of Man. Who is he? What is his *real* name?

9:28-50, The Great Children

Jesus' inner circle, Peter, James, and John, are with him on the Mount of Transfiguration. Yet, even after witnessing such an epiphany, they, like the other disciples, have so little faith in him and their relationship with him that they are ineffective in healing a demon-possessed child. Here, as in several other cases, Jesus engages children in order to teach the disciples two lessons: First, like children, they have much to learn, and time is short. Second, those with childlike openness to the movement of God in the world are the greatest.

The Children's Defense Fund (CDF) also upholds the importance of our learning from and advocating for children. For more than thirty years this organization has urgently called this nation to "leave no child behind." Advocating for housing, family support, and better education and nutrition for children, the CDF partners with businesses, the government, community-based organizations, and religious institutions to "stand in the gap" for even the youngest infant. Children are not the "least of these"; they are the models of greatness whom Jesus upholds and the world, if it would achieve the potential God has given it, must affirm.

9:51—19:27, JOURNEY TO JERUSALEM

9:51—10:42, Hospitality and/in Ministry

On the Underground Railroad, slaves "stole away" from the South to the free North. The destitute, fleeing slaves depended on the kindness and hospitality of black and white strangers for food, shelter, clothing, and a little rest.

At 10:3-16, Jesus gives instructions regarding a ministry that was also dependent on hospitality. His directives to the seventy provide a harsh window into the life of a disciple. It is an underground life whose journey toward God did not allow for familial or professional attachments or many private possessions. A person who risks her life in following Jesus must rely on the mercy of others, just as she surely had to rely in every circumstance on the mercy of God. It is a chance slaves were willing to take for freedom. It is a chance believers must take in order to be free and set the captive free.

Luke provides two examples to demonstrate the relationship between hospitality and ministry. A Samaritan helps a victim of violence (10:29-37). Luke does not designate the Samaritan as "good." Neither does he specifically identify the race of the beaten man. The Samaritan's merciful behavior is highlighted; it is paradigmatic of Jesus' own work and the work Jesus expects from and for his disciples.

In the second story, a hospitable Martha welcomes Jesus into her home and works preparing the food that will make him comfortable (10:38-42). Her sister Mary welcomes Jesus in another fashion; she converses with him and listens to his word. According to the narrative, the greatest act of hospitality a person can afford a disciple of Jesus, what Jesus calls the "better part," is not the provision for physical sustenance but the attention to the Word of God that the disciple conveys.

11:1-13, On Prayer

Luke's version of a model prayer differs substantially from Matthew's; it focuses more on addressing present human needs and less on seeking spiritual reward in the "sweet by and by." The request is for bread *today*, and for forgiveness and release from *present* indebtedness. Even the narrative about the friend who needs concentrates on attention to current physical need.

This hope for God's present intervention in a material way can also be seen in Negro spirituals like "Many Thousand Gone."

> No more auction block for me, no more, no more.
> No more auction block for me, many thousand gone.
> No more hundred lash for me, no more, no more.
> No more hundred lash for me, many thousand gone.

This song speaks to the slave's condition of oppressive physical abuse. And yet it also affirms the slave's determination to escape this downtrodden state. Many thousands have gone and left this hardship behind. The speaker intends to do the same, and through his singing encourages others to do so too.

11:14-27, What to Do with a Demon?

Jesus identifies Beelzebul as the leader of demons who authorizes and enables the overpowering possession of people and homes. Even if they are cast out, they do not go away. Into the unsuspecting and unfaithful they return with more power and more demons.

The Negro spirituals share this concern

about the might of demons. In these songs Satan and his demonic minions symbolize slavemasters who employed trickery and deceit to keep slaves ignorant and docile. In "Ezek'el Saw de Wheel," "Ol' Satan wears a club foot shoe. If you don't min', he'll slip it on you." Satan is crooked and will try to get people to be just as crooked. Just as Luke incorporates verses on the devil so that the student of Jesus might learn of the enemy, the spirituals provided a means for the slave to teach and learn about the adversary in order to defeat him in the end.

11:29-53, Of Signs and Sheba

Although Jesus has been performing miracles and giving signs, like the feeding of the five thousand, exorcisms, and other acts of great healing, his faithless generation wants a sign. In other words, they want more. Apparently, they miss the point that Jesus, as Son of Man, *is* the Sign they seek. The time will come when the Queen of Sheba, the Queen of the South, will attest to his greatness.

The Queen of Sheba (1 Kgs 10:1-13; 2 Chr 9:1-9; Matt 12:39) is the Queen of Ethiopia and Egypt. Though many maintain that she was actually from Arabia, there is evidence to support Africa as her place of origin. Because of her encounter with Solomon and the many fine gifts that she brought to him, the report of her fame was still far and wide even during the first century C.E. Luke lifts this queen as an honest witness from the past and a participant in the future judgment who will shed light on the present purpose of Jesus. In using her in this way, Jesus once again transcends society's gender barriers. A woman's witness becomes the prime witness. Just as significantly, Luke also abolishes racial-ethnic barriers when he makes an African the symbol of appropriate belief. Indeed, this will not be the last time in Luke's Gospel that an African is at the forefront.

12:1-59, Be Forewarned

There are three key warnings in this chapter. First, because the increasing crowds are intensifying in hostility against Jesus, Jesus warns his listeners about the Pharisees who try to harm the body (vv. 1-7). Second, Jesus warns the large crowd against the danger of hoarding material goods (vv. 13-34). Storing without sharing is selfish. God will provide for individual need. Stinginess and hoarding are signs of faithlessness. Third, Jesus warns against the lack of diligent watching (vv. 35-40). Just as God is careful to note the very hairs on a human head, so must the believer be careful to discern how God is acting in the present and future.

The analogy Luke uses to illustrate this last admonition is interesting. Jesus advises his hearers to act like slaves waiting for their master (vv. 41-48). The slave must be alert, ready to please the master, or else the slave will receive a severe beating. The African American history of slavery, with its numerous accounts of human selling, conscription of behavior, and gruesome beatings makes this Jesus saying a disturbing one.

13:1-17, A Woman Restored

Again reinterpreting the meaning of the Sabbath as a time "to set the captive free and let the oppressed go free," Luke narrates the Sabbath healing of a woman bent over for eighteen years. This is the second of a three-part Sabbath healings series (6:6-11;14:1-6). Luke employs agricultural language, untying an "ox or donkey" (v. 15), not only to address the negative mind-set toward women but also to show the extent of the woman's burden and thus her need for deliverance. Jesus restores her humanity by calling her to him and by touching her, thereby symbolically drawing an "untouchable" once again into community. He restores her racial and ethnic identity by referring to her as a daughter of Abraham.

Talking about the Sabbath as an entrée to addressing racial, social, and health disparities is not new or novel to the black church. The Sabbath has always been a time for not only honoring God but discerning how to honor God through love for one another and service to one another. George Barna and Harry Jackson maintain that "one of the areas that has changed little in recent years . . . is the gap between how much time blacks and whites spend at church. The idea of a Sabbath still resonates within black culture; this concept was lost more than a quarter century ago in white America."[6] The Sabbath has and must continue to be not only a time for singing, praying, teaching, silence, and preaching as forms of praise and worship of God but also a time to discern and discuss social obligations, political involvement, and emotional healing. What happens on the Sabbath must provide impetus for what happens the other six days of the week.

13:18-35, Of Little Beginnings

Jesus again employs domestic language to declare that, though the kingdom of God looks small in comparison to the "kingdom" of Herod the Fox, in the end God's reign will be great. What appears small and insignificant now will be an entity of honor and glory in the future. Something that is miniscule now can and will have a magnificent impact in the years to come.

Gabriel Prosser's rebellion, Denmark Vesey's uprising, and Nat Turner's revolt seemed small in comparison to the slave system they challenged. They were only individuals attempting to overturn a well-secured system of economic exploitation and physical maltreatment. But Prosser's actions connected with those of Vesey, and Vesey's were of the same essence as Turner's. One act of discontent led to other acts of discontent. One act of antagonism incited others. A little yeast helped to leaven the loaf of or resistance against slavery. This yeast helped produce the Emancipation Proclamation, the Reconstruction voices of Frederick Douglass and Maria Stewart, Ida B. Wells in the early twentieth century, and the civil rights movement. And now "free" African Americans have a net worth of more than $700 billion. A little goes a long way.

14:1-6, Healing on the Sabbath

In Luke's final Sabbath healing text, Jesus is eating at the house of another Pharisee (11:37). Clearly, although Luke reports the Pharisees as being hostile to Jesus and lying in wait for him (11:53-54), Jesus does not run from them. Instead in approaching the man with dropsy, Jesus stirs up more trouble and unrest with an "in your face" method of confrontation. He not only engages the Pharisees on their own turf but challenges them on their area of expertise: the law (Torah). What does the law say about curing someone? What is the lawful thing to do about a man in need?

14:7-24, Banquet Etiquette

Although he is himself just an invited guest, Jesus does not shy away from offering tips on banquet etiquette. He boldly tells guests how they must behave at a dinner party. Humility is the key to gaining the best seat in the house. Jesus then instructs the host on proper meal decorum. Instead of inviting those who can return the favor, the host must welcome persons who are most in need—the marginalized, the sick, the outcast, the man and woman whom society shuns. (See sidebar on p. 174.)

14:25-34, Specifics on Discipleship

Jesus gives specifics on the cost of discipleship. The disciple must surrender personal relationships (9:57-62), that is, parents, spouse, children, and siblings. The disciple must also surrender self. A true believer is willing to yield one's own life for the sake of the gospel. A believer must jettison all personal baggage so that he or she has room to carry the cross, that is, the message of Jesus. Like flavorless salt, a person too concerned with self is good for nothing.

Canning, "making preserves" or "preserving," is a common practice in African American culture. Canning is the planting, growing, picking, washing, cooking, mixing, and jarring of vegetables or fruit for later use. Peaches, apples, blackberries, and other edibles

Breaking Lawful Laws

Jim Crow laws and grandfather clauses established segregated accommodations for blacks and whites. These (il)legal maneuverings also prevented blacks from being able to vote. Poll taxes, reading tests, and in some case police presence scared many blacks from voting booths. Signs with "white only" relegated blacks to less than equal facilities. African American activists did not run away from these laws or the people who made them, but challenged them in the settings where the laws were supposed to function with an "in your face" method of confrontation similar to Jesus'. This was particularly the case with the sit-ins, in which African American activists sat at tables or at lunch counters with the very persons who created and supported laws banning such integrationist behavior.

Guess Who's Coming to Dinner?

Guess Who's Coming to Dinner? the 1967 Hollywood movie starring Sidney Poitier, Katharine Hepburn, Spencer Tracy, and Katharine Houghton, tells of a white woman engaged to a world-renowned black doctor. The two met in Hawaii, and after only ten days they became engaged. (African American comedian Bernie Mac stars in a contemporary remake of the film, titled *Guess Who*; he plays a father whose daughter is engaged to a white man.) At the engagement dinner in the home of the woman's parents, both Poitier's and Houghton's fathers are against this "type" of marriage. They are afraid of the racial hatred their children and possible grandchildren would endure. The mothers approve reluctantly.

This movie, produced during the height of the civil rights movement, addressed issues regarding "appropriate" behavior between blacks and whites. Is romantic love between the two races acceptable? It also addressed concerns over physical separation and segregated facilities. What is the place of an educated black man in the home of whites? Should he or any other black be invited? (In the original movie Isabel Sanford portrayed a maid in the white family's household). Luke's Jesus answers with a resounding Yes! People of every race, economic background, and social standing, and with any physical ailment, must be at our banquet table and are surely welcome at the table of the Lord.

---

are "preserved" in such a way that their flavor is enhanced. This process ensures that these items will be edible for a long time. Any misstep in the process proves detrimental to the taste and quality of the fruit.

Luke's take on discipleship is that there are not only steps to becoming a disciple but also measures a disciple must take in order to "preserve" her or his purpose, worth, or "salt." This follower must continually trust Jesus and give up ties to people and personhood that hinder the work of the gospel. If the believer is to be useful and her or his value "preserved," then the process of sacrifice is essential.

15:1-32, The Lost and Found

It is somewhat surprising to find the Pharisees grumbling because Jesus is eating with sinners. He had already established himself as one who did not adhere to rituals of purity and exclusion. Jesus previously defied cleanliness customs by not washing his hands, even when he ate with some Pharisees (11:37-38)! So why is there so much fuss? Why the steady confusion? Apparently, the Pharisees and the disciples have one rather notable and dubious trait in common: when it comes to Jesus' teaching, they "just don't get it."

Trying to show that there are more important matters than sanitation or ritual purity, Jesus shares three parables addressing the spiritually lost and the spiritually found. *Lost* is a reference either to people who have never experienced a relationship with God or to persons who have turned away from this relationship. The three stories highlight three sets of circumstances with three distinctive responses. Each circumstance is symbolic of human vicissitudes and how God responds to those who have lost their way. The sheep parable is a metaphor for persons who stray from a group and end up in the wilderness. For Luke, the wilderness is a place of physical isolation and spiritual maturation (see the comments on 4:1-13). God even goes to the dry, deserted places to redeem one human being. The parable of the lost coin demonstrates how persons may "lose" others or cause them to stray. Yet God searches until the lost treasure, the person's soul, returns to its Creator. The story of the prodigal son reminds the reader that some people forsake their spiritual foundation for immediate gratification. God does not focus on why or how the person becomes "lost." God rejoices and celebrates the individual's homecoming. Through all three examples, Jesus provides an analogy of a God who does whatever it takes to reconcile humanity to God's self.

During the 1970s, the television show *Good Times* featured an all-black family. James, the father, worked various manual jobs to pay the rent and put food on the table. Florida, the mother, often stayed home and took care of the domestic responsibilities. The three children, J. J. (the oldest), Thelma, and Michael (the youngest), completed this inner-city family living in a high-rise in Chicago.

During one episode, J. J. became engaged to his prom date, Diana. Much to the disapproval of both sets of parents, the couple ran away to elope. Diana was addicted to heroin. In a rush to carry out the elopement, J. J. mistakenly took his sister's purse instead of Diana's. Diana's purse contained her "medicine." In the midst of a withdrawal meltdown, Diana fled from their hotel. A humiliated and "lost" J. J. now had a moment to call his parents. His parents informed him about Diana's problem and begged him to come home. Although he had defied them and caused much them worry and stress, in effect, devaluing and breaking the trust he had established

with them, his parents still wanted him to come home.

Like the father of the elder son who ran away, James and Florida rejoiced when J. J. called. They accepted his collect call and welcomed him back. They were not concerned about where he was or what he was doing. They simply wanted him to come home. According to Jesus, God is not concerned about past riotous living, past straying away, or past wilderness experiences. God beckons the lost one: "Come home to me." God challenges the community: "Rejoice and do not judge."

16:1-13, Dishonest with Good Reason

In a second illustration (12:13-21) of the impact of wealth and riches in the Lukan community, Jesus tells a parable about a manager who uses "the system" for his own benefit. Facing unemployment and poverty himself, the manager reduces the debt of persons fiscally bound to his supervisor. The manager does this with the realization that he is not physically able to work and has too much pride to be found wanting. Thus he hopes those whose debts are forgiven will look kindly on him in the future.

While many have termed the manager dishonest, he merely employs capitalistic bartering for the sake of his personal well-being. He does what he has seen his supervisor do in order to survive. Luke makes it clear that there is a system of financial exploitation in place and encourages those in his community to do what they have heard and seen the rich do in order to survive.

Justin Ukpong provides an interpretation that credits the manager. He views this narrative through the lens of African peasant farmers indebted to rich produce traders. The produce traders hire managers to transact business, that is, make loans for them. The loans for medical expenses or children's school fees are refundable, with interest rates ranging from 50 percent to 100 percent.[7] Ukpong concludes his take on the story in this way:

> This perspective of reading has led to the conclusion that the rich man in the story is not the benevolent grand personage he is often thought to be, but an exploiter. The reading has also concluded that the manager of the estate is not the villain . . . but the hero of the story. . . . The approach has brought to life the image of the peasant farmers in the story, an image not generally evident when other exegetical approaches are used.[8]

This reading brings to life not only the image of African peasant farmers, but also the plight of African American *farmers*, the plight of African American *families*, and the plight of the African Americans who have *lost faith* in the American justice system. Fearing hunger and homelessness, many use a well-established, corrupt system in order to survive and meet everyday needs. For example, supposedly "retired" senior citizens receiving Social Security checks find themselves working in order to supplement their income because these monthly checks are not enough to meet needs. Yet any supplemental income is subject to taxes that seniors cannot afford. Thus some seniors receive funds from these extra jobs in cash or "under the table."

16:14-31, More Problems with Riches

In this third story on the trouble of riches, Jesus goes from addressing the earthly construct of systematic economic exploitation to addressing the eternal consequences of misused financial gain. A rich man who had all of the fine accoutrements on earth goes to Hades because he did not share his wealth. Lazarus goes to heaven and rests in the bosom of Abraham. Lazarus's needs are provided for after he dies. In heaven the poor man finds the contentment he did not have on earth. In Hades the rich man suffers, something he did not experience on earth. What a reversal this is!

The reader cannot help but ask whether the rich man is a "murderer" because he did nothing to help Lazarus in his destitute state. Just as significant is the question whether Jesus advocates that provisions for the needy only come in the afterlife. Luke suggests that there are actions on earth that can affect a person's eternal status. The rich man's refusal to provide food for Lazarus, to give him medical attention, or to offer him shelter put Lazarus in a precarious state, a state that contributed to Lazarus's demise and subsequent death. On the other hand, Luke portrays Lazarus as a recipient of "in the sweet by and by" goods. Abraham takes care of him. Although relief for Lazarus comes in eternity, Jesus still warns the rich that something must be done on earth to help the hungry, the homeless, and the helpless. The request to "warn his brothers" serves as a red flag that there are everlasting consequences for societal irresponsibility.

Through this chapter's second narrative, the author contrasts two responses to poverty and wealth. The savvy manager was able to use "the system" to advocate for himself. On the contrary, Lazarus did not verbally advocate for himself, though his daily presence at the gate spoke loudly and clearly.

There was a "system" in Luke's day, and there is a "system" today. It is a system that benefits from keeping the poor poor and the rich rich. It is a system in which some, like the manager, are able to discern how to work within it and survive, while others, like Lazarus, die trying. It is a system that says a minimum wage of $5.15 per hour, which creates a situation of "working poor," is enough. It is a system that says a family of four is not in poverty if it makes more than $20,000 a year. It is a system in which African Americans comprise

24 percent of the poor but only 12 percent of the entire U.S. population. There is a capitalistic, well-established economic "system" in place. Women and men of God must learn to use it or be abused by it.

17:1-10, Luke, the Oppressed

In a fourth narrative employing "slave" language (see 7:1-10; 12:35-48; 16:13), Luke presents an alternative view to being in bondage. Instead of a master advocating for his servant, a slave watching for his master's return, or a slave being faithful to one master, Luke now portrays slaves as groveling and gratefully carrying out their duties. Because the slave admits to his or her own worthlessness, anything that he or she does is expected but is not enough for commendation. The slave does what the slave is supposed to do.

Through this pericope Luke situates himself subversively as a slave. He is only a servant obligated to obedience. The author identifies with the marginalized state of his community, a people under Roman domination. Luke writes because, as a subject with literary ability, he is expected to write. Luke presents himself in this light so as not to arouse the suspicion of Roman authorities or to put himself or his community in danger. The subversion occurs through Luke's realization that though he is less than others, one greater than he (and others!) has come to set him and those enslaved like him free.

17:11-19, More on the Samaritans

Although Jesus' initial interaction with the Samaritans was negative (9:51-56), subsequent illustrations about and encounters with this cultural group (10:29-37) proved favorable. Not only did he heal ten lepers, but one of them, a Samaritan, returned to give thanks. Though deemed an ethnic outsider and not expected to honor a Jew, this leper prostrated himself at the feet of the "King of the Jews" in gratitude. Jesus on his way to Jerusalem to die showed that the kingdom of God is for all. His mission is for persons of all races, cultures, and geographical backgrounds.

17:20-37, Where Is the Kingdom of God?

Jesus offers another description of the kingdom of God. It is among the people. It is within the people. Previously Jesus offered the kingdom of God as something small that

Passive Resistance

Luke's actions are similar to those of African poet Phillis Wheatley. Wheatley, a native of Senegal, arrived in Boston on a slave ship in 1761. She was the first woman of African descent to have a book published. Her literary and verbal skills won her much acclaim. However, Wheatley's works did not attack, even subliminally, the slave system. They often expressed her gratitude for having met Christian missionaries who helped her find God. In addition her patriotic works also spoke highly of George Washington and other founding fathers.

Some might argue that Wheatley's writings were passive aggressive and thus still oriented toward resistance. While she did not attack slavery directly, her writings did bring attention to its brutality. His fear of Rome's power and potential retribution forced Luke to challenge Roman imperialism in the same passive aggressive manner.

would make a large impact like yeast and mustard seeds. The kingdom has secrets. It is child-friendly. This kingdom is also the good news. This good news is not some external manifestation. It is God at work within the people in order to bring the people back into right relationship with God. Luke's Jesus portrays God's reign, God's dominion, as beginning with the individual. Yes, it is small in that it starts with one person. But it is this one person who can affect the life of another, who in turn can impart the kingdom news to another, and so on ad infinitum.

The Montgomery bus boycott began because one woman, Rosa Parks, refused to surrender her seat. Sit-ins in Nashville, Tennessee; Greensboro, North Carolina; and other cities began because a few black customers decided they deserved service at all-white restaurants. The passion for freedom started within these and other movers and shakers of the civil rights movement. It was the kingdom of God within our foreparents that urged them, and it is the kingdom of God within us that stirs us to share the good news and proclaim the year of the Lord's favor for all people.

18:1-17, Justice for All

Using two parables, Jesus speaks to issues of justice. A widow represents those who continue to pray for God to resolve an unjust situation. Because of the persistent nature of the petitioner, Jesus maintains that God will act to bring resolution to the unfair circumstance. In the second parable the prayer of a humble tax collector is affirmed over the prayer of a haughty Pharisee. It is the self-identified, sinning, tax collector who "goes home justified."

It is God who defines and orchestrates justice, or fairness, according to Luke. Whether the injustice comes from human-to-human misdeeds or whether it emanates from personal wrong, God justifies or makes right

so that good may be done. Furthermore, in each instance Luke shows how important it is that people initiate the call for justice. When we call, God answers. When we cry out, God responds. When we beg and implore God to come and see about us, God comes to make it all right.

The members of the United States Supreme Court bear the title "Justice." Implied in the nomenclature is the precept that all nine of these persons will make right whatever wrong has occurred. The first African American to serve on the Supreme Court, Thurgood Marshall, had a history of "making it right" through his legal work with the NAACP. His key role in the 1954 *Brown v. Board of Education of Topeka* school desegregation case changed the course of America. From 1967 until his retirement in 1991, Justice Marshall served on the Supreme Court. His voting record shows that he heard the persistent pleas of women and African Americans and tried to "do justice."

18:18-43, Giving It All Up

In this fourth take on riches and wealth, Luke moves from the foolishness of hoarding goods (12:13-21) to an imperative to sell everything and give to the poor. Unlike the parable of poor Lazarus, who did not reap earthly benefits, Luke now advocates that the poor must reap on earth. The poor must receive here and now from the wealthy. Any rich person who gives to the needy will in turn gain treasure in heaven.

Made uncomfortable by this instruction, a vocal Peter reminds Jesus that he was one of the first to leave boat and business to follow him. Jesus assures Peter that he will get everything back now and in eternity. What family, what material goods the disciple foregoes for the kingdom of God, God will restore.

The African American church can use a text like this to address the dangers of prosperity preaching. Jesus did indeed say that whatever the disciple lost for the kingdom of God would be restored now. The key to interpreting that saying is the phrase "for the kingdom of God." Too often name-it-and-claim-it theology is rooted in a narcissistic, self-centered materialism aimed at self-betterment. Goods lost and regained for the kingdom are not goods intended for personal, self-serving use. Proper prosperity must be used instead to help the poor and thus further the work of God on earth.

19:1-10, Another Repentant Tax Collector

In Jericho Jesus meets a rich chief tax collector. Zacchaeus's job and title readily associate him with Roman culture and imperialism. Unlike the previously portrayed tax collectors, however, Zacchaeus no longer desires to be connected with ill-gotten economic gain. His desire to pay the poor shows his willingness to cleanse himself of any Roman monetary "dirt." Jesus commends Zacchaeus's character, because Zacchaeus understands that one's heavenly relationship with God is connected to the good one does on earth. It is only after the tax collector confesses his wrongdoings that God saves him. The story does not end with spiritual reconciliation. Like the woman bent over for eighteen years (13:10-17), Zacchaeus is restored socially and racially "because he too is a son of Abraham."

19:11-27, More Lessons with Slaves

Luke continues to uncover problems of social stratification. In yet another subversive comment on the Roman occupation, he admits in this parable that not all masters or rulers were liked by their subjects. The three months' wage each slave possesses should yield more money. However, the owner's encounter with a slave who does not invest provides a more honest assessment of his nature. This nobleman is not trustworthy. He takes what does not belong to him and benefits from the work of others. The slave's past experience with the master served as a backdrop for his refusal to use the owner's "gift." In the end this distrust proved accurate; the owner reneged and took back what he gave to the slave.

In an effort to boost the economy and national morale, the U.S. government issued "advance" tax refunds in 2002 and 2004. These "free" checks sent many people, particularly the poor, to banks, check cashing shops, and the malls. For some the refunds were long overdue. Others received the money with skepticism. Surely the government does nothing for free. What is the catch? Like the slave whose unpleasant experiences with his owner caused him not to trust the up-front wage, many African Americans who too have had horrifying experiences with government red tape and the Internal Revenue Service did not trust the "free" money. Free is not always free. Did the tax rebate practice of the U.S. government end up hurting the poor, and African Americans, who are disproportionately poor? Many would say yes, since the money only provided a temporary ability to buy some items, while the long-term institutional shift meant that the government now had less tax revenue to help provide the social safety net that is so important for the poor.

19:28—21:38, JESUS IN JERUSALEM: THE FUTURE AND THE FUTURE OF DEATH

19:28-47, Freedom and Death

The desire to kill Jesus intensifies now that he is in Jerusalem. The Son of Man, who has come to proclaim the good news and to do good by setting captives free, realizes that Jerusalem means him no good.

Acting on behalf of freedom is a dangerous undertaking. The more visible Martin Luther King Jr. became, the more crowds he attracted. The more the crowds lauded him, the more the enemy pursued him. Malcolm X's fiery speech about "chickens coming home to roost" spurred his assassination. Medgar Evers's fight for the poor in Mississippi resulted in his death in his own driveway. Nelson Mandela's stance against apartheid in South Africa caused him to be imprisoned for twenty-seven years. Fighting for freedom is a dangerous endeavor. These men realized it. Jesus realized it. Nonetheless, the fight for freedom must continue despite the cost. That is the message behind Luke's portrayal of Jesus' ministry.

20:1-47, What's in a Question?

Determined to trap Jesus, chief priests, scribes, and elders present three significant questions to him.

The first question is, "By what authority are you doing these things? Who is it who gave you this authority?" Jesus' temple teaching disturbed those troubled by his ministry. But who told him he could do this? Who in authority authorized his teaching? It is not important to his opponents that Jesus is doing good work.

On Whose Authority?

In some African American congregations, power struggles between pastors, official boards, and other ministry leaders can confuse and dilute any good work that takes place. Arguments over whose idea it was or who chairs the effort produce disarray and force ministry to be delayed because of pride. Disagreements over who was empowered or authorized to sign a document can manifest itself in spiritual stagnation. Thus a church does not grow, and its surrounding community does not reap the congregation's potential harvest.

The second question, "Shall we pay taxes?" is really not about paying taxes. Jesus' opponents already knew the answer. The scribes were trying to hinder the work of jubilee. It is not uncommon in the black church for budget and other financial meetings to become all-out brawls. Stances against a living wage increase for the pastor, duels that develop over a dollar increase for the maintenance staff, and fights that erupt over money for new ministries are really not about the money. The whispers about "where the tithes and offerings go" are often not really about cash flow. Such disgruntlement is often the result of a spiritual disorder that hides itself behind a fiscal facade.

The last question, "Whose wife is she?" is yet another means of entrapment. The Sadducees do not believe in the resurrection; yet they ask a question about it. The key lies not in the question but in the context that produces the question. In Luke's day, the status of a woman was tied to that of a male relative. Her identity and social belonging were situated outside of her self and her gender.

The matter of a women's identity and social belonging remains unsettled today in many contemporary societal arenas. Particularly in the black church, women are restricted from holding many high offices or performing many authoritative, which is to say, ordained, functions. Women who serve in "appropriate" places like the usher board, the choir, or the nursery cause little debate. Women pastors, however, unsettle as many "sisters" as church "brothers." This lack of support for female church and especially pastoral leadership persists, despite the impact African American women preachers like Jarena Lee, Virginia Broughton, and Maria Stewart have had on the black church and the broader American society. C. Eric Lincoln and Lawrence H. Mamiya underscore this:

Both historical and contemporary evidence underscore the fact that black churches could scarcely have survived without the active support of black women, but in spite of their importance in the life of the church, the offices of preacher and pastor of churches in the historic black churches remain a male preserve and are not generally available to women. . . . This issue continues to be a controversial one for the Black Church.[9]

21:1-4, Widows and Offerings

A widow's pension is the Social Security benefit she receives when her husband dies. In some special cases, depending on her husband's retirement status, a physically infirm wife might even be able to retire early from the assistance of "widow's benefits." In each case the wife's income is dependent on her husband's. Unfortunately, in most cases the benefits were not substantial. For a grandmother taking care of grandchildren or even great-grandchildren, the payment barely allowed for subsistence living. The pay could even have been equal to something like the two copper coins the poor widow contributes in Luke's story. Though the coins would have meant much to her, they were of little real fiscal value.

In discussing this widow's actions, however, Jesus does not condemn the amount. He says instead that what she has offered cannot be calculated. Because she has given out of her heart, what she has given is of more value than what any rich person who gives painlessly out of his or her excess could contribute. It is not the amount given but the commitment and belief of the giver that matters.

In some congregations, leaders raise offerings by asking people who can give a certain amount to stand. This "bidding" usually begins with $100, then proceeds to $75, $50,

etc. While it is fiscally profitable, spiritual shame can be involved. The implication is that the person who does nor or cannot stand has a lower degree of faith. The implication is that the person who gives at the lowest level, like $10, is less honorable than those who can afford to contribute higher amounts. Jesus reverses such inappropriate attempts to connect faith with public giving. The widow put in more, because she contributed out of what she did not have and she did so humbly.

21:5-37, Signs

Jesus addresses the ensuing crises between Rome and Judea. He gives various military, physical, and natural signs that will serve as a warning that trouble is brewing. People should heed the warning of the signs.

Common among the elderly are sayings about "signs" of things to come. Achy and/or arthritic bones often denote a coming thunderstorm. If a person's eye is jumping or shaking, bad news is headed to her or his household. For some an itchy hand means someone is about to make money. If a person has burning ears, then someone is gossiping about him or her. People want to know and understand why things are the way they are and why things happen the way they do. Signs help in this light. The words of Jesus ring true; every generation seeks a sign. From a sign that change will soon come to a sign of comfort in troubled times, every generation, even this present one, seeks a sign. We seek signs to find a sense of security about our lives, a sense of control over the precarious nature of our lives in the same way that seeking and understanding signs about the coming of the kingdom might help folk in Jesus' time feel less unsettled about the turmoil going on all around them with the Roman occupation of Palestine. This "seeking" might explain why church attendance in New York increased dramatically in the weeks and months following 9/11. People were perhaps seeking in the churches a sign that life would be normal again. Black folk, as the only super-churched community in the United States, certainly see the church as that kind of sign in lives that remain imperiled by the terrors of racism, broken families, drugs, illiteracy, high dropout rates, and unemployment.

22:1—23:56, Jesus in Jerusalem: The Presence of Death

22:1-38, Before I Go

In v. 20 Jesus says that the cup poured out is the new covenant in his blood. The Greek word for covenant (*diatheke*) means "contract" or "testament." Jesus at this last meal with his disciples leaves a will. It is a "living" will, given while he is still among them. This will gives instructions on what to do once he leaves. They are to recall his suffering and remember that they too have been called to suffer. This last meal is a memento of the time they spent in the presence of Jesus. This breaking of bread and drinking of the cup is an heirloom. Jesus passes it on to them so that they in turn may pass it to others who believe. Each time the disciples dine together, they are to remember Jesus, his mission, and his ministry.

Not only are the disciples to remember Jesus through their eating, but they are to also remember that greatness does not come from being served. True greatness occurs in service to others.

22:39-71, Prayer and Swords

Until now, Luke does not portray Jesus as a violent person. At his birth, the angels proclaim peace on earth. Jesus wishes peace on Jerusalem as he enters the city. However, death has a way of pushing other sides of a person to the surface. There is something about one's own imminent demise that brings out another side of an often-pleasant personality. In this regard, Jesus is certainly human.

Although Jesus told the disciples to depend on the hospitality and kindness of others during their mission, at the point of his betrayal he told them not to trust anyone. Although Jesus told the disciples that the community they served was to provide their food, clothing, and shelter, at the point of facing excruciating pain, mocking, and beating, Jesus warned his followers to provide for themselves. Although his message was one of release, wholeness, and deliverance, when he was on the verge of suffering, Jesus instructed those who believed in him to get not one but two swords. The swords were not to be used to defend him; Jesus wanted them to be able to protect themselves. Violence begets violence. No, Jesus did not come with a sword, but those coming after him would surely have swords. Jesus was not worried about his own safety, but in his final instruction, his last will and testament, he wanted to be sure that his disciples were secure. The swords were for them, not him. He had prayed. They had fallen asleep.

There is a prominent photo of Malcolm X holding a rifle looking out a window of his home. The picture was taken after Malcolm's house was firebombed. He, his wife, and his little girls were almost killed Though Malcolm was not a violent man, he recognized that those seeking to kill him were willing to do so by any means necessary. Malcolm believes that it was likewise necessary to use any means necessary to protect those close to him and to create the kind of liberation they sought and deserved.

23:1-31, They Conscript Simon

For only the second time in the Gospel (13:1), Luke openly portrays Roman officials in a negative light. There is no doubt about the Roman government's involvement in the trial that proceeded against Jesus. Luke specifies that the chief priests and others take Jesus to Pilate, the Roman governor. Since Jesus threatens Roman political order by claiming to be King of the Jews, he must appear before the political ruler of the Jews.

In addition, Herod Antipas of Galilee, another official appointed by Rome, is involved. Because Jesus is a Galilean, technically he falls under Herod's jurisdiction. Neither Herod nor Pilate finds fault in Jesus. Still, Pilate makes a final decision to kill Jesus. He must be crucified. A Roman governor gives Jesus to the Roman military for crucifixion.

Not only does Jesus experience Roman abuse, but an African, one Simon of Cyrene, is a victim as well. Simon is a native of Cyrene, in what is now the North African country of Libya. In Jerusalem he is far from home. Luke does not designate him specifically as a Jew visiting Jerusalem in honor of Passover. Regardless of his reason for being in the city, what happens to Simon in the city is unpleasant. He is forced or conscripted to carry the cross of Jesus. "They" seize him; the same Roman officials who grab Jesus grab Simon. Roman brutality knows no racial boundaries; it is all-inclusive.

Why is Simon chosen? Luke does not specify. Perhaps he was a dark-skinned African with distinguishing Negroid features. Perhaps he wore unusual clothing indicative of his culture. What is clear is that Luke portrays Simon of Cyrene as displaced. He is dislocated and geographically out of line. He is a distant African from a dark, distant place.[10]

What does a reader do with Simon of Cyrene? From a literary standpoint, Simon represents those in Luke's Gospel who are exploited by Roman compulsion. From a homiletical standpoint, this African serves as a harbinger of slavery. His forced presence is a reminder of the African slave trade and the Middle Passage. From a spiritual standpoint, though pressed into service, Simon still helped Jesus carry out his liberating mission by carrying his oppressive cross.

23:32-47, Peer Pressure

Dying on the cross, Jesus experiences what can only be called peer pressure. He has a dialogue with two criminals who have also been sentenced to death. They are peers, colleagues of crucifixion. One hard-hearted peer tries to get Jesus to overturn their perilous plight. Like Satan during the temptation in the wilderness (4:1-13), he pressures Jesus to perform. A peer more sympathetic to Jesus' plight intervenes on Jesus' behalf. After confessing his guilt, he seeks affiliation with Jesus in his kingdom. Jesus assures him of a place in Paradise.

Many black churches hold an annual Homecoming or Friends and Family Day. It is a day particularly designated for families to worship together, for persons who have been "absent" from the church to return, and for friends to invite their peers to church. Just as Jesus, dying on the cross, stresses the importance of peer affiliation and acceptance, so too do such church occasions highlight the need to receive all people and view all as children of God. On Family and Friends Day or Homecoming, those who have left the church as well as those who faithfully attend are given a place in "paradise," a place where they can seek God's most intimate presence.

23:48-56, Irony

There are many ironic events surrounding the crucifixion. It is ironic that, while women whom Jesus included in his traveling circle now stand at a distance, a dissenting member of the Sanhedrin council—but not a close disciple—requests the body of Jesus. It is provocative that Luke ends this segment by stating that the women, desiring to anoint the body of Jesus, wait to do so because "on the sabbath they rested according to the commandment." Jesus resisted such traditional Sabbath demands. Apparently, his attempts to redefine the Sabbath die with him.

24:1-53, DEATH'S PAST: THE RESURRECTION

24:1-53, What an Expression

African American radio "fly jock" Tom Joyner has a segment on his morning program titled "Express Yourself." Joyner poses a question or makes a statement and allows listeners to call in and give their views. In thinking of the crucifixion and its aftermath, one could ask some of the witnesses, "How do you act after a crisis?" "After a violent watershed moment, how is one to respond?" "What do you do with such bewilderment and tension after what seems like 'the end'?" Luke allows some of the witnesses to "express themselves."

The women who once accompanied Jesus try to express themselves by going to the grave to prepare the body of Jesus with oil and spices. Perhaps holding his body and giving it proper burial rites will assuage some of the displacement. However, there is heightened perplexity over the misplaced stone and the "removed" body of Jesus. They converse with an angel who assures them, and then they express what they have experienced to disciples who do not believe them.

Men on the road to Emmaus express to each other what has happened in Jerusalem. Maybe talking to each other will help. Still trying to gain some clarity, they disclose their concerns to a stranger. This stranger breaks bread with them. In the end it is this Stranger who is the source of their confusion and "expression."

Disciples gather together. Could it be that communion with one another will be the only thing to sustain them now? They are in the midst of their "expression" when a "ghost" appears and adds to the misunderstanding. This ghost is also the source of their bewilderment and fear. Yet, as was the case with the Emmaus believers, a meal serves as the backdrop for clarification.

Finally, Jesus "expresses himself." In his conversation with the men going to Emmaus, he "interprets to them the things about himself in all the scriptures." In a meeting with the disciples, Jesus "opens their minds to understand the scriptures." Even the women at the open tomb "remember how he told them." When Jesus speaks, he clarifies.

How do you act after a crisis? In the case of Luke's witnesses, the writer shows that people react differently, even to the same event. The critical, common element is that, for the believer, clarity comes when Jesus speaks or expresses himself. In trying to deal with difficult experiences, the word of God is *the* expression that brings peace and understanding. That word of God also prompts worship. After Jesus' followers had shared their horrific experience and after receiving clarity, the disciples went back to Jerusalem, with the pain of the crucifixion still fresh. But this time they went with joy so that they might worship and bless God. Now that's an expression.

Notes

1. Itumeleng J. Mosala, "Black Hermeneutic Appropriation of the Signified Practice in Luke 1-2," in *Biblical Hermeneutics and Black Theology in South Africa*, ed. Itumeleng J. Mosala, (Grand Rapids, Mich.: Eerdmans, 1989), 177.

2. Renita J. Weems, *Showing Mary: How Women Can Share Prayers, Wisdom, and the Blessings of God* (New York: Warner, 2002), 31.

3. Raymond Brown, *The Birth of the Messiah: A Commentary on the Infancy Narratives in the Gospels of Matthew and Luke* (New York: Doubleday, 1999), 237. See also Joseph A. Fitzmyer, *The Gospel According to Luke I–IX*, AB 28 (Garden City, N.Y.: Doubleday, 1981).

4. Weems, *Showing Mary*, 190.

5. Delores C. Carpenter, *A Time for Honor: A Portrait of African American Clergywomen* (St. Louis: Chalice, 2001), 63.

6. George Barna and Harry R. Jackson. *High-Impact African-American Churches* (Ventura, Calif.: Regal, 2004), 44.

7. Justin S. Ukpong. "The Parable of the Shrewd Manager (Luke 16:1-13): An Essay in Inculturation Biblical Hermeneutic," *Semeia* 73 (1996), 193.

8. Ibid., 208.

9. C. Eric Lincoln and Lawrence H. Mamiya, *The Black Church in the African American Experience* (Durham, N.C.: Duke University Press, 1990), 275.

10. Stephanie Buckhanon Crowder, *Simon of Cyrene: A Case of Roman Conscription* (New York and Oxford: Peter Lang, 2002), 50.

For Further Reading

Barna, George, and Harry R. Jackson. *High-Impact African-American Churches*. Ventura, Calif.: Regal, 2004.

Brown, Raymond. *The Birth of the Messiah: A Commentary on the Infancy Narratives in the Gospels of Matthew and Luke*. New York: Doubleday, 1999.

Carpenter, Delores C. *A Time for Honor: A Portrait of African American Clergywomen*. St. Louis: Chalice, 2001.

Crowder, Stephanie Buckhanon. *Simon of Cyrene: A Case of Roman Conscription*. New York and Oxford: Peter Lang, 2002.

Fitzmyer, Joseph A. *The Gospel According to Luke I–IX*. AB 28. Garden City, N.Y.: Doubleday, 1981.

Mosala, Itumeleng J. "Black Hermeneutic Appropriation of the Signified Practice in Luke 1–2." Pages 173–89 in *Biblical Hermeneutics and Black Theology in South Africa*. Edited by Itumeleng J. Mosala. Grand Rapids, Mich.: Eerdmans, 1989.

Thurman, Howard. *Jesus and the Disinherited*. Richmond, Ind.: Friends United, 1981.

Ukpong, Justin S. "The Parable of the Shrewd Manager (Luke 16:1-13): An Essay in Inculturation Biblical Hermeneutic." *Semeia* 73 (1996) 189–210.

Weems, Renita J. *Showing Mary: How Women Can Share Prayers, Wisdom, and the Blessings of God*. New York: Warner, 2002.

The GOSPEL *of*

JOHN

Allen Dwight Callahan

1:1-18, Prologue: The Word

The prologue of the Gospel of John is an account of the divine Word coming to dwell with, in, and through human beings. After the phrase "in the beginning," there is no hint of Genesis 1 and the creation account. The verbs "create," "make," and "form" are absent. Names, events, and vocabulary point not to the creation of the world in Genesis but to the epiphany at Sinai in Exodus 34. The vocabulary of 1:1-18, "word . . . light . . . life . . . God . . . testimony . . . glory . . . grace . . . truth," is reminiscent of the epiphany that attends the law at Sinai (Exod 33:17—34:7). According to the Targums, "amplified versions" of parts of the Hebrew Bible translated into the Aramaic language commonly spoken in Palestine at the time of Jesus, the Word, *memra*, was the mediator of divine revelation to Moses in the wilderness and on the mountain of God. Writing in Greek in the middle of the first century C.E., the Alexandrian Jewish philosopher Philo speaks of this Word (*logos*) as *theos*, "divine" (*On Dreams*, 1.229).

The witness of John the Baptist punctuates the prologue, thus firmly ensconcing the opening of the Gospel in earthly history, not heavenly pre-history. The logos became flesh and dwelt "in our midst," "in us," "with us" (1:14; translations of the Gospel of John here and in what follows are my own); the prologue is the testimony, in the words of theologian JoAnne Marie Terrell, of "with-us-ness."[1]

The incarnation has happened in history and in community; the incarnation has happened "in us." This incarnation is both human and divine, both transcendent and immanent. "The doctrines of transcendence and immanence," wrote Martin Luther King Jr., "are both half-truths in need of the tension of each other to give the more inclusive truth."[2] In this incarnation, the divine and the human sound together in a symphony of transcendence and immanence. The Gospel is its score, the prologue, its overture.

In 1:18 the nouns "father" and "son" are without an article, in spite of the long tradition of translation and interpretation that reads "a father" as "the Father" and "a son" as "the Son."[3] The "firstborn" is a Semitic idiom for being near and dear, and speaks of affection, favor, and proximity. The prologue declares that an "only begotten" son, a son who is near the heart of his father, has made the father known in the world. This language is reminiscent of what we find in Rabbinic tradition to speak of God's intimate relationship with the Mosaic law or Torah: "It [Torah] lay on God's bosom, while God sat on the throne of glory."[4] The verb *exegeomai* in 1:18 is often used to speak of the force of law; Plato writes of what "the law commands" (*ho nomos exegeitai*, *Republic* 604b). The prologue of the Gospel asserts that it is not the law that is proximate to and intimate with God, but "a beloved son of a father." This beloved son has commanded grace and truth.

1:19—12:8, SIGNIFICATIONS: "THE MANY SIGNS HE PERFORMED"

1:19-51, Transjordan

The narrative begins in earnest in Perea, on the eastern side of the Jordan River. John the Baptist speaks of "the Lamb of God who takes away the sin of the world" (1:29, 36). Jesus' first disciples call him "Rabbi" (1:38), Andrew calls him "Messiah" (1:41), and Nathaniel pronounces Jesus "Son of God" and "King of Israel" (1:49). These several titles do not add up as much as they cancel each other out. They are neither synthesized nor verified; their validity both respectively and in the aggregate is left in question. The evangelist adduces the titles to acknowledge them and, indirectly, the partisans for whom they are meaningful. But the narrative stops short of ranking or otherwise correlating the various titles. The one title that Jesus uses self-referentially is "Son of Man," that is, a Semitic phrase meaning "this person," that is, "I." The phrase also may simply mean "a person," a human being, especially in contrast to non-human principals, as in Dan 7:13. In the Gospel of John we cannot know Jesus apart from his humanity. We cannot know Jesus apart from the part of him that is like us.

2:1-12, Cana, in Galilee

With a few newly minted disciples in tow, Jesus heads north and west to the northernmost region of the Northern Kingdom of Israel, Galilee. In the Gospel of John, Galilee is the region of miracles; every time Jesus is there something miraculous happens. The first of these miraculous interventions in John, which the narrator calls a "sign," is the wine that Jesus supplies for the wedding feast in Cana of Galilee. The traditional northern Israelite wedding feast lasted seven days, and, by the time Jesus and his entourage arrive, the party has exhausted its reserves of wine. Jesus then transforms into wine the water in six stone jars used in Judean ritual ablutions, saving the wedding party from social disaster in a feat of miraculous sacrilege by turning consecrated vessels into an open bar. This "sign" is the first of several acts in which Jesus shows flagrant disregard for Judean ritual.

The "sign" of wine suddenly in plentiful supply points to the realization of ancient

Israelite hopes for a coming age of fulfillment and freedom. Classical Israelite prophecy looked forward to an abundance of wine in the time of Israel's restoration: "The time is surely coming, says the LORD, when . . . the mountains shall drip sweet wine, and all the hills shall flow with it. I will restore the fortunes of my people Israel" (Amos 9:13-14). In Judean apocalyptic literature, wine is a symbol of the coming messianic age of peace and righteousness. *Enoch* 10:19 looks forward to the vine yielding wine in abundance, and in *2 Baruch* 29:5 each vine shall have one thousand branches and each branch one thousand clusters. The abundant wine suddenly flowing at the wedding feast in Cana is a "sign" that the "day surely coming" has now arrived.

2:13—4:3, Jerusalem, in Judea

Though Jesus is seen flouting Judean observances in Galilee, it is in Jerusalem that the Gospel most dramatically portrays Jesus' opposition to Judean piety. In the Gospel of John, Jesus' attack on the temple is the main event of his first swing through Judean territory. Jesus commands, "Tear down this temple and in three days I will build it up again" (2:19). "But he was talking about his body," explains the narrator. The narrator also adduces Ps 69:9, "It is zeal for your house that has consumed me," as a scriptural warrant for Jesus' violence. In John 2:15, some of the most ancient manuscript witnesses read that Jesus wielded "something like a whip," and mention the presence of sheep and oxen. These are early scribal attempts to mitigate the violence of the incident, suggesting that Jesus used "something like a whip" and used it only on the animals. These readings are early Christian spin control on a report that Jesus, armed and dangerous, assaulted worshipers and livestock alike in the Jerusalem temple.

In the dialogue of Jesus and Nicodemus that follows the confrontation in the temple, the images of a father and his beloved son, of rebirth, of Moses' brazen serpent in the wilderness and of "things above" and "things below," are figures in a language of signs that point to the divine mystery of the God's rule. Literalism, represented in the ridiculous rejoinders of Nicodemus, does foolish violence to this language of signs. To ransack this evocative language for wooden theological propositions is to look for quadratic equations in a quatrain.

Jesus summons the image of Moses lifting up the bronze serpent in the wilderness in Num 21:8-9 to speak of his own exaltation, how he will be "lifted up" (3:14). The word in Num 21:8 for "staff" or "pole" translates elsewhere in the Hebrew Bible as "sign," including the miraculous sense of "signs and wonders." Thus, God's instruction to put the serpent "on a pole" may be understood as meaning that the serpent was to be used as, or turned into, a symbol to the people rather than directly affecting a cure.[5] Wisdom 16:5-8 recounts the snake attack in the wilderness, saying, "they were troubled for a little while as a warning, and received a symbol of deliverance to remind them of your law's command. For the one who turned toward it was saved, not by the thing that was beheld, but by you, the Savior of all." The second-century Samaritan philosopher and convert to Christianity Justin Martyr also rejected out of hand any literal interpretation of the bronze serpent: "And shall we accept such things so unintelligently," he insists, "and not as symbols?" (*Dialogue with Trypho* 112:2). The bronze serpent is not a talisman but a symbol that signifies the grace of God.

In the Gospel of John Jesus speaks a language of such symbols. To insist on the literal interpretations of the words of Jesus is futile, egregious, even ludicrous. Nicodemus makes this mistake (3:1-4). Some of these symbols had undergone development in ancient Israelite tradition long before becoming a part of the Johannine semiotic repertoire. Wind and spirit are images in Ezekiel 37 and Joel 2, and the imagery of the virtuous leader as shepherd is in Ezekiel 34. "Up" and "down," "above" and "below" are locative adverbs that had become ethical metaphors in Israelite wisdom centuries before the Gospel was written: "For the wise the path of life leads upward" (Prov 15:24).

In his paintings of the life of Jesus, African American artist Henry Ossawa Tanner (1859–1937) sought to represent Jesus as a man in history, at the same time representing in the interplay of colors and the confrontation of light and shadow the mystery of the incarnation as divine events. The great twentieth-century theologian and mystic Howard Thurman argued that we may only understand and appreciate the salvation that God wrought in Jesus when we see Jesus as a man in history, marked by his particularity as a son of Israel and by his marginality as a subject under the domination of Greek culture and Roman imperialism in first-century Palestine.

The solution that Jesus found for himself and for Israel as they faced the hostility of the Greco-Roman world becomes the word and the work of redemption for all the cast-down people in every generation and in every age. I mean this quite literally. I do not ignore the theological and metaphysical interpretation of the Christian doctrine of salvation. But the underprivileged everywhere have long since abandoned any hope that this type of salvation deals with the crucial issues by which their days are turned into despair without consolation. The basic theme is that Christianity as it was born in the mind of this Jewish teacher and thinker

---

Henry Ossawa Tanner, *Nicodemus Visiting Christ*

Henry Ossawa Tanner's painting, "Nicodemus Visiting Christ" (see fig. 1 in the gallery following page 204), signifies the manifestation of the Word. Although historical and human, it remains nevertheless mysterious. The light in the scene does not come from above but from within, from the rooftop staircase of the dwelling that is the scene of the conversation between Jesus and Nicodemus. The highlights of Jesus' face shine as he speaks and gestures in near-darkness; illumination at the same time emanates in and transcends thought and language, thought's human sound. As Jesus speaks, the light of the world enters the darkness of Nicodemus's ignorance.

The face of Jesus and the profile of Nicodemus are informed by Tanner's studies of people he encountered in his travels in the Levant and North Africa. Tanner extensively researched for himself the faces and features, the customs and costumes of Bible lands. Of that research, Tanner wrote, "My efforts have been to not only put the Biblical incident in the original setting . . . but at the same time give the human touch 'which makes the whole world kin' and which ever remains the same."

—Henry Ossawa Tanner, quoted in Linda Roscoe Hartigan, *Sharing Traditions: Five Black Artists in Nineteenth-Century America* Washington, D.C.: Smithsonian Institution, 1985), 106.

appears as a technique of survival for the oppressed.[6]

Nicodemus is a ruler of the people, yet he does not understand the dynamics of God's rule. It is only here that the phrase "rule of God" (*basileia tou theou*) appears in the Gospel of John. Jesus uses the phrase polemically here, to burst the bubble of Nicodemus's ruling-class pretensions. Jesus' metaphor of rebirth speaks of transformation not of the world but of the self. The regime change demanded by the rule of God must begin with a radical transformation of those who would rule: "You must be born again."

The invitation to transformation, offered using the inclusively indefinite relative pronoun "whosoever," henceforth is open and extends to all subsequent hearers and readers. Educator, activist, and presidential advisor Mary MacLeod Bethune recalled hearing that invitation in the text of John 3:16 as a young girl growing up in the Jim Crow South:

> My teacher had a box of Bibles and texts, and she gave me one of each for my very own. That same day the teacher opened the Bible to John 3:16, and read: "For God so loved the world, that He gave His only-begotten Son, that whosoever believeth in Him should not perish, but have everlasting life."
>
> With these words the scales fell from my eyes and the light came flooding in. My sense of inferiority, my fear of handicaps, dropped away. "Whosoever," it said. No Jew nor Gentile, no Catholic nor Protestant, no black nor white; just "whosoever." It meant that I, a humble Negro girl, had just as much chance as anybody in the sight and love of God. These words stored up a battery of faith and confidence and determination in my heart, which has not failed me to this day.[7]

John 3:16 evokes the metaphor of the doting father and the beloved son introduced in the prologue. The Gospel uses the metaphor of the traditional relationship between a father and a son, a theological image in Hos 11:1 and a political image in the royal enthronement psalms of the Psalter, to explain the relationship of God and Jesus. The Father loves the Son (3:35; 5:20). Those who honor the Father honor the Son as well (5:23), and the Father honors those who serve Jesus (12:26). Father and Son are one and the same with respect to agency: "I and my Father are one" (10:30). Yet the Son is subordinate to the Father, because his agency is coterminous with the authority of the Father: Jesus will later concede to his disciples, "the Father is greater than I" (14:28).

In contrast, gangsta rap artist Ja Rule uses the biblical language of Jesus' divine paternity in the song "Only Begotten Son" to express the anger and pain of being abandoned by his Father. The opening verse is a parody of John 3:18, where the one who stands condemned is the one who "believeth not" in Ja, the son. Likewise the title chorus plays on John 3:16; but here the father "so feared the world" that he "left" his only begotten son, in order to "show that pain is love."[8] The cover art of the album on which the track is featured, *Venni Vetti Vecci*, intimates the metaphor: Ja Rule, hands clasped, eyes closed, and head upturned, is flanked by a white statue of Jesus Christ with outstretched arms and upturned palms (see http://en.wikipedia.org/wiki/Image:Ja_Rule.jpg). The redemptive union of Father and Son in the biblical metaphor appears in rhetorical inverse video: there is no union, no redemption; the Father does not love the Son. The aesthetic effect is that of a sacred metaphor—an image from the Bible, from the mouth of Jesus speaking of God as his Father—taken over into the vulgar argot of the street. But we may appreciate the force of the inverted image only when we recognize that the biblical metaphor has been twisted so that it is no longer a figure of speech but a cry of alienation that is the metaphor's very antithesis.

The testimony of John the Baptist that follows features the metaphor of bride and bridegroom and of the two-tier universe of heaven and earth, above and below. John says, "I must decrease" (3:30), and with that he diminishes to nothing; this is the last we hear from him in the Gospel. Commentators are divided as to whether the words of 3:31-36 are the continuing testimony of John or the resumed testimony of the narrator. John is "a man sent from God" (1:6), and John's witness is from God; his testimony is thus from above, from heaven. To come from heaven is to come from above. The "above" of v. 31 links the discourse in 3:31-36 with the dialogue of Jesus and Nicodemus, which serves as concluding commentary asserting that those who are from below cannot understand those who are from above.

4:4-42, Sychar, in Samaria

John the Baptist has moved from his earlier Transjordanian location to Aenon near Salim (3:23). When Jesus becomes aware of the surveillance of the Pharisees, he moves north. His destination is again Galilee. The narrator says that Jesus "had to go through Samaria" (4:4). But this was not due to the brute fact of geography. Though Samaria lies between Galilee and Judea on the West Bank of the Jordan, Israelites from Galilee who worshiped in Jerusalem were accustomed to crossing the Jordan twice to do an end-run around hated Samaritan territory.

This day, however, Jesus takes the express route. Thirty-five miles north of Jerusalem, the road from Jerusalem in the south to Samaria in the north ran between Mount Ebal to the north and Mount Gerizim to the south. Less than a half mile from the northwestern side of Mount Gerizim lay Jacob's Well. Sychar, ancient Shechem of the Hebrew Bible, lay nestled in the valley between the two mountains in the seven-hundred-foot shadow of the holy Mount Gerizim, one of Israel's oldest sacred sites. History, however, had made of that valley road an abysmal chasm.

The Samaritans were the descendants of the Israelites, who fell to the Assyrian Empire in the seventh century B.C.E. According to 1 Chr 5:26 the tribes of Reuben, Gad, and half of Manasseh were deported. Some of the population of Perea in the time of the second temple were descended from the survivors of the part of the Israelite-Judean population that did not go into exile.[9] "The remnant of those that escaped," as 2 Chr 30:6, 10-11 calls them, continued to live on the western side of the Jordan after the destruction of the Northern Kingdom. The region assumed the name of its royal capital, Samaria, and its ethnic, religious, and political development followed a course that diverged from that of the Israelites in the Southern Kingdom of Judea. The Southern Kingdom, Judah, fell to the Babylonians a century after Samaria had succumbed to Assyria, and also suffered a deportation of its elite. Some descendants of that elite returned to Judea after the fall of the Babylonian Empire under the patronage of its Persian successor (2 Chr 36:22-23; Ezra 1:1-4; see Isa 45:1-25).

The Judean historian Josephus reports that in the fourth century B.C.E. the Samaritan ruler Sanballat built a temple on Mount Gerizim to rival that in Jerusalem. At the end of the second century John Hyrcanus, ruler of Judea, would suffer the competition with the Jerusalem sanctuary no longer; he burned the temple and Sychar to the ground. The open wound of animus between north and south that festered over the centuries had become a running sore of religious, political, and social conflict in the time of Jesus. The narrative of the encounter between Jesus and the Samaritan woman carries with it the burden of this troubled history, and we cannot appreciate the nuances of the conversation without bringing this background to the foreground.

The dialogue is also freighted with erotic overtones unavoidable to readers of the Hebrew Bible. The well was where many a great man found his mate: Isaac (Gen 24:11), Moses (Exod 2:15), and, especially important for this narrative, Jacob (Genesis 29).[10] Jesus' command to the woman to get her husband (4:16) may be understood as the phatic equivalent of the question, "Are you married?"

The woman replies to the pregnant query in the negative. But here the conversation takes an abrupt, seemingly bizarre turn. Jesus replies that she has had five husbands and is now with a man to whom she is not betrothed. Jesus seems to make a clairvoyant pronouncement, but the original Aramaic underlying the language here suggests a provocative thrust that is political, not personal. In ancient Aramaic, "five husbands" translates as "five lords (ba'alim)." The Hebrew Bible mentions that the local rulers of the Samaritans had been foreigners, "lords" from five different foreign lands: Babylon, Cuthah, Avva, Hamath, and Sepharvaim (2 Kgs 17:24; Josephus, *Antiquities* 9.14.3). "Five lords" also suggests the series of five regimes that had ruled Samaria: the Assyrian, Babylonian, Persian, Greek, and Jerusalem-based Judean.[11] Jesus speaks of the five lords of the Samaritans. The sixth lord, which is not a "husband" but which has nevertheless reduced Samaria to political concubinage, is Rome ruling from Jerusalem through the Judean high priesthood.

The woman catches the political double entendre of Jesus' rejoinder, and parries the thrust with Samaritan chauvinism. She speaks of the holy mountain of her people, the sacred traditions of her people, and Jacob, the great ancestor of her people. Jesus meets the woman's Samaritan chauvinism with what has been erroneously interpreted as Judean chauvinism of his own, claiming, "For salvation is from the Judeans." But the proper translation of this sentence is, "For it is salvation from the Judeans."[12] The salvation to which Jesus refers is deliverance from the Judeans, who began their rule over Samaria by burning down the venerable Samaritan temple on Mount Gerizim.

Later in a conversation with his disciples, Jesus uses an agrarian proverb of the harvest as a metaphor for the recruitment of the Samaritans to his project (4:35-38). In the mouth of Jesus the saying, "There are yet four months and then the harvest" (4:35), is transformed into a metaphor for the ingathering of the Samaritan Israelites. The "word" (*logos*, 4:41) that the Samaritan woman and her fellow countrymen receive so enthusiastically is liberation from the ideological and political pressure that Judea had exerted on the Samaritans for centuries. For the Samaritans, the word of Jesus is "salvation from the Judeans."

4:43-54, Second Sign: Again, in Galilee

"But after two days" (4:43) recapitulates the notice of the two-day sojourn in Samaria in 4:20. Jesus performs a second sign after "coming from Judea to Galilee." The people must see signs to know that the time of Israel's divine restoration is at hand. In the prophetic tradition of Isaiah, healing is a root metaphor for communal restoration (Isa 29:18-21; 35:5-6; 42:18-20; 43:8). In the Gospel of John, healing is signification. The accounts of the physical restoration of infirm persons in John (4:46-54; 5:1-16; 9:1-7; 11:1-45) are not so much miracle stories as signs that point to the activity of God in Israel.

The Galileans, having been at the feast and having witnessed Jesus' attack on the temple (4:45), welcome Jesus. The narrator announces Jesus' return to Galilee, citing the well-attested proverb about the prophet being without honor in his hometown.[13] The proverb makes sense in this context if Jesus was a Judean, as the Samaritan woman assumes in 4:9. Yet Jesus' visits to the Judean capital of Jerusalem are increasingly dangerous. He is warmly received and presumably safe in Samaria, Galilee, Perea, and, as we shall see, in Bethany—in every place but Jerusalem.

The nobleman who accosts Jesus in Cana is a royal official (*basilikos*) from Capernaum, and thus a Herodian official. Herod Antipas, son of Herod the Great, was tetrarch of Galilee and Perea; this nobleman was an official in Herod Antipas's court. The official is a man of privilege, accustomed to giving orders. As befits his station, he comes to Jesus making demands. The demand of the official, relayed in indirect (4:47) and again direct discourse (4:49), is that Jesus "go down" to heal his sick son. Jesus answers the demand with a command. It is then the official who must "go down": the verb that the nobleman uses in the imperative, "go down," is the same verb in genitive absolute clause recounting the official's return to Capernaum on Jesus' order. The healing is accomplished by remote control. It is the second Galilean sign.

5:1-30, The Sabbath: Jerusalem in Judea

The phrase "after these things" marks a new moment in the narrative. Jesus is again in Jerusalem for "a feast." The topographical detail of the scene shows an accurate knowledge of Jerusalem in the first half of the first century: archaeological excavations have confirmed the layout of the pool and five porches near the foot of the temple mount. In addition to one of the three annual pilgrimage festivals—Passover, Pentecost, and Tabernacles

—commentators have variously suggested one of two other feasts, Rosh Hashanah (New Year) and Purim, as the unnamed feast here. But neither Rosh Hashanah nor Purim is a pilgrimage feast, and thus they are ineligible as a narrative motivation for Jesus to make the trek from Galilee to Jerusalem.

Careful exegesis fails to establish a baptismal motif here. Indeed this is non-baptism: the lame man never gets to the healing waters. He does not even get close, let alone wet. He lies prostrate in a sea of destitute masses, "the infirm, the blind, the lame, the paralyzed" (5:4), who congregated near the temple precincts waiting for the mercy of God or the coins of generous pilgrims. The miraculous healing of the paralytic at Bethesda (or, possibly, Bethzatha) is celebrated, albeit obliquely, in the Negro spiritual "Wade in the Water": "Wade in the water, children, / Wade in the water, children, / Wade in the water, children, God's going to trouble the water." The phrase "trouble the water" echoes John 5:4 as it is rendered in the King James Version. The "Received Text" on which this is based includes the explanatory note for John 5:4, which is missing in some ancient manuscripts, that when "an angel went down at a certain season to trouble the water," the first infirm person to enter the agitated pool would be cured. This turn of phrase from the King James Bible informs the last line of the chorus of "Wade in the Water." The phrase also informs the rhetoric of Sojourner Truth's argument for women's suffrage after African American men were enfranchised following the Civil War: "I am glad to see that men are getting their rights," she said at the Convention of the American Equal Rights Association in 1867, "but I want women to get theirs, and while the water is stirring I will step into the pool. Now that there is a great stir about colored men's getting their rights is the time for women to step in and have theirs."[14]

The miracle at the pool provokes controversy, because Jesus performed it on the Sabbath. In 5:13 Jesus slips away "because of the crowd,"[15] as he does several times in the first half of the narrative (4:41; 7:33; 8:23). After confronting Jesus as an accessory to violation of the Sabbath, the Judeans resolve to kill him (5:17), the first of several notices that some Judeans are plotting Jesus' murder (7:1; 8:37, 40; 11:53). The controversy at the end of chap. 5 concludes with Jesus' counteraccusation that his interlocutors have rejected him because they lack the love of God (5:42). They have in effect rejected Moses, whom they are so quick to claim: they do not truly have faith in what Moses has written, so they cannot have faith in what Jesus has said (5:46-47).

5:31—7:9, The Feast of Passover: Across the Sea of Galilee

Jesus returns to Galilee. The crowd follows him because of "the signs that he performed," which provoked the controversy that precipitated his departure from Jerusalem. Jesus withdraws to the hills with his disciples. Jesus has enemies, and he has retreated to Galilee to establish some distance between himself and his hostile audiences in Jerusalem.

The impromptu picnic takes place "near the time of the Passover." This is precisely the time when anyone intending to observe the Passover in Jerusalem should have been en route to the city. The Galilean masses here effectively boycott "the feast of the Judeans" to be with Jesus. The notice of the Passover is juxtaposed with that of the crowd "that had come with him" from Jerusalem. The gathering in Galilee is radically different from that about to take place in Jerusalem. Unlike the festival that Jesus disrupted by armed protest earlier, no money will change hands at this feast. No animals will be sacrificed: the meat of the feast is the flesh of a ritually clean animal never sacrificed—fish. The feast in Galilee promises to be the opposite of the Jerusalem Passover: without money, without sacral victims, and without the priesthood that oversees their exchange.

The scene is ominous and, along with other narrative clues, suggests that this assemblage of hungry men in the Galilean hill country—for centuries home and hideout to bandits and brigands—may have been far from harmless. Five thousand is the head count of an army.[16] Indeed, according to this Gospel, Jesus' actions evoked an attempt to draft him as king in Galilee, a region of Palestine with a long history, stretching back to the age of Israel's judges, of charismatic military leaders spontaneously chosen by popular acclaim. But Jesus eludes the draft (6:15).

Jesus departs under cover of darkness. This entire section of the narrative is marked by stealth and efforts to avoid detection (6:15, 16, 17, 22). The scene takes place on the "sea," that is, Lake Chinnereth or Chinneroth of the Hebrew Bible, and later Lake Gennesaret or "the Sea of Galilee." The body of water also went by the name "Lake Tiberias," after Herod the Great built the lakeside city of Tiberias around 18 C.E. on the northeastern coast and dedicated it to Tiberius Caesar (thus the parenthetical notice in 6:1). Jesus' disciples go down "to the sea" (*epi tēn thalassan*), headed for Capernaum. Jesus was walking "to the sea" (*epi tēn thalassan*), the phrase describing both the departure of the disciples and Jesus' lone stroll on the beach. After initially being "spooked" by the sight of a figure walking along the shore, the disciples recognize that the mysterious figure is Jesus. He draws near the water's edge, and the disciples, still on the water and some distance from land, "were wanting to take him aboard." They redouble their efforts to row to shore, and so arrive "very soon thereafter" (*eutheōs*, 6:21).

In the discourse that follows the mass picnic and the remove to the other side of the lake, Jesus speaks of the flesh that he gives his followers to eat. Instead of *esthiein*, "eat," the verb *trogein*, "feed," appears here. The latter signifies something to eat provided by another hand, and so is used in speaking of feeding animals. "The flesh of the Son of Man" is the flesh that the Son of Man feeds to those who follow him. It is "heavenly bread," in contrast to the manna that fell in the wilderness in Moses' day. Those who ate of the manna died; but the heavenly bread eternally sustains those who eat it (6:58). Likewise "the blood of the Son of Man" is the blood that he feeds his followers, "the pure blood of the grape," in the words of Deut 32:14. The "blood of grapes" will flow in abundance, according to Gen 49:11, which by the time of Jesus had come to be understood as an oracle of the messianic age. Once again, Jesus is speaking in metaphors.

And again, dismay attends Jesus' disturbing use of metaphorical language. At the end of the discourse on the bread of life there is at the same time a great defection from Jesus and a consolidation of his inner circle, a division provoked by his tough talk (6:60). He has maligned the miraculous manna of Moses and claimed that, unlike Moses, the sustenance he offers his hearers will enable them to live forever. Jesus' deeds attract the masses, but his words repel them.

7:1—9:41, The Feast of Tabernacles: Up to Jerusalem

The Feast of Tabernacles, or Sukkoth, is the autumnal festival celebrating the summer's grain harvest. The Israelite liturgical calendar associated the feast with the wilderness sojourn after the Exodus (see Deut 16:13; Lev 23:34). In postexilic times the feast took on eschatological significance. The prophetic oracle of Zechariah 14, that there would be no rain unless the nations did obeisance in Jerusalem (14:17), came to be read on the first day of the festival. The oracle suggested the continual flow of "living" (that is, flowing in contrast to standing) waters.

As Galilean pilgrims were preparing to make the southward trek to Jerusalem, Jesus "was walking around in Galilee because the Judeans sought to kill him" (7:1; see 5:18; 7:19; 8:37, 40). As Jesus' family prepares to go up to the feast, the tension between Jesus and his unbelieving kin and the danger awaiting him in Jerusalem create another occasion for stealth and even dissimulation. In 7:8, where Jesus says, "I am not going to the feast," some ancient manuscript witnesses read, "I am not going to the feast *yet*." Jesus is described in 7:10 as going up to the feast after his family, "but in secret." The venerable ancient manuscripts Sinaiticus and Codex Bezae read "*as though* in secret." The variants of 7:8 and 7:10 attempt to rescue Jesus from appearing to be dissembling, and these apologetic readings are already in the oldest manuscript witnesses.

The crowd of 7:12 is the mass of Jesus' followers from Galilee, among them his family (see 7:10). The leaders as a group are distinguished from the masses (7:26, 48-49). Mentioned specifically are the chief priests and the Pharisees (7:45-48), who act as a police force that unsuccessfully attempts to apprehend Jesus (7:32-36). Nicodemus is a dissenting voice among them (7:50). As 7:48-49 and subsequent notices in 9:22 and 19:38 make clear, these hostile Judeans are the Jerusalem ruling class, whom commoners, including Judean commoners, fear (7:13).

The controversy amid the Jerusalem crowd in chap. 7 is a conflict of opinions about Jesus' natural origin and whether it disqualified him from being a prophet. The prophet is expected to work "signs" (7:31), as Jesus does. But Jesus' home is Galilee, which, the leaders declare, does not produce prophets (7:52)—a snide and inaccurate claim; Jonah and Nahum both were Galilean prophets. Amid speculation, the "whence" of the messiah remains unknown. Jesus' point here (7:28) is precisely that his hearers know his "whence." He has not come of himself, but has been dispatched by "the one who sent me" (7:29). It is that one who is unknown to the questioning Jerusalemites. And because they do not know "the one who sent" Jesus, they know neither his "whence" nor his "whither." The query in 7:35, "Will he go to the Dispersion?" goes unanswered, as does the delegation of "some Greeks" in chap. 12 who have come to Jerusalem for the Passover. Jesus does not go to the Diaspora: the Diaspora will come to him later by hearing his voice and joining his united flock (10:16).

7:53—8:11, The Accused

The text of John 7:53—8:11 has any one of several contexts in the manuscripts of the Bible, and so may belong properly to none of them. The vocabulary of the passage is at variance with that of the rest of the Gospel: it contains the sole mention of scribes (8:3) and elders (8:9) in the Gospel of John. In some manuscript traditions the passage appears after John 21:25, presumably one of the "many other things Jesus did" (21:24). The scene of the story is the temple in Jerusalem, which accounts for why in other manuscripts it appears after Luke 21:37-38 or after Luke 24:50-53, both of which report Jesus' activities in the temple. Modern text critics mark the passage as dubious, even spurious, and some commentators have refused to treat it.

Various early manuscript copyists were uncomfortable with what appears to be Jesus' loose morality in the story: this textually free-floating tale of adultery and absolution is poor grist for the mill of a rigorous penitential theology. But the story of the woman caught in flagrante delicto remains in the Bible and so in the Christian biblical imagination. And it remains because, even if apocryphal, it is nonetheless true: in every age, hypocrisy is always but a stone's throw away from religious zeal. Anna Julia Cooper, nineteenth-century activist, historian, and educator, writes,

> By laying down for woman the same code of morality, the same standard of purity, as for man; by refusing to countenance the shameless and equally guilty monsters who were gloating over her fall,—graciously stooping in all the majesty of his own spotlessness to wipe away the filth and grime of her guilty past and bid her go in peace and sin no more . . . [Jesus] has given to men a rule and guide for the estimation of woman as an equal, as a helper, as a friend, and as a sacred charge to be sheltered and cared for with a brother's love and sympathy.[17]

Jesus diffuses the mob by commanding, "Let him who is without sin cast the first stone" (8:7). Jesus had no takers because the erstwhile stone-throwers were former paramours. And everyone knew it. Their carnal knowledge of the woman was common knowledge.

8:12-59, Conflicting Testimony

The dispute concerning testimony in 8:12-20 harks back to the controversy with the Judeans in 5:31-48. The interlocutors are the Pharisees. Likewise 8:21 returns to the argument with the Pharisees in 7:34-36. At the same time, the narration speaks of Judeans who have believed in Jesus (8:33). The Gospel is at pains to show that "the Judeans" are not a monolith. The Judeans are divided, and they are divided over Jesus.

In the discourse that follows, Jesus takes up the theme of illumination: "I am the light of the world. The one who follows me shall in no way walk in darkness, but shall have eternal life" (8:12). The image of light is a political metaphor of judgment and liberation, common to preexilic, exilic, and postexilic oracles of Israel's deliverance in the prophetic tradition under the name of Isaiah (see Isa 5:20; 9:2; 49:6; 51:4; 58:8; 60:1; 60:19). The connection of light and judgment recapitulates and elaborates on the treatment of light in the prologue (1:5, 9-10). The metaphor of light signifies deliverance and the dawn of a just order.

The ancient manuscript witnesses, taken together, give us the sense of 8:25: "But Jesus said to them, 'I said to you at the start that I am (the one) speaking to you.'" Here and elsewhere, "I am" must be rendered according to context. Jesus' "I am" statements do not echo the self-revelatory statements of God in the Hebrew Bible. Jesus is not making claims to divinity; he is drawing a contrast between the dead past and his living presence. Jesus sharpens the point of his argument that his identity is based on what he does, and it is what he does that marks him as the Father's emissary in the world. The Father is ever with Jesus in the world (8:29); Jesus is one with the Father, in that he speaks the words that the Father has taught him to say and does the things that the Father has directed him to do. Jesus is God's Son because of his deeds, for what one does defines what one truly is.

Jesus is speaking to those Judeans "who had had confidence in him" (8:31). The perfect participle indicates that these Judeans had put their trust in Jesus at an earlier time as a consequence of his prior activities in Jerusalem. Perhaps that trust has become a thing of the past, for the conversation becomes contentious. What follows is a nasty knot of accusations against Jesus. Jesus contests the charge of being possessed (8:48-49) but passes over in silence the accusation of being a Samaritan—a slur in Jerusalem. Jesus is maligned throughout the first half of the Gospel as evil (7:12; 9:16, 24; 10:21, 33), a demagogue (7:12), and demoniacal or deranged (2:17; 6:42; 7:20; 8:48, 52; 10:20).

Jesus is compared with Abraham (8:53) just as he is compared with Jacob earlier (4:12), that is, negatively. Jesus responds in 8:58 with another "I am" predication, with the sense, "I am to be before Abraham." This is an arrogation of preeminence, not priority, consistent with the general meaning of Jesus' "I am" statements, in which he contrasts himself to someone who is not present while insisting on the importance of his own presence. Jesus also arrogates to himself the honor accorded to Jerusalem. The Feast of Tabernacles celebrates Israel's sojourn in the wilderness (Lev 23:33-34), but Zechariah associates it with the eschatological "Day of the Lord" (Zech 14:3) when there will only be light and no darkness, and living waters will flow from Jerusalem (14:8), which will be exalted (14:10, 14).[18] In the Tabernacles discourse, Jesus claims all this for himself: he is the light, and he is the source of living water. He, not the Jerusalem temple, shall be exalted. Salvation is to be found neither in a holy city nor in a sacred edifice, but in a human being, a "son of man," Jesus.

9:1-41, The Man Born Blind

The evangelist has selected this instance of healing to signify that the judgment and deliverance that Jesus renders fulfill the prophetic expectations. In Jesus' encounter with the congenitally blind man in the temple precincts, the Gospel again evokes the image of light. "I must do the deeds of him who sent me, while it is day; a night comes when no one can work" (9:4); "When I am in the world, I am the light of the world" (9:5). With the notice that it was the Sabbath (9:14), the encounter becomes a controversy. Their investigation of

Jesus' activities notwithstanding, the Pharisees cannot discover "whence he is" (9:29). The erstwhile blind beggar "has seen him" (9:37), yet Jesus continues to confound the Pharisees, "that they which do not see might see, and that they which see might be made blind" (9:39). Jesus has the last word in 9:41, which serves as preamble to the monologue of 10:1-21.

10:1-42, The Feast of Dedication: The Good Shepherd

The narrative jumps from the season of the feast of Tabernacles in the fall to the winter Feast of Dedication. Jesus is depicted as being present but not as a participant; once again, the feasts mark narrative time and not Jesus' observance. The Feast of Dedication, or Hanukkah, like Sukkoth, is an eight-day feast, which commences in winter (25 Kislev, in late November or early December) and commemorates the rededication of the Jerusalem temple after the victory of the Maccabees (1 Macc 4:52-59; 2 Macc 10:5-8). Dedication harks back to a time of crisis in Israelite history when the priesthood and aristocracy were complicit with the enemies of the Torah, when the Jerusalemite priestly elite and their nonpriestly sympathizers apostatized and supported the evil Syrian monarch Antiochus Epiphanes.

Jesus' discourse on the Good Shepherd is a polemic against the Jerusalem priestly leadership of Jesus' day, summoning the image of the shepherd and the flock—one of Israel's oldest political metaphors. John 10 is based on Ezekiel 34, which in turn is informed by the enthronement Psalms 95–99 that are followed by the metaphor of the shepherd and the flock in Psalm 100.[19] Unlike the craven hired hands (10:12-13), the Good Shepherd puts himself at the disposal of his flock: he "lays down his life for the sheep" (10:11, 14).

The narrative revisits the controversy of 5:18, where the Judeans sought to kill Jesus because his claim of divine paternity was understood as a claim to equality with God. Jesus again claims unity with the Father (10:30), and again defends himself against the charge of blasphemy and its capital penalty. Jesus adduces Ps 82:6, a biblical text that affords a scriptural precedent for human claims to divinity. The point of the proof text is to show the Judeans' accusation to be a non-issue. But the Judeans do not agree, and, in words Martin Luther King Jr. once used to

---

Henry Ossawa Tanner's painting, *The Good Shepherd*

The image of the Good Shepherd was one that Henry Ossawa Tanner treated several times in his career. His 1920 painting *The Good Shepherd* (see fig. 2 in the gallery following p. 204) shows a man in traditional Palestinian dress carrying a lamb on his shoulders, walking along a steep ridge under the naked sun. At left, a chasm between the mountains yawns perilously. Tanner's 1930 painting *The Good Shepherd (Atlas Mountains, Morocco)* (fig. 3) shows the impact of his travels to North Africa: the immense scale of the chasm now threatens to dwarf the shepherd and the band of sheep who follow him closely along its edge. The good shepherd must brave the high mountains and sheer valleys in the heat of the day for the welfare of the flock: he "lays down his life for the sheep." Jesus is beloved of his Father precisely because he puts his life at the disposal of his flock (John 10:17).

describe reactionary extremists of his day, they have not yet learned how to disagree without becoming violently disagreeable. Jesus once again beats a hasty retreat from Judea, this time across the Jordan back to Betharaba in Perea (10:40-42), where the narrative began.

11:1-44, Across the Jordan to Bethany

Jesus leaves the safety of Perea to venture back into Judea. He does so for love. Jesus loved Lazarus and his sisters. Martha and Mary loved their brother. And in love they all meet at the grave. In their disappointment Martha and Mary are two women twice deserted. In death their brother has deserted them. And in their time of desperation Jesus has deserted them. The sisters are the principal figures of the Negro spiritual "O Mary Don't You Weep": "O, Mary, don't you weep, don't you mourn, / O, Mary, don't you weep, don't you mourn, / Pharaoh's army got drownded, / O, Mary, don't you weep." Mary here must be Mary the sister of Martha and Lazarus, who weeps at Jesus' feet after her brother's death (11:28-37). This identification is confirmed by a variant of the song that mentions Mary and Martha together: "O, Mary, don't you weep, / O, Martha, don't you mourn."[20]

W. E. B. DuBois wrote that when Radical Reconstruction and the great hope of America democracy were betrayed by the Compromise of 1877, "God wept."[21] The sometimes unabashed anthropomorphism of the Hebrew Bible tells us that God laughs, rants, occasionally even changes his mind. Yet the God of the Bible does not cry. He never weeps. But the taut prose of the narrator announces, "Jesus wept." The resurrection of Lazarus begins in earnest with tears—those of Mary and those of Jesus.

This emotion is set in motion, however, with grunts. Or snorts: the verb often rendered in English translations as "groan" in 11:33 means literally "to snort" and is used of horses. It is a glossed as "deeply moved" only in the Gospels; elsewhere in Greek literature where it is accompanied by the dative of person it means "admonish, sternly rebuke."[22] The setting of public mourning has made secrecy impossible. Jesus is deeply disturbed, at the same time angered and anguished, because Lazarus's death forces him to compromise his own security. Jesus must operate openly in dangerous territory, mere kilometers from Jerusalem. The crowd comes to the tomb in despair. And Jesus comes, belatedly, in guttural dread. The resurrection of Lazarus must be spectacle as well as miracle.

And with its juxtaposition of pathos and triumph, the resurrection is spectacular. In full view of the throng of mourners, Jesus summons Lazarus, now four days dead, from the tomb. The antebellum folk song "Oh, He Raise-a Poor Lazarus" announces, "Oh, He raise-a poor Lazarus, / He raise Lazarus from the dead, / While many were standin' by, /

Charles White, O Mary Don't You Weep

The image of the forlorn sisters in John 11 informs the composition of Charles White's etching, Mary Don't You Weep (1956) (see fig. 15 in the gallery following page 76). The grim woman at left heeds the counsel of the Negro spiritual and withholds her tears. At right, the anguished but resolute woman who accompanies her is Martha, her sister in suffering. The scene holds no other figures: the women are alone in the world. Lazarus is gone, and Jesus has yet to arrive. In the hiatus, there is only the anticipation of tears.

Jesus loosen' de man from under de groun',/
An' tell him, 'Go prophesy.' / An' tell him,
'Go prophesy.' "23

11:45—12:8, The Anointed

"Jesus was about to die for the sake of the
nation, and not the nation only but also so
that the scattered children of God might be
gathered in one, from that day then they plot-
ted to kill him" (11:51-52). This notice serves
as a narrative summary of the latter half of the
Gospel.

Though the anointing at Bethany is not
reported until 12:3, it is anticipated in 11:2,
where Mary is introduced without further
notice as the woman who anointed Jesus.
When Judas objects to Mary's extravagance,
Jesus defends her actions: "Leave her along,
so that she may keep it [i.e., the aromatic
oil] for the day of my burial" (12:7). The
narrator indicts Judas as being motivated

by greed; Judas holds their common purse,
to which he is wont to help himself (12:6).
Jesus is opposed to augmenting their common treasury by selling the spikenard and
instead insists that Mary be allowed to keep
it for use after he is dead. Apparently she is
in possession of such a quantity of the precious ointment that even after anointing Jesus
now, there promises to be enough left over to
anoint Jesus later. And so Jesus speaks of what
she may do with the remaining oil later. The
question remains, what is she doing now?

Mary is not embalming Jesus. That would
be premature: Jesus, after all, is not yet dead.
She is not anointing him for burial. She is
anointing him for something else.

Unlike the respective accounts of this
event in Matthew and Mark, in the Gospel
of John a woman anoints Jesus before, not
after, his triumphal entry into Jerusalem. The
Gospel of John also reports the popular expec-

Henry Ossawa Tanner, *The Resurrection of Lazarus* (1896)

Henry Ossawa Tanner's painting of the resurrection of Lazarus (see fig. 4 in the gallery
immediately following page 204) shows the astonishment of the mourners in an ochre lumi-
nescence. A kneeling woman at right, presumably Mary, still at Jesus' feet after having prostrated herself before him (John 11:32), looks up at him as he gestures toward the recumbent
Lazarus. And in the midst of the onlookers, a man of African features looks on calmly and
intently. In other paintings of Jesus, Tanner included himself as one of the disciples, and the
artist may be the model for this figure as well. The Beloved Disciple appears in the narrative
only after the resurrection of Lazarus (13:23-26; 19:26-27; 20:2-10; 21:7-20). In Tanner's
painting, perhaps the black Beloved Disciple makes his debut here.

The Bible mentions that Lazarus was entombed in a cave (John 11:38), and the folk
song sings that "Jesus loosen' de man from under de groun'." Tanner's scene is an iconic
conflation of both notices: the crowd of mourners has accompanied Jesus into the cave; one
of them lifts Lazarus from a rectangular hole in the ground, apparently in obedience to Jesus'
command to free Lazarus of his grave clothes (11:44). All the principals, including Jesus,
are illumined from the amber glow that seems to radiate from the grave itself. As in his painting of the nocturnal rendezvous of Jesus and Nicodemus, the light comes not from above but
from the midst. Illumination is immanent; it is life as the light of humanity (1:4).

---

tation that Jesus, the man who had called a dead man back to life, would be present at the feast to receive the adulation of his many admirers. The chief priests of Jerusalem and the Pharisees shared this expectation, and they had issued an All Points Bulletin in the hope of apprehending Jesus in Jerusalem during the holidays (11:57).

For this very reason, Jesus stays out of Jerusalem and remains in the suburban villages of Ephraim (11:54) and Bethany (12:1), where the family of Lazarus and his sisters throw a party in Jesus' honor. Martha is the party's hostess (12:2), and her brother Lazarus is one of those who recline at table with Jesus. Matthew and Mark affirm that the woman's expensive gesture will be remembered wherever the gospel is preached: both evangelists, however, forget to mention her name. According to the Gospel of John, it is the other member of Jesus' beloved family in Bethany, Mary, who anoints Jesus at the party. In Bethany, at the hands of Mary, Jesus literally becomes a messiah, an "anointed one"; anointing was the Israelite ritual that marked a king. It is after his anointing—and a brief report that the priests have now decided that Lazarus too should be murdered—that Jesus enters Jerusalem to public acclaim. Jesus enters Jerusalem as a messiah. The narrative sequence of the Gospel of John shows Mary's anointing of Jesus to be what it had been in Israel for more than a millennium—a coronation.

12:9—20:29, Doxology

12:9-50, Long Live the King

Jesus arrives in Jerusalem a week before the Passover, when merchants, moneychangers, and priests are already attending to the rush of pilgrims that would clog the city in its holiest festive season. A cheering crowd waving palm fronds welcomes Jesus as he enters Jerusalem. None of the other evangelists mention this detail. Matthew tells us that the people cut branches from trees and spread them on the road. Mark mentions that people spread along the road branches that they had cut in the fields. Luke says nothing of waving branches: he reports that the people laid their cloaks along Jesus' path, much like the royal reception of Jehu in 2 Kgs 9:13. But the Gospel of John tells us what the other Gospels do not: that the people greeted Jesus with palm branches that they waved aloft in celebration of his entry into the city.

The palm frond was an ancient symbol of Israel's liberation. The Israelites had waved palms two centuries before as victorious Israelite troops, having repelled their Syrian enemies, entered Jerusalem in triumph and purified the temple that had been desecrated by the Syrians. In both revolts against Rome, the first a generation after the crucifixion of Jesus and the second a century after his crucifixion, the Judean rebels would mint coins with the image of palm fronds and the legend reading, "The Liberation of Israel." To wave palm fronds in Jerusalem was to declare the liberation of Israel. Jesus was being greeted as a royal liberator.

The palms waving in the air on either side of the road signified that Jesus' hour of exaltation had come. According to the Gospel of John, this was the fourth time that Jesus had entered Jerusalem in the course of his public career (see 2:13; 5:1; 10:22). But only here does he receive a royal reception. After causing the lame to walk, the blind to see, and the dead to rise up from the grave, the people were convinced that God was working out the salvation of the dispersed children of Israel, all Israel, through Jesus.

The acclamation "Hosanna," literally, "save us," echoes Ps 118:25-26: "Save us, we beseech you, O Lord! O Lord, we beseech you, give us success. Blessed is the one who comes in the name of the Lord." This prayer is offered traditionally at the Feast of Tabernacles, where palm fronds are used to fashion the huts from which the festival takes its name. Only now, upon hearing this acclamation, does Jesus mount a donkey in fulfillment of the oracle of the King's advent in Zech 9:9: "Rejoice greatly, O daughter Zion! Shout aloud, O daughter of Jerusalem! Lo, your king comes to you, triumphant and victorious is he, humble and riding on a donkey." The Judeans receive Jesus as a king in "the city of the great king," in Jerusalem. Jesus comes as a king because the people recognize him as a king. In taking on the role of king in the oracle of Zechariah by mounting the donkey, Jesus acknowledges the people's acclaim. This tumultuous reception of Jesus in Jerusalem on the eve of the Passover is his exaltation.

The plot to kill Jesus is hatched in reaction to the groundswell of Judean acclaim following the resurrection of Lazarus: the plot even includes the murder of Lazarus as well (12:9-10). The Gospel of John presents Jesus' popularity as a political problem: it highlights the political logic of Jesus' arrest as a genuine oracle in the mouth of the high priest (11:50-51). The "death that he was to die" is a consequence of Jesus' exaltation. It is only after having arrived in Jerusalem to acclaim that Jesus speaks of his death in a thinly veiled metaphor: a grain of wheat must fall into the ground and die to bring forth a harvest (12:24). "I'm going to die for the people," said Fred Hampton, the brilliant Black Panther Party leader who was assassinated by Chicago police in 1969, "because I'm going to live for the people."[24] Because he has lived for the people, Jesus must now die for them.

13:1—17:27, The Testament of Jesus

This meal is not the Passover. Here, as throughout the Gospel of John, Jesus does not celebrate any of the feasts of the Jerusalem cult. The Gospel never depicts him or any

of his disciples as offering sacrifices, and he attends festivals only to take advantage of the populous audience that they afford him. The festivals are reported in the Gospel as markers of narrative time and moments of conflict.

Nor is this meal the inauguration of the Eucharist. There is no upper room. There are no words of institution. Jesus commands his disciples neither to eat his flesh nor to drink his blood, but to wash one another's feet. Jesus calls what he does "an example," a *hypodeigma*, something demonstrated to be emulated. With the emulation of his demonstration, Jesus claims, comes beatitude (13:17). The disciples will be blessed by putting into practice what they have learned. This blessedness comes not on the basis of what one knows, but what one does.

Foot washing is a service customarily rendered by a slave. But the Gospel of John avoids the language of slavery to describe discipleship, and Jesus explicitly rejects slavery as a metaphor. All the proverbial sayings about slaves in the Gospel of John are pejorative.

- "The slave does not remain in the house forever, but the Son does." (8:35)
- "The slave is not greater than his master, and the messenger is not greater than the one who has sent him." (13:16)
- "The slave does not know what his master does." (15:15)
- "The slave is not greater than his master." (15:20)

Jesus is not an obedient slave; he is an obedient Son. His followers are not his slaves; they are his "little children."

The foot washing is not hindered by the imminent betrayal of Judas, foretold in 13:11. He is present until the end of the meal in 13:30, and so presumably has his feet washed along with the others, even though he is "not clean" (13:10-11). The phrase "Satan entered into him" in 13:27 reflects idiomatic Semitic speech. That Satan "entered into" Judas does not mean that Judas was possessed; the Gospel of John, which has neither exorcisms nor demonology, does not appeal to the ideation of spirit possession to understand Satan's work in the world. The verb "enter into" also means "share in," "have a part in"; the Adversary had a share in what Judas would do henceforth. The meaning of Satan's involvement is set out in 13:30: "Having then received the morsel, he went out immediately. And it was night." One in whom Satan is at work takes the bread shared in intimate fellowship, then deserts the community, and walks in darkness.

The report of the other disciples' interpretation of events as onlookers adds an element of irony to the betrayal. The Beloved Disciple, "the one who leaned upon Jesus' breast" (13:25) and so was closest to him at table, inquires at Peter's behest about the identity of the one who will betray Jesus. Even after Judas takes the sop that marks him as the traitor, the disciples remain clueless. Because Judas was the treasurer of the group, those at table assume that Judas had been sent by Jesus either to get groceries for the Passover or to give alms to the poor (13:29); apparently, providing for their own needs and the needs of the poor were the only two line items in the budget of Jesus' inner circle. Judas held the common fund for the common good. And now he who single-handedly held the funds in common would single-handedly betray and endanger the common good.

After Judas's departure, Jesus speaks of his glory. That glory is realized in love. Jesus has loved his followers so that they may love each other. This love is further defined as the concrete concern for the beloved that Jesus has for his inner circle. They are to love each other as Jesus has loved them (13:34-35). This love is the single commandment that Jesus will bequeath to them; the disciples of Jesus are

to put their very souls at each other's disposal (15:12-13).

But the love of Jesus cannot be revealed in the world without being endangered by those who do not know that love and without falling prey to the betrayal of those who do. At the risk of danger and betrayal, those who love God keep God's commandments. And those who love Jesus keep his commandments; 14:15 presents the Gospel's rigorous definition of love: love is obedience to the words of Jesus. These "words" (*rhēmata*) are words of command. Commandments are directions in the practice of love. To keep the commandments is thus to follow those directions. The spirit of truth remains with the followers of Jesus because of what they do, insofar as what they do is faithful to his words.

We expect these words of Jesus to end with 14:31. If the concluding imperative of this verse were then followed by 18:1, the narration would flow smoothly to the Passion narrative. But the Gospel uses the occasion of Jesus' testamentary speech to define and resolve the words of Jesus with more words of Jesus. The words of chaps. 15, 16, and 17 carry Jesus' promises, warnings, and instructions forward into the future. In the continuing discourse of these chapters, those promises, warnings, and instructions become Jesus' bequest.

There is some confusion among the manuscript witnesses here about the sense of 14:12b-13, "Because I go to my Father, whatever you ask in my name I would do so that the Father would be glorified in the Son." In some witnesses the following verse, "whatever you ask in my name I would do," is missing. Nevertheless we find similar phrases in 15:16 and 16:23:

- "whatever you ask in my name I would do" (14:14)
- "whatever you ask the Father in my name he would give to you" (15:16)

- "whatever you ask the Father in my name he will give to you" (16:23)

These sayings describe the means by which the Father will sustain Jesus' "little children" in a hostile word. The repetition of Jesus' promise of divine assistance testifies to the anxiety of those to whom that promise was addressed. And so the promise is repeated—recurring anxiety met with repeated assurances.

The true vine in chap. 15 is another classic Israelite metaphor: vv. 1-6 are a statement of the metaphor, vv. 7-17 its explanation. It is an agrarian metaphor of fruitfulness, and henceforth a biblical metaphor of love. Thus this chorus John Wesley Work recorded in his classic collection of African American folksongs:

> I am the true vine,
> I am the true vine,
> I am the true vine
> My Father is the husbandman.
> I know my Lord is kind and true,
> My Father is the husbandman.
> For he loves me and he loves you,
> My Father is the husbandman.[25]

Jesus has chosen his followers to be abundantly fruitful (15:16). The vine is a venerable image of fecundity and a symbol of the messianic age in the semiotic thesaurus of the classical prophets (see Isa 5:1-7; 27:2-6; Ezek 17). But the language here is not eschatological, that is, it does not speak of the end of the age. The metaphor is expressed in the proverbial present tense. The vine is not a figure of judgment at the end of time. The vine does not signify life after death; it signifies death after life.

The vine is an image of abundant fruit brought forth by diligent husbandry. In Jeremiah's parable of viticulture (2:21), the "true" vine is the cultivated vine. The metaphor of the true vine signifies love as acts of tending, of ongoing tender and not-so-tender cultivation. In northern Palestine fruitless branches are removed from late February to mid-March. By late March the vines are virtually naked, and fires burning the discarded branches dot the landscape. In August the vine dresser pinches off errant shoots of the now usufruct branches so that they receive the full benefits of sun and soil.

Unfruitful branches divert nutrients from those that are fruitful and burden the vine. Though alive, such branches are not well because they are not fruitful, and thus their very vitality compromises the fecundity of the vine. And so the vintner dispenses with them. The excised, erstwhile living branches, separated from the vine on which they had imposed for life, now dry up and die, withered and fit for the tinderbox.

To be a true disciple of Jesus is to be exceedingly fruitful (15:8)—and joyful, for the very purpose of Jesus' disclosures is joy (15:11). Yet Jesus anticipates that the world will hate his followers (15:18). It is a collateral hatred—hatred due to love. Because the world has hated Jesus, it hates those who are his (15:20-24). Those who belong to Jesus will suffer that hatred in solidarity with him. "You will no longer watch (*theoreite*) me" (16:10); that is, the disciples will no longer be spectators of Jesus' tribulation. The world will become a place of tribulation for them as well.

"The world" is the present regime, and the ruler of the present regime has been judged (16:11). He has nothing in common with Jesus, no solidarity with him whatsoever (14:30), and he shall be thrown out (12:31). There is no indication that Jesus is talking about Satan here. On the rare occasions that Jesus speaks of the devil in this Gospel he does so openly. Jesus can only be speaking here of the Roman administration in Palestine and

Fig. 1. Henry Ossawa Tanner (1859–1937), *Nicodemus Visiting Christ,*1899. Photo courtesy of the Pennsylvania Academy of Fine Arts, Philadelphia. Joseph E. Temple Fund.

Fig. 2. Henry Ossawa Tanner, *The Good Shepherd*, 1920. Oil on canvas, 32" x 24". Collection of The Newark Museum, gift of Mr. and Mrs. Henry H. Wehrhane, 1929. Inv. 29.910. Photo: © The Newark Museum/Art Resource, N.Y.

Fig. 3. Henry Ossawa Tanner, *The Good Shepherd (Atlas Mountains, Morocco)*, c. 1930. Smithsonian American Art Museum, Washington, D.C. Photo Credit: Smithsonian American Art Museum, Washington, D.C. / Art Resource, N.Y.

Fig. 4. Henry Ossawa
Tanner, *The Resurrection
of Lazarus*, 1896. Musée
D'Orsay, Paris. Photo:
© Erich Lessing / Art
Resource, N.Y.

Fig. 5. Henry Ossawa Tanner, *Two Disciples at the Tomb*, c. 1905. Oil on canvas, 129.5 x 105.7 cm. Photo: © Art Institute of Chicago.

Fig. 6. Henry Ossawa Tanner, *The Miraculous Haul of Fishes*, no date. Oil on canvas, 38" x 47.5". Permanent Collection of the National Academy, N.Y. Photo: © The National Academy of Design, New York (1236-P). Used by permission.

Fig. 7. Henry Ossawa Tanner, *Jesus and His Disciples on Their Way to Bethany (Luke 24:50)*, no date. Oil on canvas, 95 x 121.5 cm. Musée D'Orsay, Paris. Photo: © Erich Lessing / Art Resource, N.Y.

its administrator, Pontius Pilate, who was deposed only a few years after he executed Jesus. Jesus here utters an oracle of Pilate's ultimate downfall.

The image of labor pains as a metaphor for ineluctable suffering is a topos of Israelite prophecy (Isa 26:17-18; 46:7-10; Hos 13:13; Mic 4:9-10). The image does not figure in an end-time tableau here; it is not the future "tribulation period" of dispensationalist eschatology. The tribulation of the end of the present regime is the tribulation of the present. Jesus' followers will have tribulation not because the present regime is dying but because a new regime is being born. And the new regime is coming into the world the way every new human life comes into the world—with fitful pains at times so agonizing that they threaten life itself: childbirth has always been potentially lethal for women. Yet the woman in labor rejoices after her travail is over (16:21). The NIV of 16:21, "when the baby is born she forgets the anguish," is infelicitous, and flies in the face of the experience of mothers everywhere. Women who have undergone the agony of labor do not soon forget it. Jesus does not say that the woman forgets that pain. What he says is that the woman does not remember the pain. The root of the Greek word for "remember" here is a cognate of the words "memorial" and "tombstone," mnemonic devices that mark the dead past in the living present. The cause for the mother's joy is not the cessation of her pain but what that pain has wrought—a new human life. The woman's joy is at the same time the celebration of new life and the refusal to commemorate past agony. Joy, ever predicated on suffering, is the death-defying affirmation of life.

Jesus concludes his bequest, as do all the great testators of ancient Israel, with a prayer. The prayer is comprised of three petitions. In the first petition, Jesus prays for his own glorification (17:1-8). Jesus describes his own activity as having glorified the Father by completing the work that the Father has given him to do. It is only in the midst of his disciples that Jesus receives glory. It is in the midst of his disciples that he returns to the Father, that he reveals the Father's glory, and that he speaks plainly. For Jesus to be in the midst of his own and the Father's own is to be "out of the world." Outside this inner circle of love, Jesus does not reveal the Father's glory. The world, the present regime, does not and cannot know his glory. His glory may only be revealed to those whom the Father has given to the Son.

In the second petition, Jesus intercedes for his disciples (17:9-19). Eternal life is to know God. Behind the Greek verb translated "know" here, *ginōskein*, is the Semitic *yada'*, to know with ongoing and unmediated intimacy. Jesus petitions the Father that he would keep the disciples in the world and out of the grip of evil, that they might remain in the world and not of it (17:15-16). Nevertheless, those who belong to Jesus may share their joy with one another in the hostile world, and so Jesus asks that they might have this joy in all its fullness. Just as Jesus has been consecrated to the work of the Father, he now consecrates others to do that work. The verb "consecrate," or "sanctify," and its cognates here have nothing to do with sacrifice. Jesus has not consecrated his followers to die, but to live—for the Father, for him, and for one another. And so there is no mention of death. Those whom Jesus consecrates are sanctified to be safe in a dangerous world, to be joyful in a sorrowful world, to be loved in a hateful world. So commissioned, they are sent into the world just as Jesus was sent into the world.

In the third and final petition Jesus prays for those who will put their trust in his word (17:20-27). Others are added to the small, beleaguered circle that eavesdrops on Jesus' prayer—his "other sheep" (10:16). They, with the disciples and Jesus and the Father, are all to be one. Just as Jesus' word divides those who refuse and reject it, those who receive it and keep it become one. In the Gospel of John, those at one with Jesus are at one with one another. This is the unity of love.

Jesus concludes his prayer with a plea that the love that the disciples have among themselves would be the same love that the Father has had for him. Jesus prays, in effect, that their love would be divine.

18:1—19:42, The King Is Dead: Saint John's Passion

Though the Pharisees bring their hostile influence to bear in the deliberations of the Jerusalem leaders (12:42), throughout the Gospel of John the Pharisees are distinguished from the real decision makers in Jerusalem, the priestly establishment. The chief priests alone plot Jesus' death. The only Pharisees in the Passion narrative of the Gospel of John, Nicodemus and Joseph of Arimathea, are friendly toward Jesus. But the priests are of one mind that Jesus must die. According to the Gospel of John, Jesus was led bound to the priest Annas, who in turn remanded him to the high priest Caiaphas, who finally handed him over to Pilate. Jesus was neither condemned nor sentenced before his appearance in the Praetorium. Pilate alone rendered judgment and oversaw the execution.

Much of traditional Christian theology has understood the crucifixion of Jesus in this Gospel as exaltation. But this is a horrid oxymoron. By no stretch of the most perverse imagination could crucifixion have been understood this way anywhere in the Roman Empire in the first century C.E. Such an agonizing, ignominious death is many things. But it is not exaltation. After Jesus' claim that his exaltation—his being "lifted up from the earth"—would draw everyone to him, the narrator explains, "he said this signifying the kind of death he would die" (12:33). But the phrase "lifting up" in John 3:14; 8:28; 12:31-32, referring to the exaltation of "the Son of Man," does not appear anywhere in the Passion narrative. Traditionally the "lifting up" has been interpreted as Jesus' crucifixion, "the kind of death he would die." As we have seen, the fame of his resurrection of Lazarus and the subsequent acclaim by the masses at the triumphal entry ironically sealed Jesus' fate. The narrative parenthesis of 12:33, as ironic as it is prophetic, explains that the exaltation of Jesus—his fame among the Jerusalem pilgrims—would be the death of him.

The Gospel does not luxuriate attention on the gore of Jesus' ordeal and death. He is bound (18:12), slapped during questioning (18:22), flogged (19:1), and forced to march to the place of his execution bearing his own cross (19:17). Of the execution itself, the Gospel says succinctly, "they crucified him" (19:18); the reader is expected to know what that means. That Jesus was nailed to a wooden gibbet and was then hoisted aloft amid cries of agony was a gruesome detail left unmentioned, because it was so well and widely known.

One of the distinctive details of the crucifixion according to this Gospel is that while hanging on the cross Jesus is impaled by a soldier's spear. "Where you there when they pierced him in the side?" asks plaintively the Negro spiritual "Where You There?"[26] "They pierced Him in the side, / An' he nevuh said a mumblin' word," recalls another Negro spiritual.[27] Inspired by both the Bible and the Negro spirituals, the wound of Jesus appears in James Weldon Johnson's poem "The Crucifixion" (see sidebar on p. 207) and undergoes theological embellishment in the holiness preacher C. C. Lovelace's sermon "The Wounds of Jesus" as recorded by Zora Neale Hurston (see sidebar on p. 207).

The Gospel of John adduces Psalm 22 at 19:24, just after the announcement of the text of the titulus over the cross, "Jesus of Nazareth, the King of the Jews." Jesus' tunic is gambled away as he dies in fulfillment of Ps 22:18: "They divided my clothes among themselves, and for my clothing they cast lots." Psalm 22 addresses the problem of a king who suffers the scorn and derision of his enemies while weakened and defenseless. The Passion narrative makes reference to Jesus as king or Jesus' kingdom ten times in two chapters: 18:33, 36 (twice), 37, 19:3, 12, 14, 15, and 21. Though the high priests quibble about Jesus' royal pretensions, the people recognized Jesus' claims, and so did Pilate, who inflicted upon him an execution worthy of a rebel king.

The notice that Jesus' body has been pierced and his bones remain unbroken correlates with the scriptural characteristics of an innocent victim. Thus the disposition of Jesus' dead body is explained in 19:36-37 as the fulfillment of Exod 12:46; Num 9:12; and Zech 12:10. The absence of sacrificial terms in describing the death of Jesus suggests that the point of these allusions is Jesus' righteous

innocence, not his sacrificial death. That Jesus should be a sacrificial lamb offered up for Israel is the final solution of the high priest Caiaphas (11:49-53), and we are reminded of his murderous prophecy in 18:14. Only those who conspire against Jesus understand his death as a sacrifice, a heinous interpretation that the evangelist puts on the lips of the arch-villain in his narrative.

The Gospel of John uses the language of the paschal lamb and its equation with the beloved, "firstborn" Son to describe the sufferings of Jesus. It is not the language of divine sacrifice, but a metaphor of righteous

James Weldon Johnson, "The Crucifixion"

Jesus, my lamb-like Jesus,
Shivering as the nails go through his hands;
Jesus, my lamb-like Jesus,
Shivering as the nails go through his feet.
Jesus, my darling Jesus,
Groaning, the Roman spear plunged in his
   side;
Jesus, my darling Jesus,
Groaning as the blood came spurting from
   his wound.
Oh, look how they done my Jesus.

—From *God's Trombones: Seven Negro Sermons in Verse* (New York: Viking, 1927), 42.

C. C. Lovelace, "The Wounds of Jesus"

I heard the whistle of the damnation train
Dat pulled out from the Garden of Eden
   loaded with cargo goin to hell
Ran at break-neck speed all de way thru de
   law
All de way thru de prophetic age
All de way thru de reign of kings and
   judges—
Plowed her way thru the Jordan—
And on her way to Calvary when she blew
   for de switch
Jesus stood out on her track like a rough-
   back mountain
And she threw her cow-catcher in His side
   and His blood ditched the train,
He died for our sins.
Wounded in the house of His friends.
That's where I got off de damnation train
And dat's where you must get off, ha!

—C. C. Lovelace, "The Wounds of Jesus," in *The Sanctified Church*, ed. Zora Neale Hurston (Berkeley: Turtle Island, 1981), 102. Sermon delivered May 3, 1929, Eau Gallie, Florida.

innocence. The Wisdom of Solomon describes this innocence and the wrath and violence it elicits:

> Let us lie in wait for the righteous man, because he is inconvenient to us and opposes our actions. He reproaches us for sins against the law, and accuses us of sins against our training. He professes to have knowledge of God, and calls himself a child of the Lord. . . . Let us see if his words are true, and let us test what will happen at the end of his life; for if the righteous man is God's child, he will help him, and will deliver him from the hand of his adversaries. Let us treat him with insult and torture, so that we may find out how gentle he is, and make trial of his forbearance. Let us condemn him to a shameful death, for, according to what he says, he will be protected. (2:12-13, 17-20)

Jesus is just such a "righteous man." He disputes with legal authorities about his healing on the Sabbath and cites the practices of God his Father in defense of his own actions (5:2-18). It is in the context of this dispute that Judeans resolve to kill Jesus (5:18). The Sabbath controversy is revisited in 7:21-24, and Jesus invokes the authority of Moses against the law of Moses. The chief priests and the Pharisees respond with an abortive attempt to arrest Jesus (7:32). Divine paternity is the focus of the vituperative argument between Jesus and his Judean interlocutors in chap. 8. Jesus performs another healing on the Sabbath in chap. 9, provoking more legal debate. In chap. 10 Jesus claims unity with the Father, a claim that provokes yet another attempt to destroy him (10:30-31). Thus the first half of the narrative of the Gospel of John is punctuated by acrimonious conflicts over the law and claims of divine paternity. As Wisdom of Solomon puts it, "the righteous man . . . [is] a

child of the Lord" (2:12-24). This is the argument of the Gospel of John *in nuce*—not that Jesus was God's Son and thus righteous, but that Jesus was righteous and thus God's Son.

20:1-18, The First Easter

In the Synoptic tradition, women are the first to learn of the resurrection of Jesus. There is no epiphany. There is no encounter with Jesus. And there are no tears. In the Gospel of John, the tears of a single, kneeling, anguished woman summon the presence of the risen Lord. A woman's tears command that Jesus deal with this crisis of mortality in the garden as he had dealt with that of Lazarus—in person.

The text is awash in tears. Mary Magdalene stands at the tomb weeping. The verb "to weep" appears twice in v. 11, in v. 13 in the query of the angels, and again in v. 15 in the same query repeated verbatim by Jesus. There, at the tomb of Lazarus, tears inaugurated the triumph of life over death. So too, tears inaugurate the triumph of life over death here. (See sidebar on p. 209.)

With the dawn, Mary encounters the risen Jesus. Grief gives way to unabashed joy, and she embraces him. Jesus insists that she stop: "Oh, touch me not, little Mary, Good Lord, Good Lord," sings the Negro spiritual, "Touch me not, little Mary, Good Lord, I'm gwine home."[28] There is a time to embrace, says the Preacher, and a time to refrain from embracing. This moment is the latter.

Jesus dispatches Mary to announce his resurrection to his terrified comrades in hiding in Jerusalem. Mary heralds the first Easter as the first Easter herald. African American women recognized Mary Magdalene as the first to proclaim the resurrection of Jesus, and they claimed her as the patron saint of their public voice. African Methodist Episcopal preacher Jarena Lee vindicates her contested call to preach by appealing to the biblical example of Mary Magdalene: "Did not Mary first preach the risen Saviour, and is not the doctrine of the resurrection the very first climax of Christianity?"[29] In defense of her right to speak in public as a woman, antebellum essayist, orator, and political philosopher

---

Run, Mary, Run

Mary's zeal and grief are a recurring theme in the Negro spirituals. The title chorus of "Run, Mary, Run" recalls that after discovering that the stone at the mouth of the tomb had been rolled away, Mary runs to the disciples at the tomb (20:2):

> Run, Mary, run
> Run, Mary, run
> Oh, run, Mary, run
> I know de underworld is not like dis.

The song "He Arose" declares, "Sister Mary, she came running, a-looking for my Lord / And the Lord will bear my spirit home." In another Negro spiritual, "De Angel Roll de Stone Away," Mary "came a-runnin' at the break of day, / lookin' for my Saviour, tell me where he lay."*

In Henry Ossawa Tanner's *Two Disciples at the Tomb* (fig. 5 in the preceding gallery), Peter and "the other disciple, the one whom Jesus loved" have come, at Mary's behest, to the tomb and gaze in bafflement into its interior. Light from the tomb illumines the disciples' faces, but not their understanding; they are stupefied (see John 20:6-10). This light, the same amber glow we see in other of Tanner's paintings, represents the light of humanity that cannot be comprehended or conquered by surrounding shadows (see John 1:5).

*These three spirituals are in James Weldon Johnson and J. Rosamond Johnson, *The Books of American Negro Spirituals* (New York: Da Capo, 2002), 2:110.

Maria Stewart asked rhetorically, "Did not . . . Mary Magdalene first declare the resurrection of Christ from the dead?"[30]

The other survivors of Jesus' crucifixion, the disciples, are huddled together in fear (20:19), in fulfillment of Jesus' prediction of their desertion (16:32). Jesus visits the disciples twice after his resurrection to find them in hiding behind bolted doors (20:19, 26). The fear that attends the Passion and its aftermath persists through the first Easter week—and with that fear, unbelief. The disciple Thomas rejects the testimony of his colleagues that Jesus is alive (20:24-25). Though Jesus invites Thomas to touch him (20:27-28), the text says nowhere that he actually does. The Negro spiritual "Look-a How Dey Done My Lord" suggests as much. One verse, "Thomas say I won't believe / . . . won't believe, won't believe, won't believe," is then followed by the next, "He said Thomas see my han' . . . see my han', see my han', see my han'."[31] Thomas has believed because of what he has seen. But what of those who know of "the signs that Jesus performed" only because they have heard or read what is "written in this book" (see 20:30)? They have not touched Jesus. They have not seen him. But having believed, they are blessed (20:29).

21:1-19, Galilee: A Reprise

Jesus returns to Galilee to meet his disciples. Clearly, however, the disciples have not returned to Galilee to meet him. Once again Jesus appears, and once again the disciples are surprised.

The miraculous meal of chap. 21 is a tacit parody of the multiplication of the loaves and fishes in chap. 6. The scenes are a study in contrasts, from the mountain several hundred feet above to the lake several hundred feet below sea level, from a picnic of five thousand to a party of five. In chap. 21 there are no mountains;

Henry Ossawa Tanner, *The Miraculous Haul of Fishes*

In Tanner's *The Miraculous Haul of Fishes* (see fig. 6 in the gallery following p. 204), oarsmen fore and aft struggle to right their fishing boat, which tilts perilously under the weight of their catch. Two men at the edge of the port side appear to be almost pulled into the water by the ensnared fish. In the background, another fishing boat floats placidly in the distance, trawling a modest catch or none at all, its calm an understated contrast to the frenetic activity in the foreground. As in some of Tanner's other paintings, the light seems to emanate from the place where the word of Jesus affects the world. The line of sunlight reflected on the water runs just to the right of the vertical axis of the scene, and leads our eye down through the center of the boat into the draught of fish; our gaze is drawn overboard, as it were, into the miracle.

---

there are no masses. The few remaining partisans of Jesus have literally gone fishing.

These disciples, in the wake of the catastrophe of the cross, have gone into the seafood business. They are not merely throwing in lines to draw out a catch sufficient to put food on the table. They are trawling, using a net; they are capturing fish in marketable quantity. The fishermen catch fish in excess of subsistence; the surplus secured by the use of the net is then to be sold for cash. Peter has led his colleagues to turn to maritime enterprise as a way of sustaining themselves and making a profit.

But the business is a bust: the men have labored all night at their nets and have nothing to show for it (21:3, 5). At the word of Jesus, however, the business at once booms—indeed, it becomes too successful. A corollary to the miracle of the haul of fish is that the net is not destroyed in the process. Jesus' concern, however, is not that the disciples work to feed themselves but that they work to feed others. Peter has led his comrades into self-interested pursuit of survival and prosperity. Jesus now prevails upon Peter to lead them to self-availing love of others that their Lord had taught them. The superabundant catch mocks Peter's concern with quotidian survival and free enterprise. In seeking after his own welfare,

he gained nothing. With the intervention of Jesus, there is more than enough. And because Jesus has shown that there is no need for Peter to be preoccupied with his own needs, Jesus now demands that Peter, the leader, train his attention on the needs of others—the followers, the "sheep" of Jesus' flock (21:15-17).

Just as the scene of 21:1-14 is an ironic instance of superabundance, so too is Peter's promise of fealty an ironic scene of apostolic commitment—ironic, because Peter has reneged on this commitment, and the Beloved Disciple has seen him do so. There is a charcoal fire on the beach (21:9) just as there was a charcoal fire in the courtyard where Peter denied Jesus (18:18). Jesus inquires of Peter three times (21:15-19), just as Peter denied him three times before the crucifixion. Jesus does not indicate that he is satisfied with Peter's affirmations of love. Jesus commands Peter thrice to tend his flock. But not once does Peter affirm that he will do so.

20:30-31; 21:1-25, EPILOGUES

The Gospel ends with the resurrected Jesus returning from the grave to those he loves. The Gospel then concludes with two epilogues, one an announcement of the inspira-

> ### Henry Ossawa Tanner, *Jesus and His Disciples on Their Way to Bethany*
>
> Though inspired by a scene from a different Gospel, Tanner's *Jesus and His Disciples on Their Way to Bethany* (see fig. 7 in the gallery following page 204) depicts the drama of discipleship to the risen Christ in John's Gospel as well. In the scene from Luke's Gospel, the oblique stance of one figure at his side as Jesus prepares to leave his disciples suggests the same question that the disciples pose at the Last Supper in the Gospel of John: how will they know the way to the Father after Jesus has departed? Jesus' answer—"I am the way" (14:6)—is conveyed in Tanner's distinctive use of light to mark immanent revelation. The brightness of the afternoon sun illumines neither Jesus nor his disciples, who remain in shadow, but the road (*he hodos*)—the way of those who follow Jesus.

tional purpose of its written narrative and the other the last words of the anonymous disciple who has put forward the narrative as a written testimony. The first epilogue, 20:30-31, speaks of "what has been written" and why. The second epilogue treats the question of who has written. The disciple who has testified concerning the events and written of them is "the beloved disciple" (21:20, 24). But clearly there are other principals involved, too. The editorial contribution of influential women in the early tradition insured that women in the life of Jesus, otherwise forgotten, would be remembered. Their influence has given rise to an account of the life of Jesus that features women throughout.[32]

The editorial board that brought together these stories as the testimony of the beloved disciple put forward neither his persona nor their own personae. Even the beloved disciple remains anonymous. "The disciple who witnessed and wrote these things" (21:24) disappears behind those words. Like the "black and known bards of long ago" who coined the Negro spirituals, the beloved disciple and his collaborators are, in the words of James Weldon Johnson, "gone, forgot, unfamed."[33] What they have written they have written, that we, not having seen, might yet believe.

NOTES

1. JoAnne Marie Terrell, *Power in the Blood? The Cross in the African American Experience* (Maryknoll, N.Y.: Orbis, 1998), 125.

2. Martin Luther King Jr., "A Comparison of the Conceptions of God in the Thinking of Paul Tillich and Henry Nelson Wieman" (Ph.D. diss., Boston University, 1955), quoted in John J. Ansbro, *Martin Luther King, Jr.: Non-Violent Strategies and Tactics for Social Change* (New York: Madison, 2000), 52.

3. See John A. T. Robinson, "The Use of the Gospel of John for Christology Today," in *Christ and the Spirit in the New Testament*, ed. Barnabas Lindars and Stephen Smalley (Cambridge: Cambridge University Press, 1973), 70.

4. *Midrash on Psalms* 90:3 sec. 12 (Buber 196a).

5. James L. Kugel, *The Bible as It Was* (Cambridge, Mass.: Belknap, 1997), 480.

6. Howard Thurman, *Jesus and the Disinherited* (Richmond, Ind.: Friends United, 1981), 34–35.

7. Mary MacLeod Bethune, quoted in Gerda Lerner, *Black Women in White America* (New York: Vintage, 1973), 136.

8. Ja Rule, "Only Begotten Son," *Venni, Vetti, Vecci* (Def Jam Records, #538920, 1999).

9. B. Oded, "Observation on Methods of Assyrian Rule in Transjordania after the Palestinian Campaign of Tiglath-Pileser III," *JNES* 29 (1970): 183; quoted by K. Lawson Younger Jr.,

"The Deportation of the Israelites," *JBL* 117, no. 2 (1998): 213.

10. Ellen Aitken, "At the Well of Living Water: Jacob Traditions in John 4," in *The Interpretation of Scripture in Early Judaism and Christianity*, ed. Craig A. Evans, Studies in Scripture in Early Judaism and Christianity 7 (Sheffield: Sheffield Academic, 2000), 345.

11. I am indebted to Richard Horsley for suggesting to me that the five "lords" could refer to the five successive empires that ruled Samaria.

12. The same syntax appears in Luke 1:71 to speak of deliverance from enemies.

13. See Mark 6:4; Matt 13:57; Luke 4:24; *Thomas* 31; P.Oxy. 1, 5.

14. Sojourner Truth, address, Convention of the American Equal Rights Association, New York City, 1867, quoted in Lerner, *Black Women in White America*, 570.

15. I read the Greek genitive absolute here as causative.

16. See Plato, *Laws* 73.8a, 1 Macc 4:28; Herodotus 1.994.

17. Anna Julia Cooper, "Womanhood a Vital Element in the Regeneration of the Race," in *A Voice from the South* (New York: Oxford University Press, 1988), 17–18.

18. Catherine Cory, "Wisdom's Rescue: A New Reading of the Tabernacle Discourse," *JBL* 116 (1997): 113.

19. Jon Levenson, *Theology of the Program of Restoration in Ezekiel 40–48*, HSM 10 (Missoula, Mont.: Scholars), 105n57.

20. See the version of this Negro spiritual recorded by the contemporary African American a cappella group Take Six, "O Mary," (Burbank, Calif.: Reprise Records, 1988). See also Cheryl Townsend Gilkes, "'Go and Tell Mary and Martha': The Spirituals, Biblical Options for Women, and Cultural Tensions in the African American Religious Experience," *Social Compass* 43 (1996): 570–73.

21. W. E. B. DuBois, *Black Reconstruction* (New York: Atheneum, 1992), 634. The Compromise of 1877 was the agreement of Republicans and Democrats to declare Rutherford B. Hayes the winner of the 1876 presidential election despite disputed electoral votes in several Southern states. The deal was clinched after Hayes had made it known to Southern Democrats that if elected he would withdraw federal troops from the South and end federal support of Reconstruction.

22. Daniel 11:30 (LXX).

23. "Oh, He Raise-a Poor Lazarus," in *Religious Folk-Songs of the Negro*, ed. R. Nathaniel Dett (Hampton, Va.: Hampton Institute, 1927), 66.

24. Quoted by Mike Gray, "The Murder of Fred Hampton," directed by Howard Alk (Hollywood: VDI [distributor], 1971).

25. "I Am the True Vine," in John Wesley Work, *American Negro Songs* (New York: Howell Soskin, 1940), 187.

26. "Were You There?" in *Songs of Zion*, Supplemental Worship Resources 12 (Nashville: Abingdon, 1981), 126.

27. "He Never Said a Mumbalin' Word," in *Songs of Zion*, 101.

28. "Do Don't Touch-a My Garment," in Johnson, *Books*, 2:110.

29. Jarena Lee, quoted in *Afro-American Religious History*, ed. Milton Sernett (Durham, N.C.: Duke University Press, 1985), 169.

30. Marilyn Richardson, ed., *Maria Stewart: America's First Black Woman Political Writer* (Bloomington: Indiana University Press, 1987), 68.

31. "Look-a How Dey Done My Lord," in Johnson, *Books*, 2:170.

32. Elizabeth Schüssler Fiorenza, *In Memory of Her: A Feminist Theological Reconstruction of Christian Origins* (New York: Crossroad, 1989), 323–34.

33. James Weldon Johnson, "O Black and Unknown Bards," in Johnson, *Books*, 1:11–12.

FOR FURTHER READING

Brown, Raymond E. *Community of the Beloved Disciple*. Mahwah, N.J.: Paulist, 1979.

———. *The Gospel According to John*. AB. 2 volumes. Garden City, N.Y.: Doubleday, 1966.

———. *An Introduction to the Gospel of John*. Edited by F. J. Moloney. New York: Doubleday, 2003.

Callahan, Allen Dwight. *A Love Supreme: A History of the Johannine Tradition*. Minneapolis: Fortress Press, 2005.

The ACTS of the APOSTLES

Demetrius K. Williams

INTRODUCTION

The Acts of the Apostles is different in many ways from what precedes it (the Gospels) and what follows it (the letters). One feature of Acts, among many, is that it is a sequel to a Gospel, the Gospel of Luke (making it part of a two-volume work), and it assumes the genre of a *history* of the early church (Acts 1:1-5; cf. Luke 1:1-4).[1] Acts recounts the story of the expansion of the early church from the ascension of Jesus and the community of the apostles to the mission of Paul and his arrival in Rome. The work is written from the perspective of the late first century and attempts to address the various social and theological problems brought about as a result of expansion (i.e., inclusion of Gentiles), the church's

relationship with Judaism, and the cultural and political environment of Rome.[2] Tradition tells us that the author was Luke, "the beloved physician" (cf. Col 4:14; Phlm 24; 2 Tim 4:11). While neither the Gospel of "Luke" nor Acts has a name inscribed in the superscription of the earliest manuscripts indicating its author (the titles, "the Gospel according to . . .," were added in the second century in the heated debate over "the scriptures"), there is a general consensus that a single author wrote the two-volume work ("Luke" is still generally used for convenience). Scholars also generally agree that Luke-Acts was most likely composed between 80 and 90 C.E.[3] To be sure, the emergence of Christianity coincides with the period of the emerging glory of the Roman Empire, which justified its existence on the basis of an ideology of Rome as a civilizing agent.[4] Rome perceived that its purpose in history was to promote its virtues and values by means of city life throughout the empire. "Imperial temples and sanctuaries were generally located in the most prominent and prestigious positions available within the city,"[5] which constantly reminded Rome's subjects of the emperor. On any given day "one encountered pictures and statues of him everywhere, and there were also . . . the coins with his likeness, minted in almost every city." The impact of this imagery was part and parcel of Rome's ideology of world dominance.[6] On the whole, Rome's imperial cult that honored and worshiped the emperor stabilized the religious order of the world—the imperial cult, along with religion, politics and diplomacy, constructed the reality of the Roman Empire.[7] To support the material reality of its ideology throughout the empire, the production of agriculture was essential for the maintenance of cities, and Rome's ever-growing markets helped the development of *latifundia*, large agricultural estates dependent on the labor of slaves, near-slaves, and impoverished wage-laborers.[8]

The author of Luke-Acts was quite aware of the *temporal* glory and power of Rome. Jesus was born under the reign of the first emperor, Caesar Augustus (Luke 2:1; while Quirinius was governor of Syria, 2:2). His ministry began during the reign of Tiberias Caesar (Luke 3:1). He was crucified under the procurator, Pontius Pilate (Luke 23:24-25, while Tiberias is still in power). And Acts, dealing with the apostles, continues to present Roman leaders quite favorably (the book might be dedicated to a Roman patron, Theophilus; Acts 1:1; cf. Luke 1:3).[9] Moreover, Luke was not unaware that Rome too had its own "gospel" (of the *Pax Romana*, "peace of Rome"), "savior" (the reigning Caesar), and mission (to dominate and to civilize the world), as part of its ideology.[10] Nevertheless, in Luke-Acts it is clear that, although insignificant in the eyes of Rome, providence is being mediated through the traditions of Israel, not that of Rome, and it is by means of the gospel of Christ that God is bringing about a new world order.[11] Although both Peter (who dominates in chaps. 1–12) and Paul (who takes center stage in chaps. 13–28) open the way for the inclusion of the Gentiles, they are not the only ones to do so. Acts recounts the evangelistic efforts of several others, who also proclaimed the gospel to the marginalized and despised Gentiles, offering to them the new dispensation of God's love, mercy, and grace. Therefore, Luke's focus on both the unity and the inclusiveness of humanity under the sovereignty of God found welcome resonance with enslaved African Americans and their progeny.

AFRICAN AMERICAN APPROPRIATION OF THE ACTS OF THE APOSTLES

Luke's message in Acts was articulated in a world that was familiar in many ways to the "new" world in which enslaved African Americans found themselves—a world of empire-building, slavery, and dominance supported by a pervasive ruling-class ideology. The reality of *empire* (in the ancient and modern context) is important to consider, because America early on identified itself as both a "new Israel" (religiously) and a "new Rome" (politically) with an equally pervasive self-conceived "manifest destiny" to rule the world.[12] African Americans found themselves disenfranchised in the new commonwealth of America and occupying a second-class status within the church (the "new Israel"). Moreover, notwithstanding America's use of the Bible to support an ideology of oppression, there were some liberating visions in the Bible that offered an alternative model of human relations. The vision and message of Acts played a significant role in African American's articulation of an inclusive and unifying vision of freedom and equality. In Acts, as in Luke 4, the good news comes to the poor, the oppressed, and the imprisoned. Indeed Luke's message is for the oppressed and the oppressor, the high and the low, the Jew and the Gentile. His message embraces all ethnic diversity within the Roman Empire.[13]

Enslaved Africans' encounter with the Christian religion and message confirmed within them the idea of "the equality of all people before God," which Peter Paris has termed the "black Christian principle,"[14] despite whites' attempts to mute this message in the Bible and in the Christian tradition. A few early Quakers, Baptists, and Methodists made attempts to sensitize black converts to the implications of Christianity for human justice and equality, as recounted in some slavemasters' accusations: "You teach them that 'God is no respecter of persons' [Acts 10:34-36]: that 'he hath made of one blood all the nations of men' [Acts 17:36]: 'thou shalt love thy neighbor as thyself': 'all whatsoever ye would that men should do to you, do ye even so to them.'"[15] Such ideas garnered from Acts and other parts of the Bible laid the basis for the black protest tradition in the late decades of the eighteenth and early decades of the nineteenth century. This tradition was emphasized in particular, but not exclusively, by northern blacks who were formally or informally educated. They were able to find a "rhetorical space" in which to cultivate ideas, arguments, and strategies for action that would address the plight of their enslaved brothers and sisters. They applied certain biblical passages to an array of social issues in sermons, prayers, official denominational addresses, creeds, and mottoes. Some of the key themes were: (1) the kinship of humanity under the sovereignty of the one God, (2) slavery (and later segregation) as evil and in opposition to the will of God, (3) the imperatives of the teachings of Jesus to make all nations a part of God's reign, (4) the theme of Christian radical inclusion that stressed human equality and unity, and (5) judgment against all those who frustrate God's will on earth (especially those who hold others in slavery!).

It was also during this period that African Americans sought to institutionalize these ideals into a general ethical and moral principle, "all people are equal before God." This was based on a small selection of passages from Acts (among others)[16] that embodied their aim, passages that were often quoted or paraphrased in efforts to relate them to the racial situation in America.[17] Especially important were Acts 2 (Pentecost), 2:23-47 ("all things in common") and 4:32-37 ("not a needy person among them"), chap. 8 (the Ethiopian eunuch), chap. 10 (esp. vv. 34-36, "God is no respecter of persons," KJV), and chap. 17 (esp. v. 36, "God hath made of one blood all nations . . ." KJV). These were some of the passages that supported this institutionalized ideal within black churches.[18] Thus Peter Paris has remarked that black churches represent the historical embodiment of a universally significant principle: an anthropological principle grounded in the biblical understanding of the nature of humanity and its relation to God. The institutionalization of this principle constitutes the black church's uniqueness in American religious history, and "can be recognized by the fact that, for the first time, the birth of a church was not on the basis of a new theological proposition but solely on sociological grounds—social and racial equality."[19] This can be seen in Richard Allen's historic separatist black church movement that gave birth to the African Methodist Episcopal (AME) Church in Philadelphia in the early nineteenth century.

For the first time certainly in American history, there was a Christian denomination built entirely upon sociological grounds: to promote brotherhood and equality across racial lines. . . . And this was the first time in the history of western Christianity that a church included in a practical way black people on terms of equality. . . .

African Americans have also believed that the Constitution of the United States explicitly embodies the norms of racial justice. This idea, combined with the belief in America as a Christian nation, has often served as the basis for their confidence in the nation's capacity for thinking and doing the right thing.[20]

Finally, Bishop Reverdy Ransom, also of the AME Church, set forth his mandate for the church in the early twentieth century with dramatic rhetorical zeal, admonishing it to develop its own agenda and to cease following the contemptible programs and practices of white churches:

> The Church . . . must know neither race, color, nor nationality nor recognize distinctions of wealth, class or station, but only the dignity and sacredness of our common humanity. . . . It must be a prophetic Church. . . . They must proclaim liberty to the captives—those that are socially, economically, and politically disinherited—with authority of a Divine justice that will not rest until every fetter of injustice and oppression is broken.[21]

Ransom's appeal to the black church includes some of the seminal elements of its goals and objectives in society. The following examination seeks to bear out the essentials of this appeal through an exploration of African Americans' appropriation of Acts.

Bishop Tanner on Separatist Black Churches

Bishop C. M. Tanner, an AME clergyman, addressing the question of the black church practicing "reverse racism" by establishing separate churches, provided the following response in the early twentieth century:

> But the difference between . . . our Church and the churches of the other race today, is . . . in a fundamental Christian principle: *The question of the substantial oneness and brotherhood of all men.* The church which Allen founded stands today . . . as a living protest against distinction in the church of Jesus Christ on account of race or color. We hold, teach and practice that *God is no respecter of persons* (Acts 10:34) (emphasis added). This may be spoken of as the *distinctive note* of African Methodism. Our church has been on record for almost one hundred years as an advocate of this principle. Thus far her labors have been singularly blessed.

—Peter Paris, *The Social Teachings of the Black Churches* (Philadelphia: Fortress Press, 1985), 19–20.

CHAPTERS 1–7, THE GOSPEL IN THE JERUSALEM COMMUNITY

1:1-26, The Ascension and Commission

Acts 1 can be divided into two parts: vv. 1-14 and 15-26. Verses 1-14 summarize for "Theophilus" the events that took place at the end of the Gospel of Luke (Jesus' resurrection and appearances, 24:13-53) and the commissioning of the apostles, with the promise of the Holy Spirit. Important in this section is the programmatic statement of v. 8: "But you will receive power when the Holy Spirit has come upon you; and you will be my witnesses in Jerusalem, in all Judea and Samaria, and to the ends of the earth." By means of the gospel of Christ, God was inaugurating a new world order, which had begun with the ministry of Jesus, and the apostles through the power of the Spirit were to serve as God's *agents*.[22] Acts 1:8 shows that Luke was quite aware of the political and religious nature of Jesus' message regarding the inauguration of the reign of God. This message was a radical critique of all the political claims of earthly rulers, including that of the Roman Empire.[23] Moreover, while God's plan of renewal is mediated through Israel (a concern for the apostles, vv. 6-7), it would reach beyond Israel to include those who had been disenfranchised from Israel's commonwealth, the Gentiles. Hence, the reign of God for Luke would also challenge the claims of Israel regarding its exclusive rights and position within God's plan. For this reason, the inclusion of the Gentiles in the "new" people of God is an overarching concern of Acts.[24]

The second half of this opening chapter (vv. 15-26) deals with the issue of Judas, Jesus' betrayer, and the restoration of the Twelve. In vv. 15-20 Luke recounts a different version of Judas's suicide (cf. Matt 27:5, in which Judas hangs himself). The importance of recounting this story here is not just to restore the sacred number *twelve*, which represents the twelve tribes of Israel, but also to establish a chain of authority for the early church. For Luke only those who accompanied Jesus "beginning from the baptism of John until the day he was taken up" can be a witness to his resurrection (vv. 21-22).[25] The twelve apostles are also important because they have a particular function—to serve as witnesses (1:8)! Thus after casting lots, Matthias was chosen and added to the eleven apostles (vv. 21-26).

2:1-41, Pentecost: The *Democratization* of the Spirit

It has been said, "no text in Acts has received closer scrutiny than Acts 2. Whole theologies and denominations have been built up around the Acts 2 accounts."[26] To be sure, the recounting of the descent of the Holy Spirit on the day of Pentecost is a significant and pivotal event for Luke. The word "Pentecost" means "fiftieth." Greek-speaking Jews gave this name to the agricultural "festival of weeks," celebrated fifty days after Passover (after a "week of weeks"), at the completion of which a symbolic sacrifice was presented to God consisting of two loaves of bread made with the recently harvested grain, as well as certain animals prescribed by law (Lev 23:15-21). Jewish tradition also held that the law had been given on this day: but for Luke, now the Holy Spirit would be given and the birth of the church inaugurated![27] Acts 2 can be divided into three parts: (1) vv. 1-13 recount the Holy Spirit's empowering the apostles to be witnesses; (2) vv. 14-41 present Peter's sermon and the response by the crowd; and (3) vv. 42-47 depict the nature of communal relations in the early church (examined in the next section). More important than the structure of the passage itself is the manner in which Luke has made some structural parallels to his Gospel. For example, John the Baptist proclaims that the one who is coming "will baptize you with the Holy Spirit and with fire" (Luke 3:16). This is followed by the baptism of Jesus and the descent of the Holy Spirit upon Jesus (Luke 3:21-22), resulting in Jesus' inaugural sermon based on Isaiah (61:1; 58:6; 61:2; this includes the important reference to "the Spirit of the Lord is upon me . . ."), which clarifies that God's promises in the prophets are being fulfilled in Jesus' ministry (Luke 4:16-30).[28] These features are paralleled in Acts: Jesus promises the Holy Spirit (Luke 24:49; Acts 1:5), the disciples are filled with the Spirit resulting in Peter's programmatic sermon (Acts 2:14-41), and they become witnesses proclaiming the gospel to the ends of the earth (thus fulfilling Acts 1:8). Whereas Jesus' ministry and message was to the people Israel, now the message, while beginning with Israel, is to reach all nations.

After the apostles have been empowered with "tongues of fire" (vv.1-13), Peter explains the events that have just taken place in response to the accusation of drunkenness (vv. 14-41). Peter's quote of Joel (vv. 17-21) plays a significant role in the entire book. Just as a quotation from Isaiah supplies the starting point of Jesus' sermon and ministry in Luke 4, Joel's prophecy summarizes the nature of all that follows in the rest of Acts and is paradigmatic for the ministry of the apostles, actualizing what was already implicit in the quote from Joel.[29] The story of Pentecost indicates that the coming of the Holy Spirit represents a new order that is manifested as a leveling power that destroys privilege: the Spirit is poured upon "all flesh," sons and daughters, young and old, male and female servants. Peter's speech does not initiate the worldwide Gentile mission but is presented essentially to ethnic Jews from all parts of the known world. However, Luke's use of ethnic Jews in the Diaspora indicates not only that they represent every nation, but also that the Holy Spirit eventually will overcome all barriers to the gospel—language, ethnicity, class, and gender. Thus Luke appropriated and incorporated this vision into his narrative of the apostles as they spread the gospel message. Yet Luke did not implement the *full implications* of this egalitarian vision into his narrative. Acts (and the Gospel of Luke) is generally held to be one of the New Testament writings that is affirming to women, but this is not necessarily unequivocal. Luke does not portray women as missionaries and preachers. Rather they are support workers and patrons for Paul's missionary activity. Despite Luke's ambivalence regarding women's leadership roles in ministry, women played a significant role in the leadership of the church. Early Christian writers (esp. Paul's letters) provide only hints of the extent of such leadership roles.[30] Nevertheless, African American Christians have found inspiration from the message of Pentecost in Acts 2.

Excursus—African Americans and Acts 2: Dynamic Spirituality and Elusive Equality

African American Christians in general found the universalist themes in Acts 2 essential for addressing issues of slavery, human unity, racism, and segregation, while black women in particular could find justification for their practice of ministry and for challenging sexism in the church. Important is Luke's presentation of the dynamic spirituality of the event and the development of a new community. Acts 2 has been important in African American religious history not only for the experience of *glossolalia* (speaking in tongues), which was considered to be an important part of the "Latter Rain" or the "Pentecostal movement," but also with the hope of a more equal and unified humanity.

The Pentecostal movement began with the preaching of W. J. Seymour, a self-educated African American traveling Holiness preacher originally from Louisiana, at the Azuza Street Revival of 1906–1909 in Los Angeles, and it would have far-reaching implications for American spirituality. While initiated by an African American preacher, the movement was an atypical interracial movement from which whites later withdrew.[31] At Azuza, blacks, whites, Mexicans, and Asians alike sang and worshiped together: "the inter-racial character . . . on Azuza Street was indeed a kind of miracle. It was, after all, a time of growing, not diminishing, racial separation everywhere else." While observations by many whites about the interracial nature of the movement in the early day of the movement were negative, one white preacher wrote in his diary: "the color line was washed away by the blood."[32] Such positive observations were rare by whites and would soon give way to the separatist ideology of the day, causing Seymour to rethink his understanding of tongues.

Seymour's continued attacks from white preachers caused him to rethink the power of *glossolalia* alone as a force to eradicate racism and separatism. During the initial years of the movement, he put central emphasis on "tongues" both as the clearest evidence of the baptism in the Holy Spirit and as an indication of the Last Days. But discovering that folks speaking in tongues could still continue to practice racism convinced him that it was not tongues that were most important but "the *dissolution of racial barriers* that was the surest sign of the Spirit's Pentecostal presence."[33] Many white Pentecostals did not agree. Having become uncomfortable with the disgust of other whites "worshiping with niggers," early white Pentecostals opted to reject black leadership and interracial fellowship but keep the tongues. Disheartened by the behavior of many whites, Seymour began to teach

that tongue speaking was "one of the gifts of the Spirit," if indeed a gift at all. In other words, he stated: "If you get angry, or speak evil, or backbite, I care not how many tongues you may have, you have not the baptism with the Holy Spirit." The genuine fruit of the Spirit, he now recognized, were "love, joy, peace," etc. (Gal 5:22-25).[34] What becomes increasingly evident in the African American experience is that what begins as an experience of spiritual dynamism becomes tempered by social realism: the need to challenge racist attitudes and social structures. Despite this reality, the impact of the Pentecostal movement cannot be understated, because what resulted from it was the establishment of the first black denomination that did not have its roots in a white denomination—the Church of God in Christ.

Charles Harrison Mason, a former Baptist minister, had an experience of "sanctification" in 1893. He formed a Holiness church in 1897, and called it the Church of God in Christ (COGIC). In 1907, while in attendance at the Azuza Street revival, he experienced *glossolalia*, which led to the founding of the COGIC denomination in that same year. This was the first black denomination to commission and ordain white ministers. Since COGIC was the only incorporated Pentecostal body from 1907 to 1914, it was the only ecclesiastical authority to which whites could appeal. As a result, C. H. Mason ordained many white men who were initially recognized as COGIC ministers. However, these same men, on account of segregation, organized what became the Assemblies of God, the largest white Pentecostal denomination in 1914, ending the brief interracial cooperation of black and white Pentecostals by 1924.[35] The COGIC fellowship began, as with the Azuza revival under Seymour, with the hope of the dissolution of racial (but not gender!)[36] barriers between believers. For whites, Pentecostalism has been significant for "tongues," not recognizing that for blacks it also should include the divine presence that brings all people together in reconciliation, creating a new community of unity and equality. This has been the particular contribution of African Americans to the various Pentecostal manifestations in America—the Spirit *democratizes* human relationships, dissolving the old patterns of domination and separation through the egalitarianism of the Spirit. Luke, in Acts, sought to bear this out in his account of the early church. What was promised in Joel is to be realized in the community of the baptized. If African American males consistently viewed this ideal as applying to the racial situation in the United States, African American women understood it as including the gender equality issue, for the passage also says, "and your daughters shall prophesy." For several black women, and a growing number of black men,[37] this means a leveling of the barriers against women in the gospel ministry.

Early on, black women recognized the impact of Acts 2 for validating their call to ministry. The first black woman on record to make a plea for the recognition of her ministry with Richard Allen and his AME church, Jarena Lee, uses the quotation of Joel's prophecy in Acts as the opening caption to her spiritual biography.[38] Julia A. J. Foote, a member of the AME Zion Church and preacher of the nineteenth century, practiced her ministry until around 1900.[39] In her spiritual autobiography, *A Brand Plucked from the Fire* (1879), she describes her call to ministry in terms of the Spirit's prompting with reproach following, and also presented a strong argument for supporting women preachers using the Joel prophecy of Acts 2. She argues:

> I could not believe that it was a short-lived impulse or spasmodic influence that impelled me to preach. I read that on the

day of Pentecost was the Scripture fulfilled as found in Joel ii.28, 29; and it certainly will not be denied that women as well as men were at that "time filled with the Holy Ghost," because it is expressly stated that women were among those who continued in prayer and supplication, waiting for the fulfillment of the promise. Women and men are classed together, and if the power to preach the Gospel is short-lived and spasmodic in the case of women, it must be equally so in that of men; and if women have lost the gift of prophecy, so have men.[40]

Likewise Rosa A. Horn, known as Mother Horn by her followers, was an extremely effective speaker possessing great charisma, education, and culture. In her sermon "Was a Woman Called to Preach? Yes!" preached on a black radio station in New York City during the late 1930s, she used Joel's prophecy to support women's preaching.

> Note that when God said your sons and your daughters shall prophesy (preach), that meant man and woman. . . . Did not the Lord say that He would pour out His spirit upon all flesh in the last days? Yes, the last days, saith God, the last days. When you see the women preaching in the pulpit, preaching in the house, preaching in the streets, preaching everywhere, these are some of the signs of the last days. . . . Surely the Lord has called the women, under the Law and under Grace and he uses them whenever he needs them.

For Horn, scripture confirms the contemporary activity of women in ministry, and she also argues that biblical women not only were equal to men in leading godly lives but often excelled men in doing God's work.[41]

The Pentecost presentation of Acts 2 was thus important in the African American religious tradition because it supplied a basis for the black church to argue for inclusive and just practices within the church and American society. For black women it meant that the black church could not, on the one hand, argue for racial equality and, on the other hand, deny equal opportunity for women in ministry.

2:43-47; 4:32-37, "There Was Not a Needy Person Among Them": African Americans, Acts, and Socialism

At Acts 2:43-47 and 4:32-37 Luke adds brief summaries regarding the nature of the social relations among the early church community: "all who believed were together and had all things in common" (2:44); and "there was not a needy person among them, for as many as owned lands or houses sold them and brought the proceeds of what was sold . . . [and] laid it at the apostles' feet" (4:34-35). Luke's description of the early community may be a reflection of Deut 15:4-11, in which Israel is admonished to observe the law of God in such a manner that there "be no one in need among you." It is striking that in the Gospel of Luke the poor are a constant theme, but in Acts the word "poor" does not even appear. Luke operates with a prophecy-fulfillment scheme and, for him, the promise of Deuteronomy is being fulfilled in the early church. The apparent theme of the summary passages is money, but behind this theme is a particular understanding of the church and its mission: to address concretely the issue of poverty.[42] Some have suggested that the early church practiced a form of primitive communalism or socialism. While there has been no clear consensus on a descriptive term for their early practice, a few black preachers of the early twentieth century perceived in the text of Acts a scriptural validation for socialists idealism in America and a remedy to racism and poverty

within black communities and the black labor class.

The writings and speeches of black socialist preachers reflected the standard Socialist Party position on the "Negro question": it had nothing special to offer the "Negro" except the same opportunities as his white laborer. But the Socialist Party assured blacks that their plight under capitalism would be solved automatically under socialism. Unfortunately, no black socialist preacher called the Socialist Party to task for such an assumption, nor for failing to support campaigns against disfranchisement, segregation, lynching, and peonage in the South. They apparently accepted the party's position that the grievances of black workers were identical to those of white workers. Nevertheless, black socialist preachers repeatedly emphasized that blacks would have the most to gain from a socialist victory because the "colored man is the worst off of all the working class of people." Therefore it was in the basic interest of blacks to support the Socialist Party, "the party which will solve the problems of the black man, as well as those of his white brother."[43] Rev. George Washington Woodbey would add that it was in the interest of "the women, more than the men . . . if possible, to be Socialists because they suffer more from capitalism than anyone else."[44]

Although not the first African American preacher to espouse socialist ideals, Woodbey, of San Diego, became the leading black socialist preacher in the United States during the first decade of the twentieth century, and his major publications on socialism have been preserved.[45] It was Woodbey's ability to explain socialism in simple terms, however, that would make him a leader in the socialist cause and lead to his authorship of two pamphlets. The first, *What to Do and How to Do It: Socialism vs. Capitalism*, is a forty-four-page booklet consisting of a dialogue between the author and his mother. His second pamphlet, *The Bible and Socialism: A Conversation between Two Preachers*, is a ninety-six-page booklet consisting of a dialogue between Woodbey and a local pastor. Just as his mother was converted at the end of the first pamphlet, so, too, is the pastor by the close of *The Bible and Socialism*.[46] For Woodbey the Bible teaches "cooperative commonwealth." As a matter of fact, "the Bible, no more than the Socialists, holds out charity as a solution of economic difficulties."[47] Moreover, in his pamphlet *The Bible and Socialism,* Woodbey titles a section, "The Ancient Churches Cooperative Institutions." It is here that he reflects upon Acts. To the visiting pastor he says:

> Suppose, Pastor, we inquire what kind of an institution the early church was, so far as it touches the economic questions socialists and capitalists are now struggling over. . . . Now, the fact is, the church was organized on a cooperative basis, in which all shared alike. "Now the whole group of those who believed were of one heart and soul, and no one claimed private ownership of any possessions, but every-

thing they owned was held in common." [Acts 4:32, KJV]. . . . Here they ignore the so-called right of private ownership. . . . "They had all things in common." That is, they had economic equality. "Neither was there any that lacked." In other words, there was no poverty, as there need not be where the people cooperate in place of competing. This tells us how it was done: "There was not a needy person among them, for as many as owned lands or houses sold them and brought the proceeds of what was sold. They laid it at the apostles' feet, and it was distributed to each as any had need."[Acts 4:34-35][48]

Woodbey's reading of Acts 2:43-47 and 4:32-37 provided sure and convincing evidence for him that within the social practices of the early church community lay the basis for supporting socialist ideals of cooperative living. When he proffered several proof-texts from the Old Testament prophets, it could be argued that such a social arrangement was appropriate for Israel but not for the church. Luke's depiction of social arrangements in Acts, however, was solid proof that socialist

---

George Woodbey on Acts 6

"It seems that the whole burden of distribution, as well as preaching was, at first, laid on the apostles, but when complaints arose about some widows not getting fair treatment, the apostles called on the whole people to appoint seven agents, known for honesty and goodness, to take charge of the goods; one of the prominent features of the coming Cooperative Commonwealth. The people must govern everything and settle their own disputes; appoint their own men to take charge of the cooperative stores of the nation, and distribute their goods. Since the churches have ceased to be what they should be on the question of economics, these officers, known as deacons, in other parts of the scriptures, have become largely useless (see Acts vi:1-6; 1 Timothy iii:8-13)."

—Quoted in Philip S. Foner, ed. *Black Socialist Preacher: The Teachings of Reverend George Washington Woodbey and His Disciple, Reverend G. W. Slater, Jr.* (San Francisco: Synthesis, 1983), 195.

principles were compatible with Christian principles of charity and almsgiving. He also could find in Acts 6:1-6 another example of cooperative living within the first Christian community. Acts 6:1-6 supplied Woodbey with an example of how the common working people should have the privilege of self-governance. Thus, for Woodbey, people's lives and livelihood should not be imposed from above, but arise from the cooperative community.

In the end, the articles, books, speeches, and sermons of black socialist preachers (and others) attest to the fact that, although the Christian Socialist movement was short-lived, it left a deeper impression on black Americans than did any of the other organized groups seeking to achieve socialism. To be certain, while the Christian Socialist movement never addressed the question of racism, nor did it have a special message designed specifically for the black dilemma in America, it was nevertheless moderately effective for a short while to some black ministers because it harked back to the principles of early Christianity by viewing "the cooperative commonwealth as the material expression of the teachings of Christ."[49]

3:1—4:31, Power, Signs and Wonders, and Persecution

The promise that they would receive power when the Holy Spirit came upon them was fulfilled in chap. 3. Peter and John heal a lame man at the gate of the temple in the name of Jesus (vv. 3:1-10), and this healing provides an occasion for Peter's second sermon (vv. 3:11-26). This second sermon incurs the wrath of the temple authorities, because Peter and the apostles preach that in Jesus there is a resurrection of the dead (4:1-4). Since it is evening, Peter and John are kept in prison over night. On the next day Peter speaks again before the "rulers, elders, and scribes assembled in Jerusalem," prompted by the questions "By what power or by what name did you do this?" (4:6-

7). Peter's response is, "Jesus Christ of Nazareth, whom you crucified, whom God raised from the dead" (4:10). It is by this name alone that signs and wonders are performed and salvation is offered (4:12). Because the man was healed, and considering the amazing boldness of Peter and John, the rulers and elders offer no rebuttal. However, the apostles are warned again to speak no more in the name of Jesus, to which they reply, "We cannot keep from speaking about what we have seen and heard" (4:19). After returning to the community of believers, they join together in prayer (Ps 2:1-2 is applied to their current situation, 4:25-26) and are strengthened and filled with the Holy Spirit (4:23-31).

4:32—5:11, Believers and the Community of Goods

In 4:32-37 (see also the comments on 2:43-47) Luke presents a pristine picture of the early Jerusalem community through its practice of communal sharing. The sharing of possessions with the poor and less fortunate is an important concern for Luke. This idea is highlighted in Luke's account of the Beatitudes (Luke 6:20-23)[50] and the parable of the rich man and Lazarus (Luke 16:19-31). Important in this summary is how the account sets up what follows in 5:1-11, the account of Ananias and his wife, Sapphira. In 4:36-37 Luke contrasts Barnabas's positive example of selling his field and presenting it to the apostles with the negative example that follows. These examples serve to illustrate how those with possessions are to handle their possessions in the community of the faithful. While poverty cannot be solved for the world at large, for Luke it can be ameliorated within the community of the followers of Christ.

5:12-41, Signs, Wonders, and Persecution
Healing the sick and the demon-possessed (5:12-16) attracts the attention of the

authorities again (namely, the high priest and the Sadducees), and the apostles are arrested and imprisoned a second time (5:17-18). This time there is a miraculous escape during the night, and they are commanded by the Lord to enter the temple and to continue their teaching (5:19-21a; cf. 12:6-11). Not finding them in the prison but teaching in the temple (5:21b-26), the authorities bring them before the council again and remind them that they were not to teach in Jesus' name (v. 28). Peter's response is similar to that of 4:6-7: "We must obey God rather than any human authority" (v. 29). Then he bears witness to the crucifixion and exaltation of Christ (vv. 30-32), which enrages the authorities, who are tempted to murder them. However, they are counseled by one of their number, Gamaliel, not to do them harm lest they are found to be fighting against God (vv. 33-39a). After flogging the apostles, they send them away; the apostles count themselves blessed to be found worthy to suffer for Christ's sake (vv. 40-42).

6–7, Community, Conflict, and Confrontation

Unlike the pristine picture of the early community of believers summarized in 2:43-47 and 4:32-37, in 6:1-6 there is evidence of mounting tension in the community. The Greek-speaking Jewish Christians (the Hellenists) and the Aramaic-speaking Jewish Christians have a disagreement over the neglect of the Hellenists' widows in the "daily distribution of food" (v. 1), which results in the addition of new leaders within the community. This is the first "breach" in the idyllic portrayal of the community, which will providentially aid in the expansion of the gospel (cf. Acts 8:4). This episode is often seen as the institution of the deaconate in later traditions, and feminist scholars have seen the issue of "serving at table" and the specific mention of widows as more than the widows getting their

chance to serve bread to the hungry. Indeed, two important figures out of the seven are not standing by waiting tables; Stephen and Philip are powerful preachers and evangelists. The powerful example of Stephen and his witness unto death, his "martyrdom" (*martyr* is the Greek word for "witness"), is the subject of 6:8—8:1a.

In Acts 6:8-15 Luke recounts Stephen's grace, power, and performance of "wonders and signs" among the people. Stephen is the first individual outside of the Twelve to be depicted in this manner. This is an indication that the expansion of the gospel requires a larger circle of "Spirit filled" individuals. Like the apostles before him, Stephen encounters opposition. This time it is not the "authorities" but members of the synagogue (v. 9). This is where the story resembles intentionally the trial of Jesus in the Gospel of Luke. False witnesses are secretly brought in to discredit Stephen's message and mission (Acts 6:11-14): "We have heard him say that this Jesus of Nazareth will destroy this place and will change the customs that Moses handed on to us" (v. 14). When asked, "Are these things so?" (7:1), Stephen launches into a long speech (7:2-53) that contains thirty citations from the Bible (for early Christians this would be the Septuagint, the Greek version of the Hebrew Bible). In his speech he begins with the call of Abraham and the promise made to him (vv. 2-8) and the selling of Joseph and the patriarch's sojourn in Egypt (vv. 9-16). In 7:17-50 he recounts the exodus, wilderness wanderings, Moses' reception of the law at Sinai, the apostasy of the Golden Calf, and the conquest of the land of Canaan. In his recounting of the history of Israel Stephen makes special note of the children of Israel's continuous failure to comply with the plan of God for their lives. This is spelled out dramatically in vv. 51-53, wherein Stephen charges his fellow Israelites with a history of opposition to the Holy Spirit and to those whom the Spirit has commissioned (Moses, the prophets, and finally Jesus, the Righteous One). Becoming enraged at his words, mob violence ensues (vv. 7:54—8:1). Dragging him out of the city, they stone him to death. Stephen thus becomes the first Christian martyr in Holy Writ. Like Jesus, he asks for forgiveness for his assailants. Standing there in the midst is a young man named Saul (v. 68). This is the first mention of Saul (Paul) in the text.

8:1—13:3, The Gospel from Judea to Samaria and Beyond

8:1-25, Philip and the Gospel in Samaria

In Acts 8 Philip proclaims the gospel in Samaria and begins missions to the near-kinsfolk of Israel, the Samaritans, once considered outside of the covenant promises of Israel. In 8:2-40 the narrative takes a new direction. Following the programmatic outline of 1:8, the gospel is now moving toward Samaria and other non-Jewish regions. It has been suggested that this entire section is a bridge between the preceding chapters and the rest of the book. Up to this point Jerusalem has been Luke's primary focus. However, with the election of the seven (cf. 6:1-6) new leadership emerges, which is now composed mostly of Hellenistic Jews (many of whom were nurtured outside of Palestine and whose primary language is Greek). Those from this number take the message beyond the confines of Jerusalem and eventually outside of Palestine. In the next section (beginning at chap. 11), the focus of the narrative will switch to Antioch and to the mission to the Gentiles, which will occupy the rest of the book.[51]

Acts 8:5-13 depicts Philip's mission to Samaria. Scattered abroad on account of the persecution that was gaining ground under the leadership of Saul, those who departed preached the gospel beyond the borders of Jerusalem and Judea (8:3-4). Thus Luke makes it clear that the persecution had the positive effect of moving the church and the gospel into uncharted regions. Of important note is that both Stephen and Philip are "Hellenists" and thus outside the inner circle of apostles. Nevertheless, they represent an important group that will initiate the mission to the Gentiles (beginning at Antioch; cf. Acts 11), before the Twelve (and Paul as well) take part in the new missionary venture.

Proclaiming the Messiah to the Samaritans, Philip performed signs of healing and exorcism so that there was a great reception of his message (vv. 6-8). A certain Simon, known as "Magus," because he practiced such convincing magic in that city that he was known as "the power of God that is called Great," heard the message of Philip, and he too believed and was baptized and remained with Philip (v. 13). Based upon Philip's success in that region, the Jerusalem church "sent" Peter and John to Samaria (v. 14), and they prayed for the Samaritans and were "filled with the Holy Spirit" (vv. 15-17). For Luke, Philip's work required confirmation by the Jerusalem church and the apostles who were "authorized" to confer the Holy Spirit. This is important for establishing a chain of authority, which began with Jesus and then passed to the apostles and to those whom they appoint. This was part of the problem with Simon Magus's offer of money to receive the same power to confer the Holy Spirit (vv. 18-24); such gifts cannot be purchased! While rebuked by Peter and repenting of his error, Simon Magus would later be viewed as the progenitor of evil and heresy in the church.

8:26-40, The Conversion of an Ethiopian Eunuch: The Fulfillment of a Promise

Responding to the voice of the "angel of the Lord," Philip goes down to Gaza and finds an Ethiopian in his chariot reading a passage from Isaiah (vv. 27-34). Philip explains the passage to the eunuch, and, in response, the eunuch requests baptism (vv. 35-39). On baptizing this eunuch, Philip moves ahead of the rest of the church again, the implications of which will be discovered more profoundly in Acts 11. Thus he begins the mission to the Gentiles even before the actual leaders of the church have sanctioned it.[52] The leaders of the church of Jerusalem will acknowledge that "God has given even to the Gentiles the repentance that leads to life" only after the conversion of Cornelius in Acts 10 (11:18). Interestingly, contemporary scholarship has also followed this pattern of mitigating the significance of the conversion of the Ethiopian eunuch by suggesting that Luke does not follow a strictly chronological order in the presentation of the events. Rather he completes the "Acts of Philip" before moving to the next subject. In this line of argument, although the conversion of the Ethiopian appears in chap. 8 and that of Cornelius in chap. 10, the latter preceded the former.[53] This could be perceived as valuing the conversion of a European—a Roman centurion—over a *black* African—an official of the Candace.

What, then, is the significance for Luke of including a story about a recognizably black African court official? It is most probable that the story is consistent with the Lukan emphasis on universalism, a well-known and recurrent motif in both Luke and Acts.[54] The universal message of salvation accomplished in Christ is not ethnocentric but is available to both Jew and Greek.[55] This sense of the eventual geographical and ethnic expansion of the proclamation is present already in the Pentecost story (Acts 2). The Lukan theme of universal salvation and world mission unfolds throughout Acts as the gospel advances northward from Palestine through Syria (2:24), westward through Asia Minor (2:25—16:5), Europe (16:6—19:20), and finally to Rome

(19:21—28:31), the "capital" of the Gentile world. The conversion of an "Ethiopian" eunuch, then, provides a graphic illustration and symbol of the diverse persons who will constitute the church.[56] Therefore the forecast of the mission "to the end of the earth" (1:8) finds a symbolic fulfillment in 8:26-40. It is probable that the converted Ethiopian returned home, for, in ancient Greco-Roman reckoning, "Ethiopia" represented the southern "end of the earth." As a result of the expulsion of the "Hellenists" from Jerusalem, the gospel was passed on to Samaria and finally, in the figure of the Ethiopian on his way home, reached the "end of the earth" (Acts 1:8c; Zeph 3:10; Ps 68:32; Luke 11:31).[57]

The reason the geographical provenance of the Ethiopian eunuch has not received much attention and analysis is a result of an internal phenomenon within the ideological framework of the New Testament itself. There is a decided ideological and geographical shift from the southeastern region of the Mediterranean world to the northwest region. Early New Testament authors not only referred to Spain as the "limits of the West," but Rome is conceived as the capital of the Gentile world, replacing Jerusalem as the center of God's activity. Church historiography and later scholarship followed Paul westward to Rome. Thus the New Testament authors' conceptualization of the world scarcely included sub-Sahara Africa.[58] A second and more contemporary phenomenon is the failure of many Bible atlases to include the region south of Palestine and Egypt in its illustrations, which contributes to a general lack of familiarity with "Ethiopians" and their provenance for twentieth-century students of the Bible.[59] Finally, the presumptions of the Ethiopian's ethnographic identity as "marginally significant" or "inconsequential" for the Lukan theological perspective altogether may be traced to a larger problem in Western, post-

Enlightenment culture, wherein the signification and contributions of particular groups of persons have been historically marginalized or ignored. Clarice Martin calls this the "politics of omission."[60]

This is especially evident when it comes to the ethnographic identity of the Ethiopian eunuch. Is the Ethiopian Jew or Gentile? Did Luke leave his religious association purposefully ambiguous? Ernst Haenchen thinks so, stating that the story of Philip and the eunuch is simply a Hellenistic rival to that of Peter and Cornelius (Acts 10).[61] Cain Hope Felder, however, sees the possibility of racial overtones in the way that Luke has presented the story, because the Spirit does not descend upon the Ethiopian after baptism, as it does with Cornelius after Peter's sermon in Acts 10. In the end, however, Felder recognizes that this would be counter to Luke's universalist theme.[62] I do not see this as an issue representing racial overtones either, but one that has to do with Luke's theology: only legitimate apostles can confer the Holy Spirit, and for Luke Cornelius's conversion came by way of legitimation through Peter (cf. Acts 2; 8; etc.).[63] Racial overtones may be detected, however, in the way that Western scholarship has dealt with the passage. Rarely is it admitted explicitly that the Ethiopian eunuch is a *recognizable black African* from ancient Nubia. Neither does traditional scholarship develop in any detail the significance of this episode for Luke's theological perspective. As Clarice Martin states, "examination of the Ethiopian's ethnographic identity is generally perceived to be unimportant." She argues further that a survey of the literature reveals three basic approaches to the Ethiopian's ethnographic identity: (1) avoid any detailed discussion by hiding behind a veil of uncertainty, (2) provide only a cursory discussion of Nubia, and rarely with any explicit identification of Nubians or Ethiopians as black-skinned

people,[64] and (3) supply a clear and explicit appraisal of the ethnographic identity of the "Ethiopian" eunuch, with the distinguishing mark being the color of his skin.[65]

The Ethiopian eunuch's conversion on the whole reveals Luke's recurrent "witness" theme and prophecy-fulfillment character. For Luke, Isa 53:7-12 exemplifies the prophecy-fulfillment motif, which is the locus for Philip's preaching in Acts 8:26-40. First, the conversion of the Ethiopian as a *eunuch* represents the fulfillment of Isa 56:3-7, in which the prophet heralds a day when eunuchs will find acceptance into the plan of God. Second, the Ethiopian's conversion exhibits the fulfillment of the promise of an unconditional and extraordinary acceptance of foreigners into the community of the faithful in accordance with Isa 56:3-7. The Ethiopian becomes a prototype of the "foreigner" who enjoys unconditional acceptance into the new eschatological community. Thus the Church of Ethiopia, one of the most ancient in the world, claims that its origins are precisely in this encounter between Philip and the Ethiopian eunuch.[66] Finally, the conversion of the Ethiopian eunuch demonstrates for African Americans of the nineteenth and early twentieth centuries the fulfillment of Ps 68:31 that Ethiopia will "stretch out her hands to God."

EXCURSUS—THE PROMISE OF AFRICA'S REDEMPTION

The great pronouncement of Ps 68:31 ("Ethiopia will soon stretch out her hands to God") became a classic prophecy of the ultimate fulfillment of Africa and its descendants' social and cultural redemption. Numerous references to this text in sermons, speeches, and other writings during the nineteenth and early twentieth centuries related it to racial pride as a counter to racial prejudice, but it ultimately became the cornerstone of missionary emigrationism in the United States and Africa.[67] Rev. Rufus L. Perry, ex-slave Baptist pastor in Brooklyn, N.Y., refers to the theme of racial pride by arguing that American blacks have a glorious history that goes back to the ancient civilizations of Egypt and Ethiopia:

> If it be here shown beyond reasonable doubt . . . that the ancient Egyptians, Ethiopians and Libyans . . . were the ancestors of the present race of Ham, then the Negro of the 19th century may point to them with pride; and with all who would find in him a return to racial celebrity, when in the light of a Christian civilization, Ethiopia shall stretch out her hands unto God.[68]

In like manner, Dr. E. C. Morris, at the end of his National Baptist presidential address of 1898, provides the religious optimism characteristic of the hope of Africa's redemption by allusion to the Ethiopian:

> I can hear the voice of that multitude as they raise the old battle cry of "One Lord, one faith, one baptism"; and in that grand procession, as they march against the powers of darkness, I can see the Galilean Jew sitting in the chariot with the Ethiopian eunuch, and their song is: "the kingdoms of this world are become the kingdoms of our Lord, and of his Christ; and he shall reign forever and ever."[69]

Finally, Zilpha Elaw, a woman preacher of the nineteenth century, used the story of the Ethiopian eunuch to argue against notions of "black inferiority" and racial prejudice:

> The Almighty accounts not the black races of man either in the order of nature or spiritual capacity as inferior to white;

for He bestows his Holy Spirit on, and dwells in them as readily as in persons of whiter complexion: the Ethiopian eunuch was adopted as a son and heir of God; and when Ethiopia shall stretch forth her hands unto him [Ps. 68:31], their submission and worship will be graciously accepted.[70]

9:1-31, From Persecutor to Preacher: The "Conversion" and Mission of Saul of Tarsus

Luke relates the conversion of Saul in Acts 9:1-19a, which is also recounted subsequently in 22:4-16 and 26:12-18. This, however, is not the first reference to Saul. At the stoning of Stephen, Saul is the "young man" who not only approves of Stephen's stoning but also at whose feet Stephen's assailants laid their coats (7:58; 8:1). But at Saul's "conversion," he who once persecuted the faith will become its primary proponent.[71] Luke now moves closer to the character toward whom the narrative has been directed, Saul/Paul, who is the "chosen vessel" to take the gospel to the ends of the earth (cf. 9:15-16). Immediately after his life-changing experience, Saul wastes no time proclaiming Jesus in Damascus and also makes a quick visit to Jerusalem, where Barnabas helps him to gain acceptance among the apostles and the Jerusalem community (9:19b-31). To be sure, as the narrative evolves, "Luke's portrayal of Paul borders on idealism. [Paul] rarely, if ever, makes mistakes. He follows the whispers of the Holy Spirit."[72] For Luke, Paul is the ideal "convert" as well as the ideal apostle. To some degree the Paul of Acts is the "construction" of the author of the work. Regarding such a portrayal of Paul, C. K. Barrett has asserted:

> This is the legendary Paul, if the adjective may be used to describe a picture by no means wholly fictitious but one made, in

good faith, by omissions, arrangements, and emphases, so as to present to later generations the Paul that Luke, and no doubt some of his contemporaries, wished them to see. It is not quite the Paul of the letters, and it is not quite the Paul of the Pastoral Epistles, but it is fairly closely related to both.[73]

This assessment and interpretation of Paul is surprisingly similar to that in the African American religious tradition.

EXCURSUS—THE AFRICAN AMERICAN TRADITION'S APPRAISAL OF PAUL

The Paul of Acts, indefatigable defender of Gentile inclusion, offered a more acceptable picture for the African American freedom struggle than Paul as seen through the "household codes"[74] and the Pastoral Epistles (1–2 Timothy and Titus) and, of course, Philemon. Such texts supplied the backbone for the construction of the image of the "pro-slavery Paul," who was created in the likeness of the slave-holding class to support their economic exploitation of black labor and who also mandated slaves to "obey your masters in everything" (Col 3:22; cf. Eph 6:5) while having little to say to masters.[75] For this reason, "The usefulness of the Pauline letters to systems of domination and oppression is . . . clear and palpable."[76] Accordingly, African American slaves "believed that Paul religiously took away the freedom God and Jesus had so graciously offered."[77] This means that they did not simply interpret the biblical texts out of their experience; they also critiqued them by means of and because of that experience.[78]

Despite the pro-slavery portrayal of Paul, several blacks developed a more nuanced understanding of Paul: they sought to "put Paul back together again."[79] Black abolitionists believed that a different image of Paul could be reconstructed to support slavery's abolition and win Paul over for the cause of freedom by utilizing positive statements of Paul against those that were negative, and by seeking to find the general "spirit" of Paul. In African Americans' reappraisal of Paul through the lens of Acts, he can be seen as a leader in an egalitarian "integration movement." African Americans' Paul of liberation could be seen most clearly through Luke's portrayal of Paul as an egalitarian on issues of social inclusion, which provided them with a "new principle" for understanding God, humanity, and their social situation.[80]

9:32—11:18, Peter's Mission to Gentiles: Recognizing God's Impartiality—"God Is No Respecter of Persons"

It is customary in Luke's narrative that signs and wonders take place before important events. So here, before Peter's encounter with Cornelius, Peter heals Aeneas in Lydda (9:32-35) and raises a disciple named Tabitha (Greek: Dorcas) in Joppa (9:36-43). Both stories are patterned on Jesus' healings in the Gospels (Luke 5:24-25; 8:41-42, 49-56; Mark 5:22-24, 35-43). It also appears that believers were already in these areas, perhaps as a result of Philip's missionary activity in these regions (even into Caesarea; cf. 8:40). Therefore, as a result of Philip's missionary activity, which pushed the mission to those on the margins, the evangelization of the Gentiles would receive further impetus from the conversion of Cornelius (10:1-48). Although this passage is usually titled "the conversion of Cornelius," it is just as much a conversion of Peter, that is, of his attitude and opinion of Gentiles.[81]

After the outpouring of the Holy Spirit in Acts 2 and the inauguration of a "new age" of God's favor, the barriers of separation between

Jew and Gentile must now be eradicated. For this reason, several interpreters have viewed Acts 10 and 11 as comprising one of the critical turning points in the entire narrative, for it is after this episode that the Christians in Jerusalem through the testimony of Peter come to the conclusion that the gospel is also for Gentiles (11:1-18). This realization will become the fundamental thesis throughout the book of Acts; it will guide the unfolding narrative leading to and culminating in the mission of Paul.

The realization of Gentile inclusion into the people of God did not come easily. Both Cornelius in Caesarea (10:1-9a) and Peter in Joppa (10:9b-23a) received visions in order to open the way for greater inclusivity. In contrast to Cornelius, who understands the implications of his vision, Peter is simply perplexed. When Cornelius's messengers arrive at Simon the tanner's home, the Spirit tells Peter to receive the guests and go with them. A significant point in this story is that the vision takes place in Joppa. It was in Joppa that God instructed the prophet Jonah to go to Nineveh to preach to non-Israelites. Jonah instead took a ship in the opposite direction and sped toward Tarshish (Jonah 1:3). One might recall also that Peter's name is "Simon, son of Jonah" (Matt 16:17). Like the earlier prophet Jonah, this Simon, son of Jonah, in the very same city of Joppa, will be given a call to go beyond the limits of the people of Israel.[82] Thus when Peter goes to Caesarea and enters Cornelius's house (10:23b-48), he does not show great diplomacy. The first statement he makes is that it is "unlawful" for him to associate with or visit the home of Cornelius, a Gentile. Furthermore, he confesses that he has complied only because he had a vision in which God informed him, "do not call anyone profane or unclean" (10:28). Before receiving this vision "unclean" is precisely what Peter would have called Cornelius. Nev-

ertheless, Cornelius's disclosure of his own vision from God seems to astonish Peter and awakens him to a new realization (10:30-33). Peter declares that he now understands "*that God shows no partiality*, but in every nation anyone who fears him and does what is right is acceptable to him" (10:24-35). Peter comes to the conclusion that God has indeed spoken to Cornelius, and thus the gospel is opened and affirmed to all Gentiles. Peter then gives a sermon and there is a "Gentile Pentecost" (10:44-48). This is proof of their acceptance to God; the giving of the Holy Spirit is the eraser of ethnic difference.[83] Perhaps it was not coincidental that Luke tells us that Peter stayed in Joppa "for some time [lodging in the house of] a certain Simon, a tanner" (9:43). The occupation of a tanner was considered unclean by many Jews, because tanners had to work with dead animals (cf. Lev 11:39). It was precisely at the house of this Simon the tanner that God gave Peter a vision of unclean animals, which taught him not to consider anyone unclean or unacceptable to God.[84]

Peter defends this new revelation to the Jerusalem church that chides him for going to the uncircumcised and eating with them (11:1-18). Peter relates his vision on the rooftop in Joppa to the Jerusalem community, ending with a powerful challenge: "If then God gave them the same gift that he gave us when we believed in the Lord Jesus Christ, who was I that I could hinder God?" (v. 17) Therefore in Acts Peter is seen as an unwavering defender of Gentile freedom (cf. Acts 15), unlike the picture Paul portrays in Galatians 2. Luke's emphasis is that the nature and spread of the gospel is coordinated by the Jerusalem church in the initial stages (cf. 8:14; 11:1, 22). With some struggle, the Jerusalem community comes to accept Gentile membership into the community of the followers of Jesus (11:18).

Excursus—African American Appropriation of an Egalitarian Statement

As noted in the introduction, Acts 10:34-36 was a key passage in the African American protest tradition, helping to level prophetic critiques of American racism and prejudice. The Rev. Nathaniel Paul made a statement on July 5, 1827, that supplies us with examples of two statements from Acts that would become the bedrock of African American protest discourse against white racism and oppression:

> The progress of emancipation . . . is certain: It is certain because that God who has made of one blood all nations of men and, who is said to be no respecter of persons, has so decreed. . . . Did I believe that it would always continue, and that man to the end of time would be permitted with impunity to usurp the same undue authority over his fellows, I would . . . ridicule the religion of the Savior of the world. . . . I would consider my bible as a book of false and delusive fables, and commit it the flame; Nay, I would still go further: I would at once confess myself an atheist, and deny the existence of a holy God.[85]

This statement expresses the importance of Acts 10:34-36 and 17:26 for establishing the character of the biblical God of justice. Such an image of the divine could be invoked to counteract the god of slaveholding Christianity and the partial and prejudiced society in whose image the American slavocracy was created.

David Walker's famous *Appeal* of 1829 challenges this very image of the divine that would frustrate racial unity and impartial justice.[86] Walker understood Christianity and the biblical deity as mandating these very principles, which is the presupposition for both his biting prophetic critique of contemporary white Christianity and the cultivation of African American spirituality and ethics.[87]

Walker and other nineteenth-century African American Bible readers could see in Acts 10:34-36 a clear critique of racial and ethnic prejudice, which had to be rooted out directly by a revelation from God, resulting in Peter's declaration that "God is no respecter of persons" (KJV). With such a succinct and provocative statement in their arsenal, they could mold the rest of the Bible and bring it in line

---

David Walker and God's Impartiality

"Surely the Americans must believe that God is partial, notwithstanding his apostle Peter, declared before Cornelius and others that he has no respect to persons, but in every nation he that feareth God and worketh righteousness is accepted with him. [Acts 10:36]. . . . How can the preachers and people of America believe the Bible? Does it teach them any distinction on account of a man's color? . . . Can the American preachers appeal unto God, the Maker and Searcher of hearts, and tell him with the Bible in their hands, that they make no distinction on account of men's colour?"

—David Walker, "Our Wretchedness in Consequence of the Preachers of Religion," in Milton C. Sernett, *African American Religious History: A Documentary Witness*, 2nd ed. (Durham, N.C.: Duke University Press, 2000), 99.

with their cause for freedom and justice. They could find support not only in Acts' portrayal of Peter, but also in that of Paul.

11:19-26, The First Jewish-Christian Mission Center to Gentiles: Syrian Antioch

On the spread of the gospel as a result of Stephen's persecution, Acts 11:19 seems to pick up the narrative from 8:1, 4. As the gospel spreads and the geography changes, so do the characters. In 11:20 Luke reports that "some men of Cyprus and Cyrene" came to Antioch and began preaching to the Greeks. Cyrene was a city in Libya on the northern shore of Africa, where there was a strong Jewish community. We are told the names of some of the individuals in 13:1: "Simon who was called Niger" (that is, "Simon the Black") and Lucius of Cyrene. It is possible that they were leaders of the church in Antioch and even more probable these two "blacks" may have been among those who first preached the gospel to the Gentiles in Antioch. This would be the first Jewish-Christian mission center to the Gentiles, which Luke again pictures as coordinated by Jerusalem: when news arrived that the gospel had reached this region they "sent Barnabas to Antioch" (v. 22). Barnabas went to Tarsus to retrieve Paul and they stayed together there for one year teaching a great number of people, and it is at Antioch that the believers were first called "Christians" (v. 26). In 11:27-30 Luke provides the origin of the "collection for the Jerusalem saints" mentioned by Paul in his letter as a significant part of his mission to unify Jew and Gentile. For Luke it was to provide aid to the Jerusalem community on account of a famine predicted by prophets from Jerusalem.

12:1—13:3, The Apostles, Persecution, and the Death of Herod Agrippa

Unlike the earlier floggings that took place against the apostles (Acts 4 and 5), Herod Agrippa I (grandson of Herod the Great) kills one of the apostles. James, the brother of John and son of Zebedee, is martyred (v. 2). Seeking to do the same to Peter after the Passover (the parallels with Jesus' Passion are striking), Herod Agrippa has him put in prison between four squads, indicating the impossibility of escape (v. 5). Nevertheless, this is exactly what happens: Peter, believing he is having a vision, is miraculously released according to the church's earnest prayers (vv. 5, 12). But when he arrives at the home of Mary, the mother of John Mark (v. 12), where the believers had gathered to pray for Peter's release, they do not believe the report of Rhoda, the young maid who hears Peter's voice at the outer gate (v. 14). While certain elements of this episode are comedic, it must be kept in mind that Rhoda is portrayed as a stereotypical "slave" as perceived in Greco-Roman culture. Eventually Peter's continued knocking brings out the inhabitants, whom Peter instructs to tell what has happened to James (the brother of Jesus, v. 17). After this, Peter appears only one more time—at the Jerusalem conference, which is recounted in Acts 15:1-7. By the time of this conference, James, the brother of the Lord, has ascended to authority in the Jerusalem church. This episode ends with a reversal of fortune; in the beginning of the narrative, Herod killed James; now the angel of the Lord kills Herod (12:20-23).[88] Immediately after the narrative of Herod's death, Luke takes up the activities of the Antiochian church (12:24—13:4). Completing their mission there, Paul and Barnabas return with John Mark to Antioch *from* Jerusalem (12:25).[89] Just as the Jerusalem church earlier commissioned others to do the work of ministry, now the church at Antioch commissions Saul and Barnabas to the mission field (13:2-3). The important leaders in the Antiochian community included members who were of African descent (13:1, Simeon, "called Niger" and Lucius of Cyrene). This is a significant reminder of the barrier-breaking and inclusive nature of the gospel.

CHAPTERS 13–15, THE GOSPEL AND THE INCLUSION OF GENTILES

13:1—14:28, The Journey to Cyprus, Pisidian Antioch, and Iconium

While the prophets and teachers in Antioch fasted and laid hands on (ordained or commissioned) Saul and Barnabas, it was the Holy Spirit that guided and coordinated the growth and movement of the church, as 13:1-4 makes clear. As is Saul's custom according to Acts, he regularly begins mission in the synagogues of a given area before reaching out to Gentiles (13:5; cf. also 13:14; 14:1; 17:1, 10, 17; 18:4, 19; also Rom 1:16). At Acts 13:9 the name "Paul" appears for the first time: "Saul, also known as Paul." "Saul" was the name that he used among Jews, and "Paul" was his name among Gentiles.[90] Through the power of the Holy Spirit Paul also works miracles, in this case a "curse" on the false prophet and magician Bar-Jesus (v. 10). Not only do we have striking parallels with Peter's encounter with Simon in Acts 8, but also with Paul's conversion in Acts 9. After converting the proconsul (v. 12), Paul and his companions continues on to Antioch of Pisidia (in Asia Minor): but John (Mark) leaves them and returns to Jerusalem (13:13-14). This youthful decision would portend the end of the missionary relationship between Paul and Barnabas (cf. Acts 15:36-41). Nevertheless, Paul and Barnabas preach with much success to the Gentiles, although they experience opposition from their Jewish kinfolk of high standing. So they head toward Iconium.

Upon reaching Iconium, the same thing happens as in Antioch of Pisidia (14:1).

Paul: "Integrationist" Preacher and Missionary Exemplar

Beginning with Acts 13, the focus of the narrative shifts significantly. Paul's mission to the Gentiles takes center stage, while Peter and the Twelve practically disappear from the narrative. In addition, the central focus of mission shifts from Jerusalem to Antioch (11:19-30) and beyond this to Asia Minor, Greece, and ultimately Rome.[91] Two themes are underscored in Luke's unfolding narrative. First, Paul (and his companions, mainly Barnabas) can be seen as leading an "integration movement," which advocated Gentile inclusion into the newly constituting people of God on a nondiscriminatory basis (that is, without recourse to circumcision and Torah observance).[92] This theme and the image of Paul as a leader of the Gentile integration movement can be seen most clearly in Acts 15–20 (indeed, it is at Acts 20 that Paul journeys toward Jerusalem and ultimately Rome!). A key passage in the section is Acts 17, in which Paul gives the noted Areopagus speech in Athens. The second theme is the image of Paul as the great missionary who suffers many hardships in order to complete his call and mission (cf. Acts 9:16; "I myself will show him how much he must suffer for the sake of my name"). While this theme is apparent throughout Acts 13–28, the suffering motif becomes most prominent beginning at Acts 21:33, when Paul is arrested by Roman soldiers. It is such endurance and faithfulness in the face of adversity that underscores the theme (perhaps intended by Luke) that mission builds character and suffering refines it.

However, unlike in Antioch, where the Jews incited devout women and men of high standing, here the "unbelieving Jews" stir up the Gentiles. So Paul, Barnabas, and their companions flee to the surrounding country and continued preaching (14:2-7). Paul performs a miracle on a crippled man, and the crowds flock to him and Barnabas and address them as gods (14:8-18). Luke contrasts this reception with the struggle and suffering encountered when Jews from Antioch of Pisidia follow them to Lystra and stir up the crowd against them (14:19-23). Paul is stoned and dragged out of the city (v. 19; cf. 2 Cor 11:25). As they circle back through several of the cities they visited, where they proclaimed the word of God, they return to Syrian Antioch and share with the church what God is doing among the Gentiles (14:24-27).

15:1-35, The Jerusalem Conference: The Affirmation of the Gentiles

Luke's preceding account ends on a high note: "how [God] had opened a door of faith for the Gentiles" (14:27). Then some individuals, who maintain a different interpretation of the Jewish religious tradition and of the Gentiles' place within the emerging Christian community, threaten Paul's egalitarian movement. They teach, "Unless you are circumcised according to the custom of Moses, you cannot be saved" (15:1, 5). According to Acts, Philip (Acts 8), Peter (Acts 10), and now Paul and his companions had already undertaken missionary work to the Gentiles, "but now the Jerusalem church, always playing catch-up with God's plan, needed some major rethinking about what the church would be like and how it would go about its missionary work."[93] This issue is addressed in Acts 15, in a gathering that has come to be known as the Jerusalem conference. Paul and Barnabas go up to Jerusalem to confer with the Jerusalem

contingent about the matter (15:2-5; the most important figures being Peter and James, "the brother of the Lord"). Interestingly, Paul and Barnabas are not given voice in Luke's portrayal of the event. It is Peter who speaks first (Acts 15:7-11), reflecting, it would appear, on his encounter with Cornelius (in Acts 10). He is followed by James, who affirms Peter's words (Acts 15:13-21). As a result of the confirmation of the two "pillars" of the Jerusalem church (cf. Gal 2:9), Gentiles are asked only to abstain from idol meat and from the blood of strangled animals, and to avoid sexual immorality (Acts 15:23-29). Having received support from Jerusalem, Paul and Barnabas return to Antioch and read the letter regarding the resolution of the matter (15:30-35). Paul's mission among the Gentiles scores a victory for Gentile "integration" into the emerging community of Jesus followers. This event is in the center of the book, marking the pivotal event that would give the movement universal appeal. After this event, Paul, directed by the Holy Spirit, begins an amazing adventure throughout Asia Minor, Macedonia, and Achaia (Greece), which results in his famous speech in Athens (Acts 17). The Jerusalem conference is only the beginning of a long and bitter split with Judaism, which is perhaps portended by the split between Paul and Barnabas over John Mark (Acts 15:36—16:5; according to Gal 2:11-13, the issue was table fellowship with Gentiles!). After this "parting of the ways," Paul and Silas continue the mission to the Gentiles independently.

Chapters 16–20, The Gospel "to the Ends of the Earth"

Parting ways with Barnabas and leaving the Antiochian mission, Paul enlists Timothy into the mission after circumcising him (16:1-5). Guided by the Spirit, they are forbidden to enter Asia (Minor) and are sped on to Macedonia by a vision (16:6-10). Luke highlights again for us the importance of "leading women" in the reception of the gospel (and leading early house churches) and in aiding Paul's mission. Lydia (v. 14) is apparently an independent businesswoman (v. 15 says, "she and her household were baptized") who welcomes Paul into her home on his first European missionary tour. The positive action of Lydia is contrasted with the negative portrayal of the "slave girl" and Paul and Silas's subsequent imprisonment (16:16-24). While the slave girl tells the truth about Paul and his message, he exorcises the spirit of divination and yet does not offer her salvation, as he does to Lydia (v. 18). Part of this results from Luke's contrast of positive and negative examples (cf. Barnabas with Ananias and Sapphira in 4:36—5:11). Another factor is that the narrative serves as a rationale for the evangelists' imprisonment, from which they are miraculously delivered (16:25-40; a theme that has been recounted several times in Acts), and results in the salvation of the Philippian jailer and his household. After an encounter with the magistrates of Philippi, who encourage them to leave the city, they are released and return to Lydia's house (v. 40), from which they make their way to Thessalonica.

Several of Luke's literary patterns continue in the next cycle of travels (17:1-15). Going from Philippi to Thessalonica, Paul visits the Jewish synagogue first (an important missionary pattern for Paul), and many Greeks (proselytes) believe and "not a few of the leading women" (v. 4). The second literary pattern is that successful preaching can lead to opposition "from the Jews" (vv. 5-10). Finally, this negative example in Thessalonica is contrasted with a positive one in Beroea (17:10-15). In Beroea the Jews ("including not a few Greek women and men of high standing," v. 12) are receptive to their preaching. Yet again, in either case, successful preaching leads to oppo-

sition (v. 13), and the believers must speed the evangelists on to Athens.

17:16-34, The Universalist Paul in Jerusalem and Athens

In Athens, Greece, Paul is portrayed as not only the first Christian philosopher but also a proponent of human universalism. Luke's universalism has already been noted (Acts 2 and 10). It is through the portrayal of Paul, however, that it is most significantly accomplished in Acts. For this reason, Marla Selvidge concludes:

> Paul is the most important character in the Acts of the Apostles. . . . His character is portrayed as embodying most of the important lessons or ideas that the writer wants to convey to the audience. . . . His greatest achievement was his ability to step out of his sectarian past to shake hands with others throughout the Roman Empire. Paul's egalitarianism touched the lives of women from different classes, slaves, uncircumcised Jews, politicians, artisans, tent makers, followers of John the Baptist, sailors, Jewish-Christians, and even procurators and kings.[94]

Interestingly, however, compared with many of his speeches, Paul's speech at the Areopagus of Athens was apparently unsuccessful (17:15-34): there were few converts, and there is no record in the New Testament that a church developed in Athens as a result of Paul's mission there (cf. 17:34).[95] However, using Stoic and Jewish arguments, Paul expands upon the idea of Jew and Gentile unity under the sovereignty of God. Both Jews and Greeks agreed that God is the creator of the cosmos (17:24-25), that all human beings have a common origin (or are "from one blood" KJV, 17:27), and that God created all nations (17:28-29). These universalist themes aptly congeal in this speech. Such important ideals of human unity could not go unnoticed by African Americans in search of authoritative support for their arguments and rhetoric of freedom and equality. For this reason, Acts 17:21 became a touchstone for their religious-political rhetoric of human unity and equality.

EXCURSUS: THE AFRICAN AMERICAN PROTEST TRADITION AND THE "ONE BLOOD" DOCTRINE

Benjamin Banneker (1731–1806), one of the most remarkable figures of eighteenth-century America, was born free in Maryland. His *Almanacs* were published widely throughout the United States in the 1790s, and he was one of a team of three who planned and surveyed the site for the present city of Washington, D. C. In a letter sent to Thomas Jefferson, then Secretary of State, he alluded to Acts 10:34-36 and 17:26, and also employed his own personal example of intellectual excellence and nobility of character to counter claims of black inferiority. Banneker stated:

> Now Sir, if this is founded in truth [that Jefferson himself is a reasonable man, well-disposed to the black cause], I apprehend you will embrace every opportunity, to eradicate that train of absurd and false ideas and opinions, which so generally prevails with respect to us; and that your sentiments are concurrent with mine, which are, that one universal Father hath given being to us all; and that *he hath not only made us all of one flesh* [Acts 17:26] but that he hath also, *without partiality* [Acts 10:34] afforded us all the same sensations and endowed us all with the same faculties; and that however variable we may be in society or religion, however diversified in situation or color, we are all

in the same family and stand in the same relation to him.[96]

For Banneker and other blacks, it was not enough to hold a particular idea to be true, but especially for Christians, those who hold the Bible as authoritative, that conviction should compel or motivate one to action. The passages from Acts 10:34 and 17:26 aided blacks in their efforts to realize freedom and equality in a society where the odds were stacked against them. Likewise Bishop Ransom, in his speech "The Race Problem in a Christian State, 1906," perceived from Acts 17:26 the true basis for the foundation of civil government. He noted that Jesus' own ministry was carried out in the midst of racial antagonisms, and the basis of his ministry and death on the cross was to eliminate these barriers to human unity and equality. He declared:

> St. Paul, standing in the Areopagus, declared to the Athenians that, "God hath made of one blood all nations of men for to dwell on all the face of the earth [Acts 17:26]." . . . Jesus Christ founded Christianity in the midst of the most bitter and intense antagonisms of race and class. Yet he ignored them all, dealing with Jew, Samaritan, Syro-Phoenician, Greek and Roman. . . . God, through the Jew, was educating the world, and laying a moral and spiritual foundation. That foundation was the establishment of the one God idea.[97]

Ransom again, in a sermon titled, "Golden Candlesticks Shall Illuminate Darkest Africa," emphasized the unity and equality of humanity through the declaration of Acts 17:26 that all humanity stems from "one blood."

The "one blood doctrine," as Ransom termed it, was an important means of under-

Bishop Ransom and the "One Blood Doctrine"

Since all the families of the earth are now one through their daily contacts upon the land, sea, and the air, they are in a position now to receive and accept the "One Blood Doctrine," as a final link in a chain that not only reveals the sovereignty of God, but also unites all the peoples of the earth by affirmation of the "One Blood Doctrine," which means the brotherhood, freedom, and equality of all mankind.

scoring the central theme of the unity of humanity, as well as the equality of all people before God. In his speech "The Sixtieth Anniversary of the Founding of the AME Church in West Africa," Ransom could also refer to this passage with reference to the ministry of the AME church: "Ours is not a church that is born out of theological controversy, but stands upon the doctrine that all men everywhere are of one blood and that in the church there should be neither nationality, race, nor color, but all meeting together in a plain of absolute freedom and equality."[98]

After his twenty-seven consecutive years of presidential leadership in the National Baptist Convention, Dr. E. C. Morris's final address was read posthumously. Morris claimed that racial justice was a necessary condition if blacks were to remain Christians:

I may be criticized for devoting this much of my address to racial matters, but my only apology is that, unless we can in what may be termed a Christian land, secure for our race, from the dominant race such privileges to which they are entitled, we cannot hope to hold them in the Christian religion. . . . We early imbibed the religion of the white man;

we believed in it; we believe in it now, and hope never to be divorced from it; but if that religion does not mean what it says, if God did not make of one blood all nations of men to dwell on the face of the earth [Acts 17:26], and if we are not to be counted as part of that generation, by those who handed the oracle down to us, the sooner we abandon them or it, the sooner we will find our place in a religious sect in the world. . . . If the American ideal—viz. Freedom . . . guaranteed under the Constitution of the United States—is not given us, then we should in mass rise up and leave our churches, and schools, and . . . seek asylum among a people who will recognize merit in any man regardless of his color, creed or condition.[99]

Florence Spearing Randolph, a renowned AME Zion minister, missionary, suffragist, lecturer, organizer, and temperance worker, spoke out directly against racist attitudes in her sermon "If I Were White." She grounded her attack against racism on the "one blood" saying of Acts 17:26:

If I were white and believed in God, in His Son Jesus Christ, and the Holy Bible, I would speak in no uncertain words against Race Prejudice, Hate, Oppression, and Injustice. I would prove my race superiority by my attitude towards minority races; towards oppressed people. I would remember that of one blood God made all nations of men to dwell upon the face of the earth.[100]

Randolph inferred that race really means nothing in the sight of God, because all humanity shares a common ancestry, a fact that challenges those whites who claim a racial superiority. If such a thing exists, it would be based on how one treated those who are oppressed and on the fringes of society. What these and countless other expressions reveal about black Christian communities is that they understood and explained their existence not through exclusive theological propositions or dogma, but chiefly on account of social—here including political and economic and educational—realities.[101]

18:1—20:38, Paul in Corinth, Ephesus, and Greece

Leaving Athens, Paul's next stop was Corinth, where he met with a Jewish-Christian couple, Aquila and Priscilla (Prisca), recently arriving from Rome on account of an edict of Claudius expelling the Jews from the city (18:1-2).[102] As tent makers, Paul and Aquila worked together in their trade and in the gospel, preaching first in the synagogue (vv. 3-4). However, after receiving some opposition from "the Jews," Paul declared that he would go exclusively to the Gentiles (of that city!). After the conversion of Crispus, the official of the synagogue (whom Paul baptized; cf. 1 Cor 1:14), Christ confirms Paul's success in Corinth through a vision, despite more opposition from "the Jews," and Paul stays there about eighteen months (18:5-17). At the end of this period, Paul bids the believers of Corinth good-bye, returning to several areas he visited before (18-23), ending what scholars have termed his "second missionary journey" (Acts 15:36-18:23). Finally, Luke recounts in 18:24-28 how both Priscilla and Aquila (name order is reversed and important) lead Apollos, a well-versed Alexandrian Jew, more accurately in the Way of God (v. 26).

While Apollos is in Corinth (cf. 1 Cor 1:12; 3:1-9, 21-23), Paul is in Ephesus, where he stays for more than two years (19:1-20). His time in Ephesus supplies the background to his Corinthian correspondence (1 and 2 Corinthians). While in Ephesus not only does Paul preach, but he also performs "extraordi-

nary miracles" of casting out demons and curing the sick with "healing handkerchiefs" (vv. 11-12). Paul's positive example is contrasted with the negative example of the seven sons of a Jewish priest named Sceva, who as exorcists try to exorcise a demoniac in Jesus' name but are shamefully overpowered (vv. 12-20). It is in Ephesus that, according to Luke, Paul desires to see Rome (v. 21), and this is the first intimation of such, which is comparable to Jesus' journey to Jerusalem in the Gospels—this is where both meet their fate! Following the uproar in Ephesus (20:22-41), Paul makes some last visits to Greece (Philippi, Thessalonica, and Beroea) and settles for a brief while in Troas (20:1-6). While in Troas he raises Eutychus (20:7-12) and then starts a return trip to Ephesus (10:13-20). It is at this time that he calls the Ephesian elders together and makes his farewell speech (20:18-35), in which he (1) upholds his integrity in the gospel in the face of plots and opposition, knowing the fate that awaits him in Jerusalem (vv. 18-24) and (2) warns the elders of the dangers awaiting the church after his departure and gives them a charge to hold fast to the example he has provided for them (vv. 25-35). When Paul finishes his speech, he and the elders weep and embrace, and they bring him to the departing ship knowing that they will never see one another again (vv. 36-38).

CHAPTERS 21–28, THE GOSPEL AND THE ROMAN EMPIRE

21:1—23:35, Paul's Fateful Journey to Jerusalem and Personal Defense before Jewish Leaders

Paul now makes his way to Jerusalem, passing through various locales (Cos, Rhodes, Cyprus, and Syria on to Tyre; 21:1-6). When he arrives in Caesarea and visits the house of the evangelist Philip and his four "prophesying daughters," the prophet Agabus demonstrates to him his fate in Jerusalem by means of a symbolic act (he binds him hand and feet with his own belt, vv. 10-11). Nevertheless, they cannot persuade Paul to stay, for his heart is fixed (vv. 12-14): so after some days he makes his way to Jerusalem (vv. 15-16). Consistent with Luke's narrative, Paul's initial arrival is positive: the Jerusalem brothers receive him warmly (vv. 17-19) and encourage him to demonstrate his faithfulness to the law by undergoing a purification vow (vv. 20-26). Then, in vv. 27-40, the tide turns on account of "Jews from Asia" (vv. 27-30), who stir up the crowd against Paul. If not for the intervention of the tribune, who arrests and initially mistakes Paul for an Egyptian who led a recent revolt in Palestine, Paul might have succumbed to mob violence (vv. 31-40). The tribune grants Paul permission to speak, and Paul offers his defense against his accusers. He recounts his birth and upbringing, his "conversion," his subsequent ministry to the Gentiles, and his Roman citizenship, which immediately gains the attention of the tribune (22:1-29). The next day Paul is given another audience before the Sanhedrin (22:30—23:11), in which he exploits differences between the Pharisees and the Sadducees to gain support from the Pharisees. After a plot is discovered (vv. 12-25), the tribune sends Paul for an audience with Felix, procurator of Judea (52–56 c.e., vv. 26-35). Thus, in accordance with Agabus's prophecy, Paul is taken captive in Jerusalem.

24:1—26:32, Paul's Defense before Roman Magistrates and His Appeal to Rome

The narrative audience now shifts from Jewish to Roman, although some Jerusalem elders attend the hearing (24:1-27). Paul offers another speech in his defense (vv. 10-21), but Felix holds him over under limited custody until his appointment is succeeded by Porcius

Festus (appointed in 60 c.e., v. 27). Under Porcius Festus, Paul makes his appeal to Rome (the emperor's tribunal [v. 10], 25:1-12). After several more days, he offers a defense before Agrippa (25:13—26:32). In this speech Paul proffers a convincing defense of his position, and Agrippa makes a pronouncement of his innocence but detains him because of his appeal to Caesar (26:32).

27:1—28:31, Paul's Final Adventurous Journey to Rome

His fate sealed, Paul and other prisoners set sail for Rome. They pass through several locales on the way from Caesarea in the east toward Rome in the west (27:1-7). When they arrive at Fair Havens, Paul, perceiving danger, prevails upon the captain to delay the journey, but to no avail (27:8-13). Paul's perceptions are confirmed when the ship encounters a large storm at sea. An angel, however, assures Paul that no harm would come to the crew or passengers, and the ship runs aground on the island of Malta (27:14-44). Just as Paul saves the life of the Philippian jailer who supposed that the prisoner had escaped (16:27-28), so too are the lives of the prisoners aboard the ship spared on account of Paul (vv. 42-44). While on the island, a snake bites Paul, but he suffers no ill effects, which amazes the inhabitants. Moreover, after healing the father of the leading man of the island, Publius, the inhabitants bring their sick to Paul, who heals them also (28:1-10). Leaving the region, after a few more stops along the way, Paul finally arrives in Rome (28:16). Soon after his arrival, Paul calls together the leading Jews and recounts his case to them. Some believe and some do not (28:17-25). This situation leads to Paul's (or more likely, Luke's) quote of Isa 42:1, 6, which decries Israel's lack of perception, resulting in Paul's declaration that the Gentiles will hear the gospel (28:26-29). Luke ends his narrative with Paul under house arrest, preaching and teaching without hindrance (28:30-31).

EXCURSUS—THE PORTRAYAL OF PAUL AND HIS MISSION IN ACTS

Acts provides a representative picture of Paul's mission that includes a particular pattern: (1) He preaches first in the Jewish synagogue but turns to Gentiles when the synagogue preaching is no longer possible. (2) He announces the one God to Gentiles who have no contact with Jewish monotheism. (3) He repeatedly encounters persecution and moves on when necessary, but he does not abandon his mission, thus strengthening the new churches. In this mission Paul is fulfilling the Lord's prophecy that he would "bear my name before Gentiles, and kings and sons of Israel" and "must suffer for my name" (9.15-16).[103] From Acts 13 to 28 Luke presents Paul as challenging both religious and political powers; Paul's enthusiasm to fulfill the divine call brings violence to his own life and to almost every city he visits. In addition to this picture of Paul, there has been a tendency in biblical scholarship to read Acts' portrayal of Paul's activity as a series of three "missionary journeys." This arises not so much from a careful reading of the text as from the interest of missionary societies and movements in the nineteenth and twentieth centuries in finding in Acts guidelines for their own missionary work.[104] To be sure, African Americans also found in Paul's mission and journeys a paradigm for their own missionary activity. It was not lost upon them that Luke represents Paul's missionary *ethos* (character) as that of powerful words and deeds. For him "Paul represents not just the ideal Christian in the story; he is the ideal male."[105] Thus the narrative suggests that *mission builds character* and *suffering refines it*. In Luke's portrayal of

Paul the ideal of *manhood* and *mission* are combined.

EXCURSUS—AFRICAN AMERICANS AND MISSION TO AFRICA: MANHOOD AND MISSION

William H. Becker, in a seminal article, "The Black Church: Manhood and Mission," proposed two interrelated theses regarding African American missions to Africa: (1) the definition and assertion of black manhood as a conscious motive and overriding theme throughout the history of the black church, and likewise (2) the assertion of black manhood as a conscious motive in the black appropriation of the widespread nineteenth-century belief that it was black America's providential calling to convert Africa to Christianity. Thus the idea of black manhood and mission to Africa came to be united in black Christian consciousness.[106]

Toward the latter half of the nineteenth century, this idea became fused with the identity of the AME Church. This is evident in a statement of the General Conference of 1872, which adopted this report on church union:

> We are now more than ever convinced that the African Methodist Episcopal Church has yet a mission to perform, not only in the elevation and religious training of our long-neglected people in the United States, but in the perfect evangelization of Africa and the islands of the seas. . . . When prejudice on account of color shall be swept from the Church and shall disappear . . . then, and not until then, will the grand mission of the African Methodist Episcopal Church, as a separate organization, be at [an] end.

The emphasis on *African mission* is noteworthy. Why would the independent black churches, Becker asks, dependent upon the poorest classes for its support, faced with financial difficulties and a shortage of educated leaders, and also confronted in 1863 with the task of serving millions of newly freed slaves, undertake foreign missions across the seas in Africa? Why cast the net so far, when the need is so great at home in America? In short, the challenge to white prejudice necessitates the existence and constitutes the identity of the AME Church and its mission to evangelize all blacks, including those across the Atlantic in Africa. This also provided a means for black men to exercise their manhood.[107]

The idea of a providential black American mission to Africa (as already noted) was not just the opinion of the black church. This symbol of the black man as a missionary to other men of color had appeal for both black and white Americans. African American sentiment resonated with these ideas in part because they underscored the notion of black manhood. African mission provided a dramatic representation of the black man as man, as leader, as authoritative evangelist and preacher to his racial brothers. It was also a symbol that helped to make some sense of the suffering of a slave past that was viewed as a preparation for this vocation. Ultimately, from this noble endeavor, no one on earth would be able to doubt the black man's courage and effectiveness. Thus here was a symbol dramatizing the manhood of the black man *in another land*, which made it clear simultaneously that he was a man, but ironically that he had to leave America to be recognized as such.

The Reverend S. F. Flegler, who as a pastor led a group of thirty AME settlers to Liberia in 1878, addressed the South Carolina conference of the church in 1890 as follows:

Africa is the home of the Negro, the land where he is free, and where he has the best opportunity for the best development. It is much in need of the Gospel. What the Church expends in the interests of missionary operations in Liberia will return to you in glory and grandeur. The work is before us, and we will do it if we are possessed of race pride. . . . I recognize no man to be my superior, nor any race to be naturally in advance of ours. . . . God Almighty never made a soul with more elements of manhood than mine; and I thank God there is sufficient African blood in me to thrill me with aspirations of manhood.[108]

Another AME clergyman, Bishop Henry M. Turner, was convinced that there was to be a mutual exchange between Africa and African Americans, and to some degree Africa might have more to offer. For this reason, Turner concerned himself and the AME Church with Christianizing Africa and devoted great efforts to raise funds for African mission work, especially through publications such as the *Voice of Missions*, which he founded in 1893 and edited until 1900. His perception of the task, however, went beyond missions to viewing *emigration to Africa* as the only satisfactory solution to the race problem in America. Therefore, for Turner "*There is no manhood future in the United States for the Negro. He may eke out an existence for generations to come, but he can never be a man-full, symmetrical and undwarfed*" (emphasis in the original). On the contrary, the African black impressed him as embodying manliness in his very posture. He wrote from Africa: "One thing the black man has here, and that is manhood, freedom and the fullest liberty. He feels like a lord and walks the same way." Thus simple mission to Africa could not fulfill the demands of black American manhood: it required mission *in* Africa—a large-scale back-to-Africa movement by American blacks.

Turner says again: "I believe that two or three millions of us should return to the land of our ancestors, and establish our own nation, civilization, laws, customs . . . and cease to be grumblers [in] the white man's country, or the country he claims and is bound to dominate."[109]

In the same vein, Edward W. Blyden proposed uncompromisingly that black manhood and mission were not to be found in the United States but in Africa. For Blyden, God permitted African slaves to be brought to America to be educated in Christianity and then to return home to Christianize Africa: "God sent us here to be trained that we might return to the land of our fathers and take charge of it, develop it and define it."[110]

In this way, Africans could receive Christianity through the auspices of other Africans, instead of through whites. American blacks will not only teach Africa but will emigrate to Africa and also govern that land. Having this divine commission, the American black violates God's will when he seeks to deny his blackness: "I have taken so much care, says the Lord, to preserve these black skins, and they are trying to extinguish themselves. You ought to see the importance of and preserve your race as purely as you can."[111] African

mission, then, requires a pure black race, and black manhood will be fulfilled when it accomplishes its providential African mission. In this way, Blyden went beyond most black churchmen of the time in his assessment of divine providence. Overall, it was believed that African Americans developed skills in the diaspora, like the ancient Israelites, that helped them to become a nation: so too blacks have developed skills in the diaspora for the redemption of Africa.

CONCLUSION

My comments on African American appropriation of the Acts of the Apostles provide brief glimpses into the relationship between text and interpreter (or the interpretive community). In these examinations it can be seen that African Americans have read the biblical text through their social-historical experience and, conversely, their social-historical experience through the text. This *contextualized* reading of the Bible in general and Acts in particular provides a medium through which to view important issues, especially those related to black destiny, mission to Africa, black nationalism, race, class, gender, economics, and Christian spirituality. The African American interpretive tradition shows that there are no "neutral" or "disinterested" readings of biblical texts. All readings are *interested* and *contextual*. Long before this truism was acknowledged in biblical scholarship, this appeared as a self-conscious realization of the African American interpretive tradition, and it has been one of the most significant contributions of African American readings to the Acts of the Apostles.

Finally, two additional interpretive issues deserve attention for interpreters of African descent: (1) Luke's identification with and uses of certain themes of *empire* and (2) the

---

Bishop Ransom on the Mission to Africa

Bishop Reverdy Ransom had similar sentiments about the back-to-Africa movement when he stated, "God sent Africa here [to America] to go to school; his training was the most thorough and severe to be found in history."

—Quoted in Anthony B. Pinn, ed. *Making the Gospel Plain: The Writings of Bishop Reverdy C. Ransom* (Harrisburg, Pa.: Trinity Press International, 1999), 172.

limited scope of his universalism. The message and activity of the apostles are cast in conformity to the ideals of Rome (that is, the Roman *imperium*). How might it affect the African American interpretive traditions to identify with the conqueror/oppressor instead of the conquered/oppressed? Second, an examination of the narrative of Acts shows that the universalist themes have certain limits, for example, with respect to women and slaves. In both cases, this "double message" of Acts deserves further attention.

Notes

1. Justo L. González, *Acts: The Gospel of the Spirit* (Maryknoll, N.Y.: Orbis, 2001), 1–2.

2. Christopher R. Matthews, "Acts of the Apostles," in *The New Oxford Annotated Bible: NRSV with the Apocrypha*, 3rd ed., ed. Michael D. Coogan (Oxford: Oxford University Press, 2001), 183.

3. The term *common era* is used in scholarly works instead of the older designation "A.D.," *anno Domini*, "year of our Lord." On questions of authorship, date, the text of Acts, etc., see, for example, Ben Witherington III, *The Acts of the Apostles: A Socio-Rhetorical Commentary* (Grand Rapids, Mich.: Eerdmans, 1998), and Ernst Haenchen, *The Acts of the Apostles: A Commentary*, Hermeneia (Philadelphia: Fortress Press, 1971).

4. See P. A. Brunt, "*Laus Imperii*," in *Paul and Empire: Religion and Power in Roman Imperial Society*, ed. Richard A. Horsley (Harrisburg, Pa.: Trinity Press International, 1997), 25–35, on Rome's self-perception of its god-given task to conquer and civilize the world.

5. S. R. F. Price, "Rituals and Power," in Horsley, *Paul and Empire*, 61.

6. The preceding quote and statement regarding Rome's ideology of dominance comes from Paul Zanker, "The Power of Images," in Horsley, *Paul and Empire*, 74.

7. Price, "Rituals and Power," 71.

8. González, *Acts*, 10.

9. This argument has had broad appeal. Luke's address of the book to the "most excellent Theophilus" could mean one of two things: (1) He might be addressing it to a Roman administrative official (he uses "most excellent" in three other places in Acts when addressing a governor of a province—23:26; 24:3; 26:25); or (2) the name could literally be translated, "lover of God" or "beloved of God," in which case Luke's addressee could be a code name for all Christians ("beloved of God"). See Bart D. Ehrman, *The New Testament: A Historical Introduction to the Early Christian Writings*, 3rd ed. (Oxford: Oxford University Press, 2004), 115–17.

10. Richard A. Horsley, *Jesus and Empire: The Kingdom of God and the New World Disorder* (Minneapolis: Fortress Press, 2003), 12.

11. Horsley, *Paul and Empire*, 206–14, 242–52, and *Jesus and Empire*, 132–33.

12. Horsley, *Jesus and Empire*, 1–3. See also Robert Bellah, *The Broken Covenant*, 2nd ed. (Chicago: University of Chicago Press, 1992); Reinhold Niebuhr, *The Irony of American History* (New York: Scribners, 1952); and Ernest Lee Tuveson, *Redeemer Nation* (Chicago: University of Chicago Press, 1967).

13. Witherington, *The Acts of the Apostles*, 71–72.

14. Peter Paris, *The Social Teachings of the Black Churches* (Philadelphia: Fortress Press, 1985), 10–14. Paris coined the term *black Christian principle*.

15. James O. Buswell, *Slavery, Segregation and Scripture* (Grand Rapids, Mich.: Eerdmans, 1964), 34.

16. The others are chiefly Gen 1:27, which affirms that all humans are created in the image of God, and Gal 3:28, which affirms the equality of all in Christ regardless of race/ethnicity (Jew/Greek), class/status (slave/free), and gender (male/female).

17. See Vincent L. Wimbush, "Reading Texts through Worlds, Worlds through Texts," *Semeia* 62 (1993): 129–39, 132, and also his *The Bible and African Americans: A Brief History*, Facets (Minneapolis: Fortress Press, 2003), 34–37, for a brief discussion of the rise of the black protest tradition.

18. Paris, *The Social Teachings of the Black Churches*, 10–14.

19. Ibid., 17.

20. Ibid., 17–18, 34.

21. Ibid., 97.

22. David L. Tiede, "Acts 1:6-8 and the Theo-political Claims of Christian Witness," *WW* 1 (1981): 41–51. Looking at (Luke-)Acts intertextually with Roman imperial/colonial dynamics reveals some interesting results. "As Virgil's *Aeneid* presents the Romans as being ordained by the gods to take the best out of the ruins of Troy to become the rulers of the world, Luke is . . . not only imitating Virgil, but also presenting the Christians as the newly ordained conquerors of the universe." Cited in Benny Tat-siong Liew, "Acts," in *Global Bible Commentary*, ed. Daniel Patte (Nashville: Abingdon, 2004), 419–28, 425.

23. González, *Acts*, 19.

24. A cursory reading of Acts indicates that the early "Christian" communities encountered "integration" problems, which were a major concern of Acts (8:26—15:35). Nevertheless, integration into the new "Christian" community links conversion with integration into the new community, which has to do with the creation of a new social entity—the unity of Jew and Gentile into one people of God through Jesus Christ (Liew, "Acts," 420–21).

25. Thus, for Acts, while Paul is important in its narrative, he does not qualify as an apostle according to the stipulations outlined.

26. Witherington, *The Acts of the Apostles*, 128.

27. González, *Acts*, 33.

28. Witherington, *The Acts of the Apostles*, 128.

29. C. H. Talbert, ed., *Perspectives on Luke-Acts* (Edinburgh: T. & T. Clark, 1975), 195.

30. See Elisabeth Schüssler Fiorenza, *But She Said: Feminist Practices of Biblical Interpretation* (Boston: Beacon, 1992), 10, and *In Memory of Her: A Feminist Theological Reconstruction of Christian Origins* (New York: Crossroad, 1989), 161. See also Ivoni Richter Reimer, *Women in the Acts of the Apostles: A Feminist Liberation Perspective* (Minneapolis: Fortress Press, 1995), which provides a commentary on the passages related to women; and also Amy-Jill Levine, ed., *A Feminist Companion to the Acts of the Apostles* (Cleveland: Pilgrim, 2004), for other articles related to issues of women in Acts.

31. C. Eric Lincoln and Lawrence H. Mamiya, *The Black Church in the African American Experience* (Durham, N.C.: Duke University Press, 1990), 76–78. See also Harvey Cox, *Fire from Heaven: The Rise of Pentecostal Spirituality and the Reshaping of Religion in the Twenty-First Century* (Reading, Mass.: Addison-Wesley, 1995), 45–47.

32. Both quotes are in Cox, *Fire from Heaven*, 58.

33. Cox, *Fire from Heaven*, 62–63, emphasis added.

34. Ibid., 63.

35. Lincoln and Mamiya, *The Black Church in the African American Experience*, 81.

36. The Church of God in Christ still does not ordain women at the jurisdictional level, but they can "take charge" of a church until a male elder is available (Lincoln and Mamiya, *The Black Church in the African American Experience*, 90). However, W. J. Seymour was open to women preachers and exhorters; for him this was evidence of the gifts of the Spirit in the Last Days (see Estrelda Alexander's *The Women of Azusa Street* [Cleveland: Pilgrim, 2005]).

37. Arthur D. Griffin, *By Your Traditions: A Theological Perspective on Women in the Gospel Ministry* (Chicago: Black Light Fellowship, 1989). He uses Acts 2 and Acts 10 as key passages to argue for equality of role in ministry. See also Demetrius K. Williams, *An End to This Strife: The Politics of Gender in African American Churches* (Minneapolis: Fortress Press, 2004), and Ella P. Mitchell, ed., *Women to Preach or Not to Preach? 21 Outstanding Preachers Say Yes* (Valley Forge, Pa.: Judson, 1991).

38. See William L. Andrews, ed., *Sisters of the Spirit: Three Black Women's Autobiographies of the Nineteenth Century* (Bloomington: University of Indiana Press, 1986).

39. Bettye Collier-Thomas, *Daughters of Thunder: Black Women Preachers and Their Sermons 1850–1979* (San Francisco: Jossey-Bass, 1998), 57–59.

40. Andrews, *Sisters of the Spirit*, 208–9.

41. Collier-Thomas, *Daughters of Thunder*, 180–81.

42. González, *Acts*, 72–77.

43. Both quotes are from Rev. George W. Slater Jr., the first in "Race Problem's Socialist Cure," *Chicago Daily Socialist*, March 27, 1909, and the second in "The Cat's Out," *Chicago Daily Socialist*, September 29, 1908; both are in *Black Socialist Preacher: The Teachings of Reverend George Washington Woodbey and His Disciple, Reverend G. W. Slater, Jr.*, ed. Philip S. Foner (San Francisco: Synthesis, 1983), 1–2.

44. George W. Woodbey, "What to Do and How to Do It or Socialism vs. Capitalism," in *Waylands Monthly* 40 (August 1903): 37–38; cf. Foner, *Black Socialist Preacher*, 1–2.

45. Foner, *Black Socialist Preacher*, 1.

46. Ibid., 10–18.

47. Woodbey, *The Bible and Socialism*; cf. Foner, *Black Socialist Preacher*, 102–5.

48. Foner, *Black Socialist Preacher*, 193–94.

49. Quoted in ibid., 3–4.

50. Unlike Matthew's account of the Beatitudes (5:3-12), which concentrates on spiritual states, Luke's focuses on social and economic conditions that include woes against the rich.

51. González, *Acts*, 105.

52. Ibid., 117–18. As a matter of fact, Philip precedes Peter to Caesarea, where the conversion of Cornelius takes place (Acts 8:40).

53. González, *Acts*, 117–18. See also Haenchen, *The Acts of the Apostles*, 309–17.

54. Clarice J. Martin, "A Chamberlain's Journey and the Challenge of Interpretation for Liberation," *Semeia* 47 (1989): 105–35, 114; cf. John Navone, *Themes of St. Luke* (Rome: Georgian University Press, 1978), and Robert F. O'Toole, *The Unity of Luke's Theology: An Analysis of Luke-Acts* (Wilmington, Del.: Michael Glazer, 1984).

55. Martin, "A Chamberlain's Journey and the Challenge of Interpretation for Liberation," 114. Cain Hope Felder states that "New Testament perspectives eliminate all ethnic or racial criteria for determining the elect" and that "the New Testament disapproves of an ethnically focused idea of corporate election ('Israel according to the flesh')" (*Race, Racism, and the Biblical Narratives*, Facets [Minneapolis: Fortress Press, 2002], 32, 35). See also Felder's "Racial Motifs in the Biblical Narratives," in *Troubling Biblical Waters: Race, Class, and Family* (Maryknoll, N.Y.: Orbis, 1989), 37–48.

56. Martin, "A Chamberlain's Journey and the Challenge of Interpretation for Liberation," 115–16.

57. Ibid., 117. See also T. C. G. Thornton, "To the End of the Earth: Acts 1:8," *ExpTim* 89 (1978): 374–75; cf. González, *Acts*, 115.

58. Felder, *Race, Racism, and the Biblical Narratives*, 34.

59. Peter T. Nash, *Reading Race, Reading the Bible*, Facets (Minneapolis: Fortress Press, 2003), 32–40. Scholarship on the Hebrew Bible has tended to do the same by shifting research away from Africa, ignoring and altering the geographical and cultural relations among Egypt, Cush/Ethiopia, and Nubia in favor of a region known as Yemen, resulting in the de-Africanization of Egypt.

60. Martin, "A Chamberlain's Journey and the Challenge of Interpretation for Liberation," 120–21.

61. Haenchen, *The Acts of the Apostles*, 315.

62. Felder, *Race, Racism, and the Biblical Narratives*, 38.

63. Peter first admitted Gentiles because he received a direct vision to do so. See Schüssler Fiorenza, *In Memory of Her*, 163.

64. The region that was then called "Ethiopia" was not the same as the country that goes by that name today. It was rather the area of Nubia, whose church is one of the most ancient in the world and whose territories bordered the Nile south of Egypt; it was closer to what is Sudan today. In the Old Testament, its name is Cush, with its capital at Meroe. The queens of Nubia, in the region south of Egypt, were called "Candace," which was their title, not the name of a particular queen (González, *Acts*, 115).

65. Martin, "A Chamberlain's Journey and the Challenge of Interpretation for Liberation," 110–11.

66. Martin, "A Chamberlain's Journey and the Challenge of Interpretation for Liberation,"

107–9, highlights Deut 23:1, which forbade a eunuch from entry to the covenant although he was a "God-fearer."

67. Gayraud S. Wilmore, *Black Religion and Black Radicalism: An Interpretation of the Religious History of African Americans*, 3rd ed. (Maryknoll, N.Y.: Orbis, 1999), 148.

68. Wilmore, *Black Religion and Black Radicalism*, 125.

69. Paris, *The Social Teachings of the Black Churches*, 34–35. The narrative of the Ethiopian eunuch is still powerful today in the black church. The Rev. Dr. Jeremiah J. Wright Jr., pastor of the Trinity United Church of Christ in Chicago, uses this narrative for exploring the question of the diminishing number of black men in the contemporary black church, and also as a tool to evangelize them. See his *Africans Who Shaped Our Faith: A Study of 10 Biblical Personalities* (Chicago: Urban Ministries, 1995), 207–90.

70. Andrews, *Sisters of the Spirit*, 85–86.

71. Some scholars have suggested that we do not see Saul's Damascus experience as a conversion, but as a "call." There was no such thing as "Christianity" when Saul had his visionary experience, but he was commissioned by Jesus to take the gospel to the Gentiles.

72. Marla Selvidge, *Exploring the New Testament* (Upper Saddle River, N.J.: Prentice Hall, 2003), 172.

73. Witherington, *The Acts of the Apostles*, 430–31, quoting C. K. Barrett, *Paul*, 161.

74. Household codes are the hierarchical enumeration of the duties of the members of the Greco-Roman household.

75. Clarice J. Martin, "'Somebody Done Hoodoo'd the Hoodoo Man': Language, Power, Resistance, and the Effective History of Pauline Texts in American Slavery," *Semeia* 83/84 (1998): 213.

76. Neil Elliott, *Liberating Paul: The Justice of God and the Politics of the Apostle*, The Bible and Liberation (Maryknoll, N.Y.: Orbis, 1994), 9.

77. Brian K. Blount, *Then the Whisper Put on Flesh: New Testament Ethics in an African American Context* (Nashville: Abingdon, 2001), 119.

78. Ibid., 120–21.

79. Abraham Smith, "Putting 'Paul' Back Together Again: William Wells Brown's *Clotel* and Black Abolitionists Approaches to Paul," *Semeia* 83/84 (1998): 251–62.

80. See Williams, *An End to This Strife*, 75–106, for a discussion of this topic.

81. S. Wesley Ariarajah, *The Bible and People of Other Faiths* (Maryknoll, N.Y.: Orbis, 1992), 16. Ariarajah compares the accounts of Peter in Acts 10 and Jonah (13–18). The story is set up as the conversion of Cornelius but is really the conversion of Peter.

82. González, *Acts*, 131–32.

83. Liew, "Acts," 421. "Ethnic Jews" attended the Pentecost of Acts 2! No Gentiles were present.

84. González, *Acts*, 129–30.

85. Nathaniel Paul, quoted in James Cone, *Black Theology and Black Power* (New York: Seabury, 1969), 91; originally quoted in Benjamin Mays, *The Negro's God* (Boston: Chapman and Grimes, 1938), 42.

86. For a complete edition of this work in its historical setting see Herbert Aptheker, *"One Continual Cry": David Walker's Appeal to the Colored Citizens of the World (1829–1830)—Its Setting and Meaning* (New York: Humanities, 1965). References here to David Walker, "Our Wretchedness in Consequence of the Preachers of Religion," are from Milton C. Sernett, *African American Religious History: A Documentary Witness*, 2nd ed. (Durham, N.C.: Duke University Press, 2000), 193–201.

87. Wimbush, "Reading Texts through Worlds, Worlds through Texts," 133.

88. The Jewish historian Josephus has a similar account of Herod Agrippa's death, after subjects addressed him as God (*Antiquities* 19.343–53).

89. Some other ancient authorities read "Paul and Barnabas returned from Jerusalem to Antioch," presumably after their relief mission mentioned in Acts 11:29–30.

90. It is precisely at the moment of beginning his mission to the Gentiles, and later in writing his letters, that Saul uses the name "Paul." González, *Acts*, 155–56.

91. González, *Acts*, 137–39.

92. What I mean here are the kosher and purity laws that hindered social relations between Jews and Gentiles (cf. Gal 2, in which Paul recounts his debate and confrontation with Peter over eating with Gentiles). See also James D. G. Dunn, *Jesus, Paul and the Law: Studies in Mark and Galatians* (Louisville: Westminster John Knox, 1990).
93. Witherington, *The Acts of the Apostles*, 430.
94. Selvidge, *Exploring the New Testament*, 169.
95. Gonzalez, *Acts*, 203.
96. Benjamin Banneker, quoted in Herbert Aptheker, ed., *A Documentary History of the Negro People in the United States: From Colonial Times to the Civil War* (New York: Citadel, 1962), 22, emphasis added.
97. Sernett, *African American Religious History*, 338.
98. Reverdy Ransom, "Golden Candlesticks," in *Making the Gospel Plain*, ed. Anthony B. Pinn (Harrisburg, Pa. Trinity Press International, 1999), 176.
99. E. C. Morris, quoted in Paris, *The Social Teachings of the Black Churches*, 50–51.
100. Florence Spearing Randolph, "If I Were White," in Collier-Thomas, *Daughters of Thunder*, 129.
101. Vincent L. Wimbush, "Biblical Study," in *African American Religious Studies: An Interdisciplinary Anthology*, ed. Gayraud S. Wilmore (Durham, N.C.: Duke University Press, 1989), 142.
102. This is reported in Suetonius, *Claudius* 25.
103. Robert Tannehill, *The Narrative Unity of Luke-Acts: A Literary Interpretation*, vol. 2 (Philadelphia: Fortress Press, 1990), 182.
104. J. T. Townsend, "Missionary Journeys in Acts and European Missionary Societies," *AThR* 68 (1986): 99–104; cf. González, *Acts*, 152, who says that the very notion that this section of Acts has typically been outlined in terms of three "missionary journeys" of Paul is not to be found in any ancient or medieval commentary, but is rather the creation of the modern missionary movement. Wayne Meeks, *The Writings of Paul* (New York: Norton, 1972), 149, views the "'three missionary journeys' [as] part of Luke's systematic plan; we could never reconstruct them from the letters alone."

105. Todd Penner and Caroline Vander Stichele, "Gendering Violence: Patterns of Power and Constructs of Masculinity in the Acts of the Apostles," in *A Feminist Companion to the Acts of the Apostles*, ed. Amy-Jill Levine (Cleveland: Pilgrim, 2004), 208.
106. William H. Becker, "The Black Church: Manhood and Mission," in *African American Religion: Interpretive Essays in History and Culture*, ed. Timothy E. Fulop and Albert J. Raboteau (New York: Routledge, 1997); references are from this edition, which is reprinted from *JAAR* 40 (1972), 316–33. I summarize Becker's excellent overview throughout this section with additional information from Wilmore, *Black Religion and Black Radicalism*. For a critique of the notion of "manhood" see Williams, *An End to This Strife*, 107–33.
107. Becker, "The Black Church," 185–86.
108. Ibid., 187–89.
109. Ibid., 189–90.
110. "You see then the field that lies before you. You see the reason that God is giving you this schooling. It is to train you for the important duties, not here, but where there is a welcome field for your talent" (Edward W. Blyden, quoted in ibid., 190–91).
111. Ibid.

For Further Reading

Cox, Harvey. *Fire from Heaven: The Rise of Pentecostal Spirituality and the Reshaping of Religion in the Twenty-first Century*. Reading, Mass.: Addison Wesley, 1995.

Felder, Cain Hope. *Race, Racism, and the Biblical Narratives*. Facets. Minneapolis: Fortress Press, 2002.

———. *Troubling Biblical Waters: Race, Class, and Family*. Maryknoll, N.Y.: Orbis, 1989.

Foner, Philip S., ed. *Black Socialist Preacher: The Teachings of Reverend George Washington Woodbey and His Disciple, Reverend G. W. Thomas B. Slater, Jr*. San Francisco: Synthesis, 1983.

González, Justo L. *Acts: The Gospel of the Spirit*. Maryknoll, N.Y.: Orbis, 2001.

Haenchen, Ernst. *The Acts of the Apostles: A Commentary*. Hermeneia. Philadelphia: Fortress Press, 1971.

Horsley, Richard A. *Jesus and Empire: The Kingdom of God and the New World Disorder*. Minneapolis: Fortress Press, 2003.

Levine, Amy-Jill, ed. *A Feminist Companion to the Acts of the Apostles*. Cleveland: Pilgrim, 2004.

Lincoln, C. Eric, and Lawrence H. Mamiya. *The Black Church in the African American Experience*. Durham, N.C.: Duke University Press, 1990.

Martin, Clarice J. "Acts of the Apostles." Pages 763–99 in *Searching the Scriptures*, vol. 2: *A Feminist Commentary*. Edited by Elisabeth Schüssler Fiorenza. New York: Crossroad, 1994.

———. "A Chamberlain's Journey and the Challenge of Interpretation for Liberation." *Semeia* 47 (1989): 105–35.

———. *Tongues of Fire: Power for the Church Today: Studies in the Acts of the Apostles 1990–91*. Louisville: Presbyterian Church USA, 1990.

Mitchell, Ella P., ed. *Women to Preach or Not to Preach? 21 Outstanding Preachers Say Yes*. Valley Forge, Pa.: Judson, 1991.

Paris, Peter. *The Social Teachings of the Black Churches*. Philadelphia: Fortress Press, 1985.

Patte, Daniel, ed. *Global Bible Commentary*. Nashville: Abingdon, 2004.

Reimer, Ivoni Richter. *Women in the Acts of the Apostles: A Feminist Liberation Perspective*. Minneapolis: Fortress Press, 1995.

Schüssler Fiorenza, Elisabeth. *In Memory of Her: A Feminist Theological Reconstruction of Christian Origins*. New York: Crossroad, 1989.

Talbert, C. H., ed. *Perspectives on Luke-Acts*. Edinburgh: T. & T. Clark, 1975.

Williams, Demetrius K. *An End to This Strife: The Politics of Gender in African American Churches*. Minneapolis: Fortress Press, 2004.

Wilmore, Gayraud S. *Black Religion and Black Radicalism: An Interpretation of the Religious History of African Americans*. 3rd ed. Maryknoll, N.Y.: Orbis, 1999.

Wimbush, Vincent L. *The Bible and African Americans: A Brief History*. Facets. Minneapolis: Fortress Press, 2003.

Witherington, Ben, III. *The Acts of the Apostles: A Socio-Rhetorical Commentary*. Grand Rapids, Mich.: Eerdmans, 1998.

ROMANS

Thomas L. Hoyt Jr.

INTRODUCTION

The historical occasion of Romans can no longer be known with exactness, although clearly it was written after the resolution of the Corinthian crisis—quite possibly in Corinth—and before Paul's subsequent arrest in Jerusalem. Paul himself had anticipated further missionary work in the West, beyond Rome (Rom 15:22 ff.). Evidently he sought at least the good wishes of the Roman church in this endeavor. To this end, he wrote the letter to the Romans, preparing them for this forthcoming visit and further travels.

The letter serves as a theological introduction to Paul, and this is probably the purpose for which it was originally intended. The letter is the only one that Paul wrote to a congregation he had neither established nor previously visited. It was his desire to make the empire's capital city a place from which he could launch his mission to larger work in the West, namely Spain. While living in Corinth, he therefore wrote to encourage and enlighten the congregation about his understanding of the gospel he wished to convey.

CHAPTER 1

1:1-7, Salutation

Romans begins with a greeting consisting of one long sentence, 1:1-7. Paul describes himself as the *doulos* ("servant" or "slave") of Jesus Christ. *Doulos* has a long history in the prophetic faith. In the Old Testament it refers to the person or people used by God to carry forward God's purpose. This same term was used in the ancient Near East for the man who stood next to the king, namely, the prime minister. He was known as the slave of the king, because his will was bound unconditionally to the king's will, and he was the primary agent for implementing or carrying out that will.

The slave of God concept is developed most completely by the prophet who speaks in Isaiah 40–66. If the saving purpose for humankind is to be effected, God needs such a slave, and Israel is the chosen one (Isa 55:10-13). The slave of God must withstand the enmity and hatred of a world that resists God; that slave must be prepared to suffer and die (Isa 50 and 53). Ironically, such a death becomes the very means by which God breaks human resistance to God's purpose and binds humans to God's self. Paul is such a slave of Christ.

Paul is also an apostle of Christ. Although he is not one of Jesus' original twelve, he considers his apostleship as equal to theirs (1 Cor 9:1-2), in the same way that he understands his gospel to be as authoritative as the message they preach (Gal 1:11-12). He, too, was commissioned (on the Damascus road) and sent by (the risen) Christ.

Paul's apostolic task was to preach the gospel of God: the salvation that God has made possible through the death and resurrection of Jesus Christ. That salvation enables all, like the Romans, to be called "saints." "Saints" (v. 7a) is Paul's favorite way of referring to members of the Christian community. For him the word does not carry the idea of perfection that contemporary Christians often read into it. It means "those set apart." Saints are the Christ slaves set apart for the use and service of God. The term is not a description of Christian moral character but refers instead to the fact that believers belong to God.

1:8-15, Prayer of Thanksgiving

Paul gives thanks for the Christians in Rome, prays to God on their behalf, and tells of his own personal plans. He explains that he is "under obligation" (my translation; NRSV: "I am a debtor") both to "Greeks and barbarians." The word "Greeks" (v. 14) as used here includes the Romans. By the time Paul wrote, the word had lost its national and racial meaning and had become a designation for culture and language. The Greek language had spread across the Roman Empire and had divided the whole world into those who spoke it and those who did not. Even highly civilized groups on the edge of the empire were called "barbarians" because they did not speak Greek. In the same verse, "the wise and . . . the foolish" may be read as "the educated and the uneducated." Thus, Paul placed himself under obligation to every person in the whole world. His obligation was to "preach the gospel" to them all.

1:16-17, The Power of the Gospel

Just as Romans is a summary of the gospel that Paul preached, so these two verses are a summary of the letter. In them Paul answers briefly the two vital questions: (1) Who can be saved? and (2) on what condition? Those who can be saved include "every one who has faith."

These two verses include key words that recur throughout the letter:

- *Gospel.* For Paul the gospel was the good news that a merciful God opened a way of salvation for human beings. The good news is revealed as God's readiness to treat as righteous any person who comes to God in faith. Paul's statement that he is "not ashamed of the gospel" conveys his confidence in the power of the gospel as God's instrument of salvation.
- *Power.* The Greek word is *dynamis,* from which English gets *dynamo* and *dynamite.*

For Paul the word meant more than the almighty power of God revealed in nature, history, and miracles. It meant God's continuing ability and readiness to save.

- *Salvation.* Paul believed in salvation not only at the end of time but also as deliverance here and now from the power of sin and from the spiritual death that results from sin. Salvation involves a proper relation to God and the spiritual life that results.
- *Faith.* Faith is the total acceptance of God's love and complete trust in that love for one's salvation. Faith is the sole requirement for salvation (v. 17).
- *Righteousness.* Borrowed from the law courts, where its meaning had nothing to do with actual guilt or innocence but only with the way the court treated the accused, "righteousness" (translated "justification" in 5:16) refers to God's activity. It is the forgiveness afforded guilty human beings. Righteousness has two sides: mercy and wrath. Paul will show how both are expressed by the power of God.
- *Life.* This is eternal life, a quality and level of spiritual life that has been freed from the power of sin and equips a person for both time and eternity.

In this commentary, black family life will be a chief illustration. Black family life must have a posture that inculcates an attitude of love and then offers proof of that attitude. God likewise gives the good news of the Son, Jesus Christ, and asks those who respond to that good news to do so out of a repentant heart and an attitude of thanks.

1:18-32, The Guilt of Humankind

The wrath of God is upon the Gentiles because they refuse to acknowledge the sovereignty of God. This resistance leads naturally to idolatry (vv. 18-23), disgraceful passions (vv. 24-27), and approval of these unrighteous acts in others (vv. 28-32). God expresses wrath by delivering the Gentiles over to those very perversions.

CHAPTER 2

2:1-5, Let's Get Real

Paul indicts any person, even the Jew, who condemns Gentile vices but behaves similarly. The person who judges others only intensifies his own judgment (v. 3). One should not

---

We Did It Our Way, 1:18

Relationships, those with spouses and those with God, often break apart because of a desire to keep up with the Joneses. "We" haven't quite arrived until we have a two-car garage, a split-level house, the ability to go out for dinner every day if desired, and nights out on the town with plenty of spending money. "If the Joneses can do it, why can't we?" Doing what the Joneses do becomes the norm of existence. These Jones impersonators sing the song, "I Did It My Way," instead of the better one, "I Did It God's Way." Paul says the same thing about those who are seeking salvation in religion. When our agenda is set by others rather than our relationship to God's sovereignty and our conscience, we lose perspective on life. This is true for life in general and family life in particular.

misunderstand God's "wealth of kindness," "forbearance," and "patience" (v. 4). Those qualities do not imply God's indifference to sin. God's kindness (*chreston*) intends repentance. God is forgiving but not lenient. Forgiveness is creative, related to a change of mind (*metanoia*) or conversion. If change does not occur, God's wrath inevitably flows.

2:6-11, The Impartial Judgment of God

Paul stresses the impartial judgment of God by repeating the phrase "the Jew first and also the Greek" (1:16). God judges each according to her works. Two judgment results are possible: (1) eternal life for those who, "according to the steadfastness of good work," seek "glory and honor and incorruption," or (2) wrath and anger for those who out of "quarrelsomeness" are "distrusting the truth and trusting unrighteousness." Humans are saved by God's grace through faith, but they are judged according to their life of works. Hearers of the law are not the ones whom God finds righteous. Doers of the law are the ones who will be vindicated (found righteous). The same principle applies to both Jew and Gentile. Humans are saved by grace. Once saved, though, humans respond by doing.

2:12-16, The Gentile Has a Conscience

A person's destiny on judgment day will depend on whether that person has known God's will and done it, not on whether one is a Jew or a Gentile. Gentiles receive fair judgment from God because they know what the law requires instinctively, because it has been written on their hearts and is witnessed to by their conscience (vv. 14-16).

2:17-29, The Jews and the Law

Paul speaks directly to the Jews, cataloging their claims to special status and their failures. Thinking that they were the sons of Abraham, the Jews believed that even if they sinned they were God's. Paul vigorously denounces this belief. This expectation of preference before God led Jews to break the most elemental commandments of the law: they stole, committed adultery, robbed temples, just like other people without the law. Such lawbreakers would not be saved. However, the Gentiles who did not have the law but instinctively observed it would be saved. Jews and the Gentiles would be treated on their own merit by God.

In Paul's argument, the Jews are God's elect. They had the law, and yet they "dishonored God" by breaking it (v. 23). Because of their misdeeds, God's name is blasphemed. Instead of being a light to the nations, they, because of their hypocrisy (v. 24), caused God's name to be hated.

According to Paul, an obedient Gentile was better than a disobedient Jew, even if the Jew outwardly observed all the ritual traditions. This was not to say that circumcision had no value but that circumcision required a corresponding inner obedience. The mark was worthless if people broke the covenant law it symbolized. A Gentile who had never heard of Moses but lived according to the law would condemn the Jew who, despite his circumcision and knowledge of the written code, broke the law. A Jew who broke the law ceased to be the child of Abraham. The Gentile who intuitively observed the law, though having no mark on his body, was to all intents and purposes a true Israelite. It is not the external circumcision of the body but the inner circumcision of the heart that counts before God.

CHAPTER 3

3:1-8, The Jews and the Law

Rom 3:1-8 is a diatribe. Paul has a dialogue with an imaginary opponent. This form of argument is common in Paul, especially in Romans 10–11. One may easily identify the opponents' questions by underlining 3:1, 3, 5, 7, and the first eight words in 3:9. Paul's answers are found in 3:2, 4, 6, 8, 9-18.

3:9-20, None Is Righteous

No human being will be justified by works of the law (vv. 9-20). Both Gentiles and Jews are under the power of sin (v. 9). Paul quotes loosely, and apparently from memory, several Old Testament passages to make his point: the law only enables humans to recognize sin; it does not give them the power to achieve righteousness or a right relation to God (vv. 19-20).

3:21-31, Righteousness through Faith

Paul wonders how God can be merciful and forgiving without minimizing sin. The justice of God demands punishment for sin. Paul also wonders how he can describe the experience of moving from a state of sin, guilt, and condemnation to freedom from the power of sin, removal of guilt, and release from punishment. He tries to describe that experience by combining three metaphors: "justification," from the law court or covenant language; "redemption," from the institution of slavery; and "sacrifice of atonement by blood," from the sacrificial rituals of the temple. "They are justified by his grace . . . through the redemption that is in Christ Jesus . . . as a sacrifice of atonement by his blood" (vv. 3:24f.).

"Justification" amounts to an accused criminal being acquitted and released. The word "redemption," borrowed from the institution of slavery, expresses the experience of a slave who suddenly finds out that someone has purchased or ransomed his freedom. A ransom usually entailed money or some medium of exchange. Christ did better than give money. Christ gave his life as a ransom for humankind from the power of sin.

The word "expiation" derives from the practice of animal sacrifice, in which God accepts the sin offering as full payment for sin. Christ's crucifixion demonstrated God's righteousness; his death became the expiation for our sin. The power of the crucifixion is made effective through faith (vv. 22-26). Since faith is the only response necessary to a salvation freely offered, no one can boast.

3:27-31, Jew and Gentile before an Impartially Justifying God

Boasting, the radical antithesis of faith, is a form of idolatry. To boast is to have "confidence in the flesh"—in the merely human. Boasting causes one to worship the creature rather than the creator. Both Jew and Gentile stand together as creatures under the power of sin. Sin is a universal human condition. God judges Jews on the basis of the Mosaic Law and Gentiles on the basis of the light they have received.

Chapter 4

4:1-12, The Example of Abraham

Paul calls on Abraham to prove the point that it is faith rather than outward ritual, works, or legal requirements that account for one being reckoned as righteous. Abraham was judged righteous (acquitted) by God on the basis of his trust, not his works (v. 3; cf. Gen 15:6). The universal implications of Paul's argument are clear: Jews and Gentiles are bound together by a faith in Christ's death and resurrection that transcends racial, social, and cultural barriers.

God called Abraham to leave his home and go to a new land to establish a new people. He obeyed. Faith is more than intellectually believing; it is trusting and obeying. Faith entails risk; a believer acts on the basis of more than what he can see. But one must be ready to act on that which one believes. Abraham went out not knowing where he was going. Because Abraham believed God, God blotted out his sins and declared him just and righteous. To make his case, Paul picks up on the term *reckoned* in Gen 15:6 and interprets it in the light of the term's use in Ps 37:1-2. This Rabbinic-like association of words proves that Abraham was unrighteous rather than worthy when justified.

Paul follows up with a citation about David. The Israelite king is an example of the freedom that comes from unmerited divine forgiveness. Operating from a quotation of Ps 32:1-2, he argues that blessed assurance comes not from striving to live a perfect life but from the knowledge that God is forgiving.

But how is God's forgiveness related to circumcision? Does God treat the circumcised and the uncircumcised alike? Paul points out that while God pronounced Abraham righteous in Gen 15:6, the story of Abraham's circumcision is not found until Genesis 17. Therefore, God's gift of righteousness did not depend on circumcision. Circumcision was instead "a sign or seal of the righteousness which he had by faith when he was still uncircumcised" (v. 11). The rite so valued by Jews is

Outward Signs

In challenging the dependence on circumcision as an outward sign, Paul effectively discredits such external symbols as the sole markers of identity, relationship with God, and thus worth. God's relationship with humans is established through grace, not through any exterior accomplishments or markings that might designate one human as more acceptable to God and therefore acceptable within human community. Likewise, external markings of color, ethnicity, and/or gender, though important, do not indicate anything about relationship with God and therefore standing within a human community. Peter Paris speaks about this divine and its consequent human relationship through the metaphor of divine parentage that has been so eloquently expressed within the African American church. This means that God is not the parent of some elements of the human race. Instead, God is parent to all human beings, regardless of racial identity. As Peter Paris argues, "The black churches have always discerned this doctrine to be the bedrock of the biblical perspective on humanity, and they have given prominence to biblical passages that make it unequivocally clear" (Peter J. Paris, "The Bible and the Black Churches," in *The Bible and Social Reform*, ed. Ernest Sandeen [Philadelphia: Fortress Press, 1982], 135). They have also given prominence to the key implication that develops out of this primary principle. If, indeed, God is the divine parent of all, then all races must be of the same family. This kinship denies the basic premise of racism, that the different races are of different origin, and, that, therefore, some are inferior. The linkage to the same divine parent gives all races an equal standing before God that demands an equal standing before each other. It is not external marking, be it the natural marking of ethnicity or the accomplished marking of circumcision, that determines human standing before God and before other humans. It is relationship with God alone that matters, and that relationship is brokered by faith through grace.

of no advantage. Spiritual descent from Abraham is thus not based on circumcision. Abraham is therefore the father of uncircumcised Gentiles, too. (See sidebar on p. 256.)

4:13-25, God's Promise Realized through Faith

Paul's second major point is that Abraham received the promise by faith, not by works (vv. 13-25). Paul could refer to the "promise" (vv. 13, 14, 16, 20, 21) without explanation, because his Jewish Christian readers would have been quite familiar with the promises of God as seen in Gen 12:2-3; 17:4-8; 18:18; 22:17-18. Abraham believed the promises even when those promises went against logic, experience, or hope.

When Abraham was ninety-nine years old and Sarah eighty, God promised that Abraham would become the father of multitudes. Abraham trusted God, and Isaac was born. Those who believe "are blessed with Abraham who had faith." God's intent for Abraham was achieved not in the history of Israel but in the existence of a community of Jews and Gentiles whose trust in God is Abrahamic. Abraham is, therefore, the spiritual father of both the Jew and the Gentile (Ps 32:1-2; Gen 17:5; 15:6).

In order to get the full implication of the connection with Abraham, one must understand the meaning of righteousness. Righteousness/justification means right relationship. Although I have argued above that justification could mean pardon or acquittal in a legal or business sense, it could very well also represent how people relate to each other. "Relationship" is also a covenant word that specifies an attachment between persons for a common purpose. Justification means being bound to God and one another in mutual commitment. The righteousness of God is, therefore, the inner character of God that relates to people and creation by binding them together in right relationship to one another.

God manifests righteousness by blessing. The word "bless" means to share one's power, one's strength, one's life with another, to be with the other. God blesses Abraham by "accompanying" him with divine power, enabling Abraham to live and find his pilgrim way, filled with the promise of God. We too say, "Bless you," to one another. It is an instinctive way of affirming our solidarity with the other and wishing the other well.

To receive blessing, though, one must be reckoned righteous, put in the way of right

---

Romans 4:1-25: The Faith of the Fathers and Mothers Still Lives

The African American family has always had ancestors who trusted and obeyed the Word of God. This faith of ancestors through the African American experience has been grounded in the value system of proverbs that have been passed on through the years: "A hard head makes a soft bottom." "If you make your bed hard, you have to lie in it." "If you are big enough to lie, you are big enough to seek your soul salvation." "Just do what I tell you to do. I ain't going to tell you nothing wrong." "Next time I have to get on you about something, I'm going to pay you for old and new." We praise the folk wisdom of valiant and courageous men and women, our ancestors, who have shown us how to connect with the past and how to live in the present, and have established footprints for us to follow in our quest for the future. The faith of our mothers and fathers still lives.

relationship. To be in that way is to have faith. This faith is the gift of God, a work of grace, and also the act by which we respond and relate to the righteous, faithful God who has come and comes to us. This God calls us to believe, trust, and rely on the divine promises. We are called to live in faithfulness to God. This was what Abraham did. He had faith in God, and this faith was manifested in his being reckoned righteous and blessed. We who have faith participate in the life of righteousness and in the blessing of God.

CHAPTER 5

5:1-11, The Results of Justification

Chapter 5 opens with a discussion of the happy fruits of justification by faith: peace, grace, hope, and love. When the righteous decision of God becomes known to us and effective for us through our acknowledgment and grasp of it in faith, we have peace with God (v. 1). The sovereignty of sin over us is broken. This same theme is expressed throughout the chapter: "we are now reconciled with God" (v. 10); "we have now received reconciliation" (v. 11); "every alien lordship has now become for us a thing of the past" (v. 21). Because we are made right before God by God's grace through faith, we have real peace.

The work of Christ provides "access" (a word used to describe admittance into the presence of royalty) to the present blessing of grace and, through grace, to the renewed hope of glory. Humans were created to share in the glory of God; the "fall" eclipsed that hope (3:23). But now the joy of sharing in that glory is available, even in the midst of trials and tribulations.

When Christians refused to engage in immoral or idolatrous practices, such countercultural resistance made them seem socially and politically disloyal. Believers suffered as a result. Such suffering is a time of testing. (See sidebar below.) Paul calls for endurance: an active overcoming of misfortune rather than a passive acceptance of it. Such endurance produces character. "Character" is a word used of metal that has been so heated by fire that all the impurities are refined out. The hope born of suffering is the confidence that God is transforming one's character, and will continue to do so until believers share in God's glory.

Redemptive Suffering

Martin Luther King Jr. understood both the tragedy and the transformative potential of unmerited suffering. In the midst of persecution and suffering imposed on him and other civil rights activists because of their endeavors for justice, King observed: "As my sufferings mounted I soon realized that there were two ways that I could respond to my situation: either to react with bitterness or seek to transform the suffering into a creative force. . . . Recognizing the necessity for suffering I have tried to make of it a virtue. If only to save myself from bitterness, I have attempted to see my personal ordeals as an opportunity to transform myself and heal the people involved in the tragic situation which now obtains."

—Martin Luther King Jr., "Suffering and Faith," in *A Testament of Hope: The Essential Writings of Martin Luther King, Jr.*, ed. James M. Washington (San Francisco: Harper & Row, 1986), 41. For two different interpretations of this King quote, see Anthony Pinn, *Why Lord? Suffering and Evil in Black Theology* (New York: Continuum, 1995), 76, and Brian K. Blount, *Can I Get a Witness? Reading Revelation through African American Culture* (Louisville: Westminster John Knox, 2005), 84.

God's love, poured into human hearts, sustains this hope. It is the presupposition of this hope that sinners who have completely and finally fallen short can partake of God's glory (3:23). For God's love commends itself in this (v. 8), that Christ died for us while we were still weak (v. 6), still sinners (v. 8), still godless (v. 6), and still enemies (v. 10). God's love has, therefore, not waited for us to get right but has come to meet us just as we are. No one would want to die for a wicked person—no one but Christ (v. 6).

The important words "reconciled" and "reconciliation" appear in vv. 10-11 for the first time in Romans. The Greek word *katallasso*, translated "reconciliation," describes what God did in salvation. It indicates a thorough change in relationship. Enmity was given over to friendship. God opened the way for this change in relationship, bringing harmony and peace between human beings and God. God justified us through the sacrificial blood of Christ. In the death of God's Son, God intervened on our behalf with the "nevertheless" of God's free grace in the face of the apparently insurmountable power of human revolt and resistance (vv. 9-10). God has made peace. God has reconciled. God has saved. When humans put their trust in God's righteous decision as carried out in Christ Jesus, they immediately become sharers in Christ's triumph.

Romans 5:1-11 points out that in Christ the one justified by faith has peace with God. This faith is a source of hope for the future and a source of power for the present. The atoning act of Christ is cause for rejoicing because those who were "enemies" of God and had every right to fear the consequences of the wrath of God are now at peace because they are saved by that atoning work. Through Christ, humans have been reconciled to God (vv. 6-11).

5:12-21, Adam and Christ

Paul stresses the deliberate offense of the first man, his "breaking of God's command" (v. 14), his fall (vv. 15, 17-18) and above all his "disobedience" (v. 19). It is integral to Paul's thought that the sin of Adam introduces not a defective physical nature, but an existence that is blighted by a defective relationship with God. Adam does not "fall" into matter; he is matter that has sinfully asserted itself against the Creator and therefore stands under God's judgment. He stands under condemnation (vv. 16, 18) and needs grace (vv. 15ff.); his defect is remedied not by a new creation or liberation of the old nature, but by the obedience of Christ (v. 19). The new life is bestowed not by some natural process, but by justification (v. 18). It is only on the basis of a prior justification that God brings about a physical change of nature in God's creatures (8:30).

In Rom 5:17, 21, the life that Christ brings is set against the death that Adam brought and also against the death that he himself endured. His death for sinners is undoubtedly a physical fact; it is, therefore, hard to argue that the death imposed on humankind because of sin is not similarly physical. And yet death is much more than a physical reality. For Paul, it is an accursed thing (Gal 3:13). Yet it is transformed by the fact that God's own Son endured it (Rom 5:10). Now even death is the most perfect assurance of God's love and will to be reconciled with humankind (5:8, 10-11.).

So also the death that Adam brought was more than just a physical fact; it was a sign of God's judgment upon human sin. The continued existence of death as a physical fact reminds us constantly of God's "giving up" of his creation because of sin (Rom 1:18-32); it is a present judgment, part of the revealed wrath of God in this present world. Paul's view of death is thus intelligible within the categories of apocalyptic Judaism, with its stress both on the penal nature of physical death and on a final judgment. Christ's coming, death, and resurrection meant that what for apocalyptic Judaism was a secret to be revealed in the future was to a large extent already experienced in the present.

Chapter 6

6:1-14, Dying and Rising with Christ

In this chapter, Paul the pastor interprets the nature of the Christian life. What difference does the incarnation of Jesus make in the life of common folk? Some evidently argued that one should sin in order to receive more grace. Since there is nothing one can do to obtain salvation, and because a believer is already assured of acquittal on the Day of Judgment, why not sin without restraint? In emphatically rejecting this logic, Paul stresses that justifica-tion has moral implications. Right standing before God carries with it right living.

In making his case, Paul drops the terminology of faith and justification and shifts to a baptismal imagery of death, burial, and resurrection with Christ. Baptism meant union with Christ, in both his death and his resurrection. Those in Christ are therefore dead to sin. In Christ, one is freed from the power of sin and need no longer yield her body to unrighteousness. One is free to stand against sin, fight it, and offer one's body as servant of righteousness. Sin has no place at all in the life of faith.

There are various meanings of Paul's image of dying to sin. Christians have died to sin (1) in the judicial sense—in Christ's death the debt of sin is paid; (2) in the baptismal sense—a believer thereby publicly accepts Christ's death on his or her behalf; (3) in the moral sense—a believer daily resists specific sinful impulses; and (4) in the eschatological

---

"Because You Are, I Am"

The African family operates on a communal basis: "Because you are, I am." The Western mind-set is so geared to individual development as self-assertion that it is sometimes difficult to understand the corporate personality attitude of contemporary Africans or ancient Jews. The Jews thought in terms of tribe, nation, and community. It is on the basis of this communitarian perspective that Paul argues that the death of Jesus saved all, all of those in his time and in our own. The African perspective stresses ancestor reverence because of the analogous belief that its members share in the "communion of saints." This connectedness with the other extends not only in time but also into eternity. Perhaps nowhere is this connectedness of all to Jesus across even the boundary of time more explicit than in the words and meaning of the slave spiritual, "Were You There?" When the slaves asked whether a contemporary was "there" at the cross with Jesus, not only did they recognize that relationship is broader than individual connectedness—the "you" is surely as much a plural as a singular pronoun—but they also realized that time itself can through faith be transcended. The nineteenth-century slave community was, in spirit and in truth, through their own oppression and suffering, with Jesus as he agonized on the cross. Though they were of different times, they were of the same community.

sense—when one dies physically, sin no longer has any sway over the person who enters completely into resurrection life.

To live in Christ means to have died to sin; it is impossible to live in something to which one has died. In vv. 3-14, Paul discusses what it means to have died to sin. Paul uses the figures of dying and rising to illustrate the difference between the old life and the new life in Christ. Verses 3-4 contain the only references to baptism in Romans. Paul's comparison of baptism to death and resurrection is based on immersion imagery—being buried in the water and coming up out of it. The illustration may be clearer if we remember that baptism at the time was connected with adults making decisive moves from paganism to Christianity, from one way of life to another. For these adults, baptism was more than a symbolic act. It was not entering into church membership; it was actual induction into a new relationship, a personal identification with the redeemer Messiah. The one who becomes a believer breaks with sin as sharply as one who dies breaks with physical life.

Baptism signifies a union with Christ. The old preconversion life has been crucified with Christ. The "body of sin" is not destroyed, but it is deprived of its power; its domination is broken. The liberation occurs in salvific stages. First, one's former self is crucified with Christ, in order that, second, the lower part of one's nature is deprived of its power, with the result that, third, one lives no longer in bondage to sin.

God once again uses death as a tool of reconciliation (see the comments on 1:1-7). Physically, death wipes out all old accounts and frees sinners from all obligations to former masters. Metaphorically, the old self in its unredeemed state with evil thoughts, words, and actions dies. The believer is a new person, completely changed, living in a new dimension.

Verse 11 introduces the idea of being "in Christ," one of the most important themes in Paul's writings. To be "in Christ" means that a person has entered into a union with Christ, "the second Adam." The believer becomes a member of a new race of beings whose head is Christ. Christianity, though, is not only a spiritual experience of mystical union with Christ; it is a way of living. Paul therefore exhorts his readers to live the kind of sinless lives he thinks should be the believers' normal existence (vv. 2, 7, 11).

6:15-23, Slaves of Righteousness

As in v. 1, Paul begins this section with a question from an imaginary opponent in characteristic diatribe style: "Should we sin because we are not under law but under grace?" (v. 15). Many concluded that there can be no morality without law. Paul seeks to show that there is a definite change in conduct for the Christian, which is the product rather than the antithesis of grace, a true moral righteousness without being a law-centered righteousness.

Paul illustrates his point with an analogy from slavery. Masters had complete domination over their slaves, even the power of life and death. For Paul, all human beings are slaves; they are ruled either by sin or by obedience (v. 16). One's whole life is determined by which of the two masters one serves. There is no such thing as "absolute" human freedom. Humans are not free in themselves. They must live under a lordship. They are "obedient slaves" either to sin, whose end is death, or to righteousness, whose end is life (v. 16). Paul reminds his readers of Jesus' teaching that "no slave can serve two masters" (Luke 16:13). No one can serve both God and sin.

In v. 17 Paul declares that the teaching that concerns the way of life worthy of the gospel of Christ is a mold that gives to the new life its appropriate shape or pattern. Verses 17 and 18 together describe the change of lordship Paul is confident has taken place in the Romans: once slaves to sin, they are now free from its dominion. Now in obedient response to the gospel, they seek to live by its pattern. All of this has taken place through God's grace alone.

Verse 19 suggests that Paul was having some trouble making his point clear. He argued that believers are dead to sin (v. 11). He now has to recognize that they do sin (v. 13), or at least are in danger of doing so. He reconciles the two sides by saying that the believer who does occasionally sin does not love the sin and is not controlled by sin.

To be "a slave of sin" is to belong to a harsh, demanding, and degrading master. To become "a slave of God" is to enjoy the freedom to be all that one can be. But therein lies Paul's metaphor problem. "Slavery to righteousness" seems to be a contradiction in terms. There is a paradox to Christian freedom. Paul explores the meaning of this paradox by means of two prepositions, "from" and "to."

By freedom *from* sin (vv. 7, 18, 22), Paul means that the offenses that have accumulated into a vicious spiral have now, by the mighty intervention of God, been defeated. Freedom from that spiral of fear and hurtfulness is God's gift to human beings. God sets humans free. The preposition "to" completes the apostle's description. He means that God has enabled freedom *to* believe in God (v. 13), freedom *to* live (vv. 4, 13, 22), freedom *to* yield our whole selves to righteousness, to sanctification (v. 19).

The word "sanctification," a much misunderstood word, appears twice in chap. 6, and nowhere else in Romans. Even here Paul does not discuss its meaning. He merely uses it to suggest that the believers become holy. The basic meaning of the word is "holiness."

The believer's death is to sin, and the resurrection is to righteousness. Sin pays its slaves, and evil gets just what it deserves. God, on the other hand, gives God's slaves what they can never earn or deserve: the free gift of eternal life. God does not give wages, for God is not under obligation to anyone; instead, God freely gives eternal life.

CHAPTER 7

7:1-6, An Analogy from Marriage

By means of a marriage metaphor, Paul continues his argument of chap. 6 that the believer has died to the old constellation of sin and death. A critical new element is also added to the argument: the believer has died also to the law, which the apostle associates with the old constellation. For Paul, the dominion of sin and the dominion of the law constitute the same power sphere, and it is from this sphere that the Christian has been freed in his dying and rising with Christ.

According to law, a woman is required to be faithful to her husband as long as he lives. When he dies, she is released from the marriage bonds and free to marry another (vv. 2-3). The problem with this argument is that the husband does the dying. By the reasoning of v. 1, he is the one free from law. One would do well not to press Paul's illustration and realize that the only real point of comparison is that "death puts an end to obligations."

Paul applies the analogy in vv. 4-6. In union with Christ, the Christian is dissolved of former bonds to the law. Likewise, just as marriage produces fruit in children, so one expects the new union with Christ to produce offspring. The fruit of the new union is righteousness.

7:7-13, The Law and Sin

As at 6:1 and 6:15, in v. 7 Paul begins with a question raised by an imaginary opponent: If the law works the fruit of death (7:5), "What then should we say? That the law is sin?" Paul answers, "By no means!" And yet Paul knows that the law has its role in sin. It gives knowledge of sin; it establishes sin by setting forth the ethical norm whereby one can judge what is sin and what is not. It cannot, however, empower a person to resist what he knows to be wrong or do that which she knows to be right. The law therefore serves as the "catalyst" for sin (v. 8). Paul illustrates his point with an appeal to the creation accounts of Genesis. Sin was in the garden before God issued the command not to eat the fruit. And yet Adam lived in innocence before that command. Sin obtained the occasion to wreak its wretched work only with the coming of that command. The prohibition (law) fixed the object of desire (fruit) so strongly in Adam's imagination that it was thereby given a new fascination.

Just so, Paul as a boy once lived in a pre–bar mitzvah state of non-culpability prior to his instruction in the law (v. 9). But then came the law. Knowledge of the law evoked sin and death (v. 10). The commandments of God promise life; through sin's intervention they lead to death (v. 11). Still, one cannot blame the law for this failure. The failure resides in human refusal to see through the law to the desperate need humans have for God's grace. In itself the law is holy, because it derives from God. It is righteous, because it directs human beings to God's righteousness. It is good, because it teaches human beings what God's holy will really is (v. 12).

The law, however, can never produce righteousness; its work is to specify sin and arouse consciousness of guilt. While the law is therefore holy and good, it has the power to create death because it arouses the guilt that leaves humans in a state of spiritual death (vv. 7-13).

7:13-25, The Inner Conflict

Paul begins with another question from an imaginary objector: "Did what is good, then, bring death to me?" "By no means!" he responds, "It was sin, working death in me through what is good" (v. 13; 6:23). The law served to reveal the presence of sin, to

bring out its true colors. Verse 14 clarifies the dualistic thesis that runs throughout the passage—the spiritual versus the carnal. The law represents God's holy will; it is good; it is spiritual. The "fly in the ointment" is the human self, the old, self-striving ego (v. 14). It is the carnal. Paul never calls physical nature (flesh) evil in itself. Rather, it constitutes the vulnerable part of a person that sin so easily, so inevitably, seizes (v. 14).

Verses 15-17 depict a dramatic cleavage in the will of the person who seeks to follow the law. He knows what is right and is in basic agreement with the goodness of the law (v. 16). He wills what is right (v. 18), but he does what is hateful to his will (v. 15). How can this be? Verse 18 provides the answer. Human nature (flesh) has no independent power of its own. It becomes the "dwelling place" of powerful outside forces. Again, Paul has in mind the idea of two power spheres. A person in the flesh is a person apart from God. Such a person left to herself inevitably falls under the power of sin. It is like being caught in quick sand; the harder humans struggle to extricate themselves, the deeper they sink.

For such a "religious man or woman," the only remaining possibility seems a cry of despair: "Wretched man that I am! Who will rescue me from this body of death?" (v. 24). There is hope. The Christian is a complex, whole person who exhibits weakness of flesh and is in need of the inner work of God's grace (vv. 18, 22, 23). On the other hand, there is the righteous claim of God's will upon the Christian's life and the grace of God at work in one's inner life (7:25). For that Paul is thankful.

CHAPTER 8

8:1-17, New Life in the Spirit

The new life created and given by the Spirit is to be expressed in concrete living. The new covenant given "in Christ Jesus" does not nullify the call of God to the people of God to live a moral life; quite the contrary: because of the presence of the Spirit, God brings to fulfillment in the life of faith the "just requirement of the law" (vv. 1-5).

8:1-5, The Fulfillment of the Law

Paul thanks God that he need not rely on the futility of his own motive power in striving to live a holy life. Because God has sent Christ in the likeness of sinful flesh as an offering for sin, and through Christ condemned sin in the flesh (vv. 2-3), Paul and the believer now have the power of the indwelling Spirit for a righteous life (v. 4). Only a person of faith can live according to the Spirit, for only the trusting acceptance of grace opens one up to an acceptance of God's will. That is why the just requirement of the law can come to fulfillment only in those who live not according to the flesh but according to the Spirit (v. 4).

8:6-13, The Spirit Gives Life

In sounding his thanks in the Spirit, Paul leaps without clear transitions from one theme to another, as one caught up in excitement. The idea that the law comes to fulfillment through the Spirit leads to the related theme that the Spirit gives life (vv. 6-13). Sin brings death; consequently freedom from sin brings freedom from death (v. 11) Renewal of the inner life through the Spirit brings life eternal; the "Spirit is life" for the person of faith (vv. 12-13).

8:14-17, Life in Spirit as Life of Adoption

The insight that the "Spirit is life" leads into the next theme: life "in Christ" is a life of adoption. The Spirit leads one to say "Abba! Father!" In that baptismal cry, God's Spirit joins witness with our spirit so that we are children of God. The confession of faith regularly made at baptism, including the utterance

"Jesus is Lord," can be made only through the assistance of the Spirit. Paul is not advancing a predestinarian belief that God selects only some to be saved. He is affirming that human salvation is assured because it ultimately depends not on human will and power but on God. Confession of faith is a human need, and it becomes a reality in human life, but it is not a human accomplishment.

The Spirit does not bring release from present suffering but propels believers into it. Present suffering prevents confidence for the future from becoming triumphalistic. But if the Spirit does not nullify suffering, neither does suffering nullify the confidence that the community may have for the future. In Paul's mind the Spirit is connected with a universal yearning to experience the fulfillment of God's purposes. It is "adoption" that provides the motive power for speaking about the future, for children, as opposed to slaves, have a future. In v. 17 we find the transition: "if children, then heirs."

8:18-28, Future Glory

Romans 8:18-28 universalizes the glory associated with adoption and applies it to the whole creation. Present sufferings of the children of God are nothing compared to the future glory. All creation awaits the deliverance from corruption that believers now share (vv. 18-21). But even believers are in tension as they await full redemption as children. We have the assurance of having the hope of becoming children and heirs of God. Just as children of a household can look forward to sharing their portion of their parents' possessions, so Christians, as children of God through Christ, will enter into their heavenly inheritance and Christ will become their elder brother.

The human yearning to be free has a counterpart in the created order (vv. 19-23). Paul personifies creation and presents it, too, as a participant in the pain and the hope of the human community. At v. 23, Paul presents the image of the "first fruits of the Spirit," a metaphor deriving from the practice of offering the first fruits of the crop to God in the confidence that God will bring an abundant harvest (cf. 5:5). In 2 Corinthians Paul speaks of the Holy Spirit as a "guarantee" or "down payment" that God has given as an assurance of the future fulfillment of that which has been begun in promise (2 Cor 1:22; 5:5). By these images Paul affirms that the Spirit's presence in renewing human life demonstrates that the new age has been inaugurated; that demonstration carries the promise that the new age will come to full realization.

Creation is "groaning in labor pains," because it anticipates the appearance of God's children. "So also we ourselves who have received the first-fruits of the Spirit groan within ourselves as we accept with satisfaction our adoption, which is the liberation of our bodies" (vv. 22-23). The Spirit participates in the yearning by assisting the believer, who hardly knows how to prepare in anticipation of the future restoration. The Spirit puts a meaning into human sighs that they would by themselves not have. Thus, God, too, participates in the yearning for renewal that God is now accomplishing. In all this, the human yearning, the longing of creation, the intercession of the Spirit, God works for good in those who by their love of God show that they are called according to his will (vv. 26-28).

8:29-30, Chosen and Called

Verses 29-30, strongly predestinarian in tone, do not distinguish between the elect and the non-elect but affirm the confidence we may have that God will bring to completion ("glorify") what God has begun in the human community. The chain of verbs (foreknew, predestined, called, justified, glorified) expresses not a sequence of events so much as

a certainty of conviction: because of what has already begun in the new community of faith comprising Jew and Gentile, we can have full confidence in the ultimate outcome.

The community was "foreknown" or "known in advance." God's knowledge is God's election. Amos describes Israel's relation to God in terms of knowledge: "You only have I known of all the families of the earth" (3:2). Paul, in anticipating chaps. 9–11, speaks of the community of faith as being the object of God's election in order to give assurance that the future really does belong to the members of that community as God's children. God also "foreordained" them, or "set them apart." There is little or no distinction between two verbs, "foreknow" and "foreordain"; both identify the members of the community of faith as the objects of God's eternal concern. The community's hope is not in what it has become, any more than its fear should be of what it will make of itself. Hope rests in the God who has been related to the community even before it knew God's call.

In the community's call to be the people of God, it knows God's electing grace. Thus, in being called, the people of the community were also justified or set in a right relationship with God so they could begin to live as God's people. In this relationship they find their lost glory restored. In being restored in the image of God's Son, they are glorified.

8:31-39, God's Love in Christ Jesus

Grounded in God's electing grace, hope is confirmed in the resurrection of Jesus. Suffering, threats, powers, not even death itself can separate God's community from God. Chaps. 1–8 have been leading up to the climax of this triumphant hymn. The church is God's beloved people, Gentile as well as Jew. The faith of Abraham and God's promises to him are confirmed. The old age is being done away with, and a new age has dawned upon a new community composed of Abraham's descendants from among both Jews and Gentiles. Nothing can prevent the completion of that which God has already begun in history.

CHAPTER 9

The gospel of God's gracious initiative for the deliverance of all in the death of Jesus has put Jew and non-Jew on the same footing before God (3:22b-23, 30). It has even provided the non-Jew with equal access to what Paul located at the very core of Jewish identity, God's promise to Abraham and Abraham's trust in that promise (chap. 4). What then becomes of God's faithfulness to the people Israel? What about God's calling of this people as uniquely God's own?

9:1-18, Abraham and Election

In a remarkable resumption of his earlier redefinition of the authentic Jew (2:28-29) and of the authentic Abraham (cf. the comments on 4:9-12), Paul now redefines Israel in such a way as to distinguish the "children of God" and "of the promise" (v. 8) from the physical posterity of Abraham. One should take some care in interpreting Paul. He is not trying to make room for believing Gentiles among Abraham's children (as he was in 4:9-12), much less suggesting a "spiritualized" definition of the Jewish people as a pretext for substituting the church for Israel (that would reduce vv. 1-3 to posturing). Nor is he dismissing the earthly and historic continuity of the Jewish people as unauthentic; he is not abstracting an "essential" Israel from its history. Historical Israel itself is determined by "promise" rather than by "flesh." Isaac and Ishmael, one born to Abraham's wife Sarah and the other to his maidservant Hagar, were not equals.

Thus, the descendants of Abraham through Ishmael (Gen 25:12-18; cf. also *Jubi-*

lees 15:28-30; 20:11-13;) were not included in "Israel." To make the point clear, Paul moves down a generation to the twin sons of Rebecca (Jacob and Esau), "conceived from the same conjugal act with one man, Isaac" (v. 10). Here the determination of authentic Israel takes place "when they were not yet born and when they had not yet done anything good or bad, in order that God's elective intention might remain unchanged (i.e., consistent), dependent not on works but on the one who calls" (vv. 11-12a). Election, which means the calling into being of a people, exactly like the justification of the unrighteous, is God's free act, a gift.

9:19-29, God's Wrath and Mercy

To make his point, Paul introduces the image of the potter and his clay. Many readers, taking the side of the questioners in v. 19 and thinking only of the passive pliability of the clay in the potter's hands, have taken offense at what they regard as this picture of an impersonal, unfeeling, and despotic God. The point, though, is not the power of the potter but his "right" (v. 21, NRSV) to fashion each vessel for a function and to determine the use of each. A machine stamping out identical pots is "impersonal." God is not impersonal.

God's freedom and purpose lie at the heart of Paul's understanding of election. Corroboration comes in the difficult vv. 22-23. God is not simply like a potter. The purpose clauses with which both verses begin are parallel: God wishes to make Godself known by showing God's wrath and by patiently enduring, that is, by not destroying, "objects of wrath that are made for destruction" (v. 22) and then by making known "the riches of [God's] glory" on "objects of mercy" prepared for that use (v. 23). "Object" in Greek normally also means an "instrument" or piece of gear in the hands of someone (Paul himself is a "chosen instrument," NRSV, a "vessel or object of election," for God in Acts 9:15). The harshness of this language results from combining terms from the imagery of the potter with God's wrath and mercy. Paul does *not* identify the "objects of mercy" with Gentiles, much less with Christians. These phrases refer to figures in Israel's own history, Pharaoh and Moses respectively.

Verses 22-23 teach that there are two "sides" or "faces" of God, but they are never in balance and do not result in a split or mixed purpose in God's self. The hardening of Pharaoh served the deliverance of Israel under Moses, just as the revelation of wrath serves the manifestation of God's righteousness, or the "increase" of sin by the law serves the aggrandizement of grace (5:20). There is no inconsistency between God's behavior in Israel's creation and the justification of the undeserving that creates a new people from both Jew and non-Jew (v. 24).

In vv. 27-29, Paul quotes from Isa 10:22-23 and 1:9 (in that order). The texts from Isaiah return to God's reliability in the election of authentic Israel. The texts show that the prophets had seen long ago that only a few Israelites would be saved. A remnant would remain. "Remnant" in v. 27, like "seed" in v. 29, refers to that authentic line of descent from Abraham described positively in vv. 6-13. These scripture citations help explain why only a small number of Jews and a large number of non-Jews are responding to the gospel.

9:30-33, Israel's Unbelief

In the language of the race track, Paul argues that Gentiles, who were not even trying to attain God's righteousness, have arrived at that goal on proper terms because of their trust in God. Israel, on the other hand, pursuing a law that held out the promise of righteousness failed to reach even the standards of that law.

Israel's pursuit of the goal was not carried out in trust but on the supposition that righteousness can come from performance of deeds enjoined by them. God declared that "whoever believes in [Christ] will not be put to shame." That assurance had been laid down by God as a foundation stone in Zion (Isa 28:16; cf. Ps 118:22), but it has become a rock of stumbling, as promised by God to those who refuse God's message (Isa 8:14). Israel has stumbled on that rock (Rom 9:32). For that grave misstep of his own people, Paul feels great anguish.

CHAPTER 10

10:1-4, Israel's Responsibility

Paul concentrates on Israel's responsibility. Israel's genuine zeal for God turned into disobedience. Their pursuit of righteousness through law and works mutated into a search for their own righteousness rather than reliance on the righteousness of God (v. 3).

10:5-21, Salvation Is for All

In vv. 5-13, Paul follows an established Rabbinic procedure for dealing with apparently contradictory biblical texts. The law ("Moses," v. 5) does indeed invite one to establish a "righteousness of one's own" that will divide Jew from non-Jew. But the same law, when one reads Deut 30:12-14, prefixed by Deut 9:4, forbids presuming to do for oneself what God has already done (in Christ). Anyone who confesses the lordship of Christ will be brought into right relationship with God; not by deeds of the law, but by grace. "Everyone who calls on the name of the Lord shall be saved." Paul adds "everyone" to Isa 28:16. By what right? Because Joel 2:32 does just that (v. 13). Joel meant God when he referred to "Lord," but Paul applies these words to Christ.

10:14-17, There Are No Excuses

Does this passage refer to Jews or Gentiles? It is difficult to tell. If one substitutes "God" for "him" in 10:14 the text can be applied to Gentiles. If one substitutes "Christ" for "him" the text can be applied to Jews.

It may be better to apply the text to the Jews since Paul speaks to his own people in the preface to chap. 10. A questioner apparently contended that the Jews do not believe the gospel because they have not had the opportunity to hear it. Paul responds by quoting Isa 52:7 (vv. 14-15). The Jews were told about the good news. They failed to respond. He cites Isa 53:1 in v. 16 to emphasize the point.

10:18-21, God Confronts a Disobedient and Rebellious People

Can it be that Israel did not hear or understand? In v. 18, Paul cites Ps 19:4 to explain why he turned to the Gentiles. The psalmist contends that the sun and stars witness to the glory of God. Paul uses those words to argue that missionary work was started among the Jews in their synagogues and only was halted because the Jews drove Paul from the synagogues.

The Gentiles come back into view as Paul returns from Israel's role to God's. While the people of Israel considered themselves the elect people of God, Paul reminds them that God's plan extended to other nations as well (vv. 19, 20). In fact, prophets like Moses and Isaiah had spoken centuries before of God's presence being found by people who were not even looking for God (Deut 32:21; Isa 65). Was that a breakdown in God's election? On the contrary, God never ceased to reach out to Israel, even in the midst of Israel's defiance (v. 21).

In this chapter Paul issues a double claim about God. First, Israel's refusal to accept God's righteousness (10:3) serves God's purpose to bestow God's riches impartially upon all (10:12), and thus to extend salvation to non-Jews. Second, in that very action, God, by provoking Israel to anger over the matter of

these now-included outsiders (10:19), awakens and, through that awakening, recalls Israel.

CHAPTER 11

11:1-36, Israel's Rejection Is Not Final

God's word to Israel has not failed. Israel, descended through Jacob, yet defined by promise and not by the outward criterion of physical descent, called into being by the God who shows mercy (9:6-13, 16), is an actual people, not a fancy constructed out of future promises. If Israel has missed God's intent by a wide margin, and if God has had some hand in Israel's doing so (9:31-33; 10:19), does it not follow that God has repudiated God's own people? In reply, Paul uses the Hebrew scripture concept of the "remnant." "Remnant" may also be used exclusively to identify an "elite" minority within a larger whole, distinguished by special fidelity or piety. The Qumran community understood itself as such a faithful remnant. That Paul uses it in an exclusive sense here is clear from his differentiating "the elect" and "the rest" (clearly not those included in the "remnant") in v. 7, and from the analogy he draws with the seven thousand in the days of Elijah (1 Kgs 19:10, 14, 18).

The difference in nuance is important. A remnant of Israel has accepted the Messiah. God in God's deep wisdom used the disobedience of Israel to bring blessings to the Gentiles. However, God will never abandon Israel. The Gentiles ought not to boast about what they have received, which by right belonged to the Jews. If God rejected the Jews for the sake of the Gentiles, God still welcomed them for the sake of the patriarchs. God does not repent of God's gifts or calling.

11:1-5, A Remnant Remains

The preservation of a part—the remnant—gives promissory assurance for the future of the whole. Paul emphasizes that this continuity-providing remnant is "chosen by grace" (cf. 9:11-12). It is not the result of one group being any better or more deserving than the rest of Israel.

11:7-12, Why Only a Remnant?

A remnant of Israel, represented by Paul, did arrive at the goal mentioned in 9:31, but (all) the rest did not, because they sought salvation through works (cf. Deut 29:4; Isa 29:10). God therefore withdrew God's Spirit and left them to their own way because of their disobedience. The blessings bestowed upon Israel had lulled them into a false sense of security; the people thought that all was well between them and God when it was not (cf. Ps 69:22-23). They were suffering from hard hearts, spiritual blindness, and deafness. Paul's primary point, however, is a continuation of 9:33 and 10:18-21. He wants to show God's continuing presence and purpose with Israel, and so to refute the suggestion that God has abandoned Israel. Israel's "stumbling" is the occasion of riches for the world: through Israel's "stumbling," salvation has been extended to the Gentiles in order to incite Israel to jealousy (v. 11).

11:13-24, Israel's Fall Is Temporary

"Now I am speaking to you Gentiles" does not mark a change of audience; the largely Gentile Christian audience has been the same since 9:1. Paul now deliberately calls attention to the Gentiles to highlight the following verses. Paul's own calling as an "apostle to the Gentiles" (v. 13b) is in service to God. Ultimately, that service coincides with his own deep desire for his kinfolk, his "flesh" (v. 14). His desire is to preach to Gentiles to make the Jews jealous so that his own people may be saved. The beneficiaries of God's hostile treatment of Israel are the non-Jews; the beneficiary of God's reconciliation of the world is Israel.

In 11:16 Paul draws on the Jewish belief that in the consecration of the first handful of dough the whole harvest was consecrated. The part affects the whole, the dedicatory cereal consecrates the whole harvest (Num 15:17-21). In like manner, through the consecration of the ancestors Abraham, Isaac, and Jacob, the entire nation has been consecrated. Just as these ancestors were holy, so are their branches holy. What has been consecrated to God always belongs to God.

The theological point of Paul's metaphor of the olive tree is lucid and forceful. Directed to the non-Jews (v. 17), the metaphor makes clear, first, that salvation is available for them only in continuity with Israel's history and in dependence on Israel's God. The root is now Israel, and the branches are the Jews and the rest of humankind. Everything Paul has said in Romans about God's justification of the unrighteous in Jesus Christ is empty unless this means a restored relationship to the God of Abraham, Isaac, and Jacob.

Jew and Gentile are alike utterly dependent on the creative freedom of God to cut out and to graft in, to bestow life on God's own terms where it is wholly undeserved, both "according to nature" and "contrary to nature" (v. 24). This leaves no room for either pride ("do not become proud, but stand in awe," v. 20) or contempt ("God has the power to graft them in again," v. 23). The apostle rejects at every point the rigid determinism of conventional religion that divides humankind into the saved and the damned. Trust in God is the issue for men and women, for Jew (v. 23) and for non-Jew alike (v. 20).

11:25-27, Paul's First Conclusion

Paul uses the term *mystery* in a meaning shaped by the apocalyptic tradition to refer to God's ultimate purposes for the world, hidden from human perception but disclosed on God's own terms (cf. Dan 2:27-28; *1 Enoch* 9:6; 63:3). Part of Israel has been "hardened" for the sake of all non-Jewish peoples, but "in this way" (v. 26) all Israel will be saved. The end-time miracle will consist in the justification of God's own people. Paul does not here call for Jewish conversion to Christianity or a separate Christian mission to the Jewish people. The final salvation of all Israel is God's own "mystery." The certainty of that salvation, and the terms on which it must take place, are disclosed in God's revelation of God's righteousness in Jesus Christ.

11:28-32, Paul's Second Conclusion

With relation to the gospel, Jews are (God's) enemies on the non-Jew's account. Regarding election, Jews are (God's) beloved on account of the patriarchs. God does not withdraw God's gifts or call from those to whom God has given them. The Gentiles are told that, just as they had once disobeyed God but now have obtained mercy through their disobedience, so the Jews now have disobeyed the mercy extended to the Gentiles in order that they might themselves also be recipients of mercy. For God has consigned all human being to disobedience in order to bestow mercy on all (vv. 28-32). God's justification of the undeserving embraces all human beings on equal terms, but this "universalism" is one that confronts them all with both judgment and mercy.

11:33-36, Paul's Third Conclusion

In this third conclusion, Paul takes the stance of the worshiper and uses an early Christian hymn. Authentic faith and obedience, and the undergirding hope of salvation, do not rest on God's withholding God's self but on God making God's self known, on God's own terms, as a God who can be trusted.

CHAPTER 12

12:1-8, The New Life in Christ

Chapter 12 is one of the best known and most loved passages in Romans. In previous discus-

sions, Paul was concerned with the inner life of faith. Now he deals with what it means to live a justified life. The new life should be a life of worship. The person who receives God's grace lives as though his total being belongs to God. Such persons live in service to others as a way of pleasing God. The dedication and consecration of the physical being to God is the beginning of intelligent worship. Though believers have a tendency to stress the spirit and neglect the physical side of life, Paul emphasizes the connection between body and mind as crucial for worship.

Paul calls for the transformation of the mind, because he knows that actions are generated by attitudes. This transformation is not a one-time event but a constant struggle. The Christian's agenda is not to be determined by the current secular standards. The Christian's standards are determined by the coming new age as sustained by the Holy Spirit.

In vv. 3-5, Paul discourages a boastful spirit. He uses the famous image of the "body" that signifies unity in diversity. One body has many members. In the body of Christ individual gifts are to be used for the good of the whole. Verses 6-8 list gifts that may be used cheerfully in the service of the whole community. Though the list is not exhaustive or absolute, it is instructive (cf. 1 Cor 12; Eph 4:11-12). The gifts are prophesying (the gift of inspired preaching, not necessarily of predicting or foretelling), ministering (taking care of practical needs), teaching (using the authority of the Old Testament scriptures and traditions of Jesus to teach others), exhorting (encouraging others to live in obedience to God), giving (sharing possessions and performing deeds of kindness), leading (directing a congregation), and showing compassion (caring for the sick, aged, or disabled).

12:9-21, Marks of the True Christian

Paul proposes a group of vaguely attached

exhortations that focus first on relationships between Christians (vv. 9-13) and then on relationships with those outside the church (vv. 14-21).

Love (*agape*, v. 9) refers to self-giving action on behalf of others that God's Spirit makes feasible. If a person is going to practice love, she must hate evil. It is not just that she avoids evil; she must take a stand against evil (v. 9). This position is akin to the view of Martin Luther King Jr., who contended in his 1963 "Letter from Birmingham Jail": "We will have to repent in this generation not merely for the hateful words and actions of the bad people but for the appalling silence of the good people." Too many Christians have become accustomed to evil, tolerate it, bemoan it, but fail to act in love against it.

CHAPTER 13

Romans 13 has been used by governments to give theological justification for the status quo, including racism, capitalism, and totalitarianism. Injustice is thereby blessed, and the will of the powerful can dominate those who are less powerful and tyrannize them into either obedience or passivity. All of this is done in the name of a biblical mandate. But Romans 13 does not present a full outline of Paul's view of government, and even less a "doctrine of the state." Paul did not address the question of whether civil disobedience is ever called for by a Christian living under a corrupt, unjust, or racist government. He was not attempting to write a manifesto for the church's relationship to governments for all centuries. His concern was local and specific.

Romans 12:2 and Martin Luther King Jr.

Unlike many scholars and pastors who are skeptical of using Paul's writings as a resource for political engagement, Martin Luther King Jr. used the Pauline tradition to preach sermons with profound social implications. For example, his sermon, "The Transformed Nonconformist," was based on Rom 12:2: "Do not be conformed to this world, but be transformed by the renewing of your minds." King recognized the difficulty many of his contemporaries faced when trying to avoid conforming with their surrounding culture and peers. Christians, though, are called to walk to the beat of a different drum. Though they hold dual citizenship in the worlds of both time and eternity, they owe ultimate loyalty to eternity alone. That eternity is a realm ruled by Christ. Ultimately, then, the call to become a transformed nonconformist comes not only from Paul but from Jesus Christ, "the world's most dedicated non-conformist" (Martin Luther King Jr., *Strength to Love* [Philadelphia: Fortress Press, 1981], 11). King subsequently offered a variety of sayings of Jesus in order to contrast human conformist attitudes and behavior with his teachings. He used scripture as a descriptive and interpretive tool for explaining the nature of present human difficulties and as a norm for future human behavior. He depicted conformism as a tyrannical force that prevented many sincere people from taking a stand on crucial matters such as racial segregation, the cold war, the evils of capitalism and other oppressions. Conformists are afraid to act against such prevailing mores because they fear being ostracized.

Nevertheless, he was affirming that a proper understanding of, and lifestyle in relation to, the authorities is part of one's "spiritual worship" (12:1-2).

Religion and politics do meet. Paul's formulae for the mixture might be summarized as follows. (1) Desire peace, justice, and order in accordance with God's purpose for God's creation, and (2) concern oneself for that which fosters harmony and unity in the church so that the church may carry out its redemptive mission. These concerns (which are grounded in Rom 13:1-7), rather than a blind, unconditional commitment to any and every civil authority, should guide the Christian's attitude toward the authorities.

13:1-7, Being Subject to Authorities

For Paul, politics and cosmology are intricately related. Angelic powers influence political rulers. Therefore, those who are in power, even the officials with whom the ordinary Christian comes into contact, belong to the divine order. Paul thus equates obedience to the powers with obedience to God. Resistance to the powers is resistance to God's order and invites eschatological judgment. God has appointed the governing authorities for the good of society. When Paul says, "Let every person be subject . . .," he wants to say: Enlist yourselves in the given situation! Given the social order of your time, do not run away from responsibilities.

Authorities use force to punish wrong in the name of God. Rulers use terror because they are agents of wrath (v. 4). The governing authority represents God's abhorrence of evil. We may, however, detect a way of limiting obedience to rulers in vv. 1-7; Paul's servant imagery must be taken seriously. In v. 4 we are told that the ruler "is God's servant for your good." Wielding power involves both authority *and* responsibility; political institutions imply both gift and task. Government shares in the coveted God-given drive toward order. In the same breath, Paul affirms that the "good" is a task entrusted to the "powers that be." The ruler who loses

A Duty to Disobey

"You express a great deal of anxiety over our willingness to break laws. This is certainly a legitimate concern. Since we so diligently urge people to obey the Supreme Court's decision of 1954 outlawing segregation in the public schools, at first glance it may seem rather paradoxical for us consciously to break laws. One may ask: 'How can you advocate breaking some laws and obeying others?' The answer lies in the fact that there are two types of laws: just and unjust. I would be the first to advocate obeying just laws. One has not only a legal but a moral responsibility to obey just laws. Conversely, one has a moral responsibility to disobey unjust laws. I would agree with Augustine that 'an unjust law is no law at all.'"

—Martin Luther King Jr., "Letter From Birmingham Jail," *A Testament of Hope: The Essential Writings of Martin Luther King, Jr.,* ed. James M. Washington (San Francisco: Harper and Row, 1986), 293–94. Reprinted by arrangement with The Heirs to the Estate of Martin Luther King, Jr., c/o Writers House, Inc., as agent for the proprietor. Copyright © 1963 by Martin Luther King Jr., copyright renewed 1991 by Coretta Scott King.

sight of the function of serving the good loses authority.

If the ruler is truly the servant of God, then that ruler must keep within the bounds of God's will. Throughout the passage, Paul quietly sets government authority under God's authority. There is no blurring of lines between political power and divine power. The real power to be respected is God's. Government therefore has God-given responsibility for the good.

Paul's use of conscience conditions his understanding of obedience to the governing authorities. "Conscience" originally meant the pain a person feels when he does something wrong. Paul deepened this understanding into an assessing discernment amid "conflicting thoughts," an evaluating capacity that operates as a criterion for right or wrong because of the coming judgment (Rom 2:14-15). It is the reflecting and judging "I" of faith that seeks to determine God's will in various situations. If Paul appeals to such a conscience in the matter of obedience to authority, then the door is open for conscientious disobedience or selective obedience.

Christians also are to pay taxes, give dues, and show respect and honor as law-abiding citizens for the sake of conscience. In calling tax collectors "ministers of God," Paul remains consistent with what he said in v. 4. He again stresses the delegated character of civil authorities. Paul uses the language of "respect" and "honor" for the ruling authorities. Nevertheless, he does not write what emperors would have preferred him to write—that the emperor embodies a divine genius or power.

13:8-10, Love for One Another

The debt of love is to love one's neighbor as oneself. This command summarizes all the others. Verses 8-10 stress *agape*, a love that refers to mutual nurturing between believers.

Each Christian is to be a servant of the other in love (Gal 5:13).

13:11-14, An Urgent Appeal

Submission to government is set in the context of the more urgent duty to love our neighbor while we await God's justice. Living in a new transforming context, Paul calls for a new discernment (Rom 12:1-2), and he sets before and behind the text on governing authorities reminders of the eschatological situation (12:2; 13:11-14) and of the duty to love (12:9; 13:8). To love our neighbor in a world still marked by greed and injustice requires political responsibility, not disowning it. However, if our neighbor is threatened by the greed and injustice of a tyrant, the new discernment's political responsibility would acknowledge the priority of the neighbor's claims.

Chapter 14

Two categories of believers—persons of strong or weak faith—thought that they were correct in their opposing thinking and practice. The "strong" thought of themselves as persons with educated, liberated consciences. Freedom "in Christ" for them meant license to do whatever they wished. They had forgotten that freedom meant responsibility. The "weak" paid too much attention to particular cultic observances. Conservative in outlook, they obsessed about "clean" and "unclean." In speaking to the factions, Paul confronts two particular problems: food laws and holy day observances.

14:1-12, Do Not Judge Another

Two concerns of the weak take center stage: they want others to be vegetarians (vv. 2, 21) and to abstain from wine (v. 21), like themselves (cf. 1 Cor 8). Paul's advice is practical. The Jew or the Greek who could eat no meat should not be despised or ridiculed by the meat eaters, "the strong." On the other hand, neither should the vegetarians, "the weak," consider themselves superior. The abstainers cannot condemn the indulgers, since both are accepted by God (v. 3). In fact, both weak and strong Christians will stand before God as guilty defendants. God alone has the right to judge (v. 10). Paul's logic: one should be careful how one judges others in this life, since all are going to be judged ultimately by God (v. 12).

14:13-23, Do Not Make Another Stumble

Paul believes, on the authority of Christ, that nothing in itself is unclean (cf. Mark 7:15). This makes him agree with the "strong" (v. 14). And yet Paul's beliefs are conditioned by his love. One should not, out of strength, hurt another's conscience, thus putting that person's faith at risk. Food and drink do not compare to the kingdom of God. Kingdom ethics involve a community living together in righteousness, in peaceful sensitivity to one another's beliefs, and a standing in a humility before God that seeks the good of others (v. 17). Paul's hope is that any conflicts, including those involving food, drink, and day observances, that disrupt communal peace would be avoided so that there might be a literal "building up of one another" (v. 19). In other words, in order to secure peace, the strong might have to curtail their freedom in certain contexts.

Paul summarizes chap. 14 with a blessing in v. 23 that says in effect: happy is the weak or the strong person in faith who does what she does because she is fully persuaded that it is right. Those who do not act out of conviction are cursed: woe to the person who acts without being fully persuaded that his behavior is right, for that action becomes sin for that person. The latter is true because the person violates the conscience even though the act itself may be neither good nor bad

CHAPTER 15

15:1-6, Please Others, Not Yourselves

The Christian is to show "forbearance." The Greek word translated here literally means "carry" or "help carry" the burdens of the weak. The Christian who is strong must be willing to practice self-denial on behalf of weak believers. In so behaving, the Christian follows the example of Christ's sacrifice, which was motivated by love for the other. The doxology in vv. 5-6 offers a prayer of encouragement for the Roman Christians to begin to live together in harmony, following Christ's example.

15:7-13, The Gospel for Jews and Gentiles Alike

Paul highlights the example of Jesus, who became a servant to show God's faithfulness to God's promises to the Jews and to show that through the Jews God's mercy might reach the Gentiles. Paul claims that the redemption of the Gentiles had always been a part of God's plan: Ps 18:19; Deut 32:43; Ps 117:1; Isa 11:10. Verse 13 is a concluding benediction for the ethical and moral instructions of the second part of the letter.

15:14-33, Paul's Reason for Writing So Boldly

To confirm his apostleship to his Roman readers, Paul describes his divine commission in terms of priesthood. In the exercise of his preaching ministry as a prophet of God, he is also a priest who offers the sacrifice of the Gentiles made righteous unto God and consecrated by the Holy Spirit (v. 16). Slaughtered animals have been replaced with a repentant people. In other words, the success of Paul's work among the Gentiles is a mark of his apostolic commission, which authorizes him to write the epistle. His mission has prospered because Christ has been working in him (vv. 17-18). His policy had always been to pioneer with the gospel and not to build upon someone else's foundation (v. 21).

In vv. 22-29, Paul wants to give the Roman community the plan for his future journeys: first to Jerusalem, then to Rome, and then to Spain. Now that he has finished his evangelistic work in the east, he asks for their help when he reaches them in the future to support him in his missionary journey to the west. First, however, he wishes to spend a little time with them in order to know them better (vv. 22-24).

Meanwhile, Jerusalem calls for his ministry as the carrier of alms from Macedonia and Achaia for the poor (vv. 25-26). The collection for the poor at Jerusalem was a project diligently carried out by Paul (1 Cor 16; 2 Cor 8–9). We would like to know why the people in the Jerusalem church are poor, but we can only speculate: (1) the experiment in communal living may have failed (Acts 4:32—5:11); (2) the famine of 46 c.e. may have caused devastation (Acts 11:28); and (3) some who were already poor saw continual poverty as a proper response to the gospel.

Whatever may be the reason for their poverty, Paul works toward the end that poverty for the mother church might be reduced. Since the Jewish Christians have shared spiritual treasures, it is the duty of the new converts to contribute temporal things for the needs of the mother church (v. 27). We read in Acts that this offering was taken to Jerusalem (Acts 24:17). The offering was, after all, a debt that Paul owed. He wrote in Gal 2:10 that he was commissioned by the church to be the apostle to the Gentiles, but the only request they made was that he remember the poor. Paul and Barnabas had delivered a similar gift to Jerusalem from the Christians in Syrian Antioch (Acts 11:30; 12:25). This gift could not only serve as an example of appropriate response to human need, but serve as a sign of unity between Jewish and Gentile Christians.

It is not known whether Paul got to Spain. We do know that he reached Jerusalem. He was imprisoned and spent at least four years incarcerated in Caesarea and Rome.

15:30-33, Paul Makes a Prayer Request

In vv. 30-31, Paul charges the Romans to pray to God for him, that he might be "rescued from the unbelievers in Judea." "Unbeliever" literally means "disobedient." Paul was concerned about the reception he would receive from non-Christian Jews or Jews who opposed the Gospel. In Jerusalem, the Jewish Christians cautiously welcomed Paul (Acts 21:17-25). However, the Jews there mobbed him, accused him of desecrating the temple, nearly killed him, and finally imprisoned him. Still, Jewish Christian support from Rome was needed and prayed for (vv. 31-33).

Paul concluded his letter with various comments, including a benediction (15:13), travel plans (15:14-32), and another benediction (15:33).

Chapter 16

16:1-16, Personal Greetings

Phoebe is identified as a "sister" and "deaconess." The fact that she is called "sister" indicates that Paul recognized the church as an "extended family." J. Deotis Roberts clarifies how this notion of ancient Christian family must remain operative in the contemporary black church:

> When the black church is viewed as a family, all persons, whether married, single, or divorced, will come to a sense of kinship in the church as the family of God. The church is the family under the Lordship of Jesus Christ, to whom all families in heaven and earth owe their substance and health. Let us hasten the day when the church will be a family and

the family a domestic church. Then will God's Kingdom be nearer than we had believed.[1]

That Phoebe was called a deaconess, the only person so named in the New Testament, suggests that the church office of that name was emerging. She was from Cenchrae, the eastern seaport of Corinth. Paul wants her to be welcomed, because she belongs to the Lord. Members of the church, as "saints," have a duty to show hospitality, and she has helped him and many of their fellow church members.

In mentioning Prisca and Aquila, Paul's Roman readers would have noticed that the woman's name came first. The ordering suggests that her missionary role was more important than that of her husband.

16:17-24, Final Instructions

These verses are different in tone from the rest of Romans. Paul states his opposition to those who "cause dissension and offenses" (16:17). It is not clear what the teachings or emphases of these persons were, but it is clear that the dissension was destroying the community. Paul connects the disorder with the person and work of Satan. The greeting from Paul's companions—Timothy, Lucius, Sosipater, Tertius (the secretary), and Gaius—indicates that they were probably with the apostle when he was writing the epistle to the Romans from Corinth (vv. 21-24).

16:25-27, Final Doxology

In vv. 25-27 Paul gives a closing, complex sentence of praise to God for the glory shown in Jesus Christ. H. Beecher Hicks Jr. describes this act of praise for the revealed glory of God as movement in Paul from "theology to doxology." He writes: "Our religion is not complete with theology alone. We need theology, but we must also have doxology.

God Calls Whom God Will

Throughout the final chapter of Romans, Paul notes the leadership qualities and roles of women in his early churches. They serve not only as leaders in the church but as colleagues of Paul in ministry. Countless observers have recognized that the African American church must work more diligently in the encouragement, development, and support of African American women in church leadership. Though women make up the overwhelming majority of African American church membership, leadership opportunities are geared specifically toward males. Even as C. Eric Lincoln and Lawrence Mamiya recognize the regrettable present circumstance, they reflect upon the powerful voices of African American women who have, like Phoebe, Prisca, and Junia (v. 7), presented themselves as challenging object lessons to the belief that God expects only male church leaders. "If the man may preach, because the Saviour died for him, why not the woman? Seeing that he died for her also. Is he not a whole Saviour, instead of a half one? as those who hold it wrong for a woman to preach, would seem to make it appear."

—Jarena Lee, quoted in *The Black Church in the African American Experience*, ed. C. Eric Lincoln and Lawrence H. Mamiya (Durham, N.C.: Duke University Press, 1990), 275–76.

- Theology is mind power, but doxology is soul power.
- Theology asks 'why,' but doxology says 'thank you!'
- Theology is concerned about God's omniscience, but doxology affirms God's omnipotence.
- Theology is nothing more than debate and dialogue, but doxology is a hymn that takes you from hardship to hallelujah!
- Theology is something to think about, but doxology is something to shout about."[2]

Notes

1. J. Deotis Roberts, *Roots of a Black Future: Family and Church* (Philadelphia: Westminster, 1980), 132.
2. H. Beecher Hicks Jr., *Correspondence with a Cripple from Tarsus: Romans in Dialogue with the Twentieth Century* (Grand Rapids, Mich.: Zondervan, 1990), 217.

For Further Reading

Achtemeier, Paul J. *Romans*. Interpretation. Atlanta: John Knox, 1985.

Barrett, Charles Kingsley. *A Commentary on the Epistle to the Romans*. Rev. ed. Black's New Testament Commentary. Peabody, Mass.: Hendrickson, 1991.

Byrne, Brendan. *Romans*. Sacra pagina 6. Collegeville, Minn.: Liturgical, 1996.

Fitzmyer, Joseph A. *Romans*. AB 33. New York: Doubleday, 1993.

Keck, Leander. *Romans*. Nashville: Abingdon, 2005.

Stuhlmacher, Peter. *Paul's Letter to the Romans: A Commentary*. Louisville: Westminster John Knox, 1994.

Tamez, Elsa. *The Amnesty of Grace: Justification by Faith from a Latin American Perspective*. Translated by Sharon H. Ringe. Nashville: Abingdon, 1993.

Yeo, Khiok-Khng (K. K.), ed. *Navigating Romans through Cultures: Challenging Readings by Charting a New Course*. Romans through History and Culture Series. New York: T. & T. Clark, 2004.

1 CORINTHIANS

Boykin Sanders

INTRODUCTION

Reading Paul gives me a splitting head-
ache! Why? Because there are too many
stops and starts, too many interruptions
and resumptions, too many digressions!
Paul's thoughts are skewed; his directives
are confusing! When I read him, I can't
remember what I have read or what he
intended! I don't like his style!

So said a student of the Bible. First Corinthians was supposed to be clear. It permits readers a good view of what Paul was up against
and what a fledgling Christian congregation
was like in a first-century Roman city. In

1 Corinthians a reader encounters the names
and functions of some of the community's
members (see chaps. 1 and 16; cf. Acts 18;
Rom 16:1–4) and engages the congregation's
wounds and frustrations. Discord within the
assembly is noted: "I belong to Paul, and I
belong to Apollos, and I belong to Cephas,
and I belong to Christ" (1:12).[1] The strife
endured well beyond Paul's lifetime, as a later
letter from the Roman church to the Corinthian church (*1 Clement*, 96 C.E.) shows. *First
Clement* was written approximately forty-two
years after Paul wrote 1 Corinthians (54 C.E.)
from Ephesus (1 Cor 16:8). The Roman
church is shocked that the Corinthian Christians had still not quit the business of schismatic conduct (*1 Clem.* 47:1–9).

Paul also refers to Corinthian sexual practices and attendant concerns (5:1—7:40) as well as their questions about food sacrificed to idols (8:1—11:1). He addresses their concerns about the headdress of women during public worship (11:2–16), conduct befitting the celebration of the Lord's Supper (11:17–34), spiritual gifts (12:1—14:40), doubts about the resurrection of the dead (15:12), and directions about a collection for the Jerusalem assembly (16:1–24). Second Corinthians adds to this portrait. Readers know exactly who Paul's opponents are ("the super-apostles," 2 Cor 11:5; 12:11) and what those apostles think and do (cf. 2 Cor 10–13). By comparison, the opponents of Galatians are not clearly identified, and readers can only infer what they thought and did from what Paul said. In general, the doors of Paul's churches are usually closed to the public, but this is not the case with 1 Corinthians.

But are current readers any closer to understanding Paul and the Corinthians because Paul posted the raw of Corinthian life and quite a bit about his own life and thought (cf. 2 Cor 11:22—12:13)? Perhaps not! Contemporary readers face two challenges. First, they are some distance from Paul's world. Even if we translate what Paul wrote in a way that makes sense today, we would not necessarily know whether this was what Paul or the Corinthians meant in their ancient context.[2] Second, we only get one side of the Corinthian story—Paul's—despite attempts to read between and beneath the lines of 1 Corinthians. Some think that it is possible to infer the Corinthian side of things from what Paul wrote, for example, through an alleged Corinthian slogan ("I belong to Paul . . ."; 1:12; cf. 3:4) or the transitional phrase, "Now concerning the matters about which you wrote" (1 Cor 7:1, NRSV; cf. 8:1, 4; 12:1; 16:1, 12).

Employing social sciences, archaeological and anthropological methods, and insights from ancient rhetorical traditions and history, scholars of 1 Corinthians have sought to reduce the distance between the text and the contemporary reader, and in the process have enabled Paul, Apollos, the Corinthians, as well as Corinthian issues to come to life. These scholars note that the Corinthian congregation represents a cross-section of Roman society preoccupied with upward mobility. They hold that the Corinthians boast about social connections and devotion to patronage sponsors (reflected in such language as "I belong to Paul"; "I belong to Apollos").[3] For these scholars the terms *weak* and *strong* (e.g., in chaps. 1; 4; 8; 9; and 12) reflect sociopolitical differences or stratification among members of the Corinthian church. *Weak* designates persons nearest to or at the bottom of Corinth's socioeconomic pecking order, and *strong* refers to those whose higher socioeconomic standing reflects the interests and the habits of the bourgeoisie. Paul is viewed as railing against *the strong* not only because of their misdirected energies and interests, but also because of their disregard for the concerns and needs of those in the lower ranks.[4]

And there is more. Some suggest that 1 Corinthians reveals an economically well-off Paul who willfully engages in self-deprecation, refusing Corinthian financial support and engaging in manual labor (cf. 4:12; 9:12–27) in an effort to lure the bourgeois into an imitation of his example.[5] Some also view Paul as the master rhetorician, who uses various rhetorical strategies—judicial, parliamentary, and praise-and-blame rhetoric—to redirect Corinthians toward nobler ends,[6] and as a chauvinist who undermines the freedom and possibilities of women prophets.[7] Finally, Paul is viewed as straddling the fence on slavery (7:21–24), showing greater deference to slave-holding interests than to the lot of the enslaved.[8]

A major goal of these readings is to provide a clearer perspective about the Corinthian side of things. In this regard, scholars posit a decided advantage of the Corinthians over current readers.[9] The view here is that the Corinthians likely understood the meaning of "not beyond what is written" (4:6) and what being baptized on behalf of the dead implied (15:29), issues that give pause to current readers. Yet one wonders about the alleged edge of the Corinthians, since 1 Corinthians is Paul's second letter-writing attempt to discuss some of these matters with them (cf. 5:7). In this letter, his emissary, Timothy, is on his way to Corinth to discuss with the Corinthians Paul's "ways in Christ," ways the Corinthians had previously heard about from Paul himself (4:17).[10] Even now the Corinthians are loaded with concerns (cf. 7:1, 25; 8:1, 4; etc.), enlisting members from their congregation (e.g., Stephanas, Achaicus, and Fortunatus; 16:17) to ask or re-ask Paul to expound on issues that perplexed them (cf. 7:1; 8:1; 12:1).

The point is that much about 1 Corinthians remains unclear, with Paul as a likely contributor to the uncertainty regarding the Corinthian situation.[11] On one occasion, Paul tabled things the Corinthians needed to have clarified, telling them to wait for his response upon his arrival in Corinth: "About the other things I will give instructions when I come"(11:34c, NRSV). The curious reader can only wonder about what these things were. What this means is that we are left with a few things from Paul himself about the Corinthians and can reasonably infer others from the conversations taking place between the Corinthians and Paul. We know that the Corinthians registered some concerns with Paul, perhaps in the form of questions, but we do not know what the questions were. We can only infer what the questions were, if indeed Paul received questions from the Corinthians at all, by reading what Paul stated in the context of those so-called questions (e.g., 7:1–40 and 12:1–40).

The following commentary presupposes these anomalies. It is anchored in the view that Paul's utterances and directives for Corinthian proper life are initiated and sauced by

Folk Wisdom and Paul

Our African enslaved ancestors in the American south often viewed white preachers as proponents of slave-holding interests. Commonly, the economics of gains and losses determined whether Christian conversion was promoted or discouraged among the enslaved. Paul was used in the debate, often to the chagrin of the enslaved. Howard Thurman's grandmother, a former slave, noted this problem: "During the days of slavery the master's minister would occasionally hold services for the slaves. Old man McGhee was so mean that he would not let a Negro minister preach to his slaves. Always the white minister used as his text something from Paul. At least three or four times a year he used as a text: 'Slaves, be obedient to them that are your masters . . ., as unto Christ.' Then he would go on to show how it was God's will that we were slaves and how, if we were good and happy slaves, God would bless us. I promised my Maker that if I ever learned to read and if freedom ever came, I would not read that part of the Bible."

—Howard Thurman, *Jesus and the Disinherited* (Boston: Beacon, 1996), 30–31.

mystery traditions, perhaps of an apocalyptic type (2:1; cf. 2:7; 4:1; 13:2; 14:2), and that the Corinthian future, in Paul's view, whatever it is with God, will soar from a mystery: "Behold I tell you a mystery" (15:51).[12] My point is that, despite the alleged clarity of 1 Corinthians, distance still exists between contemporary readers and the text, in part due to unacknowledged scholarly commitments to Western imperialistic traditions. For this reason, I will aim for something better in commenting on the mysteries of Paul in 1 Corinthians—what is unfolding for the despised and rejected as bourgeois voices quiet (as Paul would have it) and what is coming to light as the drama of 1 Corinthians, this apocalypse (unveiling) of the end of death's reign, comes to a resounding end.[13]

In 1:1-9, the traditional salutation and thanksgiving of the letter, Paul states the shape of all parties involved in the drama of 1 Corinthians, including God. God is faithful (1:9; cf. 10:13b). All parties are defined under the grid of God, the creator/producer of the Corinthian church, and Christ Jesus, through whom the church receives its peculiar configuration. In the next section, 1:10—4:21, Paul dispenses with concerns about apostolic roles and positions to meet the Corinthians face to face (cf. 4:14). In 5:1—7:25, Paul focuses on a single theme, appropriate and inappropriate sexual conduct. The section 8:1—11:1 is devoted to another pressing concern raised by the Corinthians: eating food sacrificed to idols. In this section Paul makes himself an exemplar of apostolic freedom. The final section, 11:2—16:24, falls under the rubric of received traditions and reminders as well as current, necessary instructions (cf. 11:2, 17, 23; 12:1; 15:1, 3; 16:1-24). Because Paul expects to make a successful visit to Corinth, he ends the letter on a note of endearment: "My love be with all of you in Christ Jesus" (16:24).

1:1–9, Salutation and Thanksgiving

First Corinthians begins in conventional and customary Pauline style. The letter opens with the names of its senders (1:1) and its receivers (1:2), and a greeting (1:3), followed by words expressing Paul's hope that the letter's receivers are faring well (cf. 1:4-9). 1:1-3 comprises the salutation and greeting; 1:4-9 is the thanksgiving. Both categories honor the conventions of letter writing during Paul's lifetime.[14]

Paul, however, goes beyond convention. Rather than a single sender and a single receiver, as is more typical in letter writing of the time, Paul introduces Sosthenes as co-sender and multiple persons (the Corinthians) as receivers.[15] Then Paul goes a bit extreme. Rather than saying "Paul to the Corinthians, my people" or something similar and using the simple greeting *chairein*, "greetings," as one might expect, Paul identifies himself as an apostle of Christ Jesus through the will of God and then directs his words "to the assembly [church] of God [*tē ekklēsia tou theou*] that is in Corinth." He identifies the Corinthians as saints who are aligned with all saints everywhere who call on the name of the Lord Jesus Christ. Only then does he extend proper grace and peace, which he links with "God the Father and the Lord Jesus Christ."[16]

In 1:10—4:21, Paul's draws his apostolic self-portrait. He thinks of himself as a "servant" (*diakonos*) through whom Corinthians believe (3:5), a skilled architect laying the foundation of the Corinthian church (3:10), a house manager (steward) and minister of God's mysteries (4:1), and the father of the Corinthians in the gospel (4:15). Nonetheless, the most enduring image for Paul in 1 Corinthians is apostle of Christ Jesus, a person whose commission is bestowed by God's own choosing (cf. 4:9; 9:1, 2, 5; 12:28-29; 15:7, 9).

As for the Corinthians, Paul describes them in different terms. They are not apostles like Paul. They are God's *ekklēsia* ("assembly" or "church"), literally the "called out" group (the verb *kaleō* means "to call").[17] Paul views them as "sanctified" persons, as "saints" (1:2); they had left the ways of the Roman world for a consecrated life "in Christ Jesus." As their existence is through God their Creator, they are holy or *other*, like their Creator. In 1:10, Paul calls them "brothers" (*adelphoi*, translated in the NRSV as "brothers and sisters"), a title they receive throughout the letter (cf. 1:11, 26; 2:1; 3:1; etc). Paul also calls them God's "field" and God's "construction" (3:9), God's "temple" (3:17), and "beloved children" (4:14; cf. 10:14). They have been "enriched [by God] in every way, in speech and knowledge of every kind" (1:5) and are given spiritual gifts by God (1:7; cf. 12:1—14:40). Paul expects a blameless state for them on the day of the Lord (1:8–9).

Functionally, then, the opening and thanksgiving of 1 Corinthians introduce readers to themes that will unfold in the rest of the letter. Paul is an apostle on an irreversible divine mission to preach and perform apostolic duties on behalf of the gospel of Christ (1:17; cf. 9:16). The Corinthians' enrichment in speech and knowledge, stated as God's doing (God's grace) in 1:4, is explored especially in 1:10—3:23 and 8:1-13. God's faithfulness in 1:9, on the heels of an eschatological note regarding the day of the Lord (cf. 1:8), is met again in the context of eschatological warnings in 10:13: "Faithful is God, who does not allow you to be tempted beyond what you are able but with the testing also will make a way out in order that you are able to endure." And the eschatological reminders that close the thanksgiving section (1:7-8), which hangs over Paul's note that the congregation is a divine fellowship called into existence by God (1:9), resurface throughout the text (e.g., 3:10-17; 7:26; 10:6-13; esp. 15:50-57).

Thus the opening and thanksgiving section (1:1-9) function as an index to the letter. They foreshadow, even inform, what Paul will say about himself and the Corinthians in the body of the letter.[18]

1:10—4:21, Go Back to Your Roots

The body of the letter begins at 1:10, often called the thesis by those who view 1 Corinthians through rhetorical lenses.[19] The verse introduces the reason for the letter and also the issue that birthed it. According to 1:11-12, a group called "those of Chloe" report to Paul in Ephesus that the Corinthians are bragging about which apostle they favored. They say: "I belong to Paul," or "I belong to Apollos," or "I belong to Cephas," or "I belong to Christ" (1:12).[20] For Paul, such conduct represents a fractured body—a "division" (*schisma*, 1:10; 11:18)—of competing groups (cf. 3:5; 4:6). For Paul, this does not square with the concept of what it means to be an assembly called into being by God (1:9; cf. 12:12–14). Paul calls for a reversal of the fractured fellowship.

1:10—3:4, Your Roots

Paul makes clear in 1:10 that he wants the schismatic conduct to stop and a spirit of unity (common mind) to ensue. The meaning of the Greek verb *katartizō* is critical for understanding the apostle's point. The NRSV asserts that Paul wants the Corinthians to "*be united* in the same mind and the same purpose," that is, to become so from this point onward. The NIV translates *katartizō* in a similar fashion: "that you *be perfectly united* in mind and thought."

Lexicographically, however, *katartizō* can mean "to restore" or "to be restored to a former condition." Accordingly, I suggest that 1:10 should read: "I appeal to you, brothers and sisters, through the name of our Lord

Jesus Christ, that you all say the same thing and there be no divisions among you, but that you *be restored* (in) the same mind and the same judgment." Paul wants the Corinthians to return (come back) to a previous position, in particular a position of single-mindedness that preceded the writing of 1 Corinthians. Perhaps because of the teachings of "the many guides in Christ" (cf. 4:15) who worked the community after Paul left Corinth in 51 C.E., the "brothers and sisters" there have veered away from their singleness of mind and judgment.[21] Paul wants them to be restored to their former condition. In that sense the Corinthians are urged to find their future in the past, in the ancestral constituting ideas and practices that they had learned through Paul, their founding ancestor in Christ (4:14), whose life exhibits the mind of Christ (2:16b).[22]

Verse 10 then initiates a long section on Corinthian rectification (restoration), beginning with the admonitory language, "but I appeal to you."[23] The entire section it introduces (1:10—4:21) is a call to order to a Corinthian church that seems almost beyond Paul's reach. The church had strayed from the liberation course on which Paul had set it. In its proclivity to misjudge leaders as sources of a deliverance only God could provide (cf. 1:31), it displayed signs of past bondage.

Interestingly, the Corinthians' straying from their foundational position is mimicked in postcolonial Africa, especially in contexts where multiparty systems are encouraged and influenced by Western traditions of democracy that undermine foundational concepts such as, "I am, because we are." Community divisions along party lines often lead to war, as competing interest groups strive to achieve political ascendancy and domination.[24] To a lesser degree, divisive behavior develops among Africans in America, who divide themselves along Democratic and Republican lines of ideology. (See sidebar below.) And, as was the case with the Corinthians, Africans in America who follow the political party lines

---

Africans in America

I use the phrase "Africans in America" to underline identity concerns and to accent Paul's message to the Corinthians. Paul's message in 1 Corinthians is that Corinthians are a "called-out" group, that is, they have left the ways of Roman culture to embrace the culture of Christ crucified. They are no longer Roman globetrotting conquistadors but a community showing regard for others under the terms of *agape*. The term *African* was used to designate our enslaved ancestors until the Black Convention Movement in the 1830s, when Frederick Douglass and others, due to the politics of begging for acceptance in America, pushed the term *colored* in their bid toward that goal. My expression "Africans in America" is designed to show deference to the real Americans—the Native people of America, the "Red Indians" as they were called—and to signify that our ancestors understood themselves as exiles (strangers in a foreign land) who did not support European strategies in the Americas. Thus the language is political, as all language designations are, except here I use it to convey the idea that black people are *other* than what America became and to reflect the nature of the Christian message as Paul understood it. That is to say, Christian ways are *other* than Roman or American vis-à-vis the peoples of the world.

tend to operate with a class-consciousness that often disregards the concerns of the poor.[25]

Paul sets his own example as a prism through which the Corinthians could find their way back to the unity and "other-regard" that had given them their peculiar identity (4:14-21), the identity Paul recalled for them in 1:1-9. Paul's use of himself as an example seems awkward, since he discourages attachment to individual apostles (cf. 1:11-12 and 3:4). He does so because preconversion presuppositions led the Corinthians to think of their apostolic leaders as wisdom teachers in whom they should glory, and about whom they should boast (1:31).[26] Despite claiming that he is father of the Corinthians, Paul counters by reminding them that their communal birth took place "in Christ through the gospel" (4:15).[27] This realization provokes several key and instructive rhetorical questions. "Is Christ divided?" "Was Paul crucified for you?" "Were you baptized in Paul's name?"

The answer to all three questions is a resounding no. Christ is not divided. Corinthians are not baptized in Paul's name. Paul was not crucified for Corinthian salvation. For Paul, the focus should always be on Christ. As Christ is not divided, so Christ's people must not be divided. With those issues settled, Corinthian rectification begins. It begins with a Pauline declaration: "For Christ did not send me to baptize but to preach the gospel, not in eloquent wisdom so that the cross of Christ might not be emptied of its power" (1:17).

For Paul, to preach the gospel is to speak the word about the cross. It is a word about what the crucified Christ accomplished vis-à-vis the world, depicted here as nonbelieving Jews and Gentiles (1:23) and as the rulers of this age—rulers of the Roman world (2:6-10). The word of the cross implies the end of Greco-Roman cultural habits—expressed in this context as the divisiveness that comes from and results in a boasting in individu-

als—and the beginning of a new order under God through the Spirit (2:11-15). In the divine order, what was once viewed by the world as "foolishness" (*mōria*) is reversed. The world's foolishness becomes the wisdom and power of God (1:24). Paul expresses this reversal in several ways. First, what used to be foolishness (the word of the cross) is the very thing that saves (1:18). Second, what used to be valued as a staple of Roman culture, which the Corinthians still show signs of valuing, is overthrown in Christ. In particular, the cross disrupts Roman and worldly definitions of power (1:20). Christ crucified is the power of God and the wisdom of God (1:24). And third, what used to be dismissed as unimportant in society by Roman measures is now valued. Indeed the Corinthians, for the most part the lowly and despised on the Roman scale of value, are now newly positioned through a cross reversal. People without worldly wisdom, power, or nobility have been empowered through an act of divine liberation to be other than what the powers that dominated them intended them to be (cf. 1:26-28). For that reason, the apostle counsels the Corinthians not to take their disputes, no matter how painful, to the unjust Roman adjudicating assemblies (cf. 6:1ff.). He was perhaps mindful of the fact that the oppressed, now liberated, could not expect to receive justice in the courts of those who had once oppressed them.[28] Paul's advice seems to recognize that most Corinthians came from the underbelly of Roman society (1:26-28), as many of them were slaves or former slaves (cf. 1 Cor 7:21ff.).

While the matter of race did not factor into Paul's advice to the Corinthians when he advised them against taking disputes to Roman authorities from which they had been liberated, race has always been a factor in American discussions of justice and liberation. In the United States, slave regulations once deemed that blacks had no rights that whites, Christian or non-Christian, were duty-bound to respect. Ought not Africans to think carefully before committing their total loyalty to powerful political parties forged from the essence of the very government that once oppressed them? Ought they not to remember that the ultimate social and political allegiance is due to God and God alone, and thus to the kinds of societal agendas envisioned not by political leaders, but by the word of the cross? Can such a foolish (cross-oriented) agenda ever be wise?

No Justice Down Here

The position that blacks had no rights that whites were duty-bound to respect is actually from the 1857 Supreme Court decision *Dred Scott v. Sanford*. Scott held that he was a free person and sued for his freedom, but this was denied because he was black. If the Corinthians were being advised not to take their cases to Roman courts because of unjust judges as some proposed, then the Dred Scott decision shows the continuation of the Greco-Roman elitist pattern vis-à-vis the oppressed, who often cannot get justice in ruling-class courts due to race or political affiliations. The Corinthians made Jesus their choice and thus belonged to another kingdom. In the same way, Scott was black and thus was viewed as a person who did not belong to the kingdom of the human race.

In 2:1-5 Paul places before the Corinthians what the gospel implies via his own personal example. He reminds them of his demeanor during his first preaching tour. His choice of speech, tone, and bodily carriage were paradigmatic. He did not come to Corinth in pomp, as Romans and Roman supporters might be inclined to do, but in a manner befitting God's power for redeemed persons (2:5) and suggestive of the way of the Crucified One, who came to Jerusalem humble and mounted on a donkey. He came to Corinth in weakness, in fear, and in trembling, and his message was quite simple: "I decided to know nothing among you except Christ and him crucified" (2:2). This posture of humility defies the ways of worldly eloquence, yet it is the kind of stance (a trademark of the Christ-crucified gospel) that Paul equates with the power of God. For Paul, God's power is not exhibited in human capability (i.e., in Jewish signs or in Greek wisdom or in great oratorical skills, 1:22; 2:4). God's power is exhibited in the kind of meekness that accrues from the knowledge that God is the great commissioner of all things (1:1). In a word, the accoutrements of rhetorical skills inveigh against the gospel, breeding discord in the body of Christ.

The theme of correction or rectification is continued in 2:6—3:4. These verses call attention to Christian spirituality and its advantages, challenging the Corinthians not to walk according to worldly ways but in ways befitting the status of the liberated (the mature) in Christ (cf. 3:1-4). To that end, Paul describes the Corinthians as "babes in Christ," only able to drink milk, not yet able to eat the solid food of mature Christians. Paul's goal in using such language as "babes in Christ" or "people of the flesh" is not to put the Corinthians down. He specifically says that he did not intend to embarrass but rather to admonish (4:14). He wants the Corinthians to embrace the style of mature Christians, the style of the "perfect" (*teleioi*) who know the deep things of God (2:10) and can separate wheat from chaff in Roman Corinth. Through spiritual discernment, the perfect (the mature) know that the rulers of this age are doomed (2:6). As the rulers of this age (Roman rulers and Roman systems) had no ability to discern spiritual matters and meanings, they were unaware that the crucifixion of Christ (the hidden mystery) initiated the end of their kingdom (2:6-10).

3:5—4:5, The Ways of Founding Ancestors

The beginning of a shift in focus occurs in 3:5—4:5. Paul calls for reconsideration of apostolic roles. Toward the end of the section, at 4:1, he posits that the Corinthians are to view apostles as "ministers of Christ and stewards [house mangers] of the mysteries of God." They manage the mysteries (the meanings of the Christ-crucified gospel) within the boundaries of the will of God, the estate owner. Under the terms of estate regulations, apostles report the facts of the estate to its owner when the owner calls for an accounting on the day of the judgment (4:5). Under these terms, Paul can say that his stewardship is not under the judgment of the Corinthians but only under God who approves and disapproves his stewardship (4:4-5). Just as important is the implication that stewards are not as important as the mysteries they handle. The apostles are only servants of God who are assigned by God to their respective functions. They have no power or authority other than what was given by God.

This section not only clarifies the role and function of apostles; it also defines who the Corinthians are under the Christ-crucified gospel. The description of apostles begins in 3:5, using growth analogies to state their functions. The apostles are servant gardeners through whom Corinthians believe. These gardeners have different functions, assigned by God (3:5-6). Paul credits himself with the function of planting, and Apollos with the watering. In Paul's view, he and Apollos are one; they are wage earners, but God is the source of Corinthian existence and life (3:5-8). In addition, Paul and Apollos are coworkers (3:9a).

In his second analogy, Paul leaves Apollos out. He calls himself a master architect who laid the foundation of the Corinthian church (3:10). For Paul, Christ is that foundation (3:11). Using eschatological (end-time) language, he then warns of others who might come to Corinth to build on the foundation (Christ) that he laid. Thereafter he envisions an apocalyptic visitation wherein the Great Commissioner of the construction (i.e., God) will come to see whether the work has been carried out according to blueprint specifications.[29] Thus Paul warns of the building materials they use, whether gold, silver, precious stones, hay, or straw, since all materials will be tested by fire on the day of the inspection or the day of the Lord (3:13-15).[30]

4:6-21, Getting It Right

The subsection 4:14-21 is Paul's final volley in the search for Corinthian restoration that began in 1:10. He operates metaphorically now, as the Commissioner/Judge (the Great One) would of the Corinthian assembly. Like the eschatological Judge (God) or the Christ belonging to that Judge who assesses all creation, Paul counsels the Corinthians not to behave as if his parousia (coming) to Corinth will not take place (4:18). Paul states that he will come "soon" (*tacheōs*) if the Lord wills it (4:19a). Whether he appears as threatening or in humility will depend on whether the Corinthians change their conduct (4:21).

In that light, Paul begins a personal discussion with the Corinthians in 4:6, revealing what he has been after since his more obvious call for rectification at 1:10. The problem is that the Corinthians pitted Paul and Apollos against each other. But Corinthians should not feel puffed up because of their relationship with either Paul or Apollos, since God, through Christ, is the actual sponsor of their lives (4:6; cf. 1:31). To seal his point, Paul puts before the Corinthians a series of questions and statements. "And what do you have that you did not receive? And if you received it, why do you boast as if you did not?" (4:7). "Already you are filled. Already you are enriched. Apart from us you reigned" (4:8). A few lines later, Paul states that the Corinthians are wise in Christ, strong and glorious (4:10). In contrast, the apostles are fools on account of Christ, weak and dishonored (4:10). Indeed, the apostles are similar to the Corinthians before the great reversal of 1:26-28. The apostles are at the bottom of the social pile. They go around like persons sentenced to death, a spectacle to the world and to angels and human beings. They are hungry, thirsty, naked, buffeted, and homeless. They work with their own hands, yet in the end they are hopeful (4:12b-13). In the midst of these distinctions, the apostle says to the Corinthians, "O that you reigned in order that we might reign together with you" (4:8c).

Some scholars believe that Paul's description of the Corinthians in this context is full of irony; that is, Paul is saying one thing but means the exact opposite. The view here is that the Corinthians are none of the wonderful things Paul says in 4:8 and 4:10 (e.g., already you are filled, already you were enriched . . . ; you are wise in Christ, you are strong, you are glorious). The context, however, suggests otherwise. First, Paul stated earlier that the Corinthians were saints, called by God, and enriched in speech and in knowledge in the opening and thanksgiving of the letter (cf. 1:1-9). In 1:1-9, as shown above, the language Paul uses is serious and signifies that the Corinthians are a delivered group. As a gathering of God they are holy, meaning they are delivered from the death traps of Roman culture and its ways through the gospel of the crucified Christ and are made beautiful by God. For Paul, God has reversed their fortune and given them gifts (cf. 1:26-28). Second, in this context, Paul indicates in

no uncertain terms that he did not want to embarrass the Corinthians: "Not wishing to shame you, I write these things to you, but to admonish you as my beloved children" (4:14). "These things" (tauta) in 4:14 refers to 4:7-13, that is, the things pertaining to Paul and the Corinthians. The things pertaining to Paul are gloomy, but the things pertaining to the Corinthians are apropos for an oppressed people who have been liberated. This means that the Corinthians have the benefits of liberation. They are, in fact, wise, strong, and glorious (4:10). Paul's problem is that Corinthian behavior suggests otherwise. Their behavior is atrocious. They show signs of returning to pre-exodus desires—to behaviors reminiscent of ostentatious Greco-Roman lifestyles that, in contemporary terms, reek of megachurch lifestyles within African communities in America wherein ostentatious conduct is often affirmed with the religious declaration: "I'm blessed." In response, Paul calls out—*Exodus!*

In closing the section, Paul asks the Corinthians to imitate him (4:16). He follows up with a notation that Timothy is on his way to remind them of "his ways in Christ," "ways" that are being taught in all of Paul's churches (4:17). Since the ways to be imitated are in Christ, the Corinthians are not to infer that the imitation Paul desires is akin to the ways of worldly wisdom that Paul had denounced in the discussion so far, such as boasting in human beings. In fact, human boasting is non-spiritual in 1 Corinthians, indeed beyond the limits of the Christ-crucified spirituality (cf. 2 Cor 12:11). Nor are the Corinthians to think that Paul is asking them to return to places they had been delivered from, for their liberation would not mean a reinstatement of Roman ways. So what is it that Paul wants the Corinthians to imitate?

Some scholars think that the stark description for apostles in 4:9-13, just before the injunction "be my imitators" in 4:16, is what

Paul expects from the Corinthians. One close reader takes this to mean that Paul is asking certain Corinthians (especially those of higher social standing) to engage in his self-abasement as a way of expressing solidarity with those of lower standing.[31] Others believe that Paul outlines for the Corinthians a template of suffering in 4:9-13 and that the imitation of Paul means patient suffering.[32] The latter view is adopted by oppressed peoples and is quite pervasive in continental and diaspora African religious traditions in which embracing the Christ-like life is often thought to mean suffering patiently. The thinking is that if Jesus suffered and Paul suffered, then a good Christian must likewise suffer. But the stark images in 4:9-13 are not a template for expected Corinthian behavior. True enough, those images do convey a suffering apostle. Paul, however, never admonishes the Corinthians to suffer as he suffers. If anything, the Christ-crucified message envisions deliverance from suffering; it is a release of the despised and rejected in Corinth from the grip of Roman power and control. That release gives way to a new community of liberated people who embrace the idea that they are intricately connected as brothers and sisters in Christ through the act of baptism (cf. 12:12-13). Paul never advise them to make suffering the trademark of their liberation but only to hang together or share the sufferings of each other, should suffering come (cf. 12:26).

The fact that Christ and Paul suffer is clear enough. Christ suffered on the cross. Paul is not shy about delineating his many sufferings, including the long list of 2 Cor 11:23-27 and the fact that he was nearly killed in Asia for Christ, according to 2 Cor 1:8-9 (cf. Phil 1:15-18). But when we meet the imitation text again in this correspondence, that is, in 11:1, in which Paul qualifies his request for imitation with "just as I imitate Christ," we are able to see what imitating Paul is all about. Imitation of Paul involves primarily the willingness of redeemed persons to yield to one another vis-à-vis their personal rights for the salvation of the entire group. It means the yielding of individual preferences "to communal concerns through the principle of love (8:2, 7-13) which does not insist upon its own point of view (13:5): 'If food gives offense to my brother, then I will eat no meat to all eternity, so that I might not cause offence to my brother'" (8:13).[33] Hence, the imitation of Paul is related not to suffering, but to the kind of humility (cf. 2:1-5) that builds and fosters good corporate relations in the body of Christ. Paul's own words: "do not seek your own advantage, but the advantage of the other" (10:24; cf. Phil 2:4).

The stark images of the apostles are thus introduced not to invite the Corinthians to suffer in imitation of Christ and Paul but in an effort to tone down Corinthian boasting and arrogance—in particular to convey that God's glory and God's power reside in humility—and to differentiate the roles of apostles and the church. The church is a glorious creation of God—it is wise, strong, and peaceful; the apostles are servants who are often perplexed like carpenters, gardeners, and architects in caring for the edifice the Great Designer has designed, that is, the church.

5:1—11:1, GET OVER IT, AND MOVE ON; SHOULD I COME IN MEEKNESS OR WITH A STICK?

The section 5:1—11:1 focuses on what the crucified Christ life means for persons who leave the ways of Roman civilization. The section displays what liberation from Egypt (Roman society) means in personal and corporate terms, thus challenging the Corinthians to shake off leins against their liberation. The two issues in need of address are (1) Corinthian sexual concerns and (2) the eating of meat offered to idols.

5:1—7:40, Corinthian Sexual Issues

In 5:1—7:40 Paul deals with concerns rumored (esp. in chaps. 5–6) and with matters "formally" posted to Paul's attention in chap. 7. The first issue (a matter rumored) calls attention to a kind of conduct among Corinthians, says Paul, that even the non-Christian society of Roman Corinth does not endorse: a man is sexually involved with his father's wife. To add insult to injury, the Corinthians appear to approve of the behavior, perhaps because of the high social standing of the accused.[34] In any case, Paul classifies the conduct as *porneia* (sexual immorality), and he tells the Corinthians that they should mourn (5:2). He then calls for a return to the holiness that is appropriate for liberated people in Christ. The accused man must become persona non grata (unwelcome) and is to be excommunicated (5:4-5), because his conduct is detrimental to the body of Christ, the church. Indeed, his conduct is contaminating their liberation movement. His behavior and the threat it brings to the Corinthian community might be likened to the fate of an African tree that resides today in the Aburi Botanical Gardens in the Republic of Ghana, West Africa. In 1906, this once beautiful tree became host to a parasite. Because the life cycle of the parasite went unchecked, by 1936 the host tree had become the parasite itself. Today, though it has the appearance of a tree, it is a tree in name only.[35] For fear of a similar metamorphosis, Paul urges the Corinthians to declare non-support for the violating man. He puts before them the expectations of Christian life in paschal terms. The Corinthians are to purge themselves of things that corrupt and embrace those activities that support the way of holiness (5:7-8). As such, the Corinthian community of believers is to be like its ancestral prototype, a communion of the nonfermented or the unleavened leaving Egypt (the ways of Roman culture). For that reason Paul uses the Passover analogy (the constituting experience of the Jewish world) to convey his call for Corinthian holiness. Holiness is their ancestral blueprint. Hence the embrace of the accused is tantamount to a return to a pre-exodus lifestyle, to contamination, depicted by Paul here as Roman culture. Indeed, the Corinthians have become more Roman than the Romans (cf. 5:1, 6-8). So Paul reminds them that they are not to mix, that is, that they are to stay clear of the civilization from which the church has been exorcised (5:9-11). Paul therefore demands that they "drive out the wicked person from among you" (5:13, NRSV). In so doing, he is asserting a priestly role, in particular his duty as a steward of God to manage the mysteries of God properly and to ensure that the community is not tainted or compromised on the Day of the Lord.

6:1-20. Chapter 6 continues this discussion, though with a slight shift. The focus now turns from the accused man to the responsibility of the Corinthians to adjudicate cases among themselves that are being taken to Roman courts. The saints (*hoi hagioi*), that is, the Corinthians—not Roman officials—are to adjudicate their own cases, since Roman court adjudicators belong to another kingdom. As Roman adjudicators represent the *psychikos*, "natural or unspiritual," rather than the *pneumatikos*, "the spiritual" (cf. 2:14-15), and embody conduct the Corinthians have left behind, for example, fornication, adultery, and the like (6:9-10) and as the Corinthians are washed, sanctified, and justified in God through Christ (6:11), their cases should be handled by the saints, who will in the future judge angels (6:2). The fact that the Corinthians are taking cases to Roman officials (called unjust persons by Paul) for settlements suggests a reversion to a pre-liberated way of life.

The violation in the first case is the situation of the sexually immoral man in chap. 5.

The violation in the second case is signified in 6:7-8 by the Greek verb *apostereō*, which is usually translated, "to defraud" or "to suffer loss." For most interpreters, the court cases of chap. 6 reflect economic disputes, that is, Corinthians are taking each other to court over property rights that could have been handled in the Corinthian assembly itself. Some think that the wealthy of the Corinthian church are taking each other to court over trivial issues, which could well have been solved even by the least within the church (6:2-4). The Greek verb that is translated here as "to defraud" or "to suffer loss" reappears in 7:8 and is thought there to refer to sexual matters: "*Do not deprive* one another except perhaps by agreement for a set time" (7:5a, NRSV). In chap. 7, Paul gives advice to couples on sexual practices, advising them not to deprive each other of conjugal rights. Since chap. 6 ends with a discussion on sexual matters (6:13-20), and since the list of vices of 5:11 is reintroduced and magnified with extended attention to sexual concerns in 6:9-10, it stands to reason that the court cases referred to in chap. 6 are not

so much about property or economic issues as they are about sexual issues.[36] Hence Paul ends the section appropriately with the exhortation: "Flee from sexual immorality" (6:18). In so doing, he makes clear that Christian liberation is not a license for sexual immorality (cf. 6:9c-10). Instead, liberation means that the members of Christ's body are to stay clear of prostitution, and so Paul ends his discussion here with the same concern that he focused on in chap. 5, contamination: "Or do you not get it that the one who is sexually involved with a prostitute is one body with the prostitute? For it says, 'the two will be one flesh'" (6:16). Thus, in Paul, God's deliverance is deliverance from an oppressive state of contamination, that is, a deliverance from Roman ways (6:20; cf. 7:25). It is in that light that Paul admonishes the Corinthians not to unite with prostitutes, for prostitution is corrupting and belongs to Romanicity. (See sidebar below.) Thus the apostle calls for a divorce: "flee sexual immorality" (*pheugete tēn porneian*, 6:18a).[37]

7:1-40. Chapter 7 concludes Paul's discussion on sexual concerns with a specific

---

You Better Mind

Many scholars have used the term *paganism* to describe the values that Paul wanted the Corinthian believers to stay clear of. Some of these so-called "pagan values" are listed in 1 Cor 6:9b-10a, like idolatry and fornication. Paul condemns this lifestyle because the Corinthians have been redeemed "in the name of the Lord Jesus Christ and in the spirit of our God" (6:11b). Both the NIV and NRSV translators have translated *en tois ethnesin* in 1 Cor 5:1 to mean "among pagans," when a better translation might be "among [the] nations." I do not like using the term *pagan* here because it does not precisely name the Roman culture that Paul is railing against. Indeed, for Africans in America the term *pagan* can be offensive since it has been used in a condescending manner to typecast non-European peoples, especially persons of African descent, as savages, heathens, barbarians, and so on. I speak rather of *Romanicity* in this commentary because I find it a more appropriate label for the conduct that Paul wants his converts to avoid, since Corinth at the time of Paul's letters was under Roman rule and influenced by Roman values.

focus on appropriate sexual conduct among believers. It also initiates a series of concerns that the Corinthians evidently posted to Paul, as indicated by the transitional phrase "Now concerning the matters about which you wrote" (7:1; cf. 7:25; 8:1; 12:1; 16:1, 12). The first issue about which they asked his opinion is introduced by a rather cryptic remark: "it is good (well) for a man not to touch a woman" (7:1b), that is, for a man not to engage in sexual relations with a woman. It is difficult to determine whether the quotation refers to a position taken by the Corinthians, for example, we Corinthians hold that it is good [well] for us not to be sexually active, because to be involved distracts from what we are called to do (cf. 7:32-35), or whether the quote is Paul's response: I, Paul, state that it is not good (well) for a man to touch a woman, because to do so defeats the purpose of our assembly, that is, to be the way of the crucified Christ (the indivisible body) in the world while awaiting the coming distress (7:25).

Majority scholarly opinion adopts the first position, that is, the statement represents a Corinthian position and is generated by Corinthian asceticism, the equating of sexual activity with sin and sexual abstinence with the holy life.[38] Paul's response negates this view and is perhaps signified in the position he takes in 7:28, "But if you marry you do not sin, and if a virgin marries, she does not sin" (cf. 7:36c). Paul's position could also be indicated in his advice to married couples; they should not withhold conjugal rights from each other. If they do withhold such rights, they should make an agreement, and they should maintain such an agreement only for a season to participate in prayer. Afterwards, they should resume their normal sex lives (7:5).

The goal behind this sanctioning of marital sexuality is the avoidance of sexual immorality (*porneia*, cf. 7:2). Paul's preferred position regarding sexual involvement is

that of celibacy or non-sexual involvement. However, he realizes that in real life and in the case-based situations of Corinthian congregants in particular, *porneia* is already a live issue and thus a future threat (7:2; cf. 5:1). For that reason, Paul's position on sexual relations in chap. 7 is more often governed by concessionary considerations (in particular the meeting of minds through the Spirit) rather than by directives Paul could cull from scriptural traditions, the Lord, or even mandates or orders of his own (cf. 7:10-16, 25-40). While ideally the Corinthians would follow Paul's example of celibacy (7:7), he recognizes that not all Corinthians are gifted in this way. For example, widows and widowers are advised to remain in the status of widowhood, but if they are not able to, because of sexual desire, they should get married rather than be sexually out of control (7:8–9), and in that way ruin the conceptual framework of the Christ-crucified gathering. The same advice applies to believers who are married to other believers, believers married to nonbelievers, circumcised and uncircumcised believers, and believers who are enslaved (7:10-21). But in the case of marriages between believers and nonbelievers, and in the case of the enslaved, concessionary advice is expanded. In the case of believers who are married, Paul is less concessionary, indeed more adamant about believers remaining together in the marriage bond (7:10). In fact, he advises that if they separate, they should remain unmarried unless they are reconciled (7:11). However, in the case of marriages between believers and nonbelievers, Paul permits a divorce, but, at the same time, his hope is that this group would remain together, since the sanctified partner might lead the non-sanctified partner into Christian salvation (7:12-16). Paul expands the discussion also in the case of the enslaved. Although the enslaved are advised to remain slaves, the freedom route is offered if they are conflicted by their condition (contra the NRSV).[39]

The remainder of chap. 7, that is, vv. 25-40, focuses on virgins (*parthenoi*) and those who are desirous of marriage, and is shaped by eschatological considerations. Here, as before, concessions apply. The Corinthians are to remain in the status of their calling (7:26-28); however, because of the shortened time before Christ's coming, they are to take what seems tantamount to an otherworldly stance. Corinthians are to live in the world as if the matters of the world do not count. Paul counsels those with wives to live as if they have none, those who mourn as if they are not mourning, those who rejoice as if they are not rejoicing, those who buy as if they have no possessions, and those who deal with the world as if they have no dealings with it (7:29-31).[40] The community is not to be preoccupied with worldly concerns, depicted here by Paul as husbands who are preoccupied with concerns of their wives and vice versa (7:32-35), for worldly concerns contaminate or interfere with an undivided commitment to God (cf. 7:32-35).

For Paul, then, given the eschatological crisis that is already in progress—"the form of this world is passing away" (7:31b)—the preferred way is freedom from distractions. The Corinthian believers are to remain in the status of their calling insofar as they are able (7:40; cf. 7:7, 8, 12-24, 26, 38) and to avoid *porneia* (sexual immorality) at all costs. Hence, marriage is urged as a means of avoiding *porneia* (7:9, 36-38), and sex in marriage is no sin (7:36).

8:1—11:1, Eating Meat Offered to Idols

The second issue about which the Corinthians asked Paul by means of a letter was the question of food sacrificed to idols. There are interesting parallels between what Paul has done in 5:1—7:40 and this section. For one thing, the idea that Paul expressed in 6:12 about "all things being lawful but all things not being beneficial" is restated near the end of this section (cf. 10:23). Another interesting comparison is the exhortation "*flee* sexual immorality" in 6:18, and "*flee* from food offered to idols" (*pheugete apo tēs eidōlolatrias*) in 10:14. More importantly, the theme that comes to the surface around the issues of order and concessions regarding sexuality and life stations dominates this section also (cf. chaps. 8, 9, 10).

8:1-13. The concessionary principle guides the discussion regarding food offered to idols in chap. 8. Paul begins, "We know that all have knowledge. Knowledge puffs up, but loves builds up" (8:1). He is speaking about the knowledge that there is no idol in the world, and that there is no God but one (8:4). Both the Corinthians and Paul know that there is one God the Father, out of which all things come, and that there is one Lord Jesus Christ, through whom all things are (8:6). Paul wants this knowledge to be tempered by love (*agapē*), in particular by how God's love in Christ is expressed in the context of community. For Paul such love is communal in nature—thus concessionary.

Through love, Paul wants knowledgeable, individual Corinthians to behave in ways that are beneficial for the whole community (cf. 7:35). His particular point is that what a person eats or does not eat does not determine his or her standing with God (8:8). Knowledge affirms this point, showing that idols do not exist. But for Paul, the community is to be governed not by what one knows but by showing regard (love) for each other. He is more concerned that those who are knowledgeable vis-à-vis idols relate to those who are described by Paul as persons having a "weak conscience" (8:7, 10). Here "weak individuals" are not those of the community who are economically deprived or at the bottom of the social pecking order, as the term *weak* (*asthenēs*) might imply in 9:22 and 12:22.

Some Corinthians do not honor such persons. Not only do they eat meat offered to idols since they know idols do not exist, but they also cause persons without such knowledge to follow their example. Thereafter, the person of "weak conscience" becomes conscious of his or her mistake and convinced that this amounts to an offense against the body of Christ (8:10-12). Paul advises: "Therefore, if food is a cause of their falling, I will never eat meat, so that I may not cause one of them to fall" (8:13, NRSV). It is advice born out of love.

9:1-27. Paul expands the conversation with a literary foray into the topic of rules. He is authorized to act freely, that is, to eat meat sacrificed to idols but, for the greater good, he decides not to do so. Like an interior designer teaching students the art of window dressing, Paul uses the thematic of love-in-community as his curtain rod and hangs on it rhetorical curtain concerns: "Am I not free? Am I not an apostle? Have I not seen Jesus Christ our Lord? Are you not my work in the Lord?" (9:1).

The Corinthians, as certifiers of Paul's apostleship in the gospel (9:2), recognize that they and their apostle have rights. Paul alluded to this in 8:10, where he states that knowledge authorizes the Corinthians to eat food offered to idols precisely because idols do not exist. Paul makes the same case about his own rights here. He has a right to eat and drink and to be accompanied by a wife, as a soldier has a right to be paid for military service, a planter to part of the food he or she produces, or a shepherd for a share of the milk the flock produces (cf. 9:4-7). Further support for this stance is anchored in scriptural traditions, especially the saying about Moses not muzzling the ox while it is treading out the grain (9:8-9), which serves in this context as a basis for Paul to press upon the Corinthians that his rights are deserved (cf. 9:11). But, as in 8:9, where Paul is concerned that the knowl-edge and exercise of rights might be a cause for "stumbling" (*proskomma*), here again he renounces his rights for the greater good. He works in the gospel and deserves to be paid out of the gospel (9:14), but he renounces the right for the simple reason of wanting to exhibit the Christ-crucified message. In other words, he does not exercise his rights because the love ethic requires consideration for others as the first order of Christian responsibility (cf. 10:23). Thus, as an apology for his apostolic behavior, Paul notes here that his mentioning of his apostolic rights is not a backdoor effort to recall what he had previously renounced (cf. 9:15). Rather, it is his way of exemplifying the meaning of Christ crucified through personal example.

Paul reasserts the point when he returns to the first curtain of the designer's display, "Am I not free?" (9:1). The answer to the question is a resounding yes: "Paul, you are free." But Paul's freedom is not Roman or Western individualism: "Freedom in Paul is not thought of in individuated terms. It is not individual liberation or personal salvation—from sin or from any other binding restraint. Rather, Paul's freedom is corporately defined as Paul tends to qualify his discussions on freedom or liberation with plurals."[41] Indeed, Paul's freedom is enslavement to others for a greater gain (9:19-23)—salvation for those who would otherwise not be saved (9:22b). To illustrate the point, he applies the analogy of the runner in 9:24 as a metaphor of Christian love in community. This love is self-control in the context of a community with many runners. It is the primordial I-am-because-we-are principle of the African worldview. Freedom is an athletic engagement of runners—not a runner—whose successes on the track are defined not by individual accomplishments but by corporate considerations (9:24-27). It is the life of the "we" in which people hang together as losers and winners (cf. 12:26).

10:1—11:1. At the end of chap. 9, Paul uses the analogy of the Corinthian Isthmian games to express the ways of the Christian life. Like participants in those games, the goal is to win, and Paul used the analogies of runners and boxers to highlight the virtue of self-control if participants want to be victorious. Paul is aware that participants who fail often bear the stigma of defeat and are publicly humiliated. As a result, participants trained extensively to avoid those consequences.[42] Paul also preached the avoidance of dire circumstances in the matter of faith. The finishing point for Paul and the Corinthians is the end of the age, which is now underway (cf. 10:11) but will come to full bloom in the resurrection, when death is finally defeated (15:50-57). Paul therefore trains extensively: "But I punish my body and enslave it, so that after proclaiming to others I myself might not be disqualified" (9:27, NRSV).

In 10:1-10 Paul intensifies the concern about disqualification that he presents in the athletic analogies of 9:24-27. So concerned is he about the failure of his mission that he summons the exodus tradition. First, he reminds the Corinthians of God's act of liberation "under the cloud" (10:1). Then he lays out the exodus as a salvation story. The Corinthians' spiritual ancestors, the Hebrews, passed through the sea, were baptized by Moses under the cloud, ate spiritual food, and drank spiritual drink. Even though a rock followed them, which Paul calls Christ, God struck them down in the wilderness (10:1-5). For Paul, the striking down (judgment) had a pedagogical function: "These things happened as examples [*typoi*] for us" (10:6a). Seemingly unappreciative of deliverance by God from their Egyptian enslavement, the Israelites desired to revert back to the things of the past, that is, the things and ways of Egypt, when their journey became difficult. Paul alludes to five instances of Israelite regressions or violations in liberation: evil desires, idolatry, sexual immorality, tempting Christ, and grumbling (cf.10:6b-10). At the end of the regressions list, Paul repeats its pedagogical purpose: "These things happened to them to serve as an example, and they were written down to instruct us, on whom the ends of the ages have come" (10:11, NRSV).

Paul uses these traditions for Corinthian benefit. A great salvation had indeed taken place in Corinth. God, depicted as a shadowing cloud, led the Corinthians out of Roman enslavement via the crucifixion of Christ, an act of deliverance. They were baptized by Paul and others, signifying their salvation and incorporation into the community of the redeemed (1:13-16; 12:12-13), and they received food and drink from God as they journeyed toward their destiny, signified here as participating in the Lord's Supper (cf. 10:14-22; 11:23-34). But Corinthian deliverance could be wiped out by regressions to habits the Corinthians had been delivered from (cf. 6:9b-11). In this case, the regressions are sexual immorality and idolatry (matters that also threatened the ancestors' survival).

No Turnin' Back

First Corinthians 10:1-13 reflects the story of the Hebrews' desire to return to pre-exodus habits, presented in the Old Testament as a desire to return to Egypt. The Corinthians manifest the same behavior in their yearning to revert to ways they had renounced, and so Paul cites the exodus tradition to warn them of consequences of returning to their Roman cultural past. In African freedom traditions in the Americas, a similar thought pattern was exhibited when freed slaves desired to return to the masters from whom they had been liberated.

There is an encouraging word: "God is faithful, and he will not let you be tested beyond your strength, but with the testing he will also provide for you a way out so that you may endure it" (10:13b, NRSV). Still, Paul warns, "So, as a result, the one who thinks he stands—let him pay attention lest he falls" (10:12). In the end, Paul counsels the Corinthians to separate from the values of Roman imperial culture (10:14). The ways of Romanicity (signified in the eating of food sacrificed to idols) and the ways of the crucified Christ community (signified in the Corinthian fellowship—a holy communion) are mutually exclusive. He warns the Corinthians about a jealous God who could disqualify them (even destroy them), as that God had done in the case of their ancestors in the past (10:16-22). The theme of divine judgment hangs like a threatening cloud over Paul and the Corinthians here. Paul in particular is concerned that Corinthian conduct might be the cause for a disqualification of their work and his work on the Day of Judgment. He works on the premise that a redeemed people would be blameless on that day (cf. 1:8).

In 10:23, Paul continues his warning: "All things are lawful, but not all things are beneficial" (NRSV). He is amplifying the concerns of 8:1-13. This curious saying (first introduced in

The Living Text

Paul's stress on imitating his personal example is pervasive in 1 Corinthians as well as in his other letters, for example, 1 Thess 1:6; 2:14; cf. Eph 5:1. Sometimes he will say to his addressees, "imitate me," as in 1 Cor 4:16 and 11:1, but in most instances the imitation is implied, for example, in 2:1-5; 8:13; 9:1-27; 14:13-19. It is interesting that this imitation is promoted among Gentile converts. In the case of the Corinthians, these converts had been Christians for no more than four years when Paul wrote 1 Corinthians, which could mean that they were unaware of the requirements of a tradition with deep roots in Judaism. This could mean that Paul served as a guiding text for them until such time they were able to acquire the knowledge of scriptures. *First Clement* is a testament to the role that scriptures would eventually play in a community that depended more on personal religion as guide at the beginning of its life as compared to written traditions in its later life, that is, around the year 96 C.E. The same pattern is evident in African religious experience in America, where individuals depended more on personal example than written texts in early expressions of the black Christian tradition. This was due in part to their inability to read and also to injunctions against reading the Bible. My own great-grandfather, William Alston, who was born in 1844 as a slave and died in 1926, was fondly remembered as a person who conveyed the Christian way to others by personal example in the state of South Carolina. The word about him is that it was not what he said or taught but how he lived that helped people to embrace the way of the gospel of the crucified. (On the social and historical context of imitation during Paul's time, see Benjamin Fiore, "Paul, Exemplification, and Imitation," in *Paul in the Greco-Roman World: A Handbook*, ed. J. Paul Sampley [Harrisburg, Pa.: Trinity Press International, 2003], 228–57.)

6:12 and immediately followed by a reference to food in 6:13) becomes clearer at this point, especially in the framework of 10:24-30. The point is that it is lawful to eat meat offered to idols since idols do not exist, but it is unlawful in the Christ-crucified gospel (in the body of Christ, the church) to disregard the concerns of the body for what suits one's own whim (10:23-30; cf. 9:21; Gal 6:2). Thus Paul sauces this section on Christian social relations by means of personal example. He tells the Corinthians to measure their own conduct by his example. His conduct or liberty is determined by the measure of *others* rather than by the dictates of his own personal satisfaction (10:31-33). Indeed, it is the measure of *others first* (the meaning of Christ crucified) that informs his all-things-to-all-people position of 9:19-23, as well as his point here about eating and refusing to eat. Hence Paul comes to the end of this section in almost the same way he concluded the first section, that is, with an appeal that the Corinthians would imitate his personal example (11:1—"Be my imitators just as I also imitate Christ" [cf. 4:16]).

In 11:1 Paul ends his quest to reinstall the way of the Christ-crucified gospel through apostolic example (esp. in 1:10—4:21 and 9:1-27) and also ends his advice to the Corinthians on the ways of Christ when faced with pre-exodus snares or the death traps of Roman ways (cf. 5:1—11:1). This new world to which the Corinthians belong, this "called-out" configuration (the Corinthian church), is to be *other* than the world in every way. In the language of African slave ancestors in America, it (the new world) is heaven is where only the righteous dwell, a place where each member of the formally oppressed stands manumitted, bidding farewell to worldly ways. In a sense, it is the re-emergence of the African village world without the infiltrations and impediments of foreign influences, depicted here as idolatry and *porneia*, or the utter corruption

of the black world by individualism and Western pursuits. Having struggled to re-gather the Corinthians for a noble destiny through a sustained call for rectification, a return to charter meanings in 1:1—11:1, and through insisting that the Corinthians divest themselves of Roman ways, a hindrance to divine order and intention in 5:1—11:1, Paul now offers a mapping of the Christ-crucified way to ensure that the Corinthians arrive at the destiny the Divine Being intended: the day of the Lord (15:51-57). To that end Paul calls out with confidence in the struggle: "*Marana tha*," "Our Lord, come" (16:22), and like a Harriet Tubman, who threatened conflicted slaves on their way to freedom with death for being desirous of a return to enslavement, he insists that there should be no turning back to Romanicity: "If anyone does not love the Lord, let such one be accursed [*anathema*]" (16:22).

11:2—16:24, The Culture of Your Ancestors: What Is Best?

This final section contains reminders, instructions, and traditions Paul uses to guide Corinthian life in the Christ-crucified gospel (the primordial blueprint) until the day of the Lord, a day Paul views with a degree of urgency (*marana tha*, "Our Lord, come," 16:22). This material provides guidance on expectations in gatherings for worship (11:2-34), instructions on the value and use of spiritual gifts (12:1—14:37), traditions and instructions about the resurrection of the dead (15:1-58), instructions about the collection, information about his associates, greetings, and, finally, a benediction (16:1-24). These are the traditions Paul wants the Corinthians to remember and practice on their way to the end. They are ancestral and salvific traditions, and if kept will ensure that their future will be directed and guided by the paradigm of the Christ-crucified way.

11:2–34, Ancestral Reminders

Verse 2 indicates that Paul is pleased with the fact that the Corinthians remember him and hold to the traditions that he had delivered to (taught) them. But what follows in vv. 3-16, about appropriate worship styles for women, contradicts this assessment (compare v. 17). This is criticism, not praise. There is therefore much discussion as to whether 11:3-16 belongs here and, more important, whether it reflects Paul's views. For example, a hierarchical order is promoted that contradicts what Paul espouses about the relationship between males and females elsewhere. Males and females are depicted in a more uniform and even fashion in 7:3-4; 12:12-13; and Gal 3:28. Here there is a hierarchical structure, with God the head of Christ, Christ the head of man, and the man (husband) the head of woman (wife), for example, in 11:3. Furthermore, the male is viewed as the image and glory of God, but the female (woman) as the glory of the male (man). The text further states that the man is not created out of the woman but the woman out of the man, and that the man was not created on account of woman but the woman for the sake of man (11:7-9). The common view is that either this is an interpolation that reflects the interest of patriarchal (male-dominating) culture after Paul's time or an attempt by Paul himself to regulate women who prophesy and pray in a fashion that is disquieting to him—they prophesy and pray within the congregation with their heads uncovered.[43] The unease is seen in the fact that the text suggests that head covering is a tradition in the churches of God (11:16).[44] In any case, it seems that Paul or some other writer is trying to differentiate the culture of his or her churches from patterns that might have prevailed in circles of Greco-Roman culture, patterns from which the churches in question should have distinguished themselves.

If it is the cultural issue that is at stake here, then Paul's views regarding the next issue in 11:17-34 are understandable. The Corinthians do not keep the distinguishing culture of the Lord's Supper. Paul cannot commend such conduct because the Corinthian congregation is by definition called out of Roman society. In particular, the celebration of the supper shows evidence of social stratification (class division) and attendant practices within Roman culture; the poor are left hungry while the rich are given to splurging (cf. 11:27-32).[45] Paul views this as anti-liberation behavior. He advises the Corinthians to eat in their own homes to ensure that the Christ-crucified tradition is upheld (11:34). The community is called to exhibit the Christ-crucified message through solidarity, in particular by waiting for each other and sharing in the celebration of the Lord's Supper as a unified group, regardless of social standing. To this end, Paul inserts the supper tradition for mimetic reasons (cf. 11:23-26). The community is to remember what God has done through Christ for all of the liberated, not the privileged few: "This is my body on your behalf" (11:24). The supper tradition also reminds the community of Israel's exodus from Egyptian slavery and its own exodus through Christ from the debilitating conditions of Roman society and its suffocating ways. The community is to remember its deliverance until the Lord comes (11:26). The apostle is able to proclaim in wilderness tradition terms that those that eat and drink in an unworthy manner threaten the judgment of God, just as their spiritual ancestors, the Hebrews, did in straying from their liberation centuries ago. Here, judgment comes in the form of weakness, illness, and death (11:30).[46] The community can avert such destruction by waiting for and waiting on each other (cf. 11:33-34).

12:1—14:40, Embracing Your Ancestral Values

12:1 signifies the beginning of new subject matter for Paul: "Now concerning spiritual gifts" (*peri de tōn pneumatikōn*). This transitional phrase, like those in 7:1 and 8:1, indicates that Paul is responding to a posted Corinthian concern. Paul states that he does not want the Corinthians to be ignorant about spiritual gifts, just as he indicated in 10:1 that he did not want them to be ignorant of the things pertaining to their ancestors' deliverance. The assumption is that either the Corinthians do not know about spiritual gifts or they are not aware of what they should know. The infinitive *agnoein* can mean either "not to know" or "to be unaware" of something. In any case, Paul says that no one in the Spirit will say "*Anathema Jesus*" (cursed is Jesus), and no one is able to say "*Kyrios Jesus*" (Jesus is Lord) except in the Holy Spirit (12:3). Here we may assume that the first issue, "cursed is Jesus" is not a concern, since Paul does not elaborate on it further. His focus is on the second issue, Jesus and the Holy Spirit, the matter of concern in chap. 12. The Corinthians do not know about *spiritual* gifts, at least in the way Paul desires.

The ensuing discussion in 12:4-31 specifies the Corinthians' ignorance. They seem to be unaware that the arrangement of the members of the body of Christ is God's choice (12:18; cf. 12:11), and that all gifts are given to persons in the body of Christ by God through the one Spirit. The subtext is the matter of tongues, alluded to in 12:27 and 12:30, but will become the subject that Paul seeks to defuse in 14:1-40. Paul's point is that the one Spirit bestows all gifts of the church, whether those gifts are gifts of healing, miracle working, prophesying, discerning of spirits, kinds of tongues, or interpretation of tongues (12:8-10). Furthermore, the Spirit provides gifts for the common good of the church (12:7) through baptism. The Spirit makes the church an indivisible body of equally valued members without regard for ethnicity and social status (12:12-13).

Since the Corinthian congregants have valued some members and devalued others—thinking that some members of the body are more important than others (e.g., the hand might be more important than the foot)—Paul attempts a correction. He states that all members of the body are important and needed, that God chose the arrangement of the body's parts, and that members previously devalued should now be equally valued (12:14-24a).

The gift of speaking in tongues is causing dissension within the body. Some Corinthians believe that it is the superior gift, but Paul puts it at the bottom of the list in

Neither Male nor Female

There has been much debate in the African religious community in America concerning functions and roles of males and females in ecclesiastical settings. Paul does not promote one gender over the other, since all are one in Christ (Gal 3:28; 1 Cor 12:12-13). The book of Acts makes a similar point in chap. 10, especially in Peter's pronouncement, "I truly understand that God shows no partiality, but in every nation anyone who fears him and does what is right is acceptable to him" (vv. 34b-35, NRSV). The lesson for the black church here is that gender discrimination in the work of the church is unacceptable, and, according to Paul, a return to the ways of the world. Paul stated that the form of this world is passing away (cf. 1 Cor 7:31b). Thus, in the new world of the Christ-crucified gospel, promotion or demotion based on gender is not endorsed.

12:27-28. He places the apostles first. Some view this listing as a corroboration of rank, that is, the apostolic calling ranks first in the order of gifts; but Paul has done a turnabout here. Just as the social status of the Corinthians, through the mercies of God, had been reversed from nobodies to somebodies in the discussion about Corinthian ranking in 1:26-28, Paul puts those considered nothing by the standards of 4:9-13 (apostles) at the top of the list, and in so doing signifies the way of the kingdom of God. The "nobodies" of the Corinthian fellowship are raised up; that is, those viewed as insignificant members of their group are given top billing.

By putting the apostles first, Paul has reminded the Corinthians of the meaning of liberation in the crucified Christ, namely, that the placement of members in the body is a matter of God's choice; the least considered members are just as important as those considered most important by the measures of worldly ranking. In other words, Paul does not put apostles at the top of the list to say that they rank first in the order of gifts, as some think; he puts apostles first and tongue speakers last to develop a level playing field, indeed a field wherein status and rank are no longer relevant in the building up of the body of Christ. To that end Paul closes the discussion of spiritual gifts with a number of important questions, all designed to level the field regarding spiritual gifts: "Are all apostles? Are all prophets? Are all teachers? Do all work miracles? Do all possess the gifts of healing? Do all speak in tongues? Do all interpret?" (12:29, 30).

With these questions Paul leaves the Corinthians on the brink. Rhetorically, they know what the answer really is—or do they? What is clear is that he expects them to say, "We are not all apostles, we are not all prophets, we are not all teachers, we are not all workers of miracles. . . ." Furthermore, the Corinthians know that spiritual gifts are

a worthy pursuit (12:31a). Spiritual gifts do build up the church (14:12), but in the case of the Corinthians the pursuit of them has fractured it. So Paul seeks a redirection of the Corinthians through his meditation on love in 13:1-13, the purpose of which is to get the Corinthians to move beyond debates about spiritual gifts and focus on the real task of the church, that is, to make use of their spiritual gifts for the building up of the congregation in such a way that members would practice the indivisible Christ in real life situations: "If one member suffers, all members suffer together; if one member is glorified, all members rejoice together" (12:26).

13:1-13. Chapter 13 is Paul's way of trying to achieve the unity described in 12:26. Here Paul downsizes the significance of gifts the Corinthians considered to be of utmost importance, for example, speaking in tongues and prophecy. Acts of faith and mercy are also lowered. He makes love (*agapē*) the matchless virtue of the spiritual life (13:1-3). In so doing, the Corinthians come face to face with a meaning that shames their concern about and regard for self that are part of their thinking of spiritual gifts. Love is *other* oriented. It has none of the liabilities exhibited by the gifts the Corinthians boast about. Love is long suffering, kind, not envious, does not insist on its own way, is not boastful, does not behave disgracefully, does not seek its own thing, does not provoke to anger, does not consider the bad. Love is none of the very things that have paralyzed the Corinthian assembly in Paul's discussion thus far (13:4-6).

Paul also flashes the eternalness of love over against the temporal limitations of spiritual gifts (cf. 13:8). He states unequivocally that prophecy, tongues, and knowledge will disappear when "the perfect" (*to teleion*) comes (13:10). The perfect is love; it stands in a class of its own even in a line up of valued Christian virtues like faith and hope (13:13).

14:1-33a, 37-40. Chapter 14 addresses the matter of speaking in tongues. In 8:1, Paul extols love as a virtue: "love builds up." Having delineated the ways of love in chap. 13, he now commends it above the gift of tongues: "Pursue love" (14:1a). All spiritual gifts are gathered under the measure of love. Under this rubric the gift of prophecy is commended—even preferred—among the gifts: "Pursue love, and be zealous for spiritual gifts, but prophesy more" (14:1). Prophecy is preferred only insofar as it functions in relationship with love. Inherent in prophecy is a concern for others (the character of love), "for their building up and encouragement and consolation" (14:3). But tongue speakers are viewed as self-promoting agents of confusion. Thus, Paul goes to great lengths in chap. 14 to discourage speaking in tongues, barring the assistance of an interpreter. He compares those who speak in tongues to instruments whose sounds do not make sense and to languages perhaps known by their speakers but unknown by their hearers (cf. 14:7-10). In the Corinthian context, where the liberated need clarity on how to navigate the waters of Romanicity and its death traps, tongues are less preferred since they do not perform a major task considered in this chapter: the building up of the congregation (see 14:4, 12, 17, 26).

Paul compares speaking in tongues without an interpreter to the ways of infants and to nonbelievers (14:20-23; cf. 13:11) while comparing the ways of love to the mature or the putting away of childish things (13:11c; 14:20). Hence tongues are encouraged in the context of the gathered congregation only if an interpreter is present to convey to the audience the meaning of what is said, and especially meanings to those who are non-converts and inquirers (14:23). Otherwise, because of the need of speakers to focus on the building up of the church (14:26c), tongue speakers are to be quiet while prophecy is to occur. In the end, Paul does not forbid tongues (14:39) but presses for prophecy, since it operates more closely with and from love (cf. 14:33, 40).

14:33b-36, Should Women Be Quiet in Church? To judge from Paul's preoccupation with the subject in chaps. 12–14, tongues seems to have won the day in Corinth. Some commentators think this passage is an intrusion into this context because (1) manuscript traditions do not agree regarding its location, that is, whether it belongs in its present position or after 14:40, and (2) the passage itself is awkward, that is, it is at odds with Paul's statements about women elsewhere (cf. 7:2-16; Gal 3:28). On linguistic and conceptual grounds, however, the passage is linked with the previous discussion about order and worship (cf. 14:26-33a), which is also the focus of the larger passage. Also, in both passages an injunction to silence occurs (14:28b, 30b, and 34a). Could this mean that Paul, by incorporating the passage about the silencing of women in the church, is continuing directives about silencing, only this time focusing on women? The passage could be a response to a strong group of women prophets in the congregation at Corinth.[47] Indeed, these women were so powerful that Paul conceded to their position at the end of the chapter: "So, my friends, be eager to prophesy, and do not forbid speaking in tongues; but all things should be done decently and in order" (14:39-40, NRSV).

15:1–58, Hold on Until . . .

Chapter 15 concludes the body of 1 Corinthians. It addresses two broad issues. The first is the resurrection itself (15:1-34); the second is its nature, addressed in 15:35-57. Verse 58 concludes the section by reinforcing the tenor of the discussion in the chapter. It exhorts the Corinthians to be firm and unshakable in the gospel in view of the coming day of the Lord

(v. 58b; cf. v. 2c). It encapsulates and restates the aim of the rectification Paul had been seeking throughout the letter, and it properly exhorts the Corinthians to do the work of the Lord yet to be done between the writing of this letter and the expected consummation: "Keep your eyes open, stand firm in the faith, be courageous, be strong. Let all things among you happen in love" (16:13).

The primary issue driving the two sections in question is the disbelief by some Corinthians in the resurrection of the dead. Some say that there is no resurrection of the dead (15:12)—no coming to life of the dead body of the deceased in the future. In response, Paul reminds the Corinthians in 15:1-34 of their own faith stance. At vv. 35-57 he focuses on the concerns of detractors, while remaining aware of believers' needs. Believers need a measure to prevent further drifting of congregants in the direction of detractors. Paul responds by recalling tradition regarding the disputable issue (vv. 1-11), by airing and facing up to the detractors' concern (vv. 12-19), by offering the example of Christ in support of the believers' position (vv. 20-28), and by incorporating his own example as evidence of the reality and challenge of the resurrection (vv. 29-34). Thus 15:1-11, Paul's discussion about the gospel, is strategic. It reminds believers and doubters alike that the gospel (the proclamation of the death, burial, and resurrection) is not new for the Corinthians (cf. 2:2). Not only was it preached when Paul came to Corinth; it was accepted. Furthermore, the Corinthians stood in it (the gospel) and are being saved through it (15:1-2a).

The reminder is crafted in such a way that all Corinthian eyes are turned toward the roots of the gospel. The gospel Paul preached (concerning the death, burial, and resurrection of Christ) was older than Paul's announcement and their acceptance of it in Corinth. It was rooted in ancestral traditions "according to the scriptures" (15:3-5). The experiences of the resurrection witnesses, nearer to the Corinthian world in time, are crucial for dissuading those who lean in the direction of disbelief (15:5-7). One such witness to the resurrection is the apostle Cephas (Peter), who preceded Paul and whom the Corinthians know (cf. 1:12; 3:21); others are the twelve apostles and the five hundred *adelphoi* ("brothers and sisters," NRSV), of whom Paul declares that "some have died"—perhaps to strengthen the case for a future resurrection of the dead. But Paul is mindful of the role of living witnesses to the risen Christ, asserting, "most of whom are still alive" (15:6b). He himself belongs to that group of living witnesses of the risen Christ: "last of all as one untimely born he appeared also to me" (15:8). The point is that *the* gospel is widely embraced: "Whether then it was I or those [the other apostles], so we preach and so you believed" (v. 11).

But Paul does more. He registers what concerns him most—the veering away from tradition and belief in the resurrection of the dead by some Corinthian believers—by alluding to the possibility that what he preached is not holding in Corinth. Indeed, Paul wonders whether his work among the Corinthians might be in vain (15:2c; cf. 9:1d),[48] and he uses his own person as a means of reseeding the Corinthians for the goal of Christian life—the resurrection of the dead. Paul states that God's grace was not given to him for nothing, but that he worked harder than all the other apostles (15:10). It is his personal example of remaining in the Christ-crucified gospel that will impel the Corinthians toward the goal of Christian existence, the resurrection that is already beginning but will come in full at the coming of the Lord. So also Paul reminded the Philippians (cf. Phil 3:7-16, esp. vv. 10-16, for Paul's language about pressing toward the resurrection as the goal of the Christian life). Thus Paul counsels that the Corinthians should be undeterred on their journey toward the goal of the Christian life (15:58; 16:13), even as disbelief in the resurrection of the dead is afloat and thriving within the Corinthian assembly (15:12).

Verses 12-34 represent the additional weight and pressure Paul uses to counteract Corinthian disbelief. The evidence of Jesus' resurrection in vv. 1-11 demonstrates that the resurrection of believers is credible (cf. 15:12). But if there is no resurrection of the dead, then Christ has not been raised. Paul makes this point in vv. 12-17 via a plethora of if-then statements (protasis-apodosis style); that is, if this is true then that is true, or if this is not true then that cannot be true. If the dead are not raised, Christ is not raised. Thus, if the community adopts the position of disbelief in the resurrection of the dead, then it remains un-manumitted, having hope in this life alone (vv. 17-19).

Having recognized and carefully argued against the Corinthian view that there is no resurrection of the dead, Paul makes a case in its favor. First, using the perfect tense, he embraces the resurrection: "And now Christ is raised from the death . . ." (*nuni de Christos egēgertai . . .*), signifying that Christ had been raised, is yet raised, and will forever be raised from the dead (v. 20). Paul then calls Christ's resurrection "the first fruits" of those who are asleep (the dead). By so doing, he signifies that the resurrection, already in process, is irreversible. Thus the order (administration) of Christ ("so also in Christ all shall be made alive," v. 22b) is now replacing the administration of Adam or death (v. 22a). Significantly, "the first fruits" will be followed by other fruits (Corinthian believers) at the parousia (coming) of Christ.[49] For Paul, Christ's parousia signifies the end, a time when Christ will hand over the kingdom to God (v. 24, cf. v. 28), having subjugated and wiped out the administration of Adam (death), which in Paul's argument is

Roman civilization (Roman rulers, authorities) and death itself (v. 26).

Paul follows the rules of rhetoric by incorporating things that are closer in time to Corinthian experience, as he had done earlier in his delineation of witnesses (15:5-8). This time the proof is in Corinthian practices and in Paul's own commitment to the crucified-resurrection message. If the dead are not raised, the Corinthians are contradicting their own practices; they are baptizing on behalf of the dead.[50] Furthermore, Paul argues that his own commitment to the resurrection message, for example, through the endangering of his own life, his dying daily, and euphonically his "fighting with wild beasts at Ephesus" (15:30-32), would have been for naught. "If the dead are not being raised, let us eat and drink, for tomorrow we die" (v. 32b). But for Paul the dead will be raised because Christ has been and will forever be raised (cf. v. 20), which means that the calling of Paul by the grace of God is not in vain or an empty engagement (v. 10). Thus the exhortation at the end of this section is fitting: "*Come back* to your senses as you ought, and stop sinning; for there are some who are ignorant of God—I say this to your shame" (v. 34, NIV; emphasis added).

Verses 35-57 address concerns regarding the form of the resurrected body. An inquirer (a supporter of Paul's position) believes in the resurrection of the dead but seeks to take up with Paul the question of its form, since some within his audience do not believe that a dead body returns to life.[51] The inquirer asks: "How are the dead raised? In what kind of body do they come?" The last issue (the first for Paul) is addressed in 15:36-49; the first is focused on in 15:50-57, the closing frame of the body of this letter.

Regarding the kind of body in which the dead are raised, Paul's response, for strategic reasons, underscores the ignorance of the inquirer, who should have known that the resurrected body is unlike the physical body. For this reason the inquirer is called a *fool* (v. 36a). The inquirer's ignorance gives Paul an opportunity to provide a dissertation on what the inquirer should have known via the analogies of a planted seed, various kinds of flesh (e.g., human beings, animals, birds, fish) and the heavenly bodies (e.g., sun, moon, and stars) in support of the stance he takes (vv. 36-41). Like the seed, the body planted in death is not raised in the form it is planted.

Paul makes another, equally important point. As God designated roles in apostolic services earlier in the argument (3:5—4:5), reversed the situation of the Corinthians through a delivery from enslaved existence (1:26-28), arranged the members of the body as God wished (12:18), and made Paul an apostle by his will (1:1), so the form of the resurrected body is God's choice (15:38). The body of the dead is planted (buried) in a perishable (physical) form, but is raised in a nonperishable (spiritual) form, according to the Adam-Christ typology (15:42-48).

Verses 50-57 address the first concern of the inquirer, "How are the dead raised?" Verse 50 recognizes the points Paul has made to this point: "And I say this, brothers and sisters, that flesh and blood cannot inherit the kingdom of God, nor does the corruptible inherit the incorruptible." Thus Paul argues different modes for the man of dust and the man of heaven, the way of the first Adam and the last Adam (cf. vv. 45-49), as a matter of God's choice. Not only is the form of the resurrected body a choice of God; how the resurrection takes place is God's choice also. Thus the apostle goes back to the word "mystery" (v. 51), a word used earlier to explain the character of Corinthian emancipation through the Christ-crucified gospel and the beginning of the end of Roman rule, institutions, and ways as experienced by the Corinthians prior to their incorporation into the redeemed assembly (cf.

2:6-16). The mystery, as always, is now hidden and will be suddenly revealed. At the sound of the last trumpet, the Corinthian faithful will be changed (vv. 52-53). The perishable will put on the imperishable, and death will be swallowed up by the victory wrought by Jesus Christ (v. 54).

Thus the Corinthian letter is an apocalyptic drama cast in the form of a journey. In many ways, it reminds the reader of the Apocalypse of John. The administration of death, the Roman world that snares and saps the energy of committed Christians, is anticipated to be ending soon (cf. Rev 18:1ff.). The audience that is being addressed is on a journey toward a destiny (an apocalyptic end) where they become totally free of the death traps of the Roman world. Their emancipation came through their embrace of the crucifixion, which meant an end of Roman ways, as those ways were signified in practice and acknowledged in the cry at the beginning of Paul's conversation: "Where is the one who is wise? Where is the scribe? Where is the debater of this age? Has not God made foolish the wisdom of the world?" (1:20, NRSV). Their divorce from Romanicity (Roman cultural values and practices) signified an exodus—a no turning back to the civilization renounced. It meant a living in the world that did not show a being of the world. And it meant a destiny, a trek to a city whose builder and maker is God. It meant an otherness, to be here but not to be here and, in the world of our African ancestors, to be present and at the same time to fly away and be in another world. And it meant total rest, the feeling, "soon I'll be done with the troubles of this world, the troubles of this world, the troubles of this world, going home to be with God." It meant the end of death's reign, indeed of the sight of death laid out cold on the canvas of the world with Jesus like a heavyweight champion (Muhammad Ali at his best) dancing and calling out to the witnessing crowd, indeed taunting death as it lies there knocked out cold, "Where, O Death, is your victory; Where, O Death, is your sting?" (15: 55).

16:1–24, This and That and Love

Chapter 16 concludes the letter. It signals Paul's final directions to the Corinthians in view of his approaching visit, which he had forecast as far back as 4:18. Ahead of this visit, Paul gives two directives, evidently based on Corinthian inquiries, the first about the collection for the poor in Jerusalem (v. 1) and the second about Apollos (v. 12). Otherwise, the apostle follows the pattern of the closing of his letters in general, for example, directives about travel (vv. 5-9), associates and others (vv. 10-12, 15-18), greetings (vv. 19-20), and final remarks, including words of blessing (a benediction, vv. 21-24). Nevertheless, there are some unique features. Details are given about Paul's method of collecting the offering for the poor saints in Jerusalem. These instructions are patterned after the directives he gave to the churches in Galatia (16:1b). In particular, the Corinthians were to put aside a weekly offering for that cause and appoint delegates that would assist Paul in the delivery of their offering to the Jerusalem saints, that is, if Paul deemed it feasible to go to Jerusalem himself (vv. 1-4).

Another feature is the attention Paul gives to special persons related to his work in Corinth. First, he highlights the work of Corinthian assembly members, especially Stephanas, Fortunatus, and Achaicus. These are noted as exceptional persons for the cause of Christ, and Paul indicates that the Corinthians should esteem them highly (vv. 15-18). Aquila and Prisca are also named (cf. Acts 18:2; Rom 16:3). A church is said to be meeting in their home (v. 19), and they are with Paul in Ephesus, the place from which this letter to the Corinthians is posted (v. 19; cf. v. 8). Apollos, who has been mentioned earlier and is noted by Paul as one of the persons who built on the Christ foundation that he laid at Corinth (3:5—4:5; cf. 1:12), is mentioned here also (16:12). Paul states that Apollos has been urged by him (Paul) to visit Corinth, but he (Apollos) shows reluctance. Still another feature is the prayer *marana tha* ("Our Lord, come!"), which is placed in the context of a divine injunction: "Let anyone be accursed who has no love for the Lord" (v. 22a). Finally, rather than ending with the benediction, "The grace of our Lord Jesus Christ be with you" (16:23), Paul offers what he views as the cure-all for Corinthian ailments, an everlasting reminder of *what is best* as the Corinthians await the *parousia* of the Lord: "My love be with you all in Christ Jesus" (v. 24; cf. chap. 13 regarding the "more excellent way").

Notes

1. Translations of the text of 1 Corinthians are mine, except where noted.
2. See Bruce J. Malina, *The New Testament World: Insights from Cultural Anthropology*, 3rd ed. (Louisville: Westminster John Knox, 2001), 1–26.
3. See John K. Chow, "Patronage in Roman Corinth," in *Paul and Empire: Religion and Power in Roman Imperial Society*, ed. Richard A. Horsley (Harrisburg, Pa.: Trinity Press International, 1997), 104–25, who notes that "in order to climb the ladder of power and honor, one would have to do more than fulfill the basic property requirements. Hence it was essential for those who did not come from a good family background, like freedmen, to have proper personal connections. One of the necessary and honorable things to do was to cultivate relationships with men of influence and, if possible, the Roman authorities. Perhaps that is why many of the local notables were at the same time priests of the imperial cults" (125). Also, for social divisions within Roman society, see Ray Pickett, "Conflict at

Corinth," in *Christian Origins*, ed. Richard A. Horsley, A People's History of Christianity 1 (Minneapolis: Fortress Press, 2005), 113–37, esp. 113–20.

4. See David G. Horrell, *The Social Ethos of the Corinthian Correspondence: Interests and Ideology from 1 Corinthians to 1 Clement* (Edinburgh: T. & T. Clark, 1996), esp. 91–101, for social history approaches to studying Pauline Christianity at Corinth and in other Pauline settings, for example, Wayne A. Meeks, *The First Urban Christians: The Social World of the Apostle Paul* (New Haven and London: Yale University Press, 1983), Ronald F. Hock, *The Social Context of Paul's Ministry: Tentmaking and Apostleship* (Philadelphia: Fortress Press, 1980), and Gerd Theissen, *The Social Setting of Pauline Christianity: Essays on Corinth*, ed. and trans. John H. Schütz (Philadelphia: Fortress Press, 1982).

5. Thus Dale B. Martin, *The Corinthian Body* (New Haven and London: Yale University Press, 1995), 65–68.

6. See Mark D. Given, *Paul's True Rhetoric: Ambiguity, Cunning, and Deception in Greece and Rome*, Emory Studies in Early Christianity (Harrisburg, Pa.: Trinity Press International, 2001).

7. Thus Antoinette Clark Wire, *The Corinthian Women Prophets: A Reconstruction through Paul's Rhetoric* (Minneapolis: Fortress Press, 1990).

8. For Paul's ambiguous position, see Amos Jones Jr., *Paul's Message of Freedom: What Does It Mean to the Black Church?* (Valley Forge, Pa.: Judson, 1984), esp. 31–63, and Brad R. Braxton, *The Tyranny of Resolution: I Corinthians 7:17–24*, SBLDS 181 (Atlanta: Society of Biblical Literature, 2000), 220–34.

9. See Charles B. Puskas Jr., *The Letters of Paul: An Introduction*, Good News Studies 25 (Collegeville, Minn.: Liturgical, 1993), 6, who notes: "Letters presuppose a sender and addressee, everyone else is a third party outsider. The sender's side of the dialogue dominates the letter. The addressee's conversation can be inferred, but it is not articulated until the addressee responds in written form as a sender."

10. According to Acts 18:11 Paul preached and labored among the Corinthians for two years. According to Paul he preached a Christ-crucified message during the period of his stay (1 Cor 2:2).

11. Thus Braxton, *The Tyranny of Resolution*, 1–67.

12. In a way 1 Corinthians reads like the book of Revelation—a mystery is finally unveiled in 1 Cor 15:50–57, where death is flattened.

13. The aim of this task is, in some way, the visionary impetus that drove Brian K. Blount to produce his *Cultural Interpretation: Reorienting New Testament Criticism* (Minneapolis: Fortress Press, 1995)—to enlarge the boundary of biblical interpretation by including voices that are not usually heard, perhaps nonconventional voices.

14. For scholarly discussions about letter forms and practices, including the role of assistants and secretaries in constructing letters in Paul's time, see Puskas, *The Letters of Paul*, 5–19; Jerome Murphy-O'Connor, *Paul the Letter-Writer: His World, His Options, His Skills*, Good News Studies 41 (Collegeville, Minn.: Liturgical, 1995); and E. Randolph Richards, *Paul and First-Century Letter Writing: Secretaries, Compositions, and Collections* (Downers Grove, Ill.: InterVarsity, 2004).

15. In Greco-Roman convention, the sender of a letter is usually a person, but in this case Paul and Sosthenes appear as co-senders. Usually the letter is sent to an individual, but here it is sent to a group—the Corinthians. And there are co-senders in all undisputed letters of Paul, except Romans. For debates on the identity and role of Sosthenes, see David E. Garland, *1 Corinthians*, Baker Exegetical Commentaries on the New Testament (Grand Rapids, Mich.: Baker, 2003), 26.

16. There is some discussion on the meaning of "theirs and ours" at the end of v. 2, in particular whether it should be translated "their place and ours" or "their Lord and ours." See Garland, *1 Corinthians*, 28. The NRSV has "both their Lord and ours."

17. The term *ekklesia* is perhaps best translated as "assembly," but for my purposes it is best to translate it as "church." This term in the

context of Roman Corinth designated a political assembly, such as the gathering of the Romans and Roman subjects to hear the emperor, the reigning lord of the Roman people. Some scholars think that the term is a highly political one in Paul also, indeed anti-imperial, and that Paul used it to signify a Christian alternative world under the political lordship of Jesus Christ and under the leadership of Paul and others. It is also viewed as international in scope, considering that Paul at the end of 1 Cor 1:2 says "theirs and ours," meaning "their Lord as well as our Lord." For this view, see Neil Elliott, "The Anti-Imperial Message of the Cross," in Horsley, *Paul and Empire*, 167–83; Richard A. Horsley, "1 Corinthians: A Case Study of Paul's Assembly as an Alternative World," in Horsley, *Paul and Empire*, 242–52; and Richard A. Horsley, *1 Corinthians*; Abingdon New Testament Commentaries (Nashville: Abingdon, 1998), 40. Whether the term has the political punch that these two scholars suggest is debatable, but what is more certain is that the church is periodically viewed as anti-Roman from the mid-second century c.e., at least in the minds of Roman rulers, until the time of Constantine (fourth century c.e.).

18. See Murphy-O'Connor, *Paul the Letter-Writer*, 62.

19. See Raymond F. Collins, *First Corinthians*, Sacra Pagina 7 (Collegeville, Minn.: Liturgical, 1999), 96–70.

20. Commentators today generally hold that the basic problem is between Paul and Apollos. They believe that Jesus and Cephas are placed in the text for rhetorical affect, since only Paul and Apollos appear as concerns for Paul after this point. See Horsley, *1 Corinthians*, 44–45, a representative of this view.

21. See Bruce W. Winter, *After Paul Left Corinth: The Influence of Secular Ethics and Social Change* (Grand Rapids, Mich.: Eerdmans, 2001).

22. In African diaspora religion in the New World, the future is in the past as it was for continental African religions. African diaspora people speak of going home in the future but the home they speak of is out in front of them

in the past. So African history moves back to the future, not ahead, as Westerners tend to think. The future is the past. Paul, as a Jew, thought similarly, with a stress on ancestors (cf. Rom 9–11), and the goal of Christian history in the future is a return to the first world (cf. Rev 21). See John S. Mbiti, *African Religions and Philosophy*, 2nd ed. (London: Heinemann, 1992), for concepts of time in African religions.

23. See Boykin Sanders, "Imitating Paul: 1 Cor 4:16," *HTR* 74 (1981): 354. For a later noting of this view, see Allen R. Hunt, *The Inspired Body: Paul, the Corinthians, and Divine Inspiration* (Macon, Ga.: Mercer University Press, 1996).

24. See Boykin Sanders, *Blowing the Trumpet in Open Court: Prophetic Judgement and Liberation* (Trenton, N.J., and Asmara, Eritrea: Africa World Press, 2002), 59–60.

25. Ibid., 123–49.

26. Those who think that Apollos caused the Corinthians to think and behave in those terms base this on what Luke notes of Apollos in Acts 18, especially that Apollos was an intellectual. See Garland, *1 Corinthians*, 45.

27. See Sanders, "Imitating Paul," 356.

28. See Sanders, *Blowing the Trumpet in Open Court*, 23–42, for a similar explanation on the phenomenon of terrorism.

29. Perhaps the blueprint here is the Christ-crucified gospel, which all builders are to use in the building of the Corinthian church. The language regarding building (*oikodomē*) resurfaces in the middle of the letter, first appearing in 8:1 but especially in chap. 14. Cf. the parable of the temple construction in *The Shepherd of Hermas*, Vision 3.2.1—13.4, an allegory about the various stones used in the construction of the church. Its completion signifies the end of the age.

30. See Jay Shanor, "Paul as Master Builder: Construction Terms in First Corinthians," *NTS* 34 (1988): 461–71, who provides excellent insights about the rules of Corinthian construction practices.

31. See Martin, *The Corinthian Body*, 65–68, 103.

32. See Horsley, *1 Corinthians*, 72–73; cf. Alan

F. Johnson, *1 Corinthians*, Inter-Varsity Press New Testament Commentary (Downers Grove, Ill.: InterVarsity, 2004), 83–86, whose view is similar to Martin's.

33. See Sanders, "Imitating Paul," 361.

34. See John K. Chow, *Patronage and Power: A Study of Social Networks in Corinth*, JSNTSup 75 (Sheffield: Sheffield Academic, 1992), 139–41, who noted that the accused man is a person of means and for that reason the Corinthians accommodated his conduct. Cf. also Johnson, *1 Corinthians*, 88, who alludes to this point for the situation of the accused man, but believes that social status is especially generating the court case scenarios in chap. 6.

35. In my visits to Ghana I use this tree as a teaching tool.

36. See Andrew D. Clarke, *Secular and Christian Leadership in Corinth: A Socio-Historical and Exegetical Study of 1 Corinthians 1–6* (Leiden: Brill, 1993), 62–71, for the view that the issue is about property, in particular the wealthy taking each other to court to settle disputes; also Chow, *Patronage and Power*, 123–30. Cf. Horsley, *1 Corinthians*, 84–87, who thinks that this refers to economic issues, but there has been no discussion thus far in the Corinthian letter about property issues.

37. For Paul, mixing in this context is corrupting. He seeks to guard the purity of the church in dramatic fashion: "Do you not know that whoever unites with a prostitute is one body with her? For it is said, 'the two shall be one flesh'" (6:16, NRSV). Interestingly, in Revelation 17–18, Romanicity (i.e., the Roman government and its institutions) is considered a great whore, with which the church is urged not to get involved.

38. See Vincent L. Wimbush, *Paul the Worldly Ascetic: Response to the World and Self-Understanding According to 1 Corinthians 7* (Macon, Ga.: Mercer University Press, 1987).

39. See Orlando Patterson, *Slavery and Social Death: A Comparative Study* (Cambridge, Mass.: Harvard University Press, 1982), and Braxton, *The Tyranny of Resolution*, 220–34, but esp. 225–26, where Braxton suggests that Paul was in an awkward predicament, that is,

if he had advised that slaves be manumitted he would have been persona non grata in the eyes of the Christian slavemasters, since his welfare depended on their goodwill.

40. See Wimbush, *Paul the Worldly Ascetic*, 23–71, for discussion on the "as if" language in 1 Cor 7:29-31.

41. See Sanders, *Blowing the Trumpet in the Open Court*, 161. For me, love (*agapē*) is a concessionary concept and Paul is seeking to show the Corinthians how it works in community through his own personal example. Freedom is also communal in Paul. This is not to deny what might have influenced Paul's apostolic behavior, for example, his non-apostolic rejection of the hospitality of the Corinthians as seen in chap. 9 (especially his refusal to accept payment for his services and his all-things-to-all-people approach) and the need to explain his decisions to his critics. See Theissen, *The Social Setting of Pauline Christianity*, 138; and against Theissen's view, see Justin J. Meggitt, *Paul, Poverty and Survival* (Edinburgh: T. & T. Clark, 1998), esp. chap. 4, who is highly critical of Theissen, suggesting that he has gone too far in crediting the rich for the Corinthian social problems Paul is addressing (or is alleged to be addressing) in 1 Corinthians.

42. Thus Roman Garrison, "Paul's Use of the Athlete Metaphor in 1 Corinthians 9," in *The Graeco-Roman Context of Early Christian Literature*, JSNTSup 137 (Sheffield: Sheffield Academic, 1997), 95–104. Cf. Garland, *1 Corinthians*, 438–45.

43. See Wire, *The Corinthian Women Prophets*, 116–33; Horsley, *1 Corinthians*, 152–57.

44. See Wire, *The Corinthian Women Prophets*, 123.

45. See Meeks, *The First Urban Christians*, 63–73, for the social composition of the Corinthian church as an index to the social problems Paul addresses in the church. For specifics of the Lord's Supper celebration as reflected in the text, see Theissen, *The Social Setting of Pauline Christianity*, 145–74, especially for how Roman social stratification affected Corinthian behavior in the celebration of the Lord's Supper.

46. See Chow, "Patronage in Roman Corinth," in Horsley, *Paul and Empire*, 122–23, as a

source for this problem. Interestingly, the circumstance reflected in 1 Cor 11:17-24 shows interesting parallels to *The Shepherd of Hermas*, Vision 3.9:1–10, where the uneven relationship between the rich and the poor cause social problems that result in threats of divine judgments, which are the same afflictions (weakness, illness, and death) that Paul refers to in 1 Cor 11:17-34. In *Hermas* the afflictions are certainly due to overeating and undereating—causing illness and death.

47. See Wire, *The Corinthian Women Prophets*, 146–58.

48. Also in the context of chap. 9, Paul had reminded the Corinthians that he had seen the risen Lord (9:1c).

49. See Horsley, *1 Corinthians*, 203–4; Collins, *First Corinthians*, 547–58.

50. See Horsley *1 Corinthians*, 206–7, who thinks that the baptism on behalf of the dead means that some Corinthians were being baptized on behalf of their deceased relatives and friends; also see Garland, *1 Corinthians*, 716.

51. See J. Paul Sampley, "The First Letter to the Corinthians," NIB 10:986–87.

For Further Reading

Blount, Brian K. *Cultural Interpretation: Reorienting New Testament Criticism.* Minneapolis: Fortress Press, 1995.

Braxton, Brad R. *The Tyranny of Resolution: I Corinthians 7:17-24.* SBLDS 181. Atlanta: Society of Biblical Literature, 2000.

Chow, John K. *Patronage and Power: A Study of Social Networks in Corinth.* JSNTSup 75. Sheffield: Sheffield Academic, 1992.

Elliott, Neil. "The Anti-Imperial Message of the Cross." Pages 167–83 in *Paul and Empire: Religion and Power in Roman Imperial Society.* Edited by Richard A. Horsley. Harrisburg, Pa.: Trinity Press International, 1997.

Given, Mark D. *Paul's True Rhetoric: Ambiguity, Cunning, and Deception in Greece and Rome.* Emory Studies in Early Christianity. Harrisburg, Pa.: Trinity Press International, 2001.

Horrell, David G. *The Social Ethos of the Corinthian Correspondence: Interests and Ideology from 1 Corinthians to 1 Clement.* Edinburgh: T. & T. Clark, 1996.

Horsley, Richard A. *1 Corinthians.* Abingdon New Testament Commentary. Nashville: Abingdon, 1998.

———. "1 Corinthians: A Case Study of Paul's Assembly as an Alternative World." Pages 242–52 in *Paul and Empire: Religion and Power in Roman Imperial Society.* Edited by Richard A. Horsley. Harrisburg, Pa.: Trinity Press International, 1997.

Hunt, Allen R. *The Inspired Body: Paul, the Corinthians, and Divine Inspiration* (Macon, Ga.: Mercer University Press, 1996).

Jones, Amos Jr. *Paul's Message of Freedom: What Does It Mean to the Black Church?* Valley Forge, Pa.: Judson, 1984).

Martin, Dale B. *The Corinthian Body.* New Haven: Yale University Press, 1995.

Patterson, Orlando. *Slavery and Social Death: A Comparative Study.* Cambridge, Mass.: Harvard University Press, 1982.

Sanders, Boykin. *Blowing the Trumpet in Open Court: Prophetic Judgement and Liberation.* Trenton, N.J., and Asmara, Eritrea: Africa World Press, 2002.

———. "Imitating Paul: 1 Cor 4:16." *HTR* 74 (1981): 353–63.

Wimbush, Vincent L. *Paul, the Worldly Ascetic: Response to the World and Self-Understanding According to 1 Corinthians 7.* Macon, Ga.: Mercer University Press, 1987.

Winter, Bruce W. *After Paul Left Corinth: The Influence of Secular Ethics and Social Change.* Grand Rapids, Mich.: Eerdmans, 2001.

Wire, Antoinette Clark. *The Corinthian Women Prophets: A Reconstruction through Paul's Rhetoric.* Minneapolis: Fortress Press, 1990.

2 CORINTHIANS

Guy Nave

INTRODUCTION

There is often a tendency among people to idealize the past. Many Christians commonly romanticize the world of the New Testament and talk about the early church as though it represented a community of people who lived in complete harmony with one another. For many Christians, life was simple and uncomplicated back then. There was no bickering or disagreeing over issues of race, gender, class, or sexual orientation. God had revealed through Jesus what it meant to be a Christian, and all Christians understood that revelation in the same way. Every minister of Jesus preached the same message, and Christian congregations agreed with their ministers. The early

church was a harmonious community. In the minds of many Christians today, the church has moved away from this type of harmony. Many Christians talk about returning to the "good old days" when life was simple and believers walked with God and knew how to live in harmony with God and each another. Such a view is reflected in the song, "Give Me That Old Time Religion." A reading of biblical texts, however, clearly reveals that there were no "good old days" when life was simple. "Old time religion" was just as complicated and divisive as modern-day religion.[1] Paul's letters to the Corinthians reveal an early Christian community plagued by division and disagreement. They also portray Paul's strenuous attempt to shape the attitudes and practices of believers who not only disagreed with each other but often disagreed and diverged from Paul's teachings. Paul's so-called second letter to the Corinthians reveals intense real-life drama and conflicts between a preacher and the congregation he founded. Members of the congregation not only disagreed with Paul but also questioned his authority and credibility. The conflicts in Corinth resonate with those played out in many present-day congregations: conflicts over ministerial authority; and integrity; the right of congregations to challenge ministers and the appropriate response of ministers to such challenges; issues of financial compensation for ministers; the appropriate use of wealth and financial resources; competition between ministers; the nature, style, and definition of ministry; and the meaning of discipleship and suffering. Second Corinthians reveals that from the very beginning the church has never represented a community of people who lived in harmony and unity. It has always represented a community of diverse people who struggle to turn to God in an effort to negotiate their differences in such a way as to create a community reflective of God's love, grace, and acceptance.

While the authenticity of 2 Corinthians is unquestioned, the unity of the letter is hotly contested. Despite the fact that 2 Corinthians appears to be composed of at least two Pauline letter fragments, the overarching themes of affliction and consolation, weakness and power, and apostolic authority and integrity suggest that the letter fragments are not unrelated.

In order to better understand 2 Corinthians, it is necessary to have a general idea of the context in which it may have been written. After establishing a Christian community in Corinth, Paul wrote at least one letter to the Corinthians before writing 1 Corinthians (1 Cor 5:9). The community responded with a letter to Paul concerning issues that

had arisen since Paul's departure (1 Cor 7:1). Paul responded to that letter and to negative reports he had heard regarding the Corinthians by writing 1 Corinthians (1 Cor 1:11). Paul later received news that the Corinthians were following and being influenced by Christian leaders who were challenging his authority and leadership. Paul immediately returned to Corinth, where he had an unpleasant interaction with an unnamed individual (2 Cor 2:5-11; 7:12). Paul seemingly cut that visit short. After leaving, he immediately wrote a "tearful" letter in response to his "painful" visit (2 Cor 1:23—2:11; 7:8-12). Some scholars argue that 2 Corinthians 10–13 is part of that "tearful" letter. The tearful letter was carried to Corinth by Paul's coworker Titus. Paul later received word from Titus that the issues raised by the tearful letter had been resolved (2 Cor 7:5-16). In response to Titus's report, Paul wrote most of what is now identified as 2 Corinthians.

Readers should keep in mind that 2 Corinthians is Paul's depiction of the Corinthian situation. Much of Paul's argument is polemical, and as with all polemics—especially religious and political ones—Paul's depiction of the situation, the Corinthians, and Paul's opponents is one-sided and probably unfair (as was their depiction of him). What 2 Corinthians reveals is that neither Paul nor any religious leader speaks on behalf of all Christians or even on behalf of every member of his or her own congregation. Therefore, as interpreters of Paul's letters it is imperative that we not try to make Paul's voice *the* representative voice of Christianity. Black slaves adamantly opposed this practice when their white "Christian" slavemasters told them that the apostle Paul demanded that slaves obey their masters.[2] African Americans who fought against segregation and discrimination also opposed this practice when white "Christian" opponents of the civil rights movement told them that black people had to submit to civil authorities because the apostle Paul wrote, "Let every person be subject to the governing authorities; for there is no authority except from God, and those authorities that exist have been instituted by God" (Rom 13:1). Paul's *letters* do not represent the definitive voice of Christianity. As Paul himself asserts in this very letter, God has called us "to be ministers of a new covenant, *not of letter* but of spirit; for the *letter* kills, but the Spirit gives life" (2 Cor 3:6, emphasis added).

1:1-11, Greetings and Blessing

As with all of Paul's letters, 2 Corinthians was written for a specific audience, one with whom Paul had a particular relationship. While most of Paul's letters begin with the standard letter writing format of that time—which included an identification of the sender, an identification of the recipient, a greeting, and a thanksgiving (or blessing)—Paul did not simply write generic introductions that he used from one letter to the next. Paul individualized each opening in such a way that it addressed the issues and concerns confronting that particular audience. His opening, therefore, provides a window into the issues that he will address throughout the remainder of his letter.

1:1-2, Greetings

Paul most likely states that he was made an apostle of Jesus Christ "by the will of God" because his apostleship was being challenged in Corinth not only by Christian leaders who had recently come to Corinth (11:4-6, 22-23) but also by members of the Christian community he had founded. Paul refused to allow the criticisms of others to cause him to doubt or question the legitimacy of his ministry. He was confident of his calling, just as Richard Allen, a freed slave and the founder

of the African Methodist Episcopal Church, was confident of his calling. Despite his initial reservations and the criticisms of white Christians and even "the most respectable people of color in the city," who wanted to remain a part of the Methodist Episcopal Church, Allen became confident of his calling from God to establish an independent religious denomination that ministered to the needs of black people and recognized all people as children of God.[3]

Timothy was a coworker of Paul's who was clearly well-known to the Christians in Corinth. While it is a common tendency to give prominent movement leaders like Paul, Richard Allen, and Martin Luther King Jr. all of the credit for a movement's success, Paul's greetings often remind us that he worked very closely with associates—named and unnamed—who played key roles in founding and ministering to many of the early Christian communities. Effective ministry is always a collaborative effort, and coworkers should be recognized and acknowledged.

1:3-11, Blessings

In this section Paul presents the basic tension between suffering and hope experienced by those enduring persecution. Paul discusses "suffering" (*pathēma*) that results from "affliction" (*thlipsis*). The Greek term *thlipsis* is often used to refer to misfortune, hardship, persecution, and the experience of oppression. While Paul assures his audience that God is a God of mercy who consoles all those experiencing misfortune, oppression, and persecution, by using Jesus as an example Paul emphasizes suffering endured for the sake of securing the liberation, empowerment, and well-being of the poor and oppressed. Jesus chose to live his life on behalf of poor and oppressed people, and in so doing endured affliction and suffering that provide divine consolation for the oppressed.

Jesus: Savior of the Oppressed

In response to the search for the "historical Jesus," James Cone wrote, "Taking seriously the New Testament Jesus, black theology believes that the historical kernel is the manifestation of Jesus as the Oppressed One whose earthly existence was bound up with the oppressed of the land."

—James Cone, *A Black Theology of Liberation*, twentieth anniversary ed. (Maryknoll, N.Y.: Orbis, 1990), 113.

For Paul, while divine consolation may take the form of deliverance from hardship (vv. 8-10), it consists primarily of divine power that enables one to endure and overcome hardship (4:7-9). This is the type of consolation referred to by many when they sing, "Lord, don't move my mountain; give me the strength to climb."

The consolation of Christ enabled Paul, as an apostle of Christ, to endure affliction on behalf of his congregations—especially the Corinthians—so that they might experience divine consolation through his suffering. Paul implies here (vv. 6-8) and argues later (chaps. 10–12) that, contrary to the preaching of his Christian opponents who mock and ridicule his afflictions and boast of their material and alleged spiritual prosperity, affliction and suffering endured to secure liberation is the truest sign of Christian discipleship and Christian ministry.

Paul's belief that Christian ministry is associated with sacrifice and suffering on behalf of others not only challenged the prosperity-teaching of his opponents, but also challenges much of the teachings of the contemporary prosperity-gospel movement. One of the central tenets of the prosperity gospel is the belief that God wills the financial and material prosperity of every Christian. Individual prosperity, rather than affliction

and sacrifice on behalf of others, is presented as evidence of God's approval of one's discipleship and ministry. Suffering and affliction are often presented as a sign of living outside God's intended will.

Like the afflictions of many oppressed people, the afflictions endured by Paul and his colleagues were so great he felt they would die; however, he placed his hope and confidence in God, who raised Jesus from the dead. It was this hope and confidence in God's resurrection power that enabled Paul to endure afflictions for the well-being of others. It was also this hope that enabled and continues to enable African Americans such as Sojourner Truth, Harriet Tubman, Martin Luther King Jr., and countless other celebrated and uncelebrated men, women, and children to sacrifice and endure afflictions for the liberation and well-being of poor and oppressed people.

1:12—2:13, A Canceled Visit to Corinth

In 1 Cor 16:5-7, Paul promised to visit and spend some time with the Corinthians after passing through Macedonia. Something, however, caused Paul to change his travel plans, which apparently gave rise to accusations regarding Paul's integrity. Paul was accused of vacillating, and here he gives his version of what happened and explains why he changed his travel plans.

1:12-22, Defending His Initial Intentions

Paul's authority, integrity, and credibility are primary topics of discussion throughout 2 Corinthians. Despite accusations questioning his integrity, Paul emphasizes his genuine concern for the Corinthians. By claiming that *his* "boast" is the integrity and "sincerity" of his conduct toward the Corinthians, Paul introduces the idea of "boasting" and "sincerity" as a way of foreshadowing his condemnation of the boasting of his opponents (chaps. 10–13). Regarding his opponents, Paul claims that *they* "boast in outward appearance and not in the heart" (5:12). He also writes, "For we are not peddlers of God's word *like so many*; but in Christ we speak as persons of *sincerity*, as persons sent from God and standing in his presence" (2:17).

Paul suggests that while his swindling and insincere opponents behave and boast according to the standards of "earthly wisdom," his behavior among the Corinthians has been from the heart out of "godly sincerity." Paul's condemnation of "earthly wisdom" is also found in 1 Corinthians. According to Paul, earthly wisdom is associated with eloquent preaching and outward appearances (1 Cor 1:17—2:13; 3:18-20). All too often, eloquent preaching and a flashy appearance are the aspirations and trademarks of many preachers. While some Christians may be impressed by this, sincerity and selfless concern for others are true signs of genuine ministerial authority and integrity.

Paul asserts that his boast and the proof of his apostleship was not the eloquence of his sermons but rather his commitment to and sacrifice on behalf of the Christian communities he had established (cf. Phil 2:16; 1 Thess 2:19). On the day of judgment, he will boast and take pride in the Corinthian congregation, a community that resulted from his labor—not the labor of his opponents, who are trying to boast and take credit for his labor (10:13-16). Likewise, the boast of the Corinthian community will lie in their connection with and loyalty to Paul, not their connection and loyalty to flashy apostles who had nothing to do with establishing them. Mutual pride and respect between preacher and congregation are signs of the grace of God at work within a Christian community.

Contrary to the accusations, Paul's failure to visit the Corinthians was not a sign of vacillation or a lack of faithfulness. Just as *the* Jesus Paul and his coworkers proclaim is the demonstration of God's faithfulness, so they—through their faithfulness to *this* Jesus and their sacrifices on behalf of the Corinthians—are a demonstration of God's faithfulness to them (Paul later accuses his opponents of proclaiming "*another* Jesus"— 2 Cor 11:4; cf. Gal 1:6-7). Every promise of God is fulfilled through Jesus, and, since God established Paul in Jesus and anointed him by giving him God's Spirit, the promises of God to the Corinthians are fulfilled through Paul.

1:23—2:13, A Painful Visit and a Tearful Letter

Continuing his theme of sincere concern for the Corinthians, Paul asserts that his failure to visit the Corinthians was motivated by his love for them. Although Paul was an itinerant minister, he understood himself as working with, for, and on behalf of all the congregations he served. Itinerant ministers who are assigned to churches by bishops or who move from one church to another for other reasons sometime treat congregations as stepping stones to larger congregations or even to becoming a bishop. A minister's main priority, however, is the well-being of the congregations she or he serves, not his or her own ministerial advancement.

Not only does a minister have a responsibility to the congregation, the congregation also has a responsibility to the minister. Each is accountable to the other. Paul had made an unplanned visit to Corinth prior to his trip to Macedonia. This emergency visit was possibly in response to news that the Corinthians were being influenced by Christian leaders who were challenging Paul's authority and leadership. Apparently someone in the congregation insulted Paul during this visit. Although the nature of the insult is unclear, it was obviously offensive to Paul and led him to cut the visit short and to write a "tearful" letter to the community. Some scholars have suggested that 2 Corinthians 10–13 is part of this tearful letter. According to Paul, his objective was not to punish the Corinthians or to cause them pain but rather to convey his love for them and his disappointment at how they had mistreated him (cf. 7:8-13).

In an effort to avoid another potentially painful visit, Paul decided to go on to Macedonia without visiting the Corinthians. Paul journeyed to Troas on his way to Macedonia. While Paul's missionary outreach was apparently successful in Troas, the experience was overshadowed by the anxiety of not knowing how his tearful letter had been received by the Corinthians. He left Troas, therefore, and continued on to Macedonia to await news from Titus (2:12-13). While Paul was in Macedonia, Titus returned from Corinth with news that Paul's letter had been well received and resulted in repentance among the Corinthians (7:5-13a).

Paul most likely composed 2 Corinthians (or at least parts thereof) in Macedonia after receiving the good news from Titus. The community apparently responded to Paul's tearful letter by severely punishing the one who had insulted Paul. While it is unclear if Paul initially instructed the community to punish the offender in this manner (2:9), Paul clearly considered the punishment too severe and encouraged the community to reaffirm its love for the offender by forgiving and consoling him.

2:14—7:16, Paul's Apostolic Ministry

In this section Paul defends the legitimacy of his apostolic ministry. Virtually all of Paul's letters reveal that his apostleship was constantly being challenged. The Greek word *apostolos* (apostle) literally means, "one who is sent." An apostle was one commissioned and sent by an authoritative figure. An apostle of Jesus, therefore, was one commissioned and sent by Jesus. Paul's opponents asserted that Jesus could not have commissioned and sent Paul because Paul had never met Jesus. Paul, however, claimed that both God and Jesus commissioned and sent him as a result of God revealing the resurrected Jesus to Paul (see Gal 1:1, 15-16; cf. Acts 9:1-22; 22:1-16; 26:9-18).

2:14-17, A Worthy Apostle and Minister

These verses seem to disrupt the flow of the previous section (Paul's discussion of his journey to Macedonia continues at 7:5). The letter moves from anxiety to thanksgiving with no explanation. Paul alludes to the ceremonial procession of the Roman army after a victorious battle. In such a procession the army paraded captive prisoners through the streets, flaunting the strength of Rome and the weakness of the defeated enemy. Ironically, Paul compares himself and his apostolic coworkers to defeated enemies taken captive while resisting and fighting against Rome. Jesus, who proclaimed the kingdom of God rather than the kingdom of Rome, was stripped, beaten, paraded through the street, and publicly crucified. Challenging imperial powers by resisting and criticizing the social injustice of the status quo, while working for and advocating on behalf of oppressed people, usually results in persecution. However, it is often through such public persecution that the knowledge and vision of Christ is spread, because it is through the afflictions and suffering resulting from such persecutions that the faithfulness of Christ—revealed through Christ's sacrifice for others—is dramatized and given ongoing meaning and significance. Over the course of history, hundreds of thousands of black and brown Christians in North America, Africa, South America, the Caribbean, Europe, and other parts of the globe have endured public lynchings, burnings, beatings, mutilation, and imprisonment following Christ and resisting imperial power and oppression. Through their suffering for the liberation of oppressed people, Christ's ministry of sacrifice, resistance, and liberation is dramatized.

Paul uses the language of "fragrance" and "aroma" because the terms refer to the odor of incense used in religious sacrifices. To critics, Paul's life and message are absurd and represent nothing more than death, but to believers they represent life. Earlier Paul writes the Corinthians, "For the message about the cross is foolishness to those who are perishing, but to us who are being saved it is the power of God" (1 Cor 1:18). For Paul, the Christian life in general and the life of an apostle in particular should reflect the event that made such a life possible—the cross of Christ (i.e. the sacrifices of Christ on behalf of others). Paul writes to Christians in Galatia, "May I never boast of anything except the cross of our Lord Jesus Christ" (Gal 6:14).

While Christianity should not be understood primarily as a religion of martyrdom, too often the Western Christian avoidance of sacrifice and the quest for prosperity and success overshadow the significance and meaning of the life, message, death, and resurrection of Jesus. Paul informed the Corinthians that the message of God through Christ is one of sacrifice and self-denial for the well-being of others. The resurrection of Jesus the Christ serves to legitimate the good news of the Christian proclamation, which is that the kingdom of this world is being replaced by the kingdom of God. The resurrection affirms that oppressive powers are unable to defeat the power of God at work in resistance against injustice, oppression, and exploitation. More than two hundred years of resistance contributed to the defeat of slavery in America. Decades of resistance contributed to the defeat of Jim Crow and racial segregation. Decades of resistance

in South Africa led to the defeat of apartheid. While it is easy to become disillusioned by the continued social and economic oppression of black people around the globe, the resurrection of Jesus Christ and the successful struggles of black people throughout the world attest to the fact that oppressive powers cannot prevail forever. Weeping may endure for the night, but joy does come in the morning (Ps 30:5).

After describing the cost of apostleship, Paul makes it clear that it is he and his coworkers rather than his opponents who are "sufficient" (i.e., competent) to represent Christ and his ministry. Paul accuses his opponents of taking advantage of the Corinthians, and he criticizes the Corinthians for gladly welcoming such exploitation (11:19-21a). Those who deny and ignore Jesus' life and message of resistance and sacrifice are nothing more than charlatans and "peddlers of God's word," who preach for profit and selfish gain.

3:1-18, Ministry of a New Covenant

Paul's remarks about commending oneself are directed against his opponents. Unlike his opponents, who commend themselves (10:12) and carry letters of recommendation to and from the Corinthians, Paul and his coworkers are commended by their actions (4:2). Their actions speak louder than words, because their actions demonstrate their commitment to and sacrifices on behalf of the ministry of God (6:3-10). The Corinthian community is Paul's letter of recommendation. Paul has no need to commend himself because the fruit of his labor demonstrates the Lord's commendation, which is far more important than any self-commendation (10:17-18).

Paul uses the analogy of writing as a way of introducing the idea of a "new covenant." His reference to letters written on hearts is meant to echo the prophecy of Jeremiah regarding the new covenant the Lord will make with the house of Israel by writing the law on the people's hearts (Jer 31:31-33). Paul considered himself and his coworkers to be ministers of this new covenant, which is not based upon written requirements but upon life in the Spirit. Written requirements are rigid and inflexible and promote death. The Spirit, however, is fluid and flexible and promotes life (cf. Rom 2:27-29; 7:6).

In light of some of the historical and even contemporary tensions between the African American and Jewish communities, it is important to realize that Paul's contrast is not between Christianity and Judaism.[4] Paul never considered himself a "convert" to a new religion, and he never thought of himself as no longer being Jewish. Paul's contrast is between allegiance to a written covenant, which promotes death and condemnation, and allegiance to the Spirit of God, which promotes life and justification. While the black church has always been profoundly biblically based, African American Christians have rejected literal interpretations and an allegiance to scriptures used to promote slavery, Jim Crow, and other forms of racial oppression.[5] With regard to racial oppression, the black church has demonstrated an understanding of the fact that a covenant based upon "the letter" kills. However, when it comes to the oppression of women, the church has often been quick to abandon the "new covenant" of the spirit in order to place a veil over the minds of Christians and to return to the "old covenant" of the letter.[6] Only by turning to the ministry of Christ are we able to abandon the covenant of the letter. Only by turning to the Lord, who is the Spirit, are we able to set aside the veil and the ministry of condemnation. Unquestioning obedience to a written code promotes death and condemnation. A covenant of the letter allows no room for freedom, but "where the Spirit of the Lord is, there is freedom." While

scripture will always be important in the life of the church, ministers of the new covenant are called to be ministers of the Spirit not the letter.[7]

4:1-6, Ministers of Jesus Christ

Paul makes it clear that participation in ministry is not based on what some people may think of you. Neither is it based upon credentials or even necessarily ability. Participation in ministry is based upon "sincerity" (1:12; 2:17; cf. 1 Cor 5:8) and God's mercy. No one is a minister of God because he or she is qualified or more talented than others. It is only because of God's mercy that one is afforded the opportunity of engaging in the ministry of revealing God's glory. Realization of this fact contributes to the sincerity and humility with which one engages in ministry.

Despite the accusations and criticism made against Paul, Paul did not become discouraged. It did not matter that he was accused of being "cunning" (cf. 12:16) or trying "to falsify God's word" (cf. 2:17). It did not matter that his opponents said, "his bodily presence is weak, and his speech contemptible" (10:10), or that many of the Corinthians considered him inferior to the "super-apostles" (11:5-6; 12:11). Paul understood that it was not about him; instead it is about "Jesus Christ as Lord," and ministers as those who serve God and God's people.

Ministry is not about competing for large congregations and faithful followers by impressing people with one's skills and credentials; instead it is about proclaiming and demonstrating in one's own life the glorious image of God—revealed in the self-sacrificing life of Jesus—the image in which we were created (Gen 1:27) and into which we are being transformed (2 Cor 3:18). As in the time of Paul, this message is often "veiled" and hard to hear because the values promoted by society associate life and success with self-attainment and self-accomplishment rather than self-denial for the well-being of others.

4:7-15, Power in the Midst of Weakness

Paul continues expounding on the idea presented in the previous section that engagement in the ministry of revealing God's glory is not based on credentials, abilities, or status. Engagement in ministry is based on God's grace. While Paul's opponents boast and place confidence in their own ability and qualifications, Paul makes it clear that human beings are nothing more than clay jars and are unworthy to be entrusted with the treasure of the gospel.

Many in Corinth were boasting of their own ability and qualification (1 Cor 26–31); Paul's message, however, emphasizes that the gospel is about God's ability. God is the one who makes "light shine out of darkness" (4:6). God is the one who manifests strength in the midst of weakness. Paul asserts that the reality of human weakness and limitation clearly attests to the reality of God's extraordinary power. The afflictions suffered by Paul and his coworkers should have destroyed them. God's divine power, however, enabled them to endure and overcome.

The savage brutality and atrocities of more than 380 years of violence and injustice against African Americans—which includes 245 years of slavery, more than 100 years of Jim Crow, and ongoing systemic institutional racial oppression and exploitation—should have destroyed African American people, but God's divine power has enabled African Americans not only to endure but to overcome.

African American Christians have been able to confront, endure, and overcome hardship because of the conviction that not even the ultimate hardship of death is able to withstand God's power. The hardships and victories of African American people reveal the superiority of God's power in the same way

the suffering, death, and resurrection of Jesus revealed the superiority of God's power. The very life of Jesus—and therefore the image of God—was not only made visible in the flesh of Paul and his coworkers, but also made visible in the flesh of African American people.[8]

4:16—5:10, Living by Faith

For the second time in chap. 4 Paul says, "we do not lose heart" (4:1, 16), and each time Paul emphasizes the importance of allowing faith in God to serve as the basis for summoning the strength to endure and overcome difficult situations. Paul informs the Corinthians that no matter how difficult and hopeless things appear, the present situation is never the final word. Just as God was able to defeat death by raising Jesus from the dead, God is able to bring eternal glory out of momentary afflictions. Faith in God provides the believer with the assurance that all afflictions—including death—are temporary.

Contrary to some notions of faith, faith does not deny the reality of pain, hardship, and suffering; instead, faith declares that the present reality is not the final reality. African American slaves were more than aware of this fact when they sang the words, "I got shoes, you got shoes; all God's chil'en got shoes. When I get to heaven, I'm gonna put on my shoes and walk all over God's heaven." Shoes represented freedom, because slaves were denied shoes. Those who sang these words understood that their present reality of enslavement was temporary. God had built a city where they would walk the streets, no longer barefoot or even in work boots but wearing shoes. It was this future hope that caused them not to lose heart.

Faith points ahead to a future yet fulfilled. It provides a confident assurance of things hoped for (Heb 11:1). It is this assurance that God will make things better in the future that enables one to live with confidence in the present. It is important to realize that living with confidence in the midst of suffering is not the same thing as passively accepting suffering and waiting for one's "pie in the sky when I die." Slavemasters often encouraged slaves to passively accept their oppressive plight of slavery on the basis that they would be rewarded in heaven. The belief that one's present reality was not the final reality, however, not only empowered slaves not to lose heart and to confidently endure, but also enabled them to reject their current reality. Confident belief that a better reality was their future and God's will was based on their understanding of God's vindication of Jesus, who lived and died resisting oppression and setting captives free. Faith in God and belief that freedom is God's will empowered them to work and fight for that will, praying as Jesus had taught them, "Your will be done, *on earth* as it is in heaven."

The African American life has always been about using faith to endure and overcome hardship; that is why the collective testimony of African American people has been, "we walk by faith, not by sight." In his book *Strength to Love*, Martin Luther King Jr. describes this kind of faith when he writes, "Our refusal to be stopped, our 'courage to be,' our determination to go on 'in spite of,' reveal the divine image within us. The man who has made this discovery knows that no burden can overwhelm him and no wind of adversity can blow his hope away. He can stand anything that can happen to him."[9]

5:11-21, Living for Christ as a New Creation
Once again Paul condemned the Corinthian focus on outward appearances and emphasized living for God out of a sincere heart and a pure conscience (cf. 1:12; 2:17; 4:3). According to Paul, he was not concerned with garnering praise or admiration for himself. He was not concerned with trying to impress others.

His ministerial zeal was on behalf of God and his diligence was for the sake of the Corinthians. Paul claimed that life and ministry should be motivated by and in response to Christ's self-sacrificing love. Because Christ died on behalf of all people, those who respond in faith to Christ die to self-centered ways of living (cf. Rom 6:5-11). Followers of Christ live on behalf of Christ, which means allowing the love of God manifested in Christ to compel a life in service to others and not in judgment of others based on outward appearances.

Traits, characteristics, and appearances valued and highly esteemed by society caused the Corinthians to embrace Paul's opponents; while Paul's traits, characteristics, and appearances—which were not valued by society—caused the Corinthians to despise and reject Paul. Paul himself confesses to having once judged Jesus negatively based on outward appearances. Living for Christ, however, means abandoning old ways of thinking and living. Life in Christ represents a new creation.

For Paul, reconciliation of all humanity to God is the primary goal within this new creation. Reconciliation to God results in a life consistent or congruous with the purpose and will of God. This means that in the new creation self-centeredness and judgment based solely on external appearance no longer exists; instead God's self-sacrificing love for those in need governs all perceptions and actions.[10] It is this new creation that Dr. King envisioned when he said, "I have a dream that my four little children will one day live in a nation where they will not be judged by the color of their skin but by the content of their character."[11]

6:1-10, Commendation through Hardships
Paul cites Isa 49:8 to associate reconciliation with salvation. Salvation is not merely about individual deliverance; it is about communal reconciliation. Through Jesus' ministry of

self-denial for the well-being of others, God is "reconciling the *world*," not merely delivering individuals (cf. 5:18-21). Paul uses the passage from Isaiah to emphasize both the urgency of the situation and the present rather than future nature of salvation.

Paul challenges the cultural values esteemed by the Corinthians. Throughout the letter, Paul criticizes his opponents for commending themselves and claiming apostolic authority based on outward signs of power and glory. He implies that ministries that claim divine authority based on appearances of success are flawed and prevent access to salvation. Paul commends himself and his coworkers as "servants of God," based not on appearances but on their commitment to the ministry of reconciliation given them by God.

An unwavering commitment to the ministry of reconciliation is what Paul considers to be the mark of genuine Christian ministry. While it may be difficult to remain faithful in afflictions and hardships, the virtues of Christian ministry are revealed by the commitment demonstrated in the midst of such adversity. When it comes to ministry, it is these commitments, and not material signs of success, that are worthy of commendation.

6:11—7:3, Appeal for Reconciliation

Paul's strong appeal for reconciliation clearly indicates that all is not well in Corinth. The divine reconciliation that Paul describes in 5:18—6:2 is the reconciliation he seeks between the Corinthians and himself. The appeal for reconciliation (6:11-13; 7:2-3) is interrupted by a strong admonition for religious purity. Many interpreters see this interruption as a non-Pauline addition. While the admonition clearly interrupts the flow and contains language and themes that diverge from much of Paul's writings, it is possible to make sense of the admonition within the context of 2 Corinthians.

Many in the Corinthian congregation have turned away from Paul and are following Paul's opponents. Paul rebukes the Corinthians for turning their back on him and associating with his opponents (chaps. 10–13). He identifies his opponents as false apostles, deceitful workers, and even ministers of Satan (11:13-15). "Beliar" is a variant of "Belial," one of the many Jewish names for Satan. Paul at times speaks very strongly about and against his opponents (cf. Gal 5:7-12). It appears that Paul strongly admonishes the Corinthians to separate themselves from his opponents in Corinth.

This passage seems to suggest that reconciliation is only for those who were once close but are now alienated. It does not appear that Paul encourages reconciliation between those who are considered enemies. Earlier, however, Paul declared, "in Christ God was reconciling the *world* to himself." I would hope that even our most ardent enemies are considered part of the world. Paul, unfortunately, is not alone in this apparent hypocrisy. The author of the Gospel of Matthew depicts Jesus saying, "Love your enemies and pray for those who persecute you" and "Do not judge, so that you may not be judged" (Matt 5:44; 7:1). However, when the author deals with his enemies—the Pharisees—he depicts Jesus cursing, judging, and condemning them (Matt 23:13-36), and, like Paul, the author does not seem to be bothered by this apparent contradiction.

Because we are imperfect human beings, even the best of us fall short and are incapable of getting it right all the time. We have moments when we recognize and acknowledge that God is the God of *all* people, but we also have moments when we deny that reality through acts and words of racism, sexism, classism, xenophobia, and homophobia. Unfortunately, like our biblical predecessors, we often abandon a ministry of reconciliation in favor of a ministry of condemnation, and despite the fact that we acknowledge belief that God is the God of all people, we still use God to legitimate the rejection and renunciation of a relationship with all people—especially those with whom we disagree.

7:4-16, Corinthian Repentance

After rejecting his opponents, Paul expresses joy over the Corinthians' repentance of their rejection of him. Paul reveals that repentance is not simply a one-time act that takes place as a prerequisite for becoming a Christian. Even followers of Jesus get it wrong sometime and need to repent. Paul also reveals, however, that it is usually easier for us to see where others may have it wrong and need to repent than it is to see where we may have it wrong and need to repent. Paul rejoiced over the Corinthians' reconciliation with him while at the same time promoting the Corinthians' rejection of and alienation from Paul's opponents. Paul, however, apparently saw no reason to repent of his conduct.

In this section, Paul resumes his conversation in 1:15—2:13. Paul was unable to take advantage of a ministerial opportunity in Troas because of his anxiety regarding the Corinthians' response to his letter scolding them for the mistreatment he received during his last visit to Corinth. Titus, however, brought Paul the "good news" that the Corinthians were remorseful and had reaffirmed their loyalty to Paul.

Paul once again associates salvation with reconciliation (see the comments on 6:1-10). Paul suggests that the Corinthians' salvation was tied to their reconciliation with and loyalty to him. Paul informed the Corinthians that the real issue in Corinth transcended both the individual who had offended him and Paul's own personal feelings. According to Paul, the Corinthians' very salvation was at stake, because their salvation was based on their relationship with him. To reject Paul was

to reject God. By reaffirming their loyalty to Paul, the Corinthians reaffirmed their loyalty to God and proved themselves guiltless in the matter.

While it may be difficult for many Christians to find fault with or to criticize the apostle Paul, it is important to remember that Paul was not God. Obedience to Paul is not the same thing as obedience to God. All Christians—especially African American Christians—should reject the notion that loyalty to a minister is identical with loyalty to God, and all ministers should avoid making such claims, no matter how strongly they may feel about the righteousness of their position. Throughout the history of Christianity, slave-holding ministers sought to convince Christian slaves that obedience to their master was the same thing as obedience to God (cf. Eph 6:5-8; Col 3:22-24; 1 Tim 6:1-2; Titus 2:9-10; 1 Pet 2:18-22). No matter the intent or sincerity of a minister, all claims that loyalty to a minister is synonymous with loyalty to God are meant to force submission and subordination, and blatantly contradict the claim, "where the Spirit of the Lord is, there is freedom" (2 Cor 4:17).

8:1—9:15, The Collection for Jerusalem

In this section Paul makes an appeal on behalf of a collection for poorer Christians in Jerusalem. According to Paul, during an earlier meeting between himself and the leaders of the Jerusalem church, James, Cephas (Peter), and John agreed to Paul's mission to the Gentiles and asked only that he "remember the poor," which he claimed he was eager to do (Gal 2:1-10). The Jerusalem collection most likely was intended not only to meet the economic needs of Christians in Jerusalem but also to demonstrate unity between Jewish and Gentile Christians.

8:1-15, The Ministry of Giving

Paul previously instructed the Corinthians to put aside some money every first day of the week, probably from offerings collected when they gathered to worship. The money was to assist poorer Christians in Jerusalem. Paul planned to collect the money and take it to Jerusalem (1 Cor 16:1-4). For some reason, however, the Corinthians had not completed the collection. Since Paul explicitly addresses his apostolic opponents immediately after discussing the collection, it may be that the Corinthians failed to complete the collection for the Jerusalem church because Paul's opponents raised questions about Paul's authority and suspicions about his motives and integrity (12:14-18). Paul, however, asserts that it was his opponents who had taken advantage of the Corinthians by requiring the Corinthians to support them (11:7-12, 19-21a). As a result of the reconciliation that took place between the Corinthians and Paul, Titus was able to revive the Corinthians' commitment to the collection.

It is interesting that Paul frequently referred to the Corinthians' offering with the Greek term *charis* (grace). The financial support of Christians on behalf of poorer brothers and sisters is an act of grace analogous to the grace that God extends to us all.

Paul depicts giving as a ministry, not simply an act of charity. This idea of ministry is important, because ministry is an ongoing way of living, not a one-time event. The ministry of giving is an act of solidarity, not an act of charity. Through the ministry of giving, we enter into solidarity with those in need. We acknowledge that those in need are our brothers and sisters and that we join with them in the effort to overcome their need.

At the heart of solidarity is the notion of justice. Therefore, the ministry of giving is about justice, not charity. American Christians tend to understand giving as charity rather than justice, because America is much better at charity than at justice. The response of Americans to national and international tragedy demonstrates the willingness of Americans to sacrifice for the sake of charity, but the huge and insurmountable chasm between the haves and the have-nots demonstrates the reluctance of Americans to sacrifice for the sake of justice.

National tragedies often reveal social injustices. For some in America, Hurricane Katrina was a shocking revelation, but for others it was a tragic reminder of what it means to be poor and black in America. Hurricane Katrina pulled back the veil of a divided America and exposed the sinful truth regarding the ways in which many of the historical and ongoing social policies of this country promote and foster race-based injustices and inequities. In response to the hurricane, there was a large outpouring of charity, but not as large an outpouring of justice. Hurricane Katrina provided America with an opportunity to engage in a "ministry of giving," but America responded primarily with acts of charity. Although providing billions in so-called relief efforts, the government tried to recoup that generosity by proposing a federal budget that cut nearly a trillion dollars from vital social programs designed to protect and empower the people most ravaged by Hurricane Katrina—further promoting and perpetuating the very injustice revealed by Katrina.[12]

Since giving is ministry, it fulfills a divine purpose. That purpose is the establishment of equity between those who have and those in need. Equity and justice are partners—inseparable soul mates—and they represent the will and purpose of God.

Another important point that Paul makes is that the ministry of giving does not seek to impoverish one in order to enrich another. Often those who are unable to give are often made to feel guilty or even shamed into giving that which they do not have. With equity, however, those who are financially able are compelled to make sacrifices and to deny themselves in order to promote and establish equity between those who have and those in need.

Economic values are predominant in American society, so much so that much—if not most—of the discrimination suffered by African Americans has been economic in character, beginning with chattel slavery. The black church has and will continue to play an important role in the economic situation of black communities. While most black churches are by no means wealthy institutions, black churches are significant economic institutions within the community, with combined annual revenue that runs into multiple billions of dollars.[13] The bulk of that revenue results from the giving of church members. Through the ministry of giving, the black church must continue to lead the way in the establishment of economic justice and equity for the black underclass in America.

8:16-24, Commendation of Titus and Others

Paul places some distance between himself and the actual gathering and transporting of the money. To the Corinthians he commends Titus and two other brothers who will bear most of the responsibility for gathering and taking the money to Jerusalem. One of the brothers, who is famous for his preaching, is actually "appointed by the churches"—probably the churches in Jerusalem—to oversee the gathering and delivering of the money to Jerusalem. Paul and others want to avoid any possibility or appearance of financial impropriety and want to assure the Corinthians and possibly the Christians in Jerusalem that the money will only be used to help promote God's purpose of equity. The misuse of congregational collections for personal gain by ministerial

leaders is one of the greatest hindrances to the ministry of giving.

9:1-5, Advance Preparation for the Collection

Paul perceives that his reputation and honor are tied to the Corinthians' collection. If the Corinthians do not provide a decent collection for the ministry to fellow believers in Jerusalem, it will reflect negatively on Paul as a minister and leader of the church. A weak offering in Corinth might also negatively affect offerings collected by Paul in Macedonia. To ensure that he and the Corinthians are not embarrassed when he arrives with his entourage from Macedonia, Paul sends Titus and the other brothers to Corinth to make sure the collection is impressive and ready for Paul's arrival.

Although Paul emphasizes that the collection is voluntary and highlights that giving is ministry that seeks to establish equity (see the comments on 8:1-16), he also appeals to the Corinthians' sense of pride in an attempt to shame them into giving generously. Surely the Corinthians do not want to be embarrassed in the presence of the Macedonians, who are poorer than the Corinthians yet who are abundantly generous in their giving and faithful in their loyalty to Paul (cf. 8:1-5).

Strategies or gimmicks that promote "healthy competition" are often employed in congregations as techniques for raising money. There are many in the church who endorse such strategies, and there are many who oppose them. The merit and/or integrity of such strategies will not be debated here. However, when "ministry" is the purpose of giving, a Christian commitment to God's desire for equity rather than a concern about reputation and pride would seem to be far more in keeping with "what is right . . . in the Lord's sight" (8:21).

9:6-15, The Rewards of Generosity

At the heart of Paul's appeal for the Corinthians' generous giving is the widely accepted notion "you reap what you sow." African Americans have long associated making sacrifices with sowing seeds, and they have understood that great sacrifices ultimately result in a great harvest. At the end of the march from Selma's bloody Edmund Pettus Bridge to Montgomery's state capitol in 1965, the Reverend Dr. Martin Luther King Jr. encouraged the people by saying,

> I know some of you are asking today,
> "How long will it take?" I come to say to you this afternoon, however difficult the moment, however frustrating the hour, it will not be long, because truth pressed to earth will rise again.
> How long? Not long, because no lie can live forever.
> How long? Not long, because you still reap what you sow.
> How long? Not long, because the arm of the moral universe is long but it bends toward justice.[14]

God is a just God, and ultimately the seeds of sacrifice sown for the sake of justice will result in a corresponding harvest of justice.

Contrary to the idea that wealth is inherently evil, Paul presents a positive attitude toward possessions. When God provides one with wealth, God does so in order that the wealth may be shared. God multiplies one's wealth (i.e. seed) not so that it may be held on to but so that it may be sown (cf. Luke 12:16-21). As the most significant black-owned financial institution within the black community, black churches have a responsibility to sow wealth (seed) into the black underclass not only in America, but in Africa and throughout the world. This ministry of sowing results not only in a reward for the sower but also in a harvest of blessed, grateful, and empowered individuals thankful to God and working on behalf of others because of the grace and generosity of God manifested through God's people.

10:1—13:13, Paul's Condemnation of His Opponents

There are a number of obvious differences and conflicts between chaps. 1–9 and chaps. 10–13. While Paul alludes to his opponents in chaps. 1–9 (2:17; 3:1; 4:2, 5; 6:14-17;), in chaps. 10–13 Paul engages in an outright attack of his opponents. Although chaps. 1–9 clearly reveal that there are difficulties

---

Black Sowing . . . Black Harvest

Commenting about the responsibility of African American Christians, James M. Shopshire writes, "If African Americans fail to garner the resources of their strongest institutions, develop internal structures and relations for humane and just purposes, and work from their strengths to participate in the economic, political and cultural structures of this nation, the continent of Africa and the world, it will not otherwise happen. As a result, black folks will remain on the bottom rather than approaching par with other racial-ethnic groups in the global economy as equals before God and among the groups of humankind."

—James M. Shopshire, "The Bible as Informant and Reflector in Social-Structural Relationships of African Americans," in *African Americans and the Bible: Sacred Texts and Social Textures*, ed. Vincent L. Wimbush (New York: Continuum, 2001), 133.

and tension in the relationship between Paul and the Corinthians, these chapters depict a reconciled Paul and Corinthian community (cf. 7:2-16). Chaps. 10–13, however, portray an alienated Paul and Corinthian community. Unlike the conciliatory tone found in chaps. 1–9, the tone of chaps. 10–13 is harsh and sarcastic. Paul is on the defensive, criticizing the Corinthians and attacking his opponents. Chaps. 1–9 suggest that at the time of composition, Titus had only visited Corinth once (cf. 7:4-16). Chaps. 10–13, however, indicate that Titus had already made a second visit to collect the Jerusalem offering (12:14-18; cf. 8:16-19). These differences suggest that chaps. 1–9 and chaps. 10–13 represent separate letters that were later combined to form one letter. Chaps. 10–13 indicate that Paul planned to arrive in Corinth for a third visit, and that he was writing in anticipation of that visit (12:14; 13:1, 10).

10:1-6, Possessing Divine Power

Paul's opponents apparently make a number of accusations against him. They claim that he talks bold and tough when he is away but when he is present he is actually timid and weak (cf. 10:10). According to Paul's opponents, such practices are typical of human ministries that lack divine power and authority. Such ministries talk a good talk but manifest no power to back up their talk.

Paul, however, declares that divine power is different from human power and that his ministry demonstrates divine power. Paul understands divine power to be manifested in apparent weakness (12:8-10; 13:3-4), just as the knowledge of God is made manifest in the apparent weakness of Christ. It is the power of God manifested in weakness that destroys human strongholds. Furthermore, humility and gentleness are often much better than harsh words and actions at diffusing arguments and promoting obedience. There

was a church mother at a church where I once served who used to tell the pastor when he was on the verge of getting worked up, "A soft answer turns away wrath, but a harsh word stirs up anger" (Prov 15:1).

While African Americans appeared to many as weak and powerless during the struggle for civil rights, the stronghold of Jim Crow was ultimately destroyed by the weakness of nonviolent resistance. In response to African American opponents of King's philosophy of nonviolent resistance, King often argued that violence in the struggle for civil rights would be self-defeating. Rather than destroying the stronghold of segregation and discrimination, violence would strengthen segregation and destroy the movement itself. King and others lived out their faith in a violent racist society without allowing that violence to force them to adopt the human standards of violence. Their faith prevented them from waging war according to human standards; instead, their weapons used divine power to destroy strongholds. Those who confronted and challenged the entrenched stronghold of segregation were imbued with a power beyond the power of racial discrimination and segregation in order to defeat the power of racial segregation.

10:7-11, Paul Claims Authority

Paul asserts that "the proof is in the pudding." Both the Corinthians and Paul's opponents claim to "belong to Christ," implying that Paul does not. Throughout his ministry Paul has to defend his status as an apostle. His critics argues that since Paul has never known or even followed the historical Jesus, there is no basis for his claim to be an apostle. Apostles are those commissioned and sent by Jesus. Paul has even been an enemy of Christ, denying Jesus and persecuting his followers (Gal 1:13; Acts 8:3; 1 Cor 15:9). Paul also lacks the charisma and rhetorical skill possessed by his opponents. Paul argues, however, that both his past and his lack of charisma are irrelevant. What the Corinthians need to do is simply look at the evidence. Despite his past (and even in contrast to it) and despite his lack of charisma, Paul's commitment to ministry and to the Corinthians clearly demonstrates that he belongs to Christ (1 Cor 1:12; 2:17; 4:5; 12:14-19).

In response to arguments made by his opponents challenging Paul's authority, Paul boasts of evidence supporting his authority (cf. Gal 1:15-24; 2:6-9). While his opponents consider his boasting excessive and even arrogant, Paul considers it more than appropriate, especially in light of the criticisms made against him by his opponents. Most African Americans are familiar with the experience of having to prove themselves constantly to those who challenge their ability and qualifications. They know what it means to have their qualifications and experiences challenged and invalidated because they stray away from some predefined standard of accepted qualifications

and experiences—a standard patterned after the qualifications and experiences of those in charge. When African Americans defend their qualifications and experiences and speak confidently about their credentials and ability, they are often accused of being cocky and arrogant. Paul, however, refuses to allow the criticism of opponents to intimidate him or cause him to doubt himself (see sidebar on p. 324). Although his experiences differ from his opponents, his experiences still qualify him to serve God and to fulfill his calling with boldness and authority, not arrogance.

A Never Ending Demand for Proof

bell hooks, who published her first book, *Ain't I a Woman*, when she was a nineteen-year-old undergraduate at Stanford, talks about having to prove herself to the white academic establishment. As a writer, she established a major corpus before she was forty. She describes, however, the racist process she endured to receive tenure. "White academics, some of whom had published very little, demanded proof of my continued intention of writing. Something like the anti-bellum slave auction, when the new master demanded proof of the slave women's fertility."

—bell hooks and Cornel West, *Breaking Bread: Insurgent Black Intellectual Life* (Boston: South End, 1991), 74.

White Self-Confidence . . . Black Arrogance

In a book full of poignant personal interviews, Ellis Cose documents the anger and frustration of successful African American professionals who recount the subtle (and often non-subtle) forms of prejudice they endure, much of which is manifested as "double standards" for blacks and whites. When white males are brash, self-confident, and risk takers, they are praised as "natural leaders." When black professionals, however, exhibit the same characteristics, they are automatically labeled as arrogant, cocky, or sassy.

—Ellis Cose, *The Rage of a Privileged Class: Why Do Prosperous Blacks Still Have the Blues?* (New York: HarperCollins, 1993).

10:12-18, Divine Rather than Human Commendation

A previously defensive-minded Paul now goes on the offensive. His comment about not comparing himself with them is clearly sarcastic since he considers them to be false apostles and ministers of Satan (11:13-15). He criticizes his opponents for commending themselves. By commending themselves they

Overcoming Self-Doubt

Shelby Steele writes, "I think black Americans are today more oppressed by doubt than by racism and that the second phase of our struggle for freedom must be confrontation with that doubt. Unexamined, this doubt leads us back into the tunnel of our oppression where we reenact our victimization just as society struggles to end its victimization of us."

—Shelby Steele, "Nurturing the Believing Self," in *The African American Book of Values*, ed. Steven Barboza (New York: Doubleday, 1998), 234.

demonstrate a failure to understand that only divine commendation really matters. Divine commendation is attested by fruitful and effective ministry, because God makes one an effective minister (cf. 3:4-6).

While Paul's opponents boast of their ministerial effectiveness, it is Paul's ministry—not the ministry of his opponents—that gives birth to the Corinthian congregation (1 Cor 4:14-16). No matter how much they criticize him, Paul's opponents cannot claim responsibility for the Corinthian congregation. And though Paul acknowledges that over the course of time other ministers will have roles within a particular congregation, he warns the Corinthians that ministers should be careful not to undermine the work of an earlier minister by attempting to lay a different foundation (1 Cor 3:10-11). Paul's opponents are making just such an attempt (2 Cor 11:4).

Paul criticizes his opponents for claiming responsibility for a congregation they played no role in founding. Paul did all the work in Corinth, but his opponents want to take the credit. They are much more interested in entering a cultivated field and claiming as their own a harvest for which they have not labored. Paul believes that ministry is not about entering fields cultivated by others. Rather than building upon the labors of others, a minister should seek to take the good news of God's liberating and transformative power to places where it has not yet been delivered (Rom 15:20-21). The objective is to go where the need is greatest. Ministry is not about going where we are comfortable and where we can be blessed by the people; it is about going where we are needed and where we can be a blessing.

Over the past few decades there has been an increasing exodus of churches from inner-city America into suburban America.[15] I am not suggesting that there is no need in the suburbs; however, churches are increasingly competing with one another for the allegiance of the same middle- and upper-class population while ignoring the unmet need of a rapidly growing urban underclass in America. Churches are competing for each other's members and are measuring success by comparing themselves with one another. God's calling, however, is to take the good news of God's love and power to those who have yet to hear it or be set free by it.

11:1-15, Paul and the False Apostles

In order to defend himself and demonstrate he is not inferior to his opponents, Paul is forced by his Corinthian opponents to engage in the "foolishness" of boasting (cf. 12:11-13). Paul—not his opponents—founded the Corinthian congregation. He seeks to protect the congregation from corrupting influences just as a parent seeks to protect a child. Paul's opponents, the "super-apostles," are leading the Corinthians away from the one true Christ whom Paul preaches. According to Paul, they do so in three ways: (1) by preaching "another Jesus," (2) by invoking a "different spirit," and (3) by proclaiming a "different gospel."

Paul preaches a Jesus crucified in weakness but raised in power (2 Cor 13:4). His opponents, who boast of their own power and charisma, appear to preach a powerful, charismatic, wonder-working Jesus. Rather than invoking the spirit of the crucified Christ—which Paul exemplifies in his life and ministry—his opponents invoke a spirit of power and ecstasy, which they claim to possess and embody in their ministry (cf. 1 Cor 12:1—14:33a). Finally, instead of proclaiming the gospel of the suffering Christ, Paul's opponents proclaim a gospel of power and present glory. They are commissioned by a powerful, charismatic, wonder working Jesus, i.e., a "super Jesus." As apostles of this "super Jesus," they are "super-apostles" who bear the trademarks of the Jesus they preach.

At the refounding of Corinth as a Roman colony in 44 B.C.E. by Julius Caesar, the city was largely repopulated with ex-slaves. By the time Paul established a Christian community in Corinth in 51 C.E., the city had already become a prosperous commercial center. With so many of the now successful merchants of Corinth being former slaves and descendants of slaves, a desire to receive the respect accorded to people of high social status was likely a prominent part of the Corinthian social ethos. It is easy to understand how and why a message of power, status, wealth, and prestige—preached by Paul's opponents—would have been more appealing to many Corinthians than Paul's message of suffering, sacrifice, and voluntary servitude. Since Paul himself had never been a slave and had a somewhat privileged background, it is very likely that he was oblivious to how his message of voluntary servitude played to an audience of slaves, former slaves, and descendants of slaves, who knew all too well the pains of social death associated with slavery.[16]

It is, unfortunately, likely that Paul's failure to consider this difference in social location between himself, an educated Roman citizen of means and privilege, and the typi-cal Corinthian, someone familiar with the oppression and the marginality of slavery, contributed to the rejection of his message by the Corinthians. Paul made the grave mistake of assuming that his interpretation of the gospel, which was shaped by his privileged position within Roman society, was the only acceptable interpretation (cf. Gal 1:6-9).

While the middle-class black church has always played a prominent role within the black community, one of the reasons why its effectiveness is decreasing among the black underclass is a comparable failure to consider how its message plays to that audience. The church's preaching and biblical interpretation often emphasize the black middle-class experience. In so doing, the church alienates those whose experiences and social reality are drastically different, thereby failing to provide hope, deliverance, and empowerment where they are often most needed.

Paul was also criticized for refusing to accept financial support from the Corinthians, which Paul's opponents suggested was an indication of his lack of love for the Corinthians, especially since he had accepted support from other churches. Despite Paul's claim that he did not want to burden the Corinthians and his accusation that the "false apostles" were taking advantage of them (11:20), the Corinthians believed that Paul's repeated boasting about supporting himself made them look bad. They also considered Paul's refusal to accept financial support from them a sign of disrespect.

Although Paul is often considered the patriarch of American Christianity, it is the Jesus, spirit, and gospel proclaimed by his opponents—those "false apostles, deceitful workers," ministers of Satan—that resonate with much of the preaching of contemporary American Christianity. Afflictions, sufferings, humility, and self-sacrifice are often considered signs of weakness and are rarely promoted by contemporary preachers. Many of the most popular preachers are charismatic, eloquent, and articulate. They preach a gospel of success and prosperity—supposedly reflective of the resurrection power of God in Christ. Weakness and suffering are disassociated with a powerful God. The power of God at work among God's people is manifested in outward signs of wealth, strength, and eloquence. This "power-tripping" runs contrary to the paradoxical nature of Paul's message of "power through weakness" (2 Cor 12:8-10). For Paul, affliction and suffering are essential components of apostolic ministry, because they represent the apostle's participation in the suffering and death of Jesus. Without sharing in the weakness of suffering, there is no sharing in the power of resurrection (cf. Rom 6:5; Phil 3:10-11).

Despite the fact that Paul's message of suffering was most likely distorted by his opponents and has often been used by those in power to promote passive acquiescence to evil, Paul does not expect his believers to play the part of passive victims. The sufferer is an active agent for justice. Those who suffered during the civil rights movement were not passive victims; they were agents for justice. Those who suffered in South Africa to end apartheid were not passive victims; they were agents for justice. The suffering that Paul refers to is "redemptive suffering"—suffering that the sufferer chooses to endure as a result of his or her actions for the redemption, liberation, and well-being of others. Paul chooses—and even welcomes—this type of suffering (2 Cor 12:10; cf. Rom 5:3). He also encourages the Corinthians to do likewise (1 Cor 4:11-16).

11:16-33, A Better Apostle than His Opponents

Feeling as though he has no choice but to stoop to the level of his opponents, Paul goes against his own convictions and engages in the foolish act of boasting. He does, however, turn the act of boasting upside down by boasting of things the Corinthians and his opponents consider shameful.

He begins by boasting that he, unlike his opponents, is "too weak" to financially exploit and take advantage of the Corinthians. Paul considers his rivals to be nothing more than charlatans who tell the Corinthians what they want to hear in order to take advantage of them (2:17). Paul asserts that his purpose is to serve the Corinthians rather than to burden them (11:9).

While his opponents boast of their lineage and pedigree, Paul informs the Corinthians that he possesses the same impeccable credentials. Those credentials, however, are not a source of pride and arrogance for him. They do not cause him to lose sight of the fact that being a "minister of Christ" is always about service and self-sacrifice for the well-being of others.

In graduate school I once overheard students and professors ridiculing a former student who decided to accept a call to pastor a small, poor inner-city church. They asserted that his decision was a waste of a graduate degree from an Ivy League institution. The former student, however, realized that impeccable credentials do not alter the purpose of ministry. Being a minister of Christ is always about service and self-sacrifice. Dr. Martin Luther King Jr. realized as much when he left the ivory towers of academia and took his Boston University Ph.D. to the streets of the segregated South to experience suffering analogous to that described here by Paul.[17]

The service and sacrifices of Paul and King are not the service and sacrifices that all Christians are called to make. Service and sacrifice can be manifested in many ways, and can take place in many venues—in the academy as well as the church. Paul's words should not be used to limit the many ways and many venues in which ministry occurs. Instead, they should remind the reader that service and self-sacrifice rather than selfish ambition, pride, and arrogance lie at the heart of Christian ministry.

12:1-10, Visions and Revelations

Paul talks about his visions and revelations in the third person because, although he wants the Corinthians to be aware that he, like his rivals, has experienced spiritual visions and revelations, he also wants to distance himself from such phenomena. Paul feels he has been forced to enter the debate on his opponents' terms (v. 11). His opponents engage in self-praise and boast about spiritual signs of power and authority. For many in Corinth, life in Christ is attested by spiritual gifts (1 Cor 12). Paul is accused of lacking spiritual gifts and acting "according to the flesh" (10:2; 1:17), and he responds by appealing to his own visions and revelations. However, he avoids using such visions and revelations as indicators of his apostleship. According to Paul, because visions and revelations often serve as a source of pride and arrogance, they get in the way of genuine ministry. Evidence of a life lived in committed and faithful service to God and others is what attests to apostleship. Paul, therefore, boasts of his "weaknesses, insults, hardships, persecutions, and calamities," all of which attest to his committed and faithful service to God and the Corinthians.

The NRSV translates Paul's statement, "Therefore *I am content* with weaknesses . . . ," which should actually read, "Therefore *I delight* in weaknesses. . . ." Paul has not merely resigned himself to accepting ministerial hardships; he actually delights in hardship because he understands that in his weakness the power of God is made manifest. In his weakened state of suffering he is strong, because the strength of his sacrifices contributes to the liberation and empowerment of others.

Paul's suffering is not simply imposed upon him. His suffering results from his choice to live a life of love for and accountability to others (see the comments on 11:1-15). In the late eighteenth century a freeborn African American abolitionist named John Marrant preached that a black exodus to Africa and the restoration of a pure and covenanted black community in their Zion were elements of God's divine plan. Marrant labored hard and endured much suffering to secure the fulfillment of this providential exodus. He exhorted other African Americans to join with him by encouraging them to welcome the suffering they would endure for the fulfillment of God's plan that would deliver all African Americans, declaring, "I take pleasure in infirmities, in reproaches, in necessities, in persecutions, in distress for Christ's sake: for when I am weak, then I am strong."[18]

12:11-13, Signs of a True Apostle

Paul brings his "fool's speech" to an end (11:1—12:13). It is clear from both his speech and his conclusion that charismatic phenomena are considered signs of apostolic authority. Although Paul indicates in other letters that his ministry is accompanied by signs and wonders (Rom 15:18-19; Gal 3:1-5), throughout his fool's speech he minimizes the importance of such phenomena as proof of apostolic authority. It appears that for the Corinthians, charismatic phenomena have become the most important factor in determining authority (cf. 1 Cor 12–14).

While it is unclear exactly what happened in Corinth involving Paul, the Corinthians, and Paul's opponents, it is obvious that all of the parties feel offended. Paul feels he has been betrayed. The Corinthians are initially impressed and persuaded by the ministry of their founder (2 Cor 14; 1 Cor 4:14-16). Over the course of time, however, rival apostles enters Corinth, and the Corinthians become more impressed with them. The Corinthians are offended because they feel Paul has disrespected them by not accepting financial assistance from them (11:7-11). They also suspect that the collection for the poor in Jerusalem (8:1—9:15) is nothing more than a way for Paul to get money for himself from the Corinthians without acknowledging a debt to them (12:16-18). While Paul gives no insight into the feelings of his opponents, they surely must have been offended by the title "super-apostles" and by being labeled "false apostles, deceitful workers," and ministers of Satan (11:13-15).

The situation in Corinth reveals the destructive dangers associated with comparing ministries. Such comparisons are often based on the false assumption that there is only one correct way of doing things: my way is right, and everyone else is wrong. Such an assumption leads to hurt feelings, division, and animosity within the church (12:20; cf. 1 Cor 1:10-13). As Paul points out elsewhere, there is diversity within the church, and that diversity is needed for the church to function properly (1 Cor 12:12-31; Rom 12:3-8). There was most likely room in Corinth for the gifts of Paul and those of the so-called "false apostles," had the well-being of the community genuinely been the primary concern.

12:14-18, Allegations of Financial Wrongdoing

Despite the Corinthians' feelings regarding Paul's refusal to accept financial assistance from them (11:7-11; 12:13), Paul still is not willing to accept assistance on his next visit. Paul considers this refusal to be a sign of both his love for and his responsibility to the congregations he has founded (cf. 1 Thess 2:9; 2 Thess 3:7-9). The Corinthians, however, allege that Paul's collection for the poor in Jerusalem (8:1—9:15) is nothing more than a way for Paul to get money for himself from

the Corinthians without acknowledging a debt to them.

Accusations of financial mismanagement by church leaders are not new. Despite the tendency to romanticize the past, there has not been a marked decline of integrity among church leaders. Like many contemporary church leaders, the apostle Paul and the "super-apostles" were both accused of financial wrongdoing (11:20; 2:17a). While it is impossible to say anything about the validity of either charge, Paul's response emphasizes the importance and necessity of implementing procedures that diminish all appearances of impropriety (cf. 2 Cor 8:16-22). Contemporary church leaders also need to take the time to find out how practices are perceived by their congregations.

12:19—13:4, Paul's Motive and Final Warning

Fearing his motives might be interpreted as self-serving, Paul informs the Corinthians that he is not motivated merely by a desire to defend himself or to prove he is better than his opponents. He is motivated by a concern for the Corinthians. His objective is to build up the community by provoking repentance and preventing a recurrence of what took place during a previous visit (cf. 2 Cor 2:1-4).

Paul hopes that the harshness of his letter will prevent him from having to be harsh when he arrives in Corinth for his third visit (cf. 2 Cor 7:8-12). Despite the accusations that he projects strength in his letters but is actually weak in person (2 Cor 10:10), Paul conveys that he can and will be harsh if necessary.

Many in Corinth equated Paul's weaknesses with an absence of power and authority. Paul, however, advocated a power-in-weakness model (2 Cor 12:9). God's power is manifested through human weakness. Just as God demonstrated resurrection power in the midst of the crucifixion, God will demonstrate power in the midst of Paul's weaknesses when dealing with the Corinthians.

When I entered the ministry, a seasoned minister once told me, "Never let the people see you sweat." Many religious leaders pretend to be "super-apostles," refusing to allow the presence of weakness to crack their facade of physical strength because they are afraid that members of their congregations, like the Corinthians, will equate their weaknesses with a lack of power and spiritual authority. There unfortunately will always be those who equate weakness with a lack of authority and power. According to Paul, however, divine—not human—strength is what really matters. When faith is placed in God, human weakness is the arena for divine strength. To deny weakness is to prevent space for the power of God to be manifested. As God revealed to Paul, "My grace is sufficient for you, for power is made perfect in weakness" (2 Cor 12:9).

13:5-10, Paul's Purpose in Writing

Paul suggests that the ultimate indicator of divine authority and approval is the impact of one's ministry on the lives of others. If Jesus Christ is present and active in the lives of the Corinthians, then God must be at work in Paul's ministry since it is Paul who first came and preached Jesus to them (2 Cor 10:14; cf. 1 Cor 4:15). Paul's prayer and desire are for the spiritual strength and maturity of the Corinthians, even if their strength makes Paul appear weak.

Virtually all of the young men and women I grew up with who made it to college were raised by parents who did not attend college. Many of our parents never even finished high school. Our parents struggled, suffered, and worked long hours to provide us with opportunities they never had. Many of us are now strong, successful professionals. While most of us realize that our "strength" is a direct result of their "weakness," there are some who, as a result of their strength, are now ashamed of their parents' weakness.

A true indicator of strength is one's ability and willingness to labor, struggle, and even suffer not merely for one's own personal well-being but also for the well-being of those in need. Paul understands that the proof of his apostolic strength and authority is not found in personal trappings of rhetorical eloquence and charismatic gifts; instead the proof of his strength and authority is revealed by the presence of Christ in his congregations. The Corinthians fail to understand that the presence of Christ about which they boast is a direct result of the personal suffering Paul has chosen to endure (cf. 2 Cor 10:7). Paul chooses to appear weak for the sake of "building up" the Corinthians (v. 10; cf. 10:8; 12:19; 1 Cor 14:26; 3:10) because he understands his relationship with them to reflect the relationship between Christ and the world: through weakness and suffering on behalf of the poor, the power and salvation of God are revealed.

13:11-13, Concluding Exhortations and Benediction

Paul concludes in customary fashion with final exhortations. Throughout 2 Corinthians, Paul has emphasized that God's power is present within social contexts that are congruent with the ways of God. God's power and authority are present in Paul's ministry of sacrificial suffering because it was in the context of the cross of Christ that God revealed God's power and authority. Paul asserts that the God of love and peace is present in the midst of people who strive for and live in peace. This was the theological rationale at the heart of Martin Luther King's nonviolent resistance movement.

A common Pauline exhortation is the exhortation to "greet one another with a holy kiss" (Rom 16:16; 1 Cor 16:20; 2 Cor 13:12;

1 Thess 5:26). Paul's urban Christian congregations were comprised of extremely diverse social groups. This diversity led to much of the division within the Corinthian community (1 Cor 1:10-17). Paul's instruction for members to greet each other with a kiss is an attempt to foster within the body of Christ the love of God that promotes full acceptance and fellowship among all people. The kiss is a symbolic reminder of God's love (cf. 1 Pet 5:14).

While the church should be a place of love and acceptance, there are those in the church who, for whatever reason, refuse to speak to particular people. If they refuse to speak to someone, they surely are not about to greet that person with a kiss. Paul's exhortation, however, was to greet "each other" with a kiss. The exhortation was not simply to greet those individuals we like or get along with. The inability to greet a brother or sister with a kiss often signals an obstacle to peace and unity that needs to be overcome. A "holy kiss" can serve as a challenge to the social reality of racial, ethnic, class, and gender division by promoting—as well as providing a symbol of—an alternative social reality of love, peace, and acceptance.

Notes

1. For a critique of the role biblical texts as well as black spiritual traditions and biblical interpretations play in the ongoing construction of cultural identity, see Farah J. Griffin, "Adventures of a Black Child in Search of Her God: The Bible in the Works of Me'Shell N'Degeocello," in *African Americans and the Bible: Sacred Texts and Social Textures*, ed. Vincent L. Wimbush (New York: Continuum, 2001), 773–81.

2. See 1 Cor 7:21-24; Eph 6:5-8; Col 3:22-25; Titus 2:9-10 (cf. 1 Pet 2:18-21). According to Howard Thurman, his grandmother, who was a former slave, refused to allow him to read any of the Pauline letters to her because during the days of slavery white ministers would read from Paul and preach that slavery was God's will and that if slaves were good and obedient God would bless them. She promised that if she ever gained her freedom she would never read Paul's letters (Howard Thurman, *Jesus and the Disinherited* [Nashville: Abingdon, 1949], 30–31).

3. Richard Allen, *The Life, Experience and Gospel Labors of the Rt. Rev. Richard Allen*, ed. George A. Singleton (New York: Abingdon, 1960).

4. For an examination of black-Jewish relations and the misconceptions and misperceptions associated with those relations, see V. P. Franklin et al., eds., *African Americans and Jews in the Twentieth Century: Studies in Convergence and Conflict* (Columbia: University of Missouri Press, 1998).

5. See Albert J. Raboteau, *Slave Religion: The "Invisible Institution" in the Antebellum South* (New York: Oxford University Press, 1978), and Dwight N. Hopkins, *Down, Up, and Over: Slave Religion and Black Theology* (Minneapolis: Fortress Press, 2000).

6. While the black church opposed slavery and rejected the use of biblical passages endorsing slavery as justification for slavery, the black church frequently used and continues to use biblical passages promoting female subordination and inferiority as justification for denying women authority and leadership roles in the church; see Clarice J. Martin, "The *Haustafeln* (Household Codes) in African American Biblical Interpretation: 'Free Slaves' and 'Subordinate Women,'" in *Stony the Road We Trod: African American Biblical Interpretation*, ed. Cain Hope Felder (Minneapolis: Fortress Press, 1991), 206–31.

7. See Brian K. Blount, *Then the Whisper Put on Flesh: New Testament Ethics in an African American Context* (Nashville: Abingdon, 2001), 185–91. For an examination of the implications this has for a Christian understanding of sexual orientation, see Blount's "Reading versus Understanding: Text Interpretation and Homosexuality," in *Homosexuality: Conversations in a Christian Community*, ed.

C. Leong Seow (Louisville: Westminster John Knox, 1996), 28–83.

8. James Cone shook the foundations of Christian theology in 1970 when he identified the black experience with God's experience and declared, "God is Black" and "Jesus is the black Christ"; *A Black Theology of Liberation*, twentieth anniversary ed. (New York: Orbis, 1990), 55–81, 121.

9. Martin Luther King Jr., *Strength to Love* (Philadelphia: Fortress Press, 1981), 94.

10. In *Troubling Biblical Waters: Race, Class, and Family* (Maryknoll, N.Y.: Orbis, 1989), 162, Cain Hope Felder asserts, "The essence of Paul's 'ministry of reconciliation' is the removal of barriers imposed by the world that alienate people from God. The ministry of reconciliation recruits persons from broken households and brings them into the Household of God. Thus, while Paul envisions God's reconciling activity as opening new possibilities for Jews and Gentiles as people of God, the ministry of reconciliation has the wider purpose of reconciling humanity as a family in the Household of God."

11. "I Have a Dream" is perhaps the best-known and most-quoted address by Dr. King. It was delivered before the Lincoln Memorial on 28 August 1963 as the keynote address of the March on Washington, D.C. The speech is often credited with prompting the 1964 Civil Rights Act.

12. "Operation Offset" was the name given by the House Republican Study Committee, a group of conservative Republicans in the House of Representatives, to the $543 billion spending-cut plan they proposed to offset the cost of the Hurricane Katrina "relief and reconstruction effort" of the Gulf Coast.

13. For an examination of the economic impact of black churches within black communities, see C. Eric Lincoln and Lawrence H. Mamiya, *The Black Church in the African American Experience* (Durham, N.C.: Duke University Press, 1990), 236–73. Many of the so-called black megachurches have annual revenue in the millions. According to Mel Duvall and

Kim S. Nash, "World Changers Church: Know Thy Customer," *Baseline* 1 (December 6, 2005): 38–49, World Changer Ministries had annual revenue exceeding $80 million in 2005 (3 March 2006, http://www.baselinemag.com/article2/0,1540,1896787,00.asp) For an insider's perspective into the black megachurch phenomenon, read Milmon F. Harrison, *Righteous Riches: The Word of Faith Movement in Contemporary African American Religion* (Oxford: Oxford University Press, 2005).

14. Martin Luther King Jr., "Our God Is Marching On!" in *A Testament of Hope: The Essential Writings and Speeches of Martin Luther King, Jr.* ed. James M. Washington (San Francisco: Harper & Row, 1986), 230.

15. At present, very little research on the suburbanization of the black church has been conducted. The question of how the outmigration of middle-class blacks is changing the face of religion in urban America is examined by Gerald D. Jaynes and Robin M. Williams, eds., *A Common Destiny: Blacks and American Society* (Washington, D.C.: National Academy, 1989). See also Hamil Harris, "Growing in Glory," *Emerge* (April 1997): 49–53, and Harrison, *Righteous Riches*.

16. See Orlando Patterson, *Slavery and Social Death: A Comparative Study* (Cambridge, Mass.: Harvard University Press, 1982).

17. For an examination of the role education played in the shaping of King's ministry, see James H. Cone, *Martin and Malcolm and America* (Maryknoll, N.Y.: Orbis, 1991), 19–37.

18. John Saillant, "Origins of African American Biblical Hermeneutics in Eighteenth-Century Black Opposition," in *African Americans and the Bible*, 247.

For Further Reading

Allen, Richard. *The Life, Experience and Gospel Labors of the Rt. Rev. Richard Allen.* Edited by George A. Singleton. New York: Abingdon, 1960.

Blount, Brian K. "Reading versus Understanding: Text Interpretation and Homosexuality." Pages 28–83 in *Homosexuality: Conversations in a Christian Community*. Edited by C. Leong Seow. Louisville: Westminster John Knox, 1996.

———. *Then the Whisper Put on Flesh: New Testament Ethics in an African American Context*. Nashville: Abingdon, 2001.

Cone, James. *A Black Theology of Liberation*. twentieth anniv. ed. New York: Orbis, 1990.

Felder, Cain Hope. *Troubling Biblical Waters: Race, Class, and Family*. Maryknoll, N.Y.: Orbis, 1989.

Hopkins, Dwight N. *Down, Up, and Over: Slave Religion and Black Theology*. Minneapolis: Fortress Press, 2000.

King, Martin Luther Jr. *Strength to Love*. Philadelphia: Fortress Press, 1981.

Lincoln, C. Eric, and Lawrence H. Mamiya. *The Black Church in the African American Experience*. Durham, N.C.: Duke University Press, 1990.

Martin, Clarice J. "The *Haustafeln* (Household Codes) in African American Biblical Interpretation: 'Free Slaves' and 'Subordinate Women.'" Pages 206–31 in *Stony the Road We Trod: African American Biblical Interpretation*. Edited by Cain Hope Felder. Minneapolis: Fortress Press, 1991.

Raboteau, Albert J. *Slave Religion: The "Invisible Institution" in the Antebellum South*. New York: Oxford University Press, 1978.

Saillant, John. "Origins of African American Biblical Hermeneutics in Eighteenth-Century Black Opposition." Pages 236–50 in *African Americans and the Bible: Sacred Texts and Social Textures*. Edited by Vincent L. Wimbush. New York: Continuum, 2001.

Shopshire, James M. "The Bible as Informant and Reflector in Social-Structural Relationships of African Americans." Pages 123–37 in *African Americans and the Bible: Sacred Texts and Social Textures*, ed. Vincent L. Wimbush. New York: Continuum, 2001.

Thurman, Howard. *Jesus and the Disinherited*. Nashville: Abingdon, 1949.

Wimbush, Vincent L., ed. *African Americans and the Bible: Sacred Texts and Social Textures*. New York: Continuum, 2001.

Faces of Roman Africa

1. Funeral portrait of a young man. Egyptian-Roman period, mid-second century C.E. Tempera on wood. From Fayum, Egypt. 31.6 x 20.6 cm. Kunsthistorisches Museum, Vienna, Austria. Photo: © Erich Lessing / Art Resource, N.Y.

2. Funeral portrait of a bearded man. Egypt, Roman period, 125–250 C.E. Encaustic wax painting on beech-wood. Musée des Beaux-Arts, Dijon, France. Photo: © Erich Lessing / Art Resource, N.Y.

3. Funeral portrait of a man. Fayum. Ca. 193–235 C.E. (Severan dynasty). Encaustic on wood, 33.0 x 18.5 cm. Inv. P210(N2732). Louvre, Paris. Photo: Gérard Blot, © Réunion des Musées Nationaux /Art Resource, N.Y.

4. Mummy portrait of a young woman with gold earrings. Hawara, Egypt, first century C.E. Encaustic, 32.5 x 21.8 cm. Inv. 10974.Aegyptisches Museum, Staatliche Museen zu Berlin. Photo: © Bildarchiv Preussischer Kulturbesitz / Art Resource, N.Y.

5. By "Africa" Romans referred to the northern edge of the continent. (The name probably derived from the *Afri* peoples around Carthage, whom Josephus related to the biblical figure Epher in Genesis 25:4: *Antiquities* 1.239-41). The region beyond was known to them only dimly, through garbled reports of Greek and Roman travelers passed along by Herodotus (430 B.C.E.), Eratosthenes (200 B.C.E.), or Strabo (22 C.E.). The Romans were well aware of other peoples beyond their own borders, however, referring to the kingdoms of the *Nobotae* (Nubians) centered in Meroe, with whom they occasionally skirmished according to Strabo, and to "Ethiopians" (a Greek term apparently used generally for "blacks").

The modern tendency to think of "Bible lands" as including the northern Mediterranean and the "Middle East" (a term first coined in the twentieth century), but not Africa, results in part from the failure to recognize that biblical placenames like Egypt, Cyrene, and Libya are African. Even Palestine is geologically a part of Africa (the land to the west of the Jordan River valley, including Jerusalem, sits on the African continental plate, while land to the east is on a different plate, the Arabo-Nubian, as indicated in the map and inset.)

Another cause may be Luke's portrayal, in the Acts of the Apostles, of the spread of the gospel in an arc from Jerusalem to Syria, then Asia Minor, then Greece, and at last Rome. Luke specifies that Jews from Mesopotamia, Egypt, Libya, and Arabia were present at Pentecost (Acts 2:8-11), that Philip baptized a high-ranking Ethiopian official (8:26-39), and that an Alexandrian named Apollos had somehow been "instructed in the Way of the Lord" (18:24-25: by whom?). But Luke gives no attention to the spread of the gospel in these African lands, even though travel to and from those regions, by sea or by land, was a matter of routine under the Pax Romana.

Alexandria was a thriving center of Christian scholarship in the second century. Fervent devotion characterized African Christians throughout successive waves of imperial persecution. Unfortunately, Luke's comparative neglect of Africa has contributed, in part, to a myopic Eurocentrism in later Christian tradition.

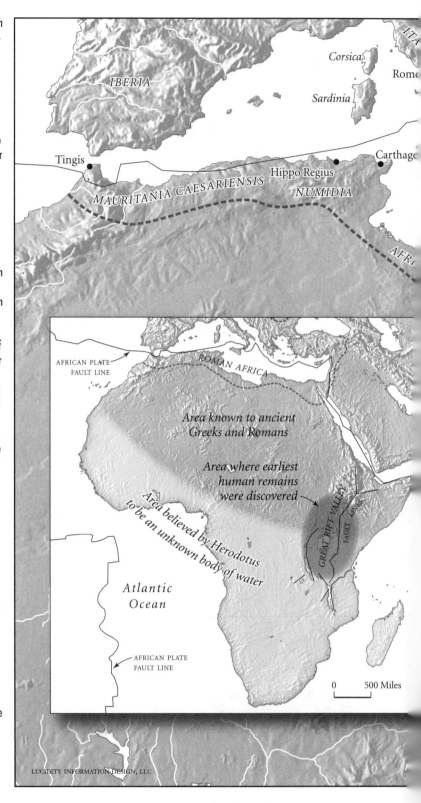

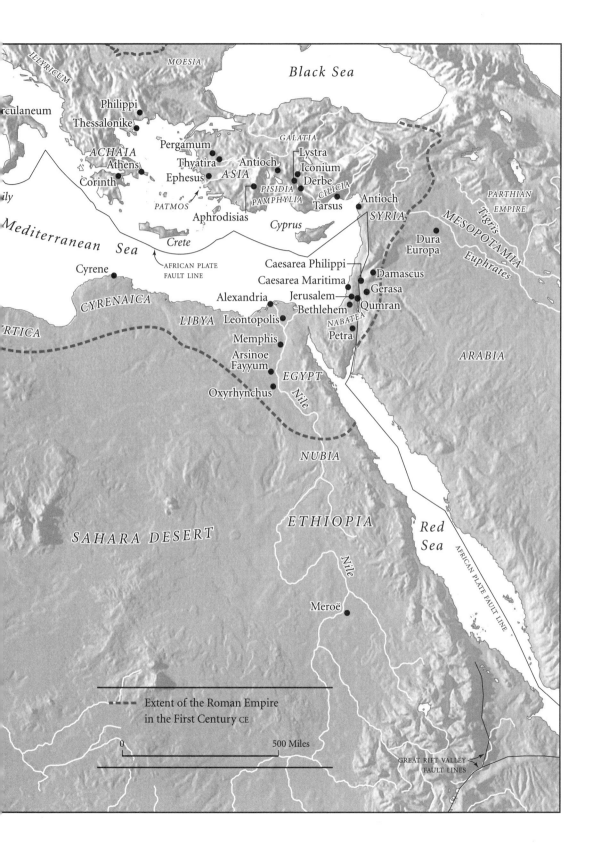

ILLYRICUM

MOESIA

Black Sea

rculaneum

Philippi

Thessalonike

GALATIA

Pergamum

Lystra

Thyatira

Antioch

Iconium

ACHAIA

Athens

Ephesus

ASIA

Derbe

Corinth

PISIDIA

CILICIA

PAMPHYLIA

Tarsus

Antioch

PATMOS

Aphrodisias

Cyprus

SYRIA

PARTHIAN
EMPIRE

Crete

MESOPOTAMIA

Tigris

Mediterranean   Sea

AFRICAN PLATE
FAULT LINE

Dura
Europa

Euphrates

Caesarea Philippi

Cyrene

Caesarea Maritima

Damascus

RTICA

CYRENAICA

Alexandria

Gerasa

LIBYA

Jerusalem

Qumran

Leontopolis

Bethlehem

NABATEA

ARABIA

Memphis

Petra

Arsinoe
Fayyum

EGYPT

Oxyrhynchus

Nile

NUBIA

SAHARA DESERT

ETHIOPIA

Red
Sea

AFRICAN PLATE FAULT LINE

Nile

Meroë

- - - Extent of the Roman Empire
in the First Century CE

0   500 Miles

GREAT RIFT VALLEY
FAULT LINES

6. The Roman theater in Alexandria. Hellenized Africa was a center of philosophical and literary culture, and home to the largest Jewish population in the Roman empire. Ethnicity, class, and religion were intertwined in complex ways: when some Jews sued for recognition as citizens of Alexandria in 38 C.E., one of their motives was to be distinguished from the non-Greek population and thus freed, as Greek citizens were, from Roman taxes. Photo: © Art Resource, N.Y.

7. Throughout the first century c.e. the corn of Egypt was a vital mainstay of the Roman imperial economy, tightly controlled from Rome. African culture captured the Roman imagination as well. Here a ceremony of the highly esteemed religion of Isis is depicted in a fresco from a private home in Pompeii. Isis had been honored for millennia as the deity guaranteeing life and fertility in the Nile valley; in the Roman era she was widely worshiped as a personal savior as well. Museo Archeologico Nazionale, Naples. Photo: © Erich Lessing / Art Resource, N.Y.

8. The ibis, the sacred bird of the Isis cult, is represented in another fresco from Pompeii with lotus flowers on its head and ears of corn in its beak, suggesting the bounty of the African god. Museo Archeologico Nazionale, Naples. Photo: © Erich Lessing / Art Resource, N.Y.

9. Portrait of a boy. Egypt, Roman period, fourth century C.E. Canvas on fig-wood, painted stucco. Louvre, Paris. Photo: © Erich Lessing /Art Resource, N.Y.

10. Greco-Roman sculpture of a young black slave. Though often minimized in contemporary classical and biblical studies, Roman slavery was ubiquitous, essential to the Roman economy, and routinely brutal. Second to third century C.E. From Aphrodisias, Turkey. Black marble, 60 cm high. Louvre, Paris. Photo: Hervé Lewandowski, © Réunion des Musées Nationaux /Art Resource, N.Y.

11. The philosopher Seneca, one of the richest men in Rome and an adviser to the emperor Nero, wrote that "we Romans are excessively haughty, cruel, and insulting" to slaves (*Moralia* 47.1). Roman herm of Seneca, first half of third century C.E. Marble, h. 28 cm. Inv. Sk 39, Antikensammlung, Staatliche Museen zu Berlin. Photo: Johannes Laurentius, © Bildarchiv Preussischer Kulturbesitz /Art Resource, N.Y.

12. Slave necklace with bulla bearing Latin inscription reading, in part, "Fugitive . . . Bring me back to my master. . . ." Roman bronze. Museo Nazionale Romano (Terme di Diocleziano), Rome. Photo: © Scala/Art Resource, N.Y.

13. An actor wears a comic mask depicting a slave, a stock character in Greek and Roman comedy. Slave characters provided "comic relief" in literature as well—as the slave Rhoda does in the Book of Acts (13:13-15). Pompeiian fresco. Museo Archeologico Nazionale, Naples. Photo: © Scala/Art Resource, N.Y.

Images of Subjugation

14. The Roman empire represented its power through images of conquered people. Here, the left pedestal of the so-called "Façade of the Captives" in Corinth depicts mourning women, bewildered children, and helmets and shields as collected trophies. The right pedestal (not shown) held the figure of Victory and a man in bonds, possibly referring to the emperor Septimius Severus's victory over the Parthians in the second century C.E. Corinth Museum Inv. No. 175. Photo: *Cities of Paul* © 2004, The President and Fellows of Harvard College.

15. Similarly, after Rome put down the Jewish revolt of 66–70 C.E., the conqueror, now emperor, Vespasian (69–79 C.E.) struck coins bearing the inscription *Judea Capta* ("Judea is vanquished"), representing the Jewish people as a subjugated woman. Bronze. Israel Museum, Jerusalem. Photo: © Erich Lessing / Art Resource, N.Y.

16. Roman imagery represented other conquered nations as helpless women as well, overpowered by Roman might. Here the emperor Claudius subdues Britannia, personified as a woman. Photo © New York University/Institute of Fine Arts Excavations at Aphrodisias.

17. The emperor Nero is depicted subjugating the nation of Armenia; from the Sebasteion in Aphrodisias. Photo © New York University / Institute of Fine Arts Excavations at Aphrodisias.

Español con India.
Mestizo.

Mestizo con Española.
Castizo.

Castizo con Española.
Español.

Español con Negra.
Mulato.

5

6

7

Mulato con Española.
Morisco.

Morisco con Española.
Chino.

Chino con India.
Salta atras.

Salta atras con Mulata.
Lobo.

9

10

11

12

Lobo con China.
Gibaro.

Gibaro con Mulata.
Albarazado.

Albarazado con Negra.
Canbujo.

Canbujo con India.
Sanbaigo.

13

14

15

16

Sanbaigo con Loba.
Calpamulato.

Calpamulato con Canbuja.
Tente en el Aire.

Tente en el Aire con Mulata.
Note entiendo.

Note entiendo con India.
Tornaatras.

18. Though Rome represented imperial power through depictions of conquered nations, the conception that races were inherently superior or inferior to one another is the relatively recent invention of European and Euro-American culture. This pseudoscientific catalog of racial combinations comes from eighteenth-century Spanish America. Anonymous: *Las Castas* (The Races). Oil on canvas; 1.04 x 1.48 m. Museo Nacional del Virreinato, Tepotzotlan, Mexico. Photo: © Schalkwijk /Art Resource, N.Y.

19. The apostle Paul remains a controversial figure in African American interpretation: his own letters and the Book of Acts emphasize his experience of Christ, but other writings appearing over his name not only accept, but reinforce the social conventions of slavery. Historically, African American interpreters have often tended to discount or marginalize these passages. *Conversion of St. Paul* by Michelangelo Merisi da Caravaggio (1573–1610). S. Maria del Popolo, Rome, Italy. Photo: © Scala / Art Resource, N.Y.

20. This late third-century Christian fresco depicts Moses bringing forth water from the rock—taken in early Christianity as a type of Christ and Christian baptism. (Paul links these themes in 1 Corinthians 10:1-40.) Such figural and typological interpretation of the Bible has been a powerful resource in African American spirituality as well, for example, in the nineteenth-century spirituals sung by African slaves in the United States. Chamber of the Four Seasons, Catacomb of SS. Marcellino e Pietro, Rome. Photo: © Scala/Art Resource, N.Y.

21. Paul regarded his imprisonments and beatings at the hands of civil magistrates as his apostolic credentials. The theme resurfaced powerfully in Martin Luther King Jr.'s nonviolent resistance. In Paul's day, rejection and punishment could be regarded as the sign of a teacher of truth; for example, here the philosopher Socrates is depicted preparing for his death after being condemned by the Athenian council for "corrupting the youth" with his teaching. First-century fresco from a villa in Ephesus, Turkey. Ephesus Archaeological Museum. Photo: © Erich Lessing/Art Resource, N.Y.

22. In other early Christian writings, outside our New Testament, Paul was remembered differently: for example, the third-century *Acts of Paul and Thecla* recount his travels with a woman companion of equal authority to his own. This eleventh-century ivory tablet depicts Saint Paul evangelizing Saint Thecla (in a tower of her home). British Museum, London. Photo: © Erich Lessing/Art Resource, N.Y.

. In contrast to their suspicion of passages in letters attributed to Paul that condone slaveholding, African American Christians have often accepted passages encouraging the subordination of women. Women played important leadership roles, however, at least in some early Christian communities. This early Christian fresco depicts scenes from the life of a deceased woman who apparently exercised leadership in her community. Second half of the third century Catacomb of Priscilla, Rome. Photo: © Scala/Art Resource, N.Y.

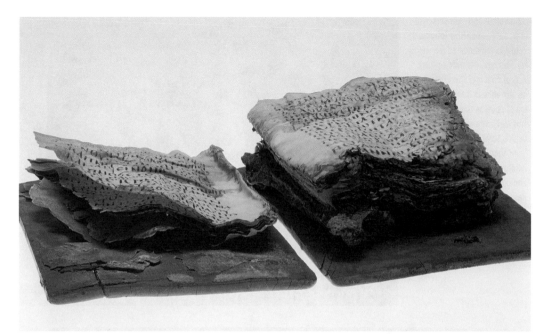

24. Africa was an early home of Christianity. The earliest extant Greek manuscripts of the New Testament come from Egypt. Early Christian writings — including those in our New Testament and others, including the Gospel of Thomas and other writings in the Nag Hammadi Library, and the recently published Gospel of Judas — were translated early on into the native language of Egypt, Coptic. This fifth-century copy of the Acts of the Apostles is written in Sahidic Coptic. MS M.910. The Pierpont Morgan Library, New York, N.Y. Photo: © The Pierpont Morgan Library /Art Resource, N.Y. Used by permission.

25. This book of Gospels (MS M.569) in Sahidic Coptic received its richly designed cover at the Monastery of St. Michael at Hamouli, Fayum, in the seventh or eighth century c.e. Textual variants in Coptic manuscripts of the Gospel of Matthew may indicate an earlier textual tradition than the Greek text represented in our New Testaments. The Pierpont Morgan Library, New York, N.Y. Photo: © The Pierpont Morgan Library /Art Resource, N.Y. Used by permission.

GALATIANS

Brad R. Braxton

INTRODUCTION

In Galatians, a storm brews! Issues of religious and social boundaries swirl at the center of the storm. The apostle Paul established a series of Gentile congregations in the Roman province of Galatia, in the central part of modern-day Turkey. Paul exhorted these Gentiles to recant their idolatrous allegiance to false gods and commit their lives to the God revealed in Jesus Christ.

> Paul likely visited Galatia in 48 or 49 C.E. and wrote Galatians in the early to mid 50s C.E.

After his life-changing encounter with Jesus Christ, Paul began preaching the gospel among the Gentiles, thereby fulfilling his commission to be the "apostle to the Gentiles." Paul proclaimed that Jesus Christ had ushered in a new age with new possibilities. By believing in Jesus Christ, the Galatians could establish a right relationship with God and thus become heirs of eternal blessings. Jesus Christ was central to the gospel Paul proclaimed to the Gentiles.

Although Jesus was a Jew, Paul insisted that faith in Jesus Christ did not obligate Gentiles to convert to Judaism through rituals such as circumcision. The Galatians accepted Paul's gospel and formed Christian congregations. The climate in the Galatian churches, however, soon changed. The winds of a competing interpretation of the gospel blew in a stormy controversy.

After Paul's departure from Galatia, other preachers arrived in the province, declaring a very different message from Paul's. Paul never specifies the identity of these preachers. He suggests that they are "agitating" his converts with distortions of the gospel. The "agitators" considered complete submission to the Jewish law—and rituals set forth therein—as requirements for Gentiles to enter the church.

For Paul, the submission of Gentile Christians to the law constituted a form of slavery. This submission implied that the Galatians could not enjoy the blessings of God's covenant unless they abandoned their ethnic identity and assumed another. If Gentile believers adopted another ethnic identity, they would deny that God had saved them *as Gentiles*.

The letter to the Galatians presents the struggles of certain early Christian communities to define the religious and social boundaries of the church. It grapples with pressing questions such as: What is the nature of the gospel? How does the gospel deal with social identity? Does church membership obligate one to adopt a particular social identity?

The relationship between this ancient letter and contemporary African American communities is fascinating. Paul struggled to liberate the Galatians from the slavery of adopting another ethnicity in order to be included in the church. Many African Americans still struggle with mental slavery—the belief that they must become "white" in order to access the blessings of the culture or church. The following interpretation of Galatians offers to contemporary readers—and especially African Americans—a manifesto of freedom. Manumission from the mental slavery that has impeded African American progress is possible.[1]

Chapter 1

1:1-5, Introduction

In v. 1 Paul identifies himself as the sender and as an apostle. He qualifies the nature of his apostolic status, asserting that his calling did not come "from people" or "through a person."[2] The agents responsible for Paul's apostolic calling are God and Jesus Christ. Paul immediately introduces his apostolic status, probably in order to re-establish his authority, which might be in jeopardy. Yet, the issue is greater than simply a personal conflict between Paul and the Galatians concerning apostolic authority. What is at stake is the question: What is the nature of the gospel?

Typically, Paul's letters contain a thanksgiving in which he expresses affection for his congregants. Galatians, however, contains no thanksgiving. This omission might indicate Paul's desire to address promptly the serious dilemma posed by a competing interpretation of the gospel.

1:6-24, Paul's Defense of the Gospel

The reader quickly senses Paul's exasperation about circumstances in Galatia. The "defection" of some Galatians from the true gospel to another has amazed Paul. The verb Paul uses to describe the Galatians' "defection" (*metatithēmi*) carries the connotation of soldiers abandoning their comrades.

In v. 7 we receive our first significant glimpse into the situation occasioning this letter. There are persons in Galatia "agitating" Paul's converts with alternative interpretations of the gospel of Jesus Christ. The "agitators" may be Jewish Christian missionaries who entered Galatia after Paul's initial evangelistic campaign. They consider full submission to the Jewish law a requirement for church membership.

In 1:6-10, Paul adamantly reminds the Galatians of the nature of the true gospel. In these few verses, Paul employs the word "gospel" multiple times. Rather than defend his apostolic calling, Paul defends the gospel that he proclaims. Paul's invocation of curses upon any who would distort the gospel demonstrates the severity of the situation for him (1:8-9).

In 1:11-24 Paul provides details about his life before and after his apostolic calling. He supplies these details to underscore the radical transformation the gospel created in him. Before encountering Christ, Paul was an enthusiastic adherent of Judaism (1:13-14). He excelled in the observances of Judaism far beyond his contemporaries. Zeal for the ancestral faith manifested itself in his extreme persecution of those who believed the gospel of Christ. After his calling, to which he alludes in 1:15-16, he proclaimed the gospel of Christ. Employing language reminiscent of the prophetic calling of Jeremiah (Jer 1:5), Paul depicts his calling as a revelatory event in which he was commissioned specifically to proclaim Christ among the Gentiles.

Paul legitimizes his gospel by declaring that Christ delivered it directly to him. Furthermore, Paul claims that he consulted no one immediately after his revelatory experience with Christ. Only after a three-year period did Paul visit with two of the leading apostles in Jerusalem, Peter and James, the brother of the Lord.

Paul concludes this section by rehearsing the reactions of Christians to the news of his calling. The report was circulating: "The one formerly persecuting us now proclaims the faith that he was formerly trying to destroy" (1:23). So potent was Paul's experience with Christ that it changed a persecutor of Christians to a Christian proclaimer.

Paul's evangelical zeal—his intense commitment to the gospel—emerges clearly in Galatians 1. The gospel is a key theme in 1:11-24. In v. 11, Paul emphatically mentions the gospel. Then, in v. 23 he uses a verb containing the word "gospel." The verb that the NRSV renders "proclaim" (*euangelizomai*) also means "to preach the gospel." This section both begins and concludes with the gospel.

African American Christians can learn much from Paul's passionate concern for the gospel. Too frequently in African American churches, secondary matters stir the passion of ministers and parishioners, while primary theological issues receive little attention. For instance, some African American congregations expend much energy discussing their construction and renovation projects, personality conflicts among church leaders, and the church constitution and by-laws. How much stronger would our congregations be if ministers and parishioners regularly engaged in passionate, thoughtful conversations about the nature of the gospel?

We live in an age where the television has become the arbiter of truth. Many African American Christians seem enamored with any Christian preaching that is televised, regardless of the theological content of the sermons. They fail to realize that not every proclamation that parades itself as the gospel is authentic.

There are many valid interpretations of the gospel. Still, we must hold accountable preachers whose messages promote practices contrary to Christianity. For example, we must courageously criticize preaching that breeds an idolatrous preoccupation with financial prosperity, a selfish abandonment of communal involvement and political responsibility, and an intellectually shallow piety that forgets the command to love God with our *minds*, as well as our hearts and souls.

CHAPTER 2

2:1-10, The Jerusalem Conference

Paul recounts his second trip to Jerusalem, which occurred fourteen years after his initial visit. His missionary colleagues, Barnabas and Titus, traveled with him. Paul was not responding to a summons from the Jerusalem apostles. In v. 2 he declares, "I came [to Jerusalem] according to revelation."

Twice already Paul has spoken about his "revelation" (1:12, 16). By invoking again the concept of revelation in 2:2, Paul emphasizes his direct connection with God. His actions and gospel are grounded in the divine, not human, sphere. Inspired by this revelation, Paul travels to the Jerusalem conference to present his version of the gospel.

The influx of Gentiles into early Christianity has occasioned a dilemma. Should Jewish Christians accept Gentile believers without requiring circumcision? Christian leaders convened at the Jerusalem Conference to address this question.

Paul attempted to create greater unity between the Jewish and Gentile segments of the church by persuading the Jerusalem leaders of the validity of his approach. In 2:6, Paul implies that the Jerusalem leaders did not intimidate him, and he emphatically denies that he needed or wanted their approval. His revelation from Christ and his successful evangelism among the Gentiles supplied all the legitimacy he needed.

According to Paul's report, his persuasive efforts were successful. The Jerusalem leaders validated his approach. These leaders further consented to Paul's approach by not compelling Titus, a Gentile, to be circumcised. At the conclusion of the meeting, Paul and the other leaders agreed to a division of labor—with the Jerusalem leaders evangelizing the Jews with a law-observant gospel, and Paul evangelizing the Gentiles with a gospel free of circumcision. The Jerusalem leaders made only one request of Paul. They asked him to raise a financial collection from his congregations to assist Christians in Jerusalem who were experiencing economic distress. Paul was eager to fulfill this request.

The Jerusalem Conference in Acts

Acts 15 provides another account of the Jerusalem conference:

> Then certain individuals came down from Judea and were teaching the brothers, "Unless you are circumcised according to the custom of Moses, you cannot be saved." And after Paul and Barnabas had no small dissension and debate with them, Paul and Barnabas and some of the others were appointed to go up to Jerusalem to discuss this question with the apostles and the elders. . . . When they came to Jerusalem, they were welcomed by the church and the apostles and the elders, and they reported all that God had done with them. But some believers who belonged to the sect of the Pharisees stood up and said, "It is necessary for them to be circumcised and ordered to keep the law of Moses." The apostles and the elders met together to consider this matter.
>
> —Acts 15:1-6, NRSV

2:11-21, The Antioch Incident

Implicit in the Jerusalem agreement concerning the division of labor was a subtle affirmation of unity. One unifying element was God. The Jerusalem apostles realized that God was operative both in those who evangelized Jews and in Paul, who evangelized Gentiles.

Another unifying element was the gospel. The gospel was deemed elastic enough to permit important cultural distinctions between Jews and Gentiles, insofar as those distinctions posed no threat to the fellowship of Jews and Gentiles. The pressures of communal life would soon put to the test the strength of the Jerusalem agreement.

Beginning in 2:11, Paul narrates an episode that occurs at some unspecified time after the Jerusalem conference. Peter comes to Antioch, an important early Christian center where Gentile converts to Christianity were not circumcised. According to Paul, Peter ate regularly with the Gentiles while in Antioch. By doing so, Peter demonstrated that the Jewish food laws, which usually prohibited fellowship between Jews and Gentiles, could also be repealed in the service of Christian unity.

Yet, when representatives from Jerusalem came to Antioch, Peter withdrew and separated himself. Following Peter's lead, Barnabas and other Jews who had been sharing table fellowship with the Gentiles separated themselves from Paul and the rest of the Gentiles. Paul charges with hypocrisy all those who withdrew.

Before the Jewish "power brokers" arrived at Antioch, Peter shared table fellowship with the Gentiles in an attempt to foster unity. Peter relinquished the ancient stereotypical views of Gentiles as "unclean," which the Jewish food laws presupposed. The representatives from Jerusalem, however, might not have shared Peter's new perspective and apparently pressured Peter into a more traditional understanding of his Jewish identity. Consequently, Peter withdrew from table fellowship with the Gentiles at Antioch.

Possibly at the root of Paul's indictment was Peter's unfortunate reclaiming of problematic stereotypes symbolized through his withdrawal from Gentile Christians. For Paul, Christ had eliminated ethnic stereotypes about the Gentiles being inherently "unclean." Furthermore, Christ had established a new common denominator by which Jews and Gentiles could be sisters and brothers in the same family. Paul must have regarded Peter's withdrawal as an affront to the unifying work of Christ.

In 2:15-21, Paul's rebuke of Peter continues. Paul espouses the common Jewish belief that no person is justified from the works of the law. Jews knew that justification—the state of being in a proper covenant relationship with God—was ultimately a result of God's grace. Jews fulfilled the works of the law mentioned in 2:16 (for example, circumcision, food laws, and the keeping of Sabbath) not to earn God's favor, but as a sign that God had already granted them favor. Divine grace and human works of the law were not mutually exclusive.

As *Jews*, Paul and Peter believed that justification was the consequence of divine grace. But as *Jewish Christians*, they believed that God, in Jesus Christ, had offered a new, once-and-for-all demonstration of grace. By investing faith *in* Jesus Christ, believers could access the saving power *of* Jesus Christ.

Since people could express faith in Jesus Christ regardless of their social identity, faith was the great social equalizer. Faith in Jesus Christ provided access to God's grace beyond any narrow social boundaries. By withdrawing from the Gentiles at Antioch, Peter insinuated that Jews were superior to Gentiles. Instead of testifying to a divine grace that removes social boundaries, Peter's action established an ethnic fence around grace.

Unfortunately, the persistence of perspectives and stereotypes that hinder genuine unity is as much a problem today as it was in this ancient incident at Antioch. Frequently, marginalized groups—whether they are ethnic "minorities," women, economically disadvantaged persons, or gay and lesbian persons—are embraced by certain dominant groups only later to be rejected by those dominant groups in crisis moments. For instance, in the frenzy of a political campaign, representatives from dominant groups shake hands and break bread with marginalized persons and make promises about building political and economic coalitions. Yet, when the time has come to fulfill the promises, these dominant groups often have withdrawn to a safe and inconspicuous political position. Instead of supporting those on the fringes and standing on the side of fairness, these dominant groups have separated themselves from the now "unclean" marginalized groups. Such action has exposed a lack of interest in genuine unity and an unwillingness to risk privilege and power for the sake of deep conviction.

The incident at Antioch reveals that from its earliest days the church has struggled to transform its exalted claims of unity into a living reality. Across history, many attempts to foster fellowship in the church have failed. Nevertheless, the goal of creating genuine Christian unity among persons of different social identities must remain central to the life of the church.

CHAPTER 3

3:1-5, The Galatians' Experience with the Holy Spirit

Galatians 3 is the theological center of the letter. This chapter advances three significant themes: (1) the Galatians' experience with the Holy Spirit, (2) the role of the Jewish law, and (3) the social boundaries of the Christian community.

Galatians 3 begins with Paul's anguished exclamation, "O foolish Galatians!" Attempting to dissuade the Galatians from their foolishness, Paul reminds them of their powerful experiences with the Holy Spirit when they initially received the gospel. The Gentiles' reception of the Holy Spirit provided an undeniable indication of their inclusion in God's covenant family.

In 3:5, Paul raises the question: "Does God, who supplies to you the Spirit and works miracles among you, do this because of the works of the law or because of your hearing the gospel?" The implied answer is that God granted the Holy Spirit to the Galatians because of their faith in the gospel.

Paul's reference to the Holy Spirit reminds contemporary churches of the *social implications* of life in the Spirit (3:1-5). Some Christians only consider the Holy Spirit a "private possession." While believers surely can have private experiences with the Spirit, the Spirit is also the active force of God moving publicly in the church and the world to create communal harmony and freedom.

On the other hand, certain Christians attempt to use the Holy Spirit as a litmus test to decide who is "genuinely" Christian. For example, some African American congrega-

---

A Practical Spirit

Many African American slaves believed that the Holy Spirit was a divine force that assisted them with practical matters like orchestrating their escapes to freedom. Concerning the Holy Spirit, Joe Oliver, a Texas slave, declared: "Dey singin' an' shoutin' till de break of day. Some goin' into trances an' some speakin' in what dey called strange tongues, dis wuz a good chance for de slaves to run away, for wen' de would rise up from dey trance some would run like de debbil wuz after him, an jes keep runnin' until he run clear off."

—Joe Oliver, quoted in Dwight N. Hopkins and George Cummings, *Cut Loose Your Stammering Tongue: Black Theology in the Slave Narratives* (Maryknoll, N.Y.: Orbis, 1991), 53.

tions insist that overtly charismatic signs, such as speaking in tongues or ecstatic praise, are criteria for being a believer. Persons whose experiences with the Holy Spirit are more subtle and serene often feel excluded by these criteria. In Galatians, God pours the Holy Spirit upon the Gentiles as evidence of their inclusion in God's family. When our appeals to the Holy Spirit become tools of exclusion, we misunderstand the Spirit's unifying task.

3:6-25, THE ROLE OF THE JEWISH LAW

In this section Paul addresses another major theme, the Jewish law. The story of Abraham provides the proper understanding of the law's role. In 3:6, Paul quotes from Gen 15:6 to emphasize the importance of Abraham's faith in establishing a covenant with God.

Paul's use of Abraham to illustrate the irrelevance of circumcision for Gentiles appears problematic. In traditional Jewish belief, Abraham demonstrated his faith by his willingness to be circumcised (Gen 17:4-14). Possibly the "agitators" introduced Abraham into the discussion, thereby compelling Paul to offer his own interpretation of Abraham. Paul certainly reads the narrative of Abraham contrary to traditional Jewish understanding. For Paul, the story of Abraham does not legitimate an ethnic practice (circumcision) that creates barriers between Jews and Gentiles. Rather, this story demonstrates that the boundaries of the covenant were wider than many Jews had thought. A life of faith, and not circumcision, brings blessings and makes persons—even Gentiles—true descendants of Abraham (vv. 7-9).

Having explained the blessings that faith brings, Paul addresses those who are cursed. He identifies the cursed ones as "all who rely on the works of the law" (v. 10). Likely, this is a reference both to the "agitators" and to the Galatians who might submit to circumcision. In Gal 3:10, Paul cites portions of Deuteronomy that highlight a negative aspect of the law.

Paul does not categorically oppose the law. Instead, he resists the Jewish imposition of the law upon Gentiles as if law observance were the only authentic manifestation of faith. The "agitators" fail to perceive that God made other provisions for the Gentiles. These provisions included a gospel free of circumcision, which Gentiles could accept through faith.

Law and Grace

Paul may have still considered the law important for Jews and, indeed, a complement to their faith. For example, Jewish Christians might interpret circumcision as a practical act of obedience, symbolizing their faithful response to God's grace.

Paul speaks negatively about the law *as it pertains to Gentile Christians*, not Jews or Jewish Christians. For Paul's positive assessment of the law, see Gal 3:21 and Rom 3:2; 7:7, 12.

To demonstrate the incompatibility of law-observance and faith for Gentiles, Paul declares in v. 12, "The law is not by faith." Paul's words are not an unconditionally negative assessment of the law. For Gentiles, faith and law observance are mutually exclusive. A preoccupation with the law causes Gentiles to misunderstand the universal nature of God's covenant, which persons enter through faith alone. According to Paul's logic, those who rely on faith are blessed, and those who rely on anything other than faith are cursed. Christ redeems both Jews and Gentiles from the curse (v. 13). Christ's redemptive work releases Jews from a provincial understanding of the law and rescues Gentiles from the necessity of becoming Jews. Christ thereby fulfills God's intent—a covenant family including both Jews and Gentiles.

Later, Paul appeals again to Abraham as justification for the primacy of faith (3:15-20). God established a covenant with Abraham on the basis of God's grace and Abraham's faith. According to Paul's calculation, this covenant predated the giving of the law on Mount Sinai by 430 years. Thus, faith is chronologically prior to the law and is the precondition upon which the law is founded.

3:26-29, The Social Boundaries of the Christian Community

In 3:28 Paul employs a confession used in baptismal services: "There is neither Jew nor Greek; there is neither slave nor free; there is neither male and female." This baptismal confession possibly indicated that "through Christ the old racial schisms and cultural divisions had been healed."[3] The confession focuses on three spheres of potential social strife: ethnic relationships ("there is neither Jew nor Greek"); economic status ("there is neither slave nor free"); and gender relationships ("there is neither male and female."). I will focus here primarily on the ethnic implications of Paul's statement in 3:28. Nevertheless, one should also apply the insights concerning ethnicity to the spheres of economic status and gender relationships.[4]

In order to understand Gal 3:28, we must correct the misconception that Christian unity entails the absence of social distinctions. If Paul advocated for the erasure of social distinction in 3:28, he would have undercut his own argument. Paul designed his evangelistic campaign to bring Gentiles into the church as Gentiles, thereby ensuring ethnic diversity in the church. Why, then, would he erase the very ethnic diversity for which he had toiled? In 3:28, Paul pleads for the eradication of *dominance*, not the erasure of *difference*. When people enter the Christian community through belief in Christ and baptism, they do not lose the social distinctions that have characterized their lives.

Even "in Christ," there is human difference. Yet Christ abolishes the dominance of one over the other based on these differences! Jews should not dominate Gentiles; free persons should not dominate slaves; men should not dominate women. Christians should foster harmonious relationships characterized by mutuality and respect for social difference.

A musical analogy further illustrates this point. Harmony is the cooperative union of opposite voices. Various vocal parts must maintain their distinctiveness, even as they unite, if harmony is to exist. Similarly, Christian unity emerges only when the social distinctions that define us are present and acknowledged but never used as a means of domination.

Paul's famous declaration in 3:28 can motivate congregations to strive for more equitable relationships across ethnic, economic, and gender lines. From a Pauline perspective, ethnic unity implies the maintenance of ethnic distinctions. Genuine unity will require deliberate, consistent, and ruggedly honest dialogue and fellowship among distinct groups.

Noble is the legacy of many African American congregations concerning the call for justice and unity among ethnic groups. There remains, however, much unfinished work concerning economic and gender justice and unity in African American congregations. For instance, persons interested in social liberation must raise a critique about the gender politics in many African American churches. As Demetrius Williams succinctly argues, African American congregations "must also become nonsexist institutions."[5]

For too long, African American congregations have cultivated a patriarchal culture, assuming that male leadership is natural. This gender apartheid relegates women to their "proper place" while denying them access to traditional symbols and systems of power (for example, the pulpit, pastoral leadership, and the right to administer the Lord's Supper). How can African American churches proclaim a liberating gospel and still place shackles on women? If churches desire to bring to life genuine unity, those who have typically held power (for example, white people, the economically advantaged, and men) will have to experience the "labor pains" of sharing power with, or even relinquishing power to, those on the margins.

> "In a recent study, 90 percent of the African American clergywomen surveyed listed sexism as the primary inhibitor of their ministries."
>
> —Delores C. Carpenter, *A Time for Honor: A Portrait of African American Clergywomen* (St. Louis: Chalice, 2001), 172.

CHAPTER 4

4:1-11, Emancipation from "The Elements"

Paul employs an illustration concerning the guardianship of minors that introduces again the theme of the inheritance of the covenant promises. The child in the illustration is a rightful heir. Yet, while under the supervision of guardians, he is no different from a slave, since he is unable to make significant decisions for himself. Similarly, Paul contends that Jews and Gentiles were in a state of slavery before the coming of Christ. Both groups are heirs of the covenant promises, but bondage under "the elements of the world" prohibited Jews and Gentiles from enjoying these promises. What are "the elements of the world"?

"The elements of the world" are (demonic) agents that enslave Jews and Gentiles. Only when Jews and Gentiles are released from this bondage can they receive the promises of the covenant. Possibly, the present age is evil because "the elements of the world" have attempted to frustrate God's plans (1:4). Christ broke the fetters of these elements, permitting believers to be adopted as God's children (4:4-5). In the legal illustration that begins the chapter, the child eventually receives the inheritance. The coming of Christ indicates that the time for Jews and Gentiles to receive their inheritance has arrived.

Just as Paul believed his culture was in bondage to evil forces, many African Americans might consider twenty-first-century America a "present evil age." Frequently, African Americans are leaders in infamous statistics. An alarming number of homicide felons and victims are African Americans. The HIV/AIDS virus is spreading in the African American community at a frightening pace. Furthermore, the average income of African Americans continues to plummet below that of our white and Asian American counterparts.

Perhaps, "the elements of the world" have contributed to America being a "present, evil age." As in the ancient case, "the elements of the world" in modern times are beings, forces, and ideologies that prohibit the promises of America from being disseminated broadly. In the context of America, "the elements" assume many forms. Surely, racist ideas and practices, which have sponsored the enduring domination of African Americans, are particular manifestations of "the elements." Although the iron shackles that formerly bound African American hands and feet have been removed, ideological shackles have remained around the psyche of many African Americans. Thus, nearly a century and a half after the end of chattel slavery, many African Americans are still in ideological bondage.

Some African Americans who are weary of this bondage are sounding the alarm and bellowing a clarion call: The fullness of time has come! Our ideological liberation draws nigh. African Americans must throw off the yoke of perspectives and behaviors, such as Eurocentrism, sexism, and self-hatred, which impede our progress as a people. Just as freedom for the Galatians entailed resisting "the elements," African Americans will experience freedom fully when we vigilantly oppose those forces that seek to enslave us.

4:12-20, A Passionate Plea

Paul bolsters his argument with strong emotional appeals. He pleads with the Galatians to remember the friendship that he has enjoyed with them. In order to befriend the Galatians, Paul became like them (v. 12). He adopted a lifestyle that no longer included law observance. Now, ironically, the Galatians are preparing to adopt a lifestyle that includes law observance. Paul passionately discourages this action, warning that the "agitators" court them for ignoble purposes (v.17).

Paul's effort to keep the Galatians from going astray is so intense that he likens it to the pains of childbirth. Paul's depiction of his apostolic work in *maternal* terms is fascinating in a letter seemingly so concerned with a male issue (circumcision). Possibly, by representing himself as a *woman*, Paul demonstrates that in the church male experience is no longer dominant (3:28).[6]

4:21-31, A Creative Reading of Hagar and Sarah

Paul concludes this chapter with a fascinating allegorical interpretation of the Hagar and Sarah saga in Genesis. Allegory is an interpretive method whereby the literal, "surface" meaning of a text is replaced by a figurative, "hidden" meaning from outside the text. Accordingly, on the surface Hagar appears to be Abraham's Egyptian concubine, and Sarah appears to be his wife. The allegory, however, reveals the hidden meanings of these "women" and their "children."

Hagar represents Mount Sinai (the place where the Jewish law was given), the earthly Jerusalem (the geographic and religious center of Jewish law observance), and slavery to law observance (the message of the "agitators"). For Paul, the allegorical meaning of Hagar is slavery. Consequently, her children—the "agitators" and those who accept their message—are enslaved. On the contrary, Sarah represents a "heavenly Jerusalem" (the realm where God's liberating Spirit reigns) and the freedom of not submitting to the law. For Paul, the hidden meaning of Sarah is freedom. Consequently, her children—Paul and those who accept his gospel—are free.

The interpretive implications of Paul's allegory of Hagar and Sarah are provocative as well. In this allegory, Paul takes considerable creative liberties with Genesis. In his contemporary moment, Paul demonstrates his serious regard for the ancient biblical text (Genesis) by reading it in fresh and unpredictable ways. He neither discards the ancient text nor assumes that the ancient meaning of the text exhausts its interpretive possibilities. Paul's current theological agenda is as determinative of biblical meaning as the historical intentions of the authors who composed Genesis.

African Americans, like Paul in this instance, have often read the Bible with a lively creativity. In sermons, songs, prayers, and testimonies, African Americans have improvised upon the Bible like seasoned jazz musicians. While respecting the Bible as a time-honored composition, African American responses to scripture have often included significant impromptu "riffs" on inherited biblical melodies. Jazz legend Miles Davis captured well the risks and rewards of improvisation and imagination: "See, if you put a musician in a place where he has to do something different from what he does all the time, then he can do that—but he's got to think differently in order to do it. He has to use the imagination, be more creative, innovative; he's got to take more risks. He's got to play above what he knows—far above it."[7] Much of the genius of African American Christianity lies in its willingness to take interpretive risks with scripture. Let us never lose the courage to improvise and "play above" what we know, even when we read the Bible.

Chapter 5

5:1-15, Moral Instructions for Freedom

Paul exhorts the Galatians to stand in the freedom that Christ has established. Through submission to the law, the Galatians would move away from, not closer to, Christ. In 5:4 Paul asserts, "You, who are trying to be justified by the law, have been separated from Christ; you have fallen away from grace." Falling from grace is to "foolishly remove oneself from Christ's sphere."[8] In Paul's estimation, separation from Christ is an exile of the worst kind.

Paul reminds the Galatians of their call to freedom (5:13). For fear that the Galatians will misuse their freedom, he offers moral instructions. In Paul's gospel, there is a strong relationship between theology and ethics.

The Galatians' desire to submit to the law might be an ironic consequence of Paul's theology. The Galatians' acceptance of the gospel exposed them to the social and religious liabilities of disassociating themselves from their families and friends who still worshiped pagan deities.[9] Having accepted Paul's message of freedom and become Christians, the Galatians found themselves dealing with the anxiety of a precarious social identity. Possibly their anxiety also stemmed from ignorance concerning the rules that should regulate their lives. In obedience to the law, they could find information and structure for daily living. The benefits of law observance were attractive, but Paul warned the Galatians against the wooing

ways of the "agitators," lest the Galatians fall into slavery.

Since Paul's preaching of freedom might have driven the Galatians to their "bondage," Paul explains his notion of freedom and establishes a paradox. Christian freedom is not unbridled but actually manifests itself in love or a "slavery" to the welfare of one's neighbors (5:13). When communities fail to accentuate the primacy of the love ethic, a destructive, competitive impulse is unleashed, which consumes individuals and erodes communal bonds (5:14-15).

Giving Paul Another Chance

Concerning Paul's ethical instructions, Brian Blount remarks:

> African Americans must ratchet up their study of Paul. The liberative benefits that can be gleaned from his counsel are legion. Too often Paul has been a target of attack and derision, not only in African American slave accounts, but . . . in the language and literature of African American scholarship as well. African American preachers too often use his words as uncritical supports for the less than liberative way in which the church works with women, gays and lesbians, church and states issues, and other matters of grave, contemporary consequence.

> —Brian K. Blount, *Then the Whisper Put on Flesh: New Testament Ethics in an African American Context* (Nashville: Abingdon, 2001), 156.

5:16-26, The Works of the Flesh and the Fruit of the Spirit

What is the safeguard against sin and the misuse of freedom? Paul responds, "The Holy

Spirit!" In 5:16, he writes, "This is what I mean, walk by the Spirit, and you will not at all perform the desires of the flesh." Throughout Galatians, Paul has signaled the importance of the Holy Spirit (3:2-5, 4:6), and here again he emphasizes it. The same Spirit who created and confirmed the Galatians' divine acceptance is also sufficient to guide their moral affairs.

Paul names vices that are characteristic of life under "the flesh." When speaking of "the flesh," Paul has in mind human existence dominated by sin. He refers to these vices as "the works of the flesh" (5:19-21). Then he names virtues that are characteristic of a Spirit-led life. These he calls "the fruit of the Spirit" (5:22-23). These vices and virtues involve behaviors that either destroy or edify the community. The works of the flesh destroy unity and community, while the fruit of the Spirit promote corporate well-being. The Spirit empowers believers to seek what is right both in their relationships with God and in their relationships with people.

Readers should notice the strong *social* emphasis of Paul's ethical admonitions. Often, discussions of Christian piety concentrate on the implications of moral transgression and transformation for individuals and not for communities and social structures. However, Paul teaches that ethics entail social, and not just individual, realities. Paul refers to the forces that destroy community in the plural: "the works of the flesh" and "the elements of the world." The forces that oppose freedom are not singular, nor do they wage war simply on the individual level. They are collective forces that attack entire cultures and institutions. The renowned African American pastor William A. Jones Jr. expresses the social nature of sin from an African American standpoint:

When sin becomes structured and inequity is institutionalized, the resultant arrangement is ineluctably wicked and nefarious, for it denies other human beings access to the tree of life. This is the continuing tragedy of America. The victims are correct when they speak of the nation in terms of "The System" for they correctly address themselves to that power arrangement in society based on wealth and whiteness, which prevents the gap between the needy and the greedy from closing. The System is racist to the very core. So deep and so pervasive is the reality that its bitter fruits multiply even without cultivation.[10]

One can easily apply Jones's observations about the social sin of racism to other social sins, such as corporate greed and environmental pollution. As scandals involving large American corporations have demonstrated, the lust for profit has "devoured" many people. This same lust has sponsored callous attitudes toward the natural environment that perpetuate a gluttonous "consumption" of precious natural resources.

Similarly, contemporary Christian understandings of salvation or sanctification that do not address social realities misrepresent the truth of the incarnation. Christ was embodied in order to liberate embodied people from embodied problems. Spiritual people do not retreat from "the world" in order to avoid moral contamination. Rather, the Holy Spirit compels believers to engage the world with the hopes of returning it to *holiness* and *wholeness*.

A congregation might examine carefully the fruit of the Spirit in Galatians 5, seeking ways to manifest each fruit concretely in the arena of social justice. A congregation's desire to bear the fruit of love or peace might compel it to lobby state legislatures for the cessation of the death penalty, or it might prompt a congregation to pursue interfaith dialogue with a neighboring synagogue or mosque.

CHAPTER 6

6:1-10, Accountability and Mutuality among Believers

Paul further amplifies the theme of communal ethics with a series of exhortations to the Galatians. Communal accountability and mutuality should characterize the behavior of Christians. Although Paul dissuades the Galatians from submitting to the Jewish law, there are standards of conduct to which Christians should adhere (for example, the fruit of the Spirit).

Paul recognizes that believers will inevitably transgress those standards. In cases of moral misconduct, the church has a responsibility to hold the offending party accountable. Yet restoration, not punishment, is the ultimate aim of church discipline. Christians correct an erring believer in order to restore that person to the fellowship of the congregation. Humility and gentleness guide all moral correction, since those who offer the correction can so easily fall prey to temptation (6:1).

If the Galatians are searching for ethical guidance, Paul offers mutuality as a moral compass. Christians have an obligation to shoulder the burdens that other believers carry. Apathy and lethargy are antithetical to Christian identity. The struggles of fellow believers should incite a congregation to compassionate and concrete responses. When the Galatians engage in loving, mutual relationships, they, indeed, fulfill *the law* that truly matters—the law of Christ. In a provocative wordplay, Paul identifies an ethic of love as the law that ultimately governs the people of Christ (6:2).

As an example of how the community can demonstrate love and mutuality, Paul urges the Galatians to provide financial support to Christian teachers. Teachers who labor among them share their spiritual gifts, wisdom, and energy with the community. In return, the community should share with those teach-ers its "good things," which include, but are not limited to, the community's financial resources.

Paul's emphasis on communal accountability tempered with gentleness can protect contemporary congregations from two dangers: moral laxity or moral hyperactivity. Some congregations rarely, if ever, hold their members to moral accountability. These congregations permit delinquent and disruptive believers, whether they are clergy or laypersons, to trample on the sanctity of the church's unity and witness. The failure of a congregation to hold its leaders and members to exacting standards of holiness lessens the credibility of the gospel.

Other congregations function as "behavior police," who harshly expose the moral failings of fellow believers. Preachers may callously trumpet the transgressions of church members from the pulpit, or parishioners may recklessly circulate the failings of others on the congregation's "grapevine." Instead of gossip on the grapevine, the gospel demands the cultivation of the fruit of the Spirit in a congregation. According to Paul, gentleness is one such fruit. As Christians address misconduct in church, they should utter the lyrics of that beloved spiritual: "Not my brother, not my sister, but it's me, O Lord, standin' in the need of prayer."[11]

Additionally, congregations should heed Paul's practical advice about the financial support of Christian teachers and ministers. Frequently, congregations expect first-class performance from ministers, while offering second-class financial support to those ministers, if any support at all. Why is it that some lay leaders in congregations will not think twice about handsomely paying a lawyer to defend them or an electrician to wire their homes, but they vehemently oppose salary raises for the ministers of their churches? By providing meaningful financial support for teachers and ministers, congregations exemplify their commitment to an ethic of mutuality.

6:11-18, Concluding Instructions

Up to this point, Paul has dictated this letter to a secretary. Paul now takes the pen and writes the conclusion in his own hand. He hurls a final assault upon the "agitators" and pleads with the Galatians to participate in the radical new creation, which Christ establishes. In the new creation, no particular social identity gives persons special privileges with God (6:15). Grace, as demonstrated in the cross, is the means of access. The present evil age about which Paul spoke at the letter's inception is rapidly giving way to God's new world order!

CONCLUSION

The impassioned conversation between Paul and the Galatians reveals that from its beginning Christianity confronted complicated issues, such as the nature of the gospel and the reconciliation of different social groups. Galatians prevents us from any Christian nostalgia—a misguided belief that there was a "Golden Age" of Christianity with little or no strife. In every generation, followers of Christ have struggled with the vast implications of accepting the gospel. It was so for Paul and the Galatians, and it is so for us.

Notes

1. For a fuller discussion, see Brad R. Braxton, *No Longer Slaves: Galatians and African American Experience* (Collegeville, Minn.: Liturgical, 2002).
2. Unless otherwise noted, all translations are mine.
3. Richard N. Longenecker, *Galatians* (Dallas: Word, 1990), 156.

4. Demetrius K. Williams, *An End to This Strife: The Politics of Gender in African American Churches* (Minneapolis: Fortress Press, 2004).
5. Ibid., 5.
6. Brigitte Kahl, "No Longer Male: Masculinity Struggles behind Galatians 3:28," *JSNT* 79 (2000): 42–43.
7. Quoted in Kirk Byron Jones, *The Jazz of Preaching: How to Preach with Great Freedom and Joy* (Nashville: Abingdon, 2004), 84.
8. Sam K. Williams, *Galatians* (Nashville: Abingdon, 1997), 138.
9. John M. G. Barclay, *Obeying the Truth: A Study of Paul's Ethics in Galatians* (Edinburgh: T. & T. Clark, 1988), 58.
10. William A. Jones Jr., "The Struggle against the System," in *The African American Church: Past, Present, and Future*, ed. Harold A. Carter, Wyatt Tee Walker, and William A. Jones Jr. (New York: Martin Luther King Fellows, 1991), 63.
11. "Standin' in the Need of Prayer," *African American Heritage Hymnal* (Chicago: GIA, 2001), 441.

For Further Reading

Blount, Brian K. *Then the Whisper Put on Flesh: New Testament Ethics in an African American Context.* Nashville: Abingdon, 2001.

Braxton, Brad R. *No Longer Slaves: Galatians and African American Experience.* Collegeville, Minn.: Liturgical, 2002.

Carpenter, Delores C. *A Time for Honor: A Portrait of African American Clergywomen.* St. Louis: Chalice, 2001.

Felder, Cain Hope. *Troubling Biblical Waters: Race, Class, and Family.* Maryknoll, N.Y.: Orbis, 1989.

Hopkins, Dwight N., and George Cummings. *Cut Loose Your Stammering Tongue: Black Theology in the Slave Narratives.* Maryknoll, N.Y.: Orbis, 1991.

Martyn, J. Louis. *Galatians.* New York: Doubleday, 1997.

Punt, Jeremy. "Towards a Postcolonial Reading of Freedom in Paul." Pages 125–49 in *Reading the*

Bible in the Global Village: Capetown. Edited by Justin S. Ukpong et al. Atlanta: Society of Biblical Literature, 2002.

Williams, Delores S. *Sisters in the Wilderness: The Challenge of Womanist God-Talk.* Maryknoll, N.Y.: Orbis, 1993.

Williams, Demetrius K. *An End to this Strife: The Politics of Gender in African American Churches.* Minneapolis: Fortress Press, 2004.

Wimbush, Vincent L. *The Bible and African Americans: A Brief History.* Facets. Minneapolis: Fortress Press, 2003.

EPHESIANS

———————

Mitzi J. Smith

INTRODUCTION

Ephesians reads like a legal document detailing a corporate merger of two major bodies—one foreign (Gentiles) and one domestic ("the circumcision").[1] The author of Ephesians, to whom I shall refer hereinafter as "Paul" in quotation marks, documents the fusion of two ethnic groups under one economical salvific plan. Ephesians maps how God accomplished the merging of the Gentile Christians with the Jewish Christians. This merger results in a united church as one body with Christ as its head. And finally, we see the ordering of the Christian household in Christ. This unification project is accomplished through God's pre-ordained and revealed salvific plan—the

mystery of God. God's plan remains a mystery until it is revealed and comprehended in and through Jesus. The plan of God incorporates both heavenly places and earthly domains.

In spite of the emphasis on unity, "Paul" at times creates distance between himself and his Gentile audience. When the author uses the first person plural pronoun "we," the reader envisions him standing among his audience. But he separates himself from his audience when he addresses them as "you" or "you Gentiles." "Paul" encourages the Gentile Christians to behave similarly when he admonishes them to distinguish themselves from other Gentiles. But in Ephesians the Gentile Christians are still referred to as "you Gentiles." It is as if a "double-consciousness" is imposed upon them. They are reminded of their Gentile roots, but they are also now incorporated into God's household and have become citizens along with the Jewish Christians.

This sense of "double-consciousness" will resonate with some African Americans. W. E. B. DuBois wrote that the American "Negro" cannot escape the "sense of always looking at one's self through the eyes of others, of measuring one's soul by the tape of a world that looks on in amused contempt and pity. One ever feels his twoness—an American, a Negro; two souls, two thoughts, two unreconciled strivings; two warring ideals in one dark body, whose dogged strength alone keeps it from being torn asunder."[2] In spite of the "twoness," African Americans maintain a sense of stability rooted in knowing we belong

---

Paul and Ephesians

The author of Ephesians is likely Jewish, and it is uncertain that the author is Paul. The apostle Paul did minister in Ephesus and was well known there. But based on theological, stylistic, and lexical differences between the authentic Pauline books (Galatians, 1 Thessalonians, 1 and 2 Corinthians, Philemon, Philippians, and Romans) and Ephesians, most scholars consider Ephesians a deuteropauline text along with other New Testament books like Colossians and 2 Thessalonians. Ephesians is labeled "deuteropauline," or secondarily Pauline, because it was probably written by a disciple of Paul in the latter part of the first century C.E. While I agree with this view, at times I will refer to the author as "Paul," particularly with respect to chaps. 3 and 4, where the author assumes the identity of Paul as a prisoner of Jesus Christ.

---

to the family of God, where our identity is certain. It is no mystery that Christ has delivered us from the insanity of this world. The strength that African Americans have found in the promise and experience of God's free grace and love through Jesus Christ has kept us from "going under." While we acknowledge that Ephesians is a book often quoted from because of the hope it offers, we must read it critically, just as our ancestors did. African Americans can salvage what is liberating and lay aside that which threatens our freedom.

1:1-23, INTRODUCTION

1:1-2, Salutation
In v. 1a, Paul, an apostle of Jesus Christ, is identified as the sender of the letter. In accordance with what is stated in the Acts of the Apostles and Galatians (1:11-12), "Paul" claims that his apostleship is not of human origin but comes through God's will (*dia thelēmatos theou*). God's will is the providential force operating in Ephesians (1:5, 9, 11). Similar to Romans (1:1) Paul is identified as the sole sender of the letter, whereas customarily Paul and another person (e.g., Timothy, 2 Cor 1:1, or Sosthenes, 1 Cor 1:1) or a group of people (Gal 1:1-2) are identified as the senders. In v.1b, the recipients of the letter are "the saints in Ephesus who believed in Jesus Christ." The prepositional phrase *in Ephesus* is absent from some of the best Greek manuscripts. Thus, the letter might originally have been addressed to a larger Christian audience, which may have included Christians in Ephesus. In v. 2, the traditional greeting "grace to you and peace from God our father and the Lord Jesus Christ" is used (see, e.g., Rom 1:1).

1:3-14, The Blessing
Verses 3-14 constitute a blessing similar to an ancient Jewish blessing (e.g., 1 Kgs 8:15,

56; Ps 41:13). In the Greek text, this blessing is one long sentence stitched together by participial and relative clauses and prepositional phrases. The most frequently occurring relative clause is "in whom," and it usually refers to Christ (1:7, 11, 13). But the blessing is addressed to "God, the Father of our Lord Jesus Christ" (v. 3). "Ephesians weaves the function of Christ as heavenly mediator into the praise of God as benefactor."[3] God is acknowledged as the giver of every blessing, including those blessings that come through Christ. It was from God that the saints received every spiritual blessing "in the heavenlies in Christ" (v. 3). The phrase "in the heavenlies" is peculiar to Ephesians. "In the heavenlies" sometimes refers to the space beyond the earth (1:20; 2:6; 6:12), and other times it may refer to the realms on earth over which God exercises all authority (3:10).

The phrase "in Christ" is sprinkled throughout this blessing and the letter (1:10, 12; 2:10, 13). All God's blessings are mediated through Christ Jesus, including the merging of the Gentiles into the family of God. In the same way that God bestows spiritual blessings upon us through Christ Jesus, God also, through Christ, pre-selected us to be God's saints and to be blameless. This election took

place before God laid the foundation of the world. In other words, God's saints were pre-ordained to be saints and to be without blame through Jesus (v. 4). Additionally, this holy and blameless condition is not according to human standards. It is dependent upon God's judgment ("before God"), which is tempered by God's love for God's saints (v. 4). While Jesus is the mediating person by which the Ephesians receive God's blessings, God's love is the mediating virtue.

Although Jesus is the mediator of our adoption as children of God, everything happens according to the intention of God's will (*tēn eudokian tou thelēmatos autou*). And everything operates within God's will specifically for the "praise of [God's] glory" (vv. 6, 12, 14). God also pre-ordained the Ephesians for adoption (v. 5). Kinship has always been important to Africans and African Americans. "Personal identity and self-esteem are integrally tied up with one's kinship relations."[4] African American slaves' view of themselves as children of God served to unite them into one family.

It is also through Jesus' blood that the Ephesians receive redemption (*apolytrōsis*) and forgiveness of offences. But still this redemption is only possible because of the riches of

Paul in Ephesus

According to the Acts of the Apostles, Paul visited Ephesus on two occasions. During his first visit, Paul had a dialogue with the Jews in the synagogue, where he was well received. In fact, they asked him to extend his stay. Paul declined the invitation but said he would return (18:19-21). In the interim between Paul's first and second visit, Apollos, a Jew born in Alexandria, Egypt, taught eloquently and boldly in the synagogue in Ephesus. When Apollos left Ephesus and went to Corinth, Paul returned to Ephesus. Twelve disciples received the Holy Spirit after Paul laid hands on them, and for three months he spoke in the synagogue. After some opposition, Paul and his disciples switch venues from the synagogue to the public lecture hall of Tyrannus. He spoke there for two more years (19:1-20).

God's grace. Yet God lavishes this abundant grace upon God's saints with wisdom and intelligence and not capriciously (v. 8).[5]

God's will for the saints is not hidden from them. God revealed the mystery of God's will. And this revelatory act is God's predetermined intention (v. 9; cf. 3:3, 4; Col 1:27-28). Every component of God's salvific plan (see the comments on 3:11-13, below), encompassing things in the heavens and on the earth, is brought together in Christ (v. 10; Col 1:20) and put into effect "according to the counsel of God's will" (v. 11). "Paul" shares two things in common with the Ephesians: (1) "we" have been redeemed, and (2) "we" have been assigned a share of the inheritance (vv. 7, 11). But the author distances himself from the Ephesians on two accounts: (1) "you heard the word of truth, the gospel of your salvation," and (2) "after you believed, you were sealed with the Holy Spirit of promise" (v. 13). By distancing, which is expressed by the use of the second person plural pronoun "you," "Paul" conveys that his reception of the word and sealing preceded theirs. Like the Ephesians, he received the corporate seal of the Spirit and thus shares in the same inheritance (v. 14; cf. 1 Thess 5:9; 2 Thess 2:14; Heb 10:39; 1 Pet 2:9). The blessing ends with a refrain that has been repeated throughout this blessing, "for the praise of His glory."

1:15-23, Report and Thanksgiving

Verse 15 begins with the words "for this reason," and they point back to the "spiritual blessings" God bestowed on the Ephesians. "Paul" and the Ephesians share much in common—salvation, reception of truth, sealing, and inheritance. He writes this letter in response to the report about their common faith in the Lord Jesus and their "love toward all the saints." He continually prays for the Ephesians. He remembers them in his prayers because their faith will be challenged (v. 16). The author's comments to the Ephesians are similar to the comments Paul made to the Romans: "your faith is proclaimed throughout the world. . . . I do not cease remembering you always in my prayers" (Rom 1:8-9; Col 1:4; 1 Thess 1:2-3).

Although "Paul" commends the Ephesians for their faith and love, these are the very virtues he encourages them to grow in. He prays that God "might give [them] a spirit of wisdom and of revelation through a knowledge of [God]" (v. 17). It is through this spirit of revelation that the saints are able to know the mysteries of God. The emphasis on revealed knowledge would be comforting to our African American ancestors who were forbidden to know the mysteries of the printed words of God in the Bible. In spite of prohibitions against African Americans reading the Bible, their status as children of God and as full human beings was no mystery to them. African American slaves came to know a Jesus Christ distinct from the one revealed to them by the handpicked preachers the slave masters commissioned to preach to them. For contemporary African Americans the emphasis on revealed knowledge demonstrates that no group holds a monopoly on knowledge or wisdom. God reveals God's mysteries to whomever God wills.

God's revelation enables the saints to know "the hope of [God's] calling" and the "riches of [God's] glorious inheritance" in them (v. 18). Significantly, the inheritance comes through Christ whom God raised from the dead. Inheritance, as we know it today, is awarded at the death of the property holder. But Christ is alive and at the right hand of God. And it is because Christ lives that the inheritance is bestowed. The revelation of the mystery also manifests the "surpassing greatness of [God's] power in *us* who believe" (v. 19). For African Americans, this has

"Heaven" Here and Now

For African American slaves heaven often symbolized Africa, Canada, or northern sections of the United States where they might be free. James Cone argues that "for black slaves, who were condemned to carve out their existence in captivity, heaven meant that the eternal God had made a decision about their humanity that could not be destroyed by white masters. . . . They have a *somebodiness* that is guaranteed by God who alone is the ultimate sovereign of the universe. . . . Black slaves are expressing the Christian contention that the death and resurrection of Christ bestows upon people a freedom that cannot be taken away by oppressors."

—James Cone, *The Spirituals and the Blues* (Maryknoll, N.Y.: Orbis, 1999), 82–83.

historically meant that a greater power is at work in us than the one at work in the world. For example, "Gullah Jack" (Jack Pritchard), a religious and political leader among black slaves in plantations outside of Charleston, South Carolina, in the early part of the nineteenth century, "knew who he was—a man guided and protected by the spiritual power of his God—a spirit far superior to all the evil present in the world."[6] For contemporary African Americans, this means that the power of God is greater than the legal and political powers wielded by the authors and supporters of anti-affirmative action initiatives and other political agendas that threaten to erode our civil rights. The efficacy of the unrivaled power residing in God's saints was the same power put into operation when God raised Christ "from the dead and seated [him] at [God's] right hand in the heavenlies" (v. 20). God's positioning of Christ "in the heavenlies"

represents a spiritual and otherworldly elevation. But God's elevation of Christ assumes a this-worldly (present and future) and political maneuver. Christ, and the unrivaled power of God mediated through him, supersedes "every ruler, authority, power, lordship (*kyriotēs*), and any name of any significance" (v. 21). It is "Paul's" prayer that God's saints will recognize that God has subordinated everything and every force to Christ. If all things everywhere are subject to Christ's power, then it follows that he is also the head (*kephalē*) of all things in the church (*ekklēsia*), which is Christ's body (*sōma*) (vv. 22, 23; cf. Col 1:18).

2:1—6:20, Body of the Letter

2:1-10, Saved by Grace

You are dead to "your transgressions (*paraptōmasis*) and sins (*hamartia*)" (v. 1). The Ephesians previously lived the same life of transgression and sin that the "children of unbelief" still live (v. 2). The author says "*we* were by nature children of wrath" (v. 3). *You* were children (*hoi huioi*) of unbelief by choice (2:2), but *we* were children (*ta tekna*) of wrath by nature. With respect to our previous lustful natures, we were all the same. God raised Christ, and, in the richness of (God's) mercy and the greatness of (God's) love, God raised us together with Christ (v. 4). This joint action on our behalf can be called salvation by God's grace. "By grace *you* have been saved" (vv. 5, 8). Our deliverance comes from God's grace, which is bound up in God's raising of Jesus Christ. "Your" deliverance or salvation is a gift of God. There are no strings attached to this inheritance—no inheritance taxes, no stipulations, no work or services to perform, and no limitations on our deliverance. Good works cannot bring about deliverance. But we are saved so that we may produce good words. We are created for the purpose of doing good works (v. 10); it is part of our destination.

In addition to God, raising us together with Christ, God "placed us together in Christ in the heavenlies" (v. 6). Here "the heavenlies" refers to more than the place where God lives beyond the earth. The term "the heavenlies" connotes an attitude, a belief, a spirit of mind and heart of knowing and experiencing the authority, power, and dominion of Jesus. God's saving action is for the benefit of future generations (v. 7). The grace of God is not just for the benefit of the present time, but its benefits are to extend into the future. This is the legacy of God's saving grace. In the same way, our African American ancestors enslaved in this country expressed hope, if not for themselves, for their children and their children's children.

"Give Us Grace," a Prayer by W. E. B. DuBois (1909–1910)

"Give us grace, O God, to dare to do the deed which we well know cries to be done. . . . Mighty causes are calling us—the freeing of women, the training of children, the putting down of hate and murder and poverty—all these and more. But they call with voices that mean work and sacrifice and death."

—W. E. B. DuBois, quoted in James Melvin Washington, *Conversations with God: Two Centuries of Prayers by African Americans* (New York: HarperCollins, 1994), 105.

2:11-22, Strangers No Longer

For the first time "Paul" identifies his audience as "you Gentiles" (*hymeis ta ethnē*). "We must not lose sight of the fact that the author is speaking about the Gentiles from the perspective of a Jew. . . . [The author has measured] the religious and social distance between himself (or other Jews) and the Gentiles."[7] "Paul" sets up a clear distinction between the Gentiles' past existence and their present status by use of the polarities "near" and "far," "once" and "now" (vv. 12-13, 17). He exhorts the Gentiles to remember their past existence and relationship to the people identified as the "circumcision in the flesh by human hands" (v. 11). Previously, the Gentiles were "in the flesh," and the circumcised ones referred to them as those of the "uncircumcision." The former life of the Gentiles is described as "without Christ," "alienated from the citizens of Israel," and "strangers of the covenant of promise" (v. 12). They were people without a deliverer, without a homeland, without hope, and without God. By remembering their past status, the Gentiles can appreciate the "now in Christ Jesus" (v. 13). For the first time the phrase "the blood of Christ" is used to describe the means by which the Gentiles are delivered from their past existence (v. 13). Christ's blood has created peace and unity. Christ's blood has destroyed the barrier (*mesotoichon*) of separation (*phragmos*), rendering ineffective any requirements that prevented the Gentiles' active and full participation in God's promises, salvation, and citizenship (vv. 14, 15). African Americans are all too familiar with "barriers of separation" that historically and currently attempt to limit our full participation as U.S. citizens. The majority of African American children have been and still are subjected to separate and unequal educational systems. When I lived in Chattanooga, Tennessee, public school test scores and other demographics were published in the local paper. The racial demographics demonstrated a clear division between predominantly black schools and predominantly white schools. Generally across the board, test scores for predominantly black schools lagged behind those of their white counterpart schools. Predominantly black and poor schools are often deficient in textbooks and other supplies. One would probably find a similar phenomenon in other large cities. Many children in inner city schools are black, and these school districts lack the tax base of more affluent and predominantly white suburban school systems.

Backs against the Wall

Howard Thurman considered the most important quest of modern religion a determination of what religion has "to say to those who stand, at a moment in human history, with their backs against the wall. . . . The masses of [people] live with their backs constantly against the wall. They are the poor, the disinherited, the dispossessed. What does our religion say to them? The issue is not what it counsels them to do for others whose need may be greater, but what religion offers to meet their own needs."

—Howard Thurman, *Jesus and the Disinherited* (Boston: Beacon, 1976), 12–13.

But such inequalities can be overcome. Jesus becomes the great equalizer and the common denominator. Jesus accomplishes peace and unity between the uncircumcised and the circumcised who are *in Christ*. Both the uncircumcised Gentiles and the Jewish Christians can only gain access to the Father through Jesus (v. 18). Because of Jesus, the Gentiles are no longer foreigners and sojourners, but counted as natives and residents. The Gentiles, through Christ, are now fellow-citizens with "the circumcision" and members of God's household, in spite of their uncircumcision (v. 19). The prophets and apostles have laid the foundation for the Gentiles' incorporation into God's family, and the corner or foundation stone (*akrogōniaios*), which is Jesus Christ, is set in place. It is to this foundation that the Gentiles are "compactly joined together" and "built together" (*synoikodomeō*), like bricks and mortar, to form with "the circumcision" a holy temple (*naos*) in the Lord (*kyrios*) and a habitation (*katoikētērion*) for God's Spirit (vv. 21-22).

African Americans have found comfort in knowing that they are members of God's family. God reserved a place at the table for them. "Such a sense of belonging has empowered African American Christians' belief that they have worth because God invited them to be participants in the ultimate family, the household of God."[8]

3:1-13, "I, Paul, Am a Prisoner of Christ for You Gentiles"

Here the reader learns that "Paul" is imprisoned. But, as is customary in the prison epistles, "Paul" considers himself a prisoner of Christ and not of the secular authorities. His incarceration resulted from his preaching the gospel to the Gentiles. For the second time, the author identifies his addressees as "you Gentiles " (v. 1). It was from Paul that "you" heard "the plan" (*oikonomia*) of God's grace (*charis*), which God gave "me" to give to "you" (v. 2). The giving of this "plan" to "Paul" constitutes God's revelation (*apokalypsis*) to him; it is the making known of the mystery (*mystērion*) (v. 3a). In Ephesians, God has kept no secrets from the Gentiles. The mystery is also known as the "mystery of Christ" (v. 4). "Paul" is certain that the Gentiles previously read about, and understood, this mystery in a brief letter that he wrote to them (v. 3b). But this secret that God's Spirit revealed to the apostles and prophets was not made known to the children of previous generations (v. 5; cf. 2:20, 22). We see that the author counts Paul among the apostles and prophets to whom the Spirit revealed the mystery of Christ. And Paul is that apostle through whom God revealed the "mystery of Christ."

Consequently, because of Paul's preaching the mystery of Christ and what was hidden in Christ, the Gentiles have become one in body, inheritance, and communion (vv. 6, 9). It is through the church that God's wisdom is revealed (v. 10). Through Christ whom Paul preached in the church, the Gentiles can approach God with boldness and confidence (v. 11).

3:14-21, A Prayer for the Gentiles

"Paul" supports his words of encouragement in v. 13 with a prayer for the Gentiles. He verbally presents a visual image of himself kneeling before the Father (*patēr*) (v. 15). The Father is identified as the one after whom the entire family (*patria*) is named. The Greek word *patria* derives from the Greek word for father, *patēr*, and it can be translated as lineage, house, or clan. The image is of many people who consider themselves of one lineage through the father's side of the family—a people with a common head of the household or with one clan chief. This family includes those in "the heavenlies" and those on "earth" (v. 14). Here the term "the heavenlies" refers to a place beyond the earth. "Paul's" prayer that God strengthen the Gentiles coincides with his desire that they not become discouraged because of his imprisonment on their behalf (v. 16; cf. v. 13).

Verses 16 and 17 are parallel in that they express the same sentiment in different ways. Verse 16 begins with a subjunctive verb expressing a wish, and v. 17 begins with an infinitive. "Paul" prays in v. 16 that the Gentiles be strengthened according to the riches of God's glory with power through his Spirit in their inner person. Verse 17 expresses the same idea of internal strengthening when it states "Paul's" desire "that Christ dwells (*katoikeō*), through faith, in your hearts, being firmly rooted and established in love." Christ dwells in the individual through the Spirit. And the one who is "firmly rooted and established" (v. 17) is the one who is "strengthened" (v. 16).

We find the same pattern of parallelism with vv. 18 and 19. Similar to vv. 16 and 17, v. 18 begins with a subjunctive verb expressing a wish, and v. 19 begins with an infinitive. In v. 18 "Paul" continues to pray that the Gentiles will be able to "fully understand, with all the saints, what is the breadth, length, height, and depth." Verse 19 expresses the same idea of comprehending the richness of God's grace when "Paul" states "that *you* know the surpassing love of the knowledge of Christ."

The author is committed to the full enfranchisement of the Gentiles. Together with "all the saints," it is his prayer that they enjoy the internal and external benefits of citizenship and of kinship. They are to experience the power of God's grace in the outward working of the Spirit's gifts and in the internal dwelling of Christ through the Spirit.

In vv. 20-21, "Paul" closes out the prayer by identifying the level of capability of the Father to whom the prayer is addressed. The qualifications of the Father show that he is fully capable of answering this prayer. The Father is "able to do superabundantly (*hyperperisseuō*) above anything we can ask or even conceive of" (v. 20a). The Father will bring about strength and understanding commensurate with the indwelling of Christ through the Spirit—"according to the power at work in us" (v. 20b). And God will be glorified in the church and in Christ Jesus in this generation and in every generation to come (v. 21).

With God on our side—in spite of all external obstacles to the enjoyment of full citizenship rights—African Americans can overcome. We do not deny the presence of institutional and individual racism. We do not deny that people, institutions, and forces will attempt to limit us in terms of where we will live, how much money we will make, access to quality education, etc. But because God is able to do superabundantly above all we ask or think, we do not offer these challenges as excuses. With God, we can move beyond the "walls." As Lee H. Butler states, "religion has provided the African American with a world-view and an integrity that enable us to continue living against all odds."[9]

4:1—5:20, Live according to Your Calling

In v. 1 the author identifies himself, for the second time, as Paul, a "prisoner of the Lord." It is as a prisoner for the sake of their inclusion that "Paul" exhorts (*parakaleō*) the Gentile Christians to conduct themselves in a manner worthy of their calling (*klēsis*). He also emphasizes that their dealings with one another should be in the spirit of love (v. 2). He emphasizes their commonalities. The Gentiles together with all the saints enjoy a common membership in "one body," permeated and empowered by "one spirit," and with one purpose (v. 4). This "one body," which is the church, is led by one Lord in whom the saints have expressed a common faith by their submission to one baptism (v. 5). Above the head, which is Christ (v. 15), God exercises ultimate dominion over all, is through all, and dwells in every member (v. 6). To each member, God has freely granted God's grace (v. 7). The gifts of God's grace are mediated through Christ. "Paul" quotes Ps 68:18 as the scriptural basis for this gift giving through Christ to support his assertion that Christ bestowed gifts on God's people when he ascended (vv. 8-9). The gifts allow the saints to function as apostles, prophets, evangelists, pastors, and teachers in the body, which is the church (vv. 11-12). The more enduring offices or gifts are those of apostles and prophets, who are the foundation of the church and those through whom God has already revealed God's plan of salvation. While most contemporary Christians affirm the end of the apostolic office with the death

of the last of the New Testament apostles, some believe the prophetic gift still operates or should operate in the church. However, in many churches, including African American churches, the silence of the prophetic voice is deafening and has resulted in the absence of a "word from the Lord." Many African American churches have relinquished the task of speaking prophetically to the politicians of our time. But in order for the African American church to effect a maturity in believers and to effect change in our larger community, we must retrieve our prophetic voice. Martin Luther King wrote, "Any discussion of the role of the Christian minister today must ultimately emphasize the need for prophecy. . . . May the problem of race in America soon make hearts burn so that prophets will rise up, saying, 'Thus said the Lord,' and cry out as Amos did, '. . . Let justice roll down like waters, and righteousness like an ever-flowing stream.'"[10] God has given us the power and gifts to speak prophetically. The building up of our community depends on our willingness and courage to exercise prophetic gifts. Many African American churches and communities have delegated the work of community empowerment and uplift to nonprofit organizations and governmental agencies. Many of these agencies are "pimping" our communities by receiving monies and not delivering services contracted. We must boldly speak out against such practices, and do what is necessary to provide the services our communities need. In order to promote community development, Robert M. Franklin asserts that black churches must bring a "prophetic perspective and imperative" to the task of developing our communities. Black churches, Franklin says, must do the following:

> Recall their mission of *prophetic* witness, of raising critical questions about the moral and social effects of market eco-

nomics. This constitutes part of Martin Luther King's unfinished agenda. Perhaps Mahatma Gandhi best expressed the prophetic spirit of religion when he described the seven deadly sins as "politics without principle, wealth without work, commerce without morality, pleasure without conscience, education without character, science without humanity, and worship without sacrifice." . . . The church should attempt to sustain a creative tension between its roles in community development and as a prophetic moral agent.[11]

The gifts God bestows upon the church have a particular purpose, which is to further promote unity and maturity among the saints (v. 14). The evidence of this maturity is that the church will not act childlike in their faith and knowledge; they will not be deceived by doctrines that are contrary to the truth (vv. 14-15). The mortar or the cement that will hold them together is expressed by the prepositional phrase "in love" (vv. 15, 16; 3:17; 5:1). "Although the particular offices refer to those who are in charge of guiding churches after [the apostle Paul's] death, Ephesians assumes that all Christians are part of the building process. Maturity involves the community as a whole, not merely particular individuals."[12]

Verse 16 is linguistically and semantically similar, if not identical, to 2:21 in that many of the same Greek words are used to convey the same message. Verse 2:21 says "in whom" (Christ) "every building joined together fitly (*synarmologeō*) grows into a holy temple (*naos*)." Verse 16 reads "from whom," meaning Christ, "every body (*sōma*) is joined together fitly (*synarmologeō*) and is united together (*symbibazō*)."

In v. 17 "Paul" distinguishes the Gentiles who are still alienated from the life of God from the Gentiles now united in Christ. The former are ignorant and obstinate, and they practice every uncleanliness and covetousness as the latter Gentiles once did. When the Gentiles who are now part of the body and family of God heard and were taught in Christ, they abandoned their old way of life, and they "clothed" themselves "in the new person" (*anthrōpos*) (vv. 21-24; 4:24; Col 3:12, 14). As members together in the same body, the saints are to imitate Christ in their treatment of one another. The emphasis is solely on how to relate to those who share the same Christian faith. But African Americans must be careful not to use this passage as an excuse not to "reach back" and help those that remain in the oppressive circumstances and lifestyles from which God has delivered us. Too many African Americans have obtained middle-class and upper-middle-class status; moved into more affluent neighborhoods, taking our tax dollars with us; enrolled our children in more financially sound school districts; attended churches in the neighborhoods we left behind; and yet become uncomfortable should people from the communities we abandoned dare to sit next to us in our pews. Too many of us are leaving, never to glance back. C. Eric Lincoln and Lawrence H. Mamiya state that "the challenge for the future is whether black clergy and their churches will attempt to transcend class boundaries and reach out to the poor, as these class lines continue to solidify with demographic changes in black communities."[13] Otherwise, what may emerge is a separate "black Church for the poor."[14]

> "A nation should not be judged by how it treats its highest citizens, but its lowest ones—and South Africa treated its imprisoned African citizens like animals."
>
> —Nelson Mandela, *Long Walk to Freedom* (Boston: Little, Brown, 1994), 201.

The Gentile saints went through several stages to arrive at their present condition in Christ. They were taught, they renewed their minds, and they clothed themselves with a new self (4:22-24). The condition of the Gentiles who are not in Christ gives the reader an indication of how the Gentiles in Christ previously lived: they eagerly surrendered themselves to immorality and impurity, became hardhearted, and alienated from God (4:18-19).

In the exhortation (*paraenesis*), significant emphasis is placed on words. Saints are admonished to "renounce lying and speak the truth with your neighbor" (*plēsios*) (4:25), to "avoid vicious talk" (4:29), to destroy all "commotion and slander" (4:31), to regard "obscenity (*aischrotēs*) and foolish talk (*mōrologia*) or buffoonery (*eutrapelia*)" as improper (5:4), and "not to be deceived by empty words (*kenois logois*)" (5:6).

5:21—6:9, Household Codes

The rules governing relationships between husband and wives, parents and children, and masters and slaves are known as the household codes (*Haustafeln*) (5:21—6:9; cf. Col 3:18—4:1; 1 Pet 3:1-7). The household codes in Ephesians reflect "an idealized notion of the hierarchical structure of the Roman household and with early Christianity as a household movement."[15] The household codes "prescribe an ideal" about how members of the Christian household ought to conduct their lives in relation to one another.[16] The household codes in Ephesians are placed within a theological framework. The relationship between Christ and the church is used as a model for prescribing familial relationships. The author provides theological justification for the ideal conduct of wives, children, slaves, and the male head of the household. Not all Christian households were headed by males (e.g., Luke 10:38-42; Acts 12:12; 16:15). But in the author's view, in the ideal Christian household the male is head of the household.

Wives are to subordinate themselves to their husbands, and children and slaves are to obey (*hypakouō*) their parents and masters, respectively. Church leaders could question whether a wife's submission to her husband was truly voluntary.[17] The church viewed a woman as less than a Christian if she did not submit to her husband in accordance with the church's interpretation (i.e., the male clergy's interpretation) of what constituted submission. Alternatively, husbands are to love (*agapaō*), nourish, and cherish their wives; fathers are to refrain from provoking children; and masters are to avoid speaking harshly to their slaves. Husbands or males determined what constituted "subordination" or "submission." Likewise, parents determined the nature of obedience. And masters determined when slaves have met the requirements of obedience. Husbands, fathers, and masters not only determined the meaning of submission and obedience of those subordinate to them, but also defined and evaluated their own behavior. Historically, it has never been the slave who determined what constituted harsh language. Likewise, it was the husband who determined what constituted love of his wife in everyday practice.

Males treated wives and children similarly. Husbands are admonished to nourish (*ektrephō*) and nurse or cherish (*thalpō*) their wives (5:29). The same Greek word *thalpō*, which can be translated "nurse," is used at 1 Thess 2:7 in reference to a nurse (*trophos*) nurturing (*thalpō*) her own children. Also similar to the admonition to husbands to nourish their wives, at 6:4 fathers are told to nourish (*ektrephō*) their children (6:4). The author uses the same Greek word to describe how husbands are to care for their wives and how parents are to nurse their children.

Although women are to be the passive recipients of nourishment, husbands are to receive respect or fear from their wives (5:33). Likewise, slaves are to obey their masters with fear (*phobos*) and trembling (*tromos*) (6:5). The Greek word for fear is *phobeō*, and it is used to describe how the saints are to submit to one another (5:21). But in the household codes, fear is only used to describe how wives are to submit to husbands. Husbands are worthy of fear or respect and wives worthy of love. The dichotomy created between love and fear makes it possible for a husband to "love" his wife without respecting her body, her opinion, or her emotions.

Scholars have only been able to find a liberating Pauline ethic by distinguishing between the authentic Pauline writings and the deuteropauline writings, such as Ephesians. The primary reason for this is the household codes of conduct for slave-master relations contained in the deuteropauline texts of Ephesians and Colossians and in 1 Peter. In 6:5-8, "Paul" tells slaves how to behave toward their masters. Only one verse is dedicated to masters' treatment of slaves (6:9). Masters are to refrain from speaking harshly to their slaves. Again, the implication is that masters' treatment of their slaves is predicated upon the slaves' obedience to their masters. The underlying assumption is that as long as a slave performs according to the master's desires and commands, the master will not need to speak harshly to the slave. Slaves are to be obedient to their master's commands and desires regardless of whether the master is present to oversee their obedience (6:6). Slaves are admonished to accommodate their master's every desire under involuntary bondage as if they are "slaves of Christ doing the will of God." Slaves are to serve their masters with the right frame of mind (*eunoia*) (6:7). If the master can convince the slave that God sanctions his subservient status, he succeeds in sacralizing slavery. This making sacred of a secular and inhumane practice guarantees the perpetuation of the system. The reality is that the slave's obedience is forced. The slave's subservient status is never voluntary, and his con-

stant obedience is expected. However, if the master can control the slave's mind by encouraging him to conceive of his bondage in terms of divine service and privilege, then he can be more certain that his slave will be a "good slave." African slaves in America categorically rejected this admonition.

Slavery Is Never Divine

In Frederick Douglass's famous Independence Day speech titled "What to the Slave Is the Fourth of July?" he asks "What then remains to be argued? Is it that slavery is not divine; that God did not establish it; that our doctors of divinity are mistaken? There is blasphemy in the thought. That which is inhuman cannot be divine. Who can reason on such a proposition?"

—Frederick Douglass, *My Bondage and My Freedom* (New York: Dover, 1969), 44.

Even though the codes of conduct for wives, husbands, children, fathers, slaves, and masters are all set in the context of service to Christ, the greater burden always lies with the subordinate members of the household, and not with the husband/father/master. Verse 6:8 attempts to present the Lord as the great equalizer between slaves and freeborn persons. But African Americans have never considered their status as Christians as mitigating the need for liberation from slavery.

These codes of conduct do not deviate from what the larger culture expected of women, children, and slaves, who were already subordinated to the husband, father, and master. In the ancient Roman patriarchal household, the husband, father, and master were the same person. So the household codes in essence relate how each member of the household is to conduct him/herself toward the male as the head of the household. The codes are primarily concerned with how the male head of the household is to reciprocate acts of submission and obedience directed at him by other members of the household.

In each set of admonitions to a member of the household, the person considered lower on the patriarchal rung is admonished first. Wives are addressed before husbands; children are addressed before parents; slaves are addressed before masters. The onus rests on the lower members of the family to behave appropriately, and then they can expect in turn to be treated in prescribed ways by those who are their husbands, fathers, and masters.

African American preachers and other church leaders, as "stewards of the [biblical] story"[18] must read the household codes critically. African American New Testament scholar Clarice Martin asks, "Should we continue to accept as binding a Christianized pattern of hierarchical domination in the marriage relationship? Or is this a case—as with the slave regulation in the *Haustafeln* genre—where a literalist interpretation of the 'letter' imposes an outmoded social ethos of another period onto the contemporary church?"[19]

Unfortunately, in the black church, black male clergy continue to interpret the biblical text so as to keep women subordinate to male leadership. Many black women in the black church acquiesce to a script generally written by black males that supports black male leaders who call for the continued subordination of black women in the church, in the home, and in the workplace. For certain, however, some black male clergy and political leaders have acted prophetically by ordaining women for pastoral ministry in the face of opposition, selecting women to preach and serve at times and in offices normally relegated to men, and refusing to participate in churches where women's role in the pulpit is limited. But, as Delores Williams states, African American churches need to take an official opposition against sexism:

African-American Christians need doctrine in their churches. But they need *doctrine that emerges from African-American people's experience with God*, not doctrine "inherited" from oppressive Eurocentric forms of Christianity, not female-exclusive doctrine formulated centuries ago by male potentates. . . . It would no doubt be helpful for black religious scholars, along with ministers and congregations, to be involved constantly in the task of "revaluing value" so that black people can root out of the African-American denominational churches the alien sexist, capitalist, class and color values black people have internalized in their process of becoming "Americanized" and "Christianized."[20]

6:10-20, Clothe Yourselves with the Armor of God

The author is clear that God's grace is freely given to saints, and he is equally certain that the saints must exercise personal accountability for their own empowerment. The notion of "clothing oneself," "putting on," and "putting away or off" is a theme throughout Ephesians. "Paul" now admonishes the saints to be empowered in the Lord (v. 10), which is the same thing he prayed for them earlier at 3:16. The straightforward statement is reiterated with a combat or military metaphor. "Clothe yourselves in the complete armor (*panoplian*) of God" (vv. 11, 13a). This metaphorical armor will protect the saints from the "scheming of the devil (*diabolos*)." The devil is "the evil one" (v. 16). The military contest to which the author refers is not an ordinary contest against named nations recognizable in the "flesh and blood." But this contest is against unnamed "rulers, authorities, worldly princes of this darkness, against spiritual things of the wicked one in the heavenlies" (v. 12). An "evil day" will arrive in which the saints will be able to stand firm because they have done everything in their power to stand (v. 13). They clothed themselves in the complete armor of God. The author continues his use of military metaphor by naming the parts of the armor and the equivalent spiritual assets they represent (vv. 14-17). The spiritual virtues that the saints must clothe themselves with are truth, righteousness, the gospel of peace, faith, salvation, and the word of God. These are represented by the girded loins, body armor, shoes, shield, helmet, and sword.

The author asks the saints to constantly pray "in the Spirit," to pray for all the saints, and to pray for him. The saints are asked to pray specifically that when "Paul" opens his mouth, "the mystery of the gospel" will be revealed (v. 19.). He is not simply incarcerated, but he is "an ambassador in chains" (v. 20).

6:21-24, Closing Greeting

"Paul's" official act as an "ambassador in chains" is to commission "Tychicus" to go and inform the saints of his status and the status of his companions. He wishes that the saints will possess all of the virtues mentioned in his letter: peace, love, faith, and grace.

CONCLUSION

African Americans as a community can take comfort in the fact that God has already ordained that the walls that separate us from our full incorporation have been torn down. The plan for our deliverance has been revealed. The realization of our full citizenship and inheritance in Jesus Christ will materialize. Just as "Paul" admonished the Ephesians, we must do our part. We must speak prophetically so that together we can "clothe" and equip our communities with the necessary tools to reach our full potential as a people.

Notes

1. All translations are mine unless otherwise noted.

2. W. E. B. DuBois, *The Souls of Black Folk*, in *Three Negro Classics* (New York: Avon, 1965), 215.

3. Pheme Perkins, *Ephesians* (Nashville: Abingdon, 1997), 36.

4. Peter J. Paris, *The Spirituality of African Peoples: The Search for a Common Moral Discourse* (Minneapolis: Fortress Press, 1995), 92.

5. The NRSV translates this verse as "that he lavished upon us. With all wisdom and insight." In the Greek text, the phrase translated "with all wisdom and understanding" is enclosed in commas so that the phrase could be interpreted with either the preceding thought or the following thought in v. 9. I have chosen to translate the phrase as follows: "that he lavished upon us with all wisdom and understanding."

6. Juan Williams and Quinton Dixie, *This Far by Faith: Stories from the African-American Religious Experience* (New York: Morrow, 2003), 29.

7. Tet-Lim N. Yee, *Jews, Gentiles and Ethnic Reconciliation: Paul's Jewish Identify and Ephesians* (Cambridge: Cambridge University Press, 2005), 53.

8. Edward P. Wimberly, *Counseling African American Marriages and Families* (Louisville: Westminster John Knox, 1997), 21.

9. Lee H. Butler Jr., *Liberating Our Dignity, Saving Our Souls* (St. Louis: Chalice, 2006), 105.

10. Martin Luther King Jr., *Stride toward Freedom* (San Francisco: HarperCollins, 1986), 210.

11. Robert M. Franklin, *Another Day's Journey: Black Churches Confronting the American Crisis* (Minneapolis: Fortress Press, 1997), 107–8.

12. Perkins, *Ephesians*, 100.

13. C. Eric Lincoln and Lawrence H. Mamiya, *The Black Church in the African American Experience* (Durham, N.C.: Duke University Press, 1990), 384.

14. Ibid.

15. Sarah J. Tanzer, "Ephesians," in *Searching the Scriptures: A Feminist Commentary*, vol. 2,

ed. Elisabeth Schüssler Fiorenza (New York: Crossroad, 1998), 332.

16. Ibid.
17. Ibid., 334.
18. James Earl Massey, *Stewards of the Story: The Task of Preaching* (Louisville: Westminster John Knox, 2006).
19. Clarice J. Martin, "The *Haustafeln* (Household Codes) in African American Biblical Interpretation: 'Free Slaves' and 'Subordinate Women,'" in *Stony the Road We Trod: African American Biblical Interpretation*, ed. Cain Hope Felder (Minneapolis: Fortress Press, 1991), 220.
20. Delores S. Williams, *Sisters in the Wilderness: The Challenge of Womanist God-Talk* (Maryknoll, N.Y.: Orbis, 1998), 217, 218–19, emphasis added.

For Further Reading

Blount, Brian K. *Then the Whisper Put on Flesh: New Testament Ethics in an African American Context*. Nashville: Abingdon, 2001.

Butler, Lee H., Jr. *Liberating Our Dignity, Saving Our Souls*. St Louis: Chalice, 2006.

Cone, James. *The Spirituals and the Blues*. Maryknoll, N.Y.: Orbis, 1999.

Douglass, Frederick. *My Bondage and My Freedom*. New York: Dover, 1969 [1855].

DuBois, W. E. B. *The Souls of Black Folk in Three Negro Classics*. New York: Avon, 1965, 215.

Franklin, Robert M. *Another Day's Journey: Black Churches Confronting the American Crisis*. Minneapolis: Fortress Press, 1997.

Harrill, J. Albert. *Slaves in the New Testament: Literary, Social, and Moral Dimensions*. Minneapolis: Fortress Press, 2006.

Howell, Donna Wyant. *I Was a Slave: True Life Stores Told by Former American Slaves in the 1930s*. Washington, D.C.: American Legacy, 1995.

King, Martin Luther, Jr. *Stride toward Freedom*. San Francisco: HarperCollins, 1986.

Lincoln, C. Eric, and Lawrence H. Mamiya. *The Black Church in the African American Experience*. Durham, N.C.: Duke University Press, 1990.

MacDonald, Margaret Y. *Colossians and Ephesians*. Sacra Pagina 17. Collegeville, Minn.: Liturgical, 2000.

Mandela, Nelson. *Long Walk to Freedom*. Boston: Little, Brown, 1994.

Martin, Clarice. J. "The *Haustafeln* (Household Codes) in African American Biblical Interpretation: 'Free Slaves' and 'Subordinate Women.'" Pages 206–31 in *Stony the Road We Trod: African American Biblical Interpretation*. Edited by Cain Hope Felder. Minneapolis: Fortress Press, 1991.

Massey, James Earl. *Stewards of the Story: The Task of Preaching*. Louisville: Westminster John Knox, 2006.

Paris, Peter J. *The Spirituality of African Peoples: The Search for a Common Moral Discourse*. Minneapolis: Fortress Press, 1995.

Perkins, Pheme. *Ephesians*. Nashville: Abingdon, 1997.

Tanzer, Sarah J. "Ephesians." Pages 326–48 in *Searching the Scriptures: A Feminist Commentary*. Volume 2. Edited by Elisabeth Schüssler Fiorenza. New York: Crossroad, 1998.

Thurman, Howard. *Jesus and the Disinherited*. Boston: Beacon, 1976.

Williams, Delores. S. *Sisters in the Wilderness. The Challenge of Womanist God-Talk*. Maryknoll, N.Y.: Orbis, 1998.

Williams, Juan, and Quinton Dixie. *This Far by Faith: Stories from the African-American Religious Experience*. New York: Morrow, 2003.

Wimberly, Edward P. *Counseling African American Marriages and Families*. Louisville: Westminster John Knox, 1997.

Yee, Tet-Lim N. *Jews, Gentiles and Ethnic Reconciliation: Paul's Jewish Identity and Ephesians*. Society for New Testament Studies Monograph Series 130. Cambridge: Cambridge University Press, 2005.

PHILIPPIANS

―――――|🔲🔲|―――――

Monya A. Stubbs

INTRODUCTION: THE LIFE-CONTEXT

God called America to be a great nation. Nobody needs to be poor whether they're Appalachian white, whether they're Mexican Americans, whether they're Puerto Ricans, whether they're Indians or whether they're Negro, nobody needs to be poor in this rich country. . . . The resources are in this nation. The question is whether the will is there . . . and up to now I haven't seen the will.[1]

In September 1967, Martin Luther King Jr. convened the Southern Christian Leadership Conference's executive staff in rural Virginia. The purpose of the retreat was to set a renewed course for the human rights nonviolent struggle. The opinions of the staff varied. Some argued for a primary focus on the resistance to the Vietnam War. Others petitioned for continued emphasis on voter registration in the South. Still others maintained the best course of action would be to rebuild SCLC's movement in the North where members could be mobilized for direct forms of protest throughout the country against targeted injustices. The suggestion that most intrigued King, however, came from a young lawyer, Marian Wright. She proposed that the movement focus its attention and resources on uplifting the invisible poor. Inspired by Robert Kennedy's remark that Congress would never address issues of the invisible poor unless it became more uncomfortable not to do so, Wright advocated introducing the country's leaders to the poor. Following the model of the Bonus Army of World War I veterans who staged sit-ins at the capital to seek relief from the Great Depression, she proposed that SCLC "transport into Washington a representative host of faces from every region and race—men who never worked, women who could not read, children who seldom ate—for educational witness until Congress provided jobs or income."[2]

Wright's idea captured King's attention. He wanted to raise class issues—"issues that relate to the privileged as over against the underprivileged."[3] He therefore embraced four umbrella truths regarding the direction of the human rights nonviolent movement. First, the movement had to move beyond an emphasis on civil and political inequities between blacks and whites. The security and equality of blacks in America depended on a "serious and irrevocable national purpose" that had to confront hard-core economic issues that called for "something of a restructuring of the architecture of American society."[4] The great revelation of King's latter years was that in order to address the civil, political, and economic disparities of America's black citizens, the nonviolent movement had to address *poverty* as the fundamental issue that negatively affected all American citizens, regardless of race or ethnicity.

The second, perhaps parallel truth King realized was that the nonviolent movement's major objective would not be "to bring the discriminated up to a limited, particular level, but to reduce the gap between them and the rest of American society."[5] To achieve this goal, King announced:

> I am now convinced that the simplest approach will prove to be the most revolutionary—the solution to poverty is to abolish it directly by a now rather widely discussed measure—the guaranteed annual income. . . . Our emphasis should shift from exclusive attention to putting people to work over to enabling people to consume. . . . We must create full employment or we must create incomes.[6]

Third, King regarded the nonviolent movement as a global human rights struggle. The human rights nonviolent movement must struggle against poverty on both a domestic and an international front, where all the world's inhabitants are each other's neighbors. What began as a struggle for the civil rights of one group of people evolved into a struggle for the dignity of humanity. King called the Western world to initiate an immediate and sustained Marshall Plan for Asia, Africa, and South America. King's concern, however, was not whether the West would in fact aid these developing countries in "conquering the ancient enemy, poverty." Rather, he worried that Western nations would initiate this aid program as a surreptitious means to control the poor nations and not as a committed effort to wipe poverty, ignorance, and disease from the face of the earth.

As the fourth umbrella truth, King advised against viewing foreign aid programs (and his domestic anti-poverty proposal) as mere charity. Rather, he emphasized the interdependence of all humanity and the contributions each nation has made to the treasury of the world's ideas, natural resources, and labor.

Poverty and the World

In 2006 some 800 million people were chronically hungry and malnourished. Every day 30,000 children die due to causes directly related to poverty.

—www.un.org

Working to End Poverty

The United Nations Millennium Development Goals, adopted by 189 Heads of State and Governments in 2000, represent a partnership between rich and poor countries with the overarching aim being to halve the number of people living in extreme poverty and hunger by 2015.

—www.un.org

"Each of us lives eternally 'in the red.' We are ever-lasting debtors to known and unknown men and women."[7] The textiles we wear, the food we eat, the electronics we play/utilize, the cars we drive, the coffee and tea we drink, the jewelry we wear, etc., create a relationship of mutual indebtedness among all nations and all citizens.

In the end, the most fascinating and revolutionary aspect of King's refocused nonviolent movement rested not only in the activities it proposed but also in the mind-set of mutual indebtedness it enlisted. That is, the movement would take on a mind-set of *other-interestedness*" in order to facilitate the self-interest of various ethnic groups and nations of the world. With these hopes and reservations, King and the SCLC organized the ill-fated Poor People's Campaign.

THEOLOGICAL ISSUES ARISING FROM THIS LIFE-CONTEXT

Philippians is a letter written to a Christian community that Paul had converted in the city of Philippi in eastern Macedonia.[8] Paul wrote the letter from an undisclosed location, seeking to address four major concerns: (1) he wanted to thank the Philippian Christians for providing him with financial support; (2) he wanted to express his joy at how well they were doing; (3) he wanted to put them at ease over their messenger Epaphroditus, who had taken ill but had recovered; and (4) he wanted to encourage them to maintain and strengthen the *unity* of their congregation.

Each of these points is woven together in an ideological web in which Paul describes how people ought to imagine themselves in relationship with others. Consider, for instance, Phil 2:3-4: "Do nothing from selfish ambition or conceit, but in humility regard others as better than yourselves. Let each of you look not to your own interests [qualities], but to the interests [qualities] of others." These two verses function as the ideological heart of Paul's letter to the Christian community at Philippi. Paul shows how members of a Christ-believing community should imagine themselves in relationship with each other and the rest of society. For Paul, human discernment and behavior that are essentially "other centered," represent both the means and the ends for an empowered and empowering communal pattern of relating.

But, as Phil 2:5 makes clear, being members of a Christ-believing community, and therefore thinking and acting in ways that are "other centered," is not to deny oneself. Rather, it is *knowing* that you are *in* Christ. And if in Christ, you produce a "harvest of righteousness" (Phil 1:11), reflecting a habit of living that demonstrates a valuable communal experience.[9] Ultimately, Paul challenges the Philippian community to subject its collective mental orientation, and therefore its very self-identification, to recognizing and affirming the power and presence of God and Christ, not merely, nor primarily, in one's individual self, but in others. As such, although each of the four central issues named above are significant thematic foci in the letter, Paul's call to communal unity, to be of the "same mind," dominates the tenor of the letter. As one reads through Philippians, one senses a joyous anxiety in Paul's tone. Like Martin Luther King Jr., Paul struggles throughout the text with the possibility of the community not living in "unity" and therefore not living in a manner that is "worthy of the gospel of Christ." In other words, he worries that the community, as individuals and as a whole, might be crippled by divisiveness and therefore prove ineffective in producing "fruits of justice"—in creating and sustaining an environment that people have reason to value.

At first glance, such a framing of Paul's message might seem counterproductive, even dangerous for the African American community. One can reasonably argue the absurdity of suggesting that a community that carries the weight and bears the scars of centuries of subjection to chattel slavery, decades of Jim Crow laws, and current forms of overt and covert discrimination must orient its identity around "humility" and "seeing others as better than yourselves" (2:3-4). It seems like an act of self-deprecation to suggest that a faithful reading of Philippians for the African American community is to understand Paul as exhorting Christian believers to reject one's ethnicity for the sake of the gospel (3:4-11). And certainly, any interpretation of Philippians that supports the claim that Christian believers must deny their "own interests" and privilege the "interest of others" (2:4) must be rejected by the African American community as an act of self-repudiation.

However, it is precisely in and through these traditionally "troubling" passages that one finds a liberating message for contemporary readers—especially those of the twenty-first-century African American community. Paul invites contemporary readers to reenvision how we recognize and evaluate leadership as those who function as "slaves of Christ" (1:1). Like the Rev. Dr. Martin Luther King Jr., Paul challenges Christian believers to move in a unified and deliber-

ate way to fully satisfy the *needs* of "others" so that "God will fully satisfy every need of [ours] according to [God's] riches in glory in Christ Jesus" (4:18-19).

To this end, Paul lays out three levels of unity into which he hopes the Philippian community will grow stronger: (1) a unity of purpose or mission in living and proclaiming the gospel, (2) a unity around the principle of "other interestedness," and (3) a unity of perspective where people understand themselves as mutually indebted to one another.

Paul presents the view that to be "slaves of Christ Jesus"—as he, Timothy, and the Philippians are—is to be grounded in unity by a certain purpose/mission, by the principle of other-interestedness and the mindset of understanding themselves as mutually indebted to one another. These ideas are interrelated throughout the four chapters, with each chapter prioritizing one over the others. For instance, although Paul spends much of his energy in chap. 1 defining the purpose of being a "slave of Christ Jesus," the chapter also functions as a general overview to each of the other two points of unity. In chap. 2 Paul primarily explores his call to a unity around the principle of "other interestedness" and spends a little time developing the perspective of mutual indebtedness. Chapter 3, however, mainly focuses on the idea of unity through "other interestedness," while chap. 4 is dedicated to more fully explaining the concept of mutual indebtedness.

CHAPTER 1, SLAVES OF CHRIST JESUS

1:1-11, Introduction: Slaves of Christ Jesus as Sharing a Unity of Purpose

Paul begins this letter not with his usual claim to apostolic authority—an apostle of Jesus Christ (1 Cor 1:1; 2 Cor 1:1; Gal 1)—but rather, as in Rom 1:1, he introduces himself and his companion Timothy as "slaves of Christ Jesus." This concept represents Paul's metaphorical self-designation and is therefore central to how he imagines himself in relation both to Christ and to the Philippian community. Paul and Timothy's relation to Christ is *like* the relationship of a "slave" to his master. Although the concept of slave can carry several connotations,[10] Paul uses the phrase in Philippians to suggest someone who acts in the name of his or her master for the sake of the household and someone totally defined by his or her mission in the name of a master. The focus is thus on Christ's mission, which the "slave" prolongs in the name of the Lord.

In vv. 3-6 this self-proclaimed "slave of Christ" expresses his joy and constant prayer for the community because of their "sharing in the gospel from the first day until now" (v. 5). In v. 6 Paul says that he is certain God will complete the "good work" God started. Paul's idea of a good work "finds its explanation in the fact that the Philippians were partners with Paul in the gospel (v. 5), and shared their resources with him to make the proclamation of the gospel possible."[11] This "good work" however, is God's work; it is God's mission, and God brings it to completion *by human means*—the Philippian community. Paul is not saying that God's grace works in passive individuals who are totally at the mercy and power of their owner. Rather, he emphasizes the mission of God that, in turn, becomes the mission of Paul and Timothy and the Philippian community. It is in this way that, at the start of the letter, Paul shapes the idea of "slave of Christ" to emphasize one who is defined by and prolongs a certain mission in the name of the master.

This idea is furthered in v. 11, where Paul describes the work of the gospel as "producing fruits of justice" (NRSV: "harvest of righteousness"), which is the *mission* of Christ. What are these "fruits of justice"? These good fruits

are not the "divine righteousness" imputed by God that humanity receives only by faith in Christ. Paul perhaps has in mind the Old Testament understanding of this phrase, in which the emphasis is on humanity's acts of justice (or injustice) toward one another (see Amos 5:7, 6:12; Prov 11:30). Paul is emphasizing the Philippians' conduct, i.e., mission. So the focus of the phrase translated "having produced fruits of justice" privileges both the qualities and the conduct of individuals. That is, it privileges the deliberate actions of the community to live in relationship with others without pretense and intention to do harm (v. 10).[12] According to Paul's logic, there is little point in possessing dormant "good qualities" that do not result in just actions. This is the mission of the gospel that has come through Jesus Christ and is prolonged by Paul and Timothy for the glory and praise of God. Therefore, Paul and Timothy are "slaves of Christ Jesus" because of their *mission*, their work to live and spread the gospel. Likewise, the Philippian community "shares" or "partners" (*koinonia*) with Paul and Timothy in this mission. In other words, they share a *unity of purpose*.

1:12-30, Living in Unity: The Paradox of Preaching Christ

Paul turns to his current predicament—his imprisonment. He is eager to explain to the community that his imprisonment is not a cause for alarm or a hindrance to the gospel movement. On the contrary, it has in fact helped to advance the gospel. Those serving the Roman Empire are being influenced by his unwavering dedication to the cause of Christ and because of his imprisonment other believers fearlessly proclaim the gospel (vv. 12-14).

In vv. 15-18, Paul addresses the motives and mind-set of those believers who are boldly preaching the gospel. He juxtaposes two groups in order to demonstrate attitudes that either frustrate or promote the unity of purpose he recommends to the Philippian community. One group preaches Christ because of envy and self-rivalry. On the other hand, there are those who preach out of love and good will because they know, appreciate, and want to share in Paul's defense of the gospel. Theirs is a preaching of Christ that unites people and works for the deepest good of others. Those who preach out of a mind-set of self-rivalry seek to increase Paul's suffering while he is in prison. Paul does not appear to have a problem with the acceptable "message" of Christ that is being proclaimed by those who seek to increase his "suffering." In fact, through the preaching of Christ, those who seek him harm actually bring him joy, because, whether in pretense or in truth, Paul finds great joy in knowing Christ is preached. Nevertheless, Paul is troubled. He understands that it is wrong to use moral means—the preaching of Christ—to preserve immoral ends—the direct and intentional harm of another (Paul).[13] He understands that the motives that inspire one to preach Christ can directly affect how the message of Christ is manifested in the world.

While we do not know the exact identity nor the exact point(s) of contention between Paul and these fellow Christians who wish him "harm," his reason for sharing the issue with the Philippian community is ideological. That is, Paul shares the story to advise the community on how *not* to imagine themselves in relationship with each other. The point is made clear in the relational structure he establishes between the concepts. For instance, people who function out of a mind-set of love (deep concern for well-being of others) express good will and truth toward others. By contrast, people who function out of a mind-set of selfish ambition promote an environment where envy, petty rivalries, and pretense characterize communal patterns of relating. Paul, however,

offers a more advantageous manner of human relating that models the unity of purpose and unity of thinking he has commended to the community.

1:19-26, Mutual Indebtedness

In v. 19 Paul writes that he is confident that his ultimate fate is freedom. The prayers of the community along with the enabling power of the Spirit of Jesus Christ will secure his deliverance from prison (v. 19). The word Paul uses here for prayer is significant. The original meaning of *deēsis* is "lack" or "need." In the New Testament it is used to designate requests and concrete prayers to God, usually from one person or group on behalf of another. We might think of intercessory prayer, where one prays for God to meet a "need" or fill some "lack" in another.[14] Therefore, the community's petitioning God on Paul's behalf is an example of sharing and love (the deep desire to effect qualitative change in the life of another). For a moment, however, Paul seems to digress into a mind-set of self-interested priorities. He maintains that it is his desire to enlarge Christ with his whole self; he is assured that if he lives, his life will reflect the cause of Christ, and if he dies, this too will magnify Christ (he has died defending the gospel). But he admits that he is torn between remaining in life or preferring death. He actually says that he prefers death: "My desire is to depart and be with Christ, for that is far better" (v. 23b). Paul, however, immediately returns to practicing the type of reasoning process into which he hopes the Philippians will grow: "but to remain in the flesh [alive] is more necessary for you. Since I am convinced of this, I know that I will remain and continue with all of you for your progress and joy in faith" (vv. 24-25).

Paul's comments here should not be read as altruistic self-denial. Paul identifies himself as a slave of Christ, acting on behalf of his master in order to prolong the mission of his master. Therefore, Paul's recognition of the need to remain alive—recognizing the necessity of his ministry to the well-being of the Philippian community—is his recognition that "part of the divine plan of salvation is committed to him, and its seriousness consists in the fact that he cannot evade it."[15] Paul is convinced of and convicted by his *divine* purpose. But this divine purpose is inherently connected to a divine mind-set that privileges the concept of *mutual indebtedness*. Paul will remain with and share in the struggles of the community because they too share in his struggles and will even help to secure his liberation from prison. Each of them (Paul and the Philippian community) privileges the "needs" of the other and therefore secures each of their individual "needs."

1:27-30, Mutuality and Interdependence

The final section of chap. 1 functions as a summation of all that Paul has explained and advised so far. He opens the section with the adverb "only," essentially saying "this one point is critical": "live your life (*politeuomai*) in a manner worthy of the gospel of Christ" (v. 27a). Here again Paul is reinforcing an ideological position that encourages people to imagine themselves in a relationship of mutuality and relational indebtedness. Having described his own struggle with opposition to his life, Paul now suggests that the Philippians find themselves in a similar situation (v. 30). His goal is to offer strategic principles on how they should confront their opponents and in turn live a life worthy of the gospel of Christ.

Paul's use of the term *politeuomai* is telling. The term means more than simply to live out one's life. It also carries the connotation "to live as a citizen of a free state," "to take an active part in the affairs of the state."[16] But, to the ancient Greek and later to the Romans, the state was

a sort of partnership formed with a view to having people attain the highest of all human good. . . . Here in the state the individual citizen developed his [her] gifts and realized his [her] potential not in isolation, but in cooperation. Here he [she] was able to maximize his [her] abilities not by himself [herself] or for himself [herself], but in community and for the good of the community. As a consequence, mutuality and interdependence were important ideas inhering in the concept of [*polis*].[17]

It is these concepts of communal mutuality and interdependence that Paul has in mind here as is evident in the remainder of the sentence.

Beyond the verb *politeuomai*, Paul uses two other significant verbs in v. 27 to describe a life worthily lived for the gospel of Christ. The first is *steko*, "stand firm," and the second is *synathleo*, "struggling together." Both of these words are action verbs characterized by a normative cognitive logic—unity. With the first term, Paul uses the adjectival forms of "one" (*heni* and *mia*) to represent his call to *unity* in spirit and *unity* in soul or mind. With the second term, Paul adds the prefix *syn* (with) as a "subtle reinforcement of his purpose, urging them towards unity."[18] Ultimately, v. 27 exhorts the community to unify itself so that it can adequately defend the faith of the gospel which is more than the Christ event, but it is also the mind-set of mutual indebtedness that should govern the course of their actions. Because they stand in *unity*, the community should not feel frightened by their opponents. Rather their unity represents the force of their power. It is the "sign" of God's "saving" work among them, and simultaneously it is an "omen" of God's wrath against their opponents (v. 28).

Chapter 1 closes with Paul reminding the Philippian community that they stand with him as "slaves of Christ," and this is both a privilege and a burden: "for he has graciously granted you the privilege not only of believing in Christ, but of suffering for him also" (v. 29). This verse, however, does not sacralize suffering. Instead, it collapses the distinction between conviction and action. It is a great gift to believe in God's salvation of humanity through the person of Christ Jesus. It is an equally wonderful gift to participate in expressing continuing manifestations of God in the world (producing fruits of justice), which is often met with "violent" resistance by those whose mind-set prioritizes earthly things (3:19), that is, those who do not seek the deepest good for others. So to live as "slaves of Christ" is to live in community with others and to be guided by a mind-set that seeks to create an environment that all people have reason to value. And, as Paul makes clear in chaps. 3 and 4, to struggle so that one might secure the well-being of others is a privilege that leads to power.

Chapter 2, Slaves of Christ Jesus: Unity through Other-Interestedness and a Sense of Mutual Indebtedness

Although the notion of unity in divine purpose and mental orientation has underlined Paul's thought throughout the letter, it is only now that he directly employs the language to express this conviction. Paul writes: "make my joy complete, be of the same mind (*autos phroneo*), having the same love, being of full accord and of one mind" (*phroneo*) (v. 2). He obviously places a high value on communal mental cohesiveness. He mentions it twice in the same breath. Paul, however, is not calling the community to a type of blind "faith." On the contrary, *phroneo* suggests one having a certain attitude based on careful consideration that is a "combination of intellectual and affective activity"[19] (see 1:9-10). Paul expects the community to be like-minded in love. This represents the heart of his discourse about how people ought to imagine themselves in relationship with each other as those who identify and function as "slaves of Christ."

According to Paul, the most dangerous mental disposition that could destroy the community's effectiveness in proclaiming and living boldly the gospel of Christ would be the lack of a unified mind-set about how to act in love. So Paul explains: "do nothing from selfish ambition or conceit." Do not be arrogant and unwilling to recognize the value and worth of others. Rather, "in humility regard others as better than yourselves" (v. 3). Even more, "Let each of you look not to your own interests, but pay careful attention (*skopeo*) to the interests of others" (v. 4, my translation).

What are these "things" of others to which Paul alludes? To answer this question we must *recall* a point and *address* a point. First, recall that believers' self-identify as slaves of Christ, as those whose mission is to prolong the purpose of the gospel. The purpose of the gospel through Christ Jesus is the manifestation of love. Within the context of Philippians, love is, on the one hand, discerning and demonstrating the deepest good for others (creating an environment so people can live a life they have reason to value). Love is also recognizing the power and presence of God and Christ in others (1:19; 2:22; 2:25-30; 3:17; 4:15). Second, we must address Paul's purpose in chap. 2, especially 2:5. Against theological interpretations that read chap. 2 as providing Christ as a moral model—be submissive as Christ was, and you will be exalted—one can also read the passage as Paul encouraging readers to identify people who are lowly and humble as Christ was. It is in these people that we find manifestations of Christ—God's presence in the world.

For instance, v. 5 is often interpreted to mean, "Have the same attitude/mind in you that Christ had in him." Following Daniel Patte, one might also translate the passage: "have this mind among yourselves, which you have in Christ Jesus." "Among yourselves" and "in Christ Jesus" are parallel phrases. This suggest the meaning, "have the same mind-set toward each other as the mind-set you have toward Christ." That is, "imagine yourselves in relationship with others the way you imagine yourselves in relationship with Christ." Understood this way, this verse summarizes well the exhortations found in the preceding verses. "In humility consider others superior to yourselves" (v. 3b). Believers imagine Christ as superior to themselves even as Christ also imagines God superior to himself (v. 6).

In the context of exhortations to overcome conflict and divisions in the community caused by rivalry and vain ambition (v. 3), "things" refers to the qualities and conduct of others: Paul exhorts the Philippians to "look attentively" for the qualities and the conduct of the others, that is, for fruits of justice (1:11). When Paul exhorts the Philippians to "look attentively" for these Christ "qualities," he is directing that they seek the qualities and manifestations of God in others.

Of course, these manifestations are exhibited in Christ, as verses 2:6-8 illustrate. Christ is an example of one who has power (v. 6). But for Paul, the more pressing question is: how does one effectively exercise power? Christ exercised his power by sharing in the human condition (v. 7). He became obedient to the point of death. But Christ became obedient to whom and for what? Christ was obedient to God in his service to humanity (v. 8). Yet, as Paul expresses in 2:9-11, obedience to the service of humanity represents both a sign of Christ's power and the means through which Christ receives power. Paul does not integrate into his argument 2:6-11, an early Christian hymn, for christological or soteriological reasons. Rather, Paul integrates the passage into his argument to illustrate his basic conviction that through their working together in a mind-set of other-interestedness, the Philippian community could transcend any challenge they might face (v. 12). Moreover, their obedience to working out of a mind-set of other-interestedness represents a sign of the empowering presence of God that enables them to continue in their service of the gospel (vv. 12-15).

Timothy and Epaphroditus

Paul offers Timothy and Epaphroditus as individual examples of concrete manifestations of those who possess an appropriate mind-set and therefore exhibit actions that manifest God and Christ in their patterns of human relating. Timothy, already identified by Paul as a "slave of Christ" (1:1), is now heralded as a unique companion to Paul because he and Paul are "like-minded" or same-souled (*isopsychos*) in their genuine concern for the "things" (qualities and conduct) that afflict the Philippian community (v. 20). The term *merimnao* (concern) suggests more than a passing interest. Rather, the term relates a state of total distraction and preoccupation over a particular issue. It reflects a state of deep concern that enlists a person's complete attention. Timothy is thus lifted up as one whose "qualities and conduct" should be "looked at attentively" and ultimately modeled. Unlike other companions of Paul who orient their will around purely selfish gains (v. 21), Timothy serves as a faithful slave of Christ who prolongs the mission of his master through his work in the gospel—helping to create and sustain an environment that people have reason to value (v. 22).

Paul also describes Epaphroditus as a "type" of person whom the Philippian community should hold in great honor for risking his life in Christ's work and for his service to Paul (v. 29). Paul employs the term *paraboleumai* to describe Epaphroditus's commitment to the gospel and to his service to Paul. Paul relates the idea that Epaphroditus knowingly and willingly "exposes himself to danger" (*paraboleumai*) in order to benefit the gospel of Christ and in service to Paul. However, Epaphroditus's actions do not speak to the "qualities and conduct" that Paul wants to emphasize to his readers merely because they portray unwarranted selfless commitment to benefit the deepest good of another. Beyond an "other-interested" mind-set, the example of Epaphroditus is significant because his actions point to the central ideological conviction in Paul's thought that prefigures a manifestation of God and Christ's activities in the world— mutual indebtedness.

Epaphroditus exposed himself to danger, nearing death, so that he might fulfill the requirements established in the partnership between Paul and the Philippian community (v. 30), a service (*leitourgos*) that, for an unnamed reason, the Philippian community could not fulfill. However, in this context, it is not the Philippians' shortcomings but Epaphroditus's service and the relationship of mutual indebtedness that Paul wishes to highlight. *Leitourgos*, used to allude to a monetary gift (4:10-20), also recalls the sacrificial language of 2:25. "Epaphroditus will finish the service the Philippians have already offered Paul."[20] And in turn, Paul will again offer the community protective and sound knowledge regarding how they ought to imagine themselves in relationship with Christ and one another. This knowledge, argues Paul, is a truth that will provide a sense of security and certainty from which they should never turn (3:1), even in the midst of unmitigated opponents who live as "enemies of the cross of Christ" (3:18).

CHAPTER 3, SLAVES OF CHRIST JESUS: UNITY IN OTHER-INTERESTEDNESS

Having presented Timothy and Epaphroditus as examples whose qualities and conduct should be "scoped out" (*skopeo*) or paid close attention to by the Philippian community, Paul now offers himself as an example of one who possesses qualities and exhibits conduct that manifest God and Christ in the world. Chapter 3 opens with Paul's description of another group he feels must also be "looked at attentively." These persons, however, are to be observed, because their "qualities and conduct" must be rejected and avoided. Paul writes in v. 2: "Beware of the dogs, beware of the evil-workers, beware of those who mutilate the flesh." These are three warnings against a group that advocates circumcision. As with his argument in Galatians (esp. Gal 5:1-12), Paul warns the Philippians against being persuaded into believing that in order to participate fully as Christ-believers they had to undergo the physical act of circumcision and thereby subject themselves to Jewish law and custom.

The concept of "flesh" is important. On the one hand, Paul uses the term to refer to the physical act of circumcision. However, Paul broadens the term's connotative meaning to describe a code of conduct or a pattern of convictions valued under Jewish law. He presents the idea of flesh, then, as an ethnic identity marker to which he once lived into faithfully (vv. 4-6). Now Paul claims that those who have "no confidence in the flesh" are the true circumcised because they worship in the Spirit of God and boast in Christ Jesus (v. 3). Having no "confidence in the flesh" is an ideological statement. It represents a pattern of human relating and just behavior that discounts the value in "knowing Christ Jesus [as] my Lord" (v. 7). Yet Paul's values that carried weight while he functioned under a mind-set in which his understanding of justice came from the law (v. 9) were antithetical to those whose source is the justice from God based on faith in Christ (v. 9b). The former privilege social status and ethnic purity characterized by individual achievements (vv. 4-6). The latter privilege being a "slave of Christ" or rather, "knowing Christ Jesus [as] my Lord." And to know Christ as my Lord is to prolong the ministry of love that recognizes and affirms the power and presence of God and Christ not merely nor primarily in self, but in others.

Moreover, to "know Christ" is to know "the power of his resurrection and the sharing of his sufferings, by becoming like him in his death" (v. 10). The knowledge Paul speaks of here is not merely intellectual but also experiential. That is, knowing the power of his resurrection actually means experiencing this power and recognizing that it is at work in one's experience with others. The same is true about knowing Christ's sufferings. Paul is not suggesting, however, that he desires to suffer as Christ suffered or to die a physical death as Christ died. Instead, Paul recognizes that he has died with Christ (see Rom 6). He is no longer guided by a pattern of human relating to which he was subject "under the law." Instead, he now privileges a pattern of human relating made possible through the Christ event, and he wishes to make the effects of Christ's death an ever-present reality in his life. This is "being conformed to his death." The believer's experience has the "same form" as Jesus' death. Thus, as Daniel Patte explains:

> knowing Christ is finding in one's experience both resurrection like events (manifestations of the power of the resurrection) and Christ-like sufferings (i.e. situations which are like Christ's death). What kind of experience is in the "form of Christ's death?" The flow of the argu-

ment suggests that this phrase is related to the preceding statements about Paul's turn away from the commitments and values he prioritized under Pharisaic Judaism. He counts his life in Pharisaic Judaism as "loss." This is being "conformed to Christ's death."[21]

For Christian believers, then, being "conformed to Christ's death" is to experience the power of Christ's resurrection. They are like-minded in their attitude of mutual indebtedness. They affirm the power and presence of God and Christ beyond their individual experience. Ultimately, they walk as heavenly citizens whose mind-set is beyond earthly things (v. 19). That is, they are like-minded in respecting the need to recognize and affirm the qualities and conduct in others that work to create an environment that people have reason to value. Yet Paul understands that "being conformed to Christ's death" and "knowing the power of his resurrection" is not an end in itself for the believer. And he does not yet fully live into the "resurrection from the dead." Rather, these *experiences* represent a means for sharing the fullness of God's power at the parousia. So Paul says he "presses on toward," "vigilantly seeks after (*dioko*) the goal for the prize of the heavenly calling of God in Christ Jesus" (v. 14). The term translated "press on," *dioko,* is the same word Paul uses in v. 6 to describe the zeal with which he pursued and persecuted the church. Now Paul "hunts down" or vigorously pursues the high calling of God in Christ Jesus, rather than pursuing a calling that works against Christ Jesus.

Paul is not attacking Judaism. He is not interested in rejecting or de-emphasizing his ethnic identity. Instead he is addressing an inadequate Jewish Christian understanding of the gospel that, in his mind, wrongly portrays how people ought to imagine themselves in relationship with God, Christ, and one another. Jesus "emptied himself" not for the purpose of denying himself, but for the purpose of including others in the divine purpose of God. In doing so, Jesus became more fully who he was intended to be—Lord to the glory of God (2:7-11). In the same way, Paul encourages believers to empty themselves. Believers must seek out, acknowledge, and affirm in others (not merely or primarily in oneself) qualities and conduct that manifest the power and presence of God and Christ in the world. This is the work of God; believers are called to live into this work: to "work out your own salvation with fear and trembling" (2:12). What might appear through an "earthly" mind-set as believers' lowly, humiliated body, is in fact, a manifestation of citizens of heaven, experiencing conformity into the body of Christ's glory (v. 21a). Just as life conducted (*politeumai*, 1:27) in a manner worthy of the gospel of Christ is characterized by communal interdependence and mutuality, life in the heavenly or future *politeumai* will also be one of mutual love. Such an expression of how people ought to imagine themselves in relationship with God, Christ, and one another is both the current expression of God's power and the future promise of God's power (v. 21b). With the assurance of this power, Paul again reminds the Philippian community to "stand firm" so that they may continue to impart the power they have received (4:1).

Chapter 4, Slaves of Christ Jesus: Unity through a Sense of Mutual Indebtedness

Verses 2-9 repeat Paul's charge for communal unity and speak to how they are to stand firm. He grounds the exhortation for communal unity in the now-familiar concept of "like-mindedness." Euodia and Syntyche, female

leaders in the Philippian community, are obviously at odds over an unnamed issue and Paul implores them to be of the same mind in the Lord. In other words, Paul begs them to come to an agreement on the point of opposition and to do so by acknowledging and affirming the gifts and graces of God and Christ in the other. Paul then appeals to another member of the community (or to the community at large) to assist Euodia and Syntyche in reaching an agreement.[22] However, we miss Paul's point if we understand his plea as disparaging to Euodia and Syntyche. On the contrary, the women are to receive help from the community out of a sense of mutual indebtedness (indebted love). Euodia and Syntyche are *worthy* of assistance because they have fought side by side with Paul and others in the struggle (*[syn]ēthlēsan*, fight together side by side with) to live and preach the gospel.

Moreover, the life of believers is to be characterized by *epieikēs* (reasonableness) that displays how the believers ought to imagine themselves in relationship with all of society (not simply each other) (v. 5). But the term also speaks to the power Paul believes the community embodies because they function as "slaves of Christ." On one level, the term reflects the give and take or compromise that is essential to the successful negotiation of human relationships. It carries the sense of moderation, not always demanding one's own way, not insisting on the letter of the law but considering special circumstances in individual cases.[23] On another level the term connotes divine gentleness. "The weak are always anxiously trying to defend their power and dignity. But the one who has heavenly authority can display saving, forgiving and redeeming clemency"[24] even to personal enemies. The Philippian community is made up of "heavenly citizens," associated with and functioning out of divine glory. They walk in power, therefore, they must display *epieikēs* (vv. 4-6).

However, this type of reasonableness is effective only insofar as it pursues the struggle of the gospel. "Reasonableness" becomes a position of weakness and a mental orientation that promotes communal chaos if the community operates out of it with disregard for acknowledging and affirming the gifts in others and not seeking to create an environment that all people have reason to value (vv. 7-9).

In vv. 10-20 Paul again describes his relationship with the Philippian community as one of mutual indebtedness. Paul rejoices in the fact that the community once again has a mind-set to support him. Paul quickly clarifies his statement, however, and comments that he realizes that the community has always had a mind-set to support him, but has lacked the opportunity to show their concern (v. 10). Paul then lapses into a reflection on his self-sufficiency in Christ, seeming strangely uncomfortable with his obvious dependence on the Philippian community (vv. 11-12). Fearing he sounds ungrateful, Paul reluctantly thanks the community for partnering with him and sharing his afflictions (v. 13). He continues to acknowledge and affirm the mutual relationship he shares with the Philippian community in the spread of the gospel. They alone shared with him in the matter of giving and receiving; they alone partnered with him in a system of reciprocity in which each was held accountable. Paul describes the relationship like a business venture with a strict accounting of expenditures and receipts.[25] The Philippian community has provided Paul "gifts" on more than one occasion to meet his physical and fiscal needs (vv. 15-16). Paul is grateful, Paul is indebted, and Paul is uncomfortable.

After acknowledging and affirming the "gifts" the community has bestowed upon him, "gifts" that are a necessary and expected part of their partnership, Paul slips into a line of thought that reflects the complexity in the pattern of mutual indebtedness he has espoused throughout the letter. The concept of indebtedness requires those who envision themselves as people who act and bring about change to recognize what others are doing for them, that is, recognize how others enable them to function as "agents" or slaves of Christ Jesus. Ultimately, as Paul reflects, this is no easy task: "Not that I seek the gift, but I seek the profit that accumulates to your account" (v. 17). Paul removes the emphasis from affirming how the community functions as agents that enable him to serve the mission of the gospel and shifts the focus to highlight his concern for their "spiritual" well-being. In other words, he implies that what the community gives him in order to sustain his physical well-being while spreading the gospel is actually not for him; it is a deposit into their lives (added interest into their savings account). Their "gifts" to him enable them better to function as "slaves of Christ" because they are able to exercise the virtue (mind-set) of not seeking something out of self-interest, recognizing and promoting only their own goodness.[26]

But in v. 18 Paul catches himself. Perhaps he remembers the idea he would go on to develop in Rom 13:7: "be indebted [to]/owe no one [for] anything except to love one another." He, therefore, again reverses focus and states that the debt the community owes to him is paid in full. The emphasis here is not to say that their partnership has ended. Rather, the point is on the excess of their giving. They have given more than enough to cover their debt to him. In fact they have given to the extent that Paul feels he has "savings" on which he can draw to meet his physical and fiscal needs. Therefore, the gifts are not only beneficial and pleasing to him but also an acceptable and pleasing sacrifice to God.

Finally, Paul concludes with God's response to the Philippians, which is also characterized by reciprocity and mutual indebtedness. Just as Paul's needs have been fully satisfied through the power of Christ Jesus and his relationship with the Philippian community, so too will God fully satisfy the "needs" of the community in accordance to God's vast resources made possible to us through our service to the gospel of Christ Jesus (v. 19).

AFTERWORD: REVISITING THE LIFE-CONTEXT

In the continued struggle against racial injustice, Martin Luther King Jr. reminds contemporary world citizens and African Americans in particular that "equality with whites will not solve the problems of either whites or Negroes if it means equality in a world society stricken by poverty and in a universe doomed to extinction by war."[27] King's legacy demands that the struggle against racial injustice be understood in relation to broader struggles within the world economic and social community. He called the struggle to eliminate world poverty a practice of freedom. He viewed the lives that are strengthened because they live in an environment that they have reason to value as an expression of justice. Freedom and justice for both Paul and King represent the core characteristics of the gospel of Christ.

King believed that an effort on the part of wealthy nations to make prosperity a reality for poorer nations would in the end enlarge the prosperity of all. Therefore, he called for full communal unification and participation on the part of all Christian believers to transform a false ideological assumption under which the world existed:

> From time immemorial [humans] have lived by the principle that "self-preservation is the first law of life." But this is a false assumption. I would say that the other-preservation is the first law of life. It is the first law of life precisely because we cannot preserve self without being concerned about preserving other selves. The universe is so structured that things go awry if [people] are not diligent in their cultivation of other-regarding dimensions.[28]

With Paul, King understood that central to a "just," "other-regarding" mind-set is the commitment to "look at others as superior to yourself" (2:3). This concept is important, because an "other-regarding" mind-set removes from the wealthy nations an attitude of arrogant selfish ambition, and at the same time it removes from the poorer nations an attitude of shame and passivity. Instead, both parties move in relationship as mutually indebted, each understanding that both have something to share with and to receive from the other. Therefore, neither is exploited, but both are respected as manifestations of Christ in the world. Each experiences justice.[29]

Paul offers a single conceptual option—communal unity—as a means for twenty-first-century readers to transform the words of the gospel into a life experience of the gospel. Perhaps Paul, long before Isaac Newton, understood that force is greatly multiplied when individual units of power are combined in a single space at a single time. That is, force is greatly multiplied when people of like minds act together to accomplish a common goal. King learned well the lessons of Philippians. In 1967, Martin Luther King Jr. and the SCLC united under a single purpose—the elimination of world poverty. For King, to function as a "slave of Christ" would mean working to ensure a livable income for every American family and "declaring eternal opposition" to world poverty.[30] The needs that Paul assured the Philippian community God would "satisfy" were not merely spiritual allowances. Rather, they were the physical and fiscal needs that are required for daily existence in the material world (food, clothing, shelter, etc.).

> Today (2006) more than a billion people subsist on less than $1 a day. Half the people of the world are living on less than $2 a day.
>
> —www.un.org

They were the needs that the Philippians supplied to Paul. King argued that creating an environment that is suitable for and committed to meeting the physical and fiscal needs of every world citizen must arrest the attention of the African American community and the world community.

The great challenge for African Americans in the twenty-first century struggling *against* suffering is to remember the strategy of liberty: African American Christian believers, those who function as "slaves of Christ," must undertake a passionate commitment to a concern for others.

An equally significant challenge, however, for African Americans in the twenty-first century struggling *against* suffering is to *know* (through intellect and experience) that the opposite of this truth is also true. The hope of the world community depends upon keeping alive the hope and meeting the "needs" of the African American community. Such is the

Paul and Suffering

One can easily read Philippians and walk away with the sense that Paul encourages people to value the experience of suffering. But such a view misreads Paul's intent. Demetrius K. Williams rightly maintains that contemporary African American Christians can benefit from the examples of committed partnership in the cause of the gospel of liberty that Paul presents in this letter. Williams also rightly observes that "such examples of proper attitudes and actions for the greater good and betterment of the community in the face of hostility and conflict can remind African American Christians of their heritage of struggle against injustice" ("Philippians," in *Global Bible Commentary*, ed. Daniel Patte [Nashville: Abingdon, 2004], 487). Paul does not privilege suffering. Rather, he values the struggle for justice. Similarly, Martin Luther King Jr. did not envision suffering as redemptive. For those who function as citizens of heaven and yet are "slaves of Christ," it is the struggle *against* suffering that is redemptive. Therefore, with Paul, King not only reminds African Americans of their heritage of struggle against injustice but also presses them to reenter the struggle and broaden its scope. The hard truth, King argued in 1967, "is that neither Negro nor white has yet done enough to expect the dawn of a new day. . . . Freedom is not won by passive acceptance of suffering. Freedom is won by a struggle *against* suffering. By this measure, Negroes have not yet paid the full price for freedom. And whites have not yet faced the full cost of justice" (Martin Luther King Jr., *Where Do We Go from Here: Chaos or Community?* [New York: Harper & Row, 1967], 20).

strange pattern of love, a pattern of mutual indebtedness, into which Philippians calls us to flourish.

Notes

1. Martin Luther King Jr., "Sleeping through a Revolution," address to the Chicago Joint Negro Appeal," 10 December 1967, Chicago, Illinois, available at King Library and Archives, King Center, Atlanta, Ga.

2. Taylor Branch, *At Canaan's Edge: America in the King Years 1965–68* (New York: Simon & Schuster, 2006), 640–41.

3. Ibid.

4. Ibid.

5. David J. Garrow. *Bearing the Cross* (New York: Morrow, 1986), 539.

6. Martin Luther King Jr. *Where Do We Go from Here: Chaos or Community?* (New York: Harper & Row, 1967), 162–63.

7. Ibid., 181.

8. According to Luke's account in the Acts of the Apostles, it was at Philippi that Paul met a group of women to whom he preached the gospel. Lydia, a merchant selling purple cloth, believed Paul's message and was baptized with members of her household.

9. For a discussion on the social and economic value of creating an environment and life circumstances that people have reason to value, see Amartya Sen, *Development as Freedom* (New York: Anchor, 1999).

10. See Michael Joseph Brown, "Paul's Use of *doulos Christou Iēsou* in Romans 1:1," *JBL* 120 (2001): 723–37.

11. Gerald F. Hawthorne, *Philippians*, World Biblical Commentary 43 (Nashville: Nelson, 1983), 21.

12. In 1:9-10 Paul describes love as a power that progressively manifests itself both in intellectual knowing and in the knowledge that comes through personal and communal experience. In addition, Paul prays that love will lead to clear perceptions how practically to exist in relation with others. He further emphasizes the idea of insight as related to practice in v. 10 with the use of *dokimazo*—a term that means to discern so as to demonstrate. The expectation is that love will enable the community not only effectively to deliberate the issues that come to their attention but also to demonstrate the most advantageous response to these issues. But what is an advantageous or excellent response? A response, Paul maintains, that does not act out of pretense and does not cause others harm.

13. Martin Luther King Jr., *Letter from Birmingham Jail* (San Francisco: Harper, 1963), 32.

14. Heinrich Greeven, "*deēsis*," *TDNT* 2:40.

15. Walter Grundmann, "*anagkē*," *TDNT*, 1:346–47.

16. W. Bauer, F. W. Danker, W. F. Arndt, and F. W. Gingrich, *Greek-English Lexicon of the New Testament and Other Early Christian Literature* (BDAG hereafter), 3rd ed. (Chicago: University of Chicago Press, 1999), 846.

17. Gerald F. Hawthorne. *Philippians*, WBC 43, ed. Bruce M. Metzger (Nashville: Nelson, 1983).

18. Bonnie B. Thurston and Judith Ryan, *Philippians and Philemon*, ed. Daniel J. Harrington, Sacra Pagina 10 (Collegeville, Minn.: Liturgical, 2005), 69.

19. Ibid., 74. See also BDAG, 1066.

20. Thurston and Ryan, *Philippians and Philemon*, 105.

21. Daniel Patte, *Paul's Faith and the Power of the Gospel: A Structural Introduction to the Pauline Letters* (Philadelphia: Fortress Press, 1983), 173.

22. Interesting here is Paul's insistence on a communal effort in effectively working to restore harmony. Consider the language Paul uses in this request. He refers to the one(s) called for additional assistance as *syzyge* (yoke fellow). The image Paul suggests is that of people being yoked together, like oxen pulling a load together in order to accomplish an important task. Even the word Paul uses for "help" (*syllambanou*) is a compound opening with *sy[n]* "together/with." Paul is asking a person or a group to pull along with another (others) to provide needed assistance.

23. Herbert Preisker, "*epieikēs*," *TDNT* 2:588–89.
24. Ibid., 589.
25. *Dosis and lēmpsis* (giving and receiving) belong to the commercial vocabulary of the ancient world, referring to the debit and credit of the ledger. See J. Moulton and G. Milligan, *The Vocabulary of the Greek Testament* (London: Hodder and Stoughton, 1930).
26. Thurston and Ryan, *Philippians and Philemon*, 155.
27. King, *Where Do We Go from Here*, 167.
28. Ibid., 180.
29. Ibid., 188.
30. Ibid., 190. King also named militarism and racism as two other issues, but he felt that the issue of poverty necessarily included the other two.

For Further Reading

Briggs, Sheila. "Can an Enslaved God Liberate? Hermeneutical Reflections on Philippians 2:6-11," *Semeia* 47 (1989): 138–53.

Hawthorne, Gerald F. *Philippians*. WBC 43. Edited by Bruce M. Metzger. Nashville: Nelson, 1983.

King, Martin Luther Jr. *Where Do We Go from Here: Chaos or Community?* New York: Harper & Row, 1967.

Patte, Daniel. *Paul's Faith and the Power of the Gospel: A Structural Introduction to the Pauline Letters*. Philadelphia: Fortress Press, 1983.

Thurston, Bonnie B, and Judith Ryan. *Philippians and Philemon*. Edited by Daniel J. Harrington. Sacra Pagina 10. Collegeville, Minn.: Liturgical, 2005.

Williams, Demetrius K. "Philippians." In *Global Bible Commentary*. Edited by Daniel Patte. Nashville: Abingdon, 2004.

COLOSSIANS

Lloyd A. Lewis

INTRODUCTION

Mark's presentation of the good news convinces us that the people of God could find hope in a Messiah who accepted the role of Isaiah's Suffering Servant. For Mark's beleaguered congregation, in the midst of confusion from within and marginalization from without, a crucified Christ constantly reminded those who were followers of the Way that indeed the Jesus they experienced did know the "trouble they'd seen."

We expect the same link between situation and Christology when we read Colossians, and we are not disappointed. The theological portrait the author paints of Jesus Christ and his work speaks directly to an actual crisis faced by a group of Gentile Christians, a group that bore the stamp of the pastoral and missionary activity of Paul's coworker Epaphras (1:7), which he nurtured while Paul himself was imprisoned (1:24; 4:3,

> **The Epistolary Structure of Colossians**
>
> Greeting: 1:1-2
> Thanksgiving: 1:3-8
> Body
>   Theological indicative: 1:9—2:33
>   Ethical imperative: 3:1—4:6
>   Final greetings and farewell: 4:7—18

18). We learn in the letter that Paul's impersonal relationship with the Colossians did not hamper his concern for them (2:1). He returns a slave, Onesimus, to his master, Philemon (4:7-9). He has Tychichus report to the Colossians and Laodiceans on his condition (2:1; 4:13). He seals his caring relationship to the church by having the letter delivered to them (4:16).

> Although the question of the attribution of this letter to Paul has in recent years stirred some controversy, given the letter's theology and diction, its place among those writings that belong to the "school of Paul" has hardly been challenged in a convincing manner.

As in the case of Mark, the centerpiece of the argument in Colossians is found in its Christology, articulated in this case in the words of a remarkable hymn (1:15-23) that proclaims Jesus Christ as preeminent in all things, the image of the invisible God, and the source and destiny of all creation.

Believers are bound to this picture of Christ just as the human body is bound to its head. This cosmic picture of Christ, standing as head over all (1:15-17), presages a church in which nothing stands above its Lord (1:18-20), neither things visible nor things invisible. Whereas in Paul's early letters, such as 1 Corinthians, the church tends to be more charismatic, more free in its nature, and more dependent on the work of the Spirit, Colossians presents a church with developing ministries, with a sacramental life grounded in baptism, and with an authoritative concept of what Christians believe and teach.

Paul's presentation of Christ and church in this letter is not without purpose. False teachers appear to have been present in the Colossian church, actively proffering a version of religion characterized as a nonchristocentric philosophy (2:8) that would "enhance" the gospel through a blend of asceticism, selective practice of elements of Judaism, and intellectual posturing. Such hyper-spirituality always finds a place in the human desire to "be better" than the average and thus to "disqualify" others with lesser experiences (2:18). Paul, writing as a prisoner stripped of the trappings of power, leans on the gospel of Christ and points his church toward it as the source of power and the determinant of its common life.

Consequently, Colossians challenges the hearts of those in the black church. Paul leaves the African American believer with a challenge about church leadership. The personal example of Paul, the former persecutor turned evangelist who is now incarcerated, confuses the normative image of a proper church leader since his social status and background do not conform to society's image of acceptability. The letter presents black believers with a challenge to the concept of "the true black church." Many of our churches draw their lifeblood from the more free Holiness and Pentecostal traditions. Colossians, on

The Scandal of the Black Church Divided

"And so this little church—it was called a union church. At a union church, the Methodists would have services one Sunday and the Baptists would have services one Sunday and [both] the Methodists and the Baptists would go every Sunday. Now, why did they have to have a Methodist and Baptist church? Why did they have to say Methodist or Baptist? Why don't they just say church?"

—Maggie Dulin, Muhlenberg County, Kentucky, quoted in William H. Chafe, Raymond Gavins, and Robert Korstad, *Remembering Jim Crow* (New York: New Press, 2001), 93.

the other hand, presents a church on its way to being ordered and structured, one with which black Roman Catholics, Anglicans, and Lutherans would be entirely comfortable. The letter thus challenges black believers to widen their concept of "church" on the basis of a common ethnic experience, thus creating a broader ecclesial canon. Lastly, the letter, in its critique of the puritanical asceticism and spiritual athleticism of the opponents, raises serious questions about those situations in which advocates of such movements in black churches today seek to disqualify others who do not share their puritanical ethic for the sake of bolstering their own superiority.

Chapter 1

1:1-2, Greeting

The letter begins with a typical Pauline introduction. Paul establishes his role for a congregation he did not found: he is nonetheless to them "the apostle," a position he holds by virtue of his appointment by Jesus Christ (1:1), despite his well-known former activity as a persecutor of the church and his absence from the community of disciples who were actual followers of the earthly Jesus (1 Cor 15:8-11). A second feature of the greeting is that Timothy accompanies Paul in sending the letter. This confirms a salient feature of his apostolic work: Paul rarely works alone. Throughout his mission he is accompanied and supported by individuals who are his coworkers: individuals who share with him the common heritage of being children of God. As a pastor and a missionary, he thrives with the active support of others.

1:3-8, Thanksgiving

The opening salutation gives way to Paul's prayer of thanksgiving. Save in the cases in which his writing overflows in an act of blessing God (2 Cor 1:3-7; cf. Eph 1:3-13) or in

the odd instance in Gal 1:6-9, where he vigorously rebukes the Galatians for defecting from the one gospel, Paul presents in summary the major themes of this letter in his thanksgiving prayer. We know from 1 Cor 13:13 his familiar triad of "faith, hope, and love" (see also Rom 1:8; 1 Cor 1:4; Phil 1:2; 1 Thess 1:2). We find that triad here, but with an emphasis on hope as the crucial ingredient. For Paul, hope is both anticipated and present. It is "laid up in the heavens" (v. 5), thus speaking a resounding no to any intimation that God's people could not expect vindication at the close of time. At the same time it is a present reality (v. 5), already inaugurated and announced in the gospel the Colossians had received.

African American believers have preserved in hymns and sermons and in their poetry this same eschatological concern and tension. In hope they anticipate the future. At the same time they see in the Good News proclaimed and enacted signs of hope visible as God's new arrangement confronts injustice and evil.

Caged Bird

The caged bird sings
With a fearful trill
Of things unknown
But longed for still
And his tune is heard
On the distant hill
For the caged bird sings of freedom.

—"Caged Bird," copyright © 1983 by Maya Angelou, from *Shaker, Why Don't You Sing?* by Maya Angelou. Used by permission of Random House, Inc.

1:9-14, Intercession

Paul's attitude of thanksgiving motivates his intercessory prayer for the Colossians. Possessors of a promise as were the children of Israel who hoped for the land of promise (Exod 6:8), the Colossians already held an inheritance as a result of their liberation by God (1:12). Their portion was marked by the fact that they have already been transferred from darkness into light (1:13). God had already moved them into the rule of his beloved Son, who like them was designated "the beloved of God" at his baptism (Mark 1:11 and parallels). And as a token of this they had already received the gift of liberation. The Colossians, however, had been freed from more than human bondage: they had been purchased back (they had received *apolytrosis*) and had been emancipated by God's forgiveness of their sins (1:14).

1:15-20, Seeking the Light: the Hymn of Christ

As with the great Christ hymn in Phil 2:6-11, numerous attempts have been made to parse this hymn into verses of poetry and to speculate how Paul reworked an already existing hymn in order to emphasize the unambiguous role of Christ in creation (1:16-17), the place of Christ in church (1:18-19), and the essential nature of the cross in God's plan (1:20-21). These variations tether the hymn so that it does not reinforce what Paul will later indicate to be the false teaching of a gospel of glory found among the false teachers.

The hymn makes the following affirmations. First, in all of creation Christ is and was and will be first (1:15-17). That is because he bears a unique stamp, being the image (*eikon*) of the creator. To see Jesus Christ, therefore, is to see God. Second, Jesus Christ is not only the image of God but also the agent of God in creation. The pertinence of this claim is astounding, and Paul elaborates upon it by saying that Christ's creative activity brought into being things visible as well as things invisible (1:15-16). Third, Paul assumes that a true understanding of Jesus Christ as God's image

involves recognizing his role in another way. By asserting that all things cohere in him, Christ also becomes the sustainer of all of creation. It is impossible to divorce the continued workings of God from the world as it is. It is also impossible to establish any power as being antecedent or superior to the power of Jesus Christ. Appeals to such intermediaries fall flat in the face of Christ, the unique creator and sustainer.

The second part of the hymn focuses on the role that Christ plays in the church, where he also is head (1:18a). Indeed he is the church's Lord (1:18b, 19). As such his creative work finds completion in his presence as the source of reconciliation not only between disparate ethnic and religious segments of society but most significantly between God and creation itself. The moment of the crucifixion signals this new era of peace: a cosmic reconciliation accomplished not by power but by the scandalous vision of the vulnerability of the Son of God (1:20).

1:21-29, Consequences of Living with the Light

If the language of the Colossians hymn focuses on creation, then the implications of the hymn focus on worship, particularly in baptism and temple service. Initiation into the church is more than a contract of membership. Baptism functions as a dynamic border, and once it is crossed, an individual is changed. Combining his belief in the power of baptism with language drawn from the temple cult of Judaism, Paul envisions baptism as an occasion when the believer offers his or her life as an act of sacrifice: a life made into the perfect sacrificial victim (holy, pure, spotless, v. 22), so that an individual might live the life of faith.

Personal example is not far behind as Paul closes this section, since the ministry he bears shares not only in the power of Christ in

Baptism

Into the furnace let me go alone;
Stay you without in terror of the heat.
I will go naked in—for thus 'tis sweet—
Into the weird depths of the hottest zone.
I will not quiver in the frailest bone,
You will not note a flicker of defeat;
My heart shall tremble not its fate to meet,
My mouth give utterance to any moan.
The yawning oven spits forth fiery spears;
Red aspish tongues shout wordlessly my name.
Desire destroys, consumes my mortal fears,
Transforming me into a shape of flame.
I shall come out, back to your world of tears,
A stronger soul within a finer frame.

—Claude McKay (1891–1948), poet of the Harlem Renaissance, in Abraham Chapman, ed., *Black Voices* (New York: New American Library, 1968), 372. Originally published in *Harlem Shadows* (New York: Harcourt Brace), 1922.

proclaiming the gospel but also in the suffering of Christ in witnessing to it. Elsewhere in his letters Paul points to the vision of the true apostle as the suffering apostle (2 Cor 1:4, 6, 8; 2:4; 6:4; Phil 1:17). The apostle-pastor thus shares in a corporate ministry of proclaiming the gospel with others who share his burden of witness and suffering (in 1:28 he switches from the first person singular to the first person plural).

The crucial nature of leadership in the church is not lost on the African American pastor, and the emergence of the pastor as leader in the congregation and community is clearly a consequence of the importance that the apostolic individual has within the church. Paul reminds us that apostolic work is not without apostolic woes. For as much as leadership is an exercise in power, the pastor finds the true model for ministry in the servant Jesus and Jesus' servant Paul. Paul reminds

us that we do disservice to the gospel he proclaims and the ministry he bears if we forget that this burden is meant to be shared in corporate solidarity with others marked as the beloved of God. Ministry involves the whole people of God, of which the apostle-pastor is one member.

CHAPTER 2

2:1-7, Preparing for Combat

Paul begins this section with a series of words of encouragement. Much as in 1 Cor 5:3, his bodily absence does not negate his spiritual presence. The purpose of his encouragement is to ward off the influence of rival teachers. His ministry of encouragement is found not in new teaching but in reminders of the faith they already possess. This is given as a strong foil to the false teachers and their influence.

2:8-23, Avoiding the Darkness

We cannot say for sure who Paul's opponents were. It is hard to determine whether they were external attackers of the church, competitors for the hearts of believers found among adherents to pagan religious groups at Colossae, or individuals engaged in jockeying for leadership during the vacuum in oversight created by the imprisonment of Epaphras. What we can note is the way Paul characterizes the opponents' beliefs. They represent a philosophy (*philosophia*) not based on the Christ presented in the hymn (2:8). They are individuals who desire to observe festivals and dietary regulations (2:16). They promote ascetic observances, insisting that their adherents "do not handle; do not taste; do not touch" (2:20-22). Finally they encourage observance of selective elements of Judaism (2:11, 14) and practice self-abasement, angelic worship, and sexual abstinence (2:18).

Behind this portrait of the false teachers stands a belief in the power of the individual to achieve perfection before God on his or her own. Thus individuals can supposedly achieve a higher spiritual status by denigrating their bodies while putting a premium on tending their spiritual lives.

Far from being a means of spiritual progress, Paul identifies such efforts as exercises in self-aggrandizement. Paul labeled such religious aspirations as exercises in self-inflation (2:18). In 1 Cor 8:1, in the controversy over the eating of meat offered to idols, Paul states that knowledge puffs up, but love (*agape*) builds up. Self-centered knowledge, which is turned in upon itself, is the opposite of love, which faces out in concern for the other.

What is remarkable in this section is Paul's uncompromisingly hostile language launched at the false teachers. They are frauds and thieves (2:4, 8) who peddle a counterfeit product. The reality they proclaim, compared to the reality of Christ, is illusory (2:17) and ephemeral.

Paul's critique of the false teachers reminds us that over the years some African American believers, as indeed has been true of believers in general, have grasped at self-attained holiness as a means of establishing superiority over their brothers and sisters and to guarantee acceptability in the face of the dominant culture. The ambivalent view that the black church has often had toward human sexuality is one clear example of this. Any sexual ethic, for example, that accepts as a norm the idea that the God-given gift of sexuality is inherently evil and therefore is to be avoided for the sake of spiritual purity or social superiority would find no home in Paul's theology or ethics. Paul's asceticism appears more tempered by pragmatism. Paul believes in holiness, but its source is found in God who makes holy, not in personal striving.

The biting nature of Paul's attack on the false teachers also warns us of the great responsibility that attends "excommunicating" others in the church who hold differing understandings of the truth. "Putting someone out of church" is not a matter to be taken lightly. Colossians speaks of a particular situation in which the very heart of the gospel was under attack. In the light of such a fundamental aberration, Paul acts swiftly and sternly, making the false teachers look to those at Colossae as unattractive as possible. The tendency, however, is to surrender a generous orthodoxy in essentials for a brand of rigid conformity. Such an act has the potential of stifling the work of that same Spirit that began with the covenant with Abraham and ended in an aggressive Gentile mission.

The series of exhortations in this section might provide what Paul identifies as an antidote in this matter. Christ, who is God,

On Understanding the Gift of Being Embodied

"The body can be a vehicle for divine presence and the means by which human beings can communicate agape. The body is the physicality of sexuality, that which signals the potential for one to be authentically human and hence to reflect the image of God in the world. A disembodied approach to God's disclosure in Jesus subverts the very radicality of God's disclosure. It negates the significance of God's presence in human history by metaphysicalizing and mystifying God's revelation in Jesus."

—Kelly Brown Douglas, *Sexuality and the Black Church: A Womanist Perspective* (Maryknoll, N.Y.: Orbis, 1999), 116.

is sufficient grounding for every believer (2:6, 9). For the individual, faith incorporates one into the story of the dying and rising of Jesus Christ (2:12-15). Finally, the highly speculative nature of the belief of the Colossian opponents stands in stark contrast with Paul's seemingly simplistic suggestion of looking to the head, Jesus Christ. Searching for a new or the latest religious "high" becomes an exercise in futility, when the individual believer focuses instead on what he or she already posseses through the free gift of God's grace.

Chapter 3

3:1-11, Living the Risen Life

Paul's theological indicative as stated in chaps. 1–2 now forms the foundation for his ethical imperative in the concluding chapters. As in his other letters, ethical exhortation hinges on the word "so" or "therefore" (*oun*) in 3:1. The implications of Paul's theology for the individual are a series of calls to "higher ground" (the virtues in 3:12-16, for example) that mark life in the ways of God's rule. For Paul, living under God's rule is something to be experienced in the present, even as it awaits completion in the future. The assertion that through dying with Christ in baptism and rising with him the believer begins life in God's new arrangement here and now emphasizes the importance of Paul's "now." It is in no way lessened in its importance by his anticipation of God's "not yet."

The list of vices to be put aside by members of the church follows a stock pattern in the New Testament and other early Christian writings associated with the rite of baptism. The first list, in 3:5, is heavily weighted toward acts of sexual misbehavior, and the second, in 3:8, toward what might be called acts of anti-social behavior. The one is focused inwardly and the other outwardly, reminding us that Paul did not count any area of human existence as exempt from the potential of disorder. This was the old life that believers put aside, like old clothes cast aside at baptism. The new indicative found in baptism demands a new imperative in terms of human existence, one as radical in its transforming effect as creation itself. Recapitulating creation returns the world to a state in which a new humanity, freed of distinctions in status by ethnicity, gender, and social status (3:11) exists.

> ### The Imperative of Life in the New Creation
>
> Then if our Father loveth all
> Mankind of every clime and hue,
> Who loveth Him must love them, too;
> It cannot otherwise befall.
>
> —Kelly Miller, *Out of the House of Bondage* (New York: Thomas Y. Crowell, 1914), 11.

3:12—4:1, Ordering the Fundamental Structures

When Paul suggests in 3:1 a pattern for the new life, he draws a line between societal structures and God's rule. They are not identical to one another. Rather, the demands of God's rule have the potential of infecting and reforming society as the qualities of the kingdom are manifested in the lives of believers. When we contrast the list of virtues in 3:12-17 with the list of vices in 3:5-11, we note that the garments of mercy, kindness, meekness, long suffering, tolerance, and forgiveness promote healthy life in a community. They build up and do not tear apart. The last garment, enfolding all, is *agape*, which binds the other gifts together.

The new life even infects the patriarchal household of Paul's world as seen in Colossians' household code. Status and consequent behavior in society could be reduced to a series of propositions in which individual responsibilities could be articulated by following the pattern "Role A was subject to Role B in order that Behavior X might exist." Classic responsibilities found in these "household codes" were linear and non-reciprocal. Duties of wives to husbands, children to parents, and slaves to masters were typical elements of such codes. But such patterns, when they encountered the affirmation of Col 3:11, could not long remain static. Paul insisted, even as he used the codes to order the church, on the importance of mutual reciprocity.

Whereas Ephesians provides a thick description of the relationship between husbands and wives, in Colossians it is the relationship between slaves and masters that garners the greater attention. Most African Americans find the letter's insistence on the "right behavior" of slaves to be at the least problematic if not blatantly insensitive to the plight of any human being who is owned by others. Though Paul's church was grounded in its own time and situation, he insists on the power of God's new arrangement. In God's new arrangement masters are exhorted not only to show justice to their slaves but to demonstrate their recognition of equality (*isotes*) (4:1) with them. Through the church of which Christ is head, the situation exists in which social stratification begins to crumble along its hardened edges. When one adds to this Paul's appeal to God as the common master of both free man and slave and his reminder that God shows no partiality (3:25), one is left with the conclusion that far more important than determining Paul's stand on slavery is his resounding message that, in the light of the gospel, God's raison d'être is not to fortify any static and human-fashioned created social order.

4:2-6, Admonishing the Faithful

Paul's final exhortations are both general and specific. In general, the Colossians are to watch and pray: activities reminiscent of the exhortations of Jesus to his followers in the face of the cataclysm of his impending crucifixion (Mark 14:38) and in their anticipation of the approaching day of the Lord (Mark 13:18, 37).

Specifically, the Colossians are to support Paul in prayer for an opportunity to proclaim unfettered the mystery (1:26; 2:2) of Christ. But Paul's mystery is no esoteric, privately possessed faith or puzzle to be solved. It was sufficiently public to motivate others to imprison him. And it was sufficiently public to provide for the Colossians a warrant to testify to that mystery by exemplary living before outsiders so that they might present in a reasonable way their own testimony as an answer to all.

4:7-18, Final Greetings

Finally we might be startled by the collection of individuals whom Paul mentions in his conclusion: coworkers, a slave, members of the circumcision party who were involved in Paul's mission, a physician, a woman who hosted a house church, and an individual who needed a reminder to persevere in his work for the church. All bore a common share in Paul's mission to the church at Colossae. But all of them in Paul's absence represent hope for the church at Colossae as they struggled against the false teachers. And Paul's choice shows us the breadth of the family of believers, for they were Jew (Jesus, called Justus) or Greek (Tychichus); slave (Onesimus) or free (Archippus); male (Luke) and female (Nympha).

For Further Reading

Francis, Fred O., and Wayne A. Meeks, eds. *Conflict at Colossae*. Missoula, Mont.: Society of Biblical Literature, 1973.

MacDonald, Margaret Y. *Colossians and Ephesians*. Collegeville, Minn.: Liturgical, 2000.

Martin, Clarice J. "The *Haustafeln* (Household Codes) in African American Biblical Interpretation: 'Free Slaves' and 'Subordinate Women.'" Pages 206–31 in *Stony the Road We Trod: African American Biblical Interpretation*. Edited by Cain Hope Felder. Minneapolis: Fortress Press, 1991.

Sampley, J. Paul, et al. *Ephesians, Colossians, 2 Thessalonians, The Pastoral Epistles*. Proclamation Commentaries. Philadelphia: Fortress Press, 1978.

Wimbush, Vincent L. *Paul: The Worldly Ascetic*. Macon, Ga.: Mercer University Press, 1987.

1 THESSALONIANS

Cain Hope Felder

INTRODUCTION

Once readers of the New Testament realize that 1 Thessalonians is its oldest document, this letter takes on much greater significance for understanding the concerns and theology of the apostle Paul. This is especially important for African Americans, because we have historically been skeptical of specific teachings traditionally attributed to Paul (for example, "slaves obey your masters" or "wives be submissive to your husbands"). Yet the historical-critical exegetical method has amply demonstrated that several of the writings attributed to Paul were probably not written or dictated by him at all. These deuteropauline documents even include 2 Thessalonians.

Indeed, once one identifies the seven "undisputed" or clearly authentic letters of Paul—1 Thessalonians, Galatians, 1–2 Corinthians, Philippians, Philemon, and Romans—it is easy to see that Paul never mentions anything about slaves obeying their masters! Put bluntly, the black church needs to liberate itself from a provincial, pre-critical view of Paul. The Thessalonian correspondence helps to move us in that direction.

First Thessalonians was composed in the immediate aftermath of Paul's first visit to the city, after he had established the Christian church on European soil at Philippi about one hundred miles away. Thessalonica, unlike Philippi, was a port city on the northeastern part of the Aegean Sea. In Paul's time, it was also the Roman provincial capital of Macedonia. Named after Alexander the Great's half-sister, Thessaloniki, the city was founded in 316 B.C.E. In 167 B.C.E., Rome became its patron; later, in 42 B.C.E., for its strong support of Caesar Augustus (Octavian), it received the coveted status of "free state," entitling it to maintain a semblance of its own government, including the permission to mint its own coins.[1] The patronage of Rome presupposed complete loyalty from Thessalonica in return. Not surprisingly, the imperial cult thrived in Thessalonica, where the inhabitants erected a statue of Caesar Augustus only a few years before Paul first arrived in the city.

Paul and his coworkers Silvanus (Silas) and Timothy enter Thessalonica, after having founded—under some duress (1 Thess 2:2)—the church at Philippi. Acts 17:1 provides a few details, not all of which are reliable: "After Paul and Silas [note that Luke does not mention Timothy's presence until v. 14] had passed through Amphipolis and Apollonia, they came to Thessalonica where there was a synagogue of Jews." Luke, author of the Acts of the Apostles, places emphasis on the Jewish presence in Thessalonica, which was, in his view, a source of much conflict with Paul. This differs considerably from the impression that 1 Thessalonians itself gives, namely, that the Jewish presence in the city was negligible and certainly not the cause of the firestorm that Luke presents in Acts 17:2-11.

On the contrary, in his letter Paul focused on the very warm welcome he received and the extraordinary success he had in winning converts through the preaching of his apocalyptic gospel and its salvific implications. He expresses great "joy" (1:6; 2:19; 2:20; 3:9) over the relationship that he establishes with these new believers. He depicts them as Gentiles rather than Jews. They "turned to God from idols" (1:9). Paul goes on to say, "You suffered . . . from your own compatriots" (2:14).

Just as the Christians in the Jerusalem church suffered at the hands of the Jews of Jerusalem, i.e., their fellow inhabitants of that city, so too did Greeks in the emerging church in Thessalonica suffer at the hands of their fellow citizens.

It is useful to classify 1 Thess as both a "family" and a "paraenetic" letter. The letter expresses deep affection for the "family" (here a kind of fictive kinship that emerged within early Christian fellowships; see 1 Thess 2:11, 14, 17; 4:1; 5:1), while sharing separation anxieties. It also provides exhortation and advice to strengthen earlier teachings and indoctrination.[2]

1:1, SALUTATION

The opening salutation, sometimes called the epistolary prescript (typically a triad in the Hellenistic idiom), indicates the sender(s), recipients, and greeting.[3] This is similar to the wording of the opening found in 2 Thess 1:1-2. Both epistles indicate that the senders are Paul and two of his coworkers, Silvanus (a Latinism for the Greek "Silas," as mentioned in Acts 15:22—18:5) and Timothy. Acts 16:1-3 relates the circumstances in which Paul first met Timothy, son of a Jewish mother, Eunice (named in 2 Tim 1:5), and a Greek father.

Historically, Timothy had a far more prominent status in Paul's last two missionary journeys than Luke concedes. This becomes most evident in the fact that two Pastoral Epistles, alleged to be written by Paul, are addressed to Timothy. That the historical Paul had Timothy circumcised at all, let alone for the reason given by Luke in Acts 16, is doubtful, since such a ritual would for Timothy seem inconsistent with the contents of the Jerusalem conference agreement just issued by James, chief elder of that church in Acts 15. Why would Paul feel constrained to circumcise Timothy when he would be joining the group now spreading the Jerusalem church's ruling that no such religious ritual was required of new converts?[4]

With his opening reference to the term "church," Paul has in mind the Greek *ekklesia*, the Hebrew equivalent to the term *qahal*, "the assembly of God's people."[5] Believers gathered in the larger of the house churches to hear the epistle read aloud. Several months had probably elapsed between their receipt of this letter from Corinth and Paul's departure from Thessalonica (see comments below on vv. 9-10).

1:2-10, THANKSGIVING

1:2-5, A Message beyond Mere Words

One of the distinguishing marks of Paul's own theology is the focus on God as the primary agent of salvation (not on Jesus, who became the Christ only through God's agency). The opening thanksgiving attests to this perspective by mentioning first "God the Father." It is God who brings about the "Christ event." The Fatherhood of God is rarely found as a theological concept in the Old Testament/Hebrew Bible.[6] There, the overwhelming tendency is to employ such ascriptions as "the God of Abraham, Isaac, and Jacob" (Exod 3:6, 15), "God of Israel" (Judg 11:23), "God of heaven" (Gen 24:7), or "God of their fathers" (Deut 29:25). In the New Testament all of that changes for three reasons: (a) the unique and deeply personal relationship that Jesus had with God as his Father (particularly evident in the prayers of Jesus that appear in the Gospels, but also see Gal 4:6), (b) the manner in which the Gospels variously present that relationship as a model for believers, and (c) the consistent ways that Paul reinforces the teachings on the necessity of this personal, quasi-filial relationship for believers to maintain. Again in 3:11, 13, Paul mentions God as "Father" (cf. 1 Cor

8:6). In 2:11, Paul compares his own relationship with the Thessalonian church as that of a father with his children.

Faith, love, and hope are used together as a veritable formula (cf. 1 Cor 13:13), both here and in 1 Thess 5:9 ("breastplate of faith and love . . . the helmet of hope of salvation"). Paul's phrase "work of faith" makes explicit what the author of the Epistle of James seems to imply in more Jewish Christian terms. Faith must work!

Power and Holy Spirit appear as two distinct entities. 1 Cor 2:4 provides a fairly close parallel: "my speech and my proclamation were not with plausible words of wisdom but with a demonstration of the Spirit and of power."[7] In Luke-Acts these two ideas coincide with one another; as opposed to being thought of as separate phenomena. Throughout Luke-Acts, the Holy Spirit is the definitive empowering agency. Paul's thought seems to move along different lines, as he demonstrates another kind of "power" (*en dynamei*) in the face of the conventional power of popular local cult leaders; one could call this courageous boldness with an electrifying effect. Yet this "power" stems from a separate source that cannot be seen, the Holy Spirit. In Paul's view the Holy Spirit is available to all believers (thus, a "priesthood of all believers"), and it potentially can produce in them the same "power."

1:6-10, At Once Imitators and Examples

In v. 6 Paul writes, "You became imitators of us and of the Lord . . . in spite of persecution." This assessment doubtlessly reflects Paul's joy over the Thessalonians' response to his original exhortations that called them to a new and different religious lifestyle. Paul was quite impressed with the willingness on the part of the Thessalonians to suffer on behalf of their newfound Christian faith (cf. 2 Cor 8:1); he regarded their acceptance of inevitable suffering as an indication of their imitating his own sufferings on behalf of the gospel. Paul's willingness to accept suffering is fundamental to his witness and testimony as shown in such passages as 2 Cor 6:3-10; 11:16-29; or Phil 1:29; 3:10. The suffering of Paul is also an important theme taken up by Luke throughout the Acts of the Apostles.

"You became an example . . . in Macedonia and Achaia" (Greece proper). The gospel had taken root among the Thessalonians, and the news of this successful planting evidently spread to other locales. Paul becomes expansive in his pride over the exemplary way in which many former idol worshipers have become Christians.

Paul recounts happily that the Thessalonians have disavowed their former practice of idol worship. The common Greek word *eidolon* in New Testament times meant "idol" or image, but in classical Greek it conveyed the sense of "shadow" or "phantom." In Paul's preaching these idols were mere pretenses to reality, "shadows" masking as reality.[8] Plato once drew a helpful distinction between "shadows" (*eidolon*) and reality, as in his "Allegory of the Cave," so familiar from *The Republic*. For Gentiles in a major Macedonian port city, to renounce idols, i.e., to consider them "false gods" or public pretenses, was a matter of some consequence, since many such idols were part of public cults whose state-appointed priests and patrons were quite wealthy and influential Romans and Greeks. These powerful locals could impose grave consequences on cultic "defectors." In spite of such potential threats, Paul challenged the Thessalonians to "serve a living God." He maintained that idols of wood and stone are inanimate objects, routinely manipulated in the public prayers of politicians.[9] Worshipers of these non-living idols are by inference also dead.

"And wait for his Son from heaven . . ." (v. 10) introduces one of the main themes in Paul's apocalyptic preaching among the Thessalonians: the second coming of the Son, who through suffering, death, and resurrection became the Christ. Throughout his letters, Paul typically uses messianic expressions like "Jesus Christ," "Lord Jesus," or "Christ Jesus." In this quick opening summary, he not only abbreviates the messianic reference to Jesus but also condenses the specific content of what he preached. Nevertheless, it is clear that what he preached was thoroughly apocalyptic as indicated by the expression "Jesus who rescues us from the wrath that is coming" in v. 10b (cf. 2:19; 5:2-5).

The name *Jesus* in Hebrew and Aramaic means "he saves" or "rescues." One of the most important occasions for the invoking of Jesus' name is at the time of the baptism of new converts (as in the early chapters of Acts, e.g., 2:38; 4:12, where converts were baptized "in the name of Jesus"). In those and other moments within the life of the primitive church, the invocation of Jesus' name had foremost in mind the saving of an individual or group from the sins of the past. Paramount here, however, is a play on the name "Jesus" to denote the future dimension of salvation. Paul thereby provides an eschatological extension of the meaning inherent in the very name of Jesus. Throughout 1 Thessalonians, the focus is on the coming "day of the Lord," now recast in Christian terms as the second coming of Jesus at the end of time and history. The progression in Paul's thought, "you turned from . . . to serve . . . to wait," conveys both approbation and comforting reassurance that the resurrected Jesus will vindicate their new allegiance to him. Beverly Roberts Gaventa correctly points out that this new allegiance is not entirely a matter of free choice; they have been chosen and are under a certain compulsion as if drafted into new military service.[10]

2:1-12, Sufferings in Philippi and Overcoming Opposition in Thessalonica

To comprehend the sufferings that Paul experienced in Philippi or the extent of the opposition with which the Thessalonians had to cope, one must appreciate that religion in Macedonian and Greek cities was not simply a private affair but part of one's civic duty.

Both Philippi and Thessalonica enjoyed privileged relationships with Rome. The imperial cult thrived in these cities. Because the emperor was proclaimed as the supreme benefactor, offering allegiance to some other "king" would not only be frowned upon; it would bring about severe punitive consequences.

Paul does not elaborate on his remarks in v. 2a that "we had already suffered and been shamefully mistreated at Philippi." However, Acts suggests some details on Paul's sufferings there (Acts 16:16-24, 37). It alleges a humiliating and painful public flogging and forced imprisonment. One should always remember that what Luke reports is a bit embellished by his own theological aims; we have no independent sources to corroborate Luke's testimony. All that one knows for certain is that Paul himself recalls a most unpleasant experience. Perhaps his offering of allegiance to a king other than the Caesar who occupied the throne in Rome was one of the reasons why.

First Thessalonians 2:2b recalls the great opposition. The social context that Paul speaks of is heavily Gentile; in Acts 17:1-9, as Luke describes Paul's opposition, it is primarily Jewish. Again, Luke pursues his own theological agenda in his sustained attempt to present the Jews as consistent obstacles to the advance of Paul's missionary. Obviously, Paul's own words should take precedence. The opposition in Thessalonica is almost exclusively from non-Jewish opponents who are supporters of the various indigenous religions, specifically the idol worshiping of the imperial and other cults, and even the craft and trade guilds, which often had religious nuances. This distinction is important, given the stern repudiation of some Jews mentioned in the controversial 1 Thess 2:14-16 segment, which is at times incorrectly appealed to as evidence of Paul's broad disdain for adherents of his former religion (see the comments below).

2:3-8, A Strategy of Integrity

The principle that converts to the early Christian movement should be as self-sufficient as possible is secured by Paul's own example in v. 9. His ability to make a living beyond his missionary work manifested itself in his leather craft, illustrated in the fabled "tent-making ministry." Paul's opponents resort to deceit, operate from impure motives, or employ trickery. The apostle intends to contrast his own integrity, approved by God, with those who, as in vv. 5-6, had come with "flattery or with a pretext for greed."

Paul's tone changes dramatically in v. 7 from condemnation of his opponents to nurturing pastoral care. According to the great number of ancient manuscripts, he describes the work of his evangelical team among the Thessalonians as that of *nepioi*, which technically means "infants." However, this awkward rendering flies in the face of Paul's more common parental self-designations. In fact, in this context he goes on to compare himself to a "nursing mother" or "wet nurse" with the term *trophos*. Therefore, the better and more sensible rendering of *nepioi*, as most commentators agree, is "gentle," coming from the Greek word *epioi*.[11] The endearing tone expressed by such a word fits much better with the image of a nursing mother who cares deeply for her child (v. 8).

2:9-12, A Self-Supportive and Non-Exploitive Evangelism

Paul extends his self-image as a "nursing mother" by referring to his willingness to "work night and day" (v. 9) on their behalf. His thoughts then turn to his own financial resources, and the lengths to which he has gone to take care of others while not becoming a burden to them. Of course, Paul did expect monetary help at times, and he received such support on several occasions. In fact, in 2:7 (as in 1 Cor 9:3-12) Paul asserts his rights as "an apostle of Christ" to such benefits, if he chooses to receive them. He, however, has strategically disavowed such rights in order not to burden the Thessalonians. Indeed, of equal and perhaps of greater significance, Paul did not want to be confused with the local religious profiteers of Thessalonica. Nevertheless, he did receive financial help from the Philippians ("For even when I was in Thessalonica, you sent me help for my needs more than once"—Phil 4:16) and later from the Thessalonians as well.

2:13-16, Renewed Thanksgiving for Their Conversion despite Local Opposition

In 2:13 the apostle returns to his sense of gratitude for the somewhat unique circumstances in which his gospel won acceptance among the Thessalonians. That their conversion took place despite local opposition is a subject that Paul introduced in 1:6 and amplified a bit in 1:9-10. By taking this topic up so soon again, Paul underscores the depth of his appreciation. However, the resumption of the words of thanksgiving is no simple repetition of earlier statements. Paul now celebrates the fact the believers in Thessalonica recognized and accepted an important distinction between the content of his preaching and the utterances of local cult leaders and other religious figures who sought their allegiance. Thus, "you accepted it not as a human word [from popular philosophy or from some idol-worshiping cult], but as . . . God's word."

Scholars have long recognized the problematic and complex nature of vv. 14-16.

Some insist that the passage is an anti-Jewish (possibly non-Pauline) interpolation, that is, a later addition to the original text. If it really is an interpolation, one might hypothesize that it was added during a time like the fall of the Jerusalem temple (70 C.E.) or the subsequent period of widespread pogroms against the diaspora Jews in the latter part of the first century. Abraham Smith, among others, is right to reject any such anti-Jewish determination. Paul does not speak against all Jews but only "some [of the] Jews—those who oppose Jesus and his movement."[12]

2:17-19, A Deep Longing to Return to Thessalonica

Paul reverses his familial images in asserting that "for a short time, we were made orphans by being separated from you." Given the apostle's earlier familial similes in 2:7 ("like a nurse tenderly caring for her own children") or in 2:11 ("like a father with his children"), it is surprising that he would now cast himself in the image of an orphan. Perhaps the reason is that orphans exist in a helpless state. Because of his many failed attempts (note the "again and again" in v. 18b) to get back to the city, Paul feels helpless. In v. 18 he identifies Satan as the chief culprit in preventing his return.

Were there some fellow travelers with Paul in Athens who made the trip with him to Corinth who are much less enthusiastic about returning to Thessalonica? Evidently so, especially in light of the continuing persecutions taking place there. Notice how Paul places what seems to be an unexpected and otherwise unnecessary emphasis in saying, "certainly, I, Paul wanted to" return to Thessalonica. In lofty terms, Paul then offers the highest compliment to the Thessalonians (v. 19). They will be his "hope, joy, crown" for boasting to Jesus when the parousia arrives.

3:1-5, Timothy Dispatched, and Continuing Persecutions at Thessalonica

Up to now Paul has indicated that others are traveling with him; indeed Silvanus (Silas) is a co-sender of the letter, and other unnamed individuals may also accompany him as he moves from city to city. Yet, in vv. 1-2, the apostle says, "we decided to be left alone in Athens and we sent Timothy . . . to strengthen and encourage you." Why is Paul silent about Silvanus and others in his party (such as, possibly, Luke)? If by dispatching Timothy, who is described in elevated terms, Paul thinks of himself as being "left alone," he is in effect making Timothy his most trusted representative!

3:6-10, Timothy Returns with Good News

Paul's fears about the possibility of defection and backsliding among the Thessalonians, as just expressed in v. 5, prove wholly unwarranted when he receives the "good news" from Timothy, who had just rejoined Paul. Though the believers in the city were under constant threat from their powerful and influential pagan neighbors, Paul is relieved; his hope is fulfilled that all is well and that Timothy has accomplished his mission in safety. In v. 6 he mentions the other two elements in his familiar triad, "faith and love" (as in 1:3; 5:8; and 1 Cor 13:13).

Throughout this segment of the letter, the guiding term is "encourage." Paul employs the first person plural of the aorist passive of the verb *parakaleo*, meaning "we have been encouraged." He refers both to the contents of Timothy's report and how that report has aided his own faithful resilience and the resilience of those with him in facing the trials and difficulties in their continuing, suffering witness.[13]

3:11-13, Literary Transition through Prayers

With Timothy's mission to Thessalonica completed and the good report submitted to Paul, the apostle seems all the more eager to visit

A Deep Commitment to the Power of Prayer

For African Americans, prayer has traditionally been that which allowed believers to cope with untold sufferings, despite the youthful cynicism of a younger, more self-absorbed, and mean-spirited generation. The protagonist "Bigger Thomas" in Richard Wright's classic novel *Native Son* wryly humors his mother's desperate appeal for him to pray after Bigger has become an unrepentant murderer: "When I heard the news of what had happened, I got on my knees and turned my eyes to God and asked Him if I had raised you wrong. I asked him to let me bear your burden if I did wrong by you. . . . Listen, son, your poor old ma wants you to promise her one thing. . . . Honey, when ain't nobody round you, when you alone, get on your knees and tell God everything. Ask Him to guide you. That's all you can do now. Son, promise me you'll go to Him." . . . Slowly he stood up and lifted his hands and tried to touch his mother's face and tell her yes; and as he did so something screamed deep down in him that it was a lie, that seeing her after they killed him would never be. But his mother believed; it was her last hope; it was what had kept her going through the long years."

—Richard Wright, *Native Son* (New York: Harper & Row, 1966), 277–78.

the Thessalonians himself. It is for this that he now prays, even as he petitions the Lord that they increase and abound in "love for one another and for all."

4:1-7, A Personal Life Pleasing to God

This unit opens with exhortations that resemble the kind of counsel one finds in Phil 1:27 ("Only live your life in a manner worthy of the gospel of Christ"). Here, in v. 1, Paul offers not so much new counsel as an approving observation about how the Thessalonians have indeed learned by his own example. Paul speaks inclusively for his coworkers, asking the Thessalonian house churches to continue living in ways (literally, "in the way it is necessary for you to walk") that please God. Paul rehearses his so-called indicative of salvation sounded in Gal 5:25 (the indicative is: "we live by the spirit"; the imperative is "let us walk/conduct ourselves by the spirit"). The teaching that informs such living is explicit in 1 Cor 11:1, where the apostle intones, "Be imitators of me as I am of Christ."

For Paul, how a person manages his or her intimate relations is a crucial factor in establishing a life pleasing to God. In his view, the Christian vocation is one of striving for a new level of personal morality manifested in sexual "purity," which must be understood against the background of unrestrained sexual liaisons that often prevailed in the ancient Hellenistic environment. Responding to the gospel with integrity therefore meant transposing the axiom of "moderation in all things" from a generalized philosophical observation into heightened self-control over one's own body and greater respect for the sanctity of the bodies of others. This would become the hallmark of Paul's emerging teachings on "sanctification." Holiness is, first and perhaps foremost, a spiritual state that emerges from within, as contrasted to measuring up to outward standards.

4:8, Paul's Holy Sentence

"Whoever rejects this rejects not human authority but God. . . ." The priority that Paul affixes to his teaching is underscored by the way in which he insists on divine warrant for it. Whereas Jesus of Nazareth, in Matt 23:23, speaks of certain spiritual and moral issues (e.g., faith, justice, and mercy) as "weightier matters of the law," here Paul considers sexual decency as a virtual "weightier matter of grace." This "weightier matter" becomes for him a foundational teaching, emanating from his own direct revelation from God, but given as if it is on the same level as the Jesus tradition that he received after his conversion.

4:9-12, Guidelines for a Beloved and Self-Sufficient Community

This unit begins with more reflections on "the law of love" that is so central for Paul (Rom 13:8; Gal 5:14). In this context he appeals to the principle as a guideline for community self-sufficiency and a coping strategy for sheer survival in hostile and potentially hostile social settings. Verse 12, "Be dependent on no one," really means "be interdependent within the Christian fellowship." To some extent, the basis for this call to interdependence is evident in Paul's own style of ministry (cf. 2:9). Even though Paul cultivated his independent "tentmaking ministries," there were times when he expected to be paid or needed freewill offerings of material support. Indeed, the apostle celebrated the financial contributions made to him personally on more than one occasion while he was in Thessalonica: "You Philippians indeed know that in the early days of the gospel, when I left Macedonia, no church shared with me in the matter of giving and receiving, except you alone. For when I was in Thessalonica, you sent me help for my needs more than once" (Phil 4:15-18). The emphasis in Phil 4:15 is on the phrase "in the early days," which means that such financial assistance that Paul needed and may have even depended upon was not a routine expectation or requirement in his ministry.

The author of 2 Thess 3:12 exhorts persons to "work quietly" and to "earn their own living." He focuses on the apparent breakdown of community solidarity and mutual self-help for which Paul so earnestly appealed here. Doubtless, 2 Thess 3:6-13 represents a later problem that had developed wherein some Thessalonians were refusing to be gainfully employed; the resulting idleness destroyed the sense of community interdependence and led to such problems as stealing bread from other Christians.

4:13-15, Concerning the Eschaton and Believers Who Have Already Died

The apocalyptic framework of Paul's thought in 1 Thessalonians should help readers understand why the apostle felt so constrained to resume his discussion about the end-time. Abraham Smith correctly notes that there are two bases for Paul's apocalyptic hope: one is the resurrection of Jesus as the Christ; the other is the parousia (the Lord's "second coming").[14] At this juncture, the primary focus is on the particular matter of the timing of the parousia. When will the second coming take place? Evidently, this has become a burning issue among the nascent Thessalonian believers, who have wondered aloud about the status of those Christians who have already died. Community members were "grieving for the dead" who once were within their ranks.[15] How would these dead believers possibly benefit from the parousia, which lies in the future? Paul delivers an unequivocal answer at v. 14b: "God will bring with him [i.e., the returning, triumphant Lord Jesus] those who have already died."

The theocentric character of Paul's thought is worthy of special mention here; God is the principal figure who effects the events of the eschaton. The return of Jesus is made possible by God—the very God who "quickens the dead" and enables deceased believers to accompany Jesus during his triumphal reentry.

4:16-18, How the Parousia (Second Coming) Will Unfold

Commentators often acknowledge the summary nature of vv. 16-17. These verses offer a concise description of the parousia.[16] The assertions of vv. 14-15 are now verified by the sequence of events now set forth. The Lord God will utter the command, confirmed by the voice of the archangel (Michael is named as an archangel in Jude 9; cf. Dan 10:13; 12:1).[17] The trumpet of God will sound as Jesus descends from heaven, first raising the dead and then "forcibly taking up" or, more commonly, "catching up" those believers who are yet alive. The aspect of implied force in the Greek verb *harpazo* ("caught up") should not be overlooked; it suggests some surprise and even resistance. The event will be sudden and alarming, inevitably prompting the human response of initial resistance. Paul's vision is colorful, imaginative, and dramatic. It is also informed by such eschatological speculation as found in contemporary Hellenistic Judaism.[18]

5:1-5, On Discerning When the End Will Come

Despite some opinions to the contrary, Paul does not envision two distinct final events—a parousia in which the Lord comes and a separate rapture in which the faithful are gathered up on the day of the Lord. He envisions a single, orchestrated final event. And he expects this comprehensive parousia moment as fervently as Jesus anticipated the imminent in-breaking of the kingdom of God.

Despite this, the greater part of the emerging church advised against trying to affix a specific timetable on the eschatological actions of God. That day will come like a thief in the night. Multiple New Testament texts urge caution, advising that it is impossible to know the time or day when the final event will occur (Mark 13:32ff.; Matt 24:36; Acts 1:7).[19]

In v. 5 Paul categorizes the believers at Thessalonica as "children of light and of the day;" he opposes them over against nonbelievers, whom he classifies as those of the night or of darkness. Of course, there is no hint of any racial association in the apostle's words; that kind of interpretive thinking would take many centuries to develop within Western civilization. Paul merely aligns his followers with the extensive religious tradition in which the insiders saw themselves as associated with "the light" and saw others as in "darkness" or "ignorance." It is well-known that the Jews of Qumran considered themselves in similar terms and "castigated those 'born of falsehood' who come from darkness (1QS 3:13–15, 20–21; 4:18–19, 22–23)."[20]

5:6-11, Encouraging Words on Vigilance

"So let us not sleep" (v. 6) is a clever metaphor similar to the provocative opening chapter of Thomas L. Friedman's book *The World Is Flat* (2005),[21] in which readers are reminded that many potentially dangerous things can occur while we allow ourselves to sleep. He notes that humans unwittingly miss how the global political economy of the world itself can change while we are caught "sleeping"!

"For you are sons of light" harks back to an image shared between early Christians and members of the Essenes at Qumran, but here Paul associates that light with daylight and the kind of moral behavior that is appropriate for those who are vigilant (fully awake), and sober (as opposed to drunk). "Breastplate, helmet . . . salvation" recurs in phraseology found in Eph 6:14-17. The expression "whether we are awake or sleep, we might live with him" (v. 10) is vintage Paul (compare Gal 2:20; 4:19; 2 Cor 13:5).

Sojourner Truth and the Second Coming

Sojourner Truth (born Isabella Bomefree [or more likely "Baumfree"] in 1797 in Ulster County) was an ardent nineteenth-century "womanist" who, like many other African American slaves, took great comfort in a literal belief in the second coming: "By the time she left New York City she was a full-fledged Millerite. Following the teachings of William Miller, a self-taught Baptist minister whom his supporters believed had calculated the exact date of the Second Coming of Christ, Sojourner Truth also thought that the end of the world was near, and that Jesus would return soon to judge the living and the dead. . . . [She] was convinced that there was no time to spare. Souls needed to be saved, which meant that the Word of God needed to be preached. She had to tell all who would listen about Christ's imminent return."

—Juan Williams and Quinton Dixie, *This Far by Faith: Stories from the African-American Religious Experience* (New York: Morrow, 2003), 78, 92–93.

5:12-22, Resumption of Ethical Instructions

The infinitive *eidenai* technically implies "knowing" in the sense of understanding the sacrifices and faith commitments of persons in leadership positions. As derived from *oida*, it is best to render the infinitive as "pay proper respect." In v. 13b, the admonition to "be at peace among yourselves" seems to imply that Paul has some knowledge of community unrest within the ranks of the believers. There are no fewer than fifteen exhortations with imperative force within this brief section. Paul's tone is now that of the concerned but stern father (2:11) rather than the maternal nurse (2:7). The content of the paraenesis to which Paul appeals is a familiar cord in Paul's rhetoric, found in the closing sections of many of his letters. The specific injunctions to "help the weak," however, are seldom found elsewhere in Paul's own writings. Even so, it is interesting that the Lukan "Paul" uses these same words in his speech to the Ephesian elders in Acts 20:35. Of course, that the strong should help the weak (the basis for building solidarity among the far-flung clusters of house churches and the foundation for the "collection for the poor among the saints at Jerusalem") was axiomatic for Paul, but the particular phrasing found here in v. 14 is atypical. More standard paraenesis for Paul is the injunction to refrain from "paying evil for evil" (cf. Rom 12:17-21).

5:23-28, Final Injunctions and Benediction

The phrase "God of peace" in v. 23, typical of Paul, is found nowhere in the Hebrew Bible, but Paul uses it in such places as Rom 15:33; 16:20; 2 Cor 13:12; Phil 4:9; it also occurs in Heb 13:20. For a final time, Paul makes a reference to the parousia, the coming of the Lord, as if to reassure the Thessalonians of its certainty. Not withstanding these teachings, serious doubts about the delayed parousia

eventually arose among the Thessalonians (2 Thess 2:1-12). The closing instruction of v. 26, "Greet one another with a holy kiss," also occurs in 2 Cor 13:12 and Rom 16:16.

Notes

1. Charles A. Wanamaker, *The Epistles to the Thessalonians: A Commentary on the Greek Text* (Grand Rapids, Mich.: Eerdmans, 1990), 4–6.

2. Cain Hope Felder, *Troubling Biblical Waters: Race, Class, and Family* (Maryknoll, N.Y.: Orbis, 1989), 150–60.

3. Abraham Smith, *First Thessalonians* in NIB 11: 687. See further Gene L. Green, *The Letters to the Thessalonians,* The Pillar New Testament Commentary (Grand Rapids, Mich.: Eerdmans, 2002) 69–71.

4. D. Edmond Hiebert, *1 and 2 Thessalonians* (Chicago: Moody, 1992), 40–41. See further Beverly Roberts Gaventa's, *First and Second Thessalonians,* Interpretation (Louisville: Westminster John Knox, 1998), 10–11.

5. Smith, First Thessalonians in NIB 11: 688.

6. Hiebert, *1 and 2 Thessalonians,* 42. See further Felder, *Troubling Biblical Waters,* 153–54.

7. G. K. Beale, *1–2 Thessalonians,* The IVP Commentary Series 13 (Downers Grove, Ill.: Inter-Varsity, 2003), 51–52.

8. Earl F. Palmer, *1 and 2 Thessalonians,* Good News Commentary (San Francisco: Harper & Row, 1983), 9.

9. Gene L. Green, *The Letters to the Thessalonians,* The Pillar New Testament Commentary (Grand Rapids, Mich.: Eerdmans, 2002), 106–7. See further Ernest Best, *A Commentary on the First and Second Epistles to the Thessalonians* (New York: Harper & Row, 1972), 82.

10. Beverly Roberts Gaventa, *First and Second Thessalonians,* Interpretation, 19–22.

11. D. Michael Martin, *1, 2 Thessalonians: An Exegetical and Theological Exposition of Holy Scripture,* New American Commentary 33 (Nashville: Broadman and Holman), 78–79. See further Gaventa, "Maternal Images in the

Letters of Paul" in *First and Second Thessalonians*, 31–34.

12. Smith, *First Thessalonians* in NIB 11:703.
13. Gaventa, *First and Second Thessalonians*, 44–45.
14. Smith, *First Thessalonians* in NIB 11:724.
15. Gaventa, *First and Second Thessalonians*, 63.
16. Martin, *1, 2 Thessalonians*, 150. See further Green, *The Letters to the Thessalonians*, 223–24.
17. Martin, *1, 2 Thessalonians*, 151.
18. Smith, *First Thessalonians* in NIB 11:723. See further Bart D. Ehrman, *The New Testament: An Historical Introduction to the Early Christian Writings* (New York: Oxford, 2000), 270.
19. Green, *The Letters to the Thessalonians*, 232.
20. Gaventa, *First and Second Thessalonians*, 71.
21. Thomas L. Friedman, *The World Is Flat: A Brief History of the Twenty-First Century*, (New York: Farrar, Straus, and Giroux, 2005).

For Further Reading

Beale, G. K. *1–2 Thessalonians,* The IVP Commentary Series 13. Downers Grove, Ill.: InterVarsity, 2003.

Best, Ernest. *A Commentary on the First and Second Epistles to the Thessalonians.* New York: Harper & Row, 1972.

Felder, Cain Hope. *Troubling Biblical Waters: Race, Class, and Family.* Maryknoll, N.Y.: Orbis, 1989.

Gaventa, Beverly Roberts. *First and Second Thessalonians.* Interpretation. Louisville: Westminster John Knox, 1998.

Green, Gene L. *The Letters to the Thessalonians.* The Pillar New Testament Commentary. Grand Rapids, Mich.: Eerdmans, 2002.

Hiebert, D. Edmond. *1 and 2 Thessalonians.* Chicago: Moody, 1992.

Malherbe, Abraham J. *The Letters to the Thessalonians: A New Translation with Introduction and Commentary.* AB 32B. New York: Doubleday, 2000.

Martin, D. Michael. *1, 2 Thessalonians: An Exegetical and Theological Exposition of Holy Scripture.* New American Commentary. Nashville: Broadman and Holman, 1995.

Palmer, Earl F. *1 and 2 Thessalonians.* Good News Commentary. San Francisco: Harper & Row, 1983.

Smith, Abraham. *Comfort One Another: Reconstructing the Rhetoric and Audience of 1 Thessalonians.* Literary Currents in Biblical Interpretation. Louisville: Westminster John Knox, 1995.

Wanamaker, Charles A. *The Epistles to the Thessalonians: A Commentary on the Greek Text.* Grand Rapids, Mich.: Eerdmans, 1990.

2 THESSALONIANS

Cain Hope Felder

INTRODUCTION

While the New Testament gives the impression that Paul penned two epistles to the Thessalonians, only 1 Thessalonians can be attributed to him with assurance. Most scholars are of the opinion that 2 Thessalonians is scarcely an authentic sequel, despite some general similarities with 1 Thessalonians in literary style (the litany of thanksgivings, prayers, and words of encouragement). The delayed parousia (the Lord's "second coming") motif in 2 Thessalonians is an unequivocal contrast to the imminent and sudden end expected in 1 Thessalonians; moreover, the nature of the internal opposition within the community of 2 Thessalonians is much more intense (3:1-15). Even more telling is the caution mentioned in 2 Thess 2:2 that the

recipients not become duped by a forged letter ("as though from us")! During the apostle's own lifetime, any such forgery could easily be exposed. Finally, the "Paulinist" who wrote 2 Thessalonians mistakenly suggests in 3:17 that every one of Paul's letters has a distinctive "mark" (handwriting style). Yet how is this possible when no such "mark" is mentioned in the Corinthian correspondence and elsewhere in some of the undisputed letters? While it is true that Paul at times claims a distinctive way of writing (e.g., "See what large letters I make when I am writing in my own hand!" Gal 6:11), he says nothing of the sort in Romans, Philemon, and, most significantly, 1 Thessalonians. Indeed, in some of Paul's undisputed letters, the document identifies the "traveling secretary" or amanuensis who actually writes Paul's words for him. Rom 16:22 constitutes a good example; the amanuensis, Tertius, identifies himself as writing for Paul. Second Thessalonians is most likely a studied attempt to imitate 1 Thessalonians. This is noticeable particularly in 2 Thess 2:5-6: "Do you not remember that I told you these things when I was with you?"

Six well-established criteria are typically used to determine the authenticity of a letter by Paul. These are (1) language and style, (2) theological or christological orientation, (3) ecclesiology, (4) eschatology, (5) the nature of the heresy, and (6) the style of ethics or paraenesis. When one measures 2 Thessalonians by these critical standards, it becomes rather unlikely that the historical apostle himself could be the author. The author's theological and eschatological perspective in 2 Thessalonians fits far more comfortably within the closing years of the first century. The document is thus closer to the ethos and time of the book of Revelation than to 1 Thessalonians. Again and again, 2 Thessalonians indicates that a number of developments must take place before the "day of the Lord" comes (this is in marked contrast to the sudden and surprising coming of that final moment as suggested in 1 Thess 5:2).

For African American preachers in these somewhat permissive times, 2 Thessalonians offers a rich venue of topics upon which many thunderous sermons could be delivered! It is difficult to dispute the evidence that suggests that "traditional values" are under attack. These so-called traditional values, like "family", often involve opposition to both abortion and any same-sex liaison, while "faith" usually becomes a conservative, evangelical code word indicating disapproval of gender and racial equality. Despite this kind of American political and religious rhetoric, there can be little question about a disturbing rise in countercultural values that threaten many sectors of American life.

Consider only the widespread undermining of close family bonds, the lack of mutuality within friendships, the frequent absence of integrity in oaths, whether taken by politicians or priests/ministers, the subversion of any reverence for life in widespread, often senseless violence seen in crimes and the persistence of warfare on virtual demand, not to mention what seems to be a mind-boggling sanctioning of promiscuity that would even at times appear to celebrate the "seven deadly sins"!

Unfortunately, African Americans are often blamed for precipitating such decadence through hip hop, especially "gangsta rap," and the illicit drug subculture. In an uncanny way, 2 Thessalonians can be seen—somewhat like the Epistle to the Hebrews or the Epistle of James—as a pep talk for complacent Christians who have become weary or beguiled by hucksters of Christian materialism and "prosperity" at any cost. For this reason, it is ironic that few of us actually preach from this little epistle that claims to have been written by Paul as a sequence to 1 Thessalonians.

In morally sterner days of overtly puritan and evangelical discourse and behavior, 2 Thessalonians could be taken up as a wonderful resource to chastise lackluster Christians, reminding them that they must "prove themselves worthy of the kingdom of God" (1:5) through spiritual disciplines and a needed work ethic rather than a sense of casual entitlement by virtue of their sense of "election." Of course, there is a big difference between the writer's ancient time and our own. Today, Christianity in the West in general and in America in particular has become the establishment religion of the prevailing political economy. Unlike today, threats from Christian leaders about moral condemnation and its dire consequences were taken much more seriously by members of newly formed house churches and congregations.

1:1, The Prescript or Salutation

The opening salutation in v. 1 reproduces the exact wording of 1 Thess 1:1, with the single exception that 2 Thessalonians omits the word "peace." Yet one finds not only the word "peace" but an elaboration on it in v. 2 in a manner that is closer to the actual style of the apostle as seen in Rom 1:7b; 1 Cor 1:3; 2 Cor 1:2; Gal 1:3; Phil 1:2 (and even Eph 1:2). Here is an initial clue for the resolution of the question of authorship. Second Thessalonians seems to be intentionally stylized even as it not only warns readers of forged Pauline epistles (2:2) but also speaks of adhering to a set of beliefs as established "tradition" (2:15; 3:6). These considerations along with an insistence that the apocalyptic end must be preceded by signs not yet revealed suggest that this epistle simply cannot be an immediate ancient sequel to 1 Thessalonians.

Indeed, the mentioning of such an expression as "a work of faith" (1:11) is far more at home in the Epistle of James than in any authentic letter of Paul's. Also of concern are the repeated references to divine revenge as God's eschatological justice. While they are reminiscent of Rom 12:19-20, Paul himself never places the kind of emphasis upon such a view as found in 2 Thessalonians 2. Finally, although the author of 2 Thessalonians claims that his letter, like all of Paul's letters, contains a distinctive mark of authentication, most scholars are at a loss when it comes to verifying this.

All of this places us more safely in the camp of those who consider 2 Thessalonians to have been written in the latter third of the first century rather than as a close sequel to 1 Thessalonians. The latter time frame provides a more coherent sociopolitical context for this epistle. That was a time that challenged believers not to be Christians in name only

or when it was convenient, but to live out the confession of their faith in their daily lives, consciously opposing competing claims to religious truth or delusional, competing spiritual entities.

1:3-12, The Occasion of the Epistle

1:3b-4, Thanksgiving

This ancient author wisely begins on a strong, positive note of thanksgiving for the reports that he has received about the apparent valiant efforts on the part of many Christian Thessalonians who are striving to keep the faith despite threats from influential opponents. He offers words of comfort and encouragement, knowing that some are still being persecuted in an urban context that was not particularly welcoming for this fledgling religious movement. The writer seems to be aware of two potentially dangerous paths for the church—either to become swayed by the contemporary popular cultural belief systems or to take one's faith as a fast track to a life of prosperity and ease. He commends those who have studiously avoided such paths that lead inevitably to self-destruction. In this sense, the author of 2 Thessalonians is a prophet for so many today in the black church who either have gone down one of these paths or stand in peril of doing so!

In the early years of this third millennium, the masses of African Americans seem to have an almost desperate need for a piece of the material "prosperity" constantly flaunted by the majority culture media and ruthlessly adopted by opportunistic African American televangelists. The poor, often gullible, and unsuspecting believers sadly tend to ignore the time-honored fact that desperate people are the most likely to be easily exploited.

1:5-10, Assurances of God's Justice: Relief and Divine Retribution

Verse 5 mentions "the righteous judgment of God" (*dikaias kriseōs tou theou*) that conveys divine intention, namely, to provide the opportunity for the Thessalonian Christians to prove themselves worthy of the kingdom of God (so also v. 11). Although Paul himself does refer to "the kingdom of God" (Rom 14:17; 1 Cor 4:20; Gal 5:21), he does so infrequently. One would have expected the text to focus more on the "righteousness of God," which would be more typical of Paul. There follows in v. 6 an explicit description of God as "just," but the author has in view two kinds of justice—reciprocal and eschatological justice. The former sets forth the principle wherein God repays affliction with affliction, whereas the latter reflects simple divine vengeance. Unlike Paul's own emphasis on grace and compassion, 2 Thessalonians envisions mainly a God of wrath who one day will settle the score with those who persecute Christians (compare v. 9), and also those Christians who disobey the gospel. That the enemies of the church would "suffer the punishment of eternal destruction" are thoughts more consistent perhaps with the book of Revelation, from much later in the first century than the historical Paul.

"When he comes to be glorified . . . on that day" clearly envisions some time in the future; and this is an important distinction that the writer insists upon as he introduces the central situational issue confronting the church at Thessalonica. Note also the stress placed on the "glory" of the Lord in vv. 9, 10, and 12. The reiteration of the Lord Jesus Christ's glory—his name and his might—points again to a later time in the first century, when the church has a more christocentric orientation that is coming into its own, with a separate, central saving figure (other than the Yahweh/Jehovah of the Hebrew Bible) in Jesus Christ as opposed to Paul's own more theocentric tone.

1:11-12, We Pray for You

This unit opens with the writer reminding the church of Thessalonica that, no matter what the circumstances, prayers are always being offered on their behalf. The author returns to the issue that God is testing them to determine the worthiness of their "call" or election (a theme continued in 2:13), presumably as the new witnessing Israel (compare 1 Pet 2:4). Indeed, just as the writer reassures the church that others are praying for them, one should note the other end of the equation in 3:1, where the Thessalonians are asked to pray for those who send this epistle and for others whom they represent.

2:1-12, The Lord's Coming and the Heresy of the Lawless One

Chapter 2 identifies what appears to be the most hotly contested issue dividing the church at Thessalonica and informing its present crisis, namely, "the coming of the Lord." Certain individuals within the Christian community are claiming that the day of the Lord (Judgment Day) has already arrived. Beverly Gaventa makes a helpful observation:

> Verses 1-2 introduce the topic of the "day of the Lord" and emphatically insists that believers should not be disturbed by any teaching to the effect that it has already arrived. Verses 3-12 then explain in detail how the writer knows that the "day of the Lord" has not arrived and what must happen before that time can come.[1]

The author of 2 Thessalonians argues that the fateful "day of the Lord" will not arrive until a set of specific events takes place. Evidently, the most significant event is the "rebellion" led by "the lawless one" who at some future time will be revealed. This is the earliest New Testament mention of a figure who will appear in the future as some mysterious "antichrist." This antichrist is also named in 1 John 2:18, 22; 4:3; and 2 John 1:7, but nowhere else in the New Testament. The frightful struggle between Christ and this "lawless one" in vv. 3-9 again conjures up more of the ethos manifested in the book of Revelation rather than the context set forth in 1 Thessalonians.

The author wishes to dispel vehemently any notion that the parousia or second coming has arrived. To do this he predicts the necessity of a dramatic prelude in which this "lawless one" or antichrist figure—doing the work of Satan—will be then destroyed by Jesus Christ at his coming (v. 9). The drama provides vivid characteristics of the antichrist figure (v. 10); he has the ability to deceive and thereby to cause many gullible Christians to fall away from the truth. He is the author of "a powerful delusion," leading persons to take the kind of pleasure in "unrighteousness" that places their salvation in peril.

Perhaps no portion of 2 Thessalonians has greater hermeneutical relevance for the African American community today than this one. Forget about Hal Lindsay's *The Late Great Planet Earth* of the early 1970s or the phenomenal popularity of more recent Christian apocalyptic novels; these are mostly otherworldly! The great threat within the black church and wider African American context today is an apocalyptic this-worldliness of extremes. On the one hand, there are masses of black Americans in lottery lines, casinos, jails, and halfway houses; on the other hand, there is an increasing number of upwardly mobile blacks caught up in a mad pursuit of creature comforts, virtually oblivious to the pain and sufferings of the desperate masses. Dare one mention many of the black millionaire entertainers or televangelists who have found their apparent kingdoms on earth to

the puzzlement of the poor and downtrodden. Who is the "lawless one" of our times who sponsors a new kind of "powerful delusion"? It might be that the "rebellion" of 2 Thessalonians that must come first (v. 3) is this very contemporary era that has spawned the meteoric rise of the "Christian media celebrity"!

Jesus Christ will vindicate the faithful on the future Day of Judgment. This kind of public assurance for Christians who suffer as a minority group in an inhospitable social contexts is alien to modern readers, because so few today really suffer such religious persecution in a context where Christianity is the accepted dominant civil religion.

According to v. 11, "God sends them a powerful delusion." Although this verse envisions some bigger than life, beguiling antichrist figure, the African American subculture

---

"Fortune Teller Blues" by Langston Hughes

I went to de gypsy,
De gypsy took hold o' my hand.
Went to the gypsy,
Gypsy took hold o' my hand.
He looked at me and tole me
Chile, you gonna lose yo' man.

These fortune tellers
Never tell me nothin' kind.
I say these fortune tellers
Never tell me nothin' kind'
I'd give a hundred dollars
To de one that would ease my mind!

—Arnold Rampersad and David Roessel, eds., *The Collected Poems of Langston Hughes* (New York: Vintage, 1994), 70. "Fortune Teller Blues" from *The Collected Poems of Langston Hughes* by Langston Hughes. Copyright © 1994 by The Estate of Langston Hughes. Used by permission of Alfred A. Knopf, a division of Random House, Inc., and Harold Ober Associates Incorporated.

has long been plagued by colorful "prophets," gypsies, and conjurers of one sort or another; more often than not these are representatives of the evil one in miniature.

2:13-17 Gratitude and Comfort

At 2:13 the author returns abruptly to his opening thanksgiving (1:3), revealing a keen pastoral skill in balancing joyous praise and stern admonition. The author makes a most important declaration: "because the Lord chose you." The appeal to the idea of special "election" or "being chosen" has been a period

---

Walker's Appeal to *the Chosen*

"Your full glory and happiness . . . shall never be consummated, but with the entire emancipation of your universal brethren all over the world . . . for I believe that it is the will of the Lord that our greatest happiness shall consist in working for the salvation of our whole body [i.e., people of African descent worldwide]. When this is accomplished a burst of glory will shine upon you, which will indeed astonish you and the whole world."

—Lerone Bennett Jr., *Before the Mayflower: A History of Black America*, 6th ed. (Chicago: Johnson, 1961), 148.

---

theme in African American history. One example of this is found in the fiery rhetoric of the celebrated "Walker's Appeal" of September 28, 1829, published in Boston by the free-born David Walker.

The African Methodist Episcopal Bishop Henry McNeal Turner provides another, more explicit illustration of African American "election" in his famous September 1895 address to the National Baptist Convention. "[He] envisioned the power of black unity under the banner of Christ. This power was not available

to former slaves in politics or through their meager pocketbooks. In his deep Southern accent he began to preach, then sing, to cry, then pray, as he told the convention that it was time for black people to claim their place as God's chosen people, called by his Son to create a miracle in the world."[2]

The Paulinist who writes in the second chapter of 2 Thessalonians appeals to the biblical idea of election to highlight a particular compelling sacred identity and other positive features of the Thessalonian Christian walk: "first fruits for salvation," "sanctification by the Spirit," and the acceptance of the "truth." These attributes were doubtlessly validated by the well-known persecutions and trials that these Thessalonian Christians had to endure (see Acts 17:1-9 and 1 Thess 2:14-16). Then, in vv. 14-15, the author reminds his readers that their very existence is the result of Paul's historic evangelical work among them. In fact, that historic preaching activity is now part of an established "tradition" that, in light of intervening "false teaching" that the day of the Lord has arrived already (mentioned in 2:2), reminds us of a community situation more akin to that which Paul and Timothy encountered at Ephesus, as reported in 2 Tim 2:18.

Verse 15 urges the recipients of this epistle to "stand firm and hold fast to the traditions." The mentioning of "tradition" (*paradosis*), both here and in 3:6, is yet another reminder that the author presumes that there exists a well-established pattern of generally accepted teachings and moral norms among the churches. This is yet another sign that the author is someone other than the apostle Paul who carefully distinguished between an authoritative tradition that he received and his own "holy sentences" or situational instructions.

3:1-17, We Too Need Prayer in This Struggle

The closing chapter of 2 Thessalonians shifts

attention from the immediate crises within the Thessalonian church to the wider evangelical mission and its ultimate purpose, "that the Lord may be glorified everywhere." Verses 1-5 are pastoral admonitions reminding the readers of the continuing dangers from unbelievers and "the evil one"—here an allusion to the devil or Satan himself (not the specific "antichrist figure" referenced in 2:9) but as in the Lord's Prayer as found in Matt 5:13b: "rescue us from the evil one." Much of the phraseology of these opening verses is reminiscent of phrases used in 1 Thessalonians.

For modern readers who revisit the ancient setting of 2 Thessalonians, the pastoral advice might appear simplistic and mundane, but the author's confidence that the Thessalonians will respond to his commands hardly finds its parallels in most of Christianity of today. The modern church, including the African American context, is one more characterized by revolt, challenges to central authority, and Christians virtually doing "what seems right in one's own eyes" rather than adhering uniformly to some "tradition." The result, in many quarters today, is a dazzling proliferation of self-styled "splinter churches" or, even worse, the clustering of ultra-conservative political advocacy churches that claim a slippery moral high ground of so-called family values that do not augur well for a coherent Christian future. Thus, these five verses serve as a fine introduction for the final paraenesis that follow.

This second section, vv. 6-15, of the closing chapter of 2 Thessalonians reminds the church of the dangers of idle hands as being the proverbial "devil's workshop." By calling attention to idlers, the author is now taking up once again the specific instructions that were offered in 1 Thess 5:14, "And we exhort you, brethren, admonish the idlers. . . ." The author appeals once again to an apparent emerging new tradition. One must keep in mind that the word "tradition" throughout this chapter does not have the sense of teachings that Paul himself reported as being passed on to him, as seen in 1 Cor 11:23-26 and 15:3. Instead, the mentioning of "tradition" here throughout this section refers to the actual practices of the apostles themselves as exemplars.

Illustrative of the foregoing concerns of 1 Thess 2:15 is the probability that apostolic practices were also passed on by "word of mouth and letter" among the churches. Note also the author's frequent references to imitation, as found in 1 Cor 4:16, "I urge you, then, be imitators of me," and 11:1, "Be imitators of me, as I am of Christ." Clearly this new meaning of the word "tradition" is an indication that 2 Thessalonians is part of the forward march toward a new emerging Christian moral orthodoxy that will be further solidified in the Pastoral Epistles (1–2 Timothy and Titus). The author brings to bear the understanding that the function of their faith must be qualified with action so that believers would be found "working" and not "idle" by Christ on the Day of Judgment. The motive of punitive repercussions as eschatological indicative today rings hollow and cannot be approached as a threat to commend a course of action.

Verses 6-15 offer clear instructions for daily moral conduct among the Thessalonians and thus direct the community's attention to their emerging dangerous signs of complacency and laziness. Such behavior belies the public profile that would be advantageous for bona fide practitioners of the faith. The tone seems intentionally similar to ideas expressed in 1 Thess 4:9-12. Furthermore, in vv. 7 and 9 the author seems to use intentionally other familiar Pauline expressions such as "be imitators of us" (1 Cor 11:1; 1 Thess 1:14), or, in v. 13, "do not be weary," which easily allows one to recall Paul's advice in Gal 6:9.

Verse 16 returns to a familiar Pauline refrain with respect to the desire for the peace of the Lord to be a constant goal for every Christian action. All must understand that in the Semitic idiom, peace is not merely the absence of hostility and open conflicts but the result of doing what is right and just. Peace, in this sense, seeks to enhance the welfare of the entire community.

Scholars have long been at a loss in trying to authenticate the Pauline claim in v. 17 that he places a distinctive mark in every one of his epistles. Perhaps this is an overzealous extension of Gal 6:11, "See what large letters I make when I am writing in my own hand!" or of 1 Cor 16:21, "I, Paul write this greeting with my own hand." There is no such indication at the end of 2 Corinthians and, more particularly, at the end of 1 Thessalonians! For this reason the final claim that a distinctive mark is present in 2 Thessalonians is yet one more pointer to the deuteropauline status of authorship, thereby indicating that the document was written by a disciple of Paul rather than by Paul himself.

Notes

1. Beverly Roberts Gaventa, *First and Second Thessalonians* (Louisville: John Knox, 1998), 107.

2. Juan Williams and Quinton Dixie, *This Far by Faith: Stories from the African American Religious Experience* (New York: Morrow, 2003), 102–3.

For Further Reading

Giblin, Charles H. *The Threat to Faith: An Exegetical and Theological Re-Examination of 1 Thessalonians 2.* AnBib 31. Rome: Biblical Institute, 1967.

Holland, Glenn S. *The Tradition That You Received from Us: 2 Thessalonians in the Pauline Tradition.* Tübingen: Mohr Siebeck, 1998.

Hughes, Frank Witt. *Early Christian Rhetoric and 2 Thessalonians.* JSNTSup 30. Sheffield: Sheffield Academic, 1989.

Jewett, Robert. *The Thessalonian Correspondence: Pauline Rhetoric and Millenarian Piety* (Philadelphia: Fortress Press, 1986).

See also Further Reading for 1 Thessalonians on pp. 399–400.

1–2 TIMOTHY AND TITUS (THE PASTORAL EPISTLES)

Clarice J. Martin

INTRODUCTION: THE PASTORAL EPISTLES

The Pastoral Epistles—1 Timothy, 2 Timothy, and Titus—hold an enduring and distinctive place within the corpus of Christian Testament writings. Purportedly written by Paul to two of his most trusted and cherished younger coworkers, Timothy and Titus, whom he left in charge of the churches in Ephesus and Crete, respectively, the letters provide incomparable glimpses into the historical situation of first-century Christian communities ("assemblies")—communities that held fast to a cherished narrative of Christian hope and the appearance of Christ in the future (Titus 2:13).

Likely written within a similar chronological frame, probably during the reign of the emperor Domitian, in Asia Minor (90–110 C.E.), the letters appear as third-generation correspondence. The first generation was represented by Timothy's grandmother Lois and the second by Timothy's mother, Eunice. Timothy, standing as a sterling representative of the third generation, appears as one determined to pass on the precious faith legacy of his ancestors (2 Tim 1:5). The Pastoral Epistles attest decisively to the resolute transmittal of the seed and tradition of faith held by Christians from generation to generation, certifying the power, vibrancy, and adaptability of the Christian gospel over time. Offering a candid glimpse of the continuing evolution of the Jesus movement within the late first century, the Pastoral Epistles provide a fascinating glimpse of the transformations and changes experienced by Christian believers who were firmly situated within the dynamic, pluralistic, and bustling Mediterranean world. It was a world that mirrored the characteristic social networks, organizations, social mores, political tensions, internecine strife and wars, and traditional and polytheistic religions of the day. It was also a world in which luxury and indulgence were largely the possession of a small governing aristocracy, or those irrepressible social climbers with lower status who eyed the prize of privilege and struggled to attain it.

The authorship of the Pastoral Epistles remains a thorny and unsettled subject. Although these documents have been designated as "Pastoral Letters" since the eighteenth century and were accepted as genuinely Pauline by generations of early Christian writers, their authorship has been debated for more than two hundred years. A clear majority of scholars today consider the Pastorals as a whole to be pseudonymous, which is to say, written by one or more Paulinists who adapted some of Paul's ideas and wrote in his name (it was a common practice in the ancient world to honor—but adapt—the idea of an earlier writer). Even those who advocate Paul's authorship concede that another hand may have produced the letters, particularly in light of significant linguistic and thematic departures from the Pauline corpus. The Greek vocabulary, style, and syntax diverge quite noticeably from that of the traditionally recognized Pauline corpus (1 Thessalonians, 1 and 2 Corinthians, Philemon, Philippians, Galatians, Romans). The notable body of scholars who hold that the Pastorals are pseudonymous nevertheless discern in the Pastorals seasoned echoes of the apostle's theology.[1] While this writer shares with a significant number of Christian Testament interpreters the view that the Pastorals are pseudonymous, I shall at various points in the essay refer to

the writer as "Paul" (using quotation marks). I do so without prejudice, in conjunction with the Pastoral author's desire to ascribe Pauline authorship to the correspondence.

As many African American believers would attest relative to the Pastoral Epistles—and to the larger canons of both the Hebrew Bible and Christian Testament literature—the interpretation of biblical texts is richly enlarged when interpreters explore the broad range of possible historical meanings of biblical texts within their own ancient cultural milieu. Similarly, subsequent readings of those texts within diverse global cultures and communities must be undertaken with an openness to appreciating the broad interpretive legacy of our biblical heritage. Dynamic and transformative faith commitment and practice more often arise from an openness to multiple, dissident, emancipatory, and revisionist readings and interpretive practices, including careful and thoughtful reassessments of the continuing impact of our biblical inheritance on ecclesial tradition and practice, and on political and social policy. One hallmark feature of African American biblical hermeneutics (practices of interpretation) through the centuries is its culturally-nuanced agreement with the rallying cry of sixteen and seventeenth-century reformers: the church is a dynamic institution, created to be the ever-reforming embodiment of the pilgrim people of God in a changing world (*ecclesia reformata, semper reformanda*—"the church reformed and ever to be reformed"). The project and enterprise of African American biblical hermeneutics has in every age fired the engines of profound change in both church and society.[2]

African American Christians have always been convinced that fidelity to God requires not only imaginative reappropriations, reinterpretations, and reconstructions of biblical traditions, but even confrontations with biblical traditions and their centuries-old interpretive legacies. Historically, one of the most imaginative African American reappropriations of biblical traditions occurred during antebellum slavery, when African Americans claimed that the Exodus tradition in the Hebrew Bible was emblematic of their experience of enslavement in America. Enslaved African Americans found glad and notable affinities with the God who delivered Israel from slavery's tyrannous and oppressive bond in Egypt, reappropriating the liberation story to reflect their own worldview and aspirations. Convinced that the God who liberated Israel from Egypt brooked no tolerance for the enslavement of some human beings by other human beings, these black enslaved pioneers blatantly rejected the duplicitous and self-serving rhetoric of pro-slavery rhetoricians who used scripture to endorse slave-holding Christianity. Ideologically and theologically informed by a black sacred cosmos which celebrated a God who was Loving, Compassionate and Just, black biblical interpreters easily denounced both the slaveholding God and the hermeneutical practices that gave rise to this God's genesis.[3]

The early twentieth century witnessed the creation of one of the most delightful, imaginative, and impassioned reinterpretations and reconstructions of biblical tradition. Famed anthropologist Zora Neale Hurston penned the compelling allegory, *Moses, Man of the Mountain* (published in 1939), a long-lived classic which blends the story of Moses, the Great Emancipator in the Hebrew Bible, with the Moses of black folklore. The political allegory brilliantly analogizes Hebrew oppression in Egypt with black oppression within the United States, with Moses functioning as a decisive liberation agent for those living under the heels of Jim Crow practices and policies. Hurston's creative revision of the sacred myths of biblical tradition with African American personalities, terms, symbols and idioms represents a monumental testament to the limitless imaginative potential and improvisational

savvy of African Americans' engagement of the Bible over the centuries.[4]

In addition to critically reappropriating, reinterpreting, and reconstructing biblical texts and traditions, African American have also confronted and critiqued an array of biblical texts and practices, challenging, for example, the interpretive legacy of biblical traditions (and their practitioners) used to reinforce such oppressive and lethal practices as colonialism and racial domination. This well-documented fact can be seen, for example, in long-standing black critiques of those ancient canonical traditions that legitimated and endorsed the submission of enslaved men and women to slave masters and slave mistresses (e.g. the pagan, Stoic *haustafeln* or domestic codes in Colossians 3:18—4:1; Ephesians 5:21—6:9; and 1 Peter 2:18—3:7). It can also be seen in the critique of a Eurocentric interpretive legacy that ignored the profoundly glaring exploitative power of the propertied Sarah over the enslaved black woman, Hagar, in Genesis 16:1-16. African American hermeneutical strategies invoking celebration, affirmation, critique, resistance, transgression, and reform have long roots within the black interpretive repertoire. As we shall see, African American engagements of the Pastoral Epistles have mandated an integration of these and other strategic approaches to these ancient letters.[5]

First Timothy, 2 Timothy, and Titus, while addressed to individuals, are clearly public epistles in scope, interweaving personal injunction and ecclesial advice with a communal orientation. Some interpreters have described the Pastoral correspondence as a type of ancient, encyclopedic "manual of church order," but one must be cautious here. No single definitive organizational structure is presupposed in the three letters, nor are the letters a "handbook for church leaders" (2 Timothy lacks reference to church order; little reference is found in Titus to church order, and what is there departs from the account in 1 Timothy). Hence, the presence of common and similar traditional material should not lead interpreters to "collapse" the letters together as a fully unitary sub-corpus. Each letter must be studied individually, even if there are common themes. One suggested model for the Pastoral correspondence is the *mandata principis* letters found in Hellenistic royal correspondence. Those letters contain directives generated by rulers to their appointed delegates who are governing regional territories. Addressed specifically to these delegates in local cities or to other representatives, the letters outline a series of instructions to be implemented. While technically "private correspondence," the instructions delivered to specific individuals were always intended for larger audiences. The "paraenesis" or moral instructions interwoven in all three Pastorals illustrate the dual function of targeting at once both individuals and the larger Christian assemblies that we see in the *mandata principis* genre.[6]

At least three broad factors should be considered in identifying a continuum of possibilities that gave rise to the historical situation of the Pastoral Epistles. First, perceived as dissident communities[7] faced with the potentially threatening intrusions of the ideologies and retributive power of Rome, the recipients of the Pastorals were keenly aware of their tenuous relationship to imperial authorities. The Pastoral writer(s) exhorts the recipients to embrace the ideals of good citizenship, conformity to prevailing social norms, and accommodation with government and worldly authorities for the sake of peace for the church (1 Tim 2:1-2; Titus 3:1).

Second, as communities facing teachings and resistance from individuals and groups who were responsible for suffering and internal divisiveness within the faith communities,

the recipients were encouraged to remember and to imitate the example and disposition of Paul—their faith model par excellence—in their quest for steadfastness and perseverance in faith and ministry. A fiery resolve to exhibit unfaltering moral virtue, holiness, and wisdom would also counter vituperative opponents (1 Tim 1:3-7; 6:3-6; 2 Tim 2:1-26).

Finally, there is some evidence that Christian traditionalists within the faith communities feared an erosion of prevailing social mores that required free Christian women and enslaved believers (males and females) *to continue to conform unqualifiedly* to their roles as "low-status subordinates" in the assemblies that met within the Greco-Roman households (*oikoi*). Such prevailing social mores were, after all, a foundation block of Roman ideology and society. In agreement with such Christian traditionalists, the author of the Pastorals issued stern warnings against what might be termed "egalitarian excess." For these Christian traditionalists, who insisted that rigid conformity to paternal power (*patria potestas*) be upheld in government and home (where the rule of the *paterfamilias*—the father/husband/slavemaster—was the ultimate authority), any deviance potentially challenging or subverting those traditional protocols from a "dissident subculture" was likely viewed as "egalitarian excess." A libertine or liberationist eschatological ethic wherein free Christian women and enslaved persons (males and females) viewed themselves as fully freed from these customary social constraints and mores likely had its roots in the more egalitarian vision of the pre-Pauline formula in Gal 3:28: "there is no longer slave or free, there is no longer male and female; for all of you are one in Christ Jesus."

African Americans have found resonance with at least four broad themes or motifs in the Pastoral letters: (1) the generational transmittal of the Christian faith (as signaled in the textual reference to Timothy's grandmother Lois and mother, Eunice); (2) the suggestions of qualities for church leaders; (3) the more contentious instruction for navigating the terrain of gender politics relative to women's leadership, agency, and service with the church; and (4) the Pauline model of fidelity and perseverance in faith portrayed in 2 Timothy.

1 TIMOTHY

1:1-2, Salutation

The opening salutation foregrounds immediately the much-cherished and valued intimacy between Paul and his "loyal child" Timothy. The father-son terminology was customarily used to express the master-disciple relationship that was then widespread in the mystery religions.[8] As Timothy's spiritual father, "Paul" here revalidates the enduring bonds of their long-established union as grounded in the vitality of the faith they held in common. Timothy was no mere "special acquaintance" by accident or "happenstance"; he was "Paul's" loyal child "in the faith" (*en pistei*). The apostle himself used the parent-child imagery to describe his relationship to his converts in other communications (1 Cor 4:14-15; Phlm 10), and referred to Timothy as a coworker (1 Thess 3:2; Phil 2:19-20). The prayer-wish for Timothy in the salutation here, invoking "grace, mercy, and peace" (*shalom*) for Timothy's unique person and distinctive being, robust faith, and loyalty, provides a sterling model for reinforcing long-standing bonds and life-giving intimacy among ministry coworkers and friends.

Marie-Noëlle Anderson, a South African expert on traditional medicine and biodiversity, has sagely remarked on the priceless and "privileged" character of life-giving intimacy: "Intimacy should be seen as a privileged

meeting of two beings: Man with woman, parent with child, pupil with teacher."[9] Such intimacy is in clear evidence in the author's narrative transaction with Timothy. Clear, too, is the author's hope that the seeds of faith that he had planted in his young charge would continue to be sown in others, producing and

---

"For Russell and Rowena Jelliffe" by Langston Hughes

And so the seed
Becomes a flower
And in its hour
Reproduces dreams
And flowers

And so the root
Becomes a trunk
And then a tree
And seeds of trees
And springtime sap
And summer shade
And autumn leaves
And shape of poems
And dreams—
And more than tree.

And so it is
With those who make
Of life a flower,
A tree, a dream
Reproducing (on into
Its own and mine
And your infinity)
Its beauty and its life
In you and me.

—"For Russell and Rowena Jelliffe" from *The Collected Poems of Langston Hughes* by Langston Hughes. Copyright © 1994 by The Estate of Langston Hughes. Used by permission of Alfred A. Knopf, a division of Random House, Inc., and Harold Ober Associates Inc.

reproducing an unbounded spiritual harvest. The African American poet Langston Hughes offers a similar perspective on seeds in the poem, "For Russell and Rowena Jelliffe" (see sidebar on p. 413).

Hughes's sonnet recalls the astonishing mystery and power of sown seed to reproduce itself and thrive. Similarly, the parable of the sower traditions in the Synoptic Gospels (Mark 4:1-9; Matt 13:1-9; Luke 8:4-8) bears witness to the mysterious sovereignty of the sown word of the gospel to explode into fruitfulness for the kingdom—a yield of thirty, sixty, one hundredfold. "Paul" here challenges Timothy to maintain his unapologetic, unfailing commitment to this divine, potentially explosive work of ministry, where nurtured seed develops deep roots and may become a flower, a trunk, or an expansive and sturdy tree, enduring firmly through the seasons and cycles of life, irrepressibly reproducing itself in every receptive soil.

Like all mentors, Paul the apostle was a "lantern" in Timothy's life. In the words of one of America's foremost civil rights leaders and child advocacy champions, Marian Wright Edelman, we do not come into or get through life alone. Our lives are often gifted with exceptional women and men, who, like Paul, function as lanterns in our lives, brilliantly illumining our pathways with wisdom and inspiration for the journey, galvanizing and fueling our energies and resolve. Her prayer in the sidebar conveys her gratitude for these rare individuals.

The model of Paul as a loving, collegial, and focused mentor and coworker in ministry, introduced here but repeated in greater detail throughout the Pastorals, highlights the importance of such life-giving relationships in identity formation. "Without identity, we are an object of history, an instrument used by others, like a utensil. Identity is an assumed role; it is like being in a theater where every-

> ### Mentors Light Our Way
>
> "O God, I thank you for the lanterns in my life who illuminated dark and uncertain paths, calmed and stilled debilitating doubts and fears with encouraging words, wise lessons, gentle touches, firm nudges, and faithful actions along my journey of life and back to You."
>
> —Marian Wright Edelman, *Lanterns: A Memoir of Mentors* (New York: HarperCollins, 2000), xiii.

one is given a role to play."[10] Joseph Ki-Zerbo, a professor of history at Dakar University in Senegal, declaratively pinpoints a key issue in the crisis of identity formation among people of every generation and of all cultures and nations. It is the awareness that the roots of our identity anchor us within the drama of life and prevent us from becoming aimless and disoriented. Timothy's clarity about his "roots" and his Christian identity was a formidable tool in facing foes from without and fears from within.

As Christians living in the post-apostolic era, seeking guidance about how to follow the apostolic teachings of Paul, the martyr apostle of an earlier generation, the recipients of 1 Timothy appeared to be preoccupied with issues related to their own identity formation as Christ-believers. Like those in Alex Haley's famed 1976 miniseries *Roots: The Saga of an American Family* (which sparked a renaissance of genealogical study and research on family origins and history among Americans of all ethnicities and cultures), the members of the late first-century Christian assemblies required a sharper, more refined photographic picture of "Paul," who had long inspired revolutionary and costly faith within an imperial context.

Christ-believers in the assemblies where Timothy had ministered had themselves been energized by the traditions regarding the apostle who had so staunchly and fearlessly proclaimed during his life and ministry: "I am hard pressed between the two: my desire is to depart and be with Christ, for that is far better; but to remain in the flesh is more necessary for you" (Phil 1:23-24). They had nodded together in affirmative, almost lock-step agreement upon hearing once again of Paul's boundless love for Christ: "Yet whatever gains I had, these I have come to regard as loss because of Christ. More than that, I regard everything as loss because of the surpassing value of knowing Christ Jesus my Lord" (Phil 3:7-8). Their spirits hushed within them when they imagined their spiritual hero in the waning, sunset years of his life proclaim in correspondence to the Roman believers in the West (whom he had never met): "For I am not ashamed of the gospel; it is the power of God for salvation to everyone who has faith, to the Jew first and also to the Greek. For in it the righteousness of God is revealed through faith for faith; as it is written, 'The one who is righteous will live by faith'" (Rom 1:16-17). For the Ephesian faithful, a "hermeneutics of memory and mimesis (imitation)" made perfect sense as a sure-fire strategy for nurturing their own identity formation in their time. The reconstructed memories and model of the apostle clarified who they were—and "whose" they were—as bearers of the deposit handed on to them.

The author of 1 Timothy was certainly a master reconstructionist and image maker, portraying Paul as *primus inter pares* (first among equals) to qualifiedly give directions for all phases of the church's life. Such image making is familiar in the lived experiences of black peoples, both within the United States and in the African diaspora. One of the monumental achievements of Toni Morrison's Nobel Prize–winning book, *Beloved*,[11] is its bellwether cry for black peoples to *remember*

the historical past—even the disheartening, traumatized past of American slavery. In her view, a "disremembered," romanticized past obfuscates the realities and terrors of enslavement. It veils and trivializes the long tradition of resistance and revolt that dogged every step of slavery's swagger. It diminishes the pertinacity of enslaved individuals, families, and communities who exhibited boundless creative potential in their pursuit of the dream of freedom and a more robust quality of life. These subaltern giants, who so often stood tall

Love the God-Given Self

"'Here,' she said, 'in this here place, we flesh; flesh that weeps, laughs; flesh that dances on bare feet in grass. Love it. Love it hard. Yonder they do not love your flesh. They despise it. They don't love your eyes; they'd just as soon pick em out. No more do they love the skin on your back. Yonder they flay it. And O my people they do not love your hands. Those they only use, tie, bind, chop off and leave empty. Love your hands! Love them. Raise them up and kiss them. Touch others with them, pat them together, stroke them on your face 'cause they don't love that either. *You* got to love it, *you*! And no, they ain't in love with your mouth. Yonder, out there, they will see it broken and break it again. What you say out of it they will not heed. What you scream from it they do not hear. What you put into it to nourish your body they will snatch away and give you leavins instead. No, they don't love your mouth. *You* got to love it. This is flesh I'm talking about here. Flesh that needs to be loved.'"

—Toni Morrison, *Beloved* (New York: Knopf, 1987), 88.

when bowed, passed on the light-torch that still illuminates the way of black peoples in the present. "Re-memorying" the past foregrounds the myriad of ways African Americans reconstructed certain kinds of stability, created life-giving strategies for survival, and much, much more.

When Sethe's mother-in-law, the inspired preacher Baby Suggs, stood tall in the hush-arbor of the outdoor church called the Clearing and recalled the evils turned loose on African Americans during slavery—affecting eyes, hands, mouth, and the totality of their physical being—her last words to her enlivened congregation were not words of lament. She helped them to create a countercanonical script and "counterstory" to the master American narrative of racial inferiority and inhumanity—a narrative which ceaselessly trivialized the integrity, beauty and worth of black bodies, and which mocked the limitless treasure of black humanity and potential. Her reverberant, grandiloquent, and captivating rhetoric commanded an unqualifiably passionate, embodied, and performative dance of self-love—a self-love with visible markers of loving fiercely every feature of the God-given self of black women, men, and children. African American homiletical, rhetorical artistry, had once again broken through the veil of slavery's stultifying mist, disrupting—for a season, at least—slavery's intrusive assault and reign of terror in African American life. (See the sidebar on p. 415.)

If Baby Suggs used a parade of graphic imperatives and spellbinding images and metaphors to frame and reconstruct slavery's horrors, she also employed a hermeneutics of memory and mimesis to remind members of her congregation that how they were imaged, constructed, and treated by others was never an indication of who they actually were and are. The "subjected" self was never the "actual self." Proactively, she challenged them to disrupt the "constructed self" of their slaveholders by celebrating the nonnegotiable grounds and integrity of their full humanity. Imperatively framed phrases exhorting the men, women, and children to "love" despised hands, mouths, and flesh dramatically externalized and embodied their resistance to slavery's tyrannous reign.

The author of the Pastorals similarly utilized a hermeneutic of memory and mimesis in service of the identity formation of Christian believers. The Pastoral writer portrays Paul as a model for teaching and suffering and a mentor for moral behavior. He achieves this reconstruction with a series of bold paraenetic injunctions, maxims, and imperatives. The fiery imperatives in 1 Timothy and Titus, in particular, are meant to place Paul himself behind the regulations, authorizing the action stated with apostolic authority. The sidebar (see p. 417) enumerates the frequency and forces of the hortatory imperatives and "must" verbs running through the letters. Cast in the first person, second person, and third person, they create an air of intimacy, personalizing further the apostolic prescriptions for appropriate behavior.[12]

1:3-7, An Internal Crisis

Verses 3-7 have in view an internal crisis arising from battles with an elite esoteric group who taught "a different doctrine" (heterodi-daskalein) in the "household of God" (oikos tou theou) within the Ephesian communities (1 Tim 1:3; 3:15; 6:3). This different doctrine stood in sharp contrast to what Paul himself had taught (6:3), and it contravened Paul's own instruction (e.g., Gal 1:6-7). Interpreters have extensively explored the precise nature of the false doctrine or heretical teaching, highlighting its speculative character arising from preoccupation with legends, tales, myths, and fables. Likely people from *within* the assemblies, and not outsiders from *without*—as was

Hortatory Imperatives (Orders to Do Something or to Be Something) in 1 Timothy and Titus

First-Person Singular Verbs

1 Tim 1:3, "I urged"

1 Tim 2:1, "I urge"

1 Tim 2:8, "I desire"

1 Tim 2:12, "I permit"

1 Tim 5:14, "So I would have"

1 Tim 5:21, "I charge"

Titus 1:5, "I directed you"

Second-Person Singular Verbs

1 Tim 5:1, "Do not rebuke . . . but exhort"

1 Tim 5:3, "Honor widows"

1 Tim 5:7, "Command this"

1 Tim 5:11, "But refuse"

1 Tim 5:19, "Never admit"

1 Tim 5:20, "Rebuke them"

1 Tim 5:22, "Do not be hasty . . . nor participate; keep"

Titus 2:1, "Teach"

Titus 2:6, ""Urge"

Titus 3:1, "Remind"

Third-Person Singular and Plural

1 Tim 2:11, "Let a woman learn"

1 Tim 3:10, "Let them be tested first . . . let them see"

1 Tim 3:12, "Let deacons be"

1 Tim 5:4, "Let them first learn"

1 Tim 5:9, "Let a widow be enrolled"

1 Tim 5:16, "Let her assist them"

1 Tim 5:17, "Let the elders . . . be considered worthy"

1 Tim 6:1, "Let all . . . regard."

1 Tim 6:2, "Let them not be disrespectful . . . let them serve" (my translation)

Impersonal "Must" or "Ought" Verbs

1 Tim 3:2, "Now a bishop must be"

1 Tim 3:7, "He must be"

1 Tim 3:15, "How one ought to behave"

Titus 1:7, "Must be blameless"

the case in Galatia (Gal 2:4) and Corinth (2 Cor 11:4; 12-15)—the troublemakers were not "external wolves" but "homegrown," disguised wolves in the midst of the communities who had lost their spiritual bearings and wandered from the faith. Presuming to be "teachers of God's law" (1:7; 5:17), they were preoccupied with seductive novelties that would yield a fallow harvest, instead of bearing the fruitful bounty of the saving and empowering work of renewal and transformation.

Scholars have spilled a great deal of ink discussing and debating the precise nature of the teaching promoted by the false teachers. There is no mention here of the aggressive missionary tactics we see in 2 Timothy, where the false teachers rove about, "going from house to house" (2 Tim 3:6), and where the activist bent of the false teachers is captured with such terms as "they stand against" (2 Tim 3:8), and "they advance" (2 Tim 2:16; 3:13). Their verbal disputations are nonetheless unprofitable, and must be opposed (1 Tim 2:14; 2:16-17).

1:8-11, USES OF THE LAW

The author here details contrasting views and uses of the law. The false teachers used the Old Testament law, likely the Torah or the Mosaic law, to buttress their claims for personal spiritual authority and spirituality, an illegitimate use of its purpose and function. For the apostle Paul, "the law is good, if one uses it legitimately" (v. 8; cf. Rom 7:7-25, 16). Providing a minitutorial for the faithful, "Paul" now reminds the audience of the primary function of the law: to expose sin in the light of God's ethical standards. Revealing sin and pointing sinners in the direction of the gospel, the law emphasizes God's demands and human needs. Hence, the law was not intended for "just" or righteous persons, or for the smug, self-congratulatory teachers who assumed they had achieved "spiritual nirvana" through special "knowledge" (6:20). Rather, it functioned to illuminate and to restrain one from the kind of violence enumerated in vv. 9-10, to lead one to repentance, and to provide a directive to the life-giving gospel.

The vice list catalogued in 1 Tim 1:9-10 bears an unmistakable resemblance to the egregious sins listed in the Ten Commandments. The author censures "those who kill" fathers or mothers instead of honoring them (v. 9c; Exod 20:12); excoriates murderers (v. 9d; Exod 20:13, "You shall not murder"); and indicts both liars and perjurers (v. 10; Exod 20:16, "You shall not give false witness against your neighbor"), and adulterers (v. 10; Exod 20:14, "You shall not commit adultery).

Quite startling in the vice list, and often surprisingly overlooked or minimized in scholarly interpretation of this particular vice list, is the censure of "slave traders" in v. 10. The Greek term used here for slave traders is "*andrapodistas*," a word occurring only here in the Christian Testament and found in neither the Septuagint (LXX) nor in other pre-Christian literature. Technically, the term means "slave dealer," or "kidnapper," and perhaps "procurer," or "thief." Hence, and in notably bold strokes, slave trading—so widespread on the Mediterranean landscape of the first century—is linked with the sins and violence of murder, "and whatever else is contrary to the sound teaching that conforms to the glorious gospel of the blessed God, which he entrusted to me" (vv. 10b-11). Within this context, slave traders are cast with those who violate the Decalogue's commandment against stealing—in this instance the theft is human lives (Exod 20:15, "You shall not steal"). As George Knight correctly observes, there is a striking inconsistency here. Both the Hebrew Bible and the Christian Testament contain traditions that appear to forbid particular practices relative to slavery, yet appear to tolerate the institution. It is certainly the case that traditions in both Testaments seek to regulate the existing state of slaves and masters (Deut 24:7; Eph 6:5-7; Col 3:22—4:1; 1 Tim 6:1; 2 Tit 2:9, 10).[13]

The Roman Slave Trade—An Economic Goldmine

"The exportation of slaves induced the Cilician pirates most of all to engage in their evil business, since it proved most profitable. For not only were the slaves easily captured, but the market, which was large and loaded with cash, was not very far away. I mean Delos, which could take in and ship out tens of thousands of slaves (*myriadas*) in a single day. From this arose the proverb, 'Merchant, sail in and unload your ship, your cargo is already sold.' The slave trade arose after the Romans became rich from the destruction of Carthage and Corinth and began to make use of numerous household slaves. Seeing easy profit in this, large numbers of pirates emerged to accommodate the demand and handled both the kidnapping of prisoners and the sale of them at Delos. The kings of both Cyprus and Egypt cooperated with them in this, because they were enemies to the Seleucids. Since the Rhodians were equally unfriendly, they too looked the other way. As a result, the pirates, posing as slave dealers, went about their evil business unchecked."

—Strabo 14.5.2 (669)

Even if, as some interpreters classically note of vice lists in general, this particular list is but one of many examples of such lists in antiquity, posted widely in tabular form, and is only descriptive (painting a broad picture of transgressive behavior) and not prescriptive (reacting to, or seeking to change behavior within a particular locale), the technical term *slave traders* nevertheless warrants further comment. Interpreters Martin Dibelius and Hans Conzelmann, for example, caution, "One must not see the list as referring to actual contemporary events or as closely related to the historical or fictitious situation of the Epistle."[14] But what the term still strikingly represents, in any case, is biting anti-slavery polemic that requires further comment.

The profitability of the sale of enslaved men, women, and children is well attested in the annals of ancient history. The geographer Strabo describes the remarkably extensive commercial activity occasioned by the exportation of slaves in Delos after 133 B.C.E. While the trans-Mediterranean slave trade had been a fact of Greco-Roman existence for centuries, its profitability has rarely been described with such remarkable candor. Strabo observes that the profitability factor made the "theft" of the enslaved in war, and within a host of other contexts, an irresistible temptation for many. Like the American slave trade of later centuries, the "economic profitability factor" only deepened the tightly intertwined roots of slavery's hold on society.[15]

In comprehensive studies of slavery from antiquity to the present, the perception of slavery as the "theft" of the integrity of human personhood and spirit is well attested. Allusions to being a "stolen" people abound in black slave narratives, music (including the Negro spirituals) and literature. Black spirituals, such as is found in the following sidebar, are quintessential markers of the lived experi-

ence of the fracture and dissolution of family networks in slavery, an experience often described as "social death."[16]

Slavery as Social Death

Sometimes I feel like a motherless child,
Sometimes I feel like a motherless child,
Sometimes I feel like a motherless child,
A long ways from home;
A long ways from home.

Sometimes I feel like I'm almost gone,
Sometimes I feel like I'm almost gone,
Sometimes I feel like I'm almost gone,
A long ways from home;
A long ways from home.

Whether the allusion to the slave traders in 1 Tim 1:10 is descriptive or prescriptive, the inference of anti-slavery critique and polemic is unmistakable. One wonders how enslaved women and men within early Christian assemblies might have heard it (see the allusion to enslaved believers in 1 Tim 6:1-2 and Titus 2:9-10). I have argued that interpreters need to limn out some of the clamorous debates blanketed within texts like 1 Tim 3:10 and Rev 18:13—texts that allude to the cry of subaltern (oppressed and marginalized) lions whose voices are muted by the thunderous victory chants of the hunters—the imperialist and colonialist "historical winners whose stories we know all too well."[17]

1:12-17, VALIDATION

The author of the Pastorals picks up the artist's brush and continues to paint his unique reconstruction of Paul. Not only did the Paul of tradition ignite and extend the revolution of faith initially inaugurated by Jesus throughout the Mediterranean, but he also validated the pragmatic rituals of Christian life—baptism, the Lord's Supper, collections for the saints, and ministry to the weak, the powerless, widows and orphans. Crisscrossing the well-worn paths of the Roman Empire, he challenged the pretentious and imperial practices of earthly kings and patrons who enabled injustice and suffering to flourish, dealing a minor blow, at least, to the idolatry of power embodied by imperial ideologues.[18] But if Paul's portrait landed him firmly in the "Hall of Faith," with his portrait hanging on the same wall as other likely and unlikely pioneers in that mighty cloud of witnesses—Abraham, Sarah, Rahab, and Gideon (Heb 11:1-40)—the reconstruction produced no unblemished saint.

Verses 12-17 signal a profound truth: Paul, a champion of the gospel, had also been a needy recipient of God's superabundant grace. The foremost sinner and violent persecutor of the nascent and struggling assemblies became a foremost example of God's redemptive mercy. Using the well-known preaching formula "once—but now," the author of the Pastorals contrasts Paul's career as a violent persecutor with the life of one who had received a salvific grace surpassing human expectation, computation, and reason. The portrayal of Paul in post-apostolic times highlighted his conversion as an example or exhibit of the inexhaustible long-suffering of God—a loving God who welcomed even the most arrogant and unflinching opponents of the good news of the gospel.

1:18-20, A Contrast of Faith and Faithlessness

Timothy's faithfulness and good conscience are contrasted with the faithless and conscienceless duo Hymenaeus and Alexander. Hymenaeus, mentioned also in 2 Tim 2:17, 18, upset the faith of others by engaging in heedless disruptions with words, senseless

controversies, and an ungodly chatter that produced a harvest of impiety or ungodliness. The infectious discourse, compared to foul-smelling, destructive gangrene (cf. 2 Tim 2:17, *gangraina*), was a malignant sore eating away at the healthy tissue of a flourishing community. Moreover, the antagonists advanced a view of realized eschatology that implied the resurrection of the body had already taken place, a pre-Gnostic or semi-Gnostic teaching denounced in 1 Corinthians 15. The apostle Paul had emphasized the futurity of the resurrection in Rom 6:5; now "Paul" recalls that teaching as a decisive blow to the teaching of Hymenaeus and Philetus, who argued that the resurrection was already past (cf. 2 Tim 2:18).

Drawing on the image of military service widely used in philosophical diatribe to emphasize the need for disciplined focus on the battle at hand, the writer commands Timothy to "fight the good fight of faith" (v. 18), suggesting that Timothy draw upon an arsenal of tools, weaponry, and strategic resources for battle in the campaign of life.[19]

2:1-7, Church and Society

The writer of 1 Timothy has in view a particular motive for accommodating worldly authorities: "that we may lead a quiet and peaceable life in all godliness and dignity" (v. 2). Here the writer launches into a treatise on the church's relationship to society, portraying Roman political powers rather positively. He enjoins implicit prayer that the work of the Christian mission not be inhibited by the imperial powers. Many commentators suggest the admonition reflects a conservative "bourgeois" or "middle-class" ethic, one that avoids challenging the established sociopolitical order in favor of adaptation and conformity to many of its prevailing ideological and cultural assumptions and norms. Perhaps this "ideal Christian citizenship" represented a strategic survival strategy for some third-generation assemblies settling down in the world within the context and reality of a delayed parousia. In fact, for some assemblies of the saints in the latter decades of the first century, the Roman Empire was no longer the "main enemy," but the welcoming earthly environment in which Christianity would have to peacefully exist until the coming of Christ. Moreover, "the image of Christ was slowly transformed from that of an alternative king to that of a model emperor presiding over a shadow government in heaven and showing by example how things should be done on earth."[20]

The ideals of peaceful Christian citizenship in the Pastorals stand in sharp contrast to the Pauline understanding of existence, which emphasized tension in the world (2 Cor 11:23-33) and opposition to the dominant order (1 Thess 4:14-18; 1 Cor 15:20-28; Rom 8:18-25). Paul, who had founded his ethic on an eschatological perspective that indicated the end of the dominant order soon, with the parousia (coming) of his Lord to follow, was willing to transgress—albeit with some limitation and inconsistency—the patriarchal social norms relative to low-status social subordinates, including married and single women and enslaved men and women (1 Cor 7:25-35). A social history of the urbanized groups of Pauline Christianity reveals a Paul who established a revolutionary countercultural ethos within the Christian assemblies, one that often contrasted sharply with prevailing cultural assumptions and hierarchical structures. Helmut Koester's insight on this point is indispensable for understanding and interpreting the Pastorals within their social and historical context. In sharp contrast to the Pauline letters, the Pastoral Epistles mark the end of Christian eschatological ethics:

> Christianity no longer looked upon itself as the community of the new ages that promised to break down social barriers, as those

between man and women, free and slaves, at least as far as its own interior organization and order was concerned. Rather, the church had become obligated to the world and society at large and had to fulfill the general norms and moral demands in an exemplary fashion. If Christians are still admonished to distinguish themselves in their moral actions from the rest of society such distinction would now be achieved through a more dignified and faithful observance of the generally accepted rules for good behavior.[21]

Quite in contrast to the Paul of the authentic Pauline letters, who emphasized the countercultural legitimacy of rational moral decisions after careful weighing and assessment of alternatives (1 Cor 7:2-7; 7:36-38; Phil 4:8-9), the author of the Pastorals championed models and protocols of behavior in the Greco-Roman households that generally maintained the power and prerogatives of both *patria potestas* (paternal power) and *paterfamilias* (the rule of the father/husband/slavemaster).

2:8-15, A Patriarchal Family Ethic

The author's insistence on the value of social conformity to promote the community's image in the world at large meant that *patria potestas* and the authority of the *paterfamilias* be upheld, in conformity with the conventions of Hellenistic moralists. Concerned that the assemblies would not become recognizably stable organizations within society, the writer articulates a family ethic wherein the piety of the *paterfamilias* frames the piety of the entire household. The conservative mind-set in evidence here emphasizes stringent instruction for social subordinates—wives, not husbands (1 Tim 2:9-15; Titus 2:4-5, 1 Tim 5:14), and for slaves, not masters (1 Tim 6:1-2; Titus 2:9-10). The presence of these regulations suggests that some free women and some enslaved men and women were likely subverting patriarchal household norms, seeking to act and live as those who had been liberated from prevailing social and cultural values and regulations in Christ.

The strict injunction to women's silence in vv. 11-12 contrasts sharply with references to women's verbal presence and agency in the Pauline letters (cf. Rom 16:3-23). In Phil 4:3 and Rom 16:3, Paul named three women with whom he labors as *synergoi*, "fellow workers": Euodia, Syntyche, and Prisca. Paul assumed as a given that women would speak in and lead early Christian worship services (1 Cor 11:5). The writer of the Pastorals, on the other hand, presses traditions about Eve as seductress and primary progenitor of sin into his argument (cf. Sir 25:24) to reinforce male prerogative in society and the *ekklesia*.[22] This position contrasts sharply with that of Paul himself, who argued that Adam preceded Eve (1 Cor 11:18), and Eve was the one deceived by the serpent (2 Cor 11:3). It was Adam's sin that brought death into the world (2 Cor 15:21-22). For the writer of 1 Timothy, who doubtless knew of the more egalitarian tradition of "no longer slave or free . . . no longer male and female" (Gal 3: 28), there would be no "egalitarian excess" overturning patriarchal household norms—as witnessed in the charismatic assemblies of Paul of earlier generations—in *his* assemblies! The Pauline model that generally welcomed free women and enslaved men and women, and often advanced their liberation from patriarchal conventions, would have absolutely no place in his community of saints.

The patriarchal ideal for relationships between husband and wife is soundly documented in Greek and Roman literature. The Greek philosopher and biographer Plutarch, who lived in Rome ca. 90 C.E., describes the ideal relationship between husbands and wives in one of his moral essays, "Expectations of Marriage" (see sidebar below).[23]

Verses 11-12, prohibiting public teaching by women, reflect an integration of traditional patriarchal norms about the public behavior and decorum for women in Greco-Roman society. The prevailing sentiment prohibiting women's public teaching and their exercise of authority, requiring them to "ask their husbands at home" if they wanted to know something, had earlier been interpolated into a genuine letter of Paul (1 Cor 14:33b-36). As the text box narrating a public speech by

---

Expectations of Marriage

"When two voices sing in unison, the melody of the deeper voice prevails. So, too, in a temperate household every activity is carried out with both parties in agreement, but every activity also makes clear the sovereignty and choice of the husband. . . . That wife is worthless and unfit who has a sad countenance when her husband is eager to make jokes and be cheerful, or who makes jokes and laughs when he is serious. The first behavior reveals an unpleasant character, the second an inconsiderate one. . . . A wife should have no emotion of her own, but should share in the seriousness and playfulness and melancholy and laughter of her husband."

—Plutarch, *Moral Advice*, 139 D, F; 140 A

Marcus Porcius Cato concerning the "unruly" behavior of Roman women who had dared to express a public opinion about a political matter attests, women could be educated, but they were not expected to express opinions on their own.[24] Cato (234–149 B.C.E.), a wealthy, prominent politician in Rome who was an established spokesperson for ultraconservatives, argued that men should retain the full power of the patriarchal household authority and restrict women's autonomy. Cato's quotation in the sidebar (on the following page) serves to remind us that traditions or practices that subvert the liberating potential of the gospel for women must be overturned.

The quotations by Plutarch and Cato remind us of the debilitating legacy of patriarchy. Patriarchy, which presupposes that males alone best and most fully represent the interest, gifts, and potential of both women and men in church and society, is a jagged blade: it not only "cuts" by distorting the human construction of reality, in which men and women together are both equally and fully created in the image of God (Genesis 1:26-31), it "cuts" and devastates by sanctifying the dominion of some human members of the human family over others—a tradition and social practice African Americans rejected outright in the evil institution of American slavery (which legitimated the dominion of whites Americans over black Americans). As the African American sociologist Patricia Hill Collins has so wisely observed, dominant groups legitimate their "right to rule" over others—and demand or encourage the submission of others—by appeals to "commonsense." Her comments are relevant to the politics of patriarchy in both church and society: "In the United States, hegemonic ideologies concerning race, class, gender, sexuality, and nation are often so pervasive that it is difficult to conceptualize alternatives to them, let alone ways of resisting the social practices they justify."[25] As African Americans know all too

well, when biblical texts and religion are used to legitimate inequities in the social construction of reality ("the way life is supposed to be or function")—as did the pro-slavery defenders who used power to endorse the subordination of some peoples to others—the results can be devastating and demonic.

A "hermeneutic of the experiences of black peoples," that foregrounds the distinct legacy and rationales of orientation, and the enduring and dynamic regimes of choice and practice within black people's lives, requires a much-needed reassessment of continued patterns and practices of patriarchy in black church theology and ecclesiology. Biblical interpretation and practice that mandate the subordination and marginalization of women, that legitimates their exclusion from ordination, and that diminishes the equalitarian use of power between women and men within twenty-first century churches, wreaks violence on homiletical and social justice rhetoric and practice that claims to liberate the whole of creation. Further, it impoverishes cherished ideals of the constructive transformation, dynamic agency, and boundless potentiality of black peoples. The imaginative and decisive creation of hermeneutical strategies that dethrone the idolatry and legacy of patriarchal conditioning are absolutely requisite for enlarging the church's authenticity, spirituality, and mission within the world. On this point, African American hermeneutical strategies must confront, critique, and overturn the legacy of the jagged edge of patriarchy in black life. Interpretive reconstruction and practice may lead to the kind of liberationist practices that can constructively radicalizing our own present and future possibilities as a people and aid us immeasureably in formulating our life projects.[26]

The extensive literature on the history of black women's leadership, agency authority, and ordination within African American churches through the centuries reveals a complex mosaic of images. Denominational histories, autobiographies, slave narratives, spiritual narratives, historical records, and other varieties of fiction and nonfiction alike all document the distinctive challenges black women face relative to their empowerment—or disempowerment—in the church, particularly as it relates to church leadership and governance. Some denominations tend to adopt a hermeneutic that affirms the more liberationist models of women's co-leadership found in Paul's authentic letters. Other denominations and interpreters favor the more conservative, patriarchal model of "ideal Christian citizenship" for women we find in the Pastoral letters. These, and a range of other models, exist across a broad continuum within African American churches, religious communities and organizations.[27]

Sociologist Cheryl Townsend Gilkes has provided a brilliant analysis of the distinctive ways in which African American women have shaped the culture and consciousness of the black religious experience in her book *If It Wasn't for the Women: Black Women's Experience and Womanist Culture in Church and Community*.[28] Theologian Kelly Brown Douglas has helpfully highlighted the implications of a Christology that takes seriously the meaning of Christ for multiple communities and audiences within the black church in her

---

The Social Control of Women

"If each of us men, fellow citizens, had undertaken to keep the right and the authority of the husband out of the hands of the women of the family, we would have less trouble with groups of women. But as it is now, at home our freedom is trampled on by feminine rages, and here in the Forum it is crushed and trod underfoot. Because we were unable to control each woman as an individual, we are now frightened by women in groups. . . .

"Indeed, it was with some embarrassment that I came a few minutes ago to the Forum right through a crowd of women. If I had not held in respect the dignity and basic decency of each woman as an individual (it would mortify them to be seen receiving a scolding from a consul), I would have said: 'What kind of behavior is this, running around in public blocking streets and talking to other women's husbands? Could you not have asked our own husbands the same thing at home? Are you more persuasive in public than in private, with others' husbands than with your own? And yet it is not right, even in your own homes (if a sense of shame and decency were to keep you within your proper limits), for you to concern yourselves about which laws are passed or repealed here.' That's what I would have said.

"Our ancestors were not willing to let women conduct any business, not even private business, without a guardian. They wanted them to remain under the control of their fathers, brothers, and husbands. We, for heaven's sake, now allow them to take part in politics and to mingle with us in the Forum and to attend assemblies. . . . To be quite honest, they desire freedom, nay rather license in all matters. And if they win in this matter, what will they not attempt?"

—Marcus Porcius Cato, quoted by Livy, *A History of Rome* 34.2.1, 2, 8–11, 14.

important book, *The Black Christ.*[29] Biblical scholar Musa W. Dube provides an illuminating anthology with contributions of African women about religion and gender in her anthology titled, *Other Ways of Reading: African Women and the Bible.*[30] Caribbean scholar and political scientist Judith Soares has contributed helpfully to our understanding of the legacy of Eve traditions in Barbados, in her essay "Eden after Eve: Christian Fundamentalism and Women in Barbados."[31] And I have challenged African American interpreters to address the unsettling paradox of *rejecting* the literalist patriarchal injunction for slaves to be submissive to masters in the domestic house tables (Col 3:18—4:1; 2:18—3:7), while still *accepting and embracing* the literalist patriarchal injunction that women should be subordinate to husbands.[32] As Gilkes's observation in the sidebar below confirms, there is much at stake in African American women and men functioning "together," and "in harness" for the benefit for the entire community.[33]

3:1-16, LEADERSHIP QUALITIES

The author here delineates leadership qualities within the community, describing ideal conduct for *episkopoi* (overseers) and *diakonoi* (deacons). He emphasizes "moral qualities" that believers should exhibit, not "qualifications." Contemporary understandings of "bishop" and "deacon" should not be read into the passage. Officers described as *episkopoi* and *diakonoi* were earlier described within the Pauline correspondence (Phil 1:1; 3:11; cf. Rom 6:1), albeit briefly. The allusions present a view of leadership positions in an early stage of development. *Episkopoi* appear to have significant administrative and teaching responsibilities (3:2), while *diakonoi* and *presbyteroi* also assume management responsibilities, and teach or preach (3:12; 4:14; 5:17). Women are included as *diakonoi* (3:11-12; cf. Rom 16:1, where Phoebe is called a *diakonos* of the church at Cenchrae). If Paul appeared to restrict women's prophesying activities in

---

The Jagged Blade of Patriarchy

"The patriarchy of the black church has never been peaceful. The content of that patriarchy—a patriarchy that can be labeled ambivalent in its various expressions—has been severely modified by the persistent tradition of conflict that black women have maintained within black religious structures. Although women remain subordinate persons in structures where males hold nearly all the highest positions, the ideologies advanced by these men in defense of their domination reflect the embattled nature of their position. Simply stated, there are certain arguments that black preachers dare not advance in public regardless of how much they believe them; for instance, those arguments assailing women's competence were lost in the debates of the nineteenth century. In interpreting any conflicts within African American religious traditions, however, it is critically important to remember that they take place in organizational settings where the operating metaphor and ideology for human relations is *family.* They take place among 'brothers' and 'sisters,' between 'fathers' and 'mothers' and 'daughters.'. . . As early as the 1830s, black women orators refuted biblical arguments demanding their silence as public speakers."

—Cheryl Townsend Gilkes, *If It Wasn't for the Women: Black Women's Experience and Womanist Culture in Church and Community* (Maryknoll, N.Y.: Orbis), 108 (emphasis mine).

1 Corinthians 11, the author of 1 Timothy appeared to restrict their functioning as teachers and authorities (2:8: "I desire, then, that in every place the men (*andras*) should pray"; 2:12). As Linda Maloney astutely observes, even wealthy women—those with the money for leisure and adornments, implicit in 1 Tim 2:9—are enjoined to silence. According to Pliny, enslaved women were exercising leadership roles as deacons in Christian churches in Asia Minor as late as 112 C.E.[34]

What the writer of 1 Timothy has in view in 3:1-16 is church leaders whose behavior is irreproachable, soundness in life and work, and a good reputation before others in the "household of God . . . the church of the living God, the pillar and bulwark of the truth" (3:15). If the author(s) of the Pastorals has no unitary, unified model of church government detailing how deacons function alongside widows, how bishops relate to elders, and how deacons relate to bishops (cf. 1 Tim 3:1-7; 5:17; Titus 1:5-9), what he is concerned to do is to preserve, hand on, and nurture an apostolic tradition that provides an effective arsenal of resources for combating heresy, and one that reinforces ideals of Christian citizenship generally consistent with prevailing cultural norms.[35]

4:1-10, FALSE TEACHINGS

The author of 1 Timothy has done his homework! With a detective's investigative skill, he compiled a detailed list of the errors the false teachers were advancing within the Christian assembly. He has already decried their preoccupation with verbal wrangling (1 Tim 1:3-4); here he critiques their ascetic practices, including the renunciation of marriage and abstention from certain foods. In earlier decades, Paul had advised some members of the Corinthian assemblies not to marry in light of the coming end (1 Cor 7:8, 25-26), but he did not forbid marriage. The writer of 1 Timothy

also held marriage in high esteem (1 Tim 5:14), a theme similarly echoed in Titus 2:4.

Rejecting the ascetic denial of food, the writer implicitly celebrates instead the bounty and varieties of food God provides for humankind, which "God created to be received with thanksgiving by those who believe and know the truth" (v. 3b). A Jewish and Christian view of reality celebrates the goodness of God's creation (Gen 1:1-31; Rom 14:14, 20; Mark 7:18, 19). Theologian Karen Baker-Fletcher reminds us of the marvelous integrity of God's created order: "As African American preachers and church mothers often say, 'God don't make no junk!' Everything has intrinsic worth and value. Every cell of an organism, each creature in an ecosystem, the very dust of stars and earth hold secrets of life and sustenance."[36] Instead of falling in line lockstep with those false teachers who abstained from foods, Christian believers were to maintain a sense of wonder and thanksgiving, with prayer, for the gift of food.

4:11-16, YOUNG LEADERS

In a church where elders were highly regarded (1 Tim 5:1-2), younger leaders within the assemblies might have experienced some intimidation. But Timothy's gift was given through a prophecy "with the laying on of hands *by* the council of elders." The writer argues that Timothy should not fear them; instead, he should boldly exercise his gift with confidence, modeling the noblest ethical ideals of appropriate speech and conduct, love, faith, and purity (v. 12).

5:1-25, RESPECT, RECIPROCITY, RESPONSIBILITY

These three terms capture dominant motifs in chap. 5. At the outset, the writer portrays the congregation as an extended family with obligations of respect, reciprocity, and honor due to one another (vv. 1-2). The familial language of fathers, brothers, mothers, and sisters centrally highlights their responsibility for one another.

Verses 3-16 and vv. 17-20 outline regulations for the conduct of two primary groups: widows (vv. 3-16) and elders (vv. 17-20). The charge to honor and care for widows echoes a long-standing moral commitment to care for women left without a husband. This motif is deeply rooted in Jewish and Christian tradition (Exod 22:22-23; Deut 10:18; 14:29; 24:17-21; 26:12, 13; Ps 68:5; Isa 1:17, 23; Mal 3:5; Acts 6:1-6; Jas 1:27).

Suggestions that the passage refers to an "order" of widows are based on vv. 9-10, but there is little consensus on this point. The behavior of younger widows appears to be of paramount concern (vv. 11-15). Widowhood is, after all, a high honor (5:3) within the community. Whether younger or older, widows were to exhibit godliness, hospitality, fidelity to God, charitable works, and a life lived above reproach.

Elders deserve "double honor" (vv. 17-18) when they rule and teach well. The backdrop of this section and the preceding section on widows is the presence of forces (false teachers) that seek to undermine the vitality of the Christian message (widows, vv. 11-15; elders, v. 20). As those who live in the presence of the triumvirate of "God, Christ Jesus, and the elect angels," the faithful should attune their moral compass to insure fair and impartial treatment of elders who labor well.

6:1-2, A MESSAGE FOR THOSE "UNDER THE YOKE"

The writer has a special message for "all" (v. 1) of the enslaved within the faith community: they must regard masters with "all" honor. The slavemasters may not be personally "worthy" of such honor, but they are to be regarded as worthy of such honor by virtue of their position (Titus 3:1-2; 1 Pet 2:13-17). The writer emphasizes the need for enslaved men and women to conform to the traditionally prescribed, submissive behavior appropriate for low-status subordinates within the Christian assemblies, as earlier prescribed of women in 1 Tim 2:1-15. This model of "ideal Christian citizenship" will insure that "the name of God and the teaching may not be blasphemed" (v. 1).

The specific lack of directives about how masters should behave reinforces the thesis that the author reflects the interests and perspectives of those in the more economically privileged, higher status, propertied class. According to the author of 2 Timothy, service to fellow Christians who are masters should be even more rigorous, for such masters are "believers and beloved" (v. 2). As in the rhetoric of the domestic household codes in Col 3:18—4:1; Eph 5:21—6:9; and 1 Pet 2:18—3:7, we hear a "male-master rhetoric" that reinforces the prevailing social assumption that conformity to high status and low status roles must be rigorously maintained for the wellbeing of the *ekklesia* and the larger society.[37]

Verses 1-2 echo the sentiment of the widely used and disseminated *exemplum* literature in Roman imperial society. Composed by males to encourage the loyalty and obedience of wives and enslaved women and men, these "loyalty tales"—popular short stories that formed a part of the symbolic universe and repertoire of the Roman elite—sought to "shore up" and reinforce the existing social construction of reality favoring male privilege and power.

Functioning as a kind of ancient "propaganda tool" for elite males, the *exemplum* literature typically portrayed free women and enslaved women and men as docile and passive, and utterly passionate about proving their unbridled loyalty to husbands and slave masters—even to the point of death. The side-bar (below), with Cassius's example of favored stories from *exemplum* literature, valorizes the devotion of the self-sacrificing slave.[38] The *exemplum* literature recalls nineteenth- and early-twentieth-century pro-slavery tracts, pamphlets, and fictional literature that circulated on the American landscape with images of presumed "happy" and loyal slaves (cf. *Uncle Tom's Cabin* by Harriet Beecher Stowe). Functioning similarly as the ancient propaganda literature, the pro-slavery literature sought to reinforce the notion that the loyal enslaved male or female would always place the well-being of his or her slave master above their own—even to the point of death.

The slave injunctions in 1 Tim 6:1-2 were part of the lexicon of biblical texts used by pro-slavery apologists in America to legitimate slavery. The Bible was, after all, the Southern church person's chief authority cited in support of slavery. Not surprisingly, pro-slavery biblical interpretation never jeopardized the privileged status and authority of the slave-master—a situation that parallels exactly the ethic in the Pastorals relative to slavery. But African Americans never accepted a literalist biblical interpretation that legitimized their status as subhuman chattel. They always countered the dialectics of negation with multiple forms of resistance.[39]

Exempla: Pro-Slavery Propaganda

In one of the two most frequently recorded stories, the slave of Antius Restio, even though he had been branded for misconduct, secretly followed his master, hid him, brought him food, and, when soldiers approached, killed an old man in his place, claiming to the soldiers that he had taken revenge on his master for branding him (Valerius Maximum 6.8.7; Appian, *Civil War* 4:43; Cassius Dio, *Roman History* 47.10.4–5; Macrobius 1.11.19–20). Contrasting this tale with two others of self-sacrificing slaves, the historian Cassius Dio (cf. Macrobius 1.11.18) makes the moral clear:

"In these incidents, perhaps the slaves, because of some previous act of kindness, were repaying those who had treated them kindly. But a certain slave who had been branded not only did not betray the man who had branded him, but enthusiastically saved him." (Cassius Dio 47.10.4)

6:3-21, On Godliness and Wealth

The chief concern of vv. 3-21 is twofold. First, godliness (*eusebeia*), or "religion," holds value for both the present life and the life to come (vv. 3, 5b, 6, 11). In v. 3 false teachers imagine godliness to be a course of great personal gain (*porismos*). *Porismos* is literally translated as "good business," a source of profit. But the "godliness," with contentment, derives from neither monetary nor material gain, but from the active pursuit of righteousness, godliness, faith, love, endurance, and gentleness (v. 11).

The second major concern of the chapter is wealth. The "love" of money is a snare (v. 10), a root of manifold evil. According to the philosopher Epictetus, "Bion the Sophist used to say that love of money is the mother city of all evil."[40] The false teachers are thoroughly preoccupied with greed (vv. 5-9). For the writer of 1 Timothy, divestiture of wealth is not an issue; rather, a life of good works and sharing with others (*koinōnikos*, v. 18) represents the model life for the wealthy within the assembly.[41]

2 TIMOTHY

INTRODUCTION

The rallying cry of 2 Timothy is "Remember!" The author of 2 Timothy presents himself as Paul, imprisoned in the very last years of his life. Framing his spiritual "last will and testament" in the form of a personal paraenetic letter, he provides distinctive contributions to the theological heritage of the church. While 2 Timothy contains themes and motifs found in 1 Timothy, the tone of 2 Timothy is much more urgent, and it is more intensely personal. Timothy is beckoned to come to "Paul" (4:9, 11, 21), but more than this, he is charged to deepen the roots of a faith legacy passed on to him by a faithful and faith-filled mother and grandmother (1 Tim 1:5). "Paul" charges his beloved child to "fan into flame" the gift of God within him (1 Tim 1:6), and to conduct his ministry with the God-given spirit of power, love, and self-discipline (1 Tim 1:7). "Paul's" incentives for action are personal; his tone is persistent.

(See also the Introduction to 1 Timothy.)

1:1-18, NOT ASHAMED, EVEN IN SUFFERING

With unceasing prayers and gratitude, "Paul" recalls the Spirit-empowered life and ministry of his young charge Timothy (vv. 6-7, 13-14). The author's appeal in the chapter is twofold. First, he charges Timothy to *never* be ashamed of either his testimony about "our Lord" or "Paul" himself. In fact, the Spirit God gives to believers fills them with power, not cowardice (v. 7). Second, Timothy is to take his part in the suffering occasioned by the proclamation of the gospel, as did Paul (vv. 8, 12). Neither "Paul's" abandonment by others in Asia (v. 15) nor his imprisonment (v. 16) dampened his confidence; rather, God's eternal plan, pur-

poses, and grace in the work of Christ ignited the fires of his ministry and recharged the batteries of his resolve (vv. 9-10). For "Paul," the key to perseverance in ministry is *knowing* "our Savior Christ Jesus, who abolished death and brought life and immortality to light through the gospel." "Paul" championed "personal knowledge" of Christ Jesus and not "heresy" as the key to the dynamism that marked his ministry: "for I *know* the one in whom I have put my trust, and I am sure that he is able to guard until that day what I have entrusted to him" (v. 12, emphasis added). Like his mother and grandmother before him, Timothy is called to pass on a faith legacy built on the sure foundation of a personal knowledge of his God.

In his acclaimed book *Mama Made the Difference: Life Lessons My Mother Taught Me*, Bishop T. J. Jakes invites respected colleagues and friends to bear witness to the motivating power of a mother's love for her children. The clear consensus is that next to God's love, a mother's love for her child can be one of the most transformative forces on earth. In the very first chapter, "Mamas Teach Us to Believe in God," he comments: "So much in our lives begins with believing—love, peace, growth, change, destiny—I am so thankful that my mother always taught me to *believe*. She taught me to believe in God . . . and she taught me to believe in myself. . . . The strong Tide of my mama's many lessons flow out of the currents of these two streams."[42] Surely Timothy would assent to the luminous wisdom of Jake's words relative to both his mother, Eunice, and his grandmother Lois.

2:1-13, MORAL VALUES

If the image of Paul as "model for suffering" and "mentor for moral behavior" was sketched in clear but faint lines in 1 Timothy (see the Introduction), the author of 2 Timothy used a finely pointed artist's brush to fill in the details of Paul's image with graphic clarity in 2:1-13. Like a doting parent who in the last days of life teaches a series of unforgettable "life lessons" to a beloved child, "Paul" now urges Timothy to "be strong" in the grace of Christ Jesus. Moreover, Timothy must entrust what he has heard from "Paul" to faithful people who will, in turn, teach others (vv. 1-2). Utilizing a "hermeneutic of memory and mimesis" (see the Introduction), the "Paul" of 2 Timothy encourages Timothy to emulate his own soldier-like suffering (v. 4), his unswerving athletic drive in pursuing his goal (v. 5), and his patient labor in sowing seed in ministry, with the optimistic expectation of a certain crop (v. 6). Above all, Timothy must, like "Paul," endure "everything" ("all things," *panta*) for the sake of fellow believers (v. 10).

2:14-26, Correcting with Gentleness

There is a significant shift here in the thematic focus of chap. 2. Timothy's mandate to (1) "remember Jesus Christ" (v. 8) and (2) imitate Paul's example as soldier, athlete, farmer, and one who perseveres in suffering recedes into the background, as the author "puts on his boxing gloves" and provides concrete strategies for engaging in combat with false teachers. The content of the false teaching is reminiscent of that which is outlined in 1 Tim 1:3-7 (see the comments there). Hymenaeus, described as one who suffered "shipwreck in the faith" in 1 Tim 1:20, is described here as "swerving from the truth," because he believes incorrectly that the resurrection has already taken place (vv. 17-18). The "job description" for the Lord's servant who corrects the opponents is clear: the diverse company of those professing to be Christians will—like various kinds of utensils

in a large, rich person's house—purify himself and herself from that which is ignoble (not noble). Further, like vessels of silver and gold, she or he will become a vessel for noble use, ready for every good work.

Verses 16 reminds us that the "mechanics of imprisonment" Christian believers would have endured included chains. This sobering allusion recalls the unimaginable brutality of "chains" or shackles endured by many African peoples during the transatlantic slave trade of the seventeenth century. Almost one hundred pairs of shackles were found at the site of the wreckage of the *Henrietta Marie*, the oldest slave ship ever found, and the only one to have been discovered and excavated in the Americas. Located thirty miles off the coast of Key West, Florida, the ship is the only merchant ship ever recovered that sank during the course of trade. Among the almost one hundred pairs of shackles found in the wreckage nearly three centuries later, were shackles so small they seem to have been deliberately forged for the wrists and ankles of a child.[43]

3:1—4:22, Exhortations and Greetings

The imprisoned "Paul" of 2 Timothy is undaunted in spirit. He devotes a portion of his last will and testament to a description of the apostasy to be experienced in both the present and future (3:1-9). Using the model of the Hellenistic vice catalogue, the writer lists eighteen vices or sins, with a nineteenth vice added in v. 5, "holding to the outward form of godliness but denying its power." Such vice lists are found elsewhere in the Christian Testament (Rom 1:29-31; Col 3:5; 1 Tim 1:9-10).

The hermeneutic of memory and mimesis is pressed into service as "Paul" recalls the experiences of his life in ministry (3:10-17). His teaching, bold faith, and endurance of suffering and desertion qualified him—whose race of life was nearly run—to exhort Timothy to imitate his practices of steadfastness in faith and endurance in suffering. Inspired by God's radical and empowering trilogy of grace, mercy, and peace, which he has experienced for so many years firsthand, and had wished for others (2 Tim 1:2), "Paul" recounts for Timothy his own experiences of distressing times and persecutions. He minces no words about the severity of his trials in 2 Tim 3:11b, pointedly recalling: "What persecutions I endured!" The sufferings and persecutions he had experienced in Antioch, Iconium, and Lystra had doubtless become the stuff of legend, not only permanently imprinted in his mind and body, but recounted in Christian assemblies far and wide. But these sufferings and persecutions were only the "tip of the iceberg." After all, Alexander the coppersmith had also done him great harm at one point, ferociously opposing the message (2 Tim 4:14-15). "Paul" had also experienced the utter loneliness and bitter dejection of desertion, when absolutely "no one" came to his support (2 Tim 4:16). His suggestion of having been "rescued from the lion's mouth" in 2 Tim 4:17b may be a reference to deliverance from the sword, as opposed to a literal deliverance from a lion in the amphitheater. In any case, we have in 2 Timothy the portrayal of the last will and testament of one who drew near to the gateway of the kingdom with audacious hope and astonishing confidence. Paul, the exemplar and model who had endured the sometimes hazardous and contentious work of ministry, who had personally felt the bite of wolves in sheep's clothing, and who had known the vulnerability, isolation, and loneliness of abandonment by friends and colleagues, is now represented as a prisoner in the waning moments of his life. But this "Paul" could still dare to point to his sacrifices and his life as an exemplar of the faithful believer who gallantly perseveres in the great race of life to the very end. Second Timothy 3:10 documents the expansive arenas of his life that could serve as resources for Timothy to emulate in his own faith and life journey. With his first-person "my" statements, "Paul" invites close scrutiny of the ways in which Christ Jesus has pervaded his life commitments and projects, his motives and goals, and the intensity of his commitment. In 2 Tim 3:10 he invites Timothy to recall, review, and emulate:

> my teaching
> my conduct
> my aim in life
> my steadfastness

In 2 Tim 4:6 "Paul" notes that the time for his "departure" has now come. The imagery is that of a ship being loosed from its moorings. Moreover, although the prospect of death looms large, his fearless and noble sentiment in 2 Tim 4:7 cannot mask his boundless joy regarding the Lord's impending return (2 Tim 4:8): "I have fought the good fight, I have finished the race, I have kept the faith. From now on there is reserved for me the crown of righteousness, which the Lord, the righteous judge, will give me on that day, and not only to me, but to all who have longed for his appearing" (2 Tim 4:6-8). The allusion to "fighting the good fight" is found in both 1 Tim 6:12 and 2 Tim 4:7a, and recalls ancient athletic contests where competition for the prize was keen, marked by an intensity of focus, discipline, and energy that could lead one to prevail in the end. Within this context, the language of a boxing context and race may be in view in 2 Tim 4:7a. Typically, a crown of laurel, pine, or olive was awarded to ancient competitors in the athletic games (2 Tim 2:5; 1 Cor 9:25-25). "Paul" views his martyrdom as a glad and sacrificial homage to the God whom he longs for (2 Tim 4:18). His prize will be the fulfillment of the eschatological hope of being present with the God in whose presence he has lived and labored, the God who has never ceased to rescue him, stand by him, and strengthen him (2 Tim 3:11; 4:17-18).

When in 4:6 "Paul" declares that he has "fought the good fight," finished the race, and kept the faith, he recalls an image to which many peoples of African descent can relate. Nelson Mandela endured three decades of solitude, but he "fought the good fight" of survival, with his faith as a notable source of strength and inspiration. Enduring hard labor, he simply refused to die, and apartheid could not eradicate or efface his life and dignity.[44] On a similar note, June Jordan, professor of African American studies at the University of California, Berkeley, shares a personal story of "fighting the good fight." In her autobiographical essay, "A Good Fight," she recalls her shock upon learning she had been diagnosed with breast cancer in 1993—with a 40 percent chance of survival. Not only did she learn to "redefine courage," she learned—as she states it—to "make this cancer thing into a fight." She comments of her physicians, colleagues, students, and neighbors: "They dared me to practice trying to lift my arm three or four inches away from my side. They dared me to go ahead and scream and cry but not to die. And so I did not die. But I have faced death. . . . I am happy beyond belief because this is a good fight. . . . And I am happy beyond belief to be here and to join with you to make things better."[45] The opportunity to "fight the good fight," whether "of faith" or "for life," is one of the greatest gifts God bequeaths to us.

TITUS

INTRODUCTION

Titus, one of Paul's coworkers, was well-known to the apostle, and he was mentioned in several of Paul's authentic letters. A Gentile (Gal 2:3), he was present with Paul at the meeting with the Jerusalem apostles. He assisted with the collection in Corinth (2 Cor 8:6, 16-17, 23). Titus intervened in a dispute between Paul and the Corinthian church (2 Cor 2:13; 7:6-7, 13-16). Generally considered a pseudonymous letter (see the Introduction), Titus centrally foregrounds Paul as responsible for Titus's ministry in Crete—the largest of the Aegean islands. As Paul's "loyal child in the faith" (1:4), Titus was charged with overseeing the affairs of the Christian assemblies "in every town" on the island (v. 5).

Theologically, the letter to Titus echoes many of the themes and motifs found in 1 and 2 Timothy: the gospel is called "the faith" (1 Tim 1:19; 2 Tim 3:8; Titus 1:13); knowing "the truth" is essential for faith (1 Tim 2:4; 4:3; 2 Tim 2:25; 3:7; Titus 1:1); in terms of Christian ethics, the ideal of Christian citizenship, reinforcing patriarchal norms and subjection to rulers, is reinforced (Titus 3:1-2; see the comments on 1 Tim 2:1-7); salvation is understood as both present and future (1 Tim 1:16; 4:8; 2 Tim 1:9-10; Titus 2:12-14). One distinct difference between Titus and 1 and 2 Timothy is the more detailed salutation in Titus that elaborates the character of Paul's apostleship (1:1-6), and offers comment on eternal life (1:23). Only the salutation in Rom 1:1b-4, 5, 6 exceeds that of Titus.

(See also the Introduction to 1 Timothy.)

1:1-16, LEADERS AND DISCIPLINE

As in 1 and 2 Timothy, the leadership qualities for elders (v. 5) and bishops (v. 7) are clearly outlined. Not "job descriptions," but evidence that leadership was shared by many people, the terms reflect a still-fluid church structure in the latter decades of the first century.

Verses 10-16 differ from 1 Timothy in the identification of false teachers. The threat is from within, not without, for the "rebellious people" actually "profess to know God" (vv. 10, 16). The "circumcision party" is the source of the error, and they must be rebuked sharply to become sound in faith (v. 13).

Verse 12 proves that stereotypes are a fact of life for all cultures, ancient and modern. Clement of Alexandria attributes the epithet that "Cretans are always liars, vicious brutes, lazy gluttons" to Epimemes, a poet in the sixth century B.C.E.[46]

We need not rehearse the long litany of "stereotypes" Americans have laid at the feet of black peoples in America—the list is long, the path well worn. As an act of self-love, African Americans counter stereotypes best the way the writer of the Pastorals did—by reconstructing the images and discourses we want to "re-memory" and model for ourselves and our children (see the discussion of Toni Morrison's book *Beloved* in the comments on 1 Tim 1:1-2). Michael S. Harper's poetic reflection "Black Cryptogram" presents an image to cherish:

> When God
> Created
> the black child
> He was
> showing off.[47]

If the memories of Timothy's mother, Eunice, and grandmother Lois sparked Timothy's resolve to pass on the golden heritage of Christian faith (see the comments on 2 Tim 1:5), Sterling Plumpp's poem "Daybreak" encircles the possibilities black men have to soar as eagles within a limitless sky of pos-

sibilities and promise—a monumental epic of triumph and fortitude:

> every day
> i find a new life.
> my love for freedom
> our right
> to wear robes
> as we please,
> never sets.
> black voices
> dance in my soul
> like anxious sparkles.
> every black man
> is an epic
> sung
> in the soft keys
> of survival.
> o i want,
> i want,
> to hear
> be near
> all my brothers
> when I die[48]

2:1-15, Morals and Manners

The developing Christian ethos in the community emphasizes living in the community in accord with sound doctrine (v. 1) and a concern to prevent the word of God from being discredited (v. 5). Older women are charged to assist younger women in conformity to their traditionally prescribed roles as "household managers" (vv. 3-5), while younger men are to be self-controlled (v. 6). Enslaved women and men—and not slave-masters—are accountable for their behavior (see the comments on 1 Tim 6:1-2).

Verses 11-14 reconfirm the glad news that "our great God and Savior, Jesus Christ," appeared in history as a human being. If the transforming power of God's grace can make salvation available to all (v. 11), it can also fire the engine of a transformed moral life in which impiety gives way to self control and uprightness, and where a preoccupation with worldly passions brakes for godliness to have the "right of way."

3:1-15, Closing Exhortations

The theme of submission to governing authorities echoes the sentiment of "ideal Christian citizenship" in 1 Tim 2:1-4, where accommodation to the prevailing social order is linked with paraenesis encouraging fellow believers to live harmoniously (vv. 3-8).

The letter closes with a charge for believers to devote themselves to good works so that everyone might benefit (vv. 8-11). The parting comment about false teachers appears to be an afterthought, but the fact that the subject is broached attests both to its importance and also to the need to address it.

Notes

1. For one of the best summations of the history of the debate, see Luke Timothy Johnson, *The Writings of the New Testament: An Interpretation* (Minneapolis: Fortress Press, 1999), 423–28.

2. For a discussion of *ecclesia reformata semper reformanda*, see John C. Purdy, ed., *Always Being Reformed: The Future of Church Education* (Louisville: Geneva, 1985).

3. Dwight Hopkins provides a succinct discussion of the God of the enslaved in Antebellum America in *Shoes That Fit Our Feet: Sources for a Constructive Black Theology* (Maryknoll, N.Y.: Orbis, 1993), 13–48.

4. Zora Neale Hurston, *Moses: Man of the Mountain* (New York: Harper, 1991).

5. Delores Williams has provided a brilliant exploration of the Hagar and Sarah tradition from a Womanist perspective in *Sisters in the Wilderness: The Challenge of Womanist God-Walk* (Maryknoll, N.Y.: Orbis, 1998).

6. Johnson, *Writings of the New Testament*, 439.

7. The history of the Jesus movement within the historical context of the Roman Empire has received much-needed attention in the literature in the last two decades. See, for example, Richard Horsley and Neil Silberman, *The Message and the Kingdom: How Jesus and Paul Ignited a Revolution and Transformed the Ancient World* (Minneapolis: Fortress Press, 2002).

8. Martin Dibelius and Hans Conzelmann, *The Pastoral Epistles*, Hermeneia (Minneapolis: Fortress Press, 1972), 13.

9. Marie-Noëlle Anderson, "April 19," in *Origins: African Wisdom for Every Day*, ed. Danielle and Oliver Föllmi (New York: Abrams, 2005).

10. Joseph Ki-Zerbo, "June 5," in Föllmi, *Origins*.

11. Toni Morrison, *Beloved* (New York: Knopf, 1987).

12. See Robert J. Karris's summation of the data in *The Pastoral Epistles* (Wilmington: Michael Glazier, 1979), 49–50.

13. George W. Knight III, *The Pastoral Epistles: A Commentary on the Greek Text* (Grand Rapids, Mich.: Eerdmans, 1992), 86.

14. Dibelius and Conzelmann, *The Pastoral Epistles*, 23.

15. Nicholas K. Rauh, *The Sacred Bonds of Commerce: Religion, Economy, and Trade Society at Hellenistic Roman Delos, 166–87 B.C.* (Amsterdam: Gieben, 1993), 422–23. See Strabo 14.5.2.

16. The experience of being "stolen" and sold like commodified property or goods is well-documented in the literature, including the autobiographical narratives of ex-slaves like Ouladah Equiano, born in 1745. See, for example, Arna Bontemps, "Ouladah Equiano: An Interesting Account," in *Great Slave Narratives* (Boston: Beacon, 1969), 24–27. See also "Spirituals and Blues," in *Black Southern Voices: An Anthology of Fiction, Poetry, Drama, Nonfiction, and Critical Essays*, ed. John Oliver Killens and Jerry W. Ward Jr. (New York: Penguin, 1992), 227–28.

17. Clarice J. Martin, "Polishing the Unclouded Mirror: A Womanist Reading of Revelation 18:13," in *From Every People and Nation: The Book of Revelation in Intercultural Perspective*,

ed. David Rhoads (Minneapolis: Fortress Press, 2005), 82–109.

18. Horsley and Silberman. *The Message and the Kingdom*, 156, 224–32.

19. Dibelius and Conzelmann, *The Pastoral Epistles,* 32–34.

20. Horsley and Silberman. *The Message and the Kingdom*, 225.

21. Helmut Koester, *Introduction to the New Testament*, vol. 2, *History and Literature of Early Christianity*, 2nd ed. (New York: de Gruyter, 2000), 305.

22. Linda M. Maloney, "The Pastoral Epistles," in *Searching the Scriptures: A Feminist Commentary*, ed. Elizabeth Schüssler Fiorenza (New York: Crossroad, 1998), 370.

23. Jo Ann Shelton, *As the Romans Did: A Sourcebook in Roman Social History*, 2nd ed. (New York: Oxford University Press, 1998), 44.

24. Ibid., 298.

25. Patricia Hill Collins, *Black Feminist Thought: Knowledge, Consciousness, and the Politics of Empowerment,* 2nd ed. (New York: Routledge, 2000), 284.

26. Lucius Outlaw's concept of a "hermeneutics of the experiences of black peoples" is a useful ideological construct for practices of biblical interpretation within African American culture. See Outlaw, *On Race and Philosophy* (New York: Rouledge, 1996), 30.

27. On the politics of gender in the religious experience of African American peoples, see, for example, Cornel West and Eddie S. Glaude, eds., *African American Religious Thought: An Anthology* (Louisville: Westminster John Knox, 2003), and Elizabeth Brooks Higginbotham, *Righteous Discontent: The Women's Movement in the Black Baptist Church, 1880–1920* (Cambridge, Mass: Harvard University Press, 1993).

28. Cheryl Townsend Gilkes, *If It Wasn't for the Women: Black Women's Experience and Womanist Culture in Church and Community* (Maryknoll, N.Y.: Orbis, 2004).

29. Kelly Brown Douglas, *The Black Christ*, The Bishop Henry McNeal Turner Studies in North American Black Religion 9 (Maryknoll, N.Y.: Orbis, 1994).

30. Musa Dube, ed., *Other Ways of Reading: African Women and the Bible*, Global Perspectives on Biblical Scholarship (Atlanta: Society of Biblical Literature, 2001).

31. Judith Soares, "Eden after Eve: Christian Fundamentalism and Women in Barbados," in *Nation Dance: Religion, Identity, and Cultural Difference in the Caribbean*, ed. Patrick Taylor (Bloomington: Indiana University Press, 2001), 104–17.

32. Clarice J. Martin, "The *Haustafeln* (Household Codes) in African American Biblical Interpretation: 'Free Slaves' and 'Subordinate Women,'" in *Stony the Road We Trod: African American Biblical Interpretation*, ed. Cain Hope Felder (Philadelphia: Fortress Press, 1991), 206–31.

33. Gilkes, *If It Wasn't for the Women*, 108–9.

34. Maloney, "The Pastoral Epistles," 369, 379n12.

35. Koester, *Introduction to the New Testament.*

36. Karen Baker-Fletcher, "Something or Nothing: An Eco-Womanist Essay on God, Creation, and Indispensability," in *This Sacred Earth: Religion, Nature, Environment*, ed. Roger S. Gottlieb, 2nd ed. (New York: Routledge, 2004), 428–37.

37. Elizabeth Schüssler Fiorenza, *In Memory of Her: A Feminist Theological Reconstruction of Early Christian Origins* (New York: Crossroad, 1985), 251–84.

38. Holt Parker, "Loyal Slaves and Loyal Wives: The Crisis of the Outsider within Roman *Exemplum* Literature," in *Women and Slaves in Greco-Roman Culture*, ed. Sandra Joshel and Sheila Murnaghan (New York: Routledge, 2001), 157.

39. Clarice J. Martin, "'Somebody Done Hoo'dood the Hoodoo Man'": Language, Power, Resistance and the Effective History of Pauline Texts in American Slavery," in *Slavery in Text and Interpretation*, ed. Allen Callahan, Richard Horsley, and Abraham Smith, *Semeia* 83/84 (Atlanta: Society of Biblical Literature, 1998). See also Donald H. Matthews, *Honoring the Ancestors: An African Cultural Interpretation of Black Religion and Literature* (New York: Oxford University Press, 1998), 24–25.

40. Dibelius and Conzelmann, *The Pastoral Epistles*, 85; cf. Diogenes Laertius 6.50.

41. For a discussion of wealth in late-first-century assemblies, see Reggie M. Kidd, *Wealth and Beneficence in the Pastoral Epistles: A "Bourgeois" Form of Christianity?* (Atlanta: Scholars Press, 1990).

42. T. D. Jakes, *Mama Made the Difference: Life Lessons My Mother Taught Me* (New York: Putnam, 2006).

43. Madeline Burnside, Rosemarie Robothan, and Cornel West, eds., *Spirits of the Passage: The Transatlantic Slave Trade in the Seventeenth Century* (New York: Simon and Schuster, 1979), 18, 121–22.

44. June Jordan, *Affirmative Acts: Political Essays* (New York: Anchor, 1998), 2–3.

45. Ibid., 66–71.

46. Dibelius and Conzelmann, *The Pastoral Epistles*, 135–36.

47. Michael S. Harper, "Black Cryptogram: For Sterling A. Brown," in *The Oxford Anthology of African American Poetry*, ed. Arnold Rampersand (New York: Oxford University Press, 2006), 237. "Black Cryptogram" originally from *Nightmare Begins Responsibility: Poems*. Copyright 1975 by Michael S. Harper. Used with permission of the poet and the University of Illinois Press.

48. Sterling Plumpp, "Daybreak," in Rampersand, *The Oxford Anthology of African American Poetry*, 362. "Daybreak" originally from *Half Black, Half Blacker* by Sterling D. Plumpp, © 1970 Sterling D. Plumpp. Reprinted by permission of the author.

For Further Reading

Dibelius, Martin, and Hans Conzelmann. *The Pastoral Epistles*. Translated by Philip Bottolph and Adela Yarbro. Hermeneia. Philadelphia: Fortress Press, 1972.

Gilkes, Cheryl Townsend. *If It Wasn't for the Women: Black Women's Experience and Womanist Culture in Church and Community*. Maryknoll, N. Y.: Orbis, 2004.

Harris, Trudier. *Saints, Sinners, Saviors: Strong Black Women in African American Literature*. New York: Pargrave, 2001.

Hill, Patricia Liggins, ed. *Call and Response: The Riverside Anthology of the African American Literary Tradition*. New York: Houghton Mifflin, 1997.

Horsley, Richard, and Neil Silberman. *The Message and the Kingdom: How Jesus and Paul Ignited a Revolution and Transformed the Ancient World*. Minneapolis: Fortress Press, 2002.

Johnson, Luke Timothy. *The Writings of the New Testament: An Interpretation*. Rev. ed. Minneapolis: Fortress Press, 1999.

Joshel, Sandra R., and Sheila Murnaghan, eds. *Women and Slaves in Greco-Roman Culture*. New York: Routledge, 2001.

Knight, George W., III, *The Pastoral Epistles: A Commentary on the Greek Text*. New International Greek Testament Commentary. Grand Rapids, Mich.: Eerdmans, 1992.

MacDonald, Dennis Ronald. *The Legend and the Apostle: The Battle for Paul in Story and Canon*. Philadelphia: Westminster, 1983.

Outlaw, Lucius T., Jr. *On Race and Philosophy*. New York: Routledge, 1996.

Thurston, Bonnie Bowman. *The Widows: A Women's Ministry in the Early Church*. Minneapolis: Fortress Press, 1989.

West, Cornel, and Eddie S. Glaude Jr., eds. *African American Religious Thought: An Anthology*. Louisville: Westminster John Knox, 2003.

Woods, Paula L., Felix H. Liddell, eds. *I Hear a Symphony: African Americans Celebrate Love*. New York: Doubleday, 1994.

PHILEMON

Lloyd A. Lewis

INTRODUCTION

Among the letters of Paul, Philemon, the shortest of Paul's unquestioned letters, is highly problematic, especially for African Americans. Unlike the other letters for which issues of literary unity, authorship, and theological consistency loom large, the very subject matter of this letter is controversial. Paul sorts out a delicate situation that had profound societal and religious implications in his time and that has enduring religious and social implications for living in the present.

The facts of the case are relatively straightforward. Paul, during a time of imprisonment (v. 1), anticipating his own eventual release (v. 22), writes to Philemon (v. 1) and to others in his household (v. 2) in anticipation of a potentially explosive situation. Paul has encountered during his imprisonment Onesimus, a slave of Philemon's household, who either ran away from his master or was lent out by his master to serve an incarcerated Paul during one of his several times of arrest. Now, however, Paul sends Onesimus back home to his master (v. 12), albeit under changed circumstances. Onesimus has been converted to the gospel during his sojourn with Paul (v. 10). Thus, Paul writes this letter to curry the favor of a potentially offended Philemon and to pave the way for the slave's return.

Given the fact that slavery was a common feature of Greco-Roman life, we can hardly imagine that Paul, who included in his memorable affirmation in Galatians that "[in Christ Jesus] there is no longer Jew or Greek, there is no longer slave or free, there is no longer male and female," was ignorant of what slavery meant in his day. Although the economic status of slaves was far more diverse than was true in the peculiar institution of American chattel slavery, a slave was nonetheless viewed as a "thing" (Latin: *res*).

Elsewhere in his writings, besides in those places where that baptismal metaphor of the reunification of societal opposites appears, Paul can speak of slavery metaphorically, or he can speak of slavery in impersonal terms in proposing general instructions (1 Cor 7:21-24). In this letter, however, the situation is very concrete and immediate. We see Paul addressing a case in which freedom and slavery and environment and the gospel collide. What African American readers look for is some vision of how as a church leader Paul understood the gospel's power in the face of this very present social situation.

The letter itself hardly provides a systematic answer. There is no carefully laid-out argument, bolstered by Romans-quality theological exposition or ethical casuistry in this terse letter. Paul's language is vague. This is particularly curious when we consider Paul's boldness in addressing the Jew-Gentile dyad or even the male-female dyad. Is Paul's hesitance based on his recognition of the impact his decision might have on the social order and beyond that on the empire? We wish he would demand or order: he chooses to appeal (v. 9). We wish that Paul would say of Onesimus, "Once he was a slave, but now he is emancipated." He says no such thing overtly. Even the somewhat vague description of Onesimus (his Greek name means "useful") as once useless (*achrestos*) but now useful (*euchrestos*) to Paul hardly clarifies the slave's status in Paul's eyes or ours (v. 11). Could Paul be suggesting by his words that Onesimus, especially if he had

run away, had simply exchanged his old slave-master for another one who was incarcerated?

Yet if what we have here is a subtly crafted but nonetheless powerful letter of personal appeal and persuasion, which like a parable invited Philemon into wrestling with the implications of the common gospel known to Paul and Philemon and Onesimus, then this very short letter is in truth a profound exposition of Paul's gospel at work. For African American believers it has the potential to affirm our thought that belief does something and has the potential to completely undermine and revise the status quo through the application of theological principles.

The African American Hermeneutic Confronts Human Slavery

"Enslaved African Americans and subsequent generations appropriated [the notion of the equality of humanity] as a revolutionary hermeneutic for understanding scripture. This African American hermeneutic was based on their existential reality: even if the scripture said, 'slaves obey your masters,' it could not be the 'word of God' because it justified the suffering of human beings, which challenged the very essence of the Divine as righteous and just. As far as African Americans were concerned, race and class oppression were evil; and against the will of God."

—Demetrius K. Williams, "The Bible and Models of Liberation in the African American Experience," in *Yet with a Steady Beat: Contemporary U.S. Afrocentric Biblical Interpretation*, ed. Randall C. Bailey (Atlanta: Society of Biblical Literature, 2003), 53.

1–3, An Incarcerated Greeting
Philemon follows classic epistolary structure. The beginning of a typical letter in antiquity announces the author and the recipient and provides an initial word of greeting. The fluid

The Epistolary Structure of Philemon

Greeting: 1–3
Thanksgiving: 4–7
Body: 8–21
Closing: 22–25

nature of this form provides room for expansion and embellishment that can divulge the author's self-understanding and tip the hand of the author in setting forth the purpose for the epistle. Paul identifies himself as the prisoner (*desmios*) of Christ Jesus. Paul has surrendered his freedom; he belongs to Christ Jesus. At the same time, he is literally in prison due to his being in Christ's service. The choice of this self-descriptive is not accidental. We know elsewhere that Paul identifies himself as an apostle (Gal 1:1; 1 Cor 1:1; 2 Cor 1:1), as the slave of Christ (Phil 1:1), or as both slave and apostle (Rom 1:1). We also see that the character of true apostleship is demonstrated in Paul's sufferings (2 Cor 11:22-29). Those sufferings mark Paul with the sign of the cross: God's inverse sign of wisdom and power (1 Cor 1:24).

A Crucified Messiah as Paradoxical Power

"Jesus did not die in order to spare us the indignities of the wounded creation. He died that we might see those wounds as our own. He died that we might live, and live fully and hopefully—please note the correct use of the adverb 'hopefully' as 'full of hope'—not in some fantastic never-never-land not yet arrived, but in ambiguous reality here and now. Look at the cross and the suffering bleeding Savior. Beyond tragedy is truth redeemed. Look and live!"

—Peter J. Gomes, *Sermons* (New York: Morrow, 1998), 72.

Yet Paul's more literal identification of himself by his criminal status places his high profile in the church to the side. Apostleship was not in this case a significant marker of Paul's rank. Philemon, therefore, hears Paul placing himself on a level comparable to that of another criminal and slave: Onesimus himself, yet to be mentioned.

Paul's correspondence, as the introduction shows us, is hardly private. When he writes, he is accompanied by Timothy, one of his trusted followers. Timothy's "calling card" is his role as a brother (*adelphos*) to Paul. Paul's use of this term is technical and certainly more than literal. What Paul does is to create in his church the concept of members as part of an extended family. This family is not bordered by physical kinship but determined by the common role members share as the children of God. Such egalitarian language eliminates the distinction between apostle and worker. Of greatest concern to Paul is stating that he writes to one who shares a common role and bond: one found in their status as children of God.

Jesus Redefines the Meaning of "Family"

"Jesus said, 'Who are my mother and my brothers?' And looking at those who sat around him, he said, 'Here are my mother and my brothers! Whoever does the will of God is my brother and sister and mother.'"

—Mark 3:33-35

When Paul writes to Philemon, he does so to one he identifies as both the "beloved" and Paul's coworker. Paul creates through his words a wide group of peers, and in this letters the presence of language of association in addition to language of family is thick; individuals are "fellow prisoners" (v. 23), "fellow soldiers" (v. 2), fellow workers (vv. 1, 24), and partners (v. 17) with Paul. Affectionate language fashions the tenor of Christian community by promoting warm relationships. But Paul's language of love becomes more complex when one considers that superior to the affection church members have toward one another is the motivating initiative of God, who loved those alienated from him. Being "the beloved" of Paul reminds us that Philemon (v. 1) (and Onesimus, v. 16) is the beloved of God because of the common status he has with other believers as a member of the church.

The greeting gives us one other insight into Paul's attitude toward the Onesimus situation. We see that the plight of Onesimus is not a private matter involving Paul and Philemon and Onesimus alone. Apphia and Archippus and the whole house church that met in Philemon's house became witness to this matter (v. 2). Paul had taken a social issue and made it an issue for the church, a church in which the shared status of its members is crucial in creating a social web that is more compelling than even blood kinship.

4–7, Giving Thanks and Setting the Stage

The thanksgiving section of Paul's letters frequently sets forth the major themes of his letter. Philemon's thanksgiving follows this pattern as he gives thanks for Philemon's love (also vv. 5, 7, 9, 16); prayer (v. 22); sharing and partnership (v. 17); doing good works (v. 14); deep affection (vv. 12, 20); refreshment (v. 20); and fraternity (v. 20). All of these are virtues Paul identifies in Philemon.

Paul praises Philemon for his faith (v. 6), a virtue he holds in common fellowship (*koinonia*) with Paul. The concept of fellowship is essential in describing the church and its common life. Members of the church actualize this common life by sharing in the Eucharist as their participation in the life and death of the Messiah with one another. But we know that for Paul *koinonia* indicates more than shared membership in a social collective. Maintaining fellowship makes one a participant in a relationship in which individuals can count upon one another to provide mutual benefits for each other. This is a crucial assertion for Paul. Philemon has already demonstrated fellowship with Paul in his faith. Now Paul, on the basis of the fellowship he and Philemon shared with one another, can expect that in the matter of Onesimus, Philemon will not disappoint Paul's anticipation of help and aid in resolving this situation.

In v. 7 Paul, however, also recognizes Philemon's acts of love. Since Philemon provides refreshment for the hearts of the saints, Paul has received joy and comfort from his friend. The little constellation of terms, "heart," "love," and "refresh," return again in the letter, for Paul identifies Onesimus as his "heart" and prays that Philemon, the beloved, will supply refreshment for him.

The Black Church as a Family in the Black Community

"We have . . . spoken of the Black family as one of the means by which we have received the Gospel of Jesus Christ, and we have urged that there can be no authentic embrace of the one without the other. The Black Story could not have been possible without the constant witness and service of church, the Black church, as the extended family in the Black community. The leaders in the churches were our extra parents and guardians. They praised us when we did right and corrected us when we did wrong because they expected great things from us."

—Pastoral letter from the Black Episcopal Bishops to Black Clergy and Laity in the Episcopal Church, 1990.

8–21, Fashioning a Change of Attitude

Paul now begins his request of Philemon. In part he builds his request on qualities found in Philemon that he has already effusively praised. We know from the introduction of the letter that Paul has voluntarily bracketed his status as an apostle. It would be perfectly possibly for Paul to command (*epitasso*) a response from Philemon out of boldness and his apostolic rank, since boldness was one of the marks of an apostolic individual (2 Cor 7:4; see also the description of the apostles in Acts 4:13, 29, 31; 28:31). Paul, however, refuses to act as a superior to Philemon. On the basis of the love Paul shares with Philemon, the apostle chooses rather to request and to make an appeal (*parakaleo*) to the Christian slaveholder in the case of Onesimus

Fraternal Organizations in the Black Community during the Jim Crow Era

"Fraternal organizations formed another center for mutual aid. Initially established as burial societies, lodges became safety nets for their members' families. Members cared for the sick and helped feed and maintain the households of ailing members. They provided resources for members who had experienced almost any kind of loss. Reflecting on the need to pool resources, A. E. Dixie talks about his fraternal lodge and the role it played in the lives of his neighbors. 'Like if you was a farmer and your mule died and you belonged to the Emancipated Order,' Dixie remembered, 'everybody that had a mule had to give you a day's work, until they could get you another mule.'"

—William H. Chafe, Raymond Gavins, and Robert Korstad, eds., *Remembering Jim Crow* (New York: New Press, 2001), 90.

(v. 9). Since Paul typically appealed to those who were fellow members of the church, by his appealing to Philemon, Paul recognizes the common lot he shares with Philemon as a church member in approaching him to solve this social dilemma.

Paul levels the arena of his appeal by taking one other action. Paul identifies himself as a *presbytes* (v. 9), a word that could be translated "ambassador" (its literal meaning is "an old man"). The contrast, however, of Paul's status of "ambassador" with his self-description as a "prisoner" heightens his attitude of self-emptying—an attitude he will want to have Philemon also adopt in considering his posture as a master toward Onesimus, the slave.

Now we turn to the person of Onesimus himself. Paul's relationship with Onesimus pivots on the conversion of the slave. Paul calls Onesimus his "child" (v. 10), thus recognizing a difference in status between the two. But we must note that in Paul's letters, he rarely calls himself "father" in his relationship to other believers. This helps us to see that his use of such parental language is not meant to create a hierarchical relationship with another but to recognize the existential fact that Paul in his evangelistic work of preaching and baptizing had brought individuals to a new life, leading them to the shores of the gospel by preaching. Paul's "fatherhood" of Onesimus during his imprisonment indicated Paul's agency in making Onesimus through preaching and baptism to be a new child of God: his most significant definition.

Now I can move to the matter of Onesimus's usefulness (v. 11). I have dispensed above with the idea that the slave through his conversion had simply become a more diligent worker. I have further dismissed the idea that Paul's praise of Onesimus came from his joy in having Onesimus do for him what he had been doing for Philemon's household. The clue may come in v. 12, in a contrast that employs early Christian stock language used when speaking of conversion. In 1 Cor 6:1-11 Paul contrasts the state of people before they were baptized with their estate after they had been initiated into the family of believers. We know that crossing the border into the church would qualify Onesimus for new work. Now, as not before, Paul recognized Onesimus as the child of God (and the brother of both Paul and Philemon). Now, as not before, Onesimus could become a model of the gospel at work—that gospel in which the ultimate distinction in worth before God between Jew and Gentile, male and female, slave and free held no more dominion over believers. And now, as not before, Onesimus could be useful to Paul and the church in fostering the church's mission. Paul's new relationship with Onesimus was guaranteed.

The God Who Liberates

"To [the American Negro] so far as he thought and dreamed, slavery was indeed the sum of all villainies, the cause of all sorrow, the root of all prejudice; Emancipation was the key to a promised land of sweeter beauty than ever stretched before the eyes of wearied Israelites. In song and exhortation swelled one refrain—Liberty; in his tears and curses the God he implored had Freedom in his right hand. At last it came,—suddenly, fearfully, like a dream. With one wild carnival of blood and passion came the message in his own plaintive cadences:

"'Shout, O children!'

"'Shout, you're free!'

"'For God has bought your liberty!'"

—W. E. B. DuBois, *The Souls of Black Folk,* quoted in Abraham Chapman, ed. *Black Voices: An Anthology of Afro-American Literature* (New York: New American Library, 1968), 497.

The critical matter in the letter, however, is the relationship between Onesimus and Philemon and the very public nature of this impending rearrangement for them. In v. 13 Paul tells us that the presence of Onesimus would make up for the absence of Philemon, who was equally useful to Paul in his ministry and mission. Based on their common kinship in Christ, Onesimus and Philemon could become interchangeable. Not only would Onesimus be able to be Paul's envoy to Philemon; the return of Onesimus to Philemon would prove that Onesimus could be the envoy of Philemon to Paul.

Paul's approach up to this point has been both subtle and tactful. In v. 14 he continues his appeal. He proposes an answer to the matter of the status of Onesimus. We need to remind ourselves of the tremendous social pressures that ranged around this situation. Paul has already called Philemon his brother (v. 1): he now uses the same term in identifying Onesimus. Onesimus is no longer a slave. Through baptism, through being made God's beloved, he has become a brother to Paul and to Philemon and to all in Philemon's house church.

Does Paul suggest, then, that conversion is tantamount to emancipation from slavery? Does Paul suggest that the household of Philemon should observe a double standard: holding one set of rules by which Philemon would wink and recognize Onesimus's brotherhood as long as they were in church, but maintaining another set of rules once they had exited the doors into the daylight of wider society?

At the end of the body of the letter, Paul returns to his subtle social mathematics. We have seen how the apostle has emphasized that Onesimus and Philemon are on a par with each another. Now Paul demonstrates that he and Onesimus are interchangeable. Paul assumes the debts of Onesimus to

Philemon as his own (v. 19). The generosity of Paul would satisfy the debtor status of Onesimus to Philemon. And Paul reminds Philemon that he stands as a debtor to Paul.

22–25, Personal Presence in Conclusion

In addition to a group of names (individuals listed also in Colossians) and a concluding benediction (v. 25) Paul adds one other request. Having prevailed on the common ground he shares with Philemon in faith (v. 6) and having prevailed on the conscience of Philemon to receive Onesimus back into his household, Paul prevails on Philemon for an act of personal hospitality. Having mentioned the indebtedness of Philemon to him, Paul now places himself in debt to Philemon. But this debt has another aspect. Paul's request for hospitality at the end of his imprisonment comes as a final stage in his relationship with both slave and slavemaster. His impending visit shows his concern that the mode of action that Philemon adopts and its execution are crucial enough that Paul would enforce them by a personal act of inspection.

CONCLUSION

In this short letter we have seen Paul at work. In truth we have been invited into seeing the gospel at work, since Paul's presentation of the facts makes the case for the gospel something that neither Philemon nor Onesimus could avoid. In the light of all that Paul says, we return to one of the original questions raised in this short commentary. Does Paul suggest that baptism and conversion are tantamount to emancipation from slavery? As we have seen, Paul does not answer this question directly. But Paul does create a situation in which Philemon is directed to experience the disquieting nature of the gospel. Paul surrounds Philemon with all the facts. In the new arrangement, Paul can identify himself so closely with Onesimus that the prisoner-apostle assumes the runaway's indebtedness. He gives Philemon a vision of a church in which equal status before God is the norm among its members. He shows Philemon and his house church that in the new arrangement an apostle, a runaway slave, and a slaveholder could be interchangeable. And then he leaves the matter with Philemon, much as Jesus would leave a parable in the ears of his disciples. Typically Jesus would say to one listening to a parable, "What do you think?" or "Let those who have ears to hear hear!" Paul's action places the burden of actually appropriating the gospel not on the success of the preacher to convince but on the willingness of the hearer, given the gospel and its power and its demands, to hear and to decide what would be the appropriate for one hearing the good news to do.

For Further Reading

Bruce, F. F. *The Pauline Circle.* Grand Rapids, Mich.: Eerdmans, 1985.

Callahan, Allen Dwight. *Embassy of Onesimus: The Letter of Paul to Philemon.* Valley Forge, Pa.: Trinity Press International, 1997.

Martin, Dale B. *Slavery as Salvation: The Metaphor of Slavery in Pauline Christianity.* New Haven: Yale University Press, 1990.

Martin, Ralph P. *Ephesians, Colossians, and Philemon.* Atlanta: John Knox, 1991.

Petersen, Norman R. *Rediscovering Paul: Philemon and the Sociology of Paul's Narrative World.* Philadelphia: Fortress Press, 1985.

Sampley, J. Paul. *Pauline Partnership in Christ.* Philadelphia: Fortress Press, 1980.

Williams, Demetrius K. "The Bible and Models of Liberation in the African American Experience." Pages 33–59 in *Yet with a Steady Beat: Contemporary U.S. Afrocentric Biblical Interpretation.* Edited by Randall C. Bailey. Atlanta: Society of Biblical Literature, 2003.

HEBREWS

James Earl Massey

INTRODUCTION

The Epistle to the Hebrews is one of the most carefully written books in the New Testament. The author was well informed and articulate about the Jewish Scriptures and the message about Jesus Christ.

The writer's extended use of the high priesthood theme suggests that his readers had a Jewish background, and his appeal to Old Testament practices and promises supports that judgment. But beyond these considerations nothing more can be affirmed with any certainty about the identity of the first readers.

The authorship of this epistle has also not been settled. From an early period, many names have been proposed: Paul, Apollos, Barnabas, Luke, Silas, Priscilla, Aquila, Philip, Timothy, Clement of Rome, and still others. Origen (184–254 C.E.) considered its teachings Pauline, yet commented, "But who wrote the epistle, in truth God [alone] knows." This writing lacks Paul's usual identifying mark (see 2 Thess 3:17; 1 Cor 16:21), but the Eastern church circulated it and canonized it largely because it was associated by tradition with the name of Paul.

Clement of Rome knew this document and quoted from it many times in his letter to Corinth, *1 Clement* (ca. 96 C.E.). Given that the epistle would need sufficient time both to gain authoritative status and to travel widely enough to reach leaders like Clement,

Hebrews should be dated in the 60s, perhaps as early as 64 C.E.

The writer addressed a distressed and discouraged people (4:14-16; 10:32-36; 12:1-3) who were feeling the strain of tensions fomented by the policies of Emperor Nero. Even though deaths had not yet been experienced (12:4), the writer sought to stir hope for the best while helping the people get ready for the worst. He used Old Testament writings, characters, and economy to illustrate the importance of faith and patience to face and handle difficult circumstances. He subsequently pushed beyond the Old Testament as he sought an even firmer faith foundation. In many graphic statements he explained that the Old Testament religious system was provisional and prophetic in character, pointing beyond itself to what was now available to all in the person and ministry of Jesus Christ.

The epistle sets forth five elemental truths about the life and ministry of Jesus:

1. His humanity relates him fully to all humans.
2. His exemplary sonship is a model and means of hope for all.
3. His life and death afford us access to God.
4. He now holds a continuing priesthood.
5. His present ministry as ascended Savior grants a ready and necessary help to all who call upon him.

These truths were and are strategic for those who are beset by life and are fretful or confused about what they see and experience in the world as it now is.

Hebrews is unique among the New Testament writings in describing Jesus as one who also lived by faith: "I will put my trust in [God]" (2:13a). He was "tested as we are, yet without sin" (4:15).[1] He offered up "prayers and supplications, with loud cries and tears, to the one who was able to save him from death, and he was heard because of his reverent submission" (5:7). Jesus was tested by life, the writer reminds us, and he handled himself obediently to the glory of God—living by faith while "he learned obedience through what he suffered" (5:8). Thus this grand declaration: "having been made perfect he became the source of eternal salvation to all who obey him" (5:9). And this one: "For we do not have a high priest who is unable to sympathize with our weaknesses, but we have one who in every respect has been tested as we are, yet without sin. Let us therefore approach the throne of grace with boldness, so that we may receive mercy and find grace to help in time of need" (4:15-16).

Hebrews honors the central fact of Jesus' passion and death—how it happened (12:3), how he handled it all (2:9-10; 5:7-8; 12:2-3), and what his experience effects for believers (2:15, 17-18; 3:4-14; 4:14-16; 5:9; 7:25; 9:26b-28; 10:10, 19-22; 13:12, 20-21). All in all, it is a bracing statement about the cost of our salvation, on the one hand, and the cost of discipleship, on the other, and the ever-present blessing of having the shoulder of Jesus underneath our cross with us.

The message about Jesus in Hebrews is that he is a Savior fully identified with us by a common humanity and by raw experience. The writer insisted that Jesus must be understood both as religious subject and as religious object, as the one who both shows us faith and sustains us in faith. This epistle gives statements, scenes, declarations, and affirmations about Jesus as tested brother, knowing sharer, concerned Savior, and exalted advocate. He is a figure of hope, the "forerunner" (*prodromos*) who has gone ahead in the interest of those still behind. Hebrews was written to strengthen faith and obedience by which to go "on towards maturity" (6:1).

The writer himself classified his writing as a "word of exhortation" (13:22, *logou tēs paraklēseōs*), and one can see in it many fundamental traits of a practical sermon. The rhetorical patterns in the epistle reflect considerable writing ability and evident skill in addressing gathered assemblies. Some sections of the writing are so polished and pointed that they might well have been used earlier on preaching occasions, especially 3:1—4:13 and chap. 11, with its many biographical miniatures about persons who succeeded through a tested faith.

Thus Hebrews is a confessional writing sent to strengthen faith, inform the will, and renew the hope of the impatient, questioning believers who needed to continue "looking to Jesus the pioneer and perfecter of our faith, who . . . endured the cross, disregarding its shame, and has taken his seat at the right hand of the throne of God" (12:2).

The writer knew that his argument carried force and relevance because it gave a statement that faith and experience can verify as the truth. The Epistle to the Hebrews is a needed word for questioning pilgrims caught in the difficulties of history.

1:1—4:13, THE SON AS GOD'S SUPREME AGENT

1:1—2:18, The Superiority of the Son over Angels

1:1-4, Introduction: A Doctrinal Manifesto about Jesus. Hebrews begins on a high note, with a doctrinal manifesto about Jesus as God's Son and God's supreme agent of ministry. The writer's beginning statement is a beautifully worded periodic sentence in Greek, but modern translators usually break that single sentence into shorter ones for easier reading (as, for example, the three-sentence format in the NRSV and in the NEB).

The contrast in vv. 1-2 between God's prophetic servants and his Son, Jesus (first named at 2:9), should be readily understood. The prophets were all limited by their humanity and historical circumstances, while the Son speaks of his Father with a full inside view of the divine will. There is thus a fullness and finality to what the Son has said, and there is an ultimacy to what he as Son has done.

Next, in vv. 3-4, all that the Son has done to make a complete "cleansing for sins" is mentioned, and his holy character and exalted status are celebrated as evidence that he is sufficient to meet all human need. Thus, to be seated now "at the right hand of the Majestic One on high" is both his privilege and his due. But the "sitting" suggests more: namely, that the work he set out to do has been done, and that it is worthily completed. His sitting with God implies both a responsibility now completed and his first estate restored. Obtaining "a more excellent honor," or "name," than any of the angels implies that God rewarded the Son for his excellent but costly ministry as the promised Suffering Servant.

1:5-14, The Son's Relation to God. After the lofty doctrinal pronouncement about Jesus as Son of God, the writer proceeds to document the Son's superior status over angels by using selected texts from the Hebrew scriptures, interpreting some of these as words spoken by God *to* the Son. Thus 1:5 quotes Ps 2:7; 2 Sam 7:14; and 1 Chr 17:13; vv. 8-9 quote Ps 45:6-7; vv. 10-12 quote Ps 102:25-27, and vv. 13 quotes Ps 110:1. Some other texts are viewed as words spoken by God *about* the Son, addressed to angels (v. 6 quotes Deut 32:43).

The writer's use of Ps 2:7 as God's utterance to the Son reflects the understanding of the early church about the God-bestowed kingship that Jesus holds. This psalm was one of many that were viewed as messianic. Originally part of an enthronement liturgy from the time of King David, the psalm reports God's pleasure with the one being installed as king over the nation. Here in Hebrews, that commendation is cited in tribute to Jesus as the kingly Son; it is an acclamation of his worthiness to receive honor and to be obeyed. The early church did so honor him, and Psalm texts were among the lively tributes utilized in worship settings as well as in church writings, such as this epistle.

The citation of Ps 45:6-7 in vv. 8-9 points to the supreme virtue of Jesus as the one who always honored the will of God in his decisions and deeds: "You have loved righteousness and hated evil." The word "righteousness" appears six times in this letter (1:9; 5:13; 7:2; 11:7, 33; 12:11), and later, in 5:13-14, the writer will make an appeal to his readers to develop character within that righteousness, so that by moral discernment and a love for what is right, genuine spiritual growth can steadily take place in their lives.

In vv. 10-12, Ps 102:25-27 is quoted, probably to emphasize the eternality of the Son over against the changing patterns and systems of human history. The faithful are reminded that they are secure through the unfailing ministry of an eternal, unchanging Lord. This emphasis will again be in view at 13:8, where the writer proclaims that "Jesus Christ is the same yesterday, and today, and throughout the ages."

2:1-4, Exhortation Based on the Contrast between Jesus and Angels. "Therefore" in 2:1 introduces an important conclusion to the writer's statement about the status of Jesus: We must give serious attention to him—or suffer the sad consequences for failing to do so. Although angels have been sent as "servant spirits," intimately involved in human ventures, God has backed their word and work, punishing all who refused to honor what those servant spirits were sent to accomplish. The word Jesus has given is the ultimate and final word from God, and it is therefore indispensable. It is the word about salvation in its richest dimensions, a salvation brought into effect and fully guaranteed only for those who

seriously listen to Jesus and look to him with right understanding about who he is. The exhortation is a warning about what is lost by those who, having heard the message about salvation, selfishly and faithlessly "drift away" from it.

2:5-18, The Son's Relation to Believers. Having completed his preliminary statement about the superiority of Jesus over angels, and having issued a warning not to be part of the awesome fate of those who neglect the witness and work provided by the Son of God, the writer moves on in 2:5-18 to begin a discussion about how the Son stands related to those who do believe in him.

In this section of Hebrews we get our first insight from the writer about the extent to which Jesus as Son fully identifies with our humanity and its attendant experiences. Like the first humans, Jesus lived for a while "lower" in condition than angels (2:9), but, unlike them, he never failed the high purpose for which he entered the world. He too had to live by faith, by a steady trust in God as he lived his way across the years. The writer documents the Son's need for faith by quoting Isa 8:17b, using it at 2:13 as a confessional word from the Son about his life under God: "I [myself] will firmly trust in him." The writer thus accents attention upon Jesus as religious *subject* in order to highlight the importance of Jesus as religious *object.* In so doing, the writer's insight into the human experience of Jesus accents his obedience in pilgrimage; it shows him as a figure of hope for those who look to him as the worthy "pioneer of their deliverance" (v. 10). In looking to Jesus, the writer asserts, we can maintain our bearings, discern our possibilities, and anticipate our future. That future will ultimately involve life within another order God has planned for his people: thus the expression "the coming world [order]" (v. 5), a world (*oikoumenē*, "inhabited, ordered community") under the manifest lordship of Jesus as exalted Son, now raised above the present world order and "crowned with glory and honor because of the [particular] death he suffered" (2:9). The sovereignty humans lost by sinning stands modeled in him in his victory over temptation, sin, and death. Jesus now heads the household of the faithful, who will inherit the new order when this old earth order passes away.

What Jesus accomplished benefits all who identify with him. Jesus was a "pioneer" in our interest, intent to lead "many sons to glory" by his delivering deed of salvation. The "many sons" are, with him, full mem-

---

Reflection: On "Seeing" Jesus

The help Jesus offers is available to all, but that help is more readily gained by those who "see" (blepomen, 2:9) him for who he is. Jesus has fulfilled the proper end of his divine assignment (1:3b), and has been "crowned with glory and honor," so he is the one human God has deemed worthy to have "all things subject" to him. Because of human sin, the subjugation of all things to the human race has not happened, but meanwhile believers are helped to manage the difficulties and disparities of life by keeping Jesus in focus.

The writer's assertion "but we do see Jesus" (2:9) emphasizes a central insight in his theological message. At 3:1-6, a passage with an artful blend of history, theology, and doctrine, the writer exhorts the readers to "consider [katanoēsate, "fix the mind upon," "discern and act wisely"] Jesus" (3:1); at 5:9, salvation is promised to all who "obey him"; and at 12:2 the need is stressed to keep "looking [aphorōntes] to Jesus." The writer's emphasis upon "seeing" Jesus and "looking to Jesus" takes the New Testament tradition of seeing the Lord to another level. The writer does not refer here to seeing Jesus by normal vision blessed with an objective appearance, such as the disciples experienced who met with the risen Lord and afterward confessed, "We have seen the Lord" (John 20:25). Our writer rather refers here to sight of another kind, namely, "insight," a spiritual perception by which the believer is actively influenced by and identifies with Jesus. This kind of seeing is a grace-assisted understanding of who Jesus is, and it includes a realization of the personal benefits Jesus makes available in the believer's experience. "Seeing" Jesus has occurred, and still occurs, in more than one way.

Influenced by the African American contemplative way of reading the scriptures and of speaking about Jesus, veteran preacher Gardner C. Taylor used Heb 2:9 to preach about Jesus as "The Christian's Dearest Sight" (Words of Gardner Taylor, vol. 2, compiled by Edward L. Taylor [Valley Forge, Pa.: Judson, 2000], 72–77.) Near the close of that sermon Taylor mentioned having preached one night, early in his ministry, in Shreveport, Louisiana, when at some point during his delivery the lights in that section of the city failed and the church was plunged into darkness. Startled by the event, Taylor stopped preaching. But a voice soon rang out from one of the pews, "Go on, Preacher; we can see Jesus in the darkness." Seeing Jesus is experienced in more than one way.

bers of the very family of God. This was the concern of the incarnation: Jesus wanted to identify fully with humans in our plight, even becoming subject to death, so that he could make death itself his victim—from *inside* the experience. According to vv. 14-16, the grand result for believers is release from the fear of death. Angels did not need such help; humans did, and Jesus eagerly made that help available.

At 2:17-18, the author introduced the theme of the high priesthood to highlight further the great ministry of Jesus to believers. The writer will continue to unfold and accent this theme across the bulk of the epistle. The rather extended treatment of this theme, together with the many details connected with the Day of Atonement ritual, provides grounds for viewing this writing as written to and for Hebrews. (This is the only New Testament writing that explains the ministry of Jesus in terms of priesthood.) As one who suffered the round of human experience, Jesus can represent us well since he understands and identifies with our needs. He is before us as a victorious winner and with us as the sympathetic helper. The believer need only cry out for his assistance.

The rich song tradition in the black church has long encouraged this faith response to Jesus as gracious Helper. The following lines are readily familiar:

> Just tell Jesus; tell him all.
> Trials great and trials small.
> He will share them, freely bear them.
> Just tell Jesus. Tell him all.

So are these lines:

> Jesus is on the mainline,
> Tell him what you want.
> Call him up
> And tell him what you want.

3:1—4:13, The Superiority of the Son over Moses and Joshua

3:1-6, The Son Greater than Servants in the Household. Having set forth the high rank and great ministry of Jesus on behalf of his people, the writer issues an exhortation: "consider Jesus." That word "consider" (*katanoēsate*) was a call to fix the mind and heart upon him. The titles that follow increase the weight of his example and importance for the believer. Jesus is "apostle" and "high priest" of our confession. This introduces a planned comparison between Jesus and Moses, the point being to show that Jesus has a superior ministry to that of Moses. Although both Moses and Jesus held appointments from God, were faithful to their calling, were deliverers of their people, established covenants, were suffering servants, and had face-to-face dealings with God, the ministry of Jesus was superior, because he is Son, while Moses was but a servant within the household of God. The confession of the church centers on Jesus, who is God's superior messenger (apostle) and the perfect representative of the needy people (high priest). In both instances of service, Jesus acts on behalf of others. Thus, however great others have been in their service to God, Jesus is worthy of greater honor. Problems abound when Jesus is not properly "considered," when his personhood and ministry are not kept in proper focus.

As Son, Jesus presides over the "house(hold) of God" (vv. 5-6). The belonging to that household is conditional; it happens through faith and steady "confidence and pride in our hope." A right pride in belonging stimulates faithfulness to the family name and leadership.

3:7-19, Exhortation Based on the Contrast. The second warning section, which begins at 3:7—4:2, recalls Israel's failure in the wilderness and the sad consequences of that failure by a people called by God to live as his nation.

The writer quotes Ps 95:7-11, reporting God's displeasure with the generation that provoked him by its waywardness and sin. It was a generation that lacked a listening ear for God's word. That generation was united in a shared sin, and its members fell in a shared fate. God let them succeed at sinning, but the gains were fleshly and destructive. The gains of sin are always deadly, making the disobedient losers. God had offered them "rest," but their sinning blocked the benefits of the offer.

4:1-10, The "Rest of God" Explained. The privilege God offered the earlier generation still remains open. The promise God originally made still holds: one can "enter God's rest." Our period of time does not make us "come short" (*hysterēkenai,* "arrive too late") of it because the promise about "rest" involved something more than settling peacefully in the geographical spot called Canaan.

The "good news" about rest involves more than a promised land; it involves a promised life in the will of God. The levels of fulfillment in the promise begin to be experienced when the promise meets with "faith in [on the part of] the hearer." Israel first heard the promise, which included cessation of warfare after victory over the enemies blocking their entrance into Canaan, but that generation did not even enter Canaan "because of unbelief" (v. 19). God was not obligated to bless those who resisted his terms, but neither did God withdraw the offer of rest. A future realization was implied in the promise, and at the highest level of fulfillment. Possessing Canaan was not all that God had in mind for ancient Israel, and salvation here and now is not all that God has planned for believers now. The people of God will enjoy a coming "Sabbath rest" at the dawning of "another day" (4:8b), the reference here being to the ultimate life with God.

4:11-13, Exhortation to Full Obedience. "Let us be eagerly diligent (*spoudazō,* 'concen-

trate with eager interest to succeed'), therefore, to enter into that rest."

A full striving will mean staying open to God in heart and mind, with eagerness to hear God's word in order to know and do God's will. The reference in vv. 2-13 to "the word of God" as a confronting sword no doubt recalls the encounter Joshua experienced with the angelic commander of the Lord's forces just before his attack upon Jericho (Josh 5:13-15). When Joshua realized that he was confronted by the Lord's angelic messenger, he fell submissively before him, listening for instructions. The writer here appeals to his readers to take the listening posture before the word of God. Openness to that word keeps one on good terms with God, to whom all are unavoidably accountable.

4:14—10:39, Jesus the Great High Priest

4:14-16, The Priesthood of Jesus Introduced. His life on earth now done, his mission here accomplished, Jesus has "passed away into heaven," where he now ministers on our behalf before God, representing us as "the great high priest" at "the throne of grace, so that we may receive mercy and obtain grace for timely help when in need" (4:16). The believer has every encouragement, then, to remain faithful and trusting: as members of God's household, there is a definite belonging and access to blessing from God. Prayer is offered to one who responds graciously, and there is an attitude of mercy that the believer meets when help is sought through prayer.

Receiving "grace" has to do with being understood, accepted, regarded, favored, and supported by God. As Henry H. Mitchell has commented, the "Black Church has never viewed 'grace' as but a theological nicety, it was and is to the black man a means of life and strength—a source of support and balance and self-certainty in a world whose approval of blacks is still in extremely short supply."[2]

5:1-4, The High Priesthood Ministry Explained. This section begins an extended discussion of the high priesthood of Jesus. First mentioned at 2:17, then restated at 3:1 and 4:14, this title and theme of the Son's high priesthood are now expanded in 5:1—6:20.

Recalling Exodus 28–29, where consecration for the priesthood is treated, the writer enumerates some of the qualifications necessary for someone to attain and hold the priestly role. The person must be "chosen from among men," actually from Aaron's lineage: "appointed to act on their behalf" in matters relating to God, primarily through the offering of "gifts and sacrifices for sin." The priest was not someone in general but someone in particular, divinely set apart for a distinctive service.

5:5-10, Jesus as Divinely Appointed High Priest. Jesus fills every requirement for the priesthood—except one: he was not from Aaron's line. Yet he supersedes the Aaronic priesthood, because he holds an eternal appointment "after the order of Melchizedek" (5:6, 10; 6:20; 7:11, 15, 17). This is a more distinctive priesthood, because Melchizedek was the first priest mentioned in Israel's history, one whose importance was not granted by human descent but by divine decree, a fact testified when Abraham offered tithes to him. The priesthood associated with Aaron and his descendants was a later and more limited order than that accorded by God to Melchizedek.

The role of the Aaronic high priesthood constantly passed on from one priest to another, because each priest died. The priestly ministry of Jesus, however, continues eternal and unchanged, unaffected by the passage of time, because "he always lives," standing before God on our behalf. His place of privilege remains his by divine right, but it was gained by his obedience to the terms of sonship. Now successful through his pilgrimage in the world, Jesus has become "the source of eternal salvation to all those who obey him" (5:9).

5:11—6:3, Exhortation to Become Mature in Understanding. The confession of Jesus as high priest is a great truth that demands a mature understanding and appreciation. Those who are spiritually sluggish and "dull of hearing" (v. 11) miss the depth of meaning this truth holds for their lives. Thus the writer's third warning passage. He chided the readers to move from a child's milk diet to the solid food of righteousness, which would prepare them for the rigors of life that believers face. He wanted them to learn how to endure stress in the spirit and manner Jesus exemplified during "the days of his flesh" (5:7). The readers needed to become "mature," trained by practice to distinguish good from evil (5:14). Maturity in faith depends upon the same logic as does any other growth: one must advance stage by stage, and not be forever preoccupied with beginning anew. As in the natural, so in the spiritual: the key to proper nurture is appetite and the will to advance.

The writer thus advised, "Let our movement be toward maturity" (6:1). He was eager to stimulate the spiritual appetite of his readers for the deeper truths about the person and ministry of Jesus. He hoped to leave behind, without mention, the foundational teachings with which they were presumably familiar, i.e., the meaning of repentance, how baptism differs from other ceremonial washings, the ritual import of laying on of hands, the resurrection hope, and the expectation of a final judgment (6:1b-2). But as he reflected further on the foundational matters, his covenantal concern stirred the writer to voice another warning. The warning this time is about the possible irremediable loss of salvation through *apostasy.*

6:4-8, The Awesome Problem of Apostasy. Although there is great danger involved in any sinning, apostasy is most devastatingly dangerous. The tragedy of apostasy is that one deliberately steps aside from the truth, with a full change of mind about it all, and with an offensive attitude toward what one once embraced as worthy of trust. Only someone who has once believed can be guilty of such a sin, which shows the spirit of rejection where faith once motivated them.

Hebrews 6:4-8 (and the similar passage 10:26-31) must be understood as the writer's pastoral concern for his readers. The warning was against "apostasy" (*parapiptō,* "to step aside deliberately"). The message here is that there must be no change of mind about the faith after one has experienced its realities and effects. No faulty or offensive attitude against the faith must be allowed to develop. There should be no loss of hope, no matter how long God takes to meet one's expectations (6:11-12). Devotion and diligence demand each other, and they indelibly mark the true disciple of the Lord.

These verses have been a problem over many centuries of church life. The writer's statement that "it is not possible to restore to repentance those who . . . have fallen away" (6:4a, 6a) has been understood in different ways: either (1) there is no second forgiveness for backsliders; (2) there are limitations to God's forgiveness; (3) this is a hypothetical situation, used to instruct believers to remain serious and growing in their faith; or (4) this is something that can actually happen to someone who has known the benefits of salvation. The wording is rather rigorous and suggests that the former believer has now changed his or her mind about following Jesus, presumably to save themselves from some situation of outward threat. Hebrews 10:26 sheds a bit more light on the matter with its wording about "sinning deliberately," implying an attitude

of contempt for what one once embraced. Hebrews 10:27 classifies the one who is guilty of apostasy as being an "adversary" (*hypenantios,* "willfully set against"), while 6:6 pictorially classifies such a one as crucifying the Son of God on their own, "exposing him to public ridicule." Only a former believer can be apostate, but this kind of sinning is not the same as lapsing or backsliding. The writer plainly warns his readers, eager that each and all avoid that selfishness of soul that can be a prelude to the radical renunciation of Christ.

6:9-12, A Call to Diligence in Faith and Service. Building on the parable he has introduced in vv. 7-8, which reminds that farmers give tender attention to land that responds well to cultivation but burn away the thorns and thistles from land that produces undesirable growth, the writer quickly registers his expectation that his readers want to be like good growth on richly productive land. Unlike undesirable growth, true and faithful believers need not fear judgment but continuing care from God.

6:13-20, The Surety of the Hope Set on Jesus. Waiting is not easy for humans who are eager for the completion or correction of things in their lives. Even waiting on God can be an experience of strain, a testing factor, an unsettling burden—except for those who set themselves to become strong, steadied, and calmed by patience. Patience is expected on the part of believers because the promises of God are always sure. The entire civilized world honors oath making as part of a valid contract. The more serious the contract, the more distinct the means for confirming it—thus God's oath to confirm his promise to us.

The Christian hope is based on the sure promises of God to his people. That hope is for us what an anchor is for a ship—a steadying factor, a tie with the depths. Actually, however, our real tie is not below but above, in the heights, "where Jesus has gone as a forerunner on our behalf" (v. 20). Not only has Jesus gone ahead of us into the presence of God; as our "forerunner" (*prodromos*, "advance agent") he has left trailing evidence about the direction we should follow to join him there.

7:1-28, Melchizedek as Type of the Son's Priesthood

This section of Hebrews details how the two priestly orders differed and why the "order of Melchizedek" was superior to that of Aaron.

Much attention is devoted to the priesthood in this letter because the religious life of the Hebrews was centered in sacrificial worship, and only priests were divinely authorized to offer sacrifices. The religious duties of the faithful demanded the services of a priest above those of any other community leader. The priesthood was a special class within the community; its boundaries were established by divine order and its membership restricted to one family line, that of Aaron (see Exod 29:9b, "and the priesthood shall be theirs by a perpetual statute").

In chap. 7 the writer explains that, despite its high purpose, even the sanctioned priesthood has severe limitations: (1) its service could not grant anyone full access to God (7:11); (2) it operated on the basis of a severely restricting set of laws (7:18); (3) it involved a succession of persons who could not continue in office because each one died and had to be replaced by someone new (7:23); (4) every Aaronic priest was a sinner and thus needed to have his own sins handled before being able to assist others by his work (7:27); and (5) God had announced earlier a plan to supersede the Aaronic priesthood at an appointed time—and that the new priest would be like the legendary Melchizedek, whose priesthood was earlier than Aaron's and not limited by family lineage (7:15-17). Thus the detailed discussion about Melchizedek as superior to Aaron and his line.

7:1-10, Melchizedek Preceded the Levitical Priesthood. Melchizedek was a king-priest, a unique appointee under God, and one whose service role was not passed on to someone else. Jesus is "like Melchizedek" in these respects and "continues a priest for ever." No succession is necessary—or possible.

Succession was inevitable among the Levitical priests, because each one died in time, leaving the work to be handled by yet another apprentice. Each one "received the priestly office" under strict terms of lineage, physical readiness, and anointing, but each one yielded that office to the common demand of death. Each one was great as to task, responsible, trust, and the receiving tithes. But the promised priest who would be greater than all the others has now come, and he continues—one "like Melchizedek" but who is the Son of God.

The discussion turns on two Old Testament passages, Gen 14:18-20 and Ps 110:4, which are the only two references in the Bible to the life and work of Melchizedek. Despite the brevity of material about the man, a considerable tradition regarding Melchizedek had developed in Hebrew thought across the centuries. Psalm 110:4 reflects his importance as a priestly type. Hebrews claims that Ps 110:4 points beyond Melchizedek to Jesus; his interest is not in Melchizedek as such but in what that first priest represents as a type, namely, (1) an earlier order of priesthood than that of Aaron; (2) an eternal ministry—he has "neither date of birth nor date of death . . . and remains a priest perpetually" (7:3); (3) someone not from Aaron's family line; and (4) his ministry is based on direct appointment by God: "You are a priest for ever" (7:21c). The one about whom these things speak most fully, the writer claims, is Jesus.

7:11-19, Imperfections of the Levitical Order. There was a restricting temporality about the Levitical priesthood, and the legal system under which that order operated. Now, in Jesus, that weak and limited system for dealing with sin has been superseded by the life and ministry of one who has an "indestructible life." It was all foretold in that prophetic word in Ps 110:4. The writer quotes that word, which is a divine decree, and announces that the reference is to Jesus—another kind of priest, hailing from another tribe, holding a higher rank, and the guarantor of a new and better covenant. The human need is fully met in such a new priest, by whose life and ministry we now have "a better hope, through which we [do] draw near to God" (7:19).

7:20-28, The Character and Perfection of Jesus as High Priest. Jesus holds a priesthood that will not change, and it holds no limitations in its effects. A new covenant (*diathēkē,* "arrangement," "settlement") is now operative, one that assures believers of a full acceptance by God because Jesus, his priest-Son, is our advocate and ally. As the Holy One, Jesus is pure enough to help us. As the heavenly one, he is powerful enough to help us. But also human, with us, he is related enough to help us.

8:1—10:39, Jesus' Sacrificial Death

After his strategic statement about the superlative character of Jesus as the eternal high priest (7:26-28), the writer summarizes the high priesthood theme in 8:1-6 and then moves ahead to develop his argument about the new covenant now in effect through the sacrificial deed of his death (chaps. 8–10).

8:1-13, The Old Covenant Contrasted with the New. Here begins the central section of Hebrews, in which the writer contrasts the old order and the new. He does so with three aspects in view: (1) covenant benefits; (2) sanctuary matters; and (3) the nature of the sacrifice demanded. The line of thought is quite detailed, demanding familiarity with the way of worship reported in the Old

Testament. An additional difficulty in the writer's argument is his use of imagery: i.e., shadow (*skia,* 8:5) as contrasted with reality (*aleēthinos,* "true," 8:2), copy (*hypodeigma,* 8:5) in relation to pattern (*typos,* 8:5), and "earthly" in contrast to what is "heavenly."

According to his argument, Jesus is now ministering in "the true tabernacle that the Lord himself erected, not man" (8:2); the earthly sanctuary that the workers had to take down and set up again every time the nation moved about during the wilderness years was the "shadow of the heavenly reality" (8:5). The full contrast between the earthly and heavenly finally involves the difference between "the blood of goats and bulls" and "the blood of Christ" (9:12-14), the benefit of the latter being "eternal redemption" for true believers.

The analogies, contrasts, and comparatives in this section of Hebrews are part of the writer's attempt to demonstrate the meaning of the eternal ministry of Jesus as the new "high priest . . . seated at the right hand of the throne of the majestic One in the heavens" (8:1). Given this real, effective, and sufficient ministry for us on his part, there is no further need for what earthly priests do in temples made with hands. The promised period of time in Jeremiah's prophecy about the true binding of the human soul with God's clear will is announced as *present* in Hebrews. True believers can now go beyond the limitations of ritual to experience what is real. The old covenant is now obsolete, dismissed to make room for the new order established by the priestly Son of God.

9:1-28, The Earthly Sanctuary Contrasted with the Heavenly. Chapter 9 opens with a description of the covenantal regulations for worship, and how the floor plan of the tabernacle (*skēnē,* "tent") is symbolic of spiritual matters. The place of worship had stipulated furniture (i.e., lampstand, table, golden altar of incense, ark of the covenant, etc.), all of which was emblematic as well as historical. Aware that some of his readers might need a further description of the full meaning of these pieces of furniture, the writer issued a demurral, stating that he could not treat everything in detail (v. 5b). He was intent to move on to treat the *reason* for mentioning that earthly sanctuary, namely, that it represented something more than itself, that it was all "a parable of the present time" (v. 9).

The earthly tabernacle was but a "copy" of the real or "heavenly," where God dwells; the inner holy place was restricted to all except the high priest, and he could enter it "only once a year" (v. 7). Even the sacrifices he was commissioned to offer on behalf of the sinful people were of limited effect, because those sacrifices could not "bring the worshipers to perfection with respect to conscience" (v. 9).

With the mention of "conscience" (*syneidēsis*, "consciousness," "a relational knowledge"), the writer has called into clear view the one real human need for which the old sacrificial system was inadequate: the offering of sacrificial animals could not secure lasting redemption for the people. The ritual duties of the priests were regularly done, but they were only ritual, always falling short of the reality to which they pointed. God had planned something better, something truly effective in dealing with sin, and that plan would be enacted at "the time for setting things right [by reform]" (v. 10). By his death, burial, resurrection, and ascension, Jesus entered once for all into the most holy place, taking not the blood of goats and bulls but "his own blood, and has secured an eternal redemption for us" (v. 12). God's final plan is to "cleanse our conscience from dead works so that we can rightly serve the living God" (v. 14).

Jesus carries believers beyond the limitations of ritual, and he breaks the limits imposed upon us by sin. For "Christ did not

enter into a holy place made by human hands, which was but a copy of the real, but [actually] into heaven itself, and he now appears in the presence of God on our behalf" (v. 24). There he will remain, ministering as the eternal high priest "after the order of Melchizedek," until the designated time when he is to "appear (*ophthēsetai*, 'will show himself') a second time, not to deal with sin, but for [their] salvation" (v. 28).

10:1-18, Animal Sacrifices Contrasted with Jesus' Sacrificial Death. Although the writer has already dwelt at some length on the theme of sacrifice, and the related sub-theme of the old covenant with its priestly ministry to deal with human sin, he extends his treatment a great deal further in chap. 10. In this section of Hebrews there is much that overlaps with chaps. 7–9, with some parts an almost verbal repetition. But this time the writer comments about sacrifices against a new background, declaring that Jesus, by his death, grants "substance" (*eikon*, "true form," 10:1; or *hyparxis*, "reality," 10:34) for our spiritual life, while the ritualism of the old covenant order restricted every worshiper to only a "shadow" (*skia*) of true reality.

No shadow fully reveals or reflects reality, so no animal sacrifice fully availed to deal adequately with human sin. Thus the constant ritual of offering animals in prescribed sacrifice to God. The pattern had to be repeated, because human failure was constant, and the need to atone for committed sins was perennial. Thus the writer's words: "For it is not possible for the blood of bulls and of goats to take away sins" (v. 4).

The incarnation and sacrificial death of Jesus corrected the human problem and met the unfulfilled need. With a body prepared for him, Jesus fulfilled the righteous will of God as the perfect sacrifice for our sins, so that all who believe "have been [truly] cleansed through the offering of the body of Jesus

Christ once for all" (v. 10). The use here of *ephapax*, meaning "once for all," shows again (as at 7:27 and 9:12) the emphatic finality of Christ's sacrificial death as our Savior. It was a single sacrifice, "offered for all time" (*eis to diēnekes*, "in perpetuity"), and so efficacious that by this "one offering [only] he has brought to perfection forever those who are [now] being sanctified" (v. 14). Believers now live under new covenant terms and experience the anticipated reality: full remission of sins.

10:19-31, Exhortation to Experience Access to God through Jesus. With the full dismissal of sins, the believer has grounds for a confident freedom to draw near to God "with a true heart and in the full assurance that faith gives" (v. 22) and hope (v. 23). The approach to God can be made with "confidence" (*parrēsia*, "openness, freedom"), the implication being that one now has the "right" to approach because privilege has been extended by what Jesus has accomplished in our interest. This notion of "confident freedom" in things pertaining to God has been touched upon earlier by the writer at 3:6 and 4:16; in the one passage that confidence stands related to "our hope," and in the other that confidence is encouraged by the expectation of "mercy and grace" from God when we approach him in prayer. According to 10:19, the grounds for such confident freedom of access to God is "the blood of Jesus."

Given the new freedom of access to God, and assurance of acceptance by him, the writer sounds his fourth major warning to believers: He encourages them never to return to a life of sinning (vv. 26-31). To return to a life of deliberate sinning, he argues, is to spurn the Son of God, profane the blood of the new covenant, and insult the Spirit of grace (v. 29).

10:32-39, Exhortation to Faith and Perseverance. Chapter 10 closes with a call for the readers to reflect on how God had helped them through a difficult period they had suffered as believers and to set themselves in readiness to deal with any further pressures they might have to undergo for their faith. He encouraged the readers to *will* endurance, to remind themselves of the promises of God, and to commit their trust to God's timely care. The promises of God have always been sure, and will remain so even when we humans fail. The crucial word is sounded: "You really need patient endurance, so that after you have done the will of God, you may receive what has been promised" (v. 36). What God promises will result, but it cannot be rushed by our impatience. When you must wait on God, don't lose your faith; *use* your faith!

11:1—12:29, THE MEANING AND NECESSITY OF FAITH

11:1-3, Faith Defined. At many points in his letter the writer has called attention to the need on the part of his readers for "faith" (4:2; 6:1, 12; 10:22). He is now ready to elaborate on what he means by this.

Earlier in this letter, the writer has used the word "faith" with two differing but related accents: first, at 10:22, as an assurance of the heart about a truth of which one is aware—a settled state of mind. Second, at 10:23, 36, and 38, the term refers to a personal response toward God's promises—an action being focused. Now he calls attention to faith as an attitude of commitment by which one persists and endures when all things seem contrary: "Now faith is firm confidence regarding what is being expected, the proof of what is not [yet] seen" (11:1). It is important to keep this working definition in mind when reading 11:6, which states that "without faith it is not possible to be pleasing to God." The writer deals at length in chap. 11 with this understanding of faith, illustrating it with many examples drawn from Old Testament narratives.

Life with God demands on our part a certain openness to truth *and* a personal commitment to experience what truth presents and makes possible. Since truth is God's agency for dealing with us, the writer describes it as the basis of trust. Faith demands "receiving the knowledge of the truth" (v. 26), an expression that was current among first-century believers and reflected their understanding of the relation between knowledge and faith, knowledge and committed trust and action. Faith, then, is a convictional stance toward life and living, a readiness to face life and deal with its circumstances armed with an attitude of trust and the spirit to endure.

11:4-40, Faith Illustrated. This section of Hebrews reports what such a faith did and does for those who dared to live by God's concerns. Intent to supply a catalogue of models for his readers, the writer parades a succession of heroes and heroines of faith. The experience of each person shows how faith worked at some crucial juncture in their life. Each person's story allows us to watch

Reflection: The Conflicts of Life Are Not Final

The beneficial precedents set by faith heroes and heroines have encouraged and sustained Christian believers of subsequent generations during hard times. The patterned accounts in Hebrews 11 meant much to believing African Americans during the slavery era as they endured the condition Miles J. Jones aptly described in one of his homilies as "historic denigration and dehumanization" (Miles J. Jones, "Homiletic Section," in *Proclamation 6: Interpreting the Lessons of the Church Year*, Series B: Lent [Minneapolis: Fortress Press, 1996], 71). Bound together with those enumerated in the biblical account, and bound with Jesus, by the cords of faith and experienced struggle, African American slaves knew what it meant to feel like "strangers and foreigners" (11:13) and to "desire a better country" (11:16), one in which God would be rightly honored and in which they could live in freedom. They "saw" the desired freedom from a distance, and greeted it, their view always ahead to the realization yet to be. Thousands "died in faith without having received" (11:13) that freedom, but their faith had grasped it because they had been grasped by the God they knew as just. Gayraud S. Wilmore has explained: "This was the basic tenet of the seminal black theology of both illiterate slave preachers and the more educated leaders of the northern black churches and community organizations created by members of the churches before 1861: God is a God of truth and justice. He will vindicate the sufferings of Black people."[3] Howard Thurman, grandson of slaves, remembered his revered maternal grandmother talk about the destructive setting and blurred future of her childhood as a slave. Musing about what she confessed to him, and about the faith that sustained her through it all, he commented that what she and other slaves discovered through faith was that "the bitter contradictions of life are not final and that hope was built into the fabric of the struggle. This meant to them that the intensity of the tragic passage in which they were pilgrims could not be separated from the God in whom their ultimate trust was placed." Thurman added, "This was their secret, and it is this they have transmitted to their children."[4]

individuals wrestle for meaning in contexts that seem crushing and unmanageable. All of the listed persons responded to life as pilgrims caught between past and future in a very demanding present, and their trust in God's concern for them gave them perspective, patience, and persistence. All were persons of their time, but stirred by the forward look; they were seekers, impelled by what was yet to be, encouraged by what they anticipated. They all sensed that the meaning of their days would be clarified in time and vindicated by God. True faith is characterized by a forward look and an openness to the pull of the future that God has planned.

The writer laments that lack of time does not allow him to deal fully with the stories of faith, that he has to leave out of his accounting many additional "cases in point" (vv. 32-38). He ends the chapter with a word that the rewards of faith are not always immediate and not always totally complete, God having planned that time at the end of history when total fulfillment will be ours (vv. 39-40).

12:1-11, Faith and Disciplined Living. Chapter 12 begins with a call to structure a personal history that honors the kind of faith illustrated by those who form the great "cloud of witnesses" that surround the present believers. The picture in 12:1-2 is that of an athletic amphitheater. The spectators seated in the gallery are the many triumphant victors mentioned in chap. 11, and those now feeling the strain and stress of living for God are called to be winners like the others: "Run with perseverance the course set before us" (v. 1). Jesus is cited as the supreme proof of what faith enables one to do, but he is also the supreme person whose work nourishes faith in those who look fully to him. Thus that all-important instruction to keep "looking to Jesus." The believer is backed by Jesus—and beckoned forward by him. Victory against sin happens with his help. Looking to him strengthens one

to remain loyal to him. "Consider him . . . so that you may not become weary and faint in your souls" (12:3).

This instruction was urgent and insistent because of the situation of stress the readers were suffering. According to v. 4, however, none of the persons in the group being addressed had yet "resisted to the point of [shedding] their blood"; none of them had been put to death for their faith. Nevertheless, the struggle was acute and demanding, and only a stalwart faith could help them to endure with loyalty. The writer suggested that the struggle be viewed as a means of "discipline" (*paideia*, "instructive training for development"), by which God would help them "share his holiness" (v. 10) (thus the quotation from Prov 3:11-12 in Heb 12:5-6). What is painful can be made purposeful, instructive, positive in its issue.

12:12-17, Exhortation to Steadfastness in Faith. Grace can be experienced, but it can also be forfeited if evil is allowed its way in the heart. The writer reminds us that an attitude of openness to present opportunity is required if divine favor is to accomplish its purpose in the believer. He illustrates how one can "fail to obtain the grace of God" by citing the shortsighted and selfish attitude of Esau, "who traded away his birthright for a single meal" (v. 16).

12:18-29, The Privileged Position of the Believer. The believer holds a privileged position that must not be lost by impatience, immorality, bitter attitudes, or lack of trust in God. Believers need to remember and regard where they stand because of the new covenant, and live with full openness and loyalty to what it all means. Given all that belongs to our salvation, and with promise of still more to come, the believer's attitude must be one of conscious thanks and a steady reverence, offering to God acceptable worship, "with reverent devotion and awe" (v. 28).

13:1-25, Concluding Remarks

The writer closes with some pertinent exhortations and a final personal word of greeting to his readers. The exhortations are all very brief, so brief indeed that it might appear the writer was rushing to complete what had by now become lengthy. Some commentators view this section as filled with disconnected injunctions only loosely related to earlier parts of the epistle, while others view it as a later addition.

Chapter 13, however, seems integral to the writing in at least four ways:

1. The injunctions listed in vv. 1-17 do have some background in what has been set forth thematically in chaps. 1–12.
2. The personal request for prayer (vv. 18-19) restates the writer's confidence in his readers and promises to visit with them again as soon as possible.
3. The formal benediction in vv. 20-21 is a final means for encouraging his readers.
4. The additional greetings from mutual friends would also provide some encouragement for them. The information shared about Timothy's release (from prison?) would also be a reason for hope and praise by that trouble-weary community of believers.

13:1-6, Christian Relationships. The injunctions about "brotherly affection" and "hospitality" aim to strengthen the community bond that belongs to the church. Their life together must be that of family love, with no selfish individualism. Those who are in trouble, suffering at the hands of people in power, must not be forsaken but sustained.

The exhortation to "remember those who are in prison" is a call to identify with them by praying for them, visiting when access is permitted, and showing solidarity with them through supportive deed—even helping with costs for their defense. The show of solidarity softens the ordeal of confinement.

The word about fidelity in marriage warns against immorality and deeds that undermine a stable family order, while the warning against "love of money" is strategic as a value word about keeping priorities clearly focused on the life of faith. The promise about the unfailing companionship of the Lord with his people relates to any felt threat of loneliness as sufferers, on the one hand, and felt "lostness" as pilgrims, on the other.

13:7-17, Christian Duties. There is an emphatic word about honor due to godly leaders (vv. 7, 17), whose work is essential for congregational health, continuance, and mission. Jesus Christ remains all he was sent to be, and does all that his priestly ministry was planned to accomplish. No teachings must be entertained or regarded that differ from what the godly leaders have shared about Jesus and his role. Although believers must be open to learn truths of the faith (5:11-14), they must take care to assess all new teaching by truth already known, so as not to be "led away" (*parapheresthē*, "carried away"). Sharing must continue, especially sharing in the sufferings of Jesus, who was treated as an "outsider" (13:12-13). The acknowledgment of his name must not cease, whatever the suffering attached to such witness and loyalty as believers.

13:18-25, Personal Expressions. A request for prayer from his readers (vv. 18-19) is soon balanced by a prayer on the writer's part for them (vv. 20-21). Such a prayer-wish was a familiar benediction in Christian worship, as other New Testament epistles abundantly show.

With his message now shared, and its long argument concluded, the writer makes a personal appeal that his "word of exhortation" be accepted in the spirit of love out of which it has been sent (v. 22). The hope is voiced that Timothy, their mutual friend, recently released from confinement, will be able to come along when the writer makes his anticipated visit with his readers. Meanwhile, his hearty greeting must suffice (v. 24), allied by greetings from other believers known and loved by them. In his final statement, a benediction, "May God's favor remain with all of you" (v. 25), the writer assures his readers that God's favor is their common provision and their mutual bond.

A Steadying Word about Jesus

Thomas Kilgore Jr., black pulpit statesman, periodically shared with the congregations he served a reminding poetic musing about Jesus Christ as their shepherd. Under the rubric "Our Need," it appeared in the Sunday bulletin as a personal expression from the pastor to his members.

> In a world of
> Alienation
> Doubt
> Lostness
> Materialism
> And Sin,
> We need a Shepherd.
> God has given us One
> In Jesus Christ, Our Lord.

—Thomas Kilgore Jr. with Jini Kilgore Ross, *God's Glory, Humanity's Praise: Materials for Worship and Meditation* (Silver Springs, Md.: Beckham, 1996), 183.

Notes

1. The NRSV translation is used, unless otherwise specified.
2. Henry H. Mitchell, *Black Belief* (New York: Harper & Row, 1975), 130.
3. Gayraud S. Wilmore, *Pragmatic Spirituality: The Christian Faith through an Afrocentric Lens* (New York: New York University Press, 2004), 161.
4. Howard Thurman, *Negro Spiritual Interprets Life and Death* (New York: Harper & Row, 1970), 4.

For Further Reading

Attridge, Harold W. *The Epistle to the Hebrews.* Hermeneia. Philadelphia: Fortress Press, 1989.

Bruce, Frederick F. *The Epistle to the Hebrews: The English Text with Introduction, Exposition and Notes.* Grand Rapids, Mich.: Eerdmans, 1964.

Craddock, Fred B. "The Letter to the Hebrews: Introduction, Commentary and Reflections." In *NIB* 12.

Jewett, Robert. *Letter to Pilgrims: A Commentary on the Epistle to the Hebrews.* New York: Pilgrim, 1981.

Johnson, William G. *Hebrews.* Atlanta: John Knox, 1980.

Lane, William L. *Hebrews 1–8, Hebrews 9–13.* Dallas: Word, 1991.

Turner, George Allen. *The New and Living Way.* Minneapolis: Bethany Fellowship, 1975.

Wilson, R. McL. *Hebrews.* Grand Rapids, Mich.: Eerdmans, 1987.

JAMES

Gay L. Byron

INTRODUCTION

James is an eclectic letter filled with moral advice, piercing wisdom, practical instruction, and socioeconomic commentary. Addressed to those scattered in the diaspora (see the comments on 1:1), this letter has been considered an "epistle of straw" and deemed insignificant and even controversial when compared to the teachings about faith in the letters of Paul. Paul emphasizes faith as an unmerited gift from God (Gal 2:16; Rom 3:28); James, on the other hand, says, "faith without works is dead" (2:17, 26). Both perspectives hold merit, but the tendency to focus on the relevance of James only in contrast to the teachings of Paul overshadows the theological treasure and unique storehouse of material contained in this letter.

James was most likely written around the end of the first century or early in the second century by a pseudonymous author who lived in one of the cities of the dispersion (diaspora). Although, on the assumption that the author was James "the brother of the Lord" (Gal 1:19) who became the leader of the church in Jerusalem (Acts 15:13; 21:18), there is now a growing body of scholarly literature to support an earlier date (ca. 61 C.E.). The "James" of this letter does not identify his familial background, his hometown, or his connection to Jesus and the church in Jerusalem. In fact, Jesus is mentioned only twice in this letter, first in the opening greeting (1:1a), and then in a rhetorical sense to discuss acts of favoritism (2:1).[1] The author does, however, make good use of Greco-Roman literary conventions,[2] offer a broad awareness of some of the challenges facing the early Christians as they expanded throughout the empire, and focus more on the "law of love" than on the Mosaic law. Thus, a later date for the letter and a place of origin beyond Jerusalem are more probable.

Because of its fragmented literary character and the multiplicity of genres utilized by the author, it is difficult to isolate one coherent theme in the letter.[3] It includes wisdom literature (1:5-8; 3:13-18), prophetic oracle (5:1-6), judgment speech (1:19-21, 26-27; 3:13-16; 4:11-12; 5:12), diatribe (2:14-17; 4:1-12),[4] apocalyptic discourse (5:7-11),

---

Who Is James?

In the New Testament there are five persons identified as "James": the son of Zebedee (Mark 1:19; 3:17; Acts 12:2), the father of Jude (Luke 6:16; Acts 1:13), the son of Alphaeus (Mark. 3:18ff.), the younger (Mark 15:40), and the brother of Jesus (Mark 6:3ff.; 1 Cor 15:7; Gal 1:19; 2:9, 12; Acts 12:17; 15:13; 21:18; Jude 1). There is no consensus among contemporary scholars regarding the author and provenance of this letter. For more information about James, the brother of Jesus, see Hershel Shanks and Ben Witherington III, *The Brother of Jesus: The Dramatic Story and Meaning of the First Archaeological Link to Jesus and His Family* (San Francisco: Harper, 2003), and Bruce Chilton and Jacob Neusner, eds., *The Brother of Jesus: James the Just and His Mission* (Louisville: Westminster John Knox, 2001).

---

warnings (4:13—5:6), and a variety of ethical teachings. All of this material is used to communicate a number of seemingly disparate topics that call attention to the circular or general nature of the letter.[5] Although it is possible the author was addressing a particular community of believers, it is more likely that James was offering general exhortations and guidelines that could be applied to any of the Jewish Christian communities dispersed throughout the Mediterranean. Many of the disparate themes—clarifying the meaning of faith, redefining relationships, cultivating spiritual discipline, recognizing and addressing socioeconomic disparities between the rich and the poor, submitting to God, guarding the tongue, and living with wisdom, humility, and unceasing prayer—are introduced in the first chapter and discussed throughout the entire letter, although not in a systematic manner. James is concerned with providing a collection of ethical teachings and practical wisdom for living with engaged faithfulness in the midst of uncertain times. In this letter, critical teachings about social protest, economic awareness, and spiritual discipline are combined with encouraging pastoral instruction to yield a paradoxical blend of simple yet challenging prescriptions for living the Christian life.

JAMES 1: WORDS OF WISDOM DURING TROUBLED TIMES

1:1, Greetings to Those in the Diaspora

James opens this letter with greetings to the twelve tribes in the diaspora.[6] The Greek term *diaspora* was used in antiquity to describe persons or groups of people who were dislocated from their places of origin. Generally, these persons were scattered throughout the Mediterranean and forced to redefine their identities and reestablish their homes. The term is specifically used in the New Testament to refer to Christians as wandering people of God and to Jewish Christian communities outside of Palestine (cf. 1 Pet 1:1).[7] The use of the term frames the importance of the social context of this letter. By recalling the Jewish experience of exile, the author emphasizes the precarious state of affairs for those who are scattered among the nations. But the negative connotations of *diaspora* in the ancient Jewish context should not preclude other interpretations of the term. The word is also connected to the omnipotence and mercy of God.[8] In Ps 147:2-3, for example, God is praised as the one who rebuilds Jerusalem, heals the wounded, and gathers the dispersed.[9]

The word *diaspora* is also used to describe the millions of Africans who are scattered and dispersed throughout various parts of North and South America, the Caribbean, and other areas of the world as a result of the trans-Atlantic slave trade.[10] This dispersion brought with it a number of problems and hardships for those in the African diaspora, especially among African Americans, the effects of which are still being felt today.[11] But many are now beginning to understand that those in the diaspora need not focus only on pain, hardship, and despair. The African diaspora is a rich collection of many persons who are an integral part of this rapidly changing world.[12] As Psalm 147 indicates, those in the diaspora are sometimes best positioned to experience the mercy and power of God.

1:2-27, General Advice and Exhortations for Living through Difficult Times

James introduces a number of different themes in vv. 2-27 that are best understood as general advice and exhortations for those living through difficult times. There are at least six different themes introduced in this chapter. The first deals with how to understand trials and tribulations as an opportunity to grow in faith; that is, to become mature (*teleios*) and complete (*holoklēros*), not lacking anything

(1:2-4; cf. 2:14-26). Because this theme could be viewed as the key for understanding the entire letter, a brief explanation of it is in order before listing the other themes.

James, who considers himself a slave (*doulos*) of God and of the Lord Jesus Christ, is challenging his brothers and sisters (*adelphoi mou*) to face their trials (*peirasmoi*) with a sense of joy. He claims that the testing of one's faith, which results from trials, produces spiritual discipline (*hypomonē*). *Hypomonē*, generally translated as patience or endurance, has been interpreted quite convincingly as "militant patience" or "nonviolent resistance."[13] But James is seeking something more foundational than patience or nonviolence, even if it is in a militant or resistant mode. James is calling for spiritual discipline that will provide strength, support, and a connection to God in the face of various hardships.

The African American mystic, theologian, and pastor Howard Thurman, the grandson of a slave, knew about such spiritual discipline (*hypomonē*). In his book *Disciplines of the Spirit*, Thurman discusses the ways in which commitment, wisdom, suffering, prayer, and reconciliation can be cultivated as spiritual resources for overcoming trials and for developing strategies for circumventing the ideological and material traps associated with racism in American society.[14] In his explanation about patience, Thurman says, "To learn how to wait is to discover one of the precious ingredients in the spiritual unfolding of life, the foundation for the human attribute of patience."[15] But Thurman goes on to say patience is more than mere passive endurance: "One has to take a hard and searching look at the environment, particularly the context in which one is functioning" and respond accordingly.[16] Thurman suggests that "tutoring the human spirit" (*hypomonē*) as a form of self-mastery and social protest leads to an "inward journey" toward freedom:

During the tumultuous years of social protest during the sixties, instead of rallying in the streets, Thurman set forth directives for self-mastery that would enable Civil Rights leaders such as Martin Luther King Jr. and Whitney Young to focus their efforts on developing resources and strategies for an inward journey toward freedom. This "inward journey" would enable them to stand firm in their faith in God who is able to tear down demonic strongholds and bring about change. Thurman wanted his students and protégés to gain a type of "strange freedom" that would empower them to meet the spiritual and political challenges of their time.[17]

Thurman is not alone in his emphasis on the contemplative aspects of the faith. Many African Americans cultivated contemplative practices and spiritual disciplines that enabled them to survive and negotiate the ambivalent and perilous forces of a racist society. Ethicist Barbara A. Holmes surveys this tradition in her book *Joy Unspeakable: Contemplative Practices of the Black Church*.[18] Highlighting the importance of "communal" contemplative practices, Holmes examines how contemplation among African American religious and political leaders inevitably leads to activism and praxis: "Always the quest for justice draws one deeply into the heart of God. In this sacred interiority contemplation becomes the language of prayer and the impetus for prophetic proclamation and action."[19]

The second theme, which James introduces in common wisdom style, is consistent and unswerving devotion to God. In this regard, double-mindedness (*dipsychos*) is to be avoided at all costs if one is to receive blessings from God (1:5-8; cf. 2:4; 4:8).[20] The third theme isolates the importance of recognizing and addressing socioeconomic disparities

between the rich and the poor (1:9-11). The author takes up this theme in several other sections (2:5-7; 4:13-17; 5:1-6); it serves as one of the most compelling aspects of the letter because of the ways in which James calls for redefining relationships. After a brief transitional blessing in v. 12 for those who endure temptation, nature imagery is used to describe two contrasting sequences: one leading to sin (vv. 13-16) and one leading to God (vv. 17-18). This material isolates the fourth theme, submitting to God, which is discussed in more detail in 4:1-12. The fifth theme focuses on guarding the tongue (1:19-27): "Let everyone be quick to listen, slow to speak, slow to anger; for your anger does not produce God's righteousness" (vv. 19-20). This section dealing with speech ethics is not limited to speech in a narrow sense, but is a precursor to 3:1-12, which describes the responsibilities and challenges of teachers (*didaskaloi*), and to 3:13-18, which describes the meaning of true or pure religion (*thrēskeia kathara*). Here James teaches the importance of being immersed in the social, economic, and political realities of the larger world, which invariably leads to being doers, and not just hearers, of the word (vv. 22-25). The final theme of prayer is not specifically mentioned in chap. 1 but is alluded to in the section dealing with double-mindedness (1:5-8). James says in 1:5: "If any of you is lacking in wisdom, *ask God*, who gives to all generously and ungrudgingly, and it will be given to you." This theme of prayer is discussed more fully in 5:12-18.

JAMES 2: WHAT IS THE TRUE MEANING OF FAITH?

2:1-13, Redefining Relationships and Economic Responsibilities

The first part of chap. 2 isolates an incident of favoritism or discrimination against a poor person (*ptōchos*).[21] Such judgments of the poor are condemned in the Old Testament (Lev 19:15; Ps 82:2), and James is likewise concerned with people making distinctions (*diakrinō*) among themselves (2:4). It is difficult to determine whether James is referring to a specific incident or whether he is constructing this scene for its rhetorical effect.[22] The latter is more likely the case, since the reader is invited to assess the ways in which such action either edifies or destroys the community as a whole. What is clear, however, is the way in which this incident is being used by James to challenge his brothers and sisters (*adelphoi mou*) to examine their perceptions and thoughts about the poor and to establish relationships that are free from biased or evil judgments (2:4).

The climax of this pericope comes in v. 5 with the use of the imperative "listen" (*akousate*), directed now to his beloved (*agapētoi*) sisters and brothers. James then raises the question, "Has not God chosen the poor in the world to be rich in faith and to be heirs of the kingdom that he has promised to those who love him?" This discussion about the poor echoes back to 1:9-11 and also to the Beatitudes of Jesus (Luke 6:20; Matt 5:3), which assert the exalted state of the poor.

In this passage, James highlights the complex cultural, social, and economic factors that influenced this writing. Although on the surface it sounds as if the author is drawing attention to the distinctions between "the rich" (*hoi plousioi*) and "the poor" (*hoi ptōchoi*), such simple categories do not reflect adequately the larger ethical and theological implications of this text or the subtle ways in which status and class are interlaced with other marks of distinction, such as ethnicity, gender, age, ability, etc. Also, as Elsa Tamez notes, the poor could be either the *ptōchoi*, the beggars who totally lacked the means of subsistence and lived from alms, or the *penētoi*, those who at least had a job but owned no property.[23] Thus, this

passage and other related texts, such as 2:14-17; 4:13-17; and 5:1-6 indicate the diverse socioeconomic composition of the early Christian communities.

This section of James also calls to mind the diverse socioeconomic composition of African American churches and the acts of partiality that take place in these churches. Contrary to what is usually broadcast through the media, all African Americans are not poor and on welfare. Moreover, African Americans do not merely accumulate wealth through careers in sports and entertainment. Indeed, there is a long history of African Americans who have been considered a part of the "upper class" in this country, a class that distinguishes itself based on family lineage, academic ties, social connections, accumulated wealth, and other "hidden" socioeconomic factors.[24] In *Our Kind of People*, Lawrence Otis Graham discusses some of the cultural and social mores of the black elite. This book shatters the stereotype of the working-class or impoverished black as the only accurate and complete expression of the African American experience. The persons and experiences documented in this book confirm that class is a major issue within black communities, and that persons from the "upper class" or "middle class" raise a number of serious challenges for leaders of the black church.

In *Preaching to the Black Middle Class*, Marvin A. McMickle describes and analyzes many of the unique dynamics and challenges associated with ministry to the black middle class.[25] He documents the variety of social classes that exist within black communities and provides many vivid examples of the ways in which the more affluent or comfortable (*hoi plousioi*) in black middle-class congregations interact or fail to interact with the poor (*penētoi*) or disenfranchised (*ptōchoi*) in their midst. The *plousioi* within African American communities often acknowledge their

465

responsibility to support or reach out to the *penētoi* and *ptōchoi*,[26] but usually this is done through charitable "politically correct" contributions to organizations that assist the "poor" instead of through genuine relationship-building with those of different classes. The letter of James may offer some insights into how such relationship-building might take place—without a trace of partiality or hypocrisy (3:17).

2:14-26, Clarifying the Meaning of Faith

The second half of chap. 2 builds on the first, in that redefining relationships and addressing economic disparities are necessary prerequisites for clarifying the meaning of faith (cf. 1:22-25). In v. 14 the author raises two probing questions: "What good is it if you say you have faith but do not have works? Can faith save you?" Once again, these questions are addressed to his brothers and sisters (*adelphoi mou*) and offer a type of deliberative rhetoric that is intended to encourage the hearer of these words to deeper reflection and action. James emphasizes his point by raising an example of a brother (*adelphos*) or sister (*adelphē*) who is naked and hungry (2:15). Just as in the preceding section with the isolation of the poor person, James is now going

even further to recognize that the poor also include women, even the widows and orphans mentioned in 1:27.[27] How is one to treat such a person? Clearly for James, simply providing encouraging words (e.g., "Go in peace, keep warm, and find some food") is not enough (2:16)! One must also fulfill the bodily needs of the brother or sister through specific actions (*erga*). Thus James unapologetically declares: faith—if it has no works (*erga*)—is dead (2:17).

Scholars have long debated the meaning of James's teachings about faith and works as compared to the teachings of Paul. In Rom 3:28 Paul states: "we hold that a person is justified by faith apart from works prescribed by the law." James, on the other hand, asserts "a person is justified by works and not by faith alone" (2:24). James goes on to provide two examples to support his argument: Abraham, the Jewish patriarch (vv. 21-24; cf. Gen 22:1-19) and Rahab, the Gentile prostitute (v. 25; cf. Josh 2:1-21).[28] It is no accident that this chapter on faith follows the preceding material dealing with economic disparities and skewed relationships. For James, one can only understand the meaning of faith in the context of a community of individuals who are seeking to

Faith and Works

James is often compared to the apostle Paul, who taught that faith is based on the righteousness of God—that one is justified by faith through grace, a salvific gift from God. For Paul, works (*erga*) do not provide justification from God (Rom 3:28; Gal 2:16). But for James "works" are necessary, indeed foundational, for anyone claiming to have faith in God. Thus, James concludes in 2:24: "a person is justified by works (*erga*) and not by faith alone." Both Paul and James appeal to the story of Abraham, who offered his son, Isaac, on the altar (Gen 22:1-19), to explain their understanding of faith. Paul demonstrates the faith of Abraham from his acceptance of God's promise (Gen 15:5-6; Rom 4; Gal 3:6-18); James, on the other hand, demonstrates the faith of Abraham by emphasizing the concrete action (*erga*) that was necessary in order for Abraham's faith to become complete (*holoklēroi*).

become mature and complete in their faith. Thus, the examples of Abraham and Rahab indicate that faith can be perfected or made mature (*teleios*) by works (*erga*).

JAMES 3: RESPONSIBLE LEADERSHIP AND "PURE" RELIGION

3:1-12, Instructions for Teachers and Guarding the Tongue

Chapter 3 opens with a startling warning to those who teach: "Not many of you should become teachers (*didaskaloi*), my brothers and sisters, for you know that we who teach will be judged with greater strictness. For all of us make many mistakes" (3:1-2a). The ethics of speech is a recurring theme in this letter (1:19-27; 4:11-12), but in chap. 3 a lengthy discourse about guarding the tongue is specifically connected to the vocation of teaching. James apparently understands himself as a *didaskalos* and so makes an exaggerated effort to convince his peers that great *power* and *responsibility* are connected to the role of teaching (cf. Eph 4:11-13; 2 Tim 4:3). In essence, those who teach (or, to use the metaphor in this text, those who rely on the tongue) ought to think carefully about how they carry out their function, particularly staying mindful of their potential to either bless the Lord or curse those who are made in the likeness of God (3:9).

This material calls to mind the challenges that church leaders and theological educators face as they attempt to teach different aspects of the Christian faith. Michael Battle, an Anglican priest and professor of spirituality and black church studies, reflecting on the task of theological educators, argues that "ceaseless prayer, practiced within a community undergirded by covenants, ought to be recovered as part of the sensibility of the theological teacher."[29] Battle further claims that "the vocation of a divinity school professor is

not only to articulate how to know God in our midst, it is also to know when to 'shut up' in the midst of God's presence. The teacher's vocation is to know how *and how not* to know God through text and experience."[30]

Applying these insights to James leads to a much more theologically informed reading of this material about the tongue. While it may appear that James is consumed with the "evil" power of the tongue in this section by saying "no one can tame the tongue—a restless evil full of deadly poison" (3:8; cf. Prov 15:4; 18:21), it is more likely that this diatribe about the tongue is being used as a way of encouraging the *didaskaloi* to practice more self-control and contemplation in the face of the myriad challenges that beset their respective communities. Moreover, the *didaskaloi* are instructed to exercise their responsibilities in light of the presence and power of God. In this way, the *didaskaloi* would be in a much better position to communicate the meaning of true religion, which is discussed in the second part of chap. 3.

3:13-18, Wisdom and True Religion

In this section James appeals to the wisdom tradition to discuss what constitutes true religion. Verses 14-18 utilize the common ancient form of virtue and vice lists (cf. Gal 5:19-23). Here, the list of virtues and vices is used to distinguish the wisdom from below, which is earthly, unspiritual, and devilish (vv. 15-16), from the wisdom from above, which is "pure, peaceable, gentle, willing to yield, full of mercy, and good fruits, without a trace of partiality or hypocrisy" (v. 17). James was most concerned with challenging his followers to what he considered true or "pure" religion (*thrēskeia kathara*): "to care for orphans and widows in their distress, and to keep oneself unstained by the world" (1:27). He also indicates his distaste for partiality or hypocrisy, which invariably keeps people from responding to the needs of those in distress. James is seeking to hold his audience accountable to doing deeds that are based on wisdom and humility.

Similar to James, many African American leaders have also sought to hold their white counterparts accountable by appealing to true or "pure" religion. The nineteenth-century abolitionist Frederick Douglass, for example, used the epistle of James in his abolitionist speeches to debunk the arguments of slave-holding Christianity.[31] Douglass appealed to a tradition of reading the Bible among African Americans that emphasized the inclusive nature of God, who is no respecter of persons (Acts 10:34). Likewise, nineteenth-century political writer Maria W. Stewart also appealed to biblical writings to support her opposition to racial suffering and evil. She, like the author of James, emphasized the connection between wisdom and pure religion: "Have you one desire to become truly great? O then become truly pious and God will endow you with wisdom and knowledge from on high. . . . Religion is pure; it is ever new; it is beautiful; it is all that is worth living for; it is worth dying for."[32] For Stewart, pure religion focused on the rights of the "widow, the fatherless, the poor and the helpless."[33]

James 4: Seek First the Kingdom of God

4:1-12, Resisting Evil and Submitting to God

The theology of James is best described in the first part of chap. 4. In this section the author uses the rhetorical technique of diatribe to discuss the importance of choosing God and rejecting the world (4:4). This section hearkens back to one of the guiding themes of the letter first introduced in 1:8: avoiding double-mindedness (dipsychos). But now James indicates that submission and devotion to God require more than good thoughts and blind acceptance of God's grace. One must be engaged in ongoing spiritual warfare, which includes resisting the devil, purifying your hearts, lamenting, mourning, weeping, and humbling yourselves before God (4:7-10). This internal struggle "to master the cravings that are at war within you" is an important way to overcome any conflicts and disputes that arise in the community.

Instead of appealing to his brothers and sisters (adelphoi) by telling them to "listen," as he does in other parts of the letter (2:5; 5:4), in this chapter James indicates the seriousness of submitting and committing to God by using the derogatory label "adulteresses" (moichalides) to call out those who claim "friendship with the world" (4:4).[34] This term is quite common in the Bible (cf. Isa 54:5; Jer 3:20; Ezek 16; 23; Matt 12:34; 16:4; Mark 8:38; Luke 18:11; 1 Cor 6:9). It is a way of saying you are falling to your lowest point; now get your act together!

By the end of this section, at vv. 11-12, the author shifts back to his language of community building by appealing to the adelphoi not to judge or speak against one another (cf. Matt 7:1). This is reminiscent of the material in James 2 dealing with partiality against a poor person; once again the author emphasizes how significant it is to love one's neighbor and to do everything possible to avoid conflicts and disputes (1:19-21).

4:13-17, A Wake-Up Call to the Merchants

The material in 4:13-17 should be understood in close connection with the material in 5:1-6, both of which open with the literary marker "come now" (age nun). This common ancient literary technique shifts the subject matter to a series of warnings addressed directly to the business merchants (emporeusometha kai kerdēsomen) and the rich (hoi plousioi). In the first section, the merchants are compared to a mist that appears for a little while and then vanishes. This is similar to the description of the rich in 1:11, who in the midst of a busy life will wither away. The theme of 4:1-12, focusing on God, is still evident in this section. Also, James reiterates his earlier theme of understanding faith as concrete action (*erga*) on behalf of the poor (2:14-26) in the same type of deliberative rhetorical style most prominent in chap. 2. James is offering a wake-up call to those who are generally consumed with their own financial gain. He wants this influential group of people to renounce their boasting and arrogance and to seek the Lord's will before making decisions.

JAMES 5: FINAL WORDS OF WARNING, CHALLENGE, AND HOPE

5:1-6, A Warning to the Rich

As indicated above, chap. 5 opens with a direct warning to "the rich" (*hoi plousioi*). This section is closely related to the material in 2:1-13, which highlights the complex nature of economic distinctions. In v. 4 the author uses the imperative "behold" to summon the attention of this group, in the same way that "listen"[35] is used to emphasize how God has chosen the poor in the world to be rich in faith (cf. 2:5).[36] But to merely focus on the distinctions between "the rich" and "the poor" would preclude any real engagement of the systems and institutions that give rise to "the privileged" and "the under-privileged" and perpetuate the injustices (based on gender, race, and class) that exist between "the dominant" and "the oppressed." Verse 4 points to the deeper systemic crisis at stake for James: "The wages of the laborers who mowed your fields, which you kept back by fraud, cry out, and the cries of the harvesters have reached the ears of the Lord of hosts." This systemic crisis of inequitable wages is also a point of contention for many African Americans and other ethnic minorities who still live in impoverished conditions in both urban and rural settings.[37] This passage is a warning and a summons to all who participate in the personal and systemic economic crisis that is plaguing the world today.

5:7-11, Waiting for the Lord

In this section, James focuses on the eschatological hope that informed the early Christians through an exhortation to "be patient (*makrothymeō*) until the coming (*parousia*) of the Lord" (5:7). This pragmatic teaching is not as dramatic as other eschatological accounts in the New Testament (cf. Mark 13:24-27; Matt 24:29-31; Luke 21:25-38; 1 Thess 4:13—5:11), but it still indicates the importance of living right until the return of the Lord (5:9). In contrast to the use of the verb *makrothymeō* in vv. 7-8, which relates to staying alert or watchful as one waits for the *parousia*; in v. 11 James also returns to his appeal to spiritual discipline (*hypomonē*), which he introduced at the beginning of the letter (1:3-4). It is clear that patience (*makrothymia*) alone is not enough in the midst of suffering and hardship. Those who are considered blessed exemplify *hypomonē*, the same virtue that leads to a mature and complete faith. Thus it is not the mere patience or endurance of Job that is significant for James; rather, Job's *hypomonē* is used as an example of how to live faithfully through suffering with much resolve and commitment to persevere and to provide a witness to the world of God's compassion and mercy.

James is often used as support for the motif of redemptive suffering that is prevalent among African American Christians. In this regard, suffering is considered a moral and spiritual virtue, and the redemptive suffering of Jesus is used as the exemplary model of faith and obedience.[38] But this motif has often wrought serious consequences for African Americans who have understood the words of James (and the teachings of Jesus) as a mandate to tolerate evil in its various manifestations of injustice and oppression. There is, however, another way to view this theme. First, suffering is a universal condition for all of humanity.[39] This condition, therefore, is best addressed when *all* those who suffer—not just African Americans—acknowledge their trials and tribulations by exercising *hypomonē* and responding to suffering and injustice with acts of compassion and kindness. As indicated earlier, the teachings of Howard Thurman offer an insightful challenge for dealing with suffering and evil in the world: "In the throes of suffering and evil, we are called to cultivate spiritually self-disciplined habits and practices, which enable us to courageously exercise moral and practical choices as we make our way through the world."[40] In this regard, James offers a beacon of hope for all who hunger and thirst for righteousness.

5:12-18, A Praying Community

The final major section of the letter is indicated by "above all else" (*pro pantōn de*). This is a common marker for signaling the closing in ancient letters (cf. Plato, *Republic* 366b; Josephus, *Jewish Antiquities* 16.187). The author once again picks up on the judgment speech previously discussed at 1:19-21, 26-27; 3:13-16; 4:11-12. This time the speech is against swearing or making an oath; one is encouraged to "let your 'Yes' mean yes and your 'No' mean no" (v. 12).

After this declaration, James raises a series of questions, which build up to what may be considered the climax of the letter: the importance of prayer (*proseucheō*) for the faithful of God. Here, the author is not solely concerned with individual prayer (v. 13); rather the potential and power of a praying community are emphasized through the call of "the elders of the church" (*tous presbyterous tēs ekklēsias*) and the summons to "confess your sins to one another and pray for one another" (vv. 14-16).

At this point in the letter, James has shifted from a specific example in the assembly (*synagōgē*, cf. 2:2) to a broader vision of the church (*ekklēsia*).

The Greek term used for prayer in v. 16, *euchē*, can also be translated as oath. This is the sense in which it is used in several places in the LXX (e.g., Gen 28:20; 31:13; Num 6:2; Deut 12:6; Ps 49:14; see also Acts 18:18; 21:23). But, given what has already been said about oaths in v. 12, it is clear that the author is now dealing with prayer in this section, using Elijah (cf. 1 Kgs 17:1; 18:42-45) to exemplify the importance of the prayer of faith (*hē euchē tēs pisteōs*). James is not talking about prayer in an abstract sense; rather, he exhorts the individual and the community to offer prayers of faith that can save the sick and redeem the sinner.

Prayer is a foundational aspect of the faith of African Americans. It is a link to the power of God—a type of "conversation" with God that exceeds anything of human origin (1:5).[41] Prayer is the catalyst for healing, the vehicle through which doors are opened, and the assurance for a brighter tomorrow. Prayer changes things! Maria W. Stewart, the nineteenth-century political writer and public orator, knew of the power of prayer. One of her prayers is quite reminiscent of the individual and communal aspects of prayer found in Jas 5:13-18. For Stewart, prayer brought the weak or sick individual (*asthenēs*) closer to God for his or her own personal healing. But the conversation with God did not stop there. The individual also had a responsibility to seek healing and wholeness for others who were "poor and needy" or separated from God in any way:

> O Lord God, as the heavens are high above the earth, so are thy ways above our ways, and thy thoughts above our thoughts. For wise and holy purposes

best known to thyself, thou hast seen fit to deprive me of all earthly relatives; but when my father and mother forsook me, then thou did take me up. I desire to thank thee, that I am this day a living witness to testify that thou art a God, that will ever vindicate the cause of the poor and needy. . . . O, continue thy loving kindness even unto the end; and when health and strength begin to decay, and I, as it were, draw nigh unto the grave, O then afford me thy heart-cheering presence, and enable me to rely entirely upon thee. Never leave me nor forsake me, but have mercy upon me for thy great name's sake. *And not for myself alone do I ask these blessings*, but for all the poor and needy, all widows and fatherless children, and for the stranger in distress; and may they call upon thee in such manner as to be convinced that thou art a prayer-hearing and prayer-answering God; and thine shall be the praise, forever, Amen.[42]

5:19-20, Final Challenge: Reclaiming the "Wanderers"

The final two verses return in a symbolic manner to the opening greeting, which referred to those in the diaspora (1:1). When these verses are separated from the previous section (5:12-18) and considered as the final section of the letter, it becomes apparent that James is once again addressing those in the "diaspora."[43] This time, however, the reference is to those who are scattered or dispersed doctrinally as opposed to those who are physically separated from their place of origin: "My brothers and sisters, if anyone among you wanders (*planaō*) from the truth (*tēs alētheias*) and is brought back by another, you should know that whoever brings back a sinner from the path of wandering (*planēs hodou*) will save the sinner's soul from death and will cover a multitude of sins" (5:19-20; cf. 2 Tim 4:3-4).

This literary move of calling attention to the "wanderers" from the truth indicates the ways in which the African American experience illuminates the James text. This "wanderers" motif also points to some of the deeper implications and consequences of diaspora for contemporary African Americans and other persons of African descent. First, there is a serious need for an open acknowledgment of the different faith practices among persons of African descent. With this in mind, Christianity should be understood as one of *many* religions practiced throughout the African diaspora, and similarly, the mere physical existence of Africans throughout the diaspora as "wanderers" has given rise to many different religious alternatives that challenge the presupposition of Christianity holding the *one and only* truth for African Americans.[44] Coupled with this reality is the need for ongoing interfaith dialogue among African Americans and persons of African descent in the United States who adhere to a variety of faith traditions beyond Christianity, including Islam, Judaism, traditional African religions, etc.

Second, the wanderer calls attention to the importance of re-evaluating what constitutes outreach ministry in African American churches. Most African American churches have some type of food pantry, soup kitchen, or clothing storehouse. Although these ministries are effective and necessary, they are not enough. A reassessment of the ways in which "outreach" ministries can combine spiritual support with physical sustenance has the potential to save the sinner's soul (*psychē*) *and* body (*sōma*) from death (see the comments on 2:14-26).

Third, African American churches generally do not devote consistent attention or resources to the *global* social, economic, and political realities of Africans throughout the diaspora. The crises affecting "others" throughout the world are now having a major impact on many African American religious communities. With this in mind, clergy and scholars are beginning to "sound the trumpet" and provide a more prophetic witness both at home and abroad.[45] Whether it is through critical readings of the Bible or through innovative social and spiritual initiatives to reach the disenfranchised, African American churches—given their diaspora realities of suffering, pain, triumph, and hope—are best positioned to reclaim the "wanderers" and to provide a witness of God's love in the world (see the comments on 1:1).

CONCLUSION

James is an ancient Greco-Roman diaspora letter that contains many parallels and implications for faith communities throughout the contemporary African diaspora. This letter shows the importance of cultivating an engaged faith that is rooted in concrete "actions" (*erga*). This engaged faithfulness is nurtured through a variety of spiritual disciplines, such as guarding the tongue, praying unceasingly, and responding to the needs of the poor and disenfranchised. This letter is instructive for people of all ages. It is a type of road map for the Christian life. One is to overcome doubt (*diakrinos*) and double-mindedness (*dipsychos*) by making an intentional choice to follow God. In this way, young and old, rich and poor, male and female, black and white may all come to a fuller knowledge of the faith; that is, to grow mature (*teleios*) and complete (*holoklēros*)—not lacking anything (1:4). James wanted all of his brothers and sisters to redefine their relationships, rebuild their communities, and re-imagine their faith.

Notes

1. For a summary of the theories about the possible addition of this material by an editor who wanted to "Christianize" the letter by inserting "Jesus Christ," see Luke Timothy Johnson, *The Letter of James: A New Translation with Introduction and Commentary*, AB 37A (New York: Doubleday, 1995), 151, and Martin Dibelius, *A Commentary on the Epistle of James*, Hermeneia (Philadelphia: Fortress Press, 1975), 126–28.

2. For a useful explanation of the Greco-Roman literary conventions used in James (e.g., diatribe, blessings, ethical exhortations, etc.), see James L. Bailey and Lyle D. Vander Broek, *Literary Forms in the New Testament: A Handbook* (Louisville: Westminster John Knox, 1992).

3. The "letter" of James resembles an ancient letter only in its opening greeting. This letter includes no thanksgiving, farewell message, or other characteristic features of ancient letters. Because of its lack of epistolary features, James is often classified as *paraenesis* (advice, counsel, or exhortation), given its general ethical content. See Frances Taylor Gench, *Hebrews and James* (Louisville: Westminster John Knox, 1996), 79–86. For more information about the literary genre of James, see Johnson, *The Letter of James*, 16–26. Johnson suggests that James is "protreptic discourse in the form of a letter" (24).

4. Diatribe ("dialogue" or "lengthy address") is a form in which the speaker confronts and debates an imaginary addressee in order to instruct his or her audience. A diatribe usually includes a rhetorical question giving a false conclusion, which is then clarified by stories, analogies, examples, or quotations. See Bailey and Vander Broek, *Literary Forms in the New Testament*, 38–42.

5. The general or "catholic" letters in the New Testament are James; 1–2 Peter; 1, 2, 3 John; and Jude.

6. *Diaspora* is usually translated "dispersion" (NRSV, NAB), "scattered among the nations" (NIV), or "scattered abroad" (KJV). I suggest it is better to maintain the Greek term *diaspora*

instead of rendering another translation. In
this way the implications of this letter for
persons of African descent who are dispersed
throughout the African diaspora become more
accessible.

7. *Diaspora* occurs also in John 7:35: "Does he
[Jesus] intend to go to the diaspora among the
Greeks and teach the Greeks?"

8. See Johannes Tromp, "The Ancient Jewish
Diaspora: Some Linguistic and Sociological
Observations," in *Strangers and Sojourners: Religious Communities in the Diaspora*,
ed. Gerrie ter Haar (Leuven: Peeters, 1998),
13–58, esp. 21–23.

9. Cf. Deut 30:4; Isa 56:8; Isa 49:6.

10. For studies on the African diaspora, see
Alusine Jalloh and Stephen E. Maizlish, eds.,
The African Diaspora (Arlington: Texas A&M
University Press, 1996), and Albert J. Rabo-
teau, *Slave Religion: The "Invisible Institution"
in the Antebellum South* (New York: Oxford
University Press, 1978), esp. chap. 1, "African
Diaspora."

11. Orlando Patterson, *Rituals of Blood: Consequences of Slavery in Two American Centuries*
(New York: Basic Civitas, 1998), and *Slavery and Social Death: A Comparative Study*
(Cambridge, Mass.: Harvard University Press,
1982).

12. See, for example, Khalid Koser, ed. *New African Diasporas* (London and New York: Routledge, 2003). Chapters in this book describe
a Francophone African settlement in London,
Senegalese in Italy, and Ghanaians in Toronto,
Canada.

13. For a discussion of "militant patience," see
Elsa Tamez, *The Scandalous Message of James:
Faith without Works Is Dead*, trans. John
Eagleson, rev. ed. (New York: Crossroad,
2002), 43–46. For a discussion of the use of
hypomonē as "nonviolent resistance" in the
book of Revelation, see pages 530 and 543 in
Brian Blount's chapter on Revelation below.
Both translations offer a more critical nuance
to the notion of simply waiting on a future
resolution of unbearable social circumstances,
but neither reflects the type of spiritual discipline that empowers people to transcend hardships by cultivating a mature and complete
faith.

14. Howard Thurman, *Disciplines of the Spirit*
(New York: Harper & Row, 1963).

15. Ibid., 42.

16. Ibid.

17. Gay L. Byron, "Holy Man/Holy Community:
Howard Thurman, Early Christian Asceticism,
and the Black Church Tradition," *Hungry-
hearts: Newsletter of the Spiritual Formation
Program of the Presbyterian Church (U.S.A.)*
12 (2003): 11. See also Howard Thurman, *The
Inward Journey* (New York: Harper & Row,
1961).

18. Barbara A. Holmes, *Joy Unspeakable: Contemplative Practices of the Black Church* (Minneapolis: Fortress Press, 2004).

19. Ibid., 138–68, esp. 138. Holmes examines several exemplary "public mystics": Rosa Parks,
Martin Luther King Jr., Fannie Lou Hamer,
Howard Thurman and his wife, Sue Bailey,
and Malcolm X.

20. Much of James reads like wisdom literature,
similar to what is found in the book of
Proverbs.

21. Most commentators discuss the issue of partiality in the text, but it is Cain Hope Felder
who first noted the ways in which the example
of "discrimination" cited in this passage can be
linked to the effects of racism among African
Americans. See Cain Hope Felder, "Class and
God's Law: The Epistle of James," in *Troubling Biblical Waters: Race, Class, and Family*
(Maryknoll, N.Y.: Orbis, 1989), 118–34.

22. The reference to *synagōgē* (assembly) in 2:2
may refer to a specific assembly, or it may be
used to heighten the rhetorical imagery of the
example.

23. Tamez, *The Scandalous Message of James*, 19.

24. Lawrence Otis Graham, *Our Kind of People:
Inside America's Black Upper Class* (New York:
HarperCollins, 1999). Graham opens his book
with the provocative and controversial quote
that reflects the views of some from the "upper
class": "Bryant Gumbel is, but Bill Cosby
isn't. Lena Horne is, but Whitney Houston
isn't. Andrew Young is, but Jesse Jackson isn't.
And neither is Maya Angelou, Alice Walker,

Clarence Thomas, or Quincy Jones. And even though both of them try extremely hard, neither Diana Ross nor Robin Givens will ever be" (1).

25. Marvin A. McMickle, *Preaching to the Black Middle Class: Words of Challenge, Words of Hope* (Valley Forge, Pa.: Judson, 2000).

26. Graham, *Our Kind of People*, xii–xiii.

27. In Mark 12:43 Jesus refers to a widow as *ptōchos*.

28. Feminist commentators have discussed the ways in which Jewish legends about Rahab circulated in early Jewish Christian communities. She was considered an archetypal convert, and her confession of faith in Josh 2:11 echoes that of Moses in Deut 4:39. She is listed in Heb 11:31 among the faithful. For a more detailed discussion, see Sharyn Dowd, "James," in *The Women's Bible Commentary*, ed. Carol A. Newsome and Sharon H. Ringe (Louisville: Westminster John Knox, 1998), 460–61.

29. Michael Battle, "Teaching and Learning as Ceaseless Prayer," in *The Scope of Our Art: The Vocation of the Theological Teacher*, ed. L. Gregory Jones and Stephanie Paulsell (Grand Rapids, Mich.: Eerdmans, 2002), 156–57.

30. Ibid., 158.

31. See Margaret Aymer, "'First Pure, Then Peaceable': Frederick Douglass Reads James," Ph.D. diss., Union Theological Seminary, New York, 2004. See also, Milton C. Sernett, *North Star Country: Upstate New York and the Crusade for African American Freedom* (Syracuse, N.Y.: Syracuse University Press, 2002).

32. Marilyn Richardson, ed., *Maria W. Stewart: America's First Black Woman Political Writer: Essays and Speeches* (Bloomington: Indiana University Press, 1987), 32–33. For an excellent analysis of Stewart's political and religious activism, see Carla L. Peterson, ed., *"Doers of the Word": African-American Women Speakers and Writers in the North (1830–1880)* (New York: Oxford University Press, 1995), 56–87.

33. Clarice J. Martin, "Biblical Theodicy and Black Women's Spiritual Autobiography," in *A Troubling in My Soul: Womanist Perspectives on Evil and Suffering*, ed. Emilie M. Townes

(Maryknoll, N.Y.: Orbis, 1993), 13–36, esp. 30.

34. The Greek noun is feminine, but it is usually translated "adulterers."

35. The Greek term *idou* is translated as "Listen!" in the NRSV.

36. Some commentators emphasize "the rich" and "the poor" in James as binary opposites almost to the point of oversimplifying the complex layers of class distinctions that existed in the ancient world. For more insights on this point, see David Hutchinson Edgar, *Has God Not Chosen the Poor? The Social Setting of the Epistle of James* (Sheffield: Sheffield Academic, 2001).

37. In 2004, approximately 28.5 percent of African American families and 25.5 percent of Hispanic families (with children under eighteen) lived below the poverty level (see www.census.gov/hhes/www/poverty/hist-pov/hstpov4.html). For an example of African American and Latino/a farm workers in upstate New York who have organized protests against unfair wages, see justice campaigns, conferences, and other projects sponsored by the Rochester Labor-Religion Coalition and the Rural & Migrant Ministry at www.rural-migrantministry.org.

38. See, for example, Martin Luther King Jr.'s 1963 "I Have a Dream" speech: "I am not unmindful that some of you have come here out of excessive trials and tribulation. Some of you have come fresh from narrow jail cells. . . . You have been the veterans of creative suffering. Continue to work with the faith that unearned suffering is redemptive" (219). See also his reflections on "Suffering and Faith" recorded in 1960: "My personal trials have also taught me the value of unmerited suffering. . . . Recognizing the necessity for suffering I have tried to make of it a virtue. If only to save myself from bitterness, I have attempted to see my personal ordeals as an opportunity to transform myself and heal the people involved in the tragic situation which now obtains. I have lived these last few years with the conviction that

unearned suffering is redemptive" (41). The full texts are included in *A Testament of Hope: The Essential Writings of Martin Luther King, Jr.*, ed. James M. Washington (San Francisco: Harper & Row, 1986).

39. Thurman, *Disciplines of the Spirit*, 64.

40. Walter Earl Fluker and Catherine Tumber, eds., *A Strange Freedom: The Best of Howard Thurman on Religious Experience and Public Life* (Boston: Beacon, 1998), 15.

41. See James M. Washington, ed., *Conversations with God: Two Centuries of Prayers by African Americans* (New York: HarperCollins, 1994), and O. Richard Bowyer, Betty L. Hart, and Charlotte A. Meade, *Prayer in the Black Tradition* (Nashville: Upper Room, 1986).

42. Maria W. Stewart, "A Prayer for Divine Companionship (1835)," in Washington, *Conversations with God*, 27, emphasis added.

43. Many commentators include these final two verses with the previous section, thus missing the potential emphasis on the diaspora that is indicated in this letter.

44. For a sample of African American "religious alternatives," such as black Judaism, Nation of Islam, and other organized religions and cults, Milton C. Sernett, ed., *Afro-American Religious History: A Documentary Witness*, second ed. (Durhanm, N.C.: Duke University Press, 2000), 379–420. For examples beyond the United States, see ter Haar, *Strangers and Sojourners*.

45. See Iva E. Carruthers, Frederick D. Haynes III, and Jeremiah A. Wright Jr., *Blow the Trumpet in Zion! Global Vision and Action for the Twentieth-Century Black Church* (Minneapolis: Fortress Press, 2005).

For Further Reading

Battle, Michael. "Teaching and Learning as Ceaseless Prayer." Pages 155–70 in *The Scope of Our Art: The Vocation of the Theological Teacher*. Edited by L. Gregory Jones and Stephanie Paulsell. Grand Rapids, Mich.: Eerdmans, 2002.

Carruthers, Iva E., Frederick D. Haynes III, and Jeremiah A. Wright Jr. *Blow the Trumpet in Zion! Global Vision and Action for the Twentieth-Century Black Church*. Minneapolis: Fortress Press, 2005.

Chilton, Bruce, and Jacob Neusner, eds. *The Brother of Jesus: James the Just and His Mission*. Louisville: Westminster John Knox, 2001.

Dibelius, Martin. *A Commentary on the Epistle of James*. Hermeneia. Philadelphia: Fortress Press, 1975.

Edgar, David Hutchinson. *Has God Not Chosen the Poor? The Social Setting of the Epistle of James*. Sheffield: Sheffield Academic, 2001.

Felder, Cain Hope. *James. International Critical Commentary*. Edinburgh: T & T Clark.

Felder, Cain Hope. *Troubling Biblical Waters: Race, Class, and Family*. Maryknoll, N.Y.: Orbis, 1989.

Holmes, Barbara A. *Joy Unspeakable: Contemplative Practices of the Black Church*. Minneapolis: Fortress Press, 2004.

Johnson, Luke Timothy. *The Letter of James*. AB 37A. New York: Doubleday, 1995.

Koser, Khalid, ed. *New African Diasporas*. London and New York: Routledge, 2003.

Tamez, Elsa. *The Scandalous Message of James: Faith without Works Is Dead*. Translated by John Eagleson. Rev. ed. New York: Crossroad, 2002.

1 PETER

Larry George

INTRODUCTION

African Americans have suffered greatly at the hands of white mobs. These Africans of the diaspora were treated with contempt and viscously captured, tortured, maimed, lynched, and then burned. All of these things happened to them before cheering crowds of white men, women, and children. James Allen, Hilton Als, Congressman John Lewis, and Leon F. Litwack in *Without Sanctuary: Lynching Photography in America* graphically depict photos, in heart-wrenching detail, of African Americans' horrendous, subhuman treatment.[1] Brave souls were martyred, yet they suffered righteously as heroes and heroines in America and as ancestors of African Americans, who were perceived as savage beasts and chattel.[2]

As the righteous, those who suffered in 1 Peter were scattered within five Roman provinces as exiles.[3] Like those early believers, members of the African diaspora, as strangers in a strange land, sought liberation in Christianity. Nonetheless, they suffered not only because of their religious conversions but also in persecutions and mistreatment as subhuman beings because of the darker hues of their beautiful skin.

Even though treated maliciously as strangers and aliens, these proud Africans understood the liberating message in the Bible. They converted to Christianity in part to secure their freedom and dignity and in part to experience the social privileges of freedom, equality, and justice afforded them by their new heavenly status. Like the addressees in 1 Peter, African Christians were continually treated with contempt. Because the American government—like the Roman government in 1 Peter—and planters or slavemasters presented far more of a physical threat, African Christians resorted to nonviolent resistance to maintain their honor, to subvert their malicious treatment, and to stride continually toward their freedom.

First Peter is in the form of a general epistle, written as a baptismal homily to initiate new converts recently baptized. It also encouraged them to deal with current and forthcoming suffering from both the community and the Romans ("Babylon").

Though some attribute 1 Peter to the apostle of Jesus named Peter, most commentators consider it pseudonymous—written by someone who assumed the name of Peter, possibly a member of the community writing in his name.[4] An "epistle" served a larger literary purpose than a personal letter; 1 Peter is thus intended for a rather broad readership. It is addressed to Christians who had been scattered abroad, likely because of persecutions and threats. Some scholars suggest that 1 Peter advocates passive suffering for these new converts, following the example of Jesus Christ, but this epistle actually encourages nonviolent resistance toward a greater end, namely, total liberation. With regard to content, this epistle functions as a baptismal homily or short sermon on baptism, seeking to demonstrate how the readers should interpret and live out the meaning of their baptism in the context of suffering. The baptismal homily here serves not only to initiate these new converts into the faith, following the example of Jesus Christ, but also as a call to prepare for their current and impending sufferings and persecutions as inhabitants of a Roman province.

Although this letter purports to be written to the Christians scattered throughout Asia Minor (1:1; present-day Turkey), it addresses a wider region than Paul visited in this area, as reported in Acts and Paul's letters. Thus, scholars have concluded that this work must have been written much later in order for these areas to have been visited by Christian missionaries. Some scholars date this work between 70 and 100 C.E., a period much later than that of the apostle Peter, who is reported to have been martyred in Rome between 62 and 64 C.E.

This epistle provides themes and motifs that could offer signifying elements to be employed for the liberation of the marginalized. On the surface, it seems to call for a continuation of the status quo—an unlikely intent of this epistle. This call focuses on a seemingly passive nonresistant response to actual and impending suffering as an end in and of itself. Rather, as a type of resistance

---

The Mourners' Bench

"An alternative claim, nearly a logical mirror of the first, is that those obliged by domination to act a mask will eventually find that their face has grown to fit that mask. The practice of subordination in this case produces, in time, its own legitimacy, rather like Pascal's injunction to those who were without religious faith but who desired it to get down on their knees five times a day to pray, and the acting would eventually engender its own justification in faith. . . . I hope to clarify this debate considerably inasmuch as it bears so heavily on the issues of domination, resistance, ideology, and hegemony."

—James C. Scott, *Domination and the Arts of Resistance: Hidden Transcripts* (New Haven: Yale University Press, 1990), 10.

literature, 1 Peter calls on Christians to resist the hegemonic systems of oppression with an active nonviolent movement toward total liberation for all.[5] To reach such an end, the new converts as readers must employ a "hermeneutic of suspension" to subvert an oppressive reading (public transcript) with a resistant inclusive liberating reading.

Indeed, several people of the African diaspora can readily identify with the theme of suffering associated with baptism because they too sought baptism or conversion to Christianity as way to subvert their status as chattel slaves and sought to become full citizens because of their newly found Christian faith. Instead, their chattel status remained the same, and some were forbidden this rite of baptism by their slavemasters. Not only did the newly converted slaves find hostility from slavemasters, but also other slaves thought that such a move was an act of treason because these converted slaves abandoned their former gods.

1 Peter 1: From Preparation for the Ministry to the Liberation of the Elect

1:1-2, To Strangers in Strange Lands from a Stranger in a Strange Land

Like other Greco-Roman letters (including the letters of Paul), 1 Peter begins with a salutation that includes the identification of the sender, the addressees, and good wishes.[6]

The sender, in the name of the apostle Peter, informs the reader of the position or authority of Peter, who was an apostle of Jesus Christ. Peter, one of the Twelve, was a member of Jesus' inner circle. He was a complex apostolic leader who suffered greatly, partly because of his threefold denial of the Lord after Jesus' arrest on the eve of his crucifixion.

The intended readers are referred to as exiles of the dispersion, who were scattered throughout five Roman provinces: Pontus,

> ### Strangers in a Strange Land: Harriet Tubman
>
> "For too long, African Americans have lived as strangers in a strange land in America and throughout the diaspora. Harriet Tubman observed this as a slave in the way that she was treated and disrespected by planters."
>
> —Kate C. Larson, *Bound for the Promised Land: Harriet Tubman: Portrait of an American Hero* (New York: Random House, 2004), 88.

Galatia, Cappadocia, Asia, and Bithynia. As exiles they were considered strangers in a strange land, on the margins of their societies as outcasts. They were set apart as resident aliens who lacked social roots and who could not readily discover their ethnic origins. They also suffered because they lost their native tongues and culture, like Africans of the diaspora, and they had no political access or religious affinities. They were also viewed as a threat to the status quo. These sojourners were forbidden to marry outside of their ranks.[7]

Despite their status and place in the society, the implied author, Peter, considered them elect, chosen and destined by God the Father, sanctified by the Spirit, and sprinkled with the very blood of Jesus Christ. Over and against their social and religious sufferings, they were secure in the Godhead, which preserved their status and position in obedience to Jesus Christ. Indeed, despite the perils that they faced, they were already the recipients of an

> ### The Structure of the Typical New Testament Letter
>
> 1. opening (sender, addressees, greeting)
> 2. thanksgiving or blessing
> 3. body
> 4. paraenesis (instruction or teaching)
> 5. closing (doxology, greeting)

Exiles

Parepidēmous. One who lives alongside of, sojourner. The word is used of those who are temporary residents, not permanent settlers in the land; who have deep attachments and a higher allegiance in another sphere. The word emphasizes both alien nationality and temporary residence.

—Fritz Rienecker, *A Linguistic Key to the Greek New Testament* (Grand Rapids, Mich.: Regency Reference Library, 1980), 743.

abundance of grace and peace to fortify them in a hostile and aggressive situation.

This salutation bears many parallels to the social status and plights of Africans scattered throughout the world. They, too, are considered strangers, aliens, and sojourners in strange lands apart from their homelands, culture, religions, and languages. Unlike the addressees in 1 Peter, Africans were stolen from their homelands, stripped of their humanity, and forcefully treated as chattel slaves to support the economic and social infrastructures of their respective societies. Faced with hegemonic forms of oppression, they found a faith that promised them a new, elect status and freedom as human beings chosen and secured by God. Indeed, like the readers of 1 Peter, African Americans felt and received God's divine favor, and experienced and exemplified God's *shalom* in a foreign land. Despite the oppression that they in some way feel each day, they have celebrated and appreciated the multitude of God's goodness in abundance in terms of grace and peace.

1:3-12, A Hope Not Deferred

To scoffers who denied the active involvement and presence of God in the world, the implied author establishes the scene with a prayer that blesses the lively hope brought about by God's greatest act, the resurrection of Jesus Christ. The implied author explicitly deals with future gifts—described as imperishable, undefiled, and unfading—which are kept in an otherworldly realm. These gifts establish the fact that the righteous believers are already blessed in heaven (v. 4), a statement that represents the active, continual protection of God's power. Moreover, in this opening blessing, Peter responds to the scoffers by saying that these things will be revealed "in the last time" (v. 5).

In v. 6 the implied author indicates the impending and actual sufferings and trials that the new converts are facing. Instead of their becoming dismayed or discouraged by these trials, Peter encourages them with a different perspective, a positive, constructive view that the readers should have during tough times. He commends them for being able to "rejoice" among such trials. He assures them that such trials will be extended only "for a little while." Moreover, he insists that such a character would be built up and fortified in a way that is more "precious than gold."

This kind of steadfastness is often exhibited in African American worship contexts, in which the stranger proceeds to thank God for possessions yet obtained, yet near, and yet real, though these have not yet been revealed to the natural eye. With such a lively hope, they also have received the outcome, the faith, which is the "salvation of your souls" (v. 9). In such a salvation, African Americans of faith are already assured of their otherworldly possessions, yet they also resist the depressing signifiers that accompany racism. They are still hoping against hope, believing without first seeing the signification of their liberated salvation, without first realizing the true justice for their tired and weary souls.

1:13-25, Summoned to Prepare for Effective Ministry

In v. 13, the implied author summons the readers to secure victory over their oppressors. This liberating action requires mental,

"Lift Ev'ry Voice and Sing" [The Black National Anthem] by James Weldon Johnson

Lift ev'ry voice and sing,
　　Till earth and heaven ring,
Ring with the harmonies of liberty;
　　Let our rejoicing rise
High as the list'ning skies,
　　Let it resound loud as the rolling sea.
Sing a song full of the faith that the dark past
　　has taught us;
Sing a song full of the hope that the present
　　has brought us,
Facing the rising sun of our new day begun,
Let us march on, till victory is won.

Stony the road we trod,
　　Bitter the chast'ning rod,
Felt in the days when hope unborn had died;
Yet with a steady beat,
　　Have not our weary feet
Come to the place for which our parents
　　sighed?
We have come over a way that with tears
　　has been watered;
We have come, treading our path through
　　the blood of the slaughtered,
Out from the gloomy past,
　　Till now we stand at last
Where the white gleam of our bright star
　　is cast.

God of our weary years,
　　God of our silent tears,
Thou who has brought us thus far on the way;
Thou who has by thy might
　　Led us into the light,
Keep us forever in the path, we pray.
Lest our feet stray from the places, our God,
　　where we met thee,
Lest, our hearts drunk with the wine of the
　　world, we forget thee;
Shadowed beneath thy hand,
　　May we forever stand.
True to our God,
　　True to our native land.

physical, and spiritual preparation. Based on the challenges that this faith community faces and will certainly continually encounter, they must spiritually prepare their "minds for action." They must also "discipline" themselves so that they might be able to resist the hegemony of the false teachers and of society. This discipline for the new converts suggests that the sufferings that they experience too shall be overcome and will necessitate a firm grasp on the traditions of the past (v. 18). Like Jews preparing for the Passover, God also called these believers to establish a spiritual base for total liberation. In v. 22 the author acknowledges that they had begun this hard work of purifying their minds, wills, and emotions in their obedience to the truth. Nonetheless, readers are summoned to an authentic life, which is prescribed as a strategy against all suffering and oppression. Because African Americans survived the horrors of years of oppression from a system that seems indestructible, they are soulful folks and continue to resist and struggle in each generation against their oppressors. They prepare their minds, souls, and bodies on a daily basis to confront whatever foe they face: economic, political, legal, social, sexist, racist, classist, homophobic, etc. They do so because of their love and devotion to the true master of their fate, obeying or giving credence to the fate of their full humanity and dignity.

In v. 13c the author instructs the reader to "hope on the grace that Jesus Christ will bring you when he is revealed." This futuristic, eschatological hope rests on the parousia of Jesus Christ; in order to survive in the present, one must have a *telos*, a goal much bigger than one can realize alone. This hope is central to this section because it is through hope that the reader is mentally and spiritually strengthened. There is also a past foundation for this hope, namely, Jesus Christ's death and resurrection, which resulted in his glory.

Like Paul's admonition to Christians in Rom 12:2,[8] Peter also urges the readers not to be conformed by worldly matters, "the desires that you formerly had in ignorance (v. 14)." Rather, Peter strings together a set of admonitions: (1) Be hospitable through giving. (2) Bless the oppressor. (3) Rejoice and weep. (4) Live in harmony, in peace with all people. Overall, Peter provides a string of instructions on how to live in a strange land (1:13—2:3). These instructions are designed as a resistance guide to secure peace and to live in reverence to God. Peter begins with preparation (of the mind and soul), moves on to virtues that the new convert needs in a foreign, alien land, and ends with a "song" that proclaims the eternal nature of the Word, representing a new disposition.

It is no secret that song has played a central role in the African American experience. From its spirituals, to blues, to jazz, to bebop, to gospel, to hip hop, and to R & B, African American music has greatly assisted us in the development, maintenance, and disposition of the African soul.[9]

1 PETER 2: RULES OF CONDUCT IN A ROMAN AND AMERICAN SOCIETY

2:1-10, A Virtuous People of God

In vv. 1-10, Peter speaks to these new converts, who were formerly lost and insignificant in their communities. Even though they were considered strangers, rejects, unacceptable waste, and chattel, Peter now considers their virtuous positions before God. In vv. 4-5 the writer stresses the fact that because Jesus was a living stone, they too will now represent the same identity. They, like Jesus, are precious and priceless in God's sight.

In this new identification, Peter does not focus on their individual status, but collectively they are living stones joined together by God through Jesus Christ. Together they represent a spiritual house, wherein they are a holy priesthood, and Jesus Christ stands as the chief cornerstone, holding the entire people in unity with God. In this section, Peter uses a number of appellations or titles to describe the status of the new converts (vv. 9-10): a chosen race, royal priesthood, a holy nation, a people of his own.

2:11-25, A Higher Bar of Expectation and Excellence: Be Subject to No One but God

Peter raises the bar of expectations concerning the private and public ethical behavior of the new converts to Christ as exiles and foreigners. They are expected to be nourished with spiritual milk and grow up into salvation. In vv. 9-10 they are considered a royal priesthood, "priests" who are called to manage their own spirituality.

This section is similar to Jeremiah 29, in which Jeremiah admonishes Jews in Babylon how to conduct themselves in a foreign land. Likewise, Peter provides ethical guidelines for the foreigners and exiles so that they can avoid further maltreatment by non-Christians. The strangers are in a strange land among strange peoples and are held in contempt and

The Prophet Jeremiah Writes to the Exiles in Babylon

"Build houses and live in them; plant gardens and eat what they produce. Take wives and have sons and daughters; take wives for your sons and give your daughters in marriage, that they may bear sons and daughters; multiply there, and do not decrease. But seek the welfare of the city where I have sent you into exile, and pray to the Lord on its behalf, for in its welfare you will find your welfare."

—Jeremiah 29:5-7

persecuted as a result. Peter provides ethical prescriptions to avoid further persecution as wrongdoers.

He instructs them to keep away from immoral desires that war against their souls. He advises them to maintain good conduct so that they can serve as witnesses and present a testimony when God appears as Judge. Seeing such good conduct also would be an occasion for the non-Christians (Gentiles or non-Jews) to praise God.

The Proper Order of the *Haustafeln*

God, kings, governors, human institutions, husbands, wives, and slaves.

See Clarice J. Martin, "The *Haustafeln* (Household Codes) in African American Biblical Interpretation: 'Free Slaves' and Subordinate Women,'" in *Stony the Road We Trod: African American Biblical Interpretation*, ed. Cain Hope Felder (Minneapolis: Fortress Press, 1991), 208.

This section focuses on the *Haustafeln*, or household codes, common rules of proper conduct within Roman society. Peter expands it in such a way that it becomes deconstructed in a non-suffering period (cf. 2:11; 3:1-22). Moreover, Peter presents the annotated household code to instruct new converts on how to resist oppression and avoid suffering wrongly as wrongdoers. The central deconstruction happens when the believer becomes subject to everyone, good or evil. On the surface, it appears to be quite oppressive and restrictive to those at the bottom of the hierarchy,[10] where they are instructed to be subject to husbands, good or evil, masters, and good and gentle or perverse. This code, however, was not intended to be relevant for all times, only those times when persecution and trials would necessitate resistance to avoid persecution as wrongdoers.

Because the Christian readers are experiencing violence from non-Christians and the Roman hegemonic system of oppression, Peter provided additional ethical guidelines that now include actions and dispositions toward the government (vv. 13-14). His desire is for them to live their lives peacefully in a hostile, foreign land. He wants them to avoid all conflict and confrontation beyond that which they will face as strangers. Since they are away from their homes, essentially homeless, Peter requires them to live as freed persons, rather than to use their freedom as a license to indulge in immoral conduct, in private or public. This will require non-Christians or foolish people to treat them as freed persons, and thereby they will eliminate any form of blame or accusations for any immoral activities (v. 15).

In the standard household code, slaves were expected to be subject to their masters. Peter, however, includes additional guidelines, in which slaves were to be subject also to their perverse masters, whose sub-human treatment of them, in the standard code, they would be expected to resist physically. Peter believes that the slaves who are subject will find God's favor, which in aforetimes would be attributed as an unmerited privilege. In vv. 20-21, Peter asks a rhetorical question, "For what credit is it if you sin and are mistreated and endure it?" to direct the newly converted slaves to follow not their own conscience but to engage Jesus' example of doing good and suffering, thereby finding favor with God. Peter quotes Isa 53:7 to indicate the manner in which Jesus suffered. By doing so, Jesus' wound will heal them; even though they once wandered, now they will "turn back to the shepherd and guardian of their souls" (v. 25).

1 PETER 3: SENSELESS SUFFERING OF THE ABUSED

3:1-12, Suffering in Domestic Situations

Peter continues the annotated household code, "In the same way, wives, be subject to your own husbands" (3:1). The social consequences of appropriating this concept of suffering righteously have tremendous calamities for African American women and others who suffer in domestic situations. Here, women would be instructed in nonsocial oppressive situations, like the readers in 1 Peter, to suffer as Christ did in order to find God's favor. This is erroneous and fatal, at worse. Rather, women who are in abusive situations should seek help and shelter away from the abuser. This principle applies to men and children as well as women in abusive contexts.

3:13-22, Unhindered Prayers

Peter instructs the new converts to be in a particular relationship with one another. Because they are called to inherit a blessing, they should bless others. They should be "harmonious, sympathetic, affectionate, compassionate, and humble" toward their fellow sufferers. Verse 7 also instructs husbands to treat women with dignity and respect so that their prayers will not be hindered. As support for this claim, in 3:10-12 Peter cites Ps 34:12-16 to suggest that God's ears are opened to the one who keeps evil from their speech. Indeed, Dr. Martin Luther King Jr. suggests that African Americans should not return evil for evil, "eye for an eye and tooth for a tooth," for in the end that would result in many toothless and eyeless people.

Christians should not only respond passively to persecution by suffering righteously. They should also "give an answer to anyone who asks about the hope you possess" (3:15). This answer may serve as a message to the persecutor that they are grounded spiritually rather than in any worldly way.

1 Peter 4: Striving toward God's Standards

4:1-11, "Those Preachin' Women"[11]

Peter provides an additional rationale for suffering. A Christian should have the same

---

The Phenomenological Nature of the Call to Christian Ministry

"The Christian's call to the Gospel preaching and teaching ministry emerges from and out of an indescribable impulse, indescribable at first to the one being called and being beckoned to an almost inconceivable, unrecognizable urge to do God's business in a hostile, socio-religious context. This divine prodding relays an inner urge that is nearly impossible to overcome because it is an inner phenomenon, unlike the common cold or heartbreak that lasts or runs its course relatively within a brief period, depending on a person's immune system or ability to rebound from a lost love. No matter how one seeks to escape, this call is inescapable, unavoidable, and difficult to pass off. In short, this experience like one of cupid's arrows cannot be easily shaken, nor can one escape from it, or seek to drown it out by abusing or misusing some sort of alcohol or drug or substance. In a sense, this inner struggle will result in a spiritual experience that either will make one whole or it will cause, if avoided, in the end, self-destruction, purposelessness, and aimlessness."

—Larry D. George, "'Something You Cannot Shake': The Culture of the Call to Ordained Ministry for Women in the National Baptist Convention, U.S.A., Inc. and the African Methodist Episcopal Church Traditions," *The AME Church Review* 117 (October–December 2002): 104.

attitude that Christ had when he suffered. Moreover, the one who has suffered in the flesh ceases from sin and spends time here on earth focusing on God (v. 1). Therefore, the time has passed for the new convert to do what non-Christians desire. They had their array of past sinful actions and activities: debauchery, evil desires, drunkenness, carousing, drinking bouts, and wanton idolatries (v. 3). The company that they once kept can no longer be because they cannot submit to non-Christians who enticed them to immoralities and vilified them when the new converts refused to bite (v. 4).

Peter assures the new converts that their persecutors will be punished and their human standards will not rule over God's standard. African Americans do not fully subscribe to the human standards of racism, which states that whites are superior to blacks, and that white skin privilege is moral and black suffering accepted with further contempt (cf. Katrina), which are lies and false teachings. Rather, when it comes to embracing the truth and the law of grace, African Americans courageously continue to turn to God's standard. The end of hegemonic oppression is far away.

After rendering several admonitions, Peter informs the new converts that they have received a gift and are expected to be good stewards or managers of "the varied grace of God." This gift is not gender inclusive in 4:10-11. In some African American denominations, women are denied this right of managing and using their gifts. Though women, like men, may experience calls from God to the gospel ministry, they are denied the privilege to preach and pastor, or they face glass-ceilings in the ministry, howsoever defined. Therefore, Peter says that whosoever speaks or serves, male or female, let them speak and serve God's Word.

4:12-19, Judgment Begins at God's House

The new converts have endured various sufferings and trials at the time of this correspondence. Peter depicts this context as a trial by fire (v. 12). He believes that these trials are to be expected and that the new converts should not think it bizarre that these trials are happening to exiles and foreigners. Likewise, African Americans also should not be astonished at all by the sufferings and trials by fire that they experience historically and on a daily

---

"Dontcha Git Weary" by Sterling A. Brown

They dragged you from homeland;
They chained you in coffles
They huddled you spoonfashion in filthy
    hatches
They sold you to give a few gentlemen ease.

They broke you in like oxen
They scourged you
They branded you
They made your women breeders
They swelled your numbers with bastards. . . .
They taught you the religion they disgraced.

You sang: Keep a inchin' along
Lak a po' inch worm. . . .

You sang: Bye and Bye
I'm gonna lay down dis heaby load. . . .

You sang: Walk together chillen
Dontcha git weary. . . .

The strong men keep a comin' on
The strong men git stronger.

— "Dontcha Git Weary" from *The Collected Poems of Sterling A. Brown*, edited by Michael S. Harper. Copyright © 1980 by Sterling A. Brown. Reprinted by permission of HarperCollins Publishers.

basis. They, too, are strangers in a strange land, suffering because they are foreigners from Africa.

Yet Peter also admonishes his readers to adjust their spiritual attitudes of gratitude by God's grace, rejoicing at their suffering because in so doing they share in Christ's sufferings. Peter instructs them not to be found guilty of certain crimes: murder, theft, criminal behavior, or troublemaking. Lastly, Peter tells them not to be ashamed because of their sufferings. African Americans all too well know the shame that comes from suffering under unjust systems of oppression.

Are We There Yet?

There are approximately thirty million African Americans. Approximately half of them survive in the Black Belt south, in abject poverty, poor housing, poor schools, high crime rate, and high unemployment, in the twenty-first century, and in America.

—See Ronald C. Wimberley and Libby V. Morris, *The Southern Black Belt: A National Perspective* (Lexington: TVA Rural Studies and the University of Kentucky, 1997), and http://en.wikipedia.org/wiki/Black_Belt_Region.

Peter issues a warning that God will begin judging the world at the house of God. All Christians within the body of Christ will pass through the judgment test, and they will be barely saved. If the so-called righteous in the church are barely saved, how much worse would it be for the ungodly and sinner? African Americans should also assess themselves concerning any form of oppression—greed, sexism, elitism, homophobia, and the like—that may exist in their midst so that they may be liberated fully with their suffering ancestors.[12]

Peter places an extremely fearful truth in front of the new converts that will aid them in their struggle to exceed the human standards of righteousness in the church. The new converts are admonished by Peter to strive toward God's standards or God's will so that they may be saved as sufferers for Christ's sake, thereby entrusting "their souls to a faithful Creator as they do good" (v. 19).

1 PETER 5: FAREWELL TO THE FAITHFUL

5:1-11, God Opposes the Proud and Gives Grace to the Humble

Peter returns to providing instructions to the faith community. As a fellow elder, Peter admonishes the elders (vv. 1-4) and the entire Christian community (v. 5c-11). He charges the elders to be good shepherds of God's flock and to exercise their role and responsibilities not as a duty but willingly under God's directions, and not for shameful profit nor as lords or dictators. If they perform God's will for the flock, then when the chief shepherd, Jesus Christ, returns, Peter assures them that they will "receive a crown of glory that never fades" (v. 4).

Crowns to Be Cast at the Chief Shepherd's Feet

"And whenever the living creatures give glory, honor, and thanks to the one who sits on the throne, who lives forever, the twenty-four elders throw themselves to the ground before the one who sits on the throne and worship the one who lives forever and ever, and they offer their crowns before his throne, saying: 'You are worthy, our Lord and God, to receive glory and honor and power, since you created all things, and because of your will they existed and were created.'"

—Revelation 4:9-11

Peter charges the rest of the community to be subject to the elder, the spiritual leader of the flock. That is, Peter expects new converts to have the same spirit as the elders and defer to them for their work as shepherds of the flock.

In Peter's instructions to the entire community, he cites Prov 3:34 (cf. Jas 4:6) to reinforce the central charge of humility toward one another. God has nothing to do with the proud, but the humble receive more of God's grace. If they humble themselves, then they will be exalted by God in due time. In vv. 8-11 Peter instructs them to be sober and alert because the devil is on the prowl, seeking whom he may devour. Peter further charges the entire community to resist the devil and stay strong in their faith, and endure the sufferings like Jesus. After they suffer for a while, God will address the question of theodicy—"Why do the righteous suffer?"—with the response that God will fully restore, confirm, strengthen, and establish them.[13]

5:12-14, From a Church in Babylon

Peter closes this correspondence with a final greeting, referring to Silvanus, his secretary; to the church in Babylon (a code name for Rome), who were chosen together with them; and to Mark, whom he calls his son. By practicing one of his admonitions to show affection, he instructs them to greet one another with a loving kiss and to be at peace.

Africans of the diaspora, especially African Americans, would do well to take seriously Pheme Perkins's words (see sidebar below) and to develop a praxis that would eliminate oppression in whatever form it presents itself—poverty, classism, elitism, and the like.

Notes

1. James Allen, Hilton Als, Congressman John Lewis, and Leon F. Litwack, *Without Sanctuary: Lynching Photography in America* (Santa Fe, N.M.: Twin, 2000), 46–163; see also

---

The Church in Babylon

Concerning the status of the church in Babylon, Pheme Perkins admonishes:

"Since 1 Peter uses the symbolic name 'Babylon' to refer to Rome (cf. Rev 14:8; 18:2), he and his associates become the primary example of a church in exile. This designation throws the opening reference to its addressees in the 'Diaspora' into a different light. Ordinarily, a letter to those in the Diaspora would have come from Jerusalem (as in Acts 15:22-29). Here the political center of the empire that controls the provinces of Asia Minor is also the epitome of a place of exile. Since the author shares the situation of his addressees, they can be confident in his advice. This warm greeting also reminds readers today of their responsibility to other churches around the world. No church that remains insolated in local or even national boundaries incarnates the vision left by the apostles. Christians must reach out to their brothers and sisters around the world with the same love and support demonstrated in this letter. The sufferings of Christians in distant regions of Asia Minor were acknowledged by their fellow believers in the capital of the empire."

—Pheme Perkins, *First and Second Peter, James, and Jude,* Interpretation (Louisville: Westminster John Knox, 1995), 81–82.

Philip Dray, *At the Hands of Persons Unknown: The Lynching of Black America* (New York: Random House, 2002), 17–52.

2. See, e.g., Cheryl J. Sanders, "Liberation Ethics in the Ex-Slave Interviews" in *Cut Loose Your Stammering Tongue: Black Theology in the Slave Narratives,* ed. Dwight N. Hopkins and George C. L. Cummings (Louisville: Westminster John Knox, 2003), 96.

3. The five Roman provinces are Pontus, Galatia, Cappadocia, Asia, and Bithynia. See John H. Elliott, *1 Peter* AB 37B (New York: Doubleday, 2000), 85.

4. Since the real flesh-and-blood author is unknown, in this commentary I refer to Peter as the implied author.

5. James C. Scott, *Domination and the Arts of Resistance: Hidden Transcripts* (New Haven: Yale University Press, 1990), 10.

6. Jerome H. Neyrey, *2 Peter, Jude*, AB 37C (New York: Doubleday, 1993), 43–44.

7. See, for example, Elliott, *1 Peter*, 97–109.

8. "Be not conformed" (*syschēmatizesthe*) functions as a passive middle, suggesting both the passive mode of resisting and the reflexive form of performing a task for the sake of oneself.

9. See, for example, Brian Ward, *Just My Soul Responding: Rhythm and Blues, Black Consciousness, and Race Relations* (Berkeley: University of California Press, 1998).

10. See, for example, Clarice J. Martin, "The *Haustafeln* (Household Codes) in African American Biblical Interpretation: 'Free Slaves' and Subordinate Women,'" in *Stony the Road We Trod: African American Biblical Interpretation*, ed. Cain Hope Felder (Minneapolis: Fortress Press, 1991), 206–31.

11. See Ella Mitchell and Jacqueline B. Glass, eds., *Those Preachin' Women: Sermons by Black Women Preacher* (Valley Forge, Pa.: Judson, 2004).

12. See, for example, Prathia Hall-Wynn, "The Challenge of True Kinship," in *What Does It Mean to Be Black and Christian? Pulpit, Pew, and Academy in Dialogue*, ed. Forrest E. Harris Sr., James T. Roberson, and Larry D. George (Nashville: Townsend, 1995), 111–23.

13. God's consolation for those who suffer is recounted in the epilogue of the book of Job (42:7-17) and at the end of Revelation (chaps. 21–22).

For Further Reading

Bell, Derrick. *Faces at the Bottom of the Well: The Performance of Racism*. New York: Basic, 1992.

Blassingame, John W. ed. *Slave Testimony: Two Centuries of Letters, Speeches, Interviews, and Autobiographies*. Baton Rouge: Louisiana State University Press, 1977.

Elliott, John H. *1 Peter*. AB 37B. New York: Doubleday, 2000.

Hall-Wynn, Prathia. "The Challenge of True Kinship." Pages 111–23 in *What Does It Mean to Be Black and Christian? Pulpit, Pew, and Academy in Dialogue*. Edited by Forrest E. Harris Sr., James T. Robertson, and Larry D. George. Nashville: Townsend, 1995.

Hopkins, Dwight N., and George C. L. Cummings, eds. *Cut Loose Your Stammering Tongue: Black Theology in the Slave Narratives*. Louisville: Westminster John Knox, 2003.

Martin, Clarice J. "The *Haustafeln* (Household Codes) in African American Biblical Interpretation: 'Free Slaves' and Subordinate Women.'" Pages 206–31 in *Stony the Road We Trod: African American Biblical Interpretation*. Edited by Cain Hope Felder. Minneapolis: Fortress Press, 1991.

Mitchell, Ella, and Jacqueline B. Glass, eds. *Those Preachin' Women: Sermons by Black Women Preacher*. Valley Forge, Pa.: Judson, 2004.

Neyrey, Jerome H. *2 Peter, Jude*. AB 37C. New York: Doubleday, 1993.

Perkins, Pheme. *First and Second Peter, James, and Jude*. Interpretation. Louisville: Westminster John Knox, 1995.

Scott, James C. *Domination and the Arts of Resistance: Hidden Transcripts*. New Haven: Yale University Press, 1990.

2 PETER

Larry George

INTRODUCTION

Second Peter is a second-century, post-apostolic general epistle. Because scholars have determined 2 Peter's dependence on Jude,[1] it is dated between 90 and 135 C.E. Although this epistle purports to be written before Peter's[2] martyrdom in Rome (62–64 C.E., see 1:12-15), its literary relationship to Jude (written between 70 and 90 C.E.), suggests that it dates it from the early to mid-second century. Since no specific reader is addressed in the salutation (1:1-2), 2 Peter was inserted among the "General Epistles" (James, 1–2 Peter, Jude, and 1–3 John) of the Second Testament canon. Moreover, though 2 Peter lacks the complete structure of a Greek letter,[3] it does address a real, urgent matter: false teachers are wreaking havoc on believers concerning the parousia (the "second" coming of Jesus Christ) and concerning the perceived lack of involvement of God in the world that God would not punish the wicked and reward the righteous.

Letter from Birmingham Jail

"While confined here in the Birmingham city jail, I came across your recent statement calling my present activities 'unwise and untimely.' Seldom do I pause to answer criticism of my work and ideas. If I sought to answer all the criticisms that cross my desk, my secretaries would have little time for anything other than such correspondence in the course of the day, and I would have no time for constructive work. But since I feel that you are men of genuine good will and that your criticisms are sincerely set forth, I want to try to answer your statements in what I hope will be patient and reasonable terms."

—Martin Luther King Jr., "Letter from Birmingham Jail," http://www.nobelprizes.com/nobel/peace/MLK-jail.html.

Like Dr. King's letter from a Birmingham jail cell, this letter deals with an urgent dilemma. Peter directly addresses the issue of the delayed parousia of Jesus to silence the false teachers concerning God's direct involvement in human affairs. This affront suggests that the false teachers were denying a future reward for the righteous and, correspondingly, the eternal persecution of the oppressors. This is a challenge to the question of theodicy—why do the righteous suffer and the wicked prosper? This question also stared African Americans in the face as they wondered whether God would ever hear their cries for freedom, equality, and justice and deal with

their oppressors, who continued to prosper economically, politically, legally, and socially.

Dr. King sought to wrestle with this question in his letter from the Birmingham jail. Rather than projecting the civil rights of African Americans into some otherworldly sense (a pie-in-the-sky spirituality), Dr. King argued that equality must happen in the here and now, so that "justice cannot be delayed."[4]

Second Peter was written from Rome sometime between 90 and 135 C.E., the latest of the Second Testament writings. It has the form of a farewell address.

Formal Elements of Farewell Addresses/Testaments

1. prediction of death or departure
2. predictions of future crises for followers
3. virtues urged; ideal behavior prescribed
4. commission
5. legacy

—Jerome H. Neyrey, *2 Peter, Jude;* AB 37C (New York: Doubleday, 1993), 164.

Its central message is an interim ethic for believers, between the present and the parousia (see, e.g., 1:5-11, 19; 3:11-18). In this region, Christians were challenged and confronted with the reality of the delayed parousia of Christ, which resulted in an internal schism.

2 PETER 1: RELATIONSHIP WITH A LIBERATING JESUS

1:1-2, Salutation

The author begins by identifying himself as Simon Peter, a member of the twelve, an apostle of Jesus Christ, and a leader in the early Christian movement. The addressees are referred to as those who are granted a faith through Jesus Christ.

Larry George

In light of its dependence on Jude and its consequent late date, this epistle is pseudonymous. Also, the identity and location of its addressees are unclear. The salutation bears several affinities with Jude, with the exception that Peter is identified as an apostle of Jesus Christ. The addressees of both epistles were at some distance from the author, consisting of these whose faith is as valuable as "ours." "Ours" may refer to other possible senders, or it could mean that the author and the readers share a common faith, which was granted by Jesus Christ.

Peter indicates in his blessing that he bids them grace and peace, multiplied on them as they grow and increase in a fuller, more complete knowledge of both God and Jesus Christ. Such knowledge is necessary for the readers to engage effectively and efficiently to refute the false teachers.

1:3-8, A Liberating Divine Prayer

Peter offers a liberating divine prayer to the readers so that they will increase their intimacy in knowing Jesus. To arrive at such status, Peter systematically and progressively guides the readers by informing them of their divine nature. Verses 3-8 provide the reader with clear escalating steps to take toward intimacy, knowing Jesus Christ. Peter employs a prayer to accomplish this objective. Peter guides the readers, informing them of their possessions: faith, excellence, knowledge, self-control, perseverance, godliness, brotherly and sisterly affection, and unselfish love (vv. 5-7). These virtues equip the readers with a divine nature, and these virtues allow the readers to be effective and productive. Emerging from a life of increasing virtue, the readers are called on to grow in godliness, knowing Jesus more intimately.

1:9-11, A Liberating Walk

Peter inserts an inverted comparison between the ones who "lack such things" and those

who have made their calling and election sure. In structure, this comparison resembles Ps 1:1-3, in which the psalmist contrasts the difference between the ones who follow a path of walking with the ungodly, standing with sinners, and sitting in the seat of the scorner with the ones who delight in the law of the Lord. Peter, on the one hand, describes the ones who lack as those who are blind or nearsighted, because they fail to recall the goodness of God in forgiving and cleansing them from sin. On the other hand, Peter stresses taking every effort to make their Christian vocation certain. As a result, unlike the ones who stumble in the darkness of blindness, knowing their calling and election, they will never stumble into sin but will be richly granted entrance into the eternal reign of the Lord Jesus Christ. Thus, Peter is concerned with the readers' spiritual walk. He does not merely desire for them to enter God's reign, but he also exhorts them to move without stumbling into sin.

1:12-21, A Liberating Testimony

The readers have some contact with Christian teachings. Peter reminds them of such teachings again so that they will be well established (v. 12). It is the testimony that they possess that contains the message for their liberation. They are not in need of any new teachings, because they are currently well established in the truth. Peter seeks to convince the readers of his involvement and role as long as he is "in this tabernacle," his body as a temporary dwelling place. Peter makes a second reference to his temporality by suggesting that he will soon die, as Jesus Christ revealed to him (vv. 13-14; see John 21:18-19). These two references to Peter's death possibly suggest that the figure Peter has already departed. Peter makes every effort to assure the readers of what they previously knew.

In 1:12-15, the author seeks to remind the readers of the true testimony. Then in

vv. 16-21 he carefully describes the process of prophecy. Here he is concerned with establishing a tradition for the truth of God. These prophecies were not cleverly conceived; they came from eyewitnesses to Jesus' transfiguration, and these witnesses possessed the prophetic word. These prophecies may have come from the mouths of human beings, but they did not originate from human imaginations; they were spoken by God and carried by the Holy Spirit—so argues the author of 2 Peter (1:20-21).

2 Peter 2: Dealing with Difficulties among the Storms of Life

2:1-3, Destructive Missives

In this chapter and in the beginning of chap. 3, Peter borrows examples from Jude in order to echo with some variation (expanding parts, eliminating material, and editing aspects of Jude) the destruction of the false teachers.[5] He expands on several Old Testament illustrations of how God judged those who thought that they were safe. Furthermore, he eliminates Jude's extra-biblical references, either because these sources are not authoritative to his addressees or because they are unfamiliar to them.

In vv. 1-3 Peter builds on the previous section, with a negative characterization of the false teachers and their destructive method and message. As false prophets emerged long ago among the people of Israel, so also will false teachers infiltrate among the readers. The methods that the false teachers employ for entering the community of faith are through destructive, heretical viewpoints. The false teachers' message also points toward destruction by denying the very existence of Jesus' work of redemption as their deliverer, which is the very foundation of the readers' and false teachers' liberation. Consequently, these false teachers are effective, causing many to follow their "debauched lifestyles" (v. 2). Their goal is divisive and destructive in that their teachings call into question and attack the very foundations of the readers' faith and liberation. Their work seems to be active while the correspondence is being written: "their destruction is not asleep" (v. 3).

2:4-11, The Question of Theodicy

Peter employs Jude's polemic against false teachers to characterize and describe the fate of these scoffers. The false teachers deny God's rewards for the righteous and deny divine punishments or judgments for the unrighteous, simply because they do not believe in Jesus' parousia. These false teachers devastate and divide the Christian community with their teachings that create doubt because of the delay of Christ's return. They argue that since Jesus will not return, as evidenced by his delay, then the wicked will not be punished and the righteous never rewarded. Because of such divisive and destructive teachings, Peter borrows Jude's polemical framework, with variations. Jude's framework is suitable for Peter's audience, since false teachers are present in both contexts. In vv. 9-10, Peter argues that the false teachers' case relies on Christ's delay, which is the central tenet of the false teachers' claim.

In the examples employed—fallen angels, the ancient world of Noah, Sodom and Gomorrah, and Lot—Peter illustrates that God protected and saved the righteous, while reserving punishment at the Day of Judgment for the wicked. The Day of Judgment is appropriate punishment for the ungodly who "indulge fleshly desires" and who "despise authority" (v. 10). These examples function as proof that Jesus Christ will return to liberate the righteous and to oppress the unrighteous. Borrowing from Jude, Peter is able to dismantle the argument of the false teachers, who are destroying the foundational belief of the faith community to encourage them to indulge in sexual immorality, which they believe is acceptable, since there will be no Day of Judgment.

2:10c-16, Shelter from the Storm

In this section Peter uses three examples to cast a negative portrayal of the nature and ways of the false teachers: wicked angels, irrational animals, and the way of Balaam. As in the previous section (2:4-10b), again echoing Jude, Peter moves to attack the character of the false teachers and then pronounces judgment and destruction on them. Because the false teachings are wreaking havoc on the faith of the community, Peter, again echoing with variation Jude's polemic against false teachers, resorts to name calling,[6] because they are insulting the "glorious ones." First, he notes that even the wicked angels refuse to insult these glorious ones, possibly God's called and elected, the readers of this epistle. Second, he compares them to irrational animals that were born to be caught and destroyed; similarly, the false teachers will be caught and destroyed for insulting the oppressed. Third, he describes how they contaminate the love feasts by seeking to fulfill their lustful desires, preying on the weak and unstable Christians. Finally, he notes how they have gone astray by sinning and forsaking the right way because they follow the way of Balaam.

2:17-22, Empty Promises of Freedom

Peter continues his sustained attack on and negative characterization of the false teachers. Borrowing again from Jude, Peter rhetorically attacks them with examples that illustrate their emptiness: waterless spring (v. 17), empty words (v. 18), empty promises of freedom (v. 19), and dogs returning to vomit and pigs returning to wallow in mud (v. 22). All of these illustrations seek to expose the

lack of substance to these false teachers' ways and teachings. Peter acknowledges that they were once on the righteous path but they have departed from it; Peter also observes that it would have been better had they never known the way of righteousness than to turn from "the holy commandments that had been delivered to them" (v. 21). This condemnation suggests that the false teachers had once received the truth from the apostles, were a part of the faith community, and now they have turned to deception and immorality.

In regard to the empty promises of freedom (2:19), the false teachers are apparently exploiting God's grace, perhaps by suggesting to some in the faith community that it is

---

Empty Promises of Freedom

"The liberation tradition stands out as the single most important characteristic of black faith from 1800 to the Civil Rights movement. It could have not been otherwise. From the landing of the first twenty Africans on the wharf at Jamestown, Virginia, in 1619, to the Emancipation Proclamation on New Year's Day, 1863, African American consciousness and culture were permeated with the idea of freedom. As tensions mounted toward the Civil War it was inevitable that the black quest for God and Salvation would be greatly conditioned by the unquenchable desire to be rid of slavery. Even when individuals were manumitted, bought their own freedom, or escaped slavery and fled north, their consuming passion was to liberate the other members of their families who had been left behind."

—Gayraud S. Wilmore, *Black Religion and Black Radicalism: An Interpretation of the Religious History of African Americans*, 3rd ed. (Maryknoll, N.Y.: Orbis, 1998), 267.

acceptable to indulge in immoralities because of their promised freedom. The false teachers wrongly teach that Christians are free to do as they will. However, when some Christians indulge in immorality, they become enslaved by it. Christians in the community previously escaped from such wrongdoings because of the rich knowledge of the Lord Jesus Christ. Thus, Peter encourages Christians to recall that they are free to do what God desires and not to use their freedom as a license to sin (cf. Rom. 6:1).

2 PETER 3: A DOXOLOGY TO EXHALE

3:1-7, Substance over Shadows

In v. 1 Peter addresses the readers as "dear friends," possibly borrowed from 1 Peter (cf. 1 Peter 2:11; 4:12), and informs them that this is the second letter written to them; the first is allegedly 1 Peter. Thus, the author of 2 Peter, though obviously writing pseudonymously several decades after the previous correspondence, is familiar with the first epistle and now writes a second. The objective of this section (3:1-7) is to remind the reader of the traditions and teachings concerning Jesus' return and the judgment of heaven and earth, a little apocalypse. This truth was well established by the holy prophets and the apostles of Jesus Christ. The false teachers ask, "Where is his promised return?" to raise doubts regarding the delayed return of Jesus. To challenge this question, Peter suggests that the delay can possibly be explained from prophetic tradition, the teachings of the apostles, and the creation and flood stories.

3:8-13, An Eschatological Warning

In this section Peter's central objective is to remind the readers again of the traditional teachings regarding the Day of Judgment. According to the testament or farewell address,

Peter provides an apocalyptic eschatological explanation on the final Day, which is not measured by human standards, because one day with the Lord is like a thousand years and a thousand years like a day. The point of this reckoning system seeks to show that God is patient and ultimately has delayed the Lord's return to give all an opportunity to repent.

The eschatological reckoning system makes it difficult to calculate with certainty a day for the Lord's return. When he returns, it will be like a thief (quick, quiet, and in secret) and will be chaotic and catastrophic, with an end-time prophetic description of the destruction and annihilation of heavenly and celestial bodies. All on earth will be judged and destroyed. Peter claims that such a day should impel the readers to conduct their lives in holiness and godliness, not using this time to indulge in sexual and other immoralities. As in Revelation 20–21, Peter affirms that there will be a new heaven and new earth, wherein righteousness is the order of the day. In the end, Peter desires his readers to live in such a way that will speed Jesus' return and the day of the Lord.

3:14-18, Waiting to Exhale

In this final section Peter seeks to end on a positive, constructive tone. He encourages them to wait in peace without any sort of defilement, until the end, when they finally come into the very presence of Jesus Christ (v. 14). In v. 15 Peter refers to Paul and all of his writings, as well as the rest of scripture, because the teachings on Jesus' return are difficult to comprehend fully, and the false teachers prey on those teachings to their own destruction. The purpose of this correspondence is stated in v. 17: to forewarn the faith community to be on guard and to avoid being deceived and led astray, falling from their firm understanding of the truth. In v. 18 Peter shares a doxology exhorting the readers to grow in grace and knowledge of the Lord and Savior Jesus Christ. He ends the epistle by acknowledging that honor "both now and on that eternal day," referring to the case he made earlier regarding the Day of the Lord.

Since women in 2 Peter and Jude seem to be merely victims of the false teachers' sexual urges and immorality, they are portrayed out of the shadows of the text as objects, second-class citizens, chattel. It is appropriate then that women be allowed to exhale after reading these two epistles, since they have been waiting to exhale since Eve, to engage in their unshakable calling to the gospel ministry. Second Peter is the last-written canonical book of the Christian scriptures, and it shows how far the church had moved away from the earlier empowerment of women to ministry in the first century, wherein women were treated as equals by the Lord and Savior Jesus Christ and by the apostle Paul.

The Invisibility of Women

"The invisibility of women in 2 Peter raises a question: Is there a relation between the pastor's polemic against dissenters and the eradication of women from the text?"

—Marie-Eloise Rosenblatt, "2 Peter," in *Searching the Scripture: A Feminist Commentary*, vol. 2, ed. Elisabeth Schüssler Fiorenza (New York: Crossroad, 1994), 398.

The movie *Waiting to Exhale* (1995), based on a screenplay by Terry McMillan, deals with the varied adversities and breathtaking relationships of four African American women in dysfunctional but commonly negative encounters with African American males.[7] In the final scene of the movie, these brave and bold women form an exhilarating moment together among themselves, ready to exhale. African American women in questionable relationships with African American men

---

"Truth Shall Prevail"

"Truth, crushed to earth, shall rise again;
    The eternal years of God are her's;
But Error, wounded, writhes in pain,
    And dies among his worshippers."

—From "The Battlefield" by William Cullen Bryant II, originally published in *The United States Democratic Review*, vol. 1, no. 1 (New York: Langley, 1837).

---

are frustrated because they cannot vent their frustration regarding their continued chattel state as women of color, who face triple jeopardy—sex, race, and class.[8] Indeed, to begin the exhaling of their prophetic voices, at the end of the movie, they must gather first among themselves to exhale, possibly hoping for greater exhalation, concerning their roles and relationships as clergy, pastors, priests, bishops, cardinals, and popes, where they can fully participate on all levels dealing with the leadership and critical operation of the church.[9] We hasten this day.

Notes

1. See Pheme Perkins, *First and Second Peter, James, and Jude*, Interpretation (Louisville: Westminster John Knox, 1995), 179–78.

2. Although the author is unknown, I will refer to Peter as the implied author.

3. See the sidebar for 1 Peter 1.

4. See, for example, Martin Luther King Jr., *Why We Can't Wait* (New York: Harper & Row, 1964).

5. See, for example, Jerome H. Neyrey, *2 Peter, Jude*, AB 37C (New York: Doubleday, 1993), 219–21.

6. Cf. "brazen and insolent," v. 10c (NRSV: "bold and willful").

7. Terry McMillan, *Waiting to Exhale* (New York: Pocket, 1993).

8. Cain Hope Felder, *Troubling Biblical Waters: Race, Class, and Family* (Maryknoll, N.Y.: Orbis, 1989), 139–49, chap. 8, "The Bible, Black Women, and Ministry."

9. See, for example, Cheryl Townsend Gilkes, *If It Wasn't for the Women: Black Women's Experience and Womanist Culture in Church and Community* (Maryknoll, N.Y.: Orbis, 2001); Renita J. Weems, "Reading *Her Way* through the Struggle: African American Women and the Bible," in *Stony the Road We Trod: African American Biblical Interpretation*, ed. Cain Hope Felder (Minneapolis: Fortress Press, 1991), 57–77; Delores S. Williams, *Sisters in the Wilderness: The Challenge of Womanist God-Talk* (Maryknoll, N.Y.: Orbis, 1993).

For Further Reading

Felder, Cain Hope. *Troubling Biblical Waters: Race, Class, and Family.* Maryknoll, N.Y.: Orbis, 1989.

Gilkes, Cheryl Townsend. *If It Wasn't for the Women: Black Women's Experience and Womanist Culture in Church and Community.* Maryknoll, N.Y.: Orbis, 2001.

Griffin, Paul R. *Seeds of Racism: In the Soul of America.* Cleveland: Pilgrim, 1999.

McMillan, Terry. *Waiting to Exhale.* New York: Pocket, 1993.

Neyrey, Jerome H. *2 Peter, Jude.* AB 37C. New York: Doubleday, 1993.

Perkins, Pheme. *First and Second Peter, James, and Jude.* Interpretation. Louisville: Westminster John Knox, 1995.

Weems, Renita J. "Reading *Her Way* through the Struggle: African American Women and the Bible." Pages 57–77 in *Stony the Road We Trod: African American Biblical Interpretation.* Edited by Cain Hope Felder. Minneapolis: Fortress Press, 1991.

Williams, Delores S. *Sisters in the Wilderness: The Challenge of Womanist God-Talk.* Maryknoll, N.Y.: Orbis, 1993.

1–3 JOHN

Thomas B. Slater

INTRODUCTION

AUTHORITY AND AUTHORSHIP

Church tradition ascribes the Gospel of John, 1, 2, 3 John, and Revelation to the apostle John and identifies this apostle as the beloved disciple of the Fourth Gospel.[1] While many Christians accept these traditions as factual, Revelation says only that it was written by a man named John (1:1), and this John never refers to himself as an apostle or to the apostles as if he were one of them.[2] Also, the tradition does not say that the apostle John actually wrote the Gospel but that he authorized it as a valid representation of the meaning of Jesus as he understood it.[3]

Moreover, considerable debate exists as to whether or not the Gospel and the epistles were written or authorized by the same person. For example, some note the absence of irony in the epistles, prevalent in the Gospel, and the presence of obscure references in 1 John not found in the Gospel. Others argue that 1 John reflects Greco-Roman society more than the Gospel and seems to be closer to Matthew, Mark, and Luke in many ways.[4] This is a difficult question. These differences might be due to the different purposes of the writings. Indeed, the letters provide too small a comparison with the Gospel to draw any hard and fast historical conclusions either way.

Additionally, some scholars debate whether the same person wrote all three epistles. Some argue correctly that 2 John and 3 John are true letters, while 1 John is not. For example, 2 and 3 John identify the sender and the recipient(s) in ways similar to other New Testament letters (e.g., Rom 1:1-7; Phil 1:1-2) as well as end with greetings (cf. Rom 16; Phil 4:21-23). However, while 1 John does not contain these epistolary features, it is clearly written as a message from a pastoral leader to parishioners (see 2:1 and 5:13). Therefore, while the form is not epistolary, 1 John still has an epistolary function.[5] Indeed, David Aune reminds us that the early church could employ any type of literary format for an epistolary function.[6]

On the other hand, it should be noted that the early church did not randomly associate the Gospel of John and 1, 2, and 3 John without good reason. For example, the Gospel of John and 1 John begin in strikingly similar ways (John 1:1 and 1 John 1:1); the love commandment is a key theme in both (see John 13:34-35 and 1 John 4:7-13). Similarities in style, language, and conceptuality run counter to arguments for different authors. Furthermore, the Gospel and epistles have different sociohistorical contexts that could account for the differences between them. Indeed, some elements recur among the epistles themselves: (1) 1 John 4:7-12 and 2 John 6 emphasize the love commandment; (2) 1 John 4:2 and 2 John 7 advocate confessing the incarnation; and, as I noted above, (3) 2 and 3 John begin and end in very similar ways.

I believe that 1, 2, and 3 John reflect continuing interpretation of the Gospel of John and the tradition behind that Gospel within a given community of early Christians. Furthermore, these Christians reside within the same general geographical area. Even so, whether or not we have one author or multiple authors is not a major historical factor in interpreting the books. If we have one author, the same author has reflected upon the significance of

Jesus for the circumstances of his/her community of faith.

In this commentary I work from the perspective that 1, 2, and 3 John were written by the current leader of the Johannine community in order to maintain social cohesion and to affirm the truth of the theological tradition as she or he understood it in light of the Gospel of John. I shall call the author "John" for the sake of convenience. Also, for the sake of convenience, I shall call these documents letters or epistles, since each has a message from the community's leader to members of the community, realizing fully that 1 John does not contain all the forms of the genre but functions in general like a letter nonetheless.[7] If the letters represent the work of two or more writers, these writings may represent the earliest example of a single, unbroken tradition in the early church for two or more generations.

DATE

There is no consensus on the precise date of the Johannine epistles. The writings reflect a time after the separation of the target audience from the synagogue. This occurred sometime late in the first century C.E.

STRUCTURE

There is no real structural pattern in 1 John. Topics overlap to such a degree that it is extremely difficult to discern a particular topic being addressed and then the author going to another topic. The book continuously repeats itself.

PURPOSE

The Nature of the Group

First John is like an extended exhortation on several themes. It is a message from the leader of a sectarian group to members of his or her particular movement. A sect is a group that emphasizes a particular doctrine and/or practice to the point that the group distinguishes itself even within its own religious tradition. Three elements in the Johannine epistles give credence to the sectarian nature of the letter.[8]

First and foremost, the community's "high Christology," the explicit reference to Jesus Christ as God (John 1:1 and 20:28), distinguished it from other movements within Judaism and also within early Christianity. While first-century Judaism could speak of messianic figures to come, they were created beings (outstanding humans or archangels). The Johannine community asserted that Jesus Christ was also God's agent of creation (see John 1)! This is clearly a development in the concept of messianic figures beyond what had been espoused previously within Judaism. On the other hand, the Christian assertion that Jesus was God's Son (Matt 3:17; 17:5) could have meant merely that he was an extraordinary being who was obedient to his Father.

Second, the community emphasized love among its members. This is often the case among sects that find themselves outside the social mainstream or who have been or believe they have been marginalized in someway. "Love is the decisive commandment and necessary sign of belonging to the community, because love is how this community have experienced God-toward-them."[9]

Other early Christian documents advocated a love that went beyond the elect community. Indeed, Jesus taught that love should be given to the one with the greatest need, regardless of whether or not that person was within the group (Luke 10:25-37). Paul holds a similar position (Rom 5:6-11). The Johannine love command has an in-group, internal function, while what we find in Luke and Romans has both internal and external consequences.[10] The Johannine love ethic probably developed in an atmosphere in which

the community's beliefs and/or practices were initially ridiculed or repressed by more traditional adherents of Jewish background. When the letters were written, this love ethic is espoused within a context of tensions within Johannine Christianity itself.

Third, dualism is found in both the Gospel and the letters. Dualism occurs when two sides perceive their perspectives to be mutually exclusive. The dualism in the Gospel of John is a prevalent feature.[11] It enables the reader to know without a doubt who is good and who is not, who is in the community and who is not. The Johannine epistles have this same type of dichotomy between good and bad (1 John 1:5-8; 4:1-6; 2 John 9; 3 John 11). Dualism enables the Johannine community to live as though it is the community assured of God's election.

Statements of Purpose

In five instances 1 John articulates reasons for the writing of the letter. The first is found in 1:4: "We are writing this that our joy may be complete." John hopes to convince his audience of the truth of his beliefs. Their adherence will bring joy to him. John speaks as a father might speak to his children: "Make me happy by behaving properly."

The second occurs in 2:1. John says that he is writing so that his readers will not sin. John states that if they do sin, Christ Jesus is their advocate (*parakletos*) before God.[12] Thus, in this passage, sin is a live option for Christians, but Christ provides the means by which sins are forgiven. He follows with an ethical exhortation to keep God's commandments in order to demonstrate that one is a child of God.

The third reason comes in 2:12-14, where John twice addresses three different groups: little children, fathers, and young men. First, he tells children that their sins are forgiven. Second, he tells fathers that they know the beginning and the history of the Christian movement. This sentence echoes 1 John 1:1-4. Finally, the young men are told that they have conquered the devil (cf. John 17:15; 1 John 3:12; 5:18). The second set of sayings parallel the first. These brief passages focus upon three themes that this commentary will demonstrate are important for 1 John: forgiveness of sins, upholding and affirming tradition, and Christ's role in human salvation.

The fourth occurs in 2:26. It warns the readers about "those who would deceive you." John encourages the recipients of his message by describing the anointing that protects and guides them. The anointing is a reference to the baptism of the Holy Spirit. This verse is a word of assurance intended to keep people within the sacred community, an important theme in 1, 2, and 3 John.[13]

Finally, in 5:13 John exhorts his parishioners to remain within the community by asserting that faith in God's Son leads to eternal life. Again, maintaining cohesion within the community is a key issue in 1 John (see 1:7; 2:25-26; 3:1-3, 11, 16-23; 4:7-17; 5:1-3, 18-20).[14]

These statements show that three topics were central to the author's purpose: (1) salvation from sin; (2) remaining true to the tradition, and (3) keeping the community intact.

THEOLOGY AND ETHICS

Ecclesiology and Christology are the main theological issues in the Johannine epistles. The ecclesiology can be summed up as "unity in the community" based upon the love command. John repeatedly exhorts his readers to remain true to its confession that Jesus Christ came in the flesh and that his ministry had saving implications for humankind. Even though some have left the community, John exhorts those who have not left to affirm its christological confession. Those who left have demonstrated by their leaving that they were not children of God and members of the sacred community.[15]

The main ethical requirement is a sectarian one: to love the brother or sister in the sacred group. A similar development occurred in the South among black Americans in the century after emancipation of the slaves. This "sectarian" development enabled a legally disenfranchised community to endure constant discrimination while attempting to sustain itself during dangerous times.

Americans of African descent have found that college degrees, financial security, good looks, and social standing do not exempt them from racism. Indeed, one could possess all of these things and still be referred to by a racial slur or be called "boy" by someone junior in social, economic, or even political status. Many southern Euroamericans practiced a common form of pernicious racism: they refused to speak to and therefore acknowledge blacks, even ones whom they knew very well, in public. Such refusal challenged the disregarded black person's existence. As a result, Americans of African descent in the South began to greet one another whenever and wherever they might be. This practice was extended to other black Americans whom they did not even know.

Moreover, some blacks refused to call another black by their first name in mixed company, using "Mrs./Sis. Smith" and "Mr./Bro. Jones" instead. For some, this practice was particularly important when addressing the clergy, educators, lawyers, and physicians. In this way, the respect denied the group in the wider society was found in abundance within the group itself. Similarly, the love denied the Johannine sect in the broader society was affirmed and nurtured within the group itself.

EXAMPLES OF INTERPRETATION

Perhaps the most widely discussed exegesis of a passage from the Johannine epistles is found in Martin Luther King Jr.'s sermon "Antidotes for Fear," in *Strength to Love*, a collection of King's sermons that has gone through many editions and has been translated into several languages. Coretta Scott King has said that this book has been mentioned to her by King's admirers more than any other as a theological resource and also as a source of inspiration.[16]

"Antidotes for Fear" is an exegetical study of 1 John 4:18. While acknowledging the helpful dimension of fear, King argues that some fears are abnormal, like imagined snakes under a carpet. "Our problem is not to be rid of fear but rather to harness and master it."[17] Love masters fear. Such love is not soft but strong and unflinching. This type of love casts out personal fears (e.g., aging) as well as widely held fears (e.g., racial injustice). "Not arms, but love, understanding, and organized goodwill can cast out fear. Only disarmament, based on good faith, will make mutual trust a living reality."[18] He continues, "If our white brothers are to master fear, they must depend not only on their commitment to Christian love but also on the Christ-like love which the Negro generates toward them."[19] King lived this love ethic, and many today continue to be influenced by his example.[20]

Another outstanding African American interpretation comes from the late Bishop Joseph A. Johnson Jr. In his magnum opus, *Proclamation Theology*, Johnson argues that the nature of God is love and that black Americans experience this divine love in spite of the discriminatory society in which they encounter life. While fully acknowledging the reality and necessity of divine wrath, Johnson asserts that divine love has healing power, is fully manifest in Christ Jesus, and is outgoing, merciful, redemptive.[21]

1 JOHN

1:1-4, Prologue

Many have correctly noted that the prologue of 1 John, 1:1-4, echoes John 1 in many ways.[22] Though 1 John is not a typical letter, it still contains a message for a specific audience.[23] Both John and 1 John refer to "the beginning." While the Gospel refers to creation, the epistle refers to the birth of the Johannine tradition. In this subtle way, the writer joins creation and tradition, the past and the present. Moreover, the writer identifies the word of life as the incarnation, the coming of the Son of God in the flesh, Jesus Christ. It is precisely the incarnation that has been heard, seen, and touched by members of the community. Repeatedly, the author stresses the need to confess (1) that the Son of God came in the flesh and (2) that Jesus was that Son. Verse 2 continues the incarnation

---

Proclamation Theology

Joseph A. Johnson Jr. was a bishop in the Christian Methodist Episcopal (CME) Church at the time of his death. Prior to that he was a professor of New Testament at the Interdenominational Theological Center (ITC) in Atlanta. He had a Ph.D. from Vanderbilt and a Th.D. from Iliff. *Proclamation Theology* is an excellent example of a black American, biblically based neo-orthodox systematic theology. It represents a strong tradition in the black church that theology must be relevant to be worthwhile. This work has not received the attention it deserves even in the African American community.

theme and then equates it with eternal life: "the eternal life that was with the Father and was made manifest to us" refers rhetorically to Jesus. Continuing in v. 3, John states that the gospel was established so that his audience might have fellowship with God and Christ by means of the Johannine tradition. If one adheres to this tradition, one's joy shall be complete (v. 4). In these four verses, John not only advocates keeping the tradition but also asserts that by adhering to it one can maintain an unbroken fellowship with God. Finally, there is an unbroken line in this tradition from God to Jesus to John and to John's audience. What we have here is an emphasis upon a given historical tradition and the importance of being faithful to it in order to be saved.[24]

Homecoming

Many black congregations celebrate annual "homecoming" to commemorate the founding of that congregation. Former members often return at this time to see family and old friends and to reminisce. A major feature of these gatherings is the reading of the church history during the afternoon service. In this way, homecoming becomes a means of passing the tradition on to the younger generation.

Moreover, many black American families have "family historians" who can retain family history for several generations. Their histories are usually transmitted orally, but more are being written. Many family historians can accurately transmit pre-emancipation history. This mode of keeping history probably goes back to the west African *griot*, who retained family histories for an entire tribe. In these and other ways, tradition plays an important role in African American culture.

1:5—2:2

John next states that the tradition comes from Jesus; however, this aspect of the tradition is not about Christ but about God the Father. John employs dualistic language by associating light with God and darkness with falsehood (cf. John 1:9).[25] Dualism is often employed when two sides believe that their positions are mutually exclusive (see v. 6). Neither side wants to compromise. Dualism has played a significant role in the African American community. American culture has said that black was bad, but African American culture has asserted that "Black is beautiful." In the process, African Americans have affirmed their dignity, researched their history, established the positive contributions by people of African descent from biblical times to the present, and contributed to a sense of self-worth in a hostile environment. John wants as much for his community.

Fellowship is an important concern in the Johannine epistles. One proves that one has fellowship with God by having fellowship with those in community (1:7a). As is often the case, 1 John connects fellowship with salvation (v. 7b). The argument goes as follows: fellowship with those in community demonstrates that one has fellowship with God, and such fellowship shall lead to one's salvation. Again, note the tradition: John passes on to his readers what has been given to him. In this way, he hopes to separate himself from his theological opponents.[26] John's argument is that Christians must live a righteous life ("walk in the light"). This implies that his adversaries did not walk in the light and that neither side wanted to compromise its position. Fellowship was effectively broken.

Black leaders in predominantly white denominations have often not received the respect their offices and their skills demand. Their ministries have been limited frequently to their own ethnic community.

Such practices have disrupted true fellowship in these denominations. What are Christians to think when their brothers and sisters in Christ treat them with the same disdain that they experience in society at large? The need for authentic Christian fellowship becomes more acute in such circumstances.

Verses 8-10 discuss sin and forgiveness. It appears as though John's opponents professed that they "have no sin" (v. 8). Some might cogently argue that it is difficult to know whether they actually espoused this, since none of their writings have survived. However, I suggest that 1:8-10 represents the teachings of John's antagonists while 2:1-2, 3:6, 8-9 and 5:18 are John's hyperbolic statements to prove a point.

The point of 1:8-10 is to show the inadequacy of his opponents' theology. First and foremost, John asserts that everyone sins. To believe otherwise is to deceive oneself (v. 8). Confession must precede God's forgiveness (v. 9). The author reiterates earlier points in different words in v. 10.

Verses 8-10 represent three parallel statements on sin and forgiveness. In these parallels, the statements in vv. 8 and 10 are about human actions, while v. 9 is about God's actions. The first parallel consists of the statements, "If we say we have no sin" (v. 8), "If we confess our sins" (v. 9), and "If we say we have not sinned" (v. 10). The first and third statements are about the human condition; the second, about God. Verse 9 tells us that if we acknowledge our transgressions, God will pardon us and put us in right relationship with God. Only God can accomplish this. This pattern is repeated in the second parallel, "We deceive ourselves" (v. 8), "he is faithful and just" (v. 9), and "we make him a liar" (v. 10). Again, the first and third statements are about humans; the second, about God. The third parallel is, "the truth is not in us" (v. 8), "he will forgive our sins and cleanse us from all unrighteousness" (v. 9), and "his word is not in us" (v. 10). Again we note that the first and last statements are about humans; the middle, about God. Verse 8 and 10 are syn-

Fellowship

Fellowship is very important within the black church. For example, the church became the place where African Americans could be themselves in music, in preaching, in response to preaching, and in many other ways in the days prior to and even after integration. Thus, in this sense the African American church became an important place where one could enjoy being black in a setting where one's culture is affirmed, confirmed, and validated. Moreover, these feelings of pride are reinforced as congregations create fellowship together across denominational lines. _Fellowship within the group has the power to compensate for being marginalized by the general society._ This is why fellowship was so important within Johannine Christianity. (For example, my home church when I was a boy was Methodist. Our choir participated in two "singing conventions," in which area choirs met on Sunday afternoons on a regular basis to sing. One convention was solely Methodist; the other ecumenical. Years after the conventions dissolved people continued to talk about the excellent fellowship at those gatherings.)

onymous parallels that address inappropriate human actions, and they sandwich v. 9, which discusses God's forgiveness of human sin.[27]

In 2:1-2, John explicitly states how forgiveness occurs. John refers to his readers as "my little children" (2:1). This is at once a term of endearment and a statement of his spiritual parentage on their behalf. He states that if they do sin, they have an advocate (*parakletos*; cf. John 14:16-17, 26; 15:26; 16:7-11) who will intercede for them with the Father, "Jesus Christ the righteous." Here is a clear example of the Paraclete concept in the Johannine community. The Paraclete is a name for the Holy Spirit in John 14–16, where Jesus promises to send the community "another Paraclete" (14:16), implying that Jesus is the first Paraclete. At the very least, some in the community understood that Jesus was the first Paraclete and the Holy Spirit the second. In other words, the first Paraclete represented the word of God in his person; the second re-presented by spiritual means the witness of Jesus to the Johannine community.

John states in 2:2 that Jesus Christ is the means by which the sins of the entire world are removed (*hilasmos*). There has been much discussion as to the precise meaning of *hilasmos*.[28] Some argue that it should be translated "expiation," while others argue for "propitiation." Raymond Brown makes a helpful distinction between the two terms: expiation refers to the offended person, propitiation to the offense itself.[29]

It is quite possible that John was not as refined a thinker as his contemporary exegetes and that he thought of Jesus as the means to remove the effects of human sin in a way that included aspects of both terms.[30] In 2:1 the author states that Christ is an advocate before God, the one who is offended; 2:2 refers to the transgression itself. Thus, both expiation and propitiation are relevant terms. A better translation might be "and he is the means of the removal of our sins." Such a translation does justice to both terms, while effectively communicating John's intended meaning. John was not a systematic theologian trained in linguistic analysis. We should not expect him to be as precise or as consistent (cf. 2:1-2 and 5:18) as we would like him to be. He was a church leader attempting to exhort his readers to remain faithful to their tradition by any means possible.

Why have others not seen this? A Eurocentric approach is often an either/or approach that imposes a post-Enlightenment, Western European/North American perspective on an ancient eastern Mediterranean text. Such an approach assumes a logic that is not always at home in John's Greco-Roman religious milieu. Religious literature, often written by non-professional or non-academic persons, is often more flexible and less precise than theological/philosophical literature written from an academic and professional perspective. A good example is Sunday school literature. Most black denominations have their own publishing houses, and Sunday school lessons are written by seminary graduates in such a way that persons with a sixth-grade education can understand them. The aim is to make sound theological principles and concepts accessible to a more general audience. The Johannine epistles are much closer to Sunday school lessons than to philosophical/theological essays.

2:3-11

In this section John contrasts those who keep God's commandments with those who do not. In particular, he refers to the love command (vv. 5, 10; see also John 13:34-35). He argues for ethics over theology, doing over merely stating, walking the walk, not just talking the talk (see also 3:18).[31] Those who say "I know him" should love their sisters and brothers in the faith as well (for God is love, 4:7). The fact that they do not love their siblings in the faith is a clear indication, if not demonstration, that they do not actually know God. However, true Christians obey God's commandments and have the truest, most complete type of love. Only this love connotes and denotes Christian discipleship (vv. 3-6). Often African Americans have not experienced Christian love from other Christians. From the trials of Richard Allen, James Pennington, H. H. Garnet, James Walker Hood, William Paul Quinn, and many others, black Christians know too well that Christian love has not been extended to them. John struggles to prevent this same lack of love from destroying his community.

John returns to tradition in vv. 7-11. He begins by addressing his readers as "Beloved." In other words, they both possess and express the love that his antagonists do not (v. 7). He then states that he is not teaching something new but something old; i.e., he is repeating the tradition ("the word that you have heard"). For some reason, he then contradicts

Grandma Theology

In the late 1970s, black seminarians at Perkins School of Theology at Southern Methodist University in Dallas began to describe their theology as "Grandma Theology." Their goal was to express their theology in terms that any African American grandmother with a third-grade education could understand and hopefully affirm with a strong "Amen!" John attempts to do the same thing for his readers. The book is relatively free of technical terms and repeats traditional expressions important to the community. In this way, John wants to his readers to say "Amen!" to his message to them.

the preceding statement by referring to a new commandment and then employs dualistic, apocalyptic imagery.[32] "The darkness is passing away" is an apocalyptic expression that means that the end of the world—or of this present age—is near. The contrast between the darkness and the light in this passage, an example of dualism, is also an apocalyptic motif. It is a symbolic means of denoting the bad from the good, evil from righteousness.[33] John's point is that Christians must love comrades within the sacred community as a sign of one's righteousness (vv. 9-11).

In the introduction I commented on the love command and the sectarian nature of the Johannine community. I now address it from a different perspective. Many African American Christians have experienced the lack of application of the love command by Christians from other ethnic communities (and, regrettably, vice versa in some cases) that have espoused a love ethic that they have enacted in limited fashion. It has been applied only to persons within one's ethnic community.

One recent development along these same lines is that some predominantly white denominations have drawn lines of theological demarcation. One example is the struggle within the Southern Baptist Convention (SBC) between the fundamentalists, who now control the SBC, and the Cooperative Baptist Fellowship (CBF), the moderate wing of the SBC. The result has been the widespread dismissal of non-fundamentalists in every segment of the denomination. The moderates have been denigrated and treated as though they are not legitimate Christians. *They have not been loved.* Time will tell whether this experience makes them more sensitive to those who have had these experiences from birth (e.g., African Americans) or if they will become more inward and/or sectarian.[34]

2:12-14

Here John emphasizes the victory of Christians over sin and Satan. The faithful members of the Johannine community truly know the Father. They live righteous lives; that is why "the word of God abides" in them (v. 14).

2:15-20

These verses contain dualist contrast, first, between love for the world and love for God; second, between the earthly and the divine. The former includes sensual lust and arrogance (*alagoneia*). Then, in v. 17, John contrasts the temporal and the eternal. The temporal world is coming to an end (an apocalyptic expectation common to the time), but the one who does the will of God shall remain forever. This is an exhortation to keep people within the sacred community. Verses 15-17 constitute additional exhortations with that same purpose.[35]

John continues the contrast in vv. 18-19. First, he states that the world's end is near as evidenced by the presence of the antichrist.[36] Many early Christians believed that just before Jesus returned the antichrist would appear. Thus, the antichrist was a precursor of sorts of the Christ's second coming. John, however, takes the expectation to another level: those who left the community are antichrists. According to John, they were never actually part of the community or they would not have left (see v. 22). Commenting upon this passage, Bishop Othal Hawthorne Lakey said that John would probably be more concerned with doctrine than the status of those who left because doctrine can have longer lasting effects.[37] The doctrine he believed John expressed was that Johannine Christians should have no fear, because they possess a divine anointing that will protect them and keep them safe during the final days of tribulation (v. 20). This anointing refers to the activity of the Holy Spirit in their lives.

Remarks that denounce one's opponents as antichrists do not indicate a mild difference of opinion. Rather, they suggest a fierce contention between two uncompromising sides. Within such a context, opposing sides attempt to demonize each other. Therefore, one cannot take for granted that one side has not misrepresented its opposite to some degree.[38]

2:21-25

These verses contrast truth and falsehood in a manner similar to the light/darkness contrast discussed earlier. The truth for John is that Jesus is the Messiah; the lie, that Jesus is not the Messiah, is revealed in v. 22. Whoever does not affirm that Jesus is the Messiah is the antichrist. John adds that the one who denies that Jesus is the Christ, the Son of God, also denies the Father. The additional warning expresses a sentiment very similar to the assertion of the unity of Jesus and God the Father in the Gospel of John. The best example is John 10:30: "The Father and I are one."[39] God the Father and Christ Jesus are "interrelated identities and, because the one implies the other, to deny one is to deny the other."[40] Thus, it is not that John is simply employing hyperbole in order to cast his opponents in a bad light. Rather, John is again reflecting upon tradition and calling to task his theological adversaries in light of that tradition. On the positive side, confessing the Father and Jesus establishes a strong, positive relationship between God and the devotees.

2:26-28

In John's second statement about his purpose for writing, he includes a warning about those who would deceive with untruths. John, however, assures the readers that their spiritual baptism will shield them. The baptism of the

Spirit has a didactic function in John 14:25-26; it is the teaching that provides protection from deception. One might ask why John feels a need to write if the Spirit keeps them safe. Most probably, John believes that they have the *potential* to remain true to the tradition. His message simply attempts to bolster their resolve. Verses 27-28 conclude with a mild word of encouragement to "keep the faith," i.e., be righteous until Christ returns.

3:1-3

Verse 1 affirms that the community comes from God. "The consequences and proof of the love of God is being, and being called, children of God."[41] This is an elevated status. The world does not recognize this status because it has not recognized the true God (cf. John 1:9-10). Because it does not know the Parent, the world is unable to recognize the children of the Parent. It is therefore unremarkable that the world is hostile to the community of faith. The community sees itself as being marginalized: it has experienced social degradation. David Rensberger writes, "This self-understanding is typical of sectarian and countercultural groups. It has obvious risks when carried to extremes; but it is also part of what enabled the early Christians, struggling against traditional and widely held social values, to persevere."[42] I concur. A similar feeling of communal ostra-cism has fueled both a sense of sectarianism and survival in African America. Indeed, it is a self-avowed self-affirmation against the judgments of the wider society that has enabled so many black Americans to succeed despite the hostility expressed and limitations imposed by explicit and implicit forms of racism.

Some might argue that John could just as easily be overreacting, that there is no evidence to prove the community was beleaguered in any way. I would counter with two questions. Where is the evidence that Christians were held in even moderate esteem in the first century C.E.? Where are the inscriptions, the letters, the essays, the works of arts to support such a claim?

Verse 2 develops the preceding verse. John does not attempt to provide details about what the future holds for God's children. It is only important that "we shall be like him." That is clearly a word of assurance.[43] John's intent is to convince his readers of the certainty of their salvation and to motivate them to remain faithful to their tradition. A reference to purity naturally follows (v. 3). John refers here to moral purity.[44]

3:4-10

Verses 4-6 constitute the case; vv. 7-10, the argument. In vv. 4-6 John contrasts sin and righteousness. First, he equates sin with law-

Arts of Survival

African American culture has enabled the community to survive and nurture outstanding citizens in the arts, the sciences, and public service. Jazz, the blues, and spirituals are original American art forms loved and appreciated around the world. In the sciences, the contributions of the likes of Charles Drew and George Washington Carver are second to none. Phillis Wheatley, Ralph Ellison, and Toni Morrison, to name a few, have received international acclaim. Ralph Bunche and Andrew Young are among the public servants whose work has wrought benefits on an international scale.

lessness and affirms that Christ could take away sin because he was sinless. His additional remark that those who abide in Christ do not sin is a direct contradiction of 1:8—2:2. The reality of human behavior of even the most ethical persons clearly makes v. 6 pure hyperbole. John overstates the case in order to distance himself from his adversaries, something that recurs throughout 1 John and is characteristic of sectarian groups.[45]

In vv. 7-10 John again employs dualistic language to distinguish those (unrighteous) who left the movement from those (righteous) who stayed. Leaving demonstrated their moral impropriety. "The separatists are those whose parentage lies with the devil, and the faithful . . . are the children of God."[46]

3:11-18

John now returns to the subject of tradition: "that we should love one another," a theme he repeats frequently (e.g., 2:7-11; 3:1, 11; 4:7-12; 5:3) and is a clear reflection of the Gospel of John (e.g., 13:34-35).[47] John again turns to dualism. Cain represents evil, not righteousness. While the world hates the Johannine community, there is love within the community; the community is passing from death into life. The dualism is an apocalyptic motif employed to encourage members of the community to remain faithful. "Life" here refers to unending life with God. The key focus is on the love found within the community, a love that requires one to love in proportion to another's needs (cf. Luke 10:25-37). The author ends by exhorting the readers not to love in words only but also in deed and in truth. This final exhortation echoes throughout the New Testament (e.g., Matt 7:24-27; Gal 5:6; Jas 1:22).[48]

"Truth" (*aletheia*) almost becomes a technical term in the Johannine epistles (see 1 John 1:6; 2:21; 3:19; 2 John 1–4; 3 John

1, 3–8).[49] It appears to mean living in accord with the tradition, at the very least, and perhaps also maintaining and sustaining communal harmony and unity. It is not employed in the same manner in every case.

3:19-24

Rensberger argues persuasively that these verses constitute a transition that introduces the main themes of chaps. 4–5: the correct Christology, keeping the love command, abiding within the community, and living in the Spirit.[50]

4:1-6

These verses discuss the relationship between pneumatology and Christology. John asserts that each spirit must be tested. The manner of the test is quite simple: the person who confesses that Jesus Christ has come in the flesh has the Spirit of God; the person who denies the incarnation has the spirit of the antichrist. This principal confession is required in the Johannine epistles.

Verse 4 contains a word of assurance that the believers are children of God (see also 3:1-2). By the power of God, they have already defeated their opponents.[51] John then contrasts those who belong to the world with those who belong to God, and the spirit of truth with the spirit of error. This passage has an ecclesiastical function: it separates the elect from those outside the elect community. Sects often see the world in this dualistic, separatist way.

4:7-12

For many readers, these verses constitute the apex of the book.[52] Here John states most succinctly the relationship between loving and being related to God. Again, he expresses himself dualistically. Those who love others within the community are children of God and know God; those who do not love those in community do not know God and by implication are not related to God. God's essential nature is love (*agape*). Thus it is not possible to be God's offspring if one does not love other persons within the community. Indeed, that is why John addresses his parishioners as "beloved" (*agapetos*). This is an example of "theological genetics." Just as a human offspring possesses characteristics of one or both parents, so too true Christians exhibit the essential characteristic of God: love. They love one another. The sending of God's Son into the world so that humans might have eternal life is proof of God's love for humankind (vv. 9-10). Believers should follow God's example and love one another (v. 11). John ends the section by reasserting the love command, the only means by which one can ascertain who is and who is not a child of God. If believers abide in love, this love will reach its maturity.[53]

Historically, the black church has provided the love and support that the wider society has not given. Young people have found the affirmation and encouragement lacking in the broader society. Adults have been given responsibilities that matched their skills and talents. They have also received praise for jobs done well. Many black Christians greet fellow Christians as "Brother Smith" and "Sister Jones," whether they are members of their denomination or not. Affirmative action, in the form of love, found a home in the black church long before it became a legal practice in America. This is the love John wants in his community.

4:13-15

The gift of the Holy Spirit assures Johannine Christians that God abides in them and that they abide in God. The Spirit leads believers to confess that Jesus is the Son of God and the Savior of the world (see also 4:1-3). John reiterates his earlier affirmation by stating that believers who confess that Jesus is the Son of God abide in God and God in them.

At the center of the debate is the role and function of Jesus. John's theological opponents spoke of Jesus and Christ as separate beings. In the second century, docetists and Gnostic Christians would hold similar positions, but it would not be prudent, given the meager evidence, to identify them as John's opponents here. There were, however, first-century philosophical/theological movements that might better explain the situation.

Greco-Roman philosophies and religions heavily influenced one another. Middle Platonism was a major philosophical movement in the first Christian century prior to the rise of Christianity. First-century proponents included Philo of Alexandria and Plutarch. Platonists believed in a transcendent God who was far removed from earth and resided in a perfect, transcendent world. In Platonism human intellect was that aspect of humans that was closest to the nature of the divine. Thus, the mind should be nurtured in order to guide one to a better life. The better life was based upon rational living. Conversely, the body was the inferior part of humans because of its tendency to be led by physical desires and not by reason. Similarly, Roman Stoicism emphasized the importance of living rationally and argued that reason is the divine aspect within humans. These two major Greco-Roman philosophical movements reinforced one another and had extensive influence on the general populace. For example, while the content differs significantly, the use of lists of virtues and vices (Gal 5:19-24) and household rules (Eph 5:21—6:9) are Stoic motifs.

Persons within the Johannine community who either advocated or were attracted to Platonic and/or Stoic concepts would be less likely to be strong advocates of the incarnation. It would be inconceivable that the divine would voluntarily confine itself within human flesh. On the other hand, such thinkers would be more likely to emphasize the divinity of Christ and advocate being more like Christ than like Jesus.

4:16-21

These verses, for the most part, simply reiterate much of what has been said previously, with some added details about the love command. Practicing love gives one confidence at the final judgment (v. 17). This is the same boldness/confidence discussed in 2:28—3:3. Verse 18 implies that confidence and fear are mutually exclusive and cannot coexist in a person.[54] If one is confident before God on Judgment Day, there literally is no need to fear anything or anyone. Fear and love are polar opposites. Those who still are fearful concerning the final judgment are not yet "perfected in love" (4:18; see also John 5:22-27). Such persons are not spiritually mature.[55] "If a man is afraid in the presence of God, it is a sign that God's love does not fill him, . . . that he belongs to 'the other side.'"[56]

The remainder of the chapter rehearses themes that we have seen previously: the centrality of the love command within community as proof of one's love for God (e.g., 4:7-15) and also the connection between Johannine tradition and the love command (4:21; cf. John 13:34-35).

5:1-12

R. A. Culpepper correctly notes that this section articulates the relationship between love and faith. Verses 1-4 relate faith to the inescapable necessity to love: the love ethic is the sign that one is a true child of God. Verses 2-3 connect the love ethic toward others with loving God and obeying God's commandments.[57] The section ends with the affirmation that those who adhere to the love command defeat the world through their faith.

Verses 5-9 discuss the three witnesses: the Spirit, the water, and the blood. The symbolism probably refers to Jesus' baptism (water), his crucifixion (blood), and the activity of the Holy Spirit in his life, the Spirit who speaks to our human spirits even now (5:10). "The three witnesses fulfill the biblical requirement that testimony must be validated by at least two witnesses (Deut 19:15)."[58]

John then argues that if one accepts human testimony, one should accept the witnesses established by God even more. He ends by stating that God has testified that Jesus Christ is his son (v. 9). At this point, a recurring theme in 1 John, the incarnation, and a recurring motif, dualism, reappear. Those who affirm the incarnation have God's witness

Inclusive Theology

Too frequently in American religious discourse, "faith" means only "correct doctrine" or "sound theology." This is a classic misrepresentation of the biblical witness that the African American church has consistently denounced. Reading the Torah, the great prophets proclaimed that religion without sound ethics was empty (e.g., Amos 5:21-24; Mic 6:6-8; Hos 6:6). Jesus (e.g., Matt 9:13; Mark 12:33) and Paul (Gal 5:6, 22-25) have the same message. African American Christians have consistently made this same connection. The most recent academic manifestations are black liberation theology and womanist theology. Neither is satisfied with inclusive language. These writers insist on an inclusive theology accompanied by inclusive love.

(presumably by means of the Holy Spirit [see 5:7-8]) and eternal life through God's Son. However, those who do not affirm the incarnation are liars whose denials have forfeited eternal life for them.

5:13-21

These nine verses conclude the book. John has written to his readers to assure them that they do indeed have eternal life (v. 13). This assurance should give them the confidence to petition God (v. 14). The key phrase in v. 14 is "according to his will." John does not say that Christians get whatever they request from God. It is not a "name it and claim it" theology. Rather, because one is a faithful child of God, one should have the faith to go to God and ask for divine favors. If one's request is not granted, it is not necessarily a sign of divine disfavor. It simply may not be within the divine plan. One's faith should not diminish. Rather, one should remain confident that God knows what is best (vv. 14-15).[59] This is a very important verse for many contemporary Christians who constantly hear from prominent preachers that God will give them whatever they ask of God. Verse 14 makes it clear that Christians should boldly approach God, but that the final decision is God's. *God shall not be manipulated, even by the most faithful persons.*

Verses 16-17 discuss intercessory prayers. Other Christians should intercede on behalf of sisters and brothers who commit sins not unto death. Unfortunately, John does not tell us what these sins are. Perhaps his readers knew, and he felt no need to identify them. These verses open the door of reconciliation to those who have disagreed with John. At the very least, John affirms the need and the efficacy of intercessory prayer. Moreover, such prayers will be heard, if not answered, if God so desires (see vv. 14-15).

2 JOHN

As I commented on 1 John 3:11-18, above, "truth" is almost a technical term in the Johannine epistles (see 2 John 1 [twice], 2, 3, 4, and 3 John 1, 3, 4, 8, 12). In most instances (2 John 2, 4; 3 John 1, 3, 4, 8, 12), it refers to the *true* tradition, from John's perspective. The content of this tradition includes (1) believing in and witnessing to the incarnation (v. 7; cf. 1 John 4:2-3); (2) keeping the love commandment, which they have had from the beginning (2 John 5–6; cf. John 13:34; 1 John 2:7; 4:7; 5:2-5).[60] It is noteworthy that 2 John repeats key themes from the Gospel and 1 John. This is evidence of the Gospel's continuing influence within the community as well as the continuation of differing, competing interpretations of that Gospel.[61]

1–3

These verses contain the type of greeting that one would expect in a Greco-Roman letter: the sender (the elder), the recipients (the elect lady and her children), and expressions of grace, mercy, and peace (cf. Gal 1:1-3; 1 Tim 1:1-2; Jude 2–3). However, neither the sender nor the recipients are specifically named. "The elder" clearly connotes one with authority (see Acts 14:23; 1 Tim 5:17-19; Jas 5:14; 1 Pet 5:1), but the degree of authority is in question.

There are almost always degrees of power in social relationships, and the parties involved do not always agree as to the degree. The key element is when and how much power to use in a given situation. A bishop in the African Methodist Episcopal (AME) Church, the African Methodist Episcopal Zion (AMEZ) or the Christian Methodist Episcopal (CME) Church is a very powerful figure. However, bishops in these denominations constantly encounter local traditions that are not Methodist, where entrenched leadership functions in ways contrary to church law and/or contrary to the best interests of the local congregation. Despite their power, these bishops cannot displace or even nullify them. This can be said of both large and small congregations. Thus, to argue that in 2 John the elder assumes an authority that he actually does not have is to misunderstand the sociopolitical dynamics of human organizations. It is quite possible that the elder is the authority figure but that he faces a personal challenge to his authority. In other words, the person, not the office of the elder, faces a challenge. Additionally, it is possible that someone else wants to be elder.

"The elect lady and her children" probably refers to the congregation and its members.

4–8

The elder expresses his delight that some persons adhere to the true tradition. He then exhorts others to do likewise (vv. 5-6). A warning follows that echoes 1 John 2:22-23. This section concludes with another admonition "to keep the faith" in order that they might receive their eternal reward (v. 8).

9–11

These verses also reiterate 1 John 2:22-23. The recipients are discouraged from showing hospitality to those who deny the incarnation. "The instruction given here is to be understood against the background of hospitality given to strangers and travelers in the ancient world."[62] Indeed, Gal 6:10 exhorts Christians to offer hospitality to travelers, especially to fellow Christians. However, there is the admonition in Matt 7:6 not to share what is good with those who cannot appreciate it.[63]

This passage of scripture must be employed with caution. It advocates an exclu-

sive attitude toward fellow Christians with different beliefs. Christian history is fraught with ethno-religious conflicts that have magnified beyond control: the Catholic-Protestant conflict in Northern Ireland, the Catholic-Muslim-Orthodox strife in the former Yugoslavia, to name a few. No side is absolutely correct, and none is absolutely incorrect. All sinfully act as if they are without error. The Johannine letters are not free of this: a central issue in 2 John is whether John's supporters should extend hospitality to their opponents; a central issue in 3 John is the lack of hospitality extended to John's supporters. Indeed, both sides of the debate need to be reminded that someone taught his disciples to treat others as they would like to be treated (Matt 7:12). Both need to remember the teachings of John 13:34-35.

On the other hand, there is a genuine danger in maintaining fellowship with persons whose beliefs and/or practices are not constructive or beneficial. How much is too much? When one begins to lose one's sense of self, it is time to re-evaluate the relationship. Some persons and/or groups have a higher tolerance than others. In any event, it is better to live by faith rather than by force. Faith helps to build relationships; force destroys them.

12–13

The letter ends with a promise of an impending visit and a final greeting from the church where the elder resides.

3 JOHN

This letter differs from the other two in that it is written to an individual. Again, one should note the references to "the truth" in vv. 3, 4, 8, and 12. In every case, the truth refers to the received tradition of the incarnation and obeying the love ethic. In addition, while 2 John tells the faithful not to extend hospitality to those who do not adhere to the tradition, 3 John decries the fact that the elder's own emissaries have not been received by Diotrephes. Finally, Demetrius is also commended for his fidelity to the tradition.

Multiplication by Division

The late Rev. Dr. Gaius Thibodeaux, long-time general secretary of evangelism for the AME Church, often stated that some Christians know how to multiply by dividing. Dr. Thibodeaux deeply regretted that too often division was the only way some Christians could resolve conflicts.

1–4

The recipient of the letter is identified as Gaius, "the beloved" brother in the faith who confesses to "the truth." The greeting continues with felicitations concerning Gaius's health. The faithful discipleship of the elder's "children" brings the elder the greatest joy. Referring to Gaius's community as "my children" denotes that the elder has some type of or degree of authority over them. However, as noted previously, authority and power are often two separate social realities.

5–7

The elder now commends their hospitality to those within the community, especially strangers. Word has reached the elder of their good deed (v. 6). These traveling ministers have worked for the cause and accepted nothing from heathens, i.e., have not affiliated with the unrighteous (see 2 John 10).

9–10

These verses discuss Diotrephes, a man who does not accept the elder's authority. He also does not entertain nor allow others to entertain the elder's emissaries. The elder describes Diotrephes as an arrogant liar. While it is easy to accept the elder's view as an accurate depiction of the events, one must face the fact that we have a one-sided picture. Rensberger states that the conflict may not have had anything to do with authority.[64] However, if this is not an authority conflict, what is it? If rejecting the elder's representatives is not an affront to the elder's authority, what is it? Indeed, by circumventing any attempts at hospitality to the elder's envoys, Diotrephes challenges the elder's authority to send envoys in the first place. Conversely, Gaius acknowledges the elder's authority by accepting his envoys.

While the full details are not available, it is clear that this is a power struggle between a regional figure (the elder) and a local figure (Diotrephes). We know that Diotrephes is a local leader with some degree of power, because he is able to stop some local members from entertaining the elder's representatives. Moreover, it is also clear that some follow Diotrephes, while others follow the elder through Gaius. It was a split community. Nothing more is definite. The mention above of bishops in black Methodist denominations illuminates this context. Many black church leaders in predominantly non-black denominations have experienced inhospitable treatment within their own communions. They know full well how the elder's representatives must have felt. A particular incident in the life of the North Texas Conference of the United Methodist Church serves as anecdotal illustration. By law, in the United Methodist Church, one can only be a district superintendent for six years. He or she must subsequently take another position. The new position must be comparable in status and in pay. When the Rev. Dr. Zan Wesley Holmes stepped down from his position as district superintendent in the early 1970s, the only comparable positions were pastorates of predominantly white congregations. None of the congregations that loved him as a district superintendent wanted him as a pastor. A dual position that was comparable was therefore created in a local church and at Perkins School of Theology especially for him.

Hospitality

It is a standing, unofficial rule in the AME Church for pastors to provide hospitality to any AME pastors in transit. This applies especially to those in need of assistance. Such fellowship only increases the sense of unity within the AME connection.

11

Here is yet another admonition against evil (see also 1 John 3:6-10; cf. 2 John 4–11).

12

Demetrius has good recommendations. He might even carry this letter and another commending him.

13–15

The letter ends with the promise of an impending visit and best wishes.

CONCLUSION

I argued in the introduction that the Johannine community was a sectarian movement, a group that emphasized a particular doctrine and/or practice more than others within its wider religious tradition. I identified the group's doctrine of Christ as the key doctrine. The emphasis on the love ethic within the community and the dualistic outlook of the community are also characteristics of sectarian movements. I have alluded to similar developments in the African American church.

Earlier in the history of the community, its doctrine of Christ caused tensions to arise between the Johannine community and more traditional Judaisms (see John 1:1; 3:31-36; 5:19-24; 10:15, 30; 16:28; 20:28). Furthermore, this probably led to the expulsion of the Johannine community from Judaism (see John 9:18-22). When 1–3 John were written, Christology continued to be a point of pain, but this time it was within Johannine Christianity. Some affirmed the incarnation, while others, perhaps under the influence of Greco-Roman philosophy, attacked it. First John was written to exhort persons who had not left to remain within the community, to affirm the incarnation, and to practice the love ethic; 2 John, to affirm the incarnation and to be weary of those who do not; and 3 John, to respect the elder's authority, the keeper of the tradition.

First and foremost, John repeatedly affirms the truth of the incarnation (e.g., 1 John 1:1-3; 2:22; 4:2-3, 15; 5:1, 5-6, 10-12; see also 2 John 7, 9). This is not done, however, to win over opponents but to exhort those still in community to remain there. Thus, Lieu is correct when she writes that sustaining community is an important goal of the Johannine letters.[65]

Second, John repeatedly refers to keeping the love ethic. It is a sign that one is a true, obedient child of God (e.g., 1 John 3:11, 14, 18, 23-24; 4:7-12, 16-21; 2 John 5–6). Indeed, "beloved" becomes an alternative expression for another Christian (see 1 John 2:7; 3:2, 21; 4:1, 7, 11; 3 John 2, 5, 11).[66] Genuine, active love is patterned after God's gracious love, defines the group collectively, and identifies its members individually. Similarly, African American Christianity has sought to establish an internal bond of love that the general society has denied African Americans. This "affirmative action" included all types of personal and communal confirmations.

Finally, John consistently employs dualistic language to clarify the situation and to identify those in the faith community. He contrast light and darkness, the Spirit of truth and the spirit of error (cf. John 14:17). The struggle between good and evil is cosmic and has profound influence upon human affairs (1 John 1:5). Furthermore, the children of God keep God's commandments and love God. Love defines true Christians (e.g., 1 John 4:7-12). On the other hand, the children of Satan hate true Christians while loving the world (e.g., 1 John 2:9-11, 15-17). John exhorts his readers to beware of antichrists and false prophets, an aspect of the dualism within the tradition (see 1 John 2:18-26; 4:1-6; 2 John 7).

Sectarianism has its positive side. Most importantly, it enables the community to persevere and survive under duress. For both the Johannine community and African American Christianity, the love ethic gives the group internal emotional reinforcement that further bolsters its steadfastness. The Johannine community's dualistic worldview explains the situation and also gives the community the resolve to remain faithful to their tradition. However, after leaving the synagogue, sectarianism contributes to the contentious nature of the group. Clearly, this is the case when in 2 John the elder advocates separation from those who do not hold theological positions like his but in 3 John decries the fact that his opponents have done that very thing to his representatives! The group has a history of solving its problems by dissociating itself from those who hold different views.[67] Unfortu-

nately, the Johannine community is unable to disagree without being disagreeable, a sin that still plagues Christian groups today. If they had found a means of coexistence, they might have set a glowing precedent and example that might have continued even to the present day.

A similar phenomenon occurred in the black church with the rise and development of African American Christian denominations. At first, the denominations were a means of pride and accomplishment. They provided an avenue for personal growth and development normally denied blacks in society. However, by the middle of the twentieth century, many African American Christians did not acknowledge the validity of sacraments in other denominations. This division within the black community was never universally accepted, and it waned considerably in the second half of the twentieth century, although, unfortunately, it continues to hold sway in some quarters.[68]

Notes

1. Dedicated to the memory of the Rev. L. T. Trammell, my "father-in-the-ministry," and the Rev. Dr. Peter David Williams, missionary, scholar, and dear friend.

2. See Rev 4:4. For the purposes of this study, I set aside the question of the relationship of Revelation to the other four books attributed to John.

3. See Rudolf Schnackenburg, *The Gospel According to St. John*, vol. 1 (New York: Crossroad, 1990), 77.

4. David Rensberger, *1 John, 2 John, 3 John* (Nashville: Abingdon, 1997), 18; Robert Kysar, *I, II, III John*. ACNT (Minneapolis: Augsburg, 1986), 12–15; see also D. Moody Smith, *First, Second, and Third John* (Louisville: John Knox 1991), 14–15.

5. See J. M. Lieu, *The Theology of the Johannine Epistles* (Cambridge: Cambridge University Press, 1991), 4.

6. David E. Aune, "The Bible and the Literature of Antiquity: The Greco-Roman Period," in *HBC*, 48. In my opinion Aune does not go far enough. He assumes without proof that form always indicates function and, in turn, indicates how to interpret. Some early Christian writings defy modern attempts of classification, and in such cases function takes priority because the message was more important than the medium for early Christians. Also, Paul's letters, the earliest known New Testament writings, which outnumber the Gospels, made the epistolary form an acceptable Christian literary genre. That is why so many "letters" came from this era and why any literary genre could be employed for epistolary purposes.

7. Smith, *First, Second, and Third John*, 35: "This is a communication from a Christian leader . . . to other Christians."

8. See R. L. Johnstone, *Religion in Society*, 5th ed. (Upper Saddle River, N.J.: Prentice-Hall, 1997), 87–89; Bryan Wilson, *Religion in Sociological Perspective* (Oxford: Oxford University Press, 1982), 91–2; J. C. Livingston, *Anatomy of the Sacred*, 4th ed. (Upper Saddle River, N.J.: Prentice-Hall, 2001), 173–77; cf. Rensberger, *1 John, 2 John, 3 John*, 37–39; Lieu, *The Theology of the Johannine Epistles*, 94.

9. Lieu, *The Theology of the Johannine Epistles*, 71.

10. Cf. Rensberger, *1 John, 2 John, 3 John* 37–39; ibid., 80–87.

11. For example, John 3:1-6, 19; 8:12; 10:1-6. See Lieu's very helpful discussions of dualism in the epistles (*The Theology of the Johannine Epistles*, 39–41, 51–4, 80–7). I agree with Lieu that the dualism is never fully developed and is not the starting point of the tensions. Rather, it is a means of expressing religious certainty and is the result of those tensions.

12. In 3:7-10 and 5:18-19, John writes that Christians do not sin. This inconsistency is not resolved by John.

13. Cf. Lieu, *The Theology of the Johannine Epistles*, 23–31.

14. Lieu is correct when arguing that community is a central issue in the Johannine epistles (*The Theology of the Johannine Epistles*, 51–54). Repeatedly, John is at pains to distinguish members of the community from those who are not (e.g., 2 John 10–11). This is also an aspect of the community's dualistic perspective.

15. Cf. Lieu, *The Theology of the Johannine Epistles*, 33–45.

16. See Martin Luther King Jr., *Strength to Love*, large print ed. (New York: Wallace, 1984), vii.

17. Martin Luther King Jr., "Antidotes for Fear," in *Strength to Love* (London: Hodder and Stoughton, 1964), 110.

18. Ibid., 112.

19. Ibid., 113.

20. See also Howard Thurman, *Jesus and the Disinherited* (Boston: Beacon, 1976), 36–57, 89–109. Thurman argues that Jesus must be understood within his ethnic and socio-economic contexts in order to be fully understood. Thurman said this a quarter of a century before "mainstream" New Testament scholarship began to recognize this. Thurman also taught King as an undergraduate.

21. J. A. Johnson Jr., *Proclamation Theology* (Shreveport, La.: Fourth Episcopal District Press, 1977), 154–75.

22. For example, J. L. Houlden, *The Johannine Epistles* (New York: Harper & Row, 1973), 49–50; Smith, *First, Second, and Third John*, 35–41; J. C. Thomas, *The Pentecostal Commentary on 1 John, 2 John, 3 John* (Cleveland: Pilgrim, 2004), 61–71.

23. Cf. Smith, *First, Second, and Third John*, 35; I. H. Marshall, *The Epistles of John* (Grand Rapids, Mich: Eerdmans, 1978), 99–100.

24. Lieu correctly writes that confidence and salvation are found in the life of the community (*The Theology of the Johannine Epistles*, 23–31).

25. On dualism in 1 John see R. A. Culpepper, *The Gospel and Letters of John* (Nashville: Abingdon, 1998), 257–58, 268; cf. Rensberger, *1 John, 2 John, 3 John*, 5–7.

26. Cf. Marshall, *The Epistles of John*, 109–11; Kysar, *I, II, III John*, 35–36; F. F. Bruce, *The Epistles of John* (Grand Rapids, Mich: Eerdmans, 1979), 41.

27. Cf. Bruce, *The Epistles of John*, 45; Rensberger, *1 John, 2 John, 3 John*, 53–57; Smith, *First, Second, and Third John*, 42–43; Marshall, *The Epistles of John*, 115.

28. It is doubtful that many exegetes have espoused an interpretation incongruent with her or his own theology since it has ramifications for one's doctrine of salvation.

29. Raymond E. Brown, *The Epistles of John* (Garden City, N.Y.: Doubleday, 1982), 219.

30. I have already noted John's inconsistency on whether Christians sin or not.

31. Many black preachers make a similar distinction between knowing about God (theology) and demonstrating a knowledge of God through one's life (ethics). Cf. Lieu *The Theology of the Johannine Epistles*, 33–8, on love as a form of corporate identity.

32. The flow of the argument is interrupted unnecessarily by the reference to a new commandment without saying why it is new.

33. One must be cognizant of the symbolic nature of this language and imagery and that this is in no way represents reality. The oversimplification and manipulation of this metaphor has had serious negative social and psychological effects upon many in the African American community, a community in which black has not always been beautiful.

34. When I was an undergraduate in the early 1970s, the only Anglo-American students who played on the intramural athletic squads with the Association of Black Students were hippies, persons who had already been marginalized on campus.

35. Cf. John 14:15.

36. One finds similar thoughts throughout the New Testament (e.g., Mark 13:3-8; John 6:40-54; 12:48; 2 Thess 2:1-12; 2 Pet 3:1-7).

37. Lakey (B.D., Drew; S.T.M., SMU), currently C.M.E. prelate in Georgia, has authored three books. He is considered an authority on American Methodist history and is a scholar-churchman in the tradition of African bishops Athanasius, Augustine, Muzarewa, and Tutu.

38. Cf. Rensberger, *1 John, 2 John, 3 John*, 83–85.

39. Similar passages are John 1:1-3, 10:31-38, 13:20, 14:6-14, 17:1-26, and 2 John 9. Cf. Rensberger, *1 John, 2 John, 3 John*, 81.

40. John Painter, *1, 2, and 3 John* (Collegeville, Minn.: Liturgical, 2002), 207.

41. Smith, *First, Second, and Third John*, 77.

42. Rensberger, *1 John, 2 John, 3 John*, 89; cf. 37–39.

43. Cf. Culpepper, *The Gospel and Letters of John*, 263; Painter, *1 John, 2 John, 3 John*, 221.

44. See Kysar, *I, II, III John*, 76; Marshall, *The Epistles of John*, 173–75; similarly Painter, *1, 2, and 3 John*, 222; Smith, *First, Second and Third John*, 80–81.

45. On this topic, see Culpepper, *The Gospel and Letters of John*, 262–65.

46. Kysar, *I, II, III John*, 81–82.

47. Cf. Culpepper, *The Gospel and Letters of John*, 265–67; Smith, *First, Second, and Third John*, 88–92.

48. Cf. Kysar, *I, II, III John*, 81–86.

49. Cf. Lieu, *The Theology of the Johannine Epistles*, 95–96.

50. Rensberger, *1 John, 2 John, 3 John*, 102–3.

51. This might be an aspect of realized eschatology, experiencing in the present a foretaste of the eschatological bliss to come, a key theological feature of John's Gospel.

52. Lieu, *The Theology of the Johannine Epistles*, 71.

53. Cf. Culpepper, *The Gospel and Letters of John*, 269–70; Kysar, *I, II, III John*, 94–98; Smith, *First, Second, and Third John*, 106–12.

54. See Houlden, *The Johannine Epistles*, 119; Painter, *1, 2, and 3 John*, 281–83.

55. Bruce, *The Epistles of John*, 113.

56. Houlden, *The Johannine Epistles*, 119.

57. Culpepper, *The Gospel and Letters of John*, 271.

58. Rensberger, *1 John, 2 John, 3 John*, 272.

59. Cf. Thomas, *The Pentecostal Commentary on 1 John, 2 John, 3 John*, 266–67; Rensberger, *1 John, 2 John, 3 John*, 139.

60. Cf. Rensberger, *1 John, 2 John, 3 John*, 149.

61. Cf. Thomas, *The Pentecostal Commentary on 1 John, 2 John, 3 John*, 39–42.

62. Painter, *1, 2, and 3 John*, 354.

63. Matthew and Galatians differ from 2 John in that neither advocates a total break in fellowship.

64. Rensberger, *1 John, 2 John, 3 John*, 162.

65. Lieu, *The Theology of the Johannine Epistles*.

66. John also consistently denounces the opposite of love (e.g., 1 John 2:7-11, 3:12-15, 4:16-21).

67. Are the seeds of Protestant Christianity within the Johannine movement?

68. I was surprised one Sunday in the late 1990s in northeast Georgia when two regular visitors to our congregation, staunch members of another local church, refused to come to receive communion.

For Further Reading

Aland, Barbara, et al., eds. *Novum Testamentum Graece*. 27th ed. Stuttgart: Deutsche Bibelgesellschaft, 1993.

Boice, J. M. *The Epistles of John*. Grand Rapids, Mich.: Zondervan, 1979.

Brown, Raymond E. *The Community of the Beloved Disciple*. New York: Paulist, 1979.

———. *The Epistles of John*. Garden City, N.Y.: Doubleday, 1982.

Bruce, F. F. *The Epistles of John*. Grand Rapids, Mich.: Eerdmans, 1979.

Bultmann, Rudolf. *Theology of the New Testament*. 2 vols. New York: Scribner, 1951, 1955.

Culpepper, R. Alan. *The Gospel and Letters of John*. Nashville: Abingdon, 1998.

Houlden, J. L. *The Johannine Epistles*. New York: Harper & Row, 1973.

Johnson, Joseph A., Jr. *Proclamation Theology*. Shreveport, La.: Fourth Episcopal District, 1977.

King, Martin Luther, Jr. *Strength to Love*. Large print edition. New York: Walker, 1984.

Kysar, Robert. *I, II, III John*. ACNT. Minneapolis: Augsburg, 1986.

Lieu, Judith M. *The Theology of the Johannine Epistles*. Cambridge: Cambridge University Press, 1991.

Marshall, I. Howard. *The Epistles of John*. Grand Rapids, Mich.: Eerdmans, 1978.

Painter, John. *1, 2, and 3 John*. Collegeville, Minn.: Liturgical, 2002.

Rensberger, David. *1 John, 2 John, 3 John*. Nashville: Abingdon, 1997.

Smith, D. Moody. *First, Second, and Third John*. Louisville: John Knox, 1991.

Thomas, J. Christopher. *The Pentecostal Commentary on 1 John, 2 John, 3 John*. Cleveland: Pilgrim, 2004.

JUDE

Larry George

INTRODUCTION

Like most of the "general" or "catholic" epistles (James, 1–2 Peter, Jude, 1–3 John), there is little certainty regarding the authorship, recipients or addressees, and the date. The epistle purports to be written by Jude[1] ("Judas," in Greek), who further claims to be the brother of James, implied author of the epistle of James, whom some scholars claim to be the brother of Jesus. Thus, these two writers, James and Jude, may represent two of Jesus' siblings.[2] Jude writes excellent Greek and is well read, as evidenced by his allusions to the Old Testament and extracanonical Jewish literature (cf. v. 9).[3] Moreover, 2 Peter borrows material from Jude, mainly concerning false teachers and their challenge to the parousia of Jesus. Because Jude is the shorter of the two epistles, scholars have concluded that Jude was used as a source for 2 Peter.[4]

Although Jude is one of the shortest books of the Christian scriptures, it delivers

Date, Place, and Author of Jude

"There is scant data for taking a firm position as to the date, place, and author. Until fresh evidence or new ways of framing the questions are introduced, we can only surmise historical judgments in this regard."

—Jerome H. Neyrey, *2 Peter, Jude,* AB 37C (New York: Doubleday, 1993), 31.

a strong exhortation.[5] It is brief and to the point, and yet it is complete with relevant and imaginative examples to argue the case. African Americans also possess relevant and profound illustrations to capture the character and essence of their plight in America. The twister tales demonstrate power in weakness and irony in the "inferior" becoming mightier than the apparent "superior" person.[6]

While Jude provides little information concerning the identity of the addressees of this pseudonymous epistle, the central thrust of Jude is to maintain the status quo, the traditions of an orderly Christian community. Even though Jude's concern for the one when preservation of the saints seems evident, this epistle launches rhetorical assaults on the false teachers who are seeking to disrupt this community.

"Feminist interpretation of the epistle ascribed to Jude is especially challenging because there are no direct references to women as wives, mothers, sisters, or daughters, to women's behavior, or even allusions to the code of domestic life that subordinated women to men."

—Marie-Eloise Rosenblatt, "Jude," in *Searching the Scriptures: A Feminist Commentary*, vol. 2, ed. Elisabeth Schüssler Fiorenza (New York: Crossroads, 1994), 393.

1–2, Salutation: From a Bondservant to the Committed

In this greeting, the writer claims to be the brother of James. In other words, Jude claims that his authority lies in his relationship to James, who was—after the death of Jesus—the leader of the church in Jerusalem. Rather than

identify himself as such—as a relative and brother—he says that he is a slave of Jesus and sibling of James. As a slave, Jude volunteered his service as Jesus' bondservant (*doulos*). A bondservant's work was one of love and devotion, which means that he possessed the passion to help the churches maintain their hope and faith in Jesus' coming.

In this greeting, contrary to what was expected in letters, Jude does not identify the addressees. Rather, Jude sends this letter to those who are "called," "wrapped," and "kept" in Christ. He assumes that all Christians have some calling on their lives, like prophets and preachers. He assures them of divine protection by informing them that they are "wrapped *in* the love of God" (v. 1d), being preserved or kept by Jesus Christ; they are sustained by Jesus so that they will perform the mission of their calling (v. 1c).

Jude concludes the salutation in an usual fashion, with a series of virtues and blessings. He advances a threefold, abundant hope: mercy, peace, and love. He intensifies this hope by suggesting that these benefits, like some libation, be lavishly poured on them who are still alive.

3–4, Striving against Difficulties

Verse 3 provides the purpose of the letter, and v. 4 represents what occasioned it. The purpose and occasion depict the difficulties that Christians must face, both within themselves, individually, and outside the faith community. When false doctrine seeks to discourage the called ones, the writer feels the necessity to encourage them to stand, struggle, fight, and act for what they firmly believe. In their struggles with false teachers, Jude assures them that he is their beloved friend, a bondservant (an egalitarian term rather than a hierarchal one), like an elder, pastor, or apostle. He notes that

519

he has longed to write to them about their common salvation. Nonetheless, he now feels pressed to write to them about their common struggle against those who seek to distort and destroy the truth.

Covert infiltration of false teachers among the readers occasions the writing of Jude. Jude describes these teachers using masculine language to reveal the nature of their activities as libertines. These condemned persons uses the grace of God as a license for all sorts of debauchery, while denying the God who provides them with grace.

5–16, Exemplars of Negative Destruction

In vv. 5-7 Jude reminds the addressees of their awareness of several Old Testament motifs on the destruction of three aberrant communities as negative exemplars: (1) the Hebrew community of the exodus were forbidden entrance into the promised land because of unbelief and faithlessness; (2) the community of fallen angels await destruction after being banished from heaven; and (3) the communities of Sodom and Gomorrah await "the punishment of eternal fire" (1:7c). These serve to remind the readers of those who once thought that they were safe in their unrighteousness but nonetheless found themselves destroyed and awaiting further punishments of the Great Day because they "did not believe" (5c).

In vv. 8-13, following the three negative exemplars, Jude turns immediately to additional examples—Cain, Korah, and, indirectly, Balaam's error—to depict further the destruction of the false teachers. "These men" represent the antagonists of the epistle, the false teachers. They employs dreams or apocalyptic visions as their source of authority, which they uses to deceive Jude's readers. Both false and true prophets/teachers are known for their

dreams and visions; the difference between the two is seen by the outcome—whether or not the dream or vision took place.

These false teachers are wreaking havoc on the community of faith as suggested by the book of Jude. They are using their authority to stain, defile, and divide the community. Verse 8 suggests the behavior and message of the false teachers: they defile the community, reject authority, and insult the glorious ones. Their teachings corrupt the flesh through sexual immorality, seek to persuade the readers to reject God-given authority, insult the angels who watch over the saints. For this, Jude condemns, rebukes, and pronounces eternal doom on them.

In vv. 14-16, Jude continues a terse assault on the behavior of the false teachers and their teachings, suggesting that Enoch, a member of the seventh generation after Adam, prophesied against them. Enoch's message is harsh and detailed, calling for a sure judgment

Jackleg Preachers

"It was not until the Revolution that black preachers were recognized by the denominations. Previously they were recognized by their own people and exercised what was later called 'jackleg' ministries whenever opportunity was given and the slaves were able to assemble under their leadership."

Jackleg preachers should not be confused with false teachers/preachers because the jackleg preachers often were the only source for prophetic truth-telling, speaking truth to power.

—Gayraud S. Wilmore, *Black Religion and Black Radicalism: An Interpretation of the Religious History of African Americans*, 3rd ed. (Maryknoll, N.Y.: Orbis, 1998), 28.

and retribution on all who mislead others and profit from such. Enoch's negative characterization reveals some of the destructive actions and words that might have been active within the community of faith that Jude is addressing. As the Hebrews who murmured in the wilderness, these false teachers' actions and words remind the readers of the result of the grumbling and fault finding of the followers of Moses, which resulted in God's promise of the land flowing with milk and honey being denied to a rebellious people.

17–23, REBUKING ROCKS, BUILDING UP BELIEFS

Jude returns to encouraging the readers of this epistle but continues to provide a negative characterization of the false teachers. Jude instructs the reader to recall Jesus' apostles' predictions of the end-times (cf. 1 Tim 4:1-5). Jude further characterizes the "scoffers" as "propelled by their ungodly desires," "divisive," "worldly," and "devoid of the Spirit" (vv. 18-19). These false teachers' actions are portrayed as lacking inner grace and godly direction. In such a disposition, Jude instructs the readers of their nature and their desire to destroy the community of faith. Jude urges that they must be rejected and avoided at all cost.

In stark contrast to these false teachers' characterization, Jude returns to his initial appellation of endearment ("dear friends"), placing him again on the levels of the readers. Jude exhorts the readers to stand fast in their faith despite the attack from without by these false teachers. He urges them to build up a most holy faith, to continue to pray in the Holy Spirit, to keep themselves in the love of God, all while awaiting the Lord's mercy. In the last lines of the body to the letter, Jude alludes to the fact that the false teachers have had some results: some of the readers waver

in the faith, others have left the community, and others are in need of mercy. Even so, Jude instructs the readers to rescue those who have fallen away because of the divisive work of the false teachers.

24–25, DOXOLOGIES

Jude concludes with a final blessing that offers further encouragement and inspiration. He assures the readers that God is able to keep them from falling to the devices of the false teachers. Not only can God do that, but also God can help them to stand among any foe, from within and outside the faith community. Moreover, God is able to present them without blemished before God's glorious presence (v. 24). To aid the reader in their final celebration of God's working grace, Jude identifies

---

Realizing God's Intentions

"More portentous was black people's indomitable and indefatigable determination and resolve to secure those benefits, and more, to respond to a higher calling and voice than those circumscribed by the limits of human transience and national interests. Some black Americans sought ever to be responding to and with the One who created peoples and nations, and so desired to ascertain and realize the divine intent for purposeful human existence in the created order. Maria W. Stewart was one of those persons."

—Clarice J. Martin, "Normative Biblical Motifs in African-American Women Leaders' Moral Discourse: Maria Stewart's Autobiography as a Resource for Nurturing Leadership from the Black Church Tradition," in *The Stone that the Builders Rejected: The Development of Ethical Leadership from the Black Church Tradition,* ed. Walter E. Fluker (Harrisburg, Pa.: Trinity Press International, 1998), 48.

the Savior, Jesus Christ, as the God who is the one to receive glory, majesty, power, and authority forever for all of God's saving works of grace (v. 25).

Notes

1. Since the real flesh-and-blood author is unknown, I will refer to Jude as the implied author.
2. Richard Bauckham, *Jude and the Relatives of Jesus in the Early Church* (Edinburgh: T. & T. Clark, 1990).
3. *The Testament of Moses*, an apocryphal story concerning the death of Moses. See, for example, vv. 4-6.
4. For contrary positions, see, for example, J. N. D. Kelly, *The Epistles of Peter and Jude* (London: Black, 1969), and Michael Green, *The Second Epistle General of Peter and the General Epistle of Jude* (Grand Rapids, Mich.: Eerdmans, 1988).
5. For the typical parts of the New Testament letter, see the sidebar at 1 Peter 1:1-2.
6. See, for example, Joel Chandler Harris (1848-1908), "Uncle Remus Initiates the Little Boy," in *The Oxford Anthology of American Literature*, edited by William Rose Benét and Norman Holmes Pearson (New York: Joel Chandler Harris, 1938), 1979–80.

For Further Reading

Bauckham, Richard. *Jude and the Relatives of Jesus in the Early Church*. Edinburgh: T. & T. Clark, 1990.

Green, Michael. *The Second Epistle General of Peter and the General Epistle of Jude*. Grand Rapids, Mich.: Eerdmans, 1988.

Kelly, J. N. D. *The Epistles of Peter and Jude*. London: Black, 1969.

Neyrey, Jerome H. *2 Peter, Jude*. AB 37C. New York: Doubleday, 1993.

REVELATION

Brian K. Blount

INTRODUCTION

Revelation reads like a piece of contemporary "pulp fiction." Consider the Quentin Tarrantino movie of that name starring Samuel L. Jackson and John Travolta. It is not the content of the movie that matters, but the plot. Like the non-sequential plot of the movie, John of Patmos's narrative does not move in a straight line. This apocalyptic director starts in the middle of the story (chap. 1), gives multiple peeks at the arrival of the end time from three unique camera angles (seventh seal, seventh trumpet, seventh bowl), flashes back to the beginning of the story in the middle of the narrative (chaps. 12–14), then pushes to a wondrous end (chaps. 20–21),

the approach to which he has already horrifically screened three times (seals, trumpets, and bowls, chaps. 1–6).

Chapters 12–14 constitute the beginning of John's apocalyptic story. Everything in the plot receives its motivation from what happens here. A reader cannot truly appreciate why the seer writes with such passion—and sometimes venom—without knowing how his church came to be in the circumstance that now threatens to devour it. A predator is on the loose in human history, a mad, mythological snake that has the church in the grip of its fangs and is, even as John writes, pumping a deadening poison into its spirit. Chapter 12 also introduces the people of God in the mythological form of a celestial woman clothed with the sun. About to give birth to a Messiah who will lead her people, she writhes in pain even as she cowers before the great red serpent, a dragon who waits to savage the child as soon as it is born. But when the child is delivered to new life on a Golgotha cross, the dragon, who is Satan in disguise, is outmaneuvered. The infant is snatched (i.e., resurrected) to the heavens, where war has broken out. The archangel Michael, leading God's angelic forces, ousts and exiles Satan from the heavenly realm onto the historical plane. On earth, no longer able to hunt the Messiah, the dragon seeks out the other children of the woman, the church. Knowing that it cannot operate alone, it seeks a surrogate, a beast it calls up from the chaos of the sea. The beast is Rome, the imperial force that sought to make itself the ruler of humankind and the plotter of human destiny. Rome and its Caesar desired to be worshiped as Lord and Savior and in so doing denied the rightful worship due exclusively to God and God's Messiah. Rome drew upon the assistance of another beast, the landed aristocracy and ruling class of Asia Minor, where John's churches were located. The Asia Minor officials demanded that all in their cities show proper worship of Rome, Rome's Caesar, and the gods of the Roman cult. Those who did not so worship were guaranteed loss of social standing, loss of economic prosperity, and perhaps even loss of life. It is at just this point that John picks up the story at chap. 1.

John's narrative is about the single revelation that comes through the many visions that populate his book. The revelation is clear and simple: Jesus Christ is Lord. This is the message that Jesus himself bore all the way to and through the cross. It is the message that John conveys in chap. 1, when he discloses Christ as a cosmic figure who walks with his churches and sustains them through every trial. It is the message the members of John's seven churches are called to bear and to live even in the midst of a circumstance where Rome and Rome's surrogate forces demand an exclusive worship of Rome instead.

In John's powerful chaps. 2 and 3, he demands that his Christ-believers become Christ-witnesses. He writes in the last decade of the first century, when Domitian is emperor, knowing that many are beginning to blend themselves into the Roman cultic, political, economic, and social landscape, and he charges them to remain defiantly and openly loyal to Christ alone. Anything they do that might suggest they condone a belief in the lordship of some other figure, anything like eating meat sacrificed to a Roman god, goddess, or Caesar at a social or trade gathering, was condemned as an idolatrous act of prostitution to a false, foreign faith. Only those who resist such accommodation to Roman ways of social and religious life can expect an eschatological relationship with God at the end of time. John demands that his people resist the fear of what they might lose in this life because of their witness to the lordship of Christ and focus instead on what they would gain in the new life that awaits them in eternity, the life he will describe so majestically in chaps. 21–22 as a new heaven and a new earth, where God dwelt directly with God's people.

Knowing that his people fear the draconian power of Rome, John shares his vision of God's power and grandeur. He sees the throne room in heaven (chap. 4); sees God majestically perched upon it, surrounded by the perpetual accolade of cosmic creatures and great angels; sees twenty-four elders who represent the believing peoples of the twelve tribes and twelve apostles; and beholds with awe an executed but still standing Lamb at God's side, who holds title to the book that bears the truth and meaning of all history (chap. 5). This Lamb is the child Messiah in chap. 12.

While this vision is helpful, John knows that it is not enough to convince his people to stand fast before the bestial pressures of Rome. His people need to know that God not only sits above them but stands among them, ready to engage their enemy and fight on their behalf. And so John also shares his vision of heavenly souls who have, like the Lamb, been executed because of their testimony to the Lamb's lordship. They cry out for God's justice against those who have butchered them. John wants his people to know that God responds—with a vengeance.

In three separate scenes that really play out simultaneously, the Lamb's breaking of the seals (6:1—8:1), the angels' blowing of the trumpets (8:2—11:19), and the angels' pouring of the devastating bowls (15:1—16:21), John conveys the vicious judgment that God rends upon a world that has idolatrously turned away from God and persecuted those who have not. The destruction is catastrophic, because the draconian forces of Rome and Asia Minor fight back against God and God's people. The resulting apocalyptic conflict is so consummate that everyone, even creation itself, is caught up in it. God does not "rapture" God's own people out of the devastation. They suffer in but through the conflict, washing their clothes to a sparkling sheen in the blood of the Lamb as they do (7:9-17). The end result will be God's conquest of the dragon's forces (chaps. 17–19) and the eventual defeat and termination of the dragon itself (20:1-15). With even death destroyed, eternal life parades into a scene so glorious that John can only describe it as a cosmic wedding in a brilliant new city whose name is Jerusalem, but whose heritage is Eden. This Eden, not death, is the lot of those who witness to the lordship of God and God's Christ. This is eternal relationship with God. This is salvation. *This* is the revelation of Jesus Christ.

CHAPTER 1

1:1-3, The Revelation of Jesus Christ

John wrote about the stripping (revelation) of Jesus Christ.[1] This *revelation* conjures the image of Jesus' crucifixion, where he was stripped naked and hung out to die. But then the image of weakness is transformed. Ultimately, this revelation isn't something someone did to Jesus; it is what Jesus did to reveal something important to everyone else. While being humiliated by hostile authorities and executed on the cross, Jesus, it turns out, stripped world history and human reality bare by clarifying something that was heretofore apparently obscure: he revealed who really is in charge.

African American slaves instinctively understood this irony about Jesus. On the one hand, they recognized the shameful horror of his death. Like him, they were weak and helpless. "Were you there," they asked in spiritual sadness, "when they crucified my Lord?" "Yes," was the implicit answer. And yet they sensed the revelation. The same folk sang, "Ride on King Jesus! No man can hinder him."

John wrote a prophecy. His focus, though, was not on future foretelling but on present preparation. He wrote about what was coming soon (1:1, 3) in the hope that his people would respond properly to that revelation in

---

Beatitudes in Revelation

The book of Revelation has beatitudes in 1:3; 14:13; 16:15; 19:9; 20:6; 22:7; 22:14. John uses the first of his seven beatitudes to declare that whoever took these words and kept them would be blessed. The best way to keep a testimony is to keep it alive. Revelation's beatitudes are apocalyptic beatitudes that focus on future expectation with hopes for present transformation in behavior.

the present. The slaves sang about the coming of God's judgment and glory in the hope that it would encourage contemporary resistance and endurance.

Spirituals: Resistance Music

"The existence of these songs is in itself a monument to one of the most striking instances on record in which a people forged a weapon of offense and defense out of a psychological shackle. By some amazing but vastly creative spiritual insight the slave undertook the redemption of a religion that the master had profaned in his midst."

—Howard Thurman, *Deep River: Reflections on the Religious Insight of Certain of the Negro Spirituals* (Port Washington, N.Y.: Kennikat, 1945), 36.

1:4-8, Faithful Witness

John's Jesus is the "faithful witness." *Martys*, the Greek term for "witness," has come to mean something quite different—*martyr*—from what it did for John and his audience. Being a witness to the lordship of Christ as opposed to the mandated lordship of Rome was actually what a Christian was often called to be in a Roman court of law. *Martyr* was a word of active engagement and nonviolent resistance, not sacrificial surrender.

1:9-20, Fear Nothing

Witnesses who testify to a counter-kingdom are bound to suffer at the hands of those who claim present kingship. John, exiled to Patmos, became an example of just such a principle. Martin Luther King Jr., passionately writing his "Letter from Birmingham Jail," became a similar example. Because of his witness for a world where divisions of race had disappeared, he was persecuted by the purveyors of prejudice, who deployed all their

resources to keep that counter-vision from becoming real. The families of slain civil rights leader Medgar Evers and the four little black girls bombed to death in 1963 in the sanctuary of their Sixteenth Street Baptist Church in Birmingham also knew the high cost of witness. They are bonded as closely to John as they are to each other.

There was a time when African Americans implicitly understood what it meant to make this kind of witness. Theirs was not a witness without cost, the kind that draws attention in the sanctuary when one stands and declares, shouts even, before one's colleagues in spiritual arms, that one will be faithful. "Preaching to the choir," testifying before a sympathetic audience that regales one's every word with celebratory and sometimes feverish acclamation, is not the kind of witness John demands and Jesus modeled.

Jesus was killed for his witness. But he did not stay dead. He dragged the keys of death up from the abyss with him and controls them securely now in his hands. The greatest symbol of a government's power is its control over life and death, symbolized most often through the specter of capital punishment. African Americans, overrepresented by grotesque margins in the cells of U.S. death row prisons, know this claim to power all too well.[2] Jesus put the lie to this claim when he rose from the dead.

John sees a "Human One" (Dan 7:14) walking amid seven lamp stands, which represent seven churches. Christ is with them. This Christ has white hair the texture of lamb's wool. In the cosmopolitan Roman empire, where people with hair like wool, that is, Africans, were well known, why does John go out of his way to depict his head this way, rather than with the straight hair commonly associated with those of European descent? This Christ has a double-edged sword. Cutting both ways, it strikes the failures of the faithful as surely as it gouges those who would harm them. It is his word of universal, impartial judgment. This Christ holds seven stars, which is to say, complete cosmic power in his hands. The spiritual had it right: "He's Got the Whole World in His Hands."

Chapter 2

2:1-7, Ephesus: You Can Be Too Good

Hypomonē is most often translated as endurance. It should be translated "nonviolent resistance." Followers resist any claim to the lordship of Rome by testifying to the lordship of Christ. African American slaves understood the integral connection between endurance and resistance. They were able to endure the horrors of slavery and resist its declarations of their bestial nature by defiantly believing in their God-ordained equality. Slaves gathered

under the cover of darkness in the hush arbors of nearby forests and celebrated a Christ who longed for their freedom. Their worship was an act of enduring, active resistance.

The Ephesians had a perceptive and critical spirit. Charismatic false prophets moved into the Ephesian church just as John was moving out.[3] African American Christian communities should be able to relate well to this kind of phenomenon. Untrained and often misinformed "jackleg" preachers have frequently taken charismatic hold of black churches and led them theologically and practically astray.

Unfortunately, the Ephesians became *too* discerning. They became a policing community. They abandoned the gracious love they had formerly shown each other by developing a kind of "works litmus test" that determined which efforts of resistance were worthy and which were not.[4]

Who Has Hair Like Lamb's Wool

"I was trying to get them to understand the images of race and color that they had been living with and what the biblical images were. In one class we discussed Rev. 1:14, where the Son of Man is described as having hair of white wool. I hadn't had a haircut for a while, and I asked, 'Who in this room has hair like lamb's wool?' They started to sweat because for them to admit that their professor, the only black person in the room, had hair like lamb's wool meant that the images of Jesus they had lived with all their lives might pose a problem. So they fidgeted and looked around the room until they finally lighted on this one student who had dark brown curly hair. (You have to understand, Colby College is not just a predominantly white liberal arts college—it is a *very* white one. Some of the white professors complain about the lack of diversity for white people, and I do have a lot of blonde-haired, blue-eyed students up in northern New England!). And he got nervous, because his racial status was coming into question. All of a sudden, the racial ambiguity, the phenotypic ambiguity that he had been carrying around was coming into crisis, and so he looked at me and said, 'Her!' It was as if he had said, 'I don't have hair like lamb's wool!' I was glad because I wanted them to struggle with that, with the iconography that runs deep into our psyche."

—Cheryl Townsend Gilkes, "We Have a Beautiful Mother," in *Living the Intersection: Womanism and Afrocentrism in Theology*, ed. Cheryl Sanders (Minneapolis: Fortress Press, 1995), 33.

The black church has too often been very "Ephesian." At times, it has focused more on the testing and purifying than on love. It has given more attention to castigating fallen members than rehabilitating and reaccepting them.

2:8-11, Smyrna: Christians and Jews

Because theirs was an ancient religion with an established tradition, Jews were not required to participate in the imperial and Greco-Roman cults. The Romans were not so accommodating to newer religions. According to John, the Jewish community told the Romans that the Christians, who were also Jews, would resist acknowledgment of Caesar's lordship. The Jews thereby offered the Christians up to persecution. This "betrayal" is why John calls them a "synagogue of Satan."

In the twenty-first century, African Americans and Jews find themselves in an often tense relationship that corresponds to the one shared by the church and synagogue communities in Smyrna. They are minority communities in an environment that can often be hostile to their racial/ethnic/religious identity and concerns. John lashed out against one minority community that tried to protect its religious turf and sought approval and status from the powerful majority community by subverting the status of a similarly situated minority group. Taken out of context his unfortunate language can and has been used to incite virulent forms of anti-Jewish feeling and behavior.

2:12-17, Pergamum: At the Foot of Satan's Throne

The Pergamum faithful are standing fast, continuing to witness to the lordship of Jesus Christ, continuing to declare his name as God's name, even though they dwell in a city determined to demand the veneration of Greco-Roman gods and Caesar instead.

African Americans know something about dwelling in situations so ominous that primary power appears to reside in Satan's hands. Surely, this was the perspective of those who were bound their entire lives to an existence of chattel slavery or shackled to a life of segregation. Even in contemporary U.S. society, where African Americans are imprisoned at epidemic rates,[5] where their numbers are disproportionately represented in the ranks of the barely subsisting underclass and working poor,[6] where racism continues to reduce housing opportunities, employment possibilities, judicial equity, and sociopolitical opportunity, the language of living in Satan's throne room strikes an ominously resonant note. No wonder African Americans created and still sing music like, "Sometimes I feel like a motherless chile, a long ways from home."

Unfortunately, though the Pergamum faithful stood fast before external pressure, they were not so successful at resisting internal seductions. Artisan, trade, and funeral associations aligned themselves with patron deities. Participation in such groups, which allowed for upward social and economic mobility, required participation in cultic activities like eating meat that had been sacrificed to those deities. Balaam and the Nicolaitans, who represented a different Christian theology that conflicted with John's, approved such practices. For John, the person who ate such food prostituted himself or herself to a foreign faith.

2:18-29, Thyatira: Do Not Accommodate

Thyatira hosted a large number of trade guilds that had strong cultic affiliations. Like Balaam, Jezebel approved eating meat that had been sacrificed to idols.[7] John was stupefied. How could believers in the exclusive lordship of Christ accommodate themselves to practices that celebrated some other divinity's rule? No doubt a similar kind of exasperation would have overwhelmed African American observers who witnessed the accommodation of slaves to the system of slavery that ravaged them.

John isn't the only visionary leader who believed that the most grave of punishments was appropriate for those who led God's people away from the goals God had set for them. Always armed, Harriet Tubman apparently considered killing any runaway whose thoughts of turning back threatened the safe conduct of her other passengers on the Underground Railroad.[8]

Tragic Accommodation

"And yet, it did happen. Consider the tragic tale of one Josiah Henson. As a trusted overseer, Henson was commissioned by his master to transport a score of slaves from Maryland to Kentucky. On the journey, Henson and his charges traveled by boat on the Ohio River and, passing along the Ohio shore, they 'were repeatedly told . . . that [they] were no longer slaves but free men, if [they] chose to be so. At Cincinnati, crowds of coloured people gathered round us, and insisted on our remaining with them.' Out of a sense of duty and pride, Henson 'sternly assumed the captain, and ordered the boat to be pushed off into the stream' and back into slavery! Later Henson rebelled, fled to Canada, and lived to regret what he came to call his 'unpardonable sin.'"

—Reported in Albert J. Raboteau, *Slave Religion: The "Invisible Institution" in the Antebellum South* (New York: Oxford University Press, 1978), 303.

CHAPTER 3

3:1-6, Sardis: Time to Wake Up

Although Sardis was the proverbial fortified city set on a hill, it was twice captured by enemy soldiers who stole in through unguarded spots in the fortifications like thieves in the night. Sardis squandered its name, its reputation of invulnerability, because its benefactors did not stay alert to the dangers around them. So did the Sardis church. Its members frittered away their reputation of witnessing for Christ by accommodating themselves to Roman cultic and social expectations.

The African American church, which has a reputation for social, economic, and political transformation, also finds itself too often accommodating to American religious and social expectations. The African American church has been the engine powering the civil rights movement, inner-city economic redevelopment, and much progressive political action. And yet it lives a sexist Christian existence that consistently denies ordained leadership roles to black women, who attend and work in far greater numbers than black men. It operates in a multi-billion-dollar environment, and yet it has no strategy for helping empower and enrich the black underclass. It is time for the black church to wake up. If the church does not, John's Christ threatens to come in judgment like a thief in the night.

The link between clothing and wakefulness is strong. Sparkling (*leukos*) clothes are the accoutrements of witness. (See sidebar on p. 530.) In their sparkling dress, witnesses stand out in a filthily clad crowd. Though *leukos* translates literally as "white," its emphasis in Revelation is more on qualitative essence than exterior pigmentation. The term is an ethical one. One is not *born leukos*, one *becomes leukos*. Black people, brown people, people of any ethnicity and hue can become *leukos*. All one needs to do is witness relentlessly for the lordship of Christ.

3:7-13, Philadelphia: Open Door Policy

In Philadelphia, the city of brotherly (*adelphos*) love (*philos*), the church maintained its witness despite the fact that it was powerless before hostile Jewish and Greco-Roman communal forces. The Philadelphia Christians "kept" Christ's word of endurance through a singular witness that refused to acknowledge any state-mandated claim to lordship for pagan deities or Roman emperors. "Endurance" (*hypomonē*) is better translated "nonviolent resistance."

Though Christ promised an open door that would give the Philadelphians access to the eschatological Davidic kingdom, he did not pledge to remove them from the circumstance that "tested" them. He did not ask that God "rapture" believers out of the difficult moment; he requested instead that God strengthen them so that they might endure and conquer it, just as Christ himself did on the cross.

This part of the message is particularly relevant for African American Christians who are preoccupied with the language and reality of being "saved." Too often the language rep-

resents an escapist inclination for "sanctuary." This "saved" existence is a kind of pre-rapture condition in which one finds comfort and protection in the assurance that one's sins are forgiven, one's eschatological future is assured, one's work is done, and one's place is in the corporate context of other saved persons just like oneself. The eschatological reality of the last day is spiritualized to the point that it can exist in the present day as a comfortable state of mind and a churchly way of being in the world without being affected by the world. Unfortunately, such separation also generally means that one no longer effects change in the world. The wording in 3:12, particularly the conditional clause "if you conquer," implies resistance behavior that engages the world.

3:14-22, Laodicea: Lukewarm Vomit

The Laodiceans are lukewarm. Christ opposes the hot *and* the cold to the lukewarm. He wishes that they were one or the other, that they knew they should stand decisively against

Defiant Dress

This clothing circumstance is exactly the kind of identity issue that resonates in the black church tradition, in which distinctive clothing often symbolizes transformation and triumph. The slaveowner had a way of dressing slaves only in the essentials necessary to any given task. Slaves were only well dressed during those times when it suited the owner, say, for example when they were placed on an auction block and paraded about like a cleaned up plantation tool.

By controlling appearance the owner demonstrated his symbolic control over the slave. The slaves used contraband opportunities to dress up for special occasions and for services of worship, whether in clothes bought by the owner or not, as a gesture of independence and defiance. It is a defiance that has remained a strong part of the black church tradition. "Hence, in the Black Church, clothing was not a sign of one's value for others as their objects; rather, it was a sign of one's value for oneself, one's community, and one's God" (Anthony B. Pinn, *Terror and Triumph: The Nature of Black Religion* [Minneapolis: Fortress Press, 2003], 97). The dress became a form of witness. Dressing up became an active form of protest and transformative challenge.

any form of accommodation to Roman imperial or pagan lordship. They should be either hot against it or cold to it.

Laodicea was a wealthy, self-sufficient town. The Laodicean Christians comprised a wealthy, self-sufficient community of faith. They believed that their wealth was an indication that they were the recipients of God's favor. John believed that their wealth was actually a sign that God did *not* favor them. Because one could only gather wealth in that Greco-Roman context by blending into the very culture that denied God's lordship, wealth was a sign of accommodation. Proponents of an African American prosperity gospel might ponder Christ's message to the Laodiceans before applauding their material wealth or extolling their search for it as an indication of a close relationship with God. Can one preoccupied by prosperity have an equal preoccupation with and for God? In Laodicea, at least, the answer was no.

Chapter 4

4:1-8a, An Opened Door (The Peek Inside)

Through an opened door, John sees the throne that symbolizes the rule of God. The heavenly council reacts to that rule by rendering glory to God. The twenty-four (double of twelve) elders symbolize the wholeness of the believing community.[9] Their sparkling robes are bestowed because they witnessed to the lordship of Christ in spite of the hostile response they expected and in turn received from the imperial force of Rome.

The shock and awe of the throne room theophany add to the majesty and glory. The seven flaming lampstands further increase the sense of grandeur; they represent the fullness (seven) of God's force in the world through the active presence of the Holy Spirit. African American worshipers use the drama and power of music and liturgical stagecraft to encourage the sense of what it would be like to stand in the midst of the roaring thunder and blinding light that John associates with the praise of God. From the ring shout of African slave worship to the throbbing beat of worship drums, shouting voices, and often pulsating, rhythmic music, many traditional African American worship services represent the ancient feel of theophany.

The sea of glass in front of the heavenly throne is a reminder of the threat to future access to God that the opened door represents. The sea is the site of chaos in the Bible.[10] Remarkably, it is closer to the throne than are the twenty-four elders. To get to God, believers must cross the torrential forces that demand celebration of the lordship of Rome.

Closer to the throne are four oddly appointed living creatures.[11] These cherubim are filled with eyes; they are all-seeing. The wings suggest that they are completely mobile. The number four symbolizes the compass points and thus their omnipresence. Genuflecting before God and not Caesar, they model appropriate witness behavior. Whether one is lifted to the highest reaches of the heavens or is crushed beneath the foot of Rome, one's primary duty is to praise God.

African American people know something about praising God even in the midst of sweltering oppressiveness. African American Christianity itself rose out of the desperate and diabolical circumstance of the American slave state. "Nobody knows de trouble I see, Lord, . . . Nobody knows like Jesus."[12] God would intervene. "Didn't my Lord deliver Daniel. . . . He delivered Daniel f'om de lion's den, Jonah f'om de belly of de whale, An' de Hebrew chillun f'om de fiery furnace, An' why not every man?"[13] Why not, indeed?

4:8b-11, A Hymn of Counter-Praise

Playing the role of heavenly liturgists, the four creatures initiate a hymn that praises

The Hymns of Revelation

Revelation is a dangerous blend of memorable music and recalcitrant rhetoric. Its liturgical hymns witness to the promise that God is relieving Rome of its historical command *right now*. Of the nine hymnic units in the Apocalypse, seven of them (4:8-11; 5:9-14; 7:9-12; 11:15-18; 16:4-6; 19:1-4; 19:5-8; see also 12:10-12; 15:3b-4) are antiphonal in form. Call and response between God, angels, cherubim, dead humans, and even the inanimate heavenly altar cascade down to earth and rise back up to the heavens in worshipful celebration of God's identity and God's purpose for human- and heaven-kind.

Proud to Be Black
Run DMC

"Ya know I'm proud to be black ya'll
And that's a fact ya'll
Now Harriet Tubman was born a slave
She was a tiny black woman when she was
    raised
She was livin' to be givin', there's a lot that
    she gave
There's not a slave in this day and age
I'm proud to be black."

—Quoted in Michael Eric Dyson, "Performance, Protest, and Prophecy in the Culture of Hip-Hop," *Black Sacred Music: A Journal of Theomusicology* 5, no. 1 (1991): 14. Copyright 1991, Duke University Press. All rights reserved. Used by permission of the publisher.

God's holy and glorious lordship. Their praise is affirmed antiphonally by the twenty-four elders. Much African American spiritual blues is antiphonal. Many spirituals developed as

the slave pastor preached and the congregation called back with a rhythmic reply. "Little by little this musical call and response became a song."[14] The music is also resistance-themed. Revelation's hymns connect with the musical genre called "rap." Rap hijacks the language and imagery of contemporary, everyday Euro-American life in order to challenge the hold American culture has over particularly young, urban, underclass African American life. The music is, in its own way, rapping against Rome.

CHAPTER 5

5:1-5, Who Is Worthy?

The scroll/book of chap. 5 is the same scroll described in chap. 10. Its location at the right hand of God, the position of special favor, indicates its importance. It contains history's ultimate plan and its ultimate meaning. God's control of the scroll symbolizes God's control over history.

Unfortunately, no one in all of creation is worthy enough to open the scroll—with a single exception. One of the twenty-four elders identifies the lion out of the tribe of Judah,[15] the "root of David."[16] He is the conquering Messiah. John builds here a powerful connection among the terms "witness," "conquer," and "worthy." A faithful *witness conquers* by testifying to the Lordship of God and Christ. The *conquering witness* is *worthy* of an eschatological relationship with God. But the conquering lion from the tribe of Judah, the root of David, already has an eschatological relationship with God; he is God's messianic emissary. His conquering testimony makes him worthy of something else; he can open the scroll sealed with the seven seals.

5:6-10, The Lamb Is Worthy

Without warning, John distances himself from the lion and focuses on a polar opposite image: a lamb, standing as if slaughtered. Christ conquers by his actions as the faithful and true witness (1:5; 3:5), which in his context resulted in, but need not always require, death. Jesus testified to a truth at his trials. He faithfully adhered to that testimony even under the threat of capital punishment. He was slaughtered. Because of the sacrificial overtones implicit in the language of slaughter, "executed" is a better term.[17] Witness may well lead to execution not because it is redemptive, but because it is resistant. Because the Lamb *is* resistant, John describes him as "standing." He means "standing up" or "standing fast." Executed because of his witness, he maintains the living, resistant force of that witness (he stands) nonetheless. His posture is itself a sign of resurrected defiance.

Womanist theologians see in Jesus' life and ministry a person who stood up. He was executed because human rulers wanted to shut down the cause for which he stood. It is not surprising that those who benefited from a society structured around the aristocratic few would target a social transformer of Jesus' capability and following for destruction. This is why Delores Williams argues that the cross and Jesus' crucifixion upon it "are reminders of what can happen to reformers who successfully challenge the status quo and try to bring about a new dispensation of love and power for the poor."[18] They are a warning that a life committed to social transformation (i.e., non-accommodating witness) will entail struggle and perhaps even great suffering.

In their praise of the Lamb, the cherubim and elders come equipped with two special props: harps and golden bowls filled with incense. The harps remind John's hearers and readers of the Levites who were responsible for the presentation of music in the Jerusalem temple. Also important are the golden bowls whose incense represents the prayers of the saints. In this context, the prayers appear to be less an offering and more a challenge to God to begin the process of vindicating God's people. In the only other significant text in which the terms *prayer* and *incense* occur in the book of Revelation, 8:3-4, they are also metaphorically connected. There the prayers of the people rise with incense to the heavens. As a result of that rising, the angels sound their seven trumpets and initiate God's judgment upon those who have persecuted the saints. 5:8 is just as provocatively positioned. It precedes the Lamb's opening of the seven seals, which also brings about catastrophic acts of judgment that operate as an answer to the peoples' prayers at 6:9-11.

The connection between cultic bowls and prayer is particularly significant in the ritual memory of many African Americans. The libation "prayer" ceremonies associated with bowls and other vessels are deployed in tribute of the "ancestors" of African heritage. Prayers are typically recited in honor of remembered forebears, as water or some other celebratory liquid is poured onto the ground. Through the libation ceremony, requests for wisdom and protection are offered to the ancestors in a manner that corresponds to the cultic petitions the saints make to God.

5:11-14, Glory to the Lamb!

In their song, the angels do not explain *why* the Lamb is worthy. Instead, they emphasize *what* the Lamb is worthy to receive: power, wealth, wisdom, might, honor, glory, and blessing. There is a relationship between the scroll and power, wealth, wisdom, et al. With knowledge and control of history (i.e., the opened scroll) comes massive power.

African Americans have held the vulnerability of Jesus as the Crucified One together with the power and majesty of Jesus as Lord in a tense but productive relationship that mirrors John's struggle to combine the lion and lamb in the Apocalypse. Jesus' suffering is real, his death horrific. "Were you there, when they crucified my Lord?" And yet this executed individual creates in the slave a real hope for social and political change. The executed Christ is also a liberating King. "Ride on King Jesus! No man can hinder him."

CHAPTER 6

6:1-8, The Four Horsemen

The opening of the four seals reinforces John's apocalyptic theology of judgment and sets up a theology of "opening." Despite the fact that the four horsemen are harbingers of destruction and death, John implies that history is not out of control. The cataclysms represent God's judgment against Rome's idolatrous claims to lordship and the accommodation of many Christians to it. John's passive verb formulation presumes that God is the controlling agent. The riders *were given* their ability and their leave.

John's "opening" language is always, even when not directly using God or the Lamb as its subject (9:2; 12:16; 13:6), salvation and/or judgment language. Key here is one's understanding of the Son of Man's warning at 2:10 that witnesses will not be "raptured" out of the coming affliction. Their faithfulness will matter as much as it does because they give it in the circumstance of such duress, just as Christ himself did on the cross. The acts of destruction and disturbance that follow the "opening" of each seal will be eschatological opportunities for believers to demonstrate the mettle of their faith.

The metaphor of the "opening" door is important in the life of the African American church. I recall the invitation extended by the pastor of the Hill Street Baptist Church of Smithfield, Virginia, immediately following every sermon: "the doors of *the* church are now open." Something had happened during the course of the worship service:

God had made our local church a gateway. One didn't merely join Hill Street Baptist Church; one enlisted in a global faith movement that understood Hill Street to be one of its many eschatological outposts. As a part of this "outpost" believers had an opportunity in the midst of whatever difficulties that beset them to demonstrate the mettle of their faith.

6:9-11, The Executed Souls

These verses provide indispensable narrative motivation for the prosecution of God's judgment. Along with 12:10-12 and 20:4-6, they contain a provocative intersection of some of the Apocalypse's most engaging images: *psychē* (soul), *martyria* (witness), and *logos* (word), as well as the revelation that the word and witness of the souls were causally linked to key narrative activity: execution, 6:9-11; beheading, 20:4-6; conquest of the dragon who instigates the killings, 12:10-11.

The critical image is that of executed souls crying out beneath the heavenly altar for

The Altars in Revelation

The heavenly altars were understood to be the cosmic prototypes for their earthly counterparts in the Jerusalem temple. The Jerusalem temple had two distinct altars. The outer one was the sacrificial altar of burnt offering. It was located in the court of priests. The inner altar was also known as the golden altar of incense. It was located just in front of the curtain that marked off the holy of holies from the rest of the sanctuary. The sacrificial altar is imaged here in this text and at 11:1; 14:18; and 16:7. The direct narrative connection to incense indicates that 8:3, 5, and 9:13 refer to the altar of incense.

God's intervention of justice and judgment. John does not picture a sacrificial slaying on the altar. The altar anticipates the divine response to slaying.

The image of executed souls surely aroused emotion and incited action. Long after the end of slavery, African American leaders continue to lay bare horrific details, stories, and even pictures of beaten, brutalized, strung up, and lynched black bodies. Do they moralize it, spiritualize it, make it somehow redemptive? No, the horror is remembered so as to provoke the kind of anger that will trigger transformative behavior. (See sidebar below.)

When the executed souls cry out for God's intervention, John pairs the words "avenge" and "judge" to demonstrate his belief that they seek justice. That clarification does not dissuade contemporary commentators from rightly flinching in the face of the harsh language. Many have complained that it is un-Christian. Speaking from the black church

---

The Revelation of Horror

The celebrated civil rights case of Emmett Till, and particularly the actions of his mother following his death, illustrate this point. Till's mother demanded that his casket remain open so that the world could see what had happened to her son. She hoped that when the horror was clearly seen so also would be seen the need for transformative behavior. "After days of lobbying state officials, Emmett's mother obtained a writ of court ordering the Mississippi sheriff to release Emmett Till's body for return to Chicago. The court order was received three hours before Emmett was to be buried in Mississippi without notice to his relatives, without ceremony, and without witnesses. Upon releasing Emmett's body, the sheriff ordered the casket pad-locked and sealed with the Mississippi State seal. He prohibited anyone from opening it. In Chicago, Funeral Home Director, A. A. Rayner, obeying [the] sheriff's order, refused to open the box containing Emmett's body. When he told Emmett's mother his decision, she demanded a hammer, because she said, 'I need to see my son.' The late Mamie Till-Mobley describes the corpse of her son she saw on September 2, 1955, in Chicago as follows: I decided that I would start with his feet, gathering strength as I went up. I paused at his mid-section, because I knew that he would not want me looking at him. But I saw enough to know that he was intact. I kept on up until I got to his chin. Then I was forced to deal with his face. I saw that his tongue was choked out. The right eye was lying midway of his chest. His nose had been broken like someone took a meat chopper and broke his nose in several places. I kept looking and I saw a hole, which I presumed was a bullet hole, and I could look through that hole and see daylight on the other side. I wondered, 'Was it necessary to shoot him?' Mr. Rayner, she says, asked me, 'Do you want me to touch the body up?' I said, 'No. Let the people see what I have seen. I think everybody needs to know what had happened to Emmett Till.'"

—Keith A. Beauchamp, "The Murder of Emmett Louis Till: The Spark That Started the Civil Rights Movement," *The Black Collegian Online*, http://www.black-collegian.com/african/till2005-2nd.shtml.

tradition in apartheid South Africa, Allen Boesak challenges that "Christians who enjoy the fruits of injustice without a murmur, who remain silent as the defenseless are slaughtered, dare not become indignant when the suffering people of God echo the prayers of the psalms and pray for deliverance and judgment."[19]

6:12-17, Final Retribution

The eschatological events that follow the opening of the sixth seal are a direct narrative response to the souls of the executed in 6:9-11. God's activity in vv. 12-17 is the eschatological preface to the coming Day of the Lord. That moment will justifiably be accompanied by all manner of cataclysmic events.

CHAPTER 7

7:1-8, An Apocalyptic Intermission and a Protective Seal

In Ezekiel 9, particularly vv. 4-8, God commissioned six executioners to slaughter the idolatrous inhabitants of Jerusalem. Just at the moment when the reader expected the bloodbath to begin, there was an intermission. God ordered that all those who grieved the abominable behavior must first be branded with a mark upon their foreheads. When an executioner saw the mark, he was to pass by the person who bore it.

Precisely the same scenario is playing itself out in Rev 7:1-8. God's fierce and final judgment awaits the Lamb's breaking of the seventh seal. This time, though, the entire world will feel the weight of God's wrath against the idolatrous celebration of Rome's satanic lordship and those who have accommodated themselves to it. Then, just when the reader expects action to begin, one of God's agents calls "time out." A group of 144,000 witnesses are to be branded on their foreheads with God's mark or seal. The seal identifies a

person as God's possession. Later, in 14:1-5, John identifies it as God's own name. The seal enables those who bear it to pass unscathed through the apocalyptic woes to come.

The 144,000 are the human wing of God's cosmic army. The number symbolizes wholeness: the number twelve is multiplied against itself and the total extended in a millenarian way (12 x 12 x 1000). This is the "whole" or "complete" remnant group.

7:9-17, An Innumerable, International Multitude

The second half of chap. 7 has two natural sections. In the first, vv. 9-12, John witnesses a horde of what are clearly believing Christians. Standing before the throne of God, they shout out a hymn of praise. That acclamation is instantly affirmed by the voices of angels, who respond antiphonally with a psalm of their own. In the second section, vv. 13-17, spurred on by a rhetorical question from one of the twenty-four elders, John learns who the singers are and why they are so motivated to sing. These are the souls of resurrected witnesses. They fall into the same characterization as the resurrected souls of 6:9-11. Unsealed, and therefore unprotected, in their earthly lives they met the fury of events that accompanied God's judgment head on. Unlike the 144,000, they were vulnerable to both the eschatological woes that attended the coming of God's new Day and the reactionary evil that human and cosmic forces of Satan pitched against it. In testifying to the lordship of the executed Lamb and suffering greatly because of it, they had washed their robes to a sparkling sheen in his blood.

In their hymns and preaching, African Americans have testified that there is indeed power in the blood of the Lamb. That blood, however, does not represent a call to martyrdom; it is an invitation to nonviolent, revolutionary action. Anthony Pinn argues for "a dissonance between the social body and the black bodies, a discord that sparks and fuels religion as historical liberation because the former operates through a process of bad faith and corrupt intentions."[20] One could argue for the same dissonance between the social body (expectation of emperor worship) and the witness body or "soul" (which symbolizes resistance to that expectation) in Revelation. The spiritual body is in extreme dissonance with the Roman social one. By definition, it is therefore resistant, and actively so. A believer must make an active choice, given the social context of Asia Minor at the end of the first century, to be one type of body or the other. John dramatizes his preference with this horde of souls clothed in robes washed to sparkling sheen in the blood of the Lamb. He has essentially reconfigured the dress of execution into the clothing of defiance. All of a sudden, what some might view as a martyr's attire has become the fine, sparkling linen of subversive witness. These dead souls, all dressed up, are a soul force.

CHAPTER 8

8:1-6, Introduction to the Trumpets

The breaking of the seventh seal commences a half hour of heavenly silence. The hush recalls the moment that preceded God's creation of heaven and earth. Here at the end, following the cataclysms of final judgment, God will create a new heaven and a new earth.

The seven angels come from the larger group of angels who stand with the elders and cherubim at 7:11. They are the seven archangels who represent the awesome power of God to punish wrongdoing. No wonder, then, that John connects them so integrally to the eschatological judgment of the trumpets and bowls.

John's use of the divine passive construction "it (the trumpet) was given" indicates that God controls the trumpets, distributes

them, and no doubt directs when and to what effect they are blown. Depending on how one has responded to God through either witness or accommodation, the sounding will signal either salvation or judgment.

Golden censer in hand, an eighth angel approaches the golden altar of incense. In the Jerusalem temple the incense altar was located just inside the holy of holies, where the presence of God was thought to reside. While John is careful to keep prayers and incense as distinct entities that rise up from the altar, he connects all three elements (prayer, incense, altar) to God's avenging, judging behavior. The altar's fire is thrown *down* as a direct response to the saints' prayers that rise *up*.

8:7-13, The First Four Trumpets

With the trumpets, John sees an escalation of God's wrath, which he conveys through the familiar imagery of the Exodus plagues.[21] What better way to assure a people who are experiencing eschatological chaos that God is in control than to remind them of a similarly desperate time in the life of Israel when, contrary to all appearances, God, who was firmly in charge, was acting to save/liberate those in God's charge.

Depending, then, on one's position vis-à-vis God, acts of judgment could also be acts of liberation. Just as the prophets called the people to remain faithful to the God who had liberated them, so John is asking his people to remain faithful to the God who is coming to judge. *They* will experience that judgment as a liberating salvation. "Each plague is God's challenge to the power of the Caesar. Each trumpet blast is a ringing command from the Liberator God: 'Let my people go!'"[22]

Like John, the African American church, existing as it does in a context of enduring racism, impoverishment, drug addiction, epidemic school dropout and imprisonment rates, disintegrating families, and underemployment, must recall in more viscerally energizing ways the fact that God did intervene in the great liberating moments of the exodus and of Jesus of Nazareth. Those past interventions are the promise of future ones. Historically, the black church's belief *that* God has intervened, does intervene, and will intervene is the spark that has ignited generations of sociopolitical activism. "African American churches and religions have been a relentless source of 'radical thrusts' for liberation. Moreover, we cannot fail to remember that the civil rights movement and the black power movement were virtually born in our churches. The history of African American churches must be told in the language of radical and revolutionary struggle for religious and secular liberty."[23] Without this tangible belief that the supernatural will intervene in a strategic way, humans feel less pressure to represent that strategic possibility tactically. The result is that too many African American churches now pursue individual, personal salvation rather than the corporate, social, and political reign of God.

CHAPTER 9

9:1-12, The Fifth Trumpet

When the fifth trumpet sounds, the execution of God's justice is so ferocious that human beings seek death in order to escape it. It begins with the angel Satan, who has fallen like a star and takes possession of the key to the great abyss. He uses it to release a demonic horde of locusts who view him as their king. His Hebrew name is *Abaddon*, "death and destruction"; his Greek name is *Apollyon*, "destroyer." Instead of aiming for the vegetation as they did in the Exodus plague (Exod 10:1-15), these scorpion-tailed locusts are ordered to sting humans relentlessly. Their lion-like teeth also produce a ferocious bite. They are the first woe.

The connection between the locusts' destruction and the judgment language of woe (8:13) is important. It indicates that Satan is not in charge. Using the divine passive formulation "it was given," John indicates that God gives Satan the key for a reason. God intervenes on behalf of those who cry out for justice (6:9-11; 8:3-5) by using evil to obliterate the very humans who operate under its employ. For a limited time of five months, the locusts torture but do not kill every human who has not been sealed with the name of God. Since only the 144,000 were sealed, many saints will also be tormented. As 3:10 instructs, the Son of Man will keep them (i.e., enable them to endure) but will not "rapture" them. What makes the saints different from their idolatrous peers is the rationale behind their suffering. Their peers suffer because they do not recognize the lordship of God and the Lamb and persecute those who do. The unsealed saints represent a kind of tragic, eschatological collateral damage.

9:13-21, The Sixth Trumpet

When the sixth trumpet sounds, the incense altar (8:3-5) orders the angel who blew it to release four angels bound by the Euphrates River. The four are released (by God) to do what they have been prepared (by God) to do, that is, to kill a third of humankind. Good news? One certainly has to search for it. No doubt, John wants his hearers and readers to recognize value in the fact that, despite what sounds like global massacre, the world has not spun out of control. God remains in charge.

Despite the ravages of the plagues, the surviving two-thirds of humankind refuse to repent from the idolatrous works of their hands. The emphasis on repentance suggests God's intent. From the very start of his work, John has made the case that his primary focus for writing has been an ethical one. For those who cannot live up to the onerous demands of witnessing—even the Jezebels and the Balaams—he exhorts repentance.

It is the combination of the theme of liberation that reverberates throughout this section of Revelation and the theme of repentance that concludes this chapter that infuses this otherwise very disturbing text with a hint of gospel. It is good news that God hears the pleas of those who have lifted their cries (6:9-11) and their prayers (8:3-5) upon the altars of sacrifice and incense (9:13). It is good news that God intends not to destroy but to reprove. Even so close to the end, there remains time to turn back toward an eschatological relationship with God.

African Americans have encountered a similarly odd circumstance that required that they plead for God's judgment in the form of a vicious war that would also devour them. Many slaves believed that God was directly responsible for that war. It was the only way to dismantle the evil empire of plantation slavery and erect something more just in its place. For the slave, it was not a matter of violence but of justice. A just God had to act by any means necessary to annihilate slavery. So indicated the vision of a certain Charles Grandy: "Den a gra' big star over in de east come right down almos to de earth. I seed it myself. 'Twas sign o' war alright. Niggers got glad. All dem what could pray 'gin to pray more 'n ever. So glad God sendin' de war."[24]

Chapter 10

10:1-3, The Angel and the Little Scroll

Both the 5:1—8:1 scroll and the one this mighty archangel holds are based on the one of Ezek 2:9-10. Indeed, they are the same scroll. True, while John calls the first scroll a *biblion,* he labels the second a *biblaridion* ("little scroll"), a diminutive for *biblios.* (*Biblion* also was originally a diminutive.) In fact,

John treats the two words as though they are synonyms. While he introduces the scroll first with the form *biblaridion* at 10:2, and follows up with the same noun form at vv. 9 and 10, at the critical point where the scroll takes narrative center stage, v. 8, he describes it as a *biblion.*

10:4-7, The Mystery of the Seven Thunders

Previous orders to publish (i.e., 1:11, 19) make this command to seal up the thunders' message intriguing. John's Ephesus letter offers direction (see also Matt 13:24-30). John celebrates the perceptive and critical spirit of the Ephesians. Unfortunately, the Ephesians became *too* discerning. If the Ephesians were segregating those who were "saved" from those who were "not" on the basis of their own spurious evaluations of witness works, how much more out of hand might such premature assessments become if they thought they could name names? What if the thunders were revealing names that were registered in or blotted out of the Lamb's scroll of life?

If John's work is to have the ethical impact that he wants it to have, so that it encourages witnessing behavior in such diverse categories as the most threatened, the most self-confident, and the most marginal believers, then no one must ever be able to claim access to such knowledge. That information must remain a mystery right up until the end. It is the "not knowing" that provokes appropriate ethical response. As long as no one's name has been revealed, no one can feel either totally in or totally out of God's eschatological future. Everyone stands equally insecure on the apocalyptic edge. Everyone is intensely motivated to live the witness *and* love worthy of one whose name is recorded in the Book of Life.

African American slaves were equally fascinated with the symbolism and power of sealed knowledge. Their mystery was the Bible.

The book could be read to slaves in the presence of an authorized agent, but slaves were forbidden to learn the skill of reading and were therefore denied their own interpretive engagement. Such "sealing" provoked in them powerful efforts of resistant, creative, witnessing discipleship. Their masters' clandestine efforts energized a relentless drive to do whatever was necessary to learn and live the liberating secrets of the book. Bible stories became an oral book that slave preachers and teachers handed down from one generation to the next. Delores Williams shares how they constructed it. "African American slaves, female and male, created an oral text from a written text (the King James Version of the Bible). They composed this oral text by extracting from the Bible or adding to biblical content those phrases, stories, biblical personalities, and moral prescriptions relevant to the character of their life situation and pertinent to the aspirations of the slave community."[25] Fusing biblical material with their own life situation and concerns, they *composed* a biblical witness that was uniquely their own. The slaves did what John no doubt hoped his hearers and readers would do. When they could not gain access to the book, they used their lives to fashion a book of their own. When one cannot know a mystery, one must divine it in the living of one's life. Like the slaves, John's people were forced to live their salvation, not overhear it.

10:8-11, The Little Scroll

John's attention is refocused on the scroll by a voice from heaven. He is told, in what comes across as eucharistic language, to take and eat it (Matt 26:26; cf. Ezek 2:8—3:3). While it embitters his stomach, it tastes like honey in his mouth. Though John reveled in the knowledge that he was interacting so closely with God's word of justice for human history, his stomach soured when he realized how much devastation that justice would bring.

Chapter 11

11:1-2, Measuring the Temple

At 10:11 John is reminded that he must prophesy; 11:1-2 conveys that prophecy as a symbolic act on the temple. "Temple" is a metaphor for the faithful believers of the seven churches. First, John measures and therefore shields the temple sanctuary. Second, he does not measure and therefore leaves vulnerable to destruction the greater part of the temple.

The inner sanctuary corresponds to the invulnerable believers whom John chronicles at 7:1-8 and 14:1-5. The terms *poimainō* ("tend like a shepherd, rule") and *rabdos* ("rod") are clarifying. Like the conquering witnesses (2:27) and Christ (12:5; 19:15), John is to prophesy in a way that will shepherd with discipline. Protection is not a reward for a special few, but another complex stage in John's exhortation. Some believers are set to do even more witnessing, not exult in a "saved" status.

The believers of 7:9-17 correspond to the unmeasured and therefore unprotected outer courtyard. Like the souls of 6:9-11, they are trampled and executed. Because they are engaged *with* the world, *in* the world, they share in the fate *of* the world. Though the believers are not responsible for the disasters, neither are they "raptured" out of them.

John uses the matter of theodicy as a teaching tool here. Nonbelievers who see the suffering of the faithful (the unprotected outer courtyard), and wonder if their God can truly be God, will nonetheless see these believers maintaining their witness to the lordship of that God. After all, God really is in control. Through yet another strategic use of the divine passive formulation "it was given," John narrates what his followers believe. The nations have the power to trample the outer courtyard only because God gives it to them.

The imagery here is particularly pertinent for African Americans, who have persisted with their faith in God's direction of human history despite the fact that their history has been fraught with trampling. Beginning in slavery, struggling through segregation, and communally disintegrating in a nascent twenty-first century still rife with the reality and effects of racism, as a minority of middle- and upper-class blacks rise above and break away from the majority black underclass, African Americans could well count their number among the tragic group John describes at 7:9-17. Throughout their generations, they have washed their robes in social, political, economic, and religious blood. And yet they remain the United States' sole "super-churched" ethnic community. Obstinately, they believe. *There* is a witness!

Super-Churched

In their highly regarded 1990 work on the black church, C. Eric Lincoln and Lawrence Mamiya found that African Americans donate more than 75 percent of all their charitable giving to the black church, and contribute more than 35 percent of their volunteer time to it. Those numbers translate into $2 billion worth of plate offerings and $35 billion worth of valued time. The economic numbers alone, however, do not tell the full story. Lincoln and Mamiya also found that the commitment of African Americans to religion and religious institutions consistently outranks that of other ethnicities in the United States. 78 percent of African Americans are "churched"; 37 percent are "super-churched"; and the weekly church attendance rates of African Americans was found to stand at 43 percent.

—C. Eric Lincoln and Lawrence H. Mamiya, *The Black Church in The African American Experience* (Durham, N.C.: Duke University Press, 1990), 260–61.

11:3-13, The Two Witnesses

Verses 3-13 are a message to the unmeasured, unprotected believers of v. 2. What John promised in v. 2 he therefore reaffirms here in v. 3; the time of such tribulation, though devastating, will be short lived.[26] Endure it. Outlast it. Witness through it.

The two witnesses are a cipher for the believing church. In them, John's hearers/readers find the model for enduring, prophetic behavior. Instead of blending into and accommodating with the Greco-Roman world in which they find themselves, these two, like Moses (turns water to blood, strikes the earth with plague) and Elijah (shuts the sky so no rain will fall), stand out by representing through their words, behavior, and identities the Lordship of Christ as an opposition to the lordship of Rome. For this testimony they pay the price of persecution. God resurrects, vindicates, and empowers them, just as God will resurrect, vindicate, and empower the unmeasured/unprotected believers who endure in their witness to that Lordship. Their story, John means to say, is the story of every faithful, unprotected, world-engaging witness.

African Americans have their own recent historic version of two representative witnesses. The Islamic tradition of Malcolm X represented a resistant African American faith that trusted God's justice when human injustice prevailed. In the mold of Moses, his powerful rhetoric threatened blood and plague against the purveyors of systemic racism. The Christian Martin Luther King Jr. operated with a nonviolent spirit that was equally powerful. Like Elijah, he withheld resources, boycotting communities until they understood that without African American participation, entire economies would dry up. Like John's two witnesses, though they were cut down in life, they have stood up in history.[27]

CHAPTER 12

12:1-6, The Woman, the Dragon, and the Son

Chapter 12 starts the story. As far as "real" (as opposed to John's narrative) time is concerned, the events in chap. 12 happened before John wrote, and, in fact, motivated his writing. Here John explains how and why the draconian siege of the church began.

In the celestial woman, John has combined many women/mother images and fashioned them into a representation of the church's corporate existence. The sun robe, moon pedestal, and twelve-star crown indicate an intimate relationship with God. Indeed, the woman is pregnant with God's Messiah (v. 5).

Is the woman, only in the story to give birth, as passive as some critics contend? I am reminded of the Vietnam War, the so-called helicopter war, which saw the highest proportion of African Americans ever to serve in an American conflict. Troops were ferried in and out of combat zones by helicopter. The active agents were the soldiers dispatched to fight and die. Yet every helicopter ingress and egress was made under the threat or reality of hostile fire. The aircraft's desperate role was to give birth to a combat force in the midst of an agonizing labor of enemy fire. John's cosmic woman, laboring against the pain of an impending birth that symbolized the persecution God's people endured as they awaited the deployment of God's messianic son and the forces who would follow him, is, metaphorically speaking, God's lead helicopter. Hers, too, is a dangerous and active role.[28]

The dragon is Satan, the evil presence behind worship-seeking empires like Rome. In a display of power, it sports seven heads and ten horns (cf. Dan 7:7, 20, 24). Upon each head is a diadem, which represents its claim to ultimate lordship. Horns represent power. The Lamb was outfitted with seven (5:6). Qualita-

tively, since the Lamb has a perfectly complete number, it has more power.

The celestial woman gives birth to a messianic Son who will shepherd not just believers but all the nations with a disciplining, iron rod (cf. Ps 2:9). The implication is that he will steer the nations to repentance. Some critics ponder why John presents the child's birth and then moves right to his ascension to the throne of God without talking specifically about his death. The birth *is* the death. His execution becomes the means to his glorification and his people's future.

12:7-9, A War in Heaven

When war breaks out in heaven, the archangel Michael represents God's combat capability. At the very moment that Jesus is historically dying on the cross, Michael and his angels are fighting mythologically in heaven. The snatching of Jesus to the throne, that is, the resurrection and ascension, is the historical metaphor that represents Michael's mythical expulsion of the dragon from heaven. As Jesus rises into the heavenly realm, the dragon is thrown down into the historical one.

12:10-11, A Victory Hymn of Praise

This hymn's praise has two rationales: Satan has been conquered; the reign of God has come. Witnesses participated in the inauguration of this reign. "They" conquered the dragon. They wielded both the blood of the Lamb and their own testimony about the transformative, revolutionary power of that blood to commence Christ's lordship. John recalls how they defeated the dragon because he wants his contemporary hearers and readers to finish the witness work they started (6:9-11).

12:13-18, The Woman, the Dragon, and the Son's Siblings

This material is a reprise of the vv. 1-6 combat between the woman and the dragon. John adds that the dragon now seeks out the other children of the woman. No longer able to target the future of God's people as a corporate community (i.e., the church) or the life of God's Son, it trains its vindictive sights on individual churches and believers instead.

Chapter 13

13:1-10, The Beast from the Sea
Daniel 7 echoes throughout John's presentation of the first draconian beast, Rome. Like the dragon, it has ten horns and seven heads (17:3, 7, 9, 12, 16). The seven heads are the seven hills and the seven emperors (17:9). The beast is the entire system of Roman rule. The ten horns are ten kings (17:12; cf. Dan 7:24). The diadems on the horns apparently lay claim to the title King of Kings, which John applies exclusively to Christ (19:12, 16). The blasphemous names are a reference to Roman coinage imprinted with the heads of emperors alongside Greek titles like "god," "son of god," "savior," or "lord."

One of the beast's heads has suffered a mortal wound. John describes its mangling with the same execution language he applies to the Lamb. The head also resurrects. John has in mind Emperor Nero, who was done in by a self-inflicted stab wound to the neck. Many feared that he would return from the dead and resurrect the evil image of Rome he had long fostered.

Operating from the background of Jer 15:2 and 43:11, John explains that if someone is destined for captivity, that person goes into captivity. The conditional statement fits John's belief that God has scripted everything. Those who witness for the Lordship of Christ can expect to be taken captive by a beast whose primary goal is to institutionalize its own exclusive lordship. John turns his attention to death by the sword. As did Jesus at Matt 26:52, he means that the proper response to bestial violence is not more violence but a faithful endurance that witnesses to one's confidence that God is in control.

Here is the *hypomonē* (endurance), which is the faith of the saints. One's ability to endure is a measure of one's faith. Some will be imprisoned, others will be slain by the sword. Keep resisting! This *hypomonē* should not be so weakly translated as "patient endurance." This kind of intransigent, obstinate trust in God's direction of human history was a hallmark of the nonviolent civil rights movement in the United States. Many civil rights leaders and followers endured social ostracism, political persecution, police brutality, and death with a faith resolve to continue the fight against segregation no matter the consequences because of their belief that ultimately God, not the beast of racism, was Lord.

13:11-18, The Beast from the Land
The second beast, symbolizing Rome's surrogate Asia Minor officials, rises from the land. It has the welcoming look of a lamb but the mouth of a dragon. No doubt John's hearers/readers recalled the Matthean Jesus' warning about false prophets who come looking like sheep but are in reality ravenous wolves (Matt 7:15). John portrays this bestial false prophet in exactly the same way (16:13; 19:20; 20:10).

The false prophet issues an identifying *charagma* (mark) on the right hand or forehead of those who responded positively to its invitation to participate in the religious, social, economic, and political rites associated with the imperial cult (13:16, 17; 14:9, 11; 16:2; 19:20; 20:4). Clearly a parody of God's seal (7:2; 14:1), the mark has a commercial connection. Without it, a person loses an ability to engage in the commerce of Asia Minor. Shut out of the economic system, one would be hard pressed to survive. John was concerned that his people were so interested in social and economic advancement that they would pass themselves off as devotees of the idolatrous rites, like eating meat sacrificed to idols (2:12-17, 18-29), that were required to maintain good standing in trade and guild associations.

Something similar happened in early African American fiction. Many novelists before and during the Harlem Renaissance dealt with the phenomenon of light-skinned African Americans passing themselves off as white to reduce social ostracism and increase social opportunity. These writers used the trope not only to describe what had actually happened, but also to demonize the societal circumstance that made it necessary. Nella Larsen's novel *Passing* (1929) makes the critical point that

---

Passing

Nella Larsen reflects upon a scene between two very light-skinned African American sisters: In a rare moment, Clare confides to Irene that the economic and psychological impact of the (white) aunts' beliefs drove her to discard her black identity and become white. She "wanted things," she tells Irene, and clearly she means not only material goods but love and emotional comfort, as well, for she wants "to be a person and not a charity or a problem, or even a daughter of the indiscreet Ham" (159). The aunts' definition of blackness attempts to rob Clare of her humanity, so she must shed that black identity to be human. To do so, she must literally turn white by passing, accepting the demands of assimilation to avoid the ramifications of what Joel Kovel refers to as the "Ham Myth of Expulsion" (79).

—Neil Sullivan, "Nella Larsen's *Passing* and the Fading Subject," in *African American Review* 32 (1998): 375. See also Joel Kovel, *White Racism: A Psychohistory* (New York: Pantheon, 1970).

---

the greater evil is not the regrettable "blending" in which some light-skinned African Americans participated, but the "evil" evolution of society that made this "passing" not only possible but in many cases preferable. In a corresponding way, John makes use of early Christian "passing." Though he clearly sees a problem with what Christians are doing in accommodating themselves to Greco-Roman life, his agenda ranges far beyond a critique of the Christians themselves. He wants the Christians to see that they are caught up in a draconian, prostituting system. The only challenge to that system resides in the will of those who refuse to participate in its many social, economic, and political benefits. Whatever it costs them, those Christians must not "pass."

The name on the bestial mark is *Neron Caesar*. When the Greek letters for Neron Caesar are transliterated into Hebrew, the numerical value of these Hebrew letters is 666 (see sidebar on p. 545). For John, perhaps, the number also suggests a desperate and futile attempt to reach completeness. Even as it flaunts its strength, the beast wallows in weakness. It is always a six, never a seven.

CHAPTER 14

14:1-5, The 144,000

John's hearers and readers already know that the 144,000 standing with the Lamb are protected (7:1-8). Their very existence is a testimony to God's ability to protect God's people in the present. That present testimony acts as a future guarantee that God will protect, that is, save God's people in the future.

The heavenly multitude in 7:9-17 sings a new song of praise to God that only the 144,000 can learn. The 144,000 have successfully resisted the lures and threats of Roman lordship. That resistance enables their learning. No doubt John means that they are the only ones *on earth* who can learn the song. Clearly, the song has already been learned by the multitude of victorious witnesses (7:9-17) who sing it. Their resistance, too, must have earned them their capability. The 144,000 are unique because they learn the song while they are still on earth. Perhaps this ability resides with their remnant status. Perhaps this is a marching song whose cadence can only be comprehended by those who parade with the Lamb on the eschatological battlefield (cf. 19:14). If the content of the song is integrally connected to its cadence, then one would expect that only by taking up the march could one learn the lines.

The 144,000 have not been "defiled" with women; they are virgins. John is working figuratively with the image of purity, in which, through abstinence, male soldiers readied themselves for holy war. John used the term *parthenos* (young woman, virgin) in a similarly figurative sense. He does not intend to exclude women from his portrait of the faithful but uses the term to convey both the male and the female faithful who resist accommodating ("defiling") themselves to the lures of the Roman imperial cult. Still, the language is disconcerting. The devaluation of both women and sexuality implied in a literal reading have borne negative consequences for more than two millennia. Affirming public readings should convey not the verse's words, but its intent: that is, "They are like virgins who would not be seduced by the idolatrous lures of the beast from the sea."

The 144,000 follow the Lamb wherever he goes. They follow him in resistance. Their status as the "sealed" or "protected" ones implies that they do not follow the Lamb to execution. The key emphasis for them is not death, but witnessing.

The 144,000 are the first fruits of the harvest. As such, they act as a guarantor that many more will be successfully harvested (cf. vv. 14-16).

14:6-13, The Gospel of Justice

John initiates a parade of six angels, three of whom come before, three after a seventh figure, one like a Son of Man (Dan 7:14). The

---

The Number of the Beast

Revelation declares that "the number of the beast . . . is the number of a person. Its number is six hundred sixty-six" (13:18).

The letters of the Hebrew alphabet also serve as numbers:

א	1	ז	7	מ	40	ק	100
ב	2	ח	8	נ	50	ר	200
ג	3	ט	9	ס	60	שׁ	300
ד	4	י	10	ע	70	ת	400
ה	5	כ	20	פ	80		
ו	6	ל	30	צ	90		

So the Greek spelling of the name "Neron Caesar," written in Hebrew letters (which do not include vowels), would be נרון קסר (NRWN QSR), the total numerical value of which adds up to 666.

ר ס ק ן ו ר נ
200+60+100 50+6+200+50

---

theme of judgment is continuous and unbearably harsh. Punishment operates as an enduring, eternal torture. The language, though, was not meant to be taken literally. John intends to dissuade believers who are considering an accommodation to Roman economic, political, social, and cultic pressures and expectations. He wants them to feel the ensuing consequences. There is a horror greater than even the worst penalty the Romans can impose.

14:14-20, Harvest Time

John presents a picture of a harvest that is both positive (for those who respond properly to the call to fear God and give God glory) and another that is negative (for those who refuse). Joel's image of the sickle reaping the grapes and the treading upon them in the wine press is surely his inspiration (Joel 3:13). In both harvest images (vv. 14-16; vv. 17-20) he includes the sickle and dramatically ends with the wine press and its horrific results. Whereas the harvesting of the vineyard includes both the reaping and treading, the harvesting of the grain fields at vv. 14-16 includes a reaping but no thrashing or winnowing (cf. Mark 4:29). There John has purposely left off the judgmental image. He expects that people of every nation and tribe and language (v. 6) can respond with repentance and find eschatological relationship with God.

This mixed language of hope for redemption, the possibility of repentance, the assurance of salvation *and* the threat of horrific judgment also existed incongruously within the language of some of the African American spirituals. One song in particular, "Sinner, Please Don't Let This Harvest Pass," simultaneously applauded God's grace while fearfully acknowledging the reality of God's judgment. First, a generous but realistic appeal: "Sinner, please don't let this harvest pass, And die and lose your soul at last." Then, an assurance of grace: "I know that my redeemer lives, Sinner,

please don't let this harvest pass." But a warning of depravity: "Sinner, Oh see the cruel tree, Where Christ died for you and me." And a final military appeal that threatens combat-like retribution: "My God is a mighty man of war, Sinner, please don't let this harvest pass."

CHAPTER 15

15:1, A Sign of War

There are only three places where a portent, a sign, appears in heaven in Revelation. The first two occurrences were the woman and dragon of chap. 12. This third one signals the end of the flashback of chaps. 12–14 and sets the narrative back to its reflection of the end-time approach in seven stages. This final perspective on the end-time will adopt the metaphor of bowls.

The bowl series kicks off with a wrathful God playing the role of cosmic prosecutor and judge. This is the language of justice that must be worked out against the injustice that has plagued the land. It is not the language of emotional, vengeful, vigilante wrath, but directed, measured, justifiable wrath against evil. When this wrath deploys, it will search out those who are deserving and pour out its full measure upon them.

Christians are typically uncomfortable with the language of God's wrath. Grace, love, and forgiveness are the preferred divine metaphors. But in a world wracked with sin and evil, wrath, while undesirable, is a necessary component of justice. For John, to eliminate wrath is to cheapen grace, to make its work meaningless. Evil cannot be allowed to prosper unchecked by regulatory force. When it does, those who are defenseless are condemned to perpetual suffering.

Writing from apartheid South Africa, Allen Boesak echoed the thoughts of many blacks around the globe who have endured the hostilities of race hatred and need God's wrathful response to it: "People who do not know what oppression and suffering is react strangely to the language of the Bible. The truth is that God *is* the God of the poor and the oppressed. . . . Because they are powerless, God will take up their cause and redeem them from oppression and violence. The oppressed do not see any dichotomy between God's love and God's justice."[29]

The good news is that God's wrath will end. A better reading would be that God's wrath will be accomplished. Once evil has been destroyed, wrath will have fulfilled its mission.

15:2-4, Songs of Praise
Circling the burning sea of glass in the heavenly throne room are the redeemed conquerors, harps in hand. The imagery recalls 14:1-5, the 144,000, and the new song sung by the multitude of witnesses. The song itself recalls the exodus; the conquerors sing the Song of Moses (Exod 15:1-18) and the song of the Lamb. John intends a parallel between the work of Moses in the exodus and the liberating work of the Lamb. The liberating, justifying wrath God displayed in the Exodus event will be replayed in the apocalyptic conquest of the Lamb.

15:5-8, The Bowl Ceremony
The bowl ceremony opens with the representatives of heaven, the seven angels, coming out to the great stadium of human history. Dressed in priestly garments, their look parallels that of the Son of Man in 1:13 (cf. Dan 10:5). One of the four living creatures gives them seven bowls of God's wrath that they are to pour out upon human history and creation. The number seven indicates that with these the wrath of God will have accomplished its goal.

CHAPTER 16

16:1-7, The First Three Bowls
Chapter 16 describes the consequences of

God's bowls of wrath in a structure that directly recalls the presentation of the seven trumpets.[30] The first trumpet and first bowl both occur over the earth. The second of each occurs over the sea. The third of each occurs over rivers and springs of water. The fourth of each occurs over the sun. The fifth of each creates darkness. The sixth of each involves the Euphrates River and the enemy troops pouring across its boundary. After the seventh of each, the reign of God arrives. The parallel message is that God's justice will prevail.

The vicious irony of the first bowl transfigures the mark of the beast that once guaranteed economic, political, and social success into a festering sore. The second bowl turns the sea to blood. When Rome does not respond, God's push for justice takes another ferociously ironic turn. The beast has drawn much blood in its execution of God's Lamb and people (cf. 11:7; 13:7). The angel in charge of the water agrees that God has executed an appropriate punishment when God also turns the fresh rivers and springs to blood. With all the drinking water fouled, Rome/Babylon chokes to death on the very liquid it has spilled.

16:8-11, The Fourth and Fifth Bowls
The fourth bowl fires a sun so hot that humans are scorched. Instead of repenting, though, the nonbelievers' hatred of God burns even hotter. Like the bestial Rome they serve, they blaspheme God instead (13:1, 5, 6; 17:3). The fifth bowl shuts the sun down. The darkness that rules is a total eclipse of the monster's imperial power. The light on empire has gone completely out.

16:12-16, The Sixth Bowl
The sixth bowl dries up the Euphrates River, which formed a natural boundary between the fearsome Parthians, whom the Romans desperately tried to keep at bay, and the Roman

Empire. This preview-premonition of Roman defeat operates simultaneously as a pledge of liberation for the witnesses of the Lamb. The dragon, bestial Rome, and the false prophet respond by conjuring demonic frog spirits whom they send forth to deceive world leaders and even Christian believers into assisting the dragon and Rome in their war with God. The dragon's lies seduce the kings of the earth to Armageddon. Armageddon is not really a place, but a symbol of the typological battle that will occur between the forces of God and the forces of the beast. The term is linked figuratively with Mount Megiddo, because in the Old Testament it is the place where righteous Israelites were often attacked by wicked nations (Judg 5:19; 2 Kgs 23:29; 2 Chr 35:20-22). The reference, then, is not a prediction of a coming war but rather the symbolism of what is already occurring in John's present. Already, God's people are besieged.

The Lamb now announces his intention to come as a thief in the night. The remark echoes Jesus' statements in the Synoptic Gospels about being watchful (e.g., Matt 24:43-44; see also 1 Thess 5:2; Rev 3:18-22). The warning alerts John's hearers and readers that they should be watchful enough to read in the signs of the times God's movement on their behalf and respond properly to that moment. God has not lost control. The chaos is a time for preparation, not fear.

16:17-21, The Seventh Bowl
With the seventh bowl God's wrath accomplishes the justice it sought. Even now, though, the truly recalcitrant refuse to repent. To the end they curse God, even as the plagues rain down upon them.

In the 1970s, a television-oriented public service project called "Scared Straight" aired. Young people at risk of being corrupted into a life of crime by social circumstances that made anti-social behavior appear heroic were confronted, in real prison settings, by hardened convicts who revealed in the harshest of terms and language the prison life that awaited them if their lives did not change. A similar "scaring straight" was often attempted in African American church revivals, where the fire and brimstone of God's judgment was vowed for all who failed to repent of broken and damaging ways of life. John's bowl presentation suggests that such harsh portraits of coming judgment are unable by themselves to turn people in the right direction. People cannot be terrified into faith or sociability. The fear must be tempered and augmented by a promising vision. Wrath disconnected from justice can foster terror but not transformation. This is why John ultimately makes the bowl series as much about God's liberating justice as the wrath required to secure it.

CHAPTER 17

17:1-6, Hard to Resist
The mention of a bowl angel recalls the severe judgment imagery of chap. 16. It also anticipates 21:9, where the emphasis surrounding another bowl angel is salvation. Both angels point John toward a city personified as a woman. Here, in chap. 17, she is both a call girl astride Rome and also Rome herself. In chap. 21 she is the wife of the Lamb. With this dramatic staging, John has positioned the city of Rome and the city of God directly against each other.

The call girl is a glamorous, finely adorned prostitute who wields the bestial power of persecution and terror wherever she rides Rome (vv. 1, 15, 16). Because of her beauty and the life of luxury and security that she promises, John is afraid that his people will accommodate themselves to her. Rome was the commercial and political epicenter of the world. He therefore mixes into his description the language of prostitution and idolatry. Any accommodation to Rome's idolatrous claims of lordship was like the leaving of a faithful spouse for a harlot.

Beneath the alluring surface, this call girl is a killer full of obscenities and filth (cf. Dan. 9:27; 11:31; 12:11; Mark 13:14). The ugliness goes unnoticed, because people are drunk on the wine of her glory. She, however, is drunk on the economic, social, and political lifeblood of other peoples. Rome has become so great drawing the life from others that it bears the likeness of a god and even admits to the parallels. Rome is the one who was, who is not, and who is to rise. Like God, it not only claims control over time itself; it intends its own parousia, or rising to eternal rule.

17:7-18, The Whore and the Beast

Once again John declares that looks deceive. The woman's beast is already dead. Its rise takes it not to heaven but to hell. In rising up, it falls down. John is writing as much for the Romans as he is for his own followers. This is not coded language; the seven heads of the beast are obviously the seven hills of Rome. He wants the Romans to know that he is talking about them. He wants them to hear and fear the imminent movement of God.

The seven heads are also seven emperors. John is living and writing during the time of the sixth one, the one who now is: Domitian (81–96 C.E.). The seventh will come, and then an eighth. John's point is that the imperial line has only a short time now until a new monstrous force, the one that will rise, the one that was mentioned at 17:1, appears, until its parousia occurs. That eighth one will try to take the place of the seventh so that it can accomplish ultimate power. It cannot see that its rise will be to its own destruction; it is quite literally dead on arrival.

The ten horns symbolize the power of kings who attempt to draw authority from Rome and ally themselves with Rome against the Lamb. Because he is the true King of Kings (19:16), the Lamb's defeat of the beast and its surrogates is certain. When it is consummated, the kings will cannibalize the beast and the woman who personifies it. The symbolism intends a potent political message. The powers that have been overwhelmed by Rome hate the beast. They only pretend to follow in order to avail themselves of its goods. When Rome can no longer deliver those goods, they will turn on it and destroy it. With the Lamb, that time is coming soon. For the person who can see clearly, Rome is in fact already dead.

In preaching and teaching this text, the African American church must approach cautiously this personification of temptation and evil in the form of woman. John's symbolic language, when taken literally, can be generally sexist and personally damaging for contemporary African American women. This is of particular concern, given the African American church's own regrettable sexist and patriarchal legacy. One need not appeal to the wealth of documentation that narrates the lack of opportunity for women in ordained or lay leadership even in a church where women outnumber men in staggering proportions. A visit to a cross-section of African American churches on any given Sunday morning will suffice. The helpful educator and preacher will not only teach John's language but also, when necessary, challenge it. African American women are neither stereotypical temptresses nor pliant brides, both of whom draw their identity and appeal solely from their sexuality. The image of woman represents not a threat to the black church but—now as throughout the life of the church—its power, its wisdom, its strength, and its future. That message must operate alongside and, if necessary, even against John's imaging of evil as a plotting, destructive whore.

CHAPTER 18

18:1-8, A Matter of Economic Injustice

"Come out of her, my people," is one of the great commands issued in the book of Revelation. Jeremiah (51:45) and Isaiah (48:20) made similar appeals to the exiled Jews on behalf of God, telling them to flee doomed Babylon before it fell. The destruction of Babylon, the prototypical destroyer of God's people, was the opportunity for the people's liberation. And so it is again when John, envisioning Rome as the new Babylon, pitches the message anew. Who, though, *are* God's people? Apparently, *everyone*. "Yet even at this late hour it is still possible for [people] to prove themselves God's people and to escape their share in Babylon's plagues by dissociating themselves from her sins. To the bitter end the miracle of grace remains open, and God never ceases to say, 'My people', to those who before were not his people."[31] Even at the end, there is still time.

Many, though, will refuse to leave Babylon / Rome, because she provides too much money and profit. This text is about economics and the power of economics to create wealth, grandeur, and the illusion of unimpeachable power. When John says that all the kings of the earth have committed fornication with her, he means that the merchants of the earth have made lavish fortunes through her. Babylon/Rome is a money machine. Wealth creates and sustains power. The face of that power is an economic imperialism that despoils the earth in pursuit of its own luxurious endowment.

Yet, as glorious as Rome's legions were in protecting the interests of Rome's economic empire, John believes there is the greater, competing glory of God. An angel commissioned through that glory declares the great Babylon's/Rome's gruesome end.

18:9-19, Lamenting Great Loss

The vision of Babylon/Rome as a wasteland provokes lament from those who prospered from its protection and intercourse. The kings of the earth who willingly allowed their countries to be resources for the Roman economic machine—selling their natural and produced resources to Rome's voracious appetite for luxury and food goods, thereby often starving their own populaces in the process while they themselves became fat with wealth—will mourn the loss. A similar scenario exists in the twenty-first-century Western world. Poorer countries sacrifice their natural and people resources in order to feed the voracious economic appetite of the prosperous countries of the Unites States, Canada, Western Europe, and Japan. In this world, U.S. military might ensures the peace that enables the trade keeping it and its kingly allies empowered through the resources poorer nations sell out from beneath the feet of their own citizens while their leaders enrich themselves on the proceeds. African Americans, like John's kings, desperate to become more fully vested in such a world, must not lose the prophetic mandate to bring more justice into such a world. In a context where a majority of African Americans still live below the poverty line, the vision of civil rights must extend passionately to the drive for global economic rights.

Merchants have goods to sell, but they lament the loss of an empire to buy them. Since no one can afford to buy, sailors mourn the loss of any need for shipping. The devastation takes a day. The swiftness of the fall indicates just how illusory Rome's power was.

18:20-24, Judgment Day

God pronounces on Rome the very judgment Rome had meted out against those like the Lamb's witnesses who resisted its rule: utter destruction. The empire sinks like the proverbial millstone into the sea (cf. Jer 51:60-63; Luke 17:2); it will go dark forever.

CHAPTER 19

19:1-11, Victory Song

Chapter 19 opens to the sound of music. A heavenly multitude of faithful witnesses

(6:9-11; 7:9-17) responds to God's destruction of the forces that would destroy God's people with a victory hymn. A succession of ensuing songs (vv. 1-3, 4, 5, 6-8) rings out in antiphonal praise. Responding to the 18:20 command to rejoice, for the only time in all of the New Testament (vv. 1, 3, 4, 6) voices sing, "Hallelujah!"

"Hallelujah!" is the praise of the "Hallel psalms," 113–118.[32] Sung partly before the Passover supper and partly afterward, they featured the exodus liberation. "Hallelujah!" also recalls Ps 104:35, where the celebration is over God's judgment of sinners. Both references relate well to this Revelation context, where the people of God are simultaneously celebrating God's judgment of the dragon and the liberation that judgment brings.

"Hallelujah!" language comes full circle with the mother of all weddings between the Lamb and the church. Invitees are those who have helped stitch together the bride's wedding garment with the righteous, resistant work of their witness. The bride's beauty will be pictured more fully at 21:2, where she appears as the New Jerusalem, a city teeming with faithful witnesses.

Overwhelmed by the spectacle, an angel shouts, "Blessed are those who are invited to the marriage supper of the Lamb." As an indicative, the statement confirms that those who have already been invited are blessed. As an imperative, it demands that those who have yet to witness must do so.

Similarly overwhelmed, John celebrates the messenger. The angel chides his intended worship and explains that he, too, is only a witness. His reprimand is a warning for contemporary believers who often make the causes they champion or the religious symbols they celebrate idols that receive an adulation due only God. In particular, many African American Christians have a profound affection for the literal reading of the King James Version of the Bible. This loyalty to a particular text and a particular reading of that text operates often like a faith whose orthodoxy rejects openness to other biblical versions or more open interpretations of even this classic version. Such devotion borders on a worship of a particular form and reading of the Bible as though it were God rather than a messenger, a medium to God. If believers absolutize anything, it takes a place reserved for God. Even faith itself can become an idol if believers become too proud of it, too boastful and full of themselves because of it.

19:11-21, The Final Horseman
John sees a rider on a sparkling horse. Unlike the other rider on a sparkling horse, who appeared following the Lamb's breaking of the first seal (6:1-2), this one brings not desecration but righteousness (cf. Isa 11:4-5). His name, "Faithful and True," identifies him as Christ (3:14). His title, "King of King and Lord of Lords," validates the testimony of those who have witnessed at such peril to his exclusive Lordship. His garment is soaked in the blood of those who have been subjected to God's judgment. His messianic identity is confirmed by the iron rod he carries (cf. Ps 2:9; Isa 11:4). A sharp sword issuing from his mouth (1:16) takes center stage. In the Old Testament the mouth like a sharp sword was the symbol of the prophet, whose utterance had a cutting edge because he spoke the word of God. This prophetic word, the same claim he made before the Sanhedrin and Pontius Pilate, is the only weapon he needs to establish God's reign of justice.

Earlier, John spoke of a great wedding feast where all who were God's witnesses were invited to dine on a great heavenly menu. Now John envisions a great feast where all those who operated against the witnesses of God are invited to *be the menu* (cf. Ezek 39:17-20). Finally, the beast from the sea and the false prophet, the representation of oppressive empire and arrogant Roman rule, are thrown into a merciless lake of fire.

Chapter 20

20:1-10, The Millennium

A thousand-year reign was not something that apocalyptic writers had to include in their works, but John included it because it was an indispensable element in his particular vision of the future. There are three general ways of assessing that particularity. The fundamentalist approach reduces the text to its literal meaning. The thousand-year reign will be a real reign with Christ and his church here on earth, a visible political reign in history before the last judgment. Christ's second coming will inaugurate it. The spiritualizing approach understands the thousand-year reign to be the time of the church between the Incarnation of Jesus and the inauguration of the last judgment. In this scenario, the first resurrection takes place at baptism, and the second one is the bodily one.

The political approach conceives of the millennium as a symbolic reign. The millennium is the utopia for all those who struggle against the idolatry and oppression of empire in order to establish God's reign on earth. Whether believers are witnessing to God's Lordship against apartheid, slavery, segregation, oppression of women, racism, heterosexism, etc., when that witnessing challenges the forces of institutionalized evil and oppression that resists the reality of God's Lordship, then the hope for a reality beyond that oppression is the hope of the thousand year reign. It is a hope that motivates transformative human activity in the present. Millennium, then, "is not about the end of the world, but about a reign of God that ends the idolatry and criminality of empires in this world."[33] It is not a passive utopia. It depends upon the witnessing activity of those who believe in it. It also cannot be spiritualized. It takes place in history. It gives direction to present history, guides human action, and marshals human witness.

The ancient Hebrews had no real concept of a resurrected afterlife. God's salvation was what God did to liberate people in history. Daniel first presented the idea that the saints of the past would be restored to life of participation in the glories of a new age (Dan 12:2-3). John sees the best of both worlds. He sees an afterlife, a resurrected life in the heavenly city, and yet he also retains an earthly paradise, which he images through the metaphor of millennium. He therefore requires two resurrections. The first one restores the witnesses so they can reign with Christ for the thousand years. The second occurs only after the thousand-year reign has ended, when the rest of the dead also come to life. But, of course, they are at that point in a precarious position, since it is also the very same time that Satan, who has been bound for those thousand years, is set free.

Satan's resurgence is not about a punishment of the people for their sins or about retribution against God's enemies, for this happens after a thousand-year period of peace. The story is a warning that evil will not stay down. Satan's rise symbolizes the power of evil to stand up (as the Lamb was still standing!) and strike back after it has itself been struck down. *Evil resurrects too!* In the end, though, Satan, like the beast and false prophet, is thrown into a fire that burns without end. Before and after the millennium, God wins.

20:11-15, Good News

Nature abhors a vacuum. So, evidently, does God. When the old heaven and the old earth flee from the presence of holiness, they will be replaced by a new heaven and a new earth. This is when the book that contains the names of those who are to be spared the second death and enjoy an eternal relationship with God is opened. Death, the final opposition to life, is itself destroyed.

CHAPTER 21

21:1-8, Transfiguration

Everything is new, heaven *and* earth. If heaven is the transcendent, invisible dimension of history and earth its empirical, visible counterpart, then history is transformed in both its physical and transcendent components. The new earth is expected. The surprise is that transcendence too will be transformed. This is what the eschatological struggles have been about: the battles with Satan, the beast, and the false prophet were not destructive, but reconstructive confrontations. God transfigured the old through the fires of conflagration so that it could become what God had always intended.

God's new creation has several notable traits. The sea, emblematic of biblical chaos, glassed over but still visibly potent even in the transcendent throne room, will be no more. Death, and the mourning that follows from it, will also be destroyed (cf. Isa 25:6-8). Salvation, eternal life lived in God's presence as God's people, will take its place. The covenant made with Israel at Sinai, renewed in the promises of the prophets and realized in the new covenant of Christ, will now be fulfilled. As prophesied, God will be with them (cf. Exod 3:12; Isa 7:14; Matt 1:23).

Negativity, presented as stereotypical catalogue of vices, will be banned from this re-creation. It is no mistake that cowardice heads the list. Throughout the narrative, John has demonstrated grave concern that a people frightened for their security, status, livelihood, and lives will compromise their faith in order not to lose them. It is cowardice that he fears the most.

21:9—22:5, The Look and Feel of the New Jerusalem

The new city in this new creation descends from the transformed, transcendent realm. Its number is twelve. There are twelve gates through which no one seeks exit but all are offered entrance. Twelve angels attend it. On the gates are carved the names of the twelve tribes of Israel. The city wall boasts twelve foundation stones that bear the names of the twelve apostles: the city is founded upon the principles of apostolic teaching. The city itself is a cube twelve thousand furlongs in length, breadth, and height. *Twelve* represents wholeness; the city is the holistic representation of God's new creation. Most important, the city combines the imagery of the twelve tribes and the twelve apostles because it is built upon both Israel and the church. Israel is not left out when the reality of the church is drawn in.

The Eden-like city needs no external or artificial lighting since God's glory illumines it. God's direct presence removes the need for a temple. The temple functioned as a mediator between God and God's people, orchestrating through its cult and ritual a way for them to connect with God. That service is no longer necessary. Even the kings of the earth who had once allied themselves with the beast and trampled the people of God are allowed (assuming the repentance John urged) inside. What a radical representation of God's grace!

Prophets and poets dream of such a transfigured, historical realm. Their beautiful rhetoric and stirring petitions conjure hope that the realization of such an existence is possible.

In the African American context, perhaps the greatest representation of such a hope in the midst of what appeared to be a hopeless situation was Martin Luther King Jr.'s timeless speech at the march on Washington, August 28, 1963. Note within it the same longing for the intervention of justice and liberation that so pervaded John's visions:

I have a dream that one day this nation will rise up and live out the true meaning of its creed: "We hold these truths to be self-evident: that all [people] are created equal." I have a dream that one day on the red hills of Georgia the sons of former slaves and the sons of former slave owners will be able to sit down together at the table of brotherhood [and sisterhood]. I have a dream that one day even the state of Mississippi, a state sweltering with the heat of injustice, sweltering with the heat of oppression, will be transformed into an oasis of freedom and justice. I have a dream that my four little children will one day live in a nation where they will not be judged by the color of their skin but by the content of their character. I have a dream today. I have a dream that one day, down in Alabama, with its vicious racists, with its governor having his lips dripping with the words of interposition and nullification; one day right there in Alabama, little black boys and black girls will be able to join hands with little white boys and white girls as sisters and brothers. I have a dream today. I have a dream that one day every valley shall be exalted, every hill and mountain shall be made low, the rough places will be made plain, and the crooked places will be made straight, and the glory of the Lord shall be revealed, and all flesh shall see it together. Hallelujah![34]

Chapter 22

22:6-21, Don't Be Late

John's intent is not to condemn. He intends instead to motivate people to seek escape from the condemnation that is coming soon for those who have worshiped and perpetuated the false witness of Satan, the beast, and the false prophet. Though stern and often frightening, the message is ultimately hopeful. He works, *by any literary means necessary,* to impress upon his people that time is short. Jesus is coming soon. Get ready. "Don't be late."

John's focus is on the language of heeding, of doing the word (22:7, 9). It is the same language that drove his exhortations at the book's opening (1:3; 2:26; 3:3, 8, 10). One prepares for the coming of Christ by working the word that witnesses to the Lordship of that Christ. The subsequent matter of whether God's punishment or vengeance is too harsh misses the point for John. God is the same God. Whether accomplishing exodus for Israel, prophetically championing the poor and downtrodden, or revealing God's self in the unflinching love of Jesus of Nazareth, God has not changed. Humans can and do change; they thereby create shifts, sometimes seismic, in the way God's presence affects them. To operate metaphorically like John himself, one might liken God to light. Light does not change. It is always light. It is always shining. It is always bright. It affects humans differently not because the properties of the light change, but because humans change their orientation to it. When one chooses to operate in the subterranean caverns of human existence, where seclusion is preferred because one does not want anyone to see the wrongs one commits, a sudden invasion of light is blinding. However, those who live in the light are not dazed by it. John's message is simple: if you live in the darkness, move immediately out. The bright eschaton is coming soon.

How does one live life in the light? One does so by not running to and hiding in the caverns of self-preservation, or in the dark alleys of clandestine deals with the economic and political powers opposed to God so that they will not hurt one or the people one loves. One lives in the light by standing up and declaring by word and action, no matter what the consequences, that God alone is Lord. Slave preacher James Smith was such a witness:

He was finally received into the church and baptized. Not long after this, he felt loudly called upon to go out and labor for the salvation of souls among the slave population with whom he was identified. At this conduct his master was much displeased, and strove to prevent him from the exercise of what the slave considered to be his duty to God and his brethren, on the Sabbath day. He was sometimes kept tied all day Sundays while the other slaves were allowed to go just where they pleased on that day. At other times he was flogged until his blood would drip down at his feet, and yet he would not give up laboring whenever he could get an opportunity, on the Sabbath day, for the conversion of souls. God was pleased to bless his labors and many were led to embrace the Saviour under his preaching. At length his master sold him to a slave trader, who separated him from his family and carried him to the State of Georgia. His parting words to his wife were that if they proved faithful to God, He would bring them together again in a more free land than Virginia.[35]

John believes that Christ is coming soon to make utopian hopes like Preacher Smith's real. His exhortation: Respond to the realization of Christ's imminent arrival. Witness! As God is directing everything that has happened, does happen, and will happen, God will not let God's people witness in vain. This is the import of the title "Alpha and Omega," which John applies to both God and Christ. Ultimately, the end is not a place or a time, but a person. History reaches its goal in Christ. John wants his followers to know that through this Christ God will bend history to God's and their favor. Perhaps this

is precisely what exiled slave preacher James Smith thought some seventeen years after he was torn away from his wife. John would have concluded that God had been faithful. Despite the odds against it happening, Smith and his wife miraculously found each other in the free land of Canada. For them, that moment, that place must have captured the essence of the symbol "new heaven and new earth." "My Lord," the apocalyptic Negro spiritual appropriately declares, "what a morning!"

Notes

1. Cf. Catherine Keller, *Apocalypse Now and Then: A Feminist Guide to the End of the World* (Boston: Beacon, 1996), 1. Keller tracks the original intent of the Greek term for revelation to the marital stripping of the veiled virgin on her wedding night.

2. "While African Americans only make up about 13 percent (13.3 percent as of 1 July 2003, according to U.S. Census Bureau) of the U.S. population, they made up 43 percent of the inmates on death row in 1999, and a little more than a third of those actually executed that year." "Death Penalty," *Almanac of Policy Issues*, http://www.policyalmanac.org/crime /death_penalty.shtml. See also "United States of America: Death by Discrimination—the Continuing Role of Race in Capital Cases," *Amnesty International*, http://web.amnesty .org/library/index/engamr510462003: "African Americans are disproportionately represented among people condemned to death in the USA. While they make up 12 per cent of the national population, they account for more than 40 per cent of the country's current death row inmates, and one in three of those executed since 1977."

3. For a comparison with a similar phenomenon that happened to Paul, see 2 Cor 11, esp. 11:4; Gal 5:1-12, esp. v. 7.

4. A similar eschatological concern exists at Matt 13:24-30, the parable of the weeds and wheat. Matthew appears to have two main points.

First, there will be an extreme judgment where the wheat and the weeds will be separated. But a second point—a unique one—is also made by Matthew. Jesus does not want a premature gathering of the weeds before God's harvest. He apparently is counseling against the rash action of those within the community who would attempt to make the determinations themselves.

5. While the African American percentage of the U.S. population in 2000 was 12.3 percent (according to the U.S. Census Bureau this figure was 13.3 percent as of July 1, 2003), the percentage of African American adults in state prisons (1997) was 45.6 percent. "Section II: Incarceration and Its Consequences," *Prison Policy Initiative*, http://www.prisonpolicy.org/prisonindex/prisoners.shtml.

6. Cf. "African Americans by the Numbers: From the U.S. Census Bureau," *Infoplease*, http://www.infoplease.com/spot/bhmcensus1.html: As of 1 July 2003, 24.4 percent of African Americans were poor. The rate was unchanged from 2002.

7. The first Jezebel was immortalized in 2 Kings as the manipulative foreign wife of the Israelite king Ahab, who tried to prop up her native Baal cult and simultaneously discredit and destroy the prophets and faith of Yahweh. John accused his rival prophet of Thyatira of trying similarly to build up the religions of Rome. He describes her evil in exactly the same way (2:20) that he described Balaam's crime (2:14).

8. See, for example, Vincent Harding, "Religion and Resistance among Antebellum Slaves, 1800–1860," in *African-American Religion: Interpretative Essays in History and Culture*, ed. Albert J. Raboteau and Timothy E. Fulap (New York and London: Routledge, 1997), 121–22: "Like [Nat] Turner she saw visions and dreamed dreams of struggle and conflict and searching for freedom. Like him she prayed and talked with God and became fully convinced that her God willed freedom. Indeed, one of her more radical biographers said that by the time she escaped from her native Maryland in 1849, 'she was ready to kill for freedom, if that was necessary, and defend the act as her religious right.'"

9. Many commentators argue that the number represents the twelve apostles and the twelve tribes of Israel and therefore the complete symbolization of the people of faith.

10. On the sea as chaos, see Job 26:12-13; Pss 74:12-15; 89:9-10; Isa 27:1; 51:9-11.

11. Clearly, the four living creatures are a composite picture drawn from the visionary recollections of Ezek 1:5-25 and Isa 6:1-4. While Ezekiel's creatures had four wings, John's, like Isaiah's, have six. The match with Isaiah is not a perfect one in this regard, however. In Isaiah's presentation, the wings are paired together as they perform certain functions. In Revelation, they apparently operate individually. The creatures are also positioned differently. In Isaiah they are situated above the throne; in Ezekiel, they appear to bear the throne (with the assistance of their adjoining wheels) from a position below. John sees them stationed right next to the throne. They are also described differently. In Ezekiel, each creature has four faces; in Revelation, there are four different creatures with four different faces. In Ezekiel, the creatures move but do not speak; in both Revelation and Isaiah, they introduce a worship of God that begins with a resounding cry of "Holy, Holy, Holy."

12. James Weldon Johnson and J. Rosamond Johnson, *The Books of American Negro Spirituals* (New York: Viking, 1969), 140–41.

13. Ibid., 148–51.

14. C. Eric Lincoln and Lawrence H. Mamiya, *The Black Church in the African American Experience* (Durham, N.C.: Duke University Press, 1990), 348.

15. See Gen 49:9-10; *Testament of Judah* 24:5; and 2 Esd 1:31-32.

16. See Isa 11:1, 10; Jer 23:5; 33:15; Zech 3:8; 6:12.

17. John may well be making such a linguistic distinction when he chooses the Greek term *sphazō*, "slaughter") rather than the more sacrificially connected term for "slaughter" (*thyō*) to describe the fate of Christ and those who follow him. Except for the anomaly of 1 John 3:12, *sphazō* is found in the New Testament exclu-

sively in the Apocalypse. Though it is prevalent elsewhere in the New Testament (cf. Mark 14:12; Luke 22:7; Acts 14:13,18; 1 Cor 5:7), the more sacrificially oriented term (*thyō*) does not occur in the Apocalypse at all. See Johannes P. Louw and Eugene A. Nida, eds., *Introduction and Domains: Greek-English Lexicon of the New Testament Based on Semantic Domains*, vol. 1, 2nd ed. (New York: United Bible Societies, 1989), 236, 534. If John does think of Christ's slaughter as an atoning sacrifice, why does he avoid the very vocabulary that would help make that connection more explicit?

18. Delores Williams, "A Crucifixion Double Cross?" *The Other Side* 29 (1993): 27.

19. Allan A. Boesak, *Comfort and Protest: The Apocalypse from a South African Perspective* (Philadelphia: Westminster, 1987), 72–73.

20. Anthony B. Pinn, *Terror and Triumph: The Nature of Black Religion* (Minneapolis: Fortress Press, 2003), 143.

21. Trumpet 1: hail and fire, mixed with blood; Exod 9:13-35, hail rains down on Egyptians. Trumpet 2: sea becomes as blood; Exod 7:14-25, Nile turns to blood. Trumpet 3: no direct parallel. Trumpet 4: darkness; Exod 10:21-29, darkness. Trumpet 5: locusts; Exod 10:1-15, locusts.

22. Boesak, *Comfort and Protest*, 76.

23. Theodore Walker Jr., *Empower the People: Social Ethics for the African American Church* (Maryknoll, N.Y.: Orbis, 1991), 36–37.

24. Dwight N. Hopkins, "Slave Theology in the 'Invisible Institution'," in *Cut Loose Your Stammering Tongue: Black Theology in the Slave Narratives*, ed. Dwight N. Hopkins and George Cummings (Maryknoll, N.Y.: Orbis, 1991), 15.

25. Delores S. Williams, *Sisters in the Wilderness: The Challenge of Womanist God-Talk* (Maryknoll, N.Y.: Orbis, 1993), 188.

26. John appeals here to the symbolic imagery of half of seven as a temporary, transient time, since seven represents wholeness. Both the forty-two months and the 1,260 days are three and a half years, just as are the 1,260 days of 12:6 and the time, two times and a half of 12:14.

27. See James H. Cone, *Martin and Malcolm and America: A Dream or a Nightmare* (Maryknoll, N.Y.: Orbis, 1991).

28. By making this unprecedented and awkward move of comparing John's metaphor with one of my own, I run many risks. Chief among them might be the perception that I intend to place God on the side of the United States and the Vietnamese people on the side of the dragon in the context of the war. I do not. I use the image only in the restricted sense of the helicopter's role, which could apply to a dropping of firefighters into a forest fire, or a ferrying of emergency medical personnel to a crisis event. In using the example above, I only choose this particular war setting because (1) a war setting fits John's understanding of the people's plight, and (2) this particular war made explicit and intentional use of the helicopter strategy. It is only that strategy and not the politics of the war itself that I wish to use as a metaphorical reference point.

29. Boesak, *Comfort and Protest*, 72.

30. As did the trumpet scourges, the bowl plagues recall the plagues Yahweh visited upon Egypt before the peoples' dramatic exodus. Bowl 1, sores: Exod 9:8-12; Bowl 2, sea to blood: Exod 7:14-25; Bowl 3, fresh water to blood: Exod 7:14-25; Bowl 5, darkness: Exod 10:21-29; Bowl 6, frogs: Exod 8:1-15; Bowl 7, Lightning, thunder, earthquake, hail: Exod 9:13-35.

31. G. B. Caird, *The Revelation of St. John the Divine* (San Francisco: Harper & Row, 1966), 224.

32. Examples of the praise language: Ps 113:1: "Praise (*hallelu*) the LORD! Praise (*hallelu*), O servants of the LORD; praise (*hallelu*) the name of the LORD." Also Ps 104:35: "Let sinners be consumed from the earth, and let the wicked be no more. Bless the LORD, O my soul. Praise (*hallelu*) the LORD!"

33. Pablo Richard, *Apocalypse: A People's Commentary on the Book of Revelation* (Maryknoll, N.Y.: Orbis, 1995), 156.

34. *A Testament of Hope: The Essential Writings of Martin Luther King, Jr.*, ed. James Melvin Washington (San Francisco: HarperCollins, 1986), 217–21.

35. John W. Blassingame, ed., *Slave Testimony: Two Centuries of Letters, Speeches, Interviews, and Autobiographies* (Baton Rouge: Louisiana State University Press, 1977), 276–77.

For Further Reading

Blount, Brian K. *Can I Get a Witness? Reading Revelation through an African American Lens.* Louisville: Westminster John Knox, 2005.

Boesak, Allan A. *Comfort and Protest: The Apocalypse from a South African Perspective.* Philadelphia: Westminster, 1987.

Boring, M. Eugene. *Revelation.* Louisville: Westminster John Knox, 1989.

Reddish, Mitchell G. *Revelation.* Macon, Ga.: Smyth & Helwys, 2001.

Rhoads, David, ed. *From Every People and Nation: The Book of Revelation in Intercultural Perspective.* Minneapolis: Fortress Press, 2005.

Richard, Pablo. *Apocalypse: A People's Commentary on the Book of Revelation.* Maryknoll, N.Y.: Orbis, 1995.

Schüssler Fiorenza, Elisabeth. *The Book of Revelation: Justice and Judgment.* 2nd ed. Minneapolis: Fortress Press, 1998.

APPENDIX:
AFRICAN AMERICAN NEW TESTAMENT SCHOLARS
HOLDING DOCTORATES

Boldface indicates contributors to this volume.

Name	*Institution*
Aymer, Albert	Drew
Aymer, Birchfield	Boston
Aymer, Margaret	Union
Blount, Brian K.	**Emory**
Braxton, Brad R.	**Emory**
Brown, Michael Joseph	**Chicago**
Burton, Keith	Northwestern
Byron, Gay L.	**Union**
Callahan, Allen D.	**Harvard**
Carson, Cottrell R.	Union
Crowder, Stephanie Buckhanon	**Vanderbilt**
Felder, Cain Hope	**Union/Columbia**
Galloway, Lincoln	Emory
George, Larry	**Vanderbilt**
Greaux, Eric	Duke
Grizzle, Trevor	Southwestern Baptist
Hendricks, Obery	Princeton
Hopkins, Jamal-Dominique	University of Manchester
Hoyt, Thomas L., Jr.	**Duke**
Lewis, Lloyd A.	**Yale**

Appendix: African American New Testament Scholars

Marbury, Carl	Harvard
Martin, Clarice J.	**Duke**
Myers, William	Pittsburgh
Nave, Guy	**Yale**
Powery, Emerson B.	**Duke**
Redding, Ann Holmes	Union
Rewolinsky, Edward	Harvard
Ridley, C. Michelle Venable	Temple
Ross, Jerome	Pittsburgh
Sanders, Boykin	**Harvard**
Scott, Thomas	Harvard
Slater, Thomas B.	**Kings College (London)**
Smith, Abraham	**Vanderbilt**
Smith, Mitzi J.	**Harvard**
St. Clair, Raquel	**Princeton Theological Seminary**
Stubbs, Monya A.	**Vanderbilt**
Waters, Kenneth	Fuller
Williams, Demetrius K.	**Harvard**
Williams, Marvin	Vanderbilt
Wimbush, Vincent L.	**Harvard**

This list builds on the one developed by Randall C. Bailey ("Academic Biblical Interpretation among African Americans in the United States," in *African Americans and the Bible: Sacred Texts and Social Textures*, ed. Vincent L. Wimbush [New York, N.Y.: Continuum, 2000], 707). We want to thank Sharon Fluker and Nikol Reed of the Fund for Theological Education for sharing their list of doctoral and dissertation fellows in biblical studies, which assisted us greatly. We apologize for any omissions; they are unintentional.

INDEX OF NAMES

▥ Index of Names

⊞ Index of Names

Index of Names